The Korean Language

This book provides a detailed survey of the Korean language, covering its speakers, genetic affiliation, historical development, dialectal variation, lexicon, writing systems, sound patterns, word structure, and grammatical structure. It is designed to be accessible to a wide readership, and provides a wealth of data in a user-friendly format that does not presuppose an in-depth knowledge of the latest linguistic theories. It will be used by general linguists and Korean linguists who are interested in the typological characteristics of the language from both synchronic and diachronic perspectives, and by undergraduates and graduate students in those disciplines who seek a comprehensive introduction to the linguistics of Korean. Likewise, advanced students of the Korean language and language educators will find it offers valuable insights into lexical, phonological, morphological and syntactic aspects of the language for their purposes.

HO-MIN SOHN is Professor of Korean Linguistics at the University of Hawaii at Manoa and President of the Korean Language Education and Research Center. He is a past president of both the American Association of Teachers of Korean (1994–7) and of the International Circle of Korean Linguistics (1979–81). He is presently the Project Director of an international collaborative project developing Korean language textbooks and a dictionary of Korean grammar and usage. His numerous publications include *Korean: Descriptive Grammar* (1994), *Korean Proficiency Guidelines (1992)*, *Linguistic Expeditions* (1986), *Woleaian-English Dictionary* (1976), *Woleaian Reference Grammar* (1975), and *A Ulithian Grammar* (1973).

THE KOREAN LANGUAGE

CAMBRIDGE LANGUAGE SURVEYS

General editors

S.R. Anderson *(Yale University)*
J. Bresnan *(Stanford University)*
B. Comrie *(Max Planck Institute for Evolutionary Anthropology, Leipzig)*
W. Dressler *(University of Vienna)*
C. Ewen *(University of Leiden)*
R. Lass *(University of Cape Town)*
D. Lightfoot *(University of Maryland)*
P.H. Matthews *(University of Cambridge)*
S. Romaine *(University of Oxford)*
N.V. Smith *(University College, London)*
N. Vincent *(University of Manchester)*

This series offers general accounts of the major language families of the world, with volumes organised either on a purely genetic basis or on a geographical basis, whichever yields the most convenient and intelligible grouping in each case. Each volume compares and contrasts the typological features of the languages it deals with. It also treats the relevant genetic relationships, historical development and sociolinguistic issues arising from their role and use in the world today. The books are intended for linguists from undergraduate level upwards, but no special knowledge of the languages under consideration is assumed. Volumes such as those on Australia and the Amazon Basin are also of wider relevance, as the future of the languages and their speakers raises important social and political issues.

Already published

The languages of Australia *R.M.W. Dixon*
The languages of the Soviet Union *Bernard Comrie*
The Mesoamerican Indian languages *Jorge A. Suárez*
The Papuan languages of New Guinea *William A. Foley*
Chinese *Jerry Norman*
The languages of Japan *Masayoshi Shibatani*
Pidgins and Creoles (volume I: Theory and structure; volume II: Reference survey) *John H. Holm*
The Indo-Aryan languages *Colin Masica*
The Celtic languages *edited by Donald MacAulay*
The Romance languages *Rebecca Posner*
The Amazonian languages *edited by R.M.W. Dixon and Alexandra Y. Aikhenvald*
The Languages of Native North America *Marianne Mithun*

The Korean language

HO-MIN SOHN

CAMBRIDGE
UNIVERSITY PRESS

PUBLISHED BY THE PRESS SYNDICATE OF THE UNIVERSITY OF CAMBRIDGE
The Pitt Building, Trumpington Street, Cambridge, United Kingdom

CAMBRIDGE UNIVERSITY PRESS
The Edinburgh Building, Cambridge CB2 2RU, UK
40 West 20th Street, New York, NY 10011–4211, USA
10 Stamford Road, Oakleigh, VIC 3166, Australia
Ruiz de Alarcón 13, 28014 Madrid, Spain
Dock House, The Waterfront, Cape Town 8001, South Africa

http://www.cambridge.org

First published 1999
Reprinted 2001
First paperback edition 2001

Printed in the United Kingdom at the University Press, Cambridge

Typeset in Times 9/13 [AU]

A catalogue record for this book is available from the British Library

ISBN 0 521 36123 0 hardback
ISBN 0 521 36943 6 paperback

For Timmy, Elliot, Miran, and Aran

CONTENTS

MAPS

PREFACE

Korean has emerged as an important world language not only for learners of Korean as a foreign/second language but also for scholars and students of general and Korean linguistics and for language pedagogists. Thousands of heritage schools, elementary, intermediate and high schools, colleges and universities, private institutes, and government agencies around the world offer all levels of Korean language instruction. The number of institutions offering Korean and consequently, the number of students learning Korean are both constantly increasing especially in Australia, Europe, China, Japan, New Zealand, the former Soviet Union, and the United States. An ever-growing number of general and Korean linguists and linguistic students as well as language educators are interested in the structure and use of Korean and its universal and typological features from diachronic, synchronic, and dynamic perspectives.

In order to meet the immediate needs of linguists working on linguistic universals and typology as well as students interested in the structure of Korean, I published a monograph entitled *Korean* in Routledge's descriptive grammar series in 1994. This volume, which consists of syntax, morphology, phonology, ideophones and interjections, and lexicon, soon became out of print in early 1996. I did not attempt to have this volume reprinted as I have been working on the current Cambridge volume, which not only encompasses most of the essential aspects touched upon in *Korean* but also widens the horizon by including chapters on genetic affiliation, historical development, dialects, and writing systems.

Through theory-neutral description and analysis, the present volume aims to present most of the major areas of Korean in as simple and widely received terms as possible, so that the book is accessible to general readers as well as linguists. I have tried not to include those recently innovated technical terms which are used only within certain theoretical frameworks. Such terms would be meaningful only among specialists and students who keep abreast of the contemporary linguistic trends. Furthermore, in order to show an unbiased and balanced picture of each major aspect with appropriate linguistic data, I deliberately avoided discussing controversial theoretical arguments that have been raised thus far by many recent and contemporary Korean linguists.

Instead, I included in the bibliography an extensive list of works in which a wide variety of theoretical issues are extensively discussed.

Thus, this volume is designed and written as a reference book for general and Korean linguists and Korean language pedagogists and as a textbook for undergraduate and graduate students interested in Korean. It can be used most profitably for university courses such as Introduction to Korean Linguistics and Structure of Korean.

This volume is a result of my many intermittent years of work at the University of Hawaii at Manoa (UHM) while teaching the undergraduate course Structure of Korean and the graduate courses History and Dialects of Korean, Korean Phonology and Morphology, Korean Syntax and Semantics, and Korean Sociolinguistics. Professor Gerald B. Mathias at UHM read the entire manuscript and provided me with many valuable comments. Ms Haejin E. Koh, one of my PhD students in Korean linguistics, gave me admirable editorial assistance. I also appreciate Dr Katharina Brett, Dr Caroline Murray, and the anonymous reviewer for many essential corrections, comments, and suggestions invaluable in improving the form and contents of this volume. I extend my appreciation to the UHM Research Relations Office and the UHM Center for Korean Studies for each awarding me a grant to help my research.

I would like to take this opportunity to specially appreciate Professor Byron W. Bender who, as my UHM academic advisor and dissertation committee chair some thirty years ago, has supported and guided me towards a career in linguistics.

As always, I thank my wife, Sook-Hi, for patiently and generously taking care of all the chores at home, giving me constant moral support, and paying much attention to my health for over forty years of our marriage.

I dedicate this volume to my beloved grandchildren, Timmy, Elliot, Miran, Aran, and those yet to be born.

Ho-Min Sohn
Honolulu

ABBREVIATIONS

The following abbreviations are used to label the linguistic terms
employed in this volume.

*	ungrammatical (when placed before a phrase or a sentence)
	reconstructed form (when placed before a phonemic form)
<	derived diachronically from
>	derived diachronically to
AC	Accusative particle
AD	Adverbial suffix; adverbializer
ADM	Admonitive (warning)
AH	Addressee honorific
APP	Apperceptive sentence-type suffix
BLN	Blunt speech level or suffix
CAS	Causative suffix
CL	Numeral classifier (counter)
CMP	Complementizer suffix
CNJ	Conjunctive suffix
DC	Declarative sentence-type suffix
DEF	Deferential speech level
DR	Directional particle
EM	emphasizer
ENDER	Sentence/clause ender
EX	Exclamatory suffix
FML	Familiar speech level or suffix
GN	Genitive particle
hon.	honorific word
HT	Honorific title
IM	Imperative sentence-type suffix
IN	Indicative mood suffix

INF	Infinitive suffix
INT	Intimate speech level or suffix
NM	Nominative case particle
NOM	Nominalizer suffix
PAS	Passive suffix
PL	Plural suffix or particle
PLN	Plain speech level or suffix
POL	Polite speech level, suffix, or particle
PR	Propositive sentence-type suffix
PRM	Promissive sentence-type suffix
PRS	Prospective modal suffix
PST	Past tense and perfect aspect suffix
Q	Question marker, i.e., interrogative sentence-type suffix
QT	Quotative particle
RL	Relativizer (or adnominal modifier) suffix
RQ	Requestive mood suffix
RT	Retrospective mood suffix
SH	Subject honorific suffix
SUP	Suppositive mood suffix
TC	Topic-contrast particle
TR	Transferentive suffix
VOC	Vocative particle

1

Introduction

Following brief notes on the transcription conventions adopted in this book, this chapter introduces the distribution of the speakers of Korean on the Korean peninsula and throughout the world, the current status of the education of Korean as a foreign language, a brief survey of linguistic studies made thus far, and an overview of the salient typological features of the language.

1.1   Transcriptions

Korean expressions in this book, including proper names, titles of books and articles, and linguistic examples, are presented in the Yale system of romanization, unless indicated otherwise. Yale and Hankul (the Korean alphabet) spelling conventions are essentially the same in that both systems follow the morphophonemic spelling principle (i.e., the principle of one phonemic form for one morpheme). That is, every romanized syllable corresponds to a Hankul syllable block, as will be observed in 6.3.

As for personal names, individualized romanizations are honored as much as possible. Since the two vowels *wu* [u] and *u* [ɨ] do not contrast after a bilabial stop consonant (*p*, *ph*, *pp*, *m*), both being pronounced as [u], *pwu* [pu], *phwu* [phu], *ppwu* [ppu], and *mwu* [mu] are abbreviated in spelling to *pu*, *phu*, *ppu*, and *mu*, respectively. Similarly, *ywu* [ju] is shortened to *yu* because the sound sequence [jɨ] does not exist in Korean. In romanized spellings, the syllable boundary marker (.) is omitted unless it is necessary. The following conventions are established instead:

(a) The sequences *ey*, *ay*, *oy*, and *uy* are inseparable single units, representing the sounds [e], [ɛ], [ø, we], and [ɨ(j), i, e], respectively, unless a syllable boundary marker (.) is placed before *y*. Thus, for instance, *peyenayta* 'cut off', *hayyo* 'does', *koyita* 'get propped', and *uyuy* 'significance' are the abbreviated forms of *pay.e.nay.ta*, *hay.yo*, *koy.i.ta*, and *uy.uy*, respectively.

(b) All pre-vowel single, geminate, or aspirate consonants (e.g., *k*, *kk*, *kh*), semivowels (*y*, *w*) other than *y* after *e*, *a*, *o*, or *u*, and consonant-semivowel sequences (e.g., *kw*, *kky*, *khw*) are the onset of the syllable to which the following vowel belongs, unless a syllable boundary marker is placed before that vowel. Thus, for instance, *salam* 'person', *akka* 'a while ago', *cokha* 'nephew', *kyeyyak* 'contract', *Sewul* 'Seoul', *sakwa* 'apple', and *ciphyey* 'paper money' are the abbreviated forms of *sa.lam*, *a.kka*, *co.kha*, *kyey.yak*, *Se.wul*, *sa.kwa*, and *ci.phyey*, respectively.

(c) Any consonant or semivowel immediately preceding the above-mentioned consonants, semivowels, or consonant-semivowel sequences is the coda of the preceding syllable. Thus, for instance, *haksayng* 'student', *Hankul* 'the Korean alphabet', *Hamkyeng* 'Hamkyeng Province', *Tayhanminkwuk* 'Republic of Korea', and *meknunta* 'eats' are the abbreviated forms of *hak.sayng*, *Han.kul*, *Ham.kyeng*, *Tay.han.min.kwuk*, and *mek.nun.ta*, respectively.

(d) The spelling *ng* represents a single consonant sound [ŋ]. It always belongs to the preceding syllable. Thus, *kangaci* 'puppy' whose phonetic form is [ka.ŋa.ɟi] is syllabified as *kang.a.ci* in its romanized form.

(e) Any consonant, vowel, or semivowel immediately preceding a syllable boundary marker belongs to the preceding syllable, as in the spellings *en.e* 'language', *kwuk.e* 'national language', *hak.kyo* 'school', *pang.en* 'dialect', *ha.yahta* 'be white', *mil.essta* 'pushed', and *po.yessta* 'was seen, showed'.

In romanization, a word boundary is marked by a space. A hyphen (-) is used to locate a morpheme boundary as needed. When phonemic or phonetic transcriptions are called for, as in chapters on genetic affiliation, historical development, writing systems, and sound patterns, the International Phonetic Alphabet (IPA) is employed along with romanized spellings.

The following table of romanization systems shows correspondences among the currently used letters of the Korean alphabet (Hankul), the Yale system, the McCune–Reischauer (M–R) system (which is widely used by non-linguists), and the IPA representations.

Table of romanization systems

Hankul letters	Phonemic value in IPA	Phonetic value in IPA	Yale	M–R
Consonants				
ㅂ	**p**	[p, b]	*p*	*p, b*
ㅍ	**ph**	[ph]	*ph*	*p'*
ㅃ	**p'**	[p']	*pp*	*pp*

ㄷ	**t**	[t, d]	*t*	*t, d*
ㅌ	**th**	[th]	*th*	*t'*
ㄸ	**t'**	[t']	*tt*	*tt*
ㅅ	**s**	[s, ʃ]	*s*	*s*
ㅆ	**s'**	[s', ʃ']	*ss*	*ss*
ㅈ	**c**	[c, ɟ]	*c*	*ch, j*
ㅊ	**ch**	[ch]	*ch*	*ch'*
ㅉ	**c'**	[c']	*cc*	*tch*
ㄱ	**k**	[k, g]	*k*	*k, g*
ㅋ	**kh**	[kh]	*kh*	*k'*
ㄲ	**k'**	[k']	*kk*	*kk*
ㅁ	**m**	[m]	*m*	*m*
ㄴ	**n**	[n, ɲ]	*n*	*n*
ㅇ*	**ŋ**	[ŋ]	*ng*	*ng*
ㄹ	**l**	[l, ɾ]	*l*	*l, r*
ㅎ	**h**	[h]	*h*	*h*

Vowels and diphthongs

ㅣ	**i**	[i]	*i*	*i*
ㅟ	**y, wi**	[y, wi]	*wi*	*wi*
ㅔ	**e**	[e]	*ey*	*e*
ㅖ	**je**	[je]	*yey*	*ye*
ㅞ	**we**	[we]	*wey*	*we*
ㅚ	**ø, we**	[ø, we]	*oy*	*oe*
ㅐ	**ɛ**	[ɛ]	*ay*	*ae*
ㅒ	**jɛ**	[jɛ]	*yay*	*yae*
ㅙ	**wɛ**	[wɛ]	*way*	*wae*
ㅡ	**ɨ**	[ɨ]	*u*	*ŭ*
ㅓ	**ə**	[ə]	*e*	*ŏ*
ㅕ	**jə**	[jə]	*ye*	*yŏ*
ㅝ	**wə**	[wə]	*we*	*wŏ*
ㅏ	**a**	[a]	*a*	*a*
ㅑ	**ja**	[ja]	*ya*	*ya*
ㅘ	**wa**	[wa]	*wa*	*wa*
ㅜ	**u**	[u]	*wu*	*u*
ㅠ	**ju**	[ju]	*y(w)u*	*yu*
ㅗ	**o**	[o]	*o*	*o*
ㅛ	**jo**	[jo]	*yo*	*yo*
ㅢ	**ɨj**	[ɨ(j), i, e]	*uy*	*ŭi*

* This letter may occur in both initial and final position of a syllable block, as in 잉 [iŋ]. The sound [ŋ] is associated with only the final ㅇ, while the initial ㅇ has a null sound value.

Spelling examples

Hankul	Phonemic	Phonetic	Yale	M–R	
한국	**hankuk**	[han.guk]	*Hankwuk*	*Han'guk*	'Korea'
한글	**hankɨl**	[han.gɨl]	*Hankul*	*Han'gŭl*	'Korean alphabet'
세종	**s:econg**	[se:.ɟoŋ]	*Seycong*	*Sejong*	'King Seycong'
대전	**tɛcen**	[tɛ.ɟən]	*Taycen*	*Taejŏn*	'Taycen city'
서울	**səul**	[sə.ul]	*Sewul*	*Sŏul*	'Seoul'
미국	**mikuk**	[mi.guk]	*Mikwuk*	*Miguk*	'America'
신라	**sinla**	[sil.la]	*Sinla*	*Silla*	'Sinla dynasty'
조선	**cosen**	[co.sən]	*Cosen*	*Chosŏn*	'Cosen dynasty'
고구려	**kokuljə**	[ko.gu.ɾjə]	*Kokwulye*	*Koguryŏ*	'Kokwulye kingdom'
백제	**pɛkce**	[pɛk.cʼe]	*Paykcey*	*Paekche*	'Paykcey kingdom'
최	**chø, chwe**	[chø; chwe]	*Choy*	*Ch'oe*	'surname Choy'
이승만	**i sɨŋman**	[i.sɨŋ.man]	*I sungman*	*I sŭngman*	'Syngman Rhee'

The following Middle Korean Hankul letters, which are no longer used in Contemporary Korean, will be represented by corresponding IPA symbols for romanization as well as for phonemic and phonetic transcriptions.

Hankul	Phonemic	Phonetic	Romanization
ㅸ	β	[β]	β
ㅿ	z	[z]	z
ㆆ	ʔ	[ʔ]	ʔ
·	ɔ	[ɔ]	ɔ

1.2   Speakers

Korean is one of the world's most common languages, with approximately 72 million speakers. In terms of the number of speakers, Korean is rated as the eleventh among over 3,000 languages existing on the globe. The current population of South Korea is over 45 million and that of North Korea around 23 million. In South Korea, over 10 million people, over a quarter of its population, live in the capital city Seoul, whereas in North Korea, the population is rather spread out, with 2 million living in the capital (Phyengyang). Some 5.3 million Koreans (7% of the total Korean population) are estimated to reside outside of the Korean peninsula, the major countries with a large Korean population being China (2 million), USA (1.9 million), Japan (700,000), and the former Soviet Union (500,000).

Korean Chinese reside mainly in the three Manchurian provinces: Jirin (1.2 million), Heilongjiang (500,000), and Liaoning (200,000), and about 44% of the entire Korean Chinese population live in the Yanbian Korean Autonomous Prefecture in Jirin Province, on the border of North Korea. In the United States, over 500,000 Koreans live in the Los Angeles area, with the rest concentrated mainly in New York, Chicago, the Washington, D.C. area, Philadelphia, San Francisco, Seattle, Atlanta, Honolulu, etc., in order of decreasing number. Korean residents in Japan reside in such cities as Osaka (250,000), Tokyo (120,000), Kobe (87,000), Nagoya (85,000), Yokohama (38,000), Fukuoka (36,000), and Shimonoseki (34,000). The Koreans of the former Soviet Union have their highest concentration (over 66%) in the Uzbekistan Republic and Kazakstan Republic (as a result of Stalin's enforced removal of Far Eastern Korean Soviets to these Central Asian regions in 1937), with some 40,000 living in Sakhalin.

Other areas where a sizable Korean population is found include the Middle East and Africa (120,000 in Saudi Arabia, Bahrain, Iran, Ghana, Gabon, etc.), Canada (40,000 in Toronto, Vancouver, etc.), Europe (26,000 in Germany, Spain, Netherlands, France, England, etc.), Central and South America (22,000 in Brazil, Argentina, Paraguay, etc.), and Australia and New Zealand where the population of Koreans is rapidly increasing.

Due to constant immigration and natural population increase, Koreans in the United States have become the fastest growing segment of the worldwide overseas Korean population. According to Barringer and Cho (1989:19), the Korean population in the United States was 5,009 (2% of all Asian Americans) in 1910; 8,568 in 1940; 69,150 in 1970; and 357,393 (10.3% of all Asian Americans) in 1980. During the past eighteen years, the Korean population in the United States has grown five-fold. If this trend continues, one can easily project the growth of the Korean American population in the 21st century. In fact, Koreans in America are expected to outnumber the Korean residents in China very soon. Unlike in America, hardly any new immigration is expected in China, Japan, or the former Soviet Union. In 1980, the Korean population in the United States ranked the fourth among the Asian minority groups, following Chinese, Filipinos, and Japanese populations. At present, Korean Americans outnumber the Japanese American population, which is approximately 800,000, and it is expected that in a few decades, only Filipinos will outnumber Koreans in the United States.

1.3   Korean as a Foreign Language

Korean as a foreign language was first taught at St Petersburg University in Russia in 1897, and subsequently in many countries in Europe, America, Asia, and the Pacific. However, it had hardly been popular among non-Koreans until quite recently. Korean has started to boom since the latter half of the 1970s when Korea began to gain visibility mainly due to its rapid economic growth, the massive overseas emigration of its people, and the South Korean government's deep concern with and commitment to globalizing Korean language and culture. Korean is now learned by an ever-increasing number of non-Koreans worldwide, as well as by ethnic overseas Koreans. Suffice it here to present the cases of four representative countries: China, the United Stages, Japan, and the former Soviet Union.

The most successful overseas Korean language education is observed in China. Despite the dark ages of Mao Tse-tung's Cultural Revolution (1966–76) when ethnic education was completely suppressed, Chinese–Korean bilingual education has been well established in the three Manchurian provinces, partly owing to the favorable minority policies of the Chinese government and also to Korean Chinese's strong motivation to maintain their ethnic identity through language and culture instruction for their children. Currently, approximately 2,000 elementary and secondary schools educate exclusively Korean minorities and offer intensive Korean language instruction. In the majority of these schools, including those in the Yanbian Korean Autonomous Prefecture, the medium of instruction is Korean, with all textbooks written in Korean. At Yanbian University, all lectures are conducted in Korean. Korean is also gaining increasing popularity among native Chinese, especially since the establishment of diplomatic ties between China and South Korea in 1992. Currently, Korean is the fourth most popular language in China, following English, Japanese, and Russian, with over two dozen universities having a Korean language department.

In the United States, no regular English–Korean bilingual education is practised. Instead, Korean is learned as a foreign language (including Korean Americans' learning of Korean as their second language). Seven Korean community schools in 1975 have grown to 830 (mostly affiliated with Korean churches), where Korean is presently taught to some 50,000 Korean American children by 5,200 teachers mainly on weekends. Ten colleges and universities in 1975, which offer Korean language courses, have grown to approximately 110, and over 20 high schools have recently started to teach Korean. A few universities including the University of Hawaii at Manoa and the University of California at Los Angeles offer BA, MA, and PhD programmes in Korean language and literature. In addition, government institutions such as the Defense Language Institute, Foreign Service Institute, Central Intelligence Agency, and National Security Agency provide intensive Korean language training for government personnel. Many private institutions have recently been established to teach Korean to the general public and to students.

In Japan, Korean is taught at over eighty colleges and universities. As of 1998, five universities have a Korean language department and offer a degree (BA or MA) in Korean. In addition, six high schools in Osaka, Tokyo, and Kobe currently offer Korean language courses. Several government agencies conduct Korean language teaching for diplomats, police officers, military personnel, and other government officials. Furthermore, Korean is taught to the general public at over sixty private institutions.

Unlike the long-standing establishment of formal foreign language education in China, Japan, and the United States, Korean language programmes have grown much more slowly in the former Soviet Union. Only since the demise of the Union have the governments, political parties, and ethnic leaders of respective Republics launched a policy of bilingualism, thus encouraging the instruction of both Russian and the ethnic language and culture to students. According to the 1989 census of the former Soviet Union, most of the younger generation ethnic Koreans are by and large monolingual and declare Russian as their native language (Myong 1991). As part of the strong movement led by many newly established Korean cultural organizations, Korean language classes are being started in an effort to revive the Korean language, culture, and tradition among young ethnic Koreans. Currently, three universities in Russia and four universities in Uzbekistan and Kazakstan offer Korean language courses.

Other countries where Korean is offered at colleges and universities include Australia, Germany, Canada, England, France, New Zealand, Indonesia, Malaysia, Thailand, the Philippines, Argentina, Austria, Belgium, Brazil, Bulgaria, Denmark, Finland, the Netherlands, Hungary, India, Israel, Italy, Mongolia, Poland, Portugal, Sweden, and Turkey. In particular, in Australia, several dozen elementary and high schools and nine universities offer formal Korean language courses. Numerous overseas students visit Korea to learn the language and culture in situ on a short or long term basis. Over ten universities and several private institutions in South Korea offer Korean language training to foreign students.

Several national or international academic organizations on Korean language education actively promote Korean as a foreign language worldwide through conferences, workshops, journals, and exchange of instructional materials. These include the International Association for Korean Language Education (IAKLE), the Korean Society of Bilingualism, and the American Association of Teachers of Korean (AATK).

For more information on the status of Korean language education throughout the world, see *Say Kwuk.e Saynghwal* 1.2 (1991) and *Gyoyug Han-Geul* 10 (1997).

1.4   Linguistic Study of Korean

The first linguistic study of Korean dates back to the ingenious work of King Seycong and his Royal Academy scholars in the fifteenth century in creating the indigenous writing system called *Hwunmin Cengum* (The Correct Sounds to Educate the People; scholar Cwu Sikyeng later proposed to call it Hankul 'the Great Writing') through an extensive analysis of the Korean sound pattern. Thus, the king's *Hwunmin Cengum* (1446) and Ceng Inci's *Hwunmin Cengum Haylyey* (Explanations and Examples of the *Hwunmin Cengum*, 1446) may be regarded as the first formal publications of Korean linguistics.

From then until the middle of the nineteenth century, only a few studies by native scholars, all related to *Hwunmin Cengum*, appeared. These are Choy Seycin's *Hwunmongcahoy Pemlyey* (Explanations of Chinese Characters with Hankul, 1527); Sin Kyengyey's *Hwunmin Cengum Wunhay* (Sound Explanations of *Hwunmin Cengum*, 1750); and Yu Huy's *Enmunci* (A Study of the Korean Native Script, 1824).

It was not until around the turn of the 20th century, however, that the Korean language was actively and extensively studied by Korean, Japanese, and Western scholars. Representative monographs by native scholars in this early period include Lee Pongwun's *Kwukmun Cengli* (A Korean Grammar, 1897); Cwu Sikyeng's *Kwukmun Munpep* (A Korean Grammar, 1905), *Kwukmun Yenkwu* (A Study of Korean, 1909), and *Mal uy Soli* (Speech Sounds, 1914); Ci Sekyeng's *Sinceng Kwukmun* (New Korean, 1905); Yu Kilcwun's *Tayhan Muncen* (A Korean Grammar, 1909); Kim Kyusik's *Cosen Munpep* (A Korean Grammar, 1912); An Hwak's 'Cosen.e uy kachi' (Values of Korean, 1915) and *Cosen.e Wenlon* (Principles of Korean, 1922); Kim Twupong's *Cosen Malpon* (A Korean Grammar, 1916) and *Kipte Cosen Malpon* (Revised Korean Grammar, 1924); Ceng Yelmo's *Cosen.ehak Kayyo* (An Introduction to Korean Linguistics, *Han-geul*, 1927–28); Kwen Tekkyu's *Cosen.emun Kyengwi* (Details of Korean Sentences, 1923); Choy Hyen-Pay's *Wuli Malpon* (Our Grammar, 1929) and *Hankul Kal* (A Study of Hankul, 1942); Pak Sungpin's *Cosen.ehak Kanguy Yoci* (Essentials of Korean Linguistics, 1931) and *Cosen.ehak* (Korean Linguistics, 1935); Gim Sheon-Gi's 'Kyengum uy poncil' (The essential nature of tensification, 1933) and *The Phonetics of Korean* (1938); Lee Hi-Sung's 'Cosen.ehak uy pangpeplon sesel' (A methodological introduction to Korean linguistics, 1938); and Kim Yunkyeng's *Cosen Munca kup Ehaksa* (A Linguistic History of Korean Writing and Language, 1938).

Among these early Korean scholars, Cwu Sikyeng was the first who studied Korean from a modern linguistic perspective; An Hwak's extensive survey of various subareas of the Korean language (1922) and Ceng Yelmo's series of works published in *Han-geul* (1927–28) are the first works that provided a scientific system to the Korean language; and Choy Hyen-Pay's extensive grammar (1929 and its revised versions) has exerted the strongest impact upon later scholars and students of the Korean language.

Representative publications by Japanese scholars in the early period before the end of the Second World War include Okagura's 'Ritogenbungo' (A study of Itwu-Korean, 1889); Kanazawa's *Nikkan Ryookokugo Dookeiron* (A Study of the Japanese–Korean Genetic Relationship, 1910); Shiratori's 'Chosengo to Ural-Altai-go to no hikaku kenkyu' (A comparative study of Korean and Ural-Altaic languages, 1914-6); and Ogura's *Kokugo oyobi Chosengo no Tame* (For Japanese and Korean, 1920), *Kyoka oyabi Rito no Kenkyu* (A Study on Hyangka and Itwu, 1929), 'Chosengo no keito' (The lineage of Korean, 1935), and *Chosengo Hogen no Kenkyu* (A Study of Korean Dialects, 2 volumes, 1944).

Early Western scholars' works include W.G. Aston's *A Comparative Study of the Japanese and Korean Languages* (1879); H.G. Underwood's *A Concise Dictionary of the Korean Language* (1890) and *Introduction to the Korean Spoken Language* (1890); G.H. Jones's 'Korean etymology' (1892); J. Edkins's 'Etymology of Korean numerals' (1898); H.B. Hulbert's *A Comparative Grammar of the Korean Language and the Dravidian Languages of India* (1905); J.S. Gale's *Korean Grammatical Forms* (1894) and *A Korean–English Dictionary* (1897); E.D. Polivanov's *K voprosu o rodstvennyx otnosenijax korejskogo i 'altajskix' jazykov* (On the Issue of the Genetic Relationship of Korean and Altaic Languages, 1927); A.A. Kholodovich's *Grammatika Koreiskogo yazyka* (A Korean Grammar, 1939) which is the first scientific grammar of Korean in Russian; and Ramstedt's *A Korean Grammar* (1939) and *Studies in Korean Etymology* (1949). Ramstedt, a Finnish scholar, made a major contribution to Korean linguistics in the West with this etymological study which established the affinity of Korean to Altaic languages. Furthermore, his morphology-oriented grammar is known as the first scientific investigation into Korean structure by a Western linguist.

In view of the scholarly enthusiasm developed for the study of Korean since the end of the nineteenth century, it may be said that the linguistic study of Korean has a history of one hundred years. Despite the efforts to promote Korean by patriotic Korean linguists and a small number of foreign scholars in the early part of the twentieth century, linguistic study of Korean was extremely limited in the academic world both in Korea and overseas during the Japanese colonial occupation of Korea from 1910 to 1945. During this thirty-five-year colonial period, the use of Korean was prohibited at Korean schools, Korean personal names were changed to Japanese names, and many distinguished scholars of Korean were imprisoned. Only since Korea's liberation from Japan in 1945 have ever-increasing linguistic studies of Korean been conducted both on the Korean peninsula and overseas.

Y.G Ko, et al. (1992, IV Bibliography) list some 4,000 linguistic books, articles, dictionaries, and textbooks of Korean, 99% of which were published after 1945. Kokuritsu Kokugo Kenkyujo's (National Language Research Institute, Japan, 1996) bibliographical monograph on Korean (covering publications from 1945 to 1993) contains 2,183 books, articles, dictionaries, and textbooks written in Japanese along with some 1,000 works written in English. Studies of Korean that have been done encompass all aspects of the language, including historical and comparative studies, phonetics and phonology, writing and transcription, morphology, syntax, lexicon, stylistics, dialects, semantics, pragmatics, sociolinguistics, language acquisition, language policies, language pedagogy, and computational linguistics. Space does not allow citation of the more recent works here. However, important studies will be cited in relevant chapters and a select bibliography is appended to this volume.

The United States has been the major arena of Korean linguistic research in the West in the latter half of the twentieth century; a brief state-of-the-art survey is in order. Modern linguistic study of Korean in America was launched by Samuel Martin's 'Korean phonemics' (1951) and *Korean Morphophonemics* (1954) and Fred Lukoff's University of Pennsylvania dissertation *A Grammar of Korean* (1954). The initial structural linguistic approach was soon replaced by unprecedentedly numerous generative studies in the 1960s and thereafter. During the past forty years, some 1,000 books, dissertations, and research papers on all aspects of the language have appeared. Thus far approximately 300 Korean-related doctoral dissertations have been produced from some 60 universities in the United States, with the University of Texas at Austin ranking as the top producer (some 40 dissertations) followed by the University of Hawaii at Manoa which has produced about 30 (cf. H.M. Sohn 1997a). In view of its characteristic typological properties, Korean is useful in testing current theories as well as constructing new hypotheses. Many graduate students and scholars come to the United States from Korea to do theoretical research on Korean, as new linguistic theories and hypotheses are being developed incessantly by a large number of linguists unparalleled anywhere else.

Many academic organizations actively promote and coordinate the linguistic studies of Korean. The International Circle of Korean Linguistics, established in 1976, holds international conferences biennially in different countries and publishes the journal *Korean Linguistics* and conference proceedings. Since 1985, the Harvard University Department of Linguistics has held biennial workshops in Korean linguistics and publishes the *Harvard Studies in Korean Linguistics* series. Initiated by the University of California system in 1990, annual conferences on Japanese–Korean linguistics are held at various American universities and selected papers are published in the *Japanese-Korean Linguistics* series (Stanford Center for the Study of Language and Information Publications). In Korea, the Korean Language Society

(*Hankul Hak.hoy*), the National Language Association (*Kwuk.e Hak.hoy*), the Linguistic Society of Korea, and the language research institutes of several major universities hold regular national meetings on Korean linguistics and publish journals. *Han-geul* (Korean Language Society), *Language Research* (Seoul National University), *Mal* (Yonsei University), and *Linguistic Journal of Korea* (Linguistic Society of Korea) are internationally circulated journals.

1.5   Salient features of Korean: an overview

What kind of a language is Korean? This section is aimed at answering this question by presenting a brief summary of the salient features Korean has.

1.5.1   *Genetic affiliation and historical development*

Both genetically and typologically, Korean and Japanese are widely regarded as each other's closest sister language although they are not mutually intelligible and their relationship is much more distant than that between, say, English and French. Since Korean and Japanese are grammatically quite similar to each other and the two peoples share many essential aspects of Asian culture, speakers of one language can learn the other language with relative facility once they become familiar with the pronunciation patterns and basic vocabulary of the other.

Many scholars claim that Korean and Japanese belong to the Altaic language family typically represented by Manchu-Tungusic, Mongolian, and Turkic languages, in that they display many Altaic features. There are also a few proposals that Korean and Japanese are genetically related to Oceanic languages, or to Dravidian languages such as Tamil. These Oceanic and Dravidian hypotheses are not as persuasive as the Altaic hypothesis.

Due to the dearth of reliable data, our knowledge about the evolution of Korean during the Old Korean period (prehistory to tenth century) is seriously limited. Only some extant linguistic fragments enable us to speculate on its shape. Korean linguists are in a better position to look at Middle Korean (eleventh to sixteenth century). The invention of the Korean alphabet by King Seycong in the fifteenth century is the greatest milestone in the history of the Korean language. It made abundant textual materials of Korean available from the fifteenth century to the Modern and Contemporary Korean period. As a result, fifteenth-century Korean and its subsequent development during the past five hundred years have been captured in a systematic manner. Furthermore, solid knowledge of fifteenth-century Korean has enabled scholars to attempt reconstruction of earlier forms of Korean, especially Early Middle Korean, on a sound basis.

1.5.2   *Dialectal variations*

The Korean language consists of seven geographically based dialects including the Central dialect (Seoul and vicinity) which has been designated the standard speech in South Korea and the Phyengan dialect (Phyengyang and vicinity) which is considered the standard speech in North Korea. Superimposed on these geographical divisions is a socio-political dialectal difference between North and South Korea as a result of the division of the country in 1945. North Koreans have replaced thousands of Chinese character-based words with newly coined native words while using many ideology-laden expressions. South Koreans use a large number of loan words borrowed recently from English. Despite such geographical and socio-political dialectal differences, Korean is relatively homogeneous, with excellent mutual intelligibility among speakers from different areas. Mass media and school education based on standard speech contribute greatly to standardizing the language.

1.5.3   *Korean vocabulary*

Although Korea and Japan are geographically, historically, and culturally close to China, Korean and Japanese do not share the same language family with Chinese, and are not genetically related to the latter. However, both Korean and Japanese have borrowed a large number of Chinese words and characters throughout the course of their long historical contacts with various Chinese dynasties. Such borrowed Chinese words and characters have become integral parts of the Korean and Japanese vocabularies. Since identical words and characters evolved independently in the three countries, however, their pronunciations have diverged considerably. Pronunciations of contemporary Chinese-character words in Korean are similar to those of Middle Chinese, especially those of the eighth-century Tang dynasty in China, although some independent vowel and consonant changes as well as the loss of tones have been made in Korean. Korean also borrowed from Japanese a large number of words that Japanese people created based on Chinese characters. Numerous words have also been created by Koreans with Chinese characters as building blocks. All of these Chinese character-based words are called Sino-Korean or Chinese-character words.

Since the end of the Second World War, Korean people have been in contact with many foreign countries and have borrowed from them thousands of words. There are about 20,000 loan words in Korean, of which almost 90% are from English. During the thirty-five-year occupation of Korea by Japan, a considerable number of Japanese native words were also borrowed. At the same time, many Western words that the Japanese had previously borrowed were reborrowed into Korean through Japanese. All such borrowed words are termed loan words.

Thus, the Korean vocabulary is composed of three components: native words and affixes (approximately 35%), Sino-Korean words (approximately 60%), and loan words (approximately 5%). Native words denote daily necessities of food, clothing, and shelter, locations, basic actions, activities and states, lower-level numerals, body parts, natural objects, animals, etc. The native stock includes thousands of sound symbolic (onomatopoeic and mimetic) words, idioms, and proverbs that reflect traditional culture and society. Most of the particles and affixes in Korean are from the native stock. Sino-Korean and loan words are generally cultural borrowings.

1.5.4 Writing systems

For centuries before the indigenous Korean phonetic alphabet called Hankul was created by King Seycong, the fourth king of the Cosen dynasty, and his assistants (scholars in the royal academy called Cip.hyencen 'Hall of Assembled Sages') in 1443, only Chinese characters were used. Currently, Korean texts are written either purely in Hankul or by means of a mixed script of Hankul and Chinese characters. While Hankul can represent any lexical items, including native, Sino-Korean, loan, and foreign words and morphemes, Chinese characters are used to represent only Sino-Korean words and morphemes. The current trend indicates an increasing use of Hankul spellings over Chinese characters, such that even in newspapers and scholarly books, use of Chinese characters is considerably limited.

Koreans are truly proud of Hankul, one of the most scientific writing systems that has been created by man. Its creation was based on an intensive analysis of the sound pattern of Korean and the phonological theory available at that time. The design of the alphabetic symbols was ingenious. Three basic vowel symbols depicted heaven (round dot: •), earth (horizontal line: —) and man (vertical line: |) following cosmological philosophy. Different combinations of these three symbols generate all vowels and semivowels existing in Korean. The round dot was later changed into a short horizontal or vertical stroke on a long line. Consonant symbols depict the shapes of speech organs: lips, teeth, tongue, and throat.

Hankul symbols are combined into syllable blocks. In forming a syllable block, a consonant symbol is placed first, then a vowel or diphthong symbol, and then a consonant symbol, if needed, in left-to-right and top-to-bottom order.

The current Hankul orthographical practice follows the principle of morphemic (i.e., morphophonemic) spelling in both South and North Korea. Thus, in principle, one morpheme is spelled in one invariant Hankul form regardless of various context-sensitive sound alternations. A series of simple phonological rules are required to obtain correct pronunciations from Hankul spellings.

1.5.5   The sound pattern

Korean has nineteen consonant, ten vowel, and two semivowel phonemes. There is a three-way contrast (lax–aspirate–tense) in stop consonants, a two-way contrast (lax–tense) in the alveo-dental fricatives, and no contrast (only aspirate) in the glottal fricative, as in lax (plain): **p, t, c, k, s** aspirate: **ph, th, ch, kh, h**; and tense: **p', t', c', k', s'**. The remaining four consonants are **l, m, n, ŋ**.

Although with dialectal variations, the Korean vowel system consists of five front vowels (three unround: **i, e, ɛ**; two round: **y, ø**) and five back vowels (three unround: **ɨ, ə, a**; two round: **u, o**). An equal set of long vowels exists distinctly in the older generation speakers, while it is obsolete in the younger generation. Tone distinctions in vowels used to be significant in fifteenth-century Korean (Middle Korean), but now exist only in southeastern (Kyengsang) and northeastern (Hamkyeng) dialects. The two semivowels are the palatal **j** and the labial **w**.

The Korean phonetic syllable structure is of the form (C)(G)V(C). That is, Korean speech allows only one optional consonant (C) and one optional glide or semivowel (G) in the onset position, and one optional consonant in the coda position. The only obligatory element is the nucleus vowel (V). Thus, for instance, the single-syllable English word *strike* is borrowed in Korean as a five-syllable loan word *suthulaikhu* **sɨthɨlaikhɨ** [sɨ.thɨ.ɾa.i.khɨ] with the insertion of the vowel [ɨ] to make it conform to the Korean syllable structure. Similarly, the Korean word *kaps* 'price' in *kaps i* **kaps-i** [kap.s'i] 'price (subject)' loses its final s when spoken before a consonant or when it occurs alone, because a spoken syllable does not allow two consonants after a vowel, thus [kap] 'price' and [kap.t'o] 'price also'.

Sound symbolism is widespread. Korean has several thousands of sound symbolic words. A large number of them show differences among lax, aspirate, and tense consonants. In these words, a lax consonant tends to connote slowness, gentleness, heaviness, and bigness, an aspirate consonant, flexibility, elasticity, crispiness, and swiftness, and a tense consonant, compactness, tightness, hardness, smallness, and extra swiftness, e.g., *pingping* **piŋ-piŋ** (as of a plane), *phingphing* **phiŋ-phiŋ** (as of a motor belt), and *ppingpping* **p'iŋ-p'iŋ** (as of a top) '(turn) round and round'. Similarly, so-called bright (Yang) vowels such as **a** and **o** tend to connote brightness, sharpness, lightness, smallness, thinness, and quickness, whereas so-called dark (Ying) vowels such as **e, u**, and **ə** indicate darkness, heaviness, dullness, slowness, deepness, and thickness, e.g., *panccak* **panc'ak** vs. *penccek* **pənc'ək** 'twinkling' and *kkolkkak* **k'olk'ak** vs. *kkwulkkek* **k'ulk'ək** 'gulping down'. Vowel harmony also occurs, without connotational differences, in stem-suffix combinations, as in *poala* **po-ala** 'Look!' and *puela* **pu-əla** 'Pour!', but not *poela **po-əla** and *puala **pu-ala**.

1.5.6 Agglutinative morphology

Korean is called an 'agglutinative' language, in that a long chain of particles or suffixes with constant form and meaning may be attached to nominals (nouns, pronouns, numerals, noun phrases, etc.) or predicate (verb or adjective) stems. In *yeca-tul man uy kolphu* 'the golf (played) by females only', for instance, the plural suffix *-tul*, the delimiter particle *man* 'only', and the genitive particle *uy* follow the head noun *yeca* 'female'. Similarly, in *ka-si-ess-keyss-sup-ni-ta* '(a respectable person) may have gone', the subject honorific suffix *-si*, the past tense suffix *-ess*, the presumptive modal suffix *-keyss*, the addressee honorific suffix *-sup*, the indicative mood suffix *-ni*, and the declarative suffix *-ta* occur in that order after the head verb stem *ka* 'go'. As observed in these examples, numerous Korean suffixes and particles do not have counterparts in many non-agglutinative languages such as English and Chinese. On the other hand, there are many particles and suffixes in Korean that do correspond to independent words in other languages. For instance, many English conjunctive words are equivalent to Korean conjunctive suffixes, as in *ka-ko* 'go and' and *ka-myen* 'if (one) goes' where *-ko* 'and' and *-myen* 'if' are conjunctive suffixes.

1.5.7 SOV syntax

Korean, like Japanese, is an SOV language. That is, it is a predicate-final language with the basic word order of Subject–Object–Predicate. In normal speech, the predicate (verb or adjective) comes at the end of a sentence or a clause, while all other elements, including the subject and object, must appear before the predicate. Korean particles (equivalent to English prepositions) always occur *after* the elements they are associated with. Thus, Korean particles are all postpositions. Also, all modifying elements such as determiners, adjectives, phrases, and clauses precede the elements they modify, as illustrated in *nay ka tani-nu-n hak.kyo* (I NM attend-IN-RL school) 'the school that I attend'.

In Korean, although the subject tends to appear first in a sentence in normal situations, it and the other major constituents preceding the predicate can be scrambled rather freely for emphatic or other figurative purposes, as long as the predicate retains the final position.

Korean is often called a situation- or discourse-oriented language, in that contextually or situationally understood elements (including subject and object) are left unexpressed more frequently than not. Thus, for instance, in *eti ka-sey-yo?* (where go-SH-POL) 'Where are you going?', the subject does not appear. Using a word denoting 'you' in this expression would sound awkward in normal contexts, unless 'you' is emphasized or contrasted with someone else, as in 'as for you'.

Korean, like Japanese, is a 'macro-to-micro' language, in that the universe is represented in the order of a set (macro) and then its members (micro). Thus, for instance, Koreans say or write the family name first and then the given name followed by a title; say or write an address in the order of country, province, city, street, house number, and personal name; and refer to time with year first and seconds last. So-called multiple subject (or topic) constructions also follow the 'macro-to-micro' order, as in *nay ka kho ka khu-ta* (I NM nose NM big-DC) 'I have a big nose.'

1.5.8   Honorifics

Korean is an honorific language, in that sentences can hardly be uttered without the speaker's approximate knowledge of his social relationship with his addressee and referent in terms of age category (adult, adolescent, or child), social status, kinship, in- or out-groupness, and/or the speech act situation. The grammatical pattern of Korean honorifics seems to be the most systematic among all known languages. Honorific forms appear in the following categories: address-reference terms (e.g., *Kim kyoswu* [plain] vs. *Kim kyoswu-nim* [hon.] 'professor Kim'); nouns and verbs (e.g., *pap* [plain] vs. *cinci* [hon.] 'rice, meal'; *cata* [plain] vs. *cwumusita* [hon.] 'sleep'; *issta* [plain] vs. *kyeysita* [hon.] 'stay, exist'); pronouns (e.g., *na* [plain] vs. *ce* [humble] 'I'); case particles (e.g., *ka/i* [neutral] vs. *kkeyse* [hon.] (nominative)); verbal suffixes (e.g., ZERO [plain] vs. *-(u)si* [hon.] (subject honorific); ZERO [plain] vs. *-(su)p* [hon.] (addressee honorific)), and six speech levels based on the speaker–addressee perspective (e.g., declarative sentence enders such as deferential level *-(su)pnita*, polite level *-e.yo* or *-a.yo*, blunt level *-so* or *-o*, familiar level *-ney*, intimate level *-e* or *-a*, and plain level *-ta*). Non-verbal behavior parallels the above-mentioned hierarchical verbal expressions. For instance, one bows to a senior person such as one's professor when greeting or leave-taking. The senior person does not bow to a junior. An in-group junior is not supposed to smoke in front of a senior person.

All the above salient features of the Korean language will be elaborated in great detail in the relevant chapters that follow.

2

Genetic affiliation

This chapter surveys several major hypotheses on the prehistory and genetic affiliation of Korean. While Korean proper names in the main body are romanized according to the Yale system, the phonemic forms of Korean and other languages, whether contemporary, ancient, or reconstructed, are transcribed by and large with the IPA system for comparative purposes.

2.1   Prehistory of Korean

Little authentic documentation is available on the origin of the Korean language. Thus, inferences to the genetic affiliation of the language have been made on the basis of various degrees of linguistic resemblances, often supported by archaeological or ethnological findings. Also, earlier forms of the language are not readily accessible because written historical data for internal reconstruction or comparative work are scarce and cannot be traced far back. Some old language fragments are available only in the literature dating from the eleventh century, such as *Kyun.ye Cen* (Life of the Great Master Kyun.ye, 1075) by Hyeklyen Ceng, *Kyeylim Yusa* (Things on Korea, 1103–4) by Chinese Sung dynasty scholar Sun Mu, *Samkwuk Saki* (Historical Record of the Three Kingdoms, 1145) by Kim Pusik, and *Samkwuk Yusa* (Memorabilia of the Three Kingdoms, 1285) by Monk Il.yen, all of which are written in Chinese characters. Moreover, much of the earlier vocabulary has been either irretrievably lost or obscured by succeeding waves of linguistic contacts, including a massive influx of Chinese loan words.

Lacking solid evidence in establishing the genealogy of Korean, innumerable attempts have been made to relate the language to diverse language families such as the Indo-European, the Tibeto-Burman, the Dravidian, the Altaic, the Austronesian, and the Paleosiberian. While there are many ingenious studies based on the widely accepted principles of comparative method and internal reconstruction, there are also numerous amateurish attempts based merely on accidental lexical resemblances, linguistic borrowings, shared typological features, or anthropological similarities. For instance, Koppelmann (1933) and Eckardt (1966) attempt to relate Korean to Indo-European, observing certain accidental lexical and anthropological resemblances. Hulbert (1905) maintains that Korean is related to the Dravidian languages in India in view of such shared syntactic features as word order and the lack of a gender system. Rahder's (1956–61) etymological dictionary of Chinese, Japanese, Korean, and Ainu lists, for each of his lexical entries, forms from a vast variety of the world's languages not compared in accordance with the established principles of comparative linguistics. This evidential opacity leads some linguists to treat Korean, together with Japanese, as a separate language family along with other major language families such as Indo-European, Afro-Asiatic, Uralic, Altaic, Sino-Tibetan, Dravidian, Austronesian, and Amerind (Pei 1954:31).

2.2   Altaic hypothesis

The Altaic hypothesis is the most persuasive explanation yet proposed given the available data and methodological refinements. It includes Korean and Japanese in the Altaic family which is composed mainly of Turkic, Mongolian, and Manchu-Tungus groups that range widely in the regions west and north of China. Altaic is thought to be a linguistic unity spoken sometime during the Neolithic period, and its original homeland is assumed to be somewhere in northern or north-central Eurasia (Miller 1976:341). The Ryukyuan language of the Okinawa prefecture of Japan and the islands belonging to the former Ryukyuan kingdom was considered by some scholars (e.g., Miller 1971) as a sister language of Japanese but is now considered to be a Japanese dialect by most Japanese scholars (cf. Shibatani 1990).

The first noteworthy comparative study of Korean is by Shiratori (1914–6) who compiled a 595-entry vocabulary comparing Korean and other Altaic languages, claiming their genetic relationship. Polivanov (1927), noticing the existence of vowel harmony in Korean, proposed the affinity of Korean to Altaic. It is Ramstedt (1928, 1949, 1952, 1957), however, who first assigned Korean into the Altaic family in a systematic way. Ramstedt deals with the entire field of Altaic comparative linguistics. Partly due to the etymological contributions of Ramstedt and others, Poppe (1960) demonstrates the linguistic unity among the Altaic languages, reconstructing the proto-Altaic phonology, morphology, and lexicon of some 570 roots based on regular sound correspondences among many of these languages. Poppe's reconstructions are summarized and indexed in Street (1974). According to the Altaic hypothesis, the dominant original Koreans and Japanese were Altaic people who migrated to Korea and Japan, bringing with them the basic elements of their languages.

Ramstedt, Poppe, and others found that the proto-Altaic word-initial *p had the following development: *$p > f > h > ZERO$. While Old Mongolian had p and Middle

Mongolian had *h*, most Modern Mongolian dialects have ZERO (except Monguor, which retains *f*). In the Manchu-Tungus group, the Nanay, Olcha, and Orok dialects retain the original *p* and Manchu has *f*, whereas Orochen, Evenki, Lamut, etc. have *h*, and Solon has ZERO. Turkish has ZERO in general. Korean is regarded as retaining the original *p*. These are illustrated below (e.g., Ramstedt 1949 and Poppe 1960).

(1)   to pray: Manchu *firu-*, Evenki *hiruge-*, Mongolian
                              iryge-, Middle Mongolian *hiryge-*, Korean *pil-*
        village, plain: Manchu *falga*, Mongolian *ail*, Turkish *al*,
                              Korean *pəl*
        to blow: Manchu *fulgije*, Lamut *hu-*, Mongolian *ulije-*,
                              Middle Mongolian *hulie-*, Korean *pul-*
        season, year, spring: Manchu *fon*, Middle Mongolian *hon*,
                              Mongolian *on*, Monguor *fan*, Korean *pom*

Japanese may be included in the above set in view of its having *h* in such putatively cognate words as *hara* 'plain', *huk-* 'to blow', and *haru* 'spring'.

Miller (1971), a strong defender of the Altaic affinity of Korean and Japanese, includes Korean materials (mainly from Martin 1966) in thirty-six of his fifty-eight sets of phonological correspondences that relate Japanese to the Altaic (pp. 305–6). In a recent historical-linguistic study of some ten Old Korean fragments of the Paykcey dynasty which are preserved largely in Japanese sources, Miller (1979) shows their etymological relationship to Altaic (see 3.3).

Skeletal vowel correspondences between reconstructed proto-Altaic (pA) and Old Korean (OK) (in particular, the language of Unified Sinla, 677–935 AD) are presented by K.M. Lee (1976:16–9) as in (2), with phonemic transcriptions slightly modified to conform to the IPA system. A somewhat similar correspondence set is proposed by B.H. Kim (1984:154) based on pA and Middle Korean (MK).

(2)

	1	2	3	4	5	6	7	8	9
proto-Altaic	*a	*o	*u	*ɨ	*e	*è	*ø	*y	*i
Old Korean	a	ɔ	u	i	æ	i	ə	ɨ	i

The lexical examples that K.M. Lee presents as evidence of vowel correspondences between Korean and Altaic languages include: (1) MK *alaj* (< *al) 'below', Evenki *alas* 'leg', Mongolian *ala* 'groin', and Old Turkish *al* 'below'; (2) MK *mɔl* 'horse', Manchu *morin*, and Mongolian *morin*; (3) MK *ula-* 'long lasting', Evenki *uri-pti* 'previously', and Mongolian *urida* 'previously'; (4) MK *ilang* 'ridge', Manchu *irun* 'ridge', Mongolian *iraγa* 'ridge', Chuvash *jəran* 'ridge', and Tartar *ɨzan* 'ridge'; (5) MK *kæsk* 'to break', Mongolian *keseg* 'pieces', and Turkish *kes-* 'to break'; (6) MK *il* 'early', Manchu *erde* 'early', Mongolian *erte* 'early', and Chuvash *ir* 'early'; (7) MK *məl* 'water', Manchu *mu-ke* 'water', Evenki *mu* 'water', and Mongolian *møren* 'river'; (8) MK *pɨl-* 'to blow', Manchu *fulgije-* 'to blow', Mongolian *ylije-* (< Middle Mongolian *hyli'e-* < **pylige-*) 'to blow'; and (9) MK *pil-* 'to pray', Manchu *firu-* 'to pray', Evenki *hiruge-* 'to pray', Mongolian *iryge-* 'to pray'. For a discussion on pA **o* in Korean, see Obayashi 1997.

As for consonants, K.M. Lee (ibid.:18) and B.H. Kim (ibid.:178) propose slightly different correspondence sets. The following is from Lee.

(3)

pA	*p *b	*t *d	*k *g	*c *ɟ	*s	*m	*n	*ŋ	*r^1 *r^2 *l^1 *l^2
OK	p	t	k	c	s	m	n	ŋ	l

Middle Korean had an aspirate consonant series (*h, ph, th, kh*) which Old Korean is assumed to have had. It is not determined, however, whether these aspirate consonants correspond regularly to the corresponding proto-Altaic voiceless or voiced series.

Notice in (3) that all four liquid proto-Altaic consonants correspond to Korean *l*, which phonetically alternates between [l] (occurring word-finally or before a consonant) and the flap [ɾ] (occurring before a vowel). The pA **r^1* corresponds to Manchu-Tungus *r*, Mongolian *r*, Turkic *r*, and Korean *l*, as shown in present-day Korean *(nun)pola* 'snowstorm', Mongolian *boroɣan* 'rain', and Yakut *burxan* 'snowstorm'. The pA **r^2* corresponds to Manchu-Tungus *r*, Mongolian *r*, Turkic *z*, and Korean *l*, as shown in MK *ilaŋ* 'ridge', Manchu *irun* 'ridge', Mongolian *iraɣa* 'ridge', and Tartar *ɨzan* 'ridge'. The pA **l^1* corresponds to Manchu-Tungus *l*, Mongolian *l*, Turkic *l*, and Korean *l*, as shown in MK *alaj* 'below', Evenki *alas* 'leg', Mongolian *ala* 'groin', and Old Turkish *al* 'below'. Finally, the pA **l^2* corresponds to Manchu-Tungus *l*, Mongolian *l*, Turkic *ʃ*, and Korean *l*, as shown in MK *tulh* 'stone', Mongolian *cilaɣun* 'stone', and Old Turkish *taʃ* 'stone'.

As shown in Ramstedt 1949, a considerable number of putative cognates are shared by the Altaic languages and Korean. K.M. Lee (1958) attempts to demonstrate a close affinity between Manchu and Korean based on a total of 236 lexical sets. K. Hong (1959) presents some lexical correspondences between Mongolian and Korean, while Gim (1968a, 1968b) compares vocabulary (including numerals) of Korean, Japanese, and Altaic languages, and B.H. Kim (1984) makes some Altaic-Korean lexical and morphological comparisons. The following examples from K.M. Lee and others demonstrate several regular consonant correspondences between Manchu (M) and Contemporary Korean (K). Parenthesized forms are either MK or other earlier forms that are reflected in contemporary dialects.

(4) M:K   Manchu   Korean

	Manchu	Korean	
h:k	*holo*	*kol*	'valley'
	halu	*kalu*	'powder'
	hulan	*kul*	'cave'
	hasaha	*kawi* (< *kasikaj*)	'scissors'
s:h	*se*	*ha-*	'to do'
	sonio	*hana*	'one'
	ʃun	*hɛ*(< *hɔj*)	'sun'
f:p	*fatha*	*pal*	'foot'
	fulgijan	*pulk-* (< *pylk-*)	'red'
	fulihe	*p'uli* (< *pulhwi* < *pulɔku*)	'root'
	fusihe	*s'i* (< *psi* < *pisiku*)	'seeds'
m:m	*mulu*	*mø* (< *mɔlɔ*)	'mountain'
	muke	*mul*	'water'
n:n	*ni*	*ni*	'to go'
	na	*nala* (< *na-lah*)	'(M) earth, (K) country'

Some case endings, verbal nominalizers, and other suffixes are also believed to be shared by Korean and Altaic languages. For instance, K.M. Lee (1976:20–2) presumes that the Korean topic-contrast particle *(n)ɨn* 'as for' is related to the Mongolian *-ni* which developed from the post-nominal third-person genitive particles *inu* (singular) and *anu* (plural), and the Korean directional particle *lo* to proto-Altaic **ru/*ry*. He also assumes that the Korean inflectional suffixes *-(ɨ)l* (prospective), *-(ɨ)n* (past relativizer), and *-(ɨ)m* (nominalizer) are the reflexes respectively of the proto-Altaic predicate nominalizers **-r*, **-n*, and **-m*. Lee further assumes that the Middle Korean locative particle *aj/ɘj* and the prosecutive particle *li* (e.g., *ili* 'hither', *tjɘli* 'thither') correspond to the proto-Altaic dative **a/*e* and prosecutive **li*, respectively. Itabashi (1987) presents some Altaic evidence in the Japanese and Korean case system.

H.K. Kim (1972:227–8) relates the Korean 'person' suffix *-chi* (e.g., *i-chi* 'this guy') with Manchu *-ci* (e.g., *caga-ci* 'clerk', *unde-ci* 'errand boy'), Mongolian *-chi* (e.g., *holda-chi* 'merchant', *yam-chi* 'guide'), and Turkish *-ci* (e.g., *karak-ci* 'thief', *ala-ci* 'murderer'). The Korean instrumental nominalizer *-kɛ* (e.g., *c'ip-kɛ* 'tweezers', *pe-kɛ* 'pillow') is regarded as being related to Manchu *-ku,* etc. (e.g., *chiri-ku* 'pillow', *eli-ku* 'broom'), Mongolian *-ge, -gei,* etc. (e.g., *ger-gei* 'wife', *kygy-ge* 'drum'), and Turkish *-ga, -ke,* etc. (e.g., *seber-ga* 'broom', *meik-ke* 'knife').

While a systematic establishment of sound correspondences between Korean and Altaic or proto-Altaic is lacking, the similarities among the languages, not only in many individual lexical items but in various levels of linguistic systems, cannot be ascribed merely to accidental correspondence, genuine borrowing, or pure typology.

In the same vein, many linguists have argued for the Japanese relationship to the Altaic, notably Boller (1857), Prohle (1916–17), Ramstedt (1924), Murayama (1962, 1974), Miller (1971), Street and Miller (1975), Street (1978), and Starostin (1991). Thus, the Altaic origin of Korean and Japanese is a generally accepted hypothesis, although the hypothesis must be further refined and verified. In terms of the number of seeming cognates, it is safe to say that, among the Altaic groups, Manchu-Tungus is the closest to Korean, followed by Mongolian and then Turkish. It must be noted, however, that there are scholars such as Haguenauer (1956), P. Kim (1960), H. Kwon (1962), Kawamoto (1974), and Kiyose (1986) who are sceptical about the affinity.

Many typologically shared features have been cited to relate Korean to Altaic (e.g., Fujioka 1908; Ogura 1935; K.M. Lee 1976). Although typological relationships help support genetic relationships especially when exclusively shared among the languages being compared, they are generally considered of secondary importance in comparative work. Some salient typological features are as follows.

Korean, Japanese, and Altaic languages manifest striking syntactic similarities. The basic word-order common to them is Subject–Object–Verb (SOV). Conforming to the general tendencies of SOV languages, modifiers such as adjectives, adverbs, and conjunctive, relative, and complement clauses precede the elements they modify, while postpositions occur in place of prepositions. In all of these languages, the singular and plural forms of nouns are not strictly distinguished; articles and conjunctions are not developed; no affix exists in adjectives to express the comparative or superlative degree; relative pronouns do not exist; the endings indicating sentence-types such as declarative, interrogative, propositive, and imperative are placed at the end of the sentence; and sentences may consist only of a predicate, with the subject and other cases contextually or situationally understood. Further, possession is expressed by an existential predicate in these languages. For the syntactic parallelism regarding grammatical cases, see J. Sohn 1973.

The morphological structure common to Korean, Japanese, and Altaic languages is agglutinative in that words are formed by adding one or more semantically clear-cut suffixes or particles to an unchanging stem, as illustrated below. The Mongolian example is from B.H. Kim (1984:65).

(5)   Mongolian: *[bari-ldu-ɣa-ci-d]-tur-ijan*   'to his wrestlers'
                               hold-each other-NOM-person-PL-to-his
                               [-----wrestlers----]

         Korean: *[s'il-ɨm-k'un-tɨl]-e-ke-lo*   'to the wrestlers'
                               throw down-NOM-person-PL-to-ANIMATE-to
                               [----wrestlers-----]

At the phonological level, vowel harmony is a shared feature. The Altaic harmony is characterized as both front–back (vertical) harmony and the advancement/retraction of tongue root (+/–ATR) harmony. In Turkic and western Mongolic languages, front-back harmony holds in that front vowels may cooccur only among themselves and so may back vowels, whereas in eastern Mongolic languages and all Tungusic languages, ATR applies. Bing (1996) presents arguments that the canonical Tungusic vowel harmony is characterized by ATR. Middle Korean vowel harmony is diagonal and is subject to ATR. Compare the two types of harmony systems below.

(6)   Mongolian   Middle Korean
           Group 1 (back):   *a, o, u*   Group 1 (low):   *a, o, ɔ*
           Group 2 (front):   *e, ø, y*   Group 2 (high):   *ə, u, ɨ*
           Group 3 (neutral): *i*   Group 3 (neutral): *i*

The high front vowel *i*, termed 'neutral', occurs with both Group 1 and Group 2 vowels. W.J. Kim (1971) proposes that the diagonal scheme of Korean vowel harmony is the result of a 'Great Vowel Shift' from an earlier vertical arrangement similar to the Mongolian type. In view of the fact that Korean is genetically closer to Tungusic than to Mongolian and Turkic languages, however, the simpler assumption is that no such sound changes took place in Korean. For a phonological argument against postulating such a vowel shift, see S.S. Oh 1998a.

Another common phonological feature of Altaic, Japanese, and Korean is the lack of liquid sounds (*r* and *l*) in the initial position of native words. This restriction is so strong that even the initial *l* in Sino-Korean words is bound to change either to ZERO (before *i* or *j*) or *n* (elsewhere), except in northern dialects where the Sino-Korean initial *l* is retained. Lack of initial consonant clusters is a further common typological feature (see 7.3 for sound combination patterns).

Proliferation of sound symbolic expressions is often quoted as a lexical feature common to Altaic, Japanese, and Korean, although such expressions are found across unrelated languages as well. Examples are Manchu *derden-dardan* 'tremblingly', *ger-gar* 'noisily', *her-har* 'thunderingly', and *kekte-kakta* 'unevenly'; Japanese *pikapika* 'sparklingly', *sarasara* 'gently', *zuruzuru* 'slipperily', and *garagara* 'bang, clash'; and Korean *t'alkak-t'alkak* 'clatteringly', *pancil-pancil* 'smoothly', *ulthuŋ-pulthuŋ* 'unevenly', and *sallaŋ-sallaŋ* 'gently' (cf. see 5.3 and H.M. Sohn 1994).

There are many obvious typological differences too. A morphological example is that nouns and verbs in many Altaic languages are inflected according to person and number, although person–number agreement is usually absent in Mongolic. Turkish *kɨr-ɨl-ma-dɨ-lar-mɨ?* 'Were they not broken?' has the suffix *-lar* (3rd person plural actor) and Turkish *ana-m* 'my mother' and *ana-n* 'thy mother' contain *-m* 'my' and *-n* 'thy' respectively (Ohno 1970:112–3). This is a pattern that Korean and Japanese do not generally have, although W. Huh (1983:7) maintains that in Middle Korean there existed vowel alternation in verbal suffixes to indicate grammatical person (see 3.4).

Tentative attempts have been made for subgrouping within Altaic. Without reference to Japanese, Ramstedt (1957:15) views Korean as the fourth member of the Altaic family, along with Turkic, Mongolian, and Manchu-Tungus. Poppe (1960:8, 147), also excluding Japanese, sees in his reconstruction of proto-Altaic indications that proto-Altaic was divided into Old Korean and the language that later diverged into the Chuvash–Turkic unity and the Mongolian–Manchu-Tungus unity.

Street (1962:95) places the oldest ancestor of Korean, and probably also of Japanese and Ainu, as a sister to proto-Altaic, as shown in (7). Poppe, in his foreword to Miller (1971), also indicates this possibility.

(7)

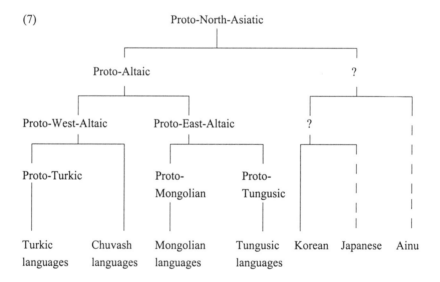

On the other hand, Martin's (1966) account of the Korean–Japanese relationship and his own research on the Altaic elements in Japanese inspired Miller (1971:44–6) to place Korean, Japanese, and Ryukyu (a divergent dialect of Japanese) quite close to the Manchu-Tungus languages, as represented in his diagram (reproduced in (8) with slight modifications). Miller hypothesizes a common heritage for Korean, Japanese, and Ryukyu, despite the fact that Ryukyu is widely regarded as a dialect of Japanese. He believes that the special relationship between this group and Manchu-Tungus, as evidenced in several important shared features, is due to close geographical association or common habitation. He thereby postulates a unity of proto-Northern and Peninsular Altaic (Mathias 1972 provides some comments on Miller's hypothesis).

(8)   Proto-Altaic

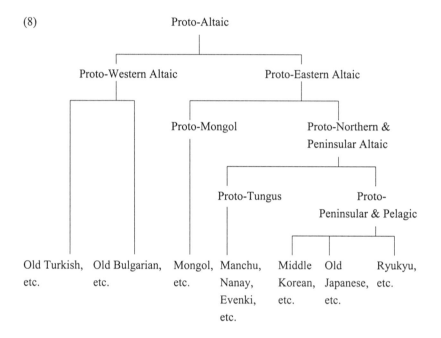

Proto-Western Altaic   Proto-Eastern Altaic

Proto-Mongol   Proto-Northern &
                          Peninsular Altaic

Proto-Tungus   Proto-
                          Peninsular & Pelagic

Old Turkish, Old Bulgarian, Mongol, Manchu,   Middle   Old   Ryukyu,
etc.   etc.   etc.   Nanay,   Korean,   Japanese, etc.
                                       Evenki,   etc.   etc.
                                       etc.

Admitting the prematurity of theorizing on subgrouping, Street and Miller (1975:10) prefer to treat West Altaic (Turkic and Chuvash), Mongolian, Tungus, Korean, and Japanese as coordinate descendants of proto-Altaic. Similarly, Starostin (1991) classifies Altaic languages into the same five language groups. For an extensive survey of the present state of the comparative study of Korean and the Altaic languages, see B. Seong 1997.

2.3   Austronesian and Dravidian hypotheses

In addition to the Altaic hypothesis, suggestions have been made for a genetic affiliation of Korean to Austronesian languages on the one hand and to Dravidian languages on the other. The Austronesian linguistic family, consisting of Indonesian, Melanesian, Polynesian, and Micronesian groups, embraces over five hundred languages spoken in the great archipelagos of the Pacific and Indian Oceans, ranging between Madagascar to the west, Easter Island to the east, Formosa to the north, and New Zealand to the south. Dempwolff (1934, 1937, 1938) provides a reconstructed sound system for proto-Austronesian, a reconstructed vocabulary of over two thousand words, and an analysis of sound correspondences between his proto-Austronesian and eleven daughter languages, thus furnishing a sound basis for comparative Austronesian linguistics.

While many authors have argued strongly for the Austronesian hypothesis with regard to Japanese, only a few scholars have suggested an affiliation of Korean to Austronesian languages. Indeed, Japanese shares some obvious phonological and lexical similarities with Oceanic languages, although with conspicuous disparity in syntax: open syllables, lack of consonant clusters, and, above all, quite a few putative cognate sets. For instance, Polivanov (1918, 1960) regards Japanese as a hybrid language made up of Altaic, Austronesian, and some undetermined elements. For 113 Japanese lexical items, Matsumoto (1928, 1948) presents Austronesian words thought to resemble them in form and meaning, and a set of eight sound correspondences based on his lexicon. Izui (1953), after associating a large number of Japanese words to Austronesian forms and establishing the sound correspondences therein, speculates that a southern language was already being spoken in Japan when a northern one entered. Ohno (1970) maintains essentially the same view on the basis of the available anthropological, archaeological, and linguistic data. He concludes that an Altaic language came to be spoken in Japan in the Yayoi period (200 BC – 250 AD) some 2,000 years ago, while an Austronesian language had been spoken in the Jomon period (until 200 BC). That is, with the introduction of the Yayoi culture that brought weaving, rice cultivation, bronze tools, and ironware, the language of southern Korea, with its dominant Altaic characteristics, began to be spoken in North Kyushu and subsequently spread east to Honshu and south to the Ryukyu islands. Ohno (ibid.:143–4) ascribes the presence of considerable Austronesian elements in the Japanese vocabulary to his assumption that the new language (i.e., the language from Korea) was unable to replace all of the native words, although it imposed its grammatical structure on the native language. He further speculates that Korean also had already absorbed quite a few Austronesian words before it was brought into Japan.

Murayama (1974, 1976), originally a strong proponent of the Altaic connections of Japanese, argues that Japanese is to be viewed as a 'mixed language' whose major structural elements consist of Austronesian and Altaic. He rejects, for instance, Shinmura's (1935) claim that the Austronesian elements in Japanese are simply loan words and also the prevalent view (e.g., Kindaichi, et al. 1951) that Austronesian elements constitute a linguistic substratum in Japanese upon which an Altaic superstratum was predominantly imposed. Presenting seventy-nine proto-Austronesian (PA) forms for which he claims to be able to establish Japanese reflexes, Murayama (1976:419, 432–5) claims that a much larger portion of the Japanese vocabulary is of the Austronesian origin. Some of his PA and Old Japanese (OJ) correspondence sets are: PA *apui : OJ *fï* 'fire'; PA *bakul : OJ *fako* 'basket, box';

PA *baji* : OJ *fafa* 'mother'; PA *buŋa* : OJ *fana* 'flower'; PA *papah* : OJ *fa* 'leaf'; PA *put'əg'* : OJ *fɔsɔ* 'navel'; PA *putih* : OJ *futi* 'white'; PA *kahui* : OJ *kɨ* 'tree'; PA *taŋan* : OJ *ta-* 'hand'; PA *inum* : OJ *nɔmi* 'drink'; PA *namnam* : OJ *namè* 'taste'; PA *mata* : OJ *ma-* 'eye'; PA *ivak* : OJ *iwo* 'fish'; and PA *vat'a* : OJ *wata* 'ocean'. Murayama also attempts to establish some tentative phonological correspondences between proto-Indonesian and Old Japanese, illustrates the parallelism in verb formation between Indonesian languages and Old Japanese, and points out that at least ten of Martin's (1966) proto-Korean–Japanese forms are shared also by Austronesian languages. He regards, for instance, Japanese *abura* 'fat, cooking oil' and *abur-u* 'broil, boil' as related to PA *apui* 'fire' to which he believes the Tungus verbal aorist suffix *-ra* was attached. He also links OJ *fako* 'box' and Middle Korean *pakuloi* 'basket' to PA *bakul* 'basket'. Murayama's view of the development of Japanese is that the Austronesian elements encountered a Tungus group somewhere in the northern part of Kyushu; and in the course of this encounter, the Austronesian elements were grammatically restructured.

Kawamoto (1974, 1977) attempts to establish a set of rules of phonological correspondences between Japanese and Austronesian by modifying and further elaborating Izui's (1953). Kawamoto undertakes some morphological comparisons, and collects several hundred Old Japanese words paired with look-alikes in proto-Austronesian or one of its branches. Refuting the Altaic hypothesis of Japanese and the Japanese–Korean relationship as unacceptable in view of 'the scarcity of lexical cognates and the lack of reliable sound correspondences', Kawamoto (e.g., 1974:127–8) suggests that Japanese is a creolized language formed from a pidgin of an Austronesian language superimposed on a Subject–Object–Verb language. Kawamoto is undecided whether this SOV language was an Altaic language, Ainu, an ancient Korean language, or some other language.

The foregoing observations lead us to conclude that while an Austronesian stratum is quite dense in Japanese, any hypothesis associating Korean to Austronesian is premature in view of the lack of persuasive phonological, lexical, or grammatical evidence. For instance, most of the putative cognate sets that have been proposed for Austronesian and Japanese (e.g., those for 'hand', 'eye', 'drink', 'tree', and 'leaf') do not have reflexes in Korean. Only a very small number of proto-Austronesian forms (e.g., 'ocean', 'fire', and 'basket') appear to resemble the corresponding Korean forms (e.g., *pata* 'sea', *pul* 'fire', and *pakuli* 'basket').

We mentioned at the beginning of this section that as early as 1905 Hulbert proposed the existence of a genetic relationship between Korean and Dravidian languages in view of their shared grammatical features. Recently, Ohno (1981) has advanced an interesting hypothesis that in Japanese and Korean there is yet another stratum between those of Altaic and Austronesian. It is the stratum of Tamil, one of the four Dravidian languages currently spoken in southern India. The original homeland of the Dravidian people was along the Indus River in northern India. He presents some 400 pairs of seeming Japanese–Tamil lexical correspondences, covering basic verbs, body parts, kinship terms, emotion words, farming and weaving terms, as well as many similar typological features. Based on certain Austronesian, Tamil, and Altaic cutural features, including farming practices, that are found in Japan, Ohno postulates the following linguistic layers in Japanese: (a) an Austronesian language was spoken in Japan in the early stages of the Jomon period (until 200 BC); (b) Tamil people migrated into southern Korea and Kyushu in the early and middle stages of the Jomon period; and (c) an Altaic people came to northern Kyushu from Korea in the Yayoi period (200 BC – 250 AD), pushing the native Tamil people to the east and south, where he finds more Japanese–Tamil lexical correspondences.

Clippinger (1984) proposes a Korean–Dravidian connection by presenting 408 putative cognates and some 60 phonological correspondence pairs. For the lexical comparison, Clippinger uses the earliest attested forms (generally Middle Korean forms) for Korean words and the entries in Burrow and Emeneau (1966) for the words of Dravidian languages (including reconstructed proto-Dravidian forms). His observation that some cognates are very close while others suggest a much earlier link leads him to speculate that Korean and Dravidian shared a common heritage at a very ancient period and that this heritage was reinforced much later by migration to the Korean peninsula, presumably in the later years of the first millennium BC. Some of the vocabulary sets that Clippinger considers cognates are given below in IPA transcriptions. Reconstructed forms are marked by *.

(9)   Korean (early forms)   Dravidian
        al 'grain'   *ari* 'grain'
        ama-, əmə- 'mother'   *amma* 'mother'
        ənni 'older sibling'   *anni* 'older brother, female'
        **əraha* 'king'   *eraja* 'king, master'
        cəc 'breasts'   *caci* 'breasts'
        kal- 'plow, cultivate'   **kar-* 'dig'
        kalaj 'phlegm'   *karaja* 'phlegm'
        kalɨchi- 'teach'   **kalc-* 'teach'
        kalɔl 'foot, leg'   *karal* 'foot'
        kolani 'deer, elk'   *kuran* 'hog deer'
        kolɨm 'pus'   *kollum* 'pus'
        kuɲtuɲi 'buttocks'   *kunti* 'buttocks'
        kjəlɔj 'kindred relations'   **kelai* 'kindred relations'
        kɨli- 'draw'   **kiru-* 'draw, scratch'

mancaɲi 'big boat'	*manci* 'cargo boat'
mo 'seedling'	*mola* 'seedling'
mok 'neck'	*mak* 'neck'
molo 'mountain'	*mala-* 'mountain, forest'
məl 'urine, feces'	*mollu* 'urine'
məj 'shoulder'	*muj* 'shoulder'
pat- 'receive'	**pat-* 'acquire, obtain'
phɨl 'grass'	*pul* 'grass'
pi 'rain'	*pej* 'rain'
psi 'seed'	*bici* 'seed'
pəjam 'snake'	*pampu* 'snake'
pəl 'bee'	*pera* 'bee'
sola 'pot, bowl'	*sola* 'earthen pot'
tal- 'burn'	**tar-* 'be hot, burn'
tali 'leg'	*tal* 'leg, thigh'
tanti 'pot'	*tanti* 'medium size pot, jar'
tolaci 'Chinese bellflower'	*tolaci* 'sacred basil'
toljən 'husband's brother'	*toren* 'younger brother'
tɔl 'moon'	*til* 'moon'
tɨl- 'enter'	**tur-* 'enter'
uthɨj 'clothes'	*utai* 'clothes'

As for syntactic similarities, Clippinger points out that in both Korean and Dravidian, there are two main word classes (nouns and verbs); nominal particles and verbal suffixes specify syntactic and other relations; particles are postpositional; modifiers always precede the modified words; word-formation is agglutinative; the basic word-order is SOV; nominal and adjectival phrases are formed in similar ways; etc. Clippinger also presents some similar phonological patterns. Despite arguments to the contrary (e.g., Murayama 1982), the Dravidian hypothesis deserves further investigation in view of the large number of lexical look-alikes and many interesting typological similarities.

2.4   Genetic linkage between Korean and Japanese

A genetic link, however remote, between Korean and Japanese (including the Ryukyu dialect) is widely accepted. Notwithstanding scepticism (e.g., Haguenauer 1956, H. Kwon 1962, Kawamoto 1974), a sizable number of shared cognates, partially attested phonological correspondences, and some already obvious uniquely shared morphological, syntactic, and semantic characteristics support the existence of a genetic relationship. Some Korean linguists offer arguments in favour of the supposition that Korean may be more closely related to Altaic languages than to Japanese, but available evidence appears to indicate that the two languages are closer to one another than to any other language.

The common origin of Korean and Japanese was proposed as early as 1717 by Arai Hakuseki, a Tokugawa Confucian, and again in 1781 by Fujii Teikan, a pioneer of modern archaeology in Japan (Miller 1967:61–2; Hattori 1974:36). But it is Aston (1879) who first made a serious comparative study exclusively of Japanese and Korean. He attempted to set up some ten consonant correspondences on the basis of approximately seventy lexical items, as well as by comparing the Chinese sounds borrowed in Japanese with those borrowed in Korean. Aston also points out similarities in grammatical categories and word-formational characteristics. Later his views were methodologically refined and expanded by other Japanese scholars such as Ooya (1889), Shiratori (1897), and Kanazawa (1910). In particular Kanazawa, whose study was partly politically motivated, claimed that Korean and the native language of the Ryukyu Islands are branches of Japanese. Some of the 146 lexical pairs he presented as cognates are: J *ba* : K *pa* 'place'; J *ha* 'tooth' : K *p'jə* 'bone'; J *a* : K *a* 'I'; J *na* : K *nə* 'you'; J *ka* : K *kɨ* 'he, she, it'; J *kati* : K *kət* 'walk'; J *kah-u* 'buy' : K *kap* 'price'; J *kata* : K *kjət* 'side'; and J *kata* : K *kut* 'hard'. Though they may be important contributions to scholarship, Kanazawa's lexical comparisons are linguistically unappealing in that they are not based on regular phonological correspondences. He also proposes correspondences in word-formation and some fifteen grammatical markers.

Ramstedt (1949, 1952, 1957), who contributed greatly to the comparison of Korean and Japanese with Altaic, was very cautious in defending linguistic affinity between the two languages. So have been many other linguists, including Ogura (1920, 1935), Shinmura (1935), Kono (1949), Hattori (1974), and B.H. Kim (1981, 1984). Their caution arises mainly from the incompleteness of available evidence. On the other hand, scholars like Ohno (1970) postulate a close relationship between Japanese and Korean, as mentioned earlier.

The most significant breakthrough is no doubt the work of Martin (1966) who systematically compares 320 sets of seeming cognates, reconstructs their hypothetical protoforms, establishes the proto-Korean–Japanese (*KJ) phonemic system, includes suprasegmental features (pitch accents), and provides phonological rules of correspondences. Let us observe some of Martin's consonant correspondences below, with irrelevant information omitted and Korean phonemic transcriptions slightly modified to conform to the IPA system adopted in this book. In Middle Korean (MK), prime (ʹ) and double prime (ʺ) indicate high and low-rising pitch accents, respectively, while in Modern Korean, double prime indicates vowel length. The

Japanese and proto-Korean–Japanese pitch accents are marked on the vowels concerned. While the Korean words used are modern and available Middle (15th century) Korean forms, most of the Japanese words used are modern or slightly antiquated forms, where, for instance, the modern *h* is written as the old *p* (> *hw* > *h*).

(10)

*KJ	K:J	*KJ	K	J
*p...	p:p	*pal(j)i 'bee'	"pəl, MK pəli	pati
		*pɔlɤ 'blow'	pul- < MK pɨl-<*pɔl-	púk-
		*pudje 'brush'	pus < MK 'put	pude
		*pör(a)- 'desire'	pala- < MK 'pɔ'la-	OJ por-
		*pataxje 'field'	path < MK path	patake
		*pjal 'fire'	pul < MK 'pɨl	pí
		*parjɔl 'needle'	panɨl < MK palɔl	pári
		*pár- 'paste it'	palɨ- < pɔlɔ-	par-
		*par(a) 'plain'	pəl	pára
		*pJezji 'star'	"pjəl	posi
		*párja 'stomach'	pɛ < MK 'pɔj	pará
*...b(...)	p:b	*tabal 'bunch'	tapal	tába
		*sjibxa 'brushwood'	səph, MK səp	siba
		*ɟörökeb- 'enjoy'	cɨlkəp-	jorokób-
*...mp(...)	p:m	*txumpje 'claw'	MK thop	tume
		*nɔmpxa 'marsh'	nɨph	numá
		*cump- 'pick up'	"cup-	tum-
		*pɔlmp- 'tread'	palp- < MK "pɔlp	pum-
*m...	m:m	*mjom 'body'	mom < MK 'mom	mi
		*mats(a)- 'correct'	mac- < MK mac-	masa
		*mazu 'measure'	mal < MK 'mal	masú
		*mac- 'meet'	mac- < MK mac-	mát-
		*máxj- 'tie up'	"mɛ- < MK mɔj-	mak-
*v...	p:#	*vazji 'foot'	pal < MK 'pal	así
		*válk(a)- 'red'	pulk- < MK pɔlk-	aka-
*k...	k:k	*kuma 'bear'	"kom < MK "kom	kumá
		*kani 'crab'	ke < kəj	kani
		*kez 'filter it'	kəlɨ-	kos-
		*kalɤ 'hang'	"kəl-	kák(e)-
		*kwat(a)- 'hard'	kut-	kata-
		*kazji 'oak'	kal	kási
		*kes 'thing'	kəs < MK kəs	kotó
		*kura 'valley'	kol < MK "kol	kura

*...ɣ...	h:g	*taɣja 'hoop'	the < MK 'thəj	tagá
		*tsáɣats- 'look for'	chac- < MK 'chɔc-	sagas-
*Cx	Ch:C	*sjibxa 'brushwood'	səph, MK səp	siba
		*txumpje 'claw'	thop	tume
		*txexe 'place'	thə < MK 'thə	toko
		*bxɔr- 'sell'	phal- < MK 'phəl-	(w)ur-
		*cxumba 'spittle'	chim < MK 'chum	tubá
*t...	t:t	*tɔrj- 'accompany'	tali- < MK tɔ'li-	tur(e)-
		*tɔx- 'arrive'	"tah-, MK tah-	túk-
		*taxje 'bamboo'	tɛ < MK 'taj	take
		*törkji 'chicken'	talk < MK tɔlk	tori
		*töd- 'close it'	tat- < MK tat-	tód(i)-
		*tɔr- 'hang'	tal- < MK tɔl-	tur(e)-
		*tɔm- 'heap'	"tam- < MK tɔm-	tum-
		*tör- 'hold'	tɨl-	tór-
		*tɔlɣji 'moon'	tal < MK 'tɔl	tukí
		*tö 'place'	-te < təj < MK tɔ(j)	do < -to
*n	n:n	*nöz 'carry'	nalɨ < nɔlɔ-	nos(e)-
		*nɔmpxa 'marsh'	nɨph	numá
		*nJalɔm 'summer'	jəlɨm< MK njə(')lɔm	natú
*d...	t:j	*djar- 'enter'	tɨl- < MK 'tɨl-	jir-
		*dar- 'give'	"tal-	jar-
		*djoz 'stone'	'tol < MK "tolh	jisí
*c...	c:t	*cjic(ji) 'breasts'	cəc	tití
		*cál- 'cut off'	calɨ-<MK cɔlɨ-	tát-
		*cur(u) 'string'	cul	turú
		*car(a)- 'suffice'	cala-<MK 'cɔla-	tar(i)-
		*cekji 'time'	-cək<MK cək	tokí
*ts...	c:s	*tsuldji 'line'	cul	súdi
		*tsáɣats- 'look for'	chac- < MK 'chɔc-	sagas-
		*tsxjori 'tail'	MK choli	sirí
*ɟ...	c:j	*ɟipje 'house'	cip < MK cip	jipê
		*ɟörökeb- 'enjoy'	cɨlkəp-	jorokób-
*r...	l:r	*parjɔl 'needle'	panɨl < MK palɔl	pári
		*bar(j)- 'split open'	palɨ-< 'pɔli-	war-
		*erj(o)- 'stupid'	əli- < MK ə'li-	óro-ka
		*párj- 'sweep away'	pəli- < MK pɔ'li-	paráp-
*...l...	l:t	*pal(j)i 'bee'	"pəl, MK pəli	pati
		*palál 'sea'	MK palɔl	OJ wata

...lɣ...	*l:k*	**swalɣje* 'liquor'	*sul* < MK *suɨl*	*sake*
		*kwalɣji 'oyster'	*kul* < MK *'kul*	*kaki*
...ɹ(...)	*l:j*	**keɹ* 'fertile'	*kəl-*	*kój(e)-*
		*piɹòm 'pigweed'	*pilɨm* < MK *pilɔm*	*píju*
		*puɹ- 'swell'	*pul-/pulɨ* < MK *pɨlɨ-*	*púj(e)-*
*s...	*s:s*	**(a-)sam* 'hemp'	*sam* < MK *sam*	*asa*
		*sJjima 'island'	*"səm* < MK *"sjəm*	*sima*
		*sarja 'new'	*sɛ* < MK *'saj*	*sára*
		*sJebxa 'side'	*jəph* <*sjəph	*sóba*
		*salpji 'spade'	*sap* < MK *'salp*	OJ *sapi*
*z...	*l:s*	**nöz-* 'carry'	*nalɨ-* <**nɔlɔ-*	*nos(e)-*
		*mazu 'measure'	*mal* < MK *'mal*	*masú*
		*kuzja 'stinking'	*kuli-*	*kusá-/kúsa-*
		*pJezji 'star'	*"pjəl*	*posi*
		*xezi 'waist'	*həli* < MK *hə'li*	*kosi*

Martin's work has provided a new footing not only for Korean–Japanese comparative linguists but also for those who attempt to relate Korean and Japanese to Altaic or some other language families, as evidenced in Miller 1971. On the other hand, some alternative solutions to or criticisms of certain aspects of Martin's work have been advanced by Miller (1971), Osada (1972), K.M. Lee (1973), Mathias (1973), and Sato (1974), among others. Martin's treatment of protovowels has received much criticism. For instance, Japanese *a* corresponds to as many as six different Korean vowels. Another comment is on his matching of Korean *l* to Japanese *r, t, k,* and *s*. Also, Martin's selection of the lexical items that are compared is called into question by some authors. It is also pointed out that Martin's method is too mechanical, with the reconstructions appearing somewhat unrealistic (e.g., his **mp* and **mb* are 'non-Altaic' and **J* is not realistic). K.M. Lee's (ibid.) comment is that without introducing other Altaic languages into the comparison of Korean and Japanese as checks, we can neither achieve comprehensive reconstructions nor guarantee the legitimacy of any reconstruction. Moreover, as K.M. Lee maintains and Martin (1975) himself admits, a major shortcoming of his work is that the comparisons were based not on the oldest forms of the languages nor on reconstructed proto-Korean and proto-Japanese, but largely on the modern or late premodern forms. In spite of such weaknesses, Martin's conclusions are generally regarded as valid.

Martin (1968a) also looked into several grammatical elements that are likely to have a common origin, including subject and genitive particles, infinitive and other suffixes, and interrogatives. Furthermore, Martin (1975) claims that the most striking similarity between Korean and Japanese, which is not shared by any other Altaic language, is the many common features in their accentual systems. He maintains that the accent patterns for proto-Korean and proto-Japanese can be reconstructed with reasonable accuracy from some modern dialects as well as from available philological records dating back to the fifteenth century for Korean and to the twelfth century for Japanese. As will be observed in 3.4, Middle Korean had three significant tones (low, high, and rising), whereas Japanese has two significant pitch accents (low and high). Observing that a number of rising-tone words of Middle Korean go back to disyllables, Martin suggests that interpreting the Middle Korean rising tone as a result of the application of pitch accents to long vowels would make the Korean accentual patterns look very similar to those of Japanese. As one may conclude, however, the fact that Korean and Japanese have common accentual features does not contribute to their external genetic relationship unless Altaic or other putatively related linguistic families are proven to have had a similar accentual system.

Another strong defender of the kinship of Korean and Japanese is Osada (1972) who claims that both languages belong to a branch of 'Ancient Altaic' while admitting the presence of Oceanic elements in the Japanese language and people. S. Kim (1974) presents some 1,270 pairs of lexical look-alikes, but due to his speculative method, his work does little to prove the relationship. N.D. Lee 1985–6 provides an extensive etymological study comparing Korean with Japanese and Altaic languages.

Whitman (1985a) compares Korean and Japanese based on results from an internal historical study of Middle Korean and Old Japanese sound patterns. Whitman analyses correspondences in vowels, consonants, and accents, presenting 352 lexical correspondence sets that illustrate his reconstructed proto-Korean–Japanese phonemes. He claims that the main problem areas of Korean–Japanese comparative linguistics (i.e., the vowel system and the sources of aspiration and spirantization in Middle Korean) provide strong support for the existence of a genetic relationship between the two languages once they are examined through rigorous internal reconstruction. Many of his putative cognate pairs are shared by Martin (1966), but he also introduces many new ones which are not in Martin's list. For comments on Whitman's treatment of vowels, see Serafim 1994.

Both Martin and Whitman include some pairs which are earlier borrowings from Chinese. For instance, from MK *cək* and OJ *toki* 'time', Martin and Whitman reconstruct *JK *cekji* and *cek*, respectively. Both Korean and Japanese forms must have developed from Middle Chinese *tieg* (cf. J. Shim 1983:51). Similarly, their *taxje* (Martin) and *tagi* (Whitman) reconstructed from MK *taj* and OJ *take* seem to be related to Middle Chinese *tjek*. Martin's *pudje* from MK *put* and OJ *pude* 'calligraphy brush' must have derived from Middle Chinese *piət* (cf. J. Shim ibid.).

Obviously, an extensive search for reliable regular sound correspondences is the surest way to prove a genetic relationship of the languages compared. This task is not an easy one, however, if the two languages diverged long ago, followed by frequent contacts with other languages. Forms and meanings constantly change, and loan words from all sources and substratal elements not only destroy the original sound patterns but replace native or superstratal words. This is the case with Korean and Japanese, which are assumed to have been separated for several thousand years. Ohno (1970) postulates about 2,300 years of divergence, while Hattori (1974) estimates at least 4,700 years. The two languages must have independently absorbed a large number of external elements through early contacts with various languages. See Hattori ibid. for some Ainu elements in Japanese and B.H. Kim 1976 for Gilyak (also named Nivkh) elements in Korean. See earlier pages of this chapter for a discussion of Austronesian and Dravidian elements.

Although a portion of the plausible Korean–Japanese cognate pairs may be either external or mutual borrowings, we cannot deny the existence of a genetic relationship given the correspondences in so many content words and a sizable number of functors such as J *i* : K *i* 'this'; J *ka* : K *ka* (question particle); J *tati* : K *tɨl* (plural particle); and J *-i, -mi, -ku* : K *-i, -m, -ki* (nominalizer suffixes) (e.g., Ohno 1970:129–31; K.M. Lee 1976:25). K.M. Lee (1963, 1976) regards Old Japanese as manifesting a remarkable relationship with the Kokwulye language spoken in Manchuria and the northern part of Korea before and around the beginning of the Christian era. There is some linguistic and archaeological evidence to suggest that the Yayoi culture (characterized by rice farming) was brought by the ancestors of Kokwulye to northern Kyushu in Japan. According to K.M. Lee, *Samkwuk Saki* contains some eighty Kokwulye words which may be compared with thirty-four Old Japanese, thirty-one Middle Korean, seventeen Tungus, and thirteen Mongol and Turkish words (cf. Lewin 1976:408). K.M. Lee (1976:34–5) postulates the following correspondences.

(11)

Kokwulye language	Old Japanese	
i	*ir-*	'enter'
mie	*midu*	'water'
nua	*na*	'earth'
nuami 'sea, pond'	*nami*	'wave'
namar	*namari*	'lead'
tan, tuan	*tani*	'valley'
kuc	*kuti*	'mouth'
nanən	*nana-*	'seven'
tək	*tɔwo*	'ten'
mir	*mi-*	'three'
ɨc	*itu-*	'five'
usaxam	*wusagi*	'rabbit'

The wall paintings of Takamatsuzuka tomb (late seventh to early eighth century) located in the southern hills of Asuka, Nara Prefecture in Japan, are known to be similar to those found in Kokwulye graves of the fifth century. A portion of the wall paintings on the east wall of the tomb (excavated in 1972) shows that a group of four women, thought to represent mourners, are dressed in jackets and pleated skirts of the Kokwulye type.

K.M. Lee (ibid.) and others assume that the predecessor of proto-Japanese and the Kokwulye language is the language of Pu.ye (100 BC – 200 AD), a dominant state in Manchuria before the Christian era. Together with the Samhan (Three Korean Han States) language(s) of the southern part of Korea, Pu.ye is viewed as having descended from an early branch of the Altaic family. The Three Kingdoms (Sinla, Paykcey, and Kokwulye) succeeded the Samhan states in the first century of our era, and subsequently Sinla unified Korea. The other old Korean languages or dialects are assumed to have either become extinct or been incorporated into the Sinla language, which was essentially the predecessor of Contemporary Korean.

B.H. Kim (1984:135–7), on the other hand, proposes that there existed in central and southern Korea a genetically undetermined linguistic substratum upon which the Altaic stratum was superimposed. Kim terms this substratum Primitive Peninsular Korean and maintains that it contained 'non-Altaic' numeral forms such as *mir* 'three', *ic* 'five', *nanɔn* 'seven', and *tɔk* 'ten'. This proposal is a significant challenge to K.M. Lee who consider these numeral forms fragments of the Kokwulye language, an Altaic descendant.

The circumstances observed thus far in regard to the genetic affiliation of Korean call for continued careful etymological investigations, covering not only material from Japanese and Korean, but that from their neighbouring languages as well. At the same time, attention must be directed to hitherto largely neglected areas such as the comparison of morphological and syntactic features and grammaticalization processes. For instance, Martin (1995) argues that the modern systems of Korean and Japanese verb endings have developed by incorporating certain auxiliary stems and delexicalized nouns, and many of these have etymologies that are shared by both languages. K.C. Kim 1995 is a study of phonological, lexical, and grammatical similarities between Korean and Japanese in comparison with Ainu. On the basis of verbal and nominal morphology Vovin (1997) attempts to demonstrate that Tungusic, Korean, and Japanese are genetically related. If we codify a sufficiently large number of uniquely shared morpho-syntactic innovations, we will have a much stronger ground on which to reconstruct a genetic relationship. The genetic affinity between Japanese and Korean and their relationship to other languages are problems to be tackled from all possible directions.

3

Historical development

This chapter deals with the historical development of the Korean language based on written records. Since the overall picture of the structure and lexicon of the language became much clearer only after abundant data became available from the fifteenth century due to the invention of Hankul (the Korean alphabet), emphasis is naturally placed on the evolution made during the past five hundred years. All Korean linguistic data appearing in this chapter are transcribed in IPA symbols.

3.1 Bird's-eye view of Korean history

As described in many works on Korean history (e.g., K.B. Lee 1984; A. Nahm 1993), archaeological findings suggest that Paleolithic people first came to Korea over 30,000 years ago and the Neolithic culture emerged in the Korean peninsula around 6000 BC. The Neolithic period was followed by the Bronze Age around 1200 BC. According to *Samkwuk Yusa* (Memorabilia of the Three Kingdoms) written by the Buddhist monk Il.yen in 1285, Ancient Cosen, one of the first tribal leagues of the Bronze culture, was established in 2333 BC by the legendary king Tankwun in northern Korea and southwestern Manchuria. Ancient Cosen is subdivided into three periods: the Tankwun Cosen, the Kica Cosen, and the Wiman Cosen periods. According to *Samkwuk Yusa*, the Kica Cosen period was initiated around 1120 BC by Kica, a scion of the fallen Shang Dynasty of China who fled to Ancient Cosen; and the Wiman Cosen period was begun around 194 BC by Wiman, a Chinese military leader of Yen who fled to Ancient Cosen and usurped the throne. Ancient Cosen dominated the territory between the Liao River in southern Manchuria and the Taytong River in central North Korea until Emperor Wu of the Han dynasty in China invaded Wiman's Ancient Cosen and placed the new territory under his administrative control in 108 BC.

By the fourth century, there existed Tungusic tribal states such as Pu.ye on the Sungari River in Manchuria, Kokwulye on the Thwungcia River (a tributary of the Yalu), Okce on the plains of Hamhung in the northeastern part of the peninsula, and

Yeymayk along the eastern coast south of Okce, while in the regions south of the Han River, Mahan was in the west, Cinhan in the east, and Pyenhan in the south. These three tribal leagues are called Samhan (Three Korean Han States). Among the northern tribal nations, Kokwulye (37 BC – 668 AD) matured into a kingdom, conquering and annexing Pu.ye, Okce, and Yeymayk. Kokwulye also routed the Chinese in 313 AD and put an end to their 400-year colonial rule over Ancient Cosen. By this time, Kokwulye bordered Paykcey (18 BC – 660 AD) to the south, a kingdom founded by immigrants from Kokwulye who controlled the Mahan tribes. Kokwulye also faced to the south the Sinla kingdom (57 BC – 935 AD) which was founded on the Cinhan region. On Pyenhan soil, a group of six small states called Ka.ya (42 AD – 562 AD) prevailed, but they were eventually subjugated to Sinla. Kokwulye, Paykcey, and Sinla are referred to as the Three Kingdoms.

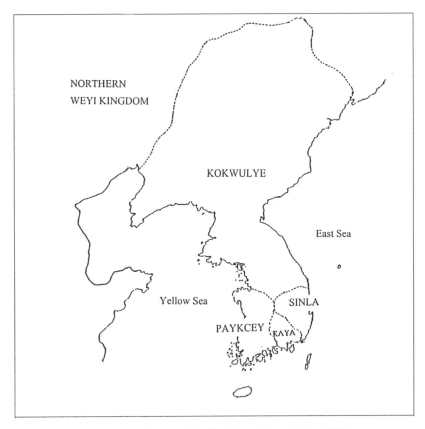

Map 1 Three Kingdoms Period, ca. 450 AD (adapted from Nahm 1993)

Chinese culture had a great impact on the Three Kingdoms and Japan. The Three Kingdoms successfully assimilated Chinese culture with their own traditions. Envoys, political refugees, and emigrants from the Three Kingdoms, especially from Paykcey, contributed greatly to the early Japanese civilization and culture by transmitting Chinese literature, Buddhism, farming methods, weaving, medicine, painting, and music to the Japanese people.

Sinla subjugated Kokwlye and Paykcey, unifying the Korean peninsula as a single political entity in 668 AD, with a territory including only Phyengyang and Wensan to the north. The Kolye dynasty (918–1392), which succeeded Sinla, restored part of the former territories once possessed by Kokwulye, expanding the northern frontier as far as the Yalu River on the western coast and including most of today's South Hamkyeng Province on the eastern coast. The English name Korea is derived from the Kolye dynasty.

Kolye was succeeded by the Cosen dynasty (1392–1910). It was during the reign of King Seycong (1397–1450) that the northern frontier was expanded to the Tumen River on the eastern coast, thus establishing Korea's borders where they remain today. In 1910, Japan annexed Korea, putting an end to the Cosen dynasty. The Japanese occupation lasted for thirty-five years, until 1945 when the Second World War ended. Subsequently, Korea gained her independence but was divided into North and South Korea.

3.2   Evolvement of Korean

The nature of the Korean language prior to the period of the Kokwulye kingdom in the north and the Samhan states (Mahan, Cinhan, and Pyenhan) in the south of the Korean peninsula is difficult to access due to a lack of written materials. The few fragmentary records lead us to believe that the Kokwulye language was Tungusic, along with the languages of Pu.ye, Okce, and Yeymayk; that the languages of the Samhan states in the southern part of the peninsula were merely dialects of each other; and that Kokwulye and other northern languages (called the Pu.ye group by K.M. Lee 1976) on the one hand and the Samhan languages on the other were considerably different. The few records are contained in Weyi Chih (Records of Weyi, written by Chen Shou in the third century), Houhan Shu (History of Later Chinese Han, written by Fan Yeh in the latter half of the fifth century), and Chou Shu (History of Chou, compiled at the beginning of the seventh century). According to Chou Shu, the language of the dominating class of Paykcey, who were Kokwulye people, was not the same as that of the commoners, who were Mahan people. This indicates that there was a noticeable difference between the languages of the northern group to which Kokwulye belonged and those of the southern group which consisted of the Samhan states. Based on the remark in Weyi Chih that the language of the tribe called Sushen in the northern part of the continent was considerably different from the languages of the northern group (Kokwulye, Pu.ye, etc.), K.M. Lee (1976:30) assumes that the Sushen language belonged to Manchu-Tungus, further speculating that the northern group had already diverged from Manchu-Tungus languages around the beginning of the Christian era. It is widely held that the Sushen tribe is the ancestor of the Yojin (Jurchen) tribe. The terms Sushen, Yojin, Nüchen, and Jurchen might have been derived from the same word that refers to the same Manchurian tribe.

Scanty records, such as the *Samkwuk Saki* (1145) and *Samkwuk Yusa* (1285), allow a glimpse of the nature of the Sinla language and lead us to regard Contemporary Korean as the descendant of the language of Unified Sinla and the succeeding dynasties. The language of Unified Sinla is assumed to have been composed mainly of the Samhan dialects with very little influence from the northern languages. In support of this assumption, H.K. Kim (1972:21–2) advances the following points.

(1)   a. The fragments of the Sinla language that are contained in existing records are reflected in present-day Korean. For instance, the name of a Sinla king *julinisakɨm*, which appears in *Samkwuk Saki*, is interpreted as *nuli* 'world' and *nimkɨm* 'king'.

           b. Many northern place names reflect the Kokwulye language and are related not to present-day Korean but to the Manchu language.

           c. There is no record indicating that Sinla's unification of the Three Kingdoms was impeded by difficulty in communication among the three peoples, suggesting that their languages were mutually intelligible.

           d. Since Unified Sinla was comprised of the region south of the Taytong River and South Hamkyeng Province, the people who occupied the area north of this borderline are assumed to have spoken the Kokwulye language.

The few records of the language of the Kolye dynasty that succeeded Unified Sinla include *Kyun.ye Cen* (1075) and *Kyeylim Yusa* (a book listing 350 Kolye words, 1103–4). However, the detailed structures of the languages of Kokwulye, Sinla, and Kolye are extremely difficult to ascertain since all the old records are not only scanty but also written in Chinese characters.

It is with the creation of Hankul in the Cosen dynasty during the fifteenth century that the structure of the Korean language began to reveal itself fairly accurately. The large amount of material written in Hankul over the past five centuries enables linguists to observe the evolvement of the language. In particular, the structure of fifteenth century Korean has been revealed through literature published during the fifteenth century. *Yongpi Echenka* (Songs of flying dragons, a eulogy cycle in 125 cantos comprising 248 poems, 1447) represented the first experimental use of Hankul. Song books written in Hankul praising Buddha and Hankul translations of Buddhist scriptures include *Sekpo Sangcel* (A life of Buddha, 1449), *Wel.in Chenkangci Kok* (Eulogistic songs for Buddha, 1449), *Wel.in Sekpo* (a combined volume of *Wel.in Chenkangci Kok* and *Sekpo Sangcel*, 1458), *Pep.hwakyeng Enhay* (Korean translations of the Lotus scripture, 1463), and *Wenkak.kyeng Enhay* (Korean translations of the scriptures for Buddha and Buddhist saints, 1464). Earlier Hankul materials also include *Twusi Enhay* (Korean translations of the poems of the Chinese poet Tu Fu, 1481).

Although linguists do not agree on the details, the widely accepted chronological divisions of the Korean language are based on certain historical events relevant to the language (e.g., H.K. Kim 1962, K.M. Lee 1976). Besides the historical evolvement discussed in the preceding section, significant events also include the creation of the Korean alphabet (1446), the Japanese invasion (1592–8), and the appearance of various significant books, such as *Kyeylim Yusa, Samkwuk Saki, Enmunci* (A manual of vernacular Korean, written by Yu Huy in 1824), and *Tayhan Muncen* (A Korean grammar, written by Choy Kwangok in 1908). The following periodization of the developmental stages of Korean is based on K.M. Lee (1976) and I.S. Lee, et al. (1997).

(2)   a. Prehistoric Korean: proto-Altaic to the Pu.ye–Han period (until around the beginning of the Christian era)

             b. Old Korean: the Three Kingdoms period to the end of the Unified Sinla dynasty (from around the beginning of the Christian era until early tenth century)

             c. Middle Korean (tenth century–sixteenth century) which ranges over the Kolye dynasty period (tenth century–fourteenth century) and the first 200 years of the Cosen dynasty, i.e., until the Japanese invasion in 1592 (fifteenth century–sixteenth century)

             d. Modern Korean (seventeenth century–nineteenth century) which ranges over the period after the Japanese Invasion to the end of the nineteenth century

             e. Contemporary Korean (twentieth century)

Some of the established linguistic characteristics of each stage of development are presented below.

3.3   Prehistoric and Old Korean

As discussed in 2.1, original Korean is regarded as having branched off from original Altaic in prehistoric times. Although very little is known about the structural nature of the languages of Pu.ye in the north and the Samhan languages in the south, K.M. Lee (1976) and others assume that the following sound changes, among other things, occurred in Korean during this prehistoric period: loss of the proto-Altaic contrast between voiced and voiceless stop consonants (e.g., *b* vs. *p*); development of the aspirated consonant series (*ph, th, ch, th, h*); and loss of many word-final vowels, i.e., *apocope*, as in *kul* 'cave, tunnel' (< proto-Altaic *kura*) and *mɔl* 'horse' (< proto-Altaic *mori*). A large portion of the morphological and syntactic differences existing between Korean and proto-Altaic may be ascribed to this prehistoric period. For instance, Prehistoric Korean developed the nominative case particle *i* which has not been reconstructed as a proto-Altaic form.

As for Old Korean, not many useful linguistic data exist about the three Old Korean languages – Sinla (57 BC – 935 AD), Paykcey (18 BC – 660 AD), and Kokwulye (37 BC – 668 AD). Only fragmentary reflexes have been observed in some existing records written in the Itwu script of Chinese characters, such as the proper nouns in *Samkwuk Saki*, fourteen vernacular poems in *Samkwuk Yusa*, and eleven poems in *Kyun.ye Cen* (for the Itwu script, see 6.2). Old Korean forms have been reconstructed from these linguistic fragments written in Itwu. While very little is known about Kokwulye and Paykcey, information about the Sinla language is relatively abundant. As has been discussed, the languages of Sinla and Paykcey are regarded as much more similar to each other than they are to the Kokwulye language. It is also assumed that the connection between Kokwulye and Altaic was far closer than that between the Sinla language and Altaic. An extensive study of the reconstruction of the Old Korean sound system based on the existing data written in Chinese Itwu is found in B.C. Park 1982.

Distinctly Altaic, the Kokwulye language is the only one of the northern (or Pu.ye) group with extant fragments of linguistic data (e.g., K.M. Lee 1976). Our knowledge about this language is limited to a vocabulary of about eighty words which appear mainly in *Samkwuk Saki*. While showing a similarity to Tungus languages (e.g., Kokwulye *nuami* vs. Tungus *namu* 'sea', Kokwulye *nanən* vs. Tungus *nadan* 'seven'), Kokwulye also reveals a certain likeness to Japanese (as discussed in 2.4) and to the Sinla language.

The Paykcey language was a Samhan dialect. Although the ruling class came from Kokwulye, evidence does not indicate an extensive influence of the northern (or Pu.ye) group. For instance, according to a record in Chou Shu, the word for 'king' was *woraka* in the language of the ruling class and *kici* in the language of the commoners. The latter appears to correspond to the Sinla word *kyesye* or *kese* 'king' (B.H. Kim 1984:104–5). Some data in *Samkwuk Saki* reveals that the Paykcey language was similar to the Sinla language and Middle Korean (MK), as shown in *turak* 'stone' (MK *tolh*), *sa* 'new' (MK *saj*), *məlke* 'clean, clear' (MK *mɔlk*), *pɨri* 'fire' (MK *pɨl*), and *muraŋ* 'ridge, high' (MK *mɔlɔ*) (e.g., I.S. Lee, et al. 1997:289). One example that the Paykcey language does not share with the Sinla language and Middle Korean is *kɨ* 'castle' whose counterpart is found in the Old Japanese word *kɨ* 'castle' (K.M. Lee 1976:37).

In an etymological study of some ten Old Korean fragments from the Paykcey dynasty that are preserved mostly in Japanese sources, Miller (1979) claims that at least six of them have clear-cut Altaic etymologies, and some show inheritance in Old Japanese (OJ), as in *kuti* 'falcon' (Tungusic *gusi, gosi*), *togan, togar* 'east' (Old Turkish *toɣar*), *tohel* 'field, land' (proto-Altaic **topar* 'dust, earth'), *oko-* 'upper, top' (proto-Altaic **øg-*; OJ *øk-* 'rise'), *ala-* 'lower, bottom' (proto-Altaic **ala* 'lower or front part'; OJ *ør-* 'to descend'), *omo* 'mother' (proto-Altaic **əm(ə)-*; OJ *omo*), *sima* 'high, soaring' (OJ *sema*), *suki* 'village', and *sugul* 'village chief' (OJ *suguri*). Extensive studies on the Paykcey language are found in Toh 1984. Toh's studies are based on place names and the geographical distribution of certain lexical items.

The Sinla language is assumed to have had the following phonological characteristics (K.M. Lee 1976:65–72; I.S. Lee, et al. 1997:290): (a) the aspirated consonant series was maintained; (b) the tensed consonant series (*p', t', c', k', s'*) was not yet developed; (c) unlike in Middle and present-day Korean, syllable-final consonants were probably released, as evidenced in Old Korean *niskɔm* 'king' (Contemporary Korean *(n)imkɨm*), where *s* appears to have had its fricative quality; (d) the current allophonic variants *r* and *l* were probably phonemically distinct in Old Korean; (e) word-internal *r* was frequently dropped, i.e., syncopated (e.g., *kəru > kəju* 'goose', *mori > moi* 'mountain', *nari > nai* 'river'); (f) the word-final Chinese sound *t* changed to *l*; and (g) there may have been a seven-vowel system as follows.

(3)

	Front	Central	Back
HIGH	*i*	*ɨ*	*u*
MID		*ə*	*ɔ*
LOW		*æ*	*a*

The Sinla language also had case and delimiter particles such as nominative *i*, genitive *ɨj/ɔj*, *s*, accusative *l*, *hɔl*, instrument *rɨ*, delimiter *n* (topic-contrast), delimiter *tɨ* 'also', etc. (K.M. Lee ibid.:14; I.S. Lee, et al. ibid:291). In addition, most inflectional suffixes that are currently in use were already developed then. Thus, the past relativizer was *-n* as in *ka-n pom* 'the spring that passed', the prospective suffix was *-l* as in *kɨli-l mɔzɔm* 'the mind that will long for', conjunctive suffixes were *-ko* 'and', *-myɔ* 'and', *-taka* 'and then', etc., and the interrogative ender was *-ko*. Even the honorific system of the Sinla language corresponds largely to that of Contemporary Korean. The subject honorific suffix was *-si* and the object honorific suffix was *-sɔlp* from which the current addressee honorific suffix *-(su)p* developed. The lexicon was also generally in agreement with that of Middle Korean.

The period of Old Korean was the initial stage of the influx of Chinese character words. In the sixth century, the titles of the kings were changed from pure Korean to Sino-Korean terms, with the use of the term *waŋ* 'king'. In the middle of the eighth century, i.e., during the Unified Sinla period, native place names were altered and modelled after the Chinese tradition, so that they consisted of two Chinese characters as they do now.

3.4   Middle Korean

With the founding of the Kolye dynasty (918–1392) in the early tenth century, the capital was moved from Kyengcwu (in the Kyengsang province) to Kaykyeng (present Kayseng in North Korea) which became the new political and cultural centre. Early Middle Korean data were recorded in Chinese characters, whereas Late Middle Korean data were recorded in the newly originated Korean alphabet Hankul. Indeed, the creation of Hankul in the early fifteenth century made extensive and exact transcriptions of the Korean language possible for the first time.

The Middle Korean period may be characterized by, among other things, the influx of a huge number of Chinese words into the Korean vocabulary. Before this period, Chinese words were limited, in general, to the names of places, people, and government ranks. But starting with the Kolye dynasty, Chinese words also pervaded the spoken language, along with their exclusive use in writing. Due to the massive importation of words from this predominant and prestigious non-Altaic language, Korean has undergone a wide range of changes, not only in its vocabulary but also to a lesser degree in the sound system, morphology, and syntax, as we shall see in detail in chapter 5 (lexicon).

Major phonological developments considered to have occurred during the early period of Middle Korean include the following: (a) addition of the voiced fricative *z* to the consonant system, as shown in *kɔzɔl* 'autumn', *azɔ* 'younger brother', and *mɔzɔm* 'mind'; (b) addition of the voiced bilabial fricative *β* to the consonant system, as shown in *nuβi* 'younger sister', *suβəl* 'liquor', and *tuβəl* 'two'; (c) development of the tensed consonant series (*p'*, *t'*, *c'*, *k'*, *s'*, *h'*), as observed in *p'ulhwi* 'root', *t'ɔl* 'daughter', *k'əzə* 'to draw', and *h'yə* 'to pull'; and (d) maintenance of the seven-vowel system with a slight sound shift (K.M. Lee ibid.:93–9). It has been assumed that the newly arranged vowel system looks like the following.

(4)   Front   Central   Back
  HIGH   *i*   *ɨ*   *u*
  MID   *e*   *ə*   *ɔ*
  LOW   *a*

In addition to the predominant inflow of Chinese lexical items, quite a few words, especially governmental, military, and animal terms, were borrowed from Mongolian as a result of Kolye people's contact with Mongolians (1206–1367) (K.M. Lee ibid.:99–103). Examples are *picijeci* 'clerk', *kalamɔl* 'black horse', *cjəltamɔl* 'red horse', *kalcike* 'yellow hawk', *paotal* 'military camp', and *patul* 'hero'. Some place names reflect Yecin (Jurchen) words, as shown in the word *Tumen* River (borrowed from the Yecin word *tɨmen* '10,000').

The later period of Middle Korean (from the fifteenth century) observed a flood of literature written in Hankul, most of which reflected the language used in the capital, i.e., the Kaykyeng dialect. Based on such literature, numerous Korean linguists have observed a wide variety of linguistic characteristics attributable to this period (cf. C.D. Yu 1962; K. Hong 1966; S.B. Cho 1967; W.J. Kim 1967, 1971, 1973; B.H. An 1971, 1992; W. Huh 1972, 1975, 1983; Y.S. Moon 1974; K.M. Lee 1976, 1977; Ramsey 1978; S.N. Lee 1981; N. Chang 1982; B.H. Kim 1984; An and Lee 1990; J.I. Kwon 1992; I.S. Lee, et al. 1997). In particular, Huh 1975 is a monumental piece of work on Middle Korean morphology. Major phonological properties are summarized below.

First of all, the phonemic system of fifteenth century Korean consisted of twenty-two (*à la* W. Huh 1983) or twenty-three (*à la* K.M. Lee 1976) consonants, seven vowels, and two semivowels. As will be discussed in chapter 6 (writing systems), K.M. Lee (1976:128–9) and a few earlier Korean linguists include *ɦ* in the Middle Korean consonant system. K.M. Lee assumes that contemporary standard words like *kasɛ* (or *kawi*) 'scissors' and *molɛ* 'sand' have been derived from the fifteenth century words *kɔzɦaj* and *molɦaj*, respectively, in view of the fact that forms such as *kasikɛ* 'scissors' and *molkɛ* 'sand' exist in southern and some other dialects.

(5)   Phonemic system of Middle Korean

         Consonants
         Stops: lax   *p*   *t*   *c*   *k*
                   aspirated   *ph*   *th*   *ch*   *kh*
                   tensed   *p'*   *t'*   *c'*   *k'*

Fricatives:	lax-voiced	β	z			$(\hbar)$
	lax-voiceless		s			h
	tensed		s'			h'
Nasal:		m	n		η	
Liquid			l			

Vowels	High:	i	$\dot{i}$	u
	Mid:		θ	o
	Low:		a	o

Semivowels	j		w

Due to their limited distribution and low functional load, the voiced fricative consonants β and $\hbar$ disappeared some time between the middle of the fifteenth century and early sixteenth century. The consonant β changed primarily to w, as in *kɨlβal* > *kɨlwal* 'sentence' and *təβi* > *təwi* 'hotness' (temperature), but also merged with p in the Kyengsang dialect. The voiced glottal fricative $\hbar$ is assumed to have been dropped in all dialects.

The vowels were classified into three groups: the bright or 'Yang' vowels *a*, *ɔ*, *o*, the dark or 'Yin' vowels *ə*, *ɨ*, *u*, and the neutral vowel *i*. The vowel system is asymmetrical with only one vowel in the front series. To account for this asymmetry, a Great Vowel Shift is assumed to have taken place as the vowel system evolved from Early to Late Middle Korean (W.J. Kim 1971, K.M. Lee 1976:138), as in *e* > *ə* > *ɨ* > *u* > *o*, and mid *ɔ* > low *ɔ*. However, more solid evidence must be shown before this assumption can be accepted as valid.

Second, there was a set of consonant clusters, each consisting of two or three phonemes, as shown in (6) (W. Huh 1983:6). Unlike in Contemporary Korean, these clusters occurred in syllable- or word-initial positions.

(6)	Sequence of two consonants:	*pt*	*pth*	*ps*	*pc*
		sp	*st*	*sn*	*sk*
	Sequence of three consonants:	*pst*	*psk*		

The phonetic values of *sp*, *st*, and *sk* are still under dispute as to whether they were pronounced as written or were simply written variants of the tensed *p'*, *t'*, and *k'*, respectively. There is evidence that these consonant clusters were indeed pronounced as clusters from left to right as they were written. For instance, current standard *t'ək* 'rice cake' and *t'oŋ* 'dung' are still pronounced as *sitəku* in some northern dialects and *sitoŋ* (in the sense of dung-manure) in some southern dialects. The changes involved are assumed to be *sitəku* > *stək(u)* > *t'ək* and *sitoŋ* > *stoŋ* > *t'oŋ*, which suggest that *st* was once pronounced as [st] before it was changed to the tensed consonant.

Linguists generally agree that the other consonant clusters were pronounced as they were written. For instance, the Middle Korean word *psɔl* 'hulled rice' contains the initial cluster *ps*. The initial *p* has subsequently disappeared, and the contemporary form is *s'al*. However, *p* is retained in other words such as *co-ps'al* (*co* 'millet' + *s'al*) 'hulled millet', where the contemporary syllable boundary falls between *cop* and *s'al*. Other examples include *ptɨt* 'will, intention', *psi* 'seed', *psɨ* 'use', *pcak* 'pair', *pskul* 'honey', and *pstaj* 'time'. Such clusters are believed to have been carried until the end of Middle Korean, until they changed to simple tensed stops in early Modern Korean, as in *t'ɨs* 'will, intention', *s'i* 'seed', *s'ɨ* 'use', *c'ak* 'pair', *k'ul* 'honey', and *t'ɛ* 'time'.

Third, fifteenth century Korean also observed the implosivization or unrelease of syllable-final consonants. Thus, all bilabial consonants were neutralized to *p*, all dental, palatal, and glottal consonants to *t*, and all velar consonants to *k* in the syllable-final position. As a result, only *p*, *t*, *k*, *m*, *n*, *ŋ*, and *l* could occur in the syllable-final position, as they do now. K.M. Lee (1976) presumes that this implosivization was responsible for *r* and *l* becoming a single phoneme in Middle Korean, *l* occurring in the syllable-final position and *r* elsewhere.

Fourth, there were eighteen compound vowels (diphthongs and triphthongs), as given in (7). There were no *w* off-glides, as is the case with Contemporary Korean.

(7)   Diphthongs

On-glides:	*ja*	*jə*	*jo*	*ju*		
	wa	*wə*				
Off-glides:	*aj*	*əj*	*oj*	*uj*	*ɨj*	*ɔj*

Triphthongs

On–off glides:	*jaj*	*jəj*	*joj*	*juj*
	waj	*wəj*		

While compound vowels of the on-glide type are still pronounced as such, those of the off-glide type have subsequently been monophthongized from the late eighteenth to the early nineteenth century, i.e., during the Modern Korean period, as we shall see later. For instance, Middle Korean *saj* 'bird' is now *sɛ:*. The monophthongization applies also to the off-glide part of triphthongs, as in *jəj* > *je*.

Fifth, Middle Korean was a tonal language. There were three tonemes: high tone (indicated by one dot to the left of the Hankul syllable block), rising tone (by two dots to the left), and low tone (by the absence of dots) as illustrated in (8). A rising tone is viewed as the combination of a low tone and a high tone as evidenced in (8d). For tone-marked Hankul letters, see chapter 6.

(8)   a. ·*kil* 'road'   ·*son* 'hand'   ·*pal* 'foot'
           ka·ci 'variety'   ·*kaci* 'branch'   ·*mal* 'a unit of measure'
       b. :*saj* 'bird'   :*pal* 'the blinds' :*mal* 'word'
       c. *cip* 'house'   *son* 'guest'   *mal* 'horse'
       d. *pulhuj* 'root' + ·*i* (subject) → *pul:huj*
           tɔli 'bridge' + ·*i* (subject) → *tɔ:li*

The existence of tone-indicating side dots in the documents issued in Seoul in the fifteenth century proves that Middle Korean had tonemes. Tones ceased to exist in the sixteenth century, however, except in the Kyengsang and Hamkyeng dialects. All vowels that had a rising tone became (and still are) long, whereas vowels with a high or low tone remained short. Middle Korean tones have been studied in numerous works such as Mun 1965, 1966; Y.C. Jeong 1971, 1972; W.J. Kim 1971, 1973; W. Huh 1972; Ramsey 1975; S.O. Lee 1978; and Martin 1992:60-86.

Sixth, fifteenth century Korean had more rigid vowel harmony than Contemporary Korean. That is, Yang (bright) vowels *o, a, ɔ* occurred only with Yang or neutral (*i*) vowels, and Yin (dark) vowels *u, ɨ, ə* occurred only with Yin or neutral vowels. Yang vowels are characterized as having more sonority than the other vowels in that they are pronounced with a retracted tongue root. Vowel harmony in Middle Korean was observed within a word (9a), across a nominal and a particle (9b), and across a predicate stem and a suffix (9c). Notice that contemporary counterparts do not necessarily manifest vowel harmony.

(9)   Middle Korean   Contemporary Korean
       a. *namo*   *namu*   'tree'
           kamakoj   *kamaky*   'crow'
           talɔ   *talɨ*   'different'
           kulɨm   *kulɨm*   'clouds'
           nilkup   *ilkop*   'seven'
           halmi   *halmi*   'old woman'

       b. *son ɔlo*   *son ɨlo*   'with a hand'
           skum ɨlo   *k'um ɨlo*   'with a dream'
           salɔm ɔl   *salam ɨl*   'person' (object)
           skum ɨl   *k'um ɨl*   'dream' (object)

son ɔj	*son ɨj*	'hand' (genitive)
cip ɨj	*cip ɨj*	'house' (genitive)

c. | *mak-ɔni* | *mak-ɨni* | 'as one blocks' |
|------------------------|--------------|---------------------|
| *mək-ɨni* | *mək-ɨni* | 'as one eats' |
| *mak-ɔmjən* | *mak-ɨmjən* | 'if one blocks' |
| *mək-ɨmjən* | *mək-ɨmjən* | 'if one eats' |
| *salɔm (< sal-ɔm)* | *salam* | 'person' |
| *jəlɨm (< jəl-ɨm)* | *jəlɨm* | 'fruit' |
| *nɔl-kaj* | *nalkɛ* | 'wing' |
| *təp-kəj* | *təphkɛ* | 'cover' |

Seventh, palatalization of alveo-dental consonants before *i* and *j* did not occur at this time. Thus, present-day *coh* 'good' and *cə* 'that' were *tjoh* and *tjə*, respectively. Similarly, word-initial deletion of *n* before *i* and *j* did not occur at this time, as shown in *nima* 'forehead' (present *ima*), and *nimkɨm* 'king' (present *imkɨm*).

In addition to the phonological aspects discussed thus far, the Hankul literature of the fifteenth century was the first and oldest data to show the comprehensive grammatical system of Korean. Some of the salient morphological and syntactic properties of this period are presented in the following.

The case system included the following case particles. Notice that the forms of genitive, locative, accusative, and instrumental–directional particles began with a Yang or Yin vowel (marked by a slash). Occurrence of these forms was conditioned by the final vowel of the preceding words in terms of vowel harmony. Contemporary Korean forms are also given for comparison. C stands for a consonant and V a vowel.

(10)		Middle Korean	Contemporary Korean
	Nominative:	*i* (after C and V)	*i* (after C)
		ka (used after V since 16th century)	*ka* (after V)
	Genitive:	*ɔj/ɨj* (for neutral animate possessor)	*ɨj, e*
		s (for honorific animate or inanimate possessor)	*ɨj, e*
	Locative:	*aj/əj*	*e*
	Accusative:	*ɔl/ɨl* (after C)	*ɨl* (after C)
		l/lɔl/lɨl (after V)	*lɨl* (after V)

Instrumental– Directional:	*ɔlo/ɨlo* (after C) *lo* (after V)	*ɨlo* (after C) *lo* (after V)
Comitative:	*wa* (after V and *l*) *kwa* (elsewhere)	*wa* (after V) *kwa* (after C)
Vocative:	*ha* (honorific) *a* (plain, after C) *ja* (plain, after V)	*a* (plain, after C) *ja* (plain, after V)

Fifteenth century Korean had *i* (with a high tone as in ·*i*) as the only nominative case particle, lacking the present *ka*. Thus, the present-day Korean phrases *namu-ka* 'tree' (nominative) and *so-ka* 'cow' (nominative) were *namo-j* and *sjo-j*, respectively, until *ka* was introduced in the sixteenth century. Notice that *i* was written (and pronounced) as a semivowel coda of the preceding vowel ending syllable. After the vowel *i* or the semivowel *j*, the nominative particle did not appear, but its reflex was indicated by a tonal difference, as in *tɔli* + ·*i* → *tɔ:li* 'bridge' (nominative). After a consonant, *i* was used as a separate syllable, as in *salɔm-i* 'person' (nominative).

The nominative case particle *ka*, which is an allomorph (occurring after V) of *i*, first appeared in the literature in 1572 (K.M. Lee 1976: 155) and has been used productively since the seventeenth century. One can only speculate that it could have been borrowed from Japanese nominative *ga*. This newly introduced particle has been redundantly attached to the already nominative-marked *na-j* (< *na* + *i*) 'I' (plain nominative), *cə-j* (< *cə* + *i*) 'I' (humble nominative), and *nə-j* (< *nə* + *i*) 'you' (plain nominative), resulting in *nɛ-ka*, *ce-ka*, and *ne-ka*, respectively.

The genitive case particles *ɔj* (after a Yang vowel) and *ɨj* (after a Yin vowel) were used for plain animate possessors, as in *salɔm-ɔj ptɨt* 'a person's intention' (present *salam-ɨj t'ɨs*) and *kəpup-ɨj thəli* 'turtle's hair' (present *kəpuk-ɨj thəl*). The form *s* was used for honorific animate possessors as in *puthjə-s toli* 'Buddha's principle' and for inanimate possessors as in *nala-s mals'ɔm* 'the language of the country'.

The honorific vocative particle *ha*, which is no longer available in Contemporary Korean, was used to address the king or Buddha, as in *nimkɨm-ha* 'Honorable King!' and *səjcon-ha* 'Honorable Buddha!'. In Contemporary Korean, the obsolete superpolite vocative form *i(si)ə* is used for God, Christ, Buddha, etc., as in *cu-jə* 'Lord!', *im-iə* 'Oh, my beloved!', and *hana-nim-isiə* 'God!'. The use of the plain vocative particles in Middle Korean is the same as in Contemporary Korean.

The present-day animate dative–locative–goal particles *eke* (neutral) and *kke* (honorific) developed respectively from Middle Korean neutral animate genitive *ɔj/ɨj* + *k(ɨ)-ə(kɨ)j* 'that place' and from Middle Korean honorific genitive *s* + *k(ɨ)-ə(kɨ)j* as illustrated in *nam-ɔj-kɨ-əj* 'to another person', *alahan-ɔj-kəkɨj* 'to an Alahan saint', *waŋ-s kɨ-əj* 'to the king', and *jəlaj-s kəkɨj* 'to Sakyamuni' (cf. K.M. Lee ibid.:171).

In addition to case particles, numerous delimiter particles were used or newly developed (cf. K.M. Lee ibid.:172-6). For instance, the topic-contrast delimiter particle alternated between *ɔn* and *ɨn* (after C) and between *nɔn* and *nɨn* (after V) to conform to vowel harmony with the cooccurring nominals. These have been reduced to *ɨn* (after C) and *nɨn* (after V) in Contemporary Korean. The delimiter *kɔcaŋ* (present *k'aci* and *k'əs*) 'until, even, to the best of' developed from the noun *kɔcaŋ* 'edge, extremity'. The delimiter *pɨthə* (present *puthə*) '(beginning) from' was formed from the verb stem *pɨth* 'stick to' and the infinitive suffix *-ə*, and the delimiter *cocha* 'even' from the verb stem *coch* 'follow' and the infinitive suffix *-a*. The comparative delimiters *tuko* and *lawa* and the enumerative delimiter *yə* existed in Middle Korean, but have since disappeared. The emphatic delimiter *za* 'as only for' evolved into *ja* in the standard speech around the end of sixteenth century, although it is still retained as *sa* in certain dialects, as shown in the present-day *na-ja/na-sa an ka* 'As for me, I am not going' in which *sa* is dialectal.

The initial vowels of many inflectional and derivational suffixes of predicates alternated between Yang and Yin sounds. Such harmonic pairs include *-a/ə* (infinitive suffix or intimate sentence ender), *-ato/əto* 'although', *-ala/əla* (plain imperative ender); *-oni/ɨni* 'because', *-ɔmjən/ɨmjən* 'if', *-ɔsi/ɨsi* (subject honorific); *-ɔm/ɨm* (nominalizer), *-ɔj/ɨj* (nominalizer, as in *noph-ɔj* 'height', *nəp-ɨj* 'width'), *-kaj/kəj* (instrument), and *-pɔ/pɨ* (adjectivizer, as in *alphɔ* (< *alh-pɔ*) 'sick' and *sɨlphɨ* (< *sɨlh-pɨ*) 'sad'). These alternating suffixes were used for vowel harmony with the cooccurring stem-final vowels as observed earlier. There were causative and passive suffixes *-hi*, *-β*, *-h*, *-ɔ*, etc. some of which are no longer in use in Contemporary Korean.

There were so-called person suffixes (W. Huh 1983:7). For instance, the verb stem *mək* 'eat' was conjugated as *mək-uni* 'as I eat' when the subject was the first person and as *mək-ɨni* when the subject was not a first person. Similarly, the past tense suffix *-tə* became *-ta* when the subject was the first person. Alternating vowels like *u* and *a* functioned as inflectional suffixes indicating the grammatical first person. This ablaut phenomenon ceased to appear in the latter part of the sixteenth century.

There were three kinds of honorific suffixes: the subject honorific *-(ɨ)si* (as in Contemporary Korean), the object honorific *-sɔβ* (corresponding to the present addressee honorific *-sɨp*), and the addressee honorific *-(ɨ)ŋi* and *-sjosjə*, both obsolete in Contemporary Korean. The semantic property of the suffix *-sɔβ* is controversial, i.e., whether it denotes the speaker's humility towards the addressee or the speaker's deference towards the object referent. While the majority of scholars seem to favour the former interpretation, W. Huh (1972) convincingly argues in favour of the latter, saying that the suffix underwent a semantic change, becoming the addressee honorific in the latter part of the sixteenth century. Huh (ibid.:28–9) observes that this suffix had six variants *-soβ*, *-coβ*, *-zoβ*, *-sop*, *-cop*, and *-zop* which alternated depending on the kinds of the cooccurring neighbouring sounds. That is, *-soβ* occurred after *k*, *p*, *s*, and *h*; *-coβ* after *t*, *c*, and *ch*; and *-zoβ* after *n*, *l*, and *m*. The final *β* changes to *p* when the following sound is a consonant. In *tɨt-coβ-ɔmjən* 'if (one) listens to (a respected person)', for instance, *-coβ* occurs because it is preceded by the consonant *t* and followed by a vowel.

As for the addressee honorifics in Middle Korean, Huh (ibid.:25; 1984:428–30) maintains that the suffix *-(ɨ)ŋi* appeared in the declarative, interrogative and propositive sentence enders, whereas the suffix *-sjosjə* was used as a requestive sentence ender. Examples include *koβɔ-ni-ŋi-ta* 'is pretty', *in-nɔ-ŋi-k'a* 'does (it) exist?', and *nimkɨm-ha alɔ-sjosjə* 'Your Majesty, please tell us!'

The past tense suffixes were *-kə*, *-a/ə*, and *-tə*. Only the last form is used in Contemporary Korean, as a retrospective mood suffix. The prospective suffix indicating futurity as well as the speaker's conjecture was *-li* as it is today. The present-day past tense forms *-as'/əs'* and the modal suffix *-kes'* (volition, presumption, and futurity) had not yet developed in Middle Korean.

Interrogative sentence enders included alternative question *-ka*, *-a*, *-njə* as in *saŋ-ka pəl-a?* 'Is (it) a prize or a punishment?' and *ha-njə cjəkɨ-njə?* 'Is (it) big or small?' and explanatory question *-ko* and *-njo* as in *mjəs salɔm-ko?* 'How many people (are there)?' and *ətɨj-za silɨm əpsɨn tɔj isnɔ-njo?* 'Is there any place where there is no worry?' Exclamatory enders included *-tota* and *-tosoita*, which have become obsolete (cf. I.S. Lee, et al. 1997:302).

The subject of an embedded relative clause was often marked by a genitive case particle, as in *pumo-ɔj nah-ɨn mom-ɔn* 'the body that the parents gave birth to' where the embedded subject *pumo* is marked by the genitive *ɔj*. This use has been discontinued since the early twentieth century.

As for the lexicon, there were already a large number of Chinese loan words in the Korean lexicon, as is still the case today. Middle Korean also had a host of other linguistic characteristics which are essentially the same as those in Modern and Contemporary Korean.

3.5   Modern and Contemporary Korean

Already by the early seventeenth century, Modern Korean showed itself as being sharply different from Middle Korean, as a result of the accumulated changes that occurred during the Middle Korean period. Modern Korean underwent even further changes, probably expedited by the social and political disorder in the wake of the seven-year Japanese invasion that started in 1592, the popularization of vernacular literature, contact with foreign languages, and the importation of Western civilization. Since the latter half of Modern Korean is much the same as Contemporary Korean, only the changes that happened primarily in its early half will be taken into account in the following (cf. K.M. Lee ibid.:185-235; W. Huh 1995).

First, word-initial consonant clusters such as *pt-*, *ps-*, and *pc-* were all reduced to tensed consonants, as already indicated. As a result, Korean syllable structure became simplified, not going beyond the *CGVC* pattern, where *C* is a consonant, *G* a glide or semivowel, and *V* a vowel.

Second, the voiced fricative phoneme *z* disappeared in the early part of the seventeenth century, becoming ZERO in most words but (rarely) also *s* in other words (W. Huh 1983:10). This consonant was completely dropped in most dialects, as in *əpəzi* > *əpəi* 'parents'. Exceptions have occurred in the southern dialects (Cenla, Kyengsang, and Ceycwu), where in many words it has merged with *s*, as in *mɔzɔl* > *masil*, *mosil* (southern dialects), *maɨl* (elsewhere) 'village' and *cizɨmjən* > *cisɨmjən* (southern dialects), *ciɨmjən* (elsewhere) 'if (he) builds'.

Third, the vowel *ɔ* became extinct in the latter part of the eighteenth century. The general rule for this change in Modern Korean was that *ɔ* merged to *ɨ*, *o*, or *a*, as shown in *palɔ* > *palɨ* 'correct', *hɔlk* > *hɨlk* 'soil', *talɔ* > *talɨ* 'different', *olɔ* > *olɨ* 'climb', *motɔn* > *motɨn* 'all', *nakɔnaj* > *nakɨnɛ* 'guest', *sɔmaj* > *somɛ* 'sleeve', *tɔlphaŋi* > *talphaŋi* 'snail', *thɔta* > *thata* 'beat, play on' *nɔmɨl* > *namul* 'vegetable', *stɔl* > *t'al* 'daughter', and *pɔlɔm* > *palam* 'wind'.

Fourth, the rarely occurring consonant *h'* disappeared, although linguists disagree about the time of its disappearance. Some claim that it took place around the latter part of the seventeenth century, while others insist that it had disappeared as early as the latter part of the fifteenth century. It has merged with *kh* as in *h'jəta* > *khjəta* 'pull' or with *h* as in *hhong* > *hong* 'wide'.

Fifth, all off-glide diphthongs were monophthongized and all triphthongs were diphthongized, with the off-glide *j* being fused with the preceding vowel. Thus, *aj* was reduced to *ɛ*, *əj* to *e*, *oj* to *ø* and *uj* to *y*, adding four front vowels to the vowel system. However, monophthongization of the two off-glide diphthongs *oj* and *uj* is not complete, in that they were also pronounced by many speakers in some dialects as on-glide diphthongs *we* and *wi*, respectively. The off-glide diphthong *ɨj* has changed to three monophthongs: *ɨ* in the word-initial syllable when not preceded by a consonant, *e* when used as a genitive case particle, and *i* elsewhere. It is often pronounced as *ɨj* by younger generation speakers when it occurs in the word-initial position, as in *ɨjsa* [ɨj.sa] 'medical doctor'. The diphthong *ɔj* and the triphthongs *joj* and *juj* have been out of use since the latter part of the eighteenth century.

Sixth, the unrounded high vowel *ɨ* became rounded after a bilabial consonant (i.e., *p*, *ph*, *p'*, *m*), being neutralized with *u*, as shown in *pɨl > pul* 'fire', *phɨl > phul* 'grass', *p'ɨl > p'ul* 'horn', *mɨl > mul* 'water', *pɨlk > pulk* 'red', and *nɔmɨl > namul* 'vegetable'.

Seventh, vowel harmony started to break down due to two major causes. As observed above, the vowel *ɔ* began to shift to *ɨ*, *o*, or *a*. The collapse of vowel harmony was inevitable because the low vowel *ɔ* is a bright vowel and the high vowel *ɨ* is a dark vowel. The other major cause may have been the influx of Chinese words where no vowel harmony was observed.

Eighth, the umlaut phenomenon occurred, i.e., non-front vowels became fronted, as in *məki > meki* 'feed' and *olchaɲi > olchɛɲi* 'tadpole'.

Ninth, palatalization of *t*, *th*, and *t'* to *c*, *ch*, and *c'*, respectively, before *i* or *j* occurred around the late seventeenth and early eighteenth century, as in *ti > ci* 'fall', *t'ih > c'ih* 'pound', *kotisik > kocisik* 'simple-mindedness', and *tikhɨjta > cikhita* 'guard against'.

Tenth, word-initial *n* was deleted in pronunciation when it occurred before *i* or *j*, as in *ni > i* 'tooth', *nimkɨm > imkɨm* 'king', and *nilɨ > ilɨ* 'inform, tell'.

Finally, a large number of words changed their lax consonants to tensed or aspirated counterparts, as in *koskoli > k'ojk'oli > k'øk'oli* 'nightingale', *kɔtkɔt.ha > k'ɛk'ɨt.ha* 'clean', *kokhili > khokhili > khok'ili* 'elephant', and *tɔstɔsha > t'at'ɨsha* 'warm'.

Some of the above phonological changes affected the phonemic system, while others merely affected the phonotactic patterns. The resulting phonemic system of Modern Korean consisted of nineteen consonants, ten vowels, two semivowels, and eleven (twelve in writing) diphthongs, as it does today.

(11)   Consonants

Stops:	lax	*p*	*t*	*c*	*k*	
	aspirated	*ph*	*th*	*ch*	*kh*	
	tensed	*p'*	*t'*	*c'*	*k'*	
Fricatives:	lax		*s*			*h*
	tensed		*s'*			
Nasals:		*m*	*n*		*ŋ*	
Liquid:			*l*			

Vowels:	High	*i*	*y*	*ɨ*	*u*
	Mid	*e*	*ø*	*ə*	*o*
	Low	*ɛ*		*a*	

Semivowels: *j*   *w*

Diphthongs: *ja*   *jə*   *jo*   *ju*   *jɛ*   *je*
                  wa   *wə*   *wɛ*   *we*   *wi*
                  (*ɨj*)

During this period, some new morphological and syntactic devices developed. For instance, the nominalizer suffix *-i* (< *-oj/ɨj*) which had been used productively in Middle Korean ceased to be productive. Instead, *-(ɨ)m* and *-ki* began to be widely used, as in *tɨlm* (*tɨl-m*) 'entering' and *kaki* (*ka-ki*) 'going'. Many nominal stems were considerably simplified, as observed in the loss of the word-final *h* in many Middle Korean words, such as *tolh* (> *tol*) 'stone' and *kilh* (> *kil*) 'road'. The nominative case particle *ka*, which had been developed only in written Korean at the end of the Middle Korean period, came to be used widely in both spoken and written Korean.

The new past tense suffix *-as'/əs'* which had been grammaticalized from the existential construction *-ə/a isi* (> *-ə/a is'*) 'be in the state of' during the Middle Korean period began to be used generally, as in *ponɛ-əs'-ta* 'sent'. Similarly, the modal verbal suffix *-kes'* which denotes the speaker/hearer's volition, conjecture, or futurity derived from the past periphrastic causative construction *-ke hoj-əs'* 'to have caused to' in the eighteenth century. A host of case and delimiter particles as well as verbal suffixes have also derived through grammaticalization from a verbal or nominal construction following a pattern similar to the Middle Korean derivation of *cocha* 'even' (< *coch* 'follow' + the infinitive suffix *-a*) and *puthə* 'from' (< *pɨth* 'stick to' + the infinitive suffix *-ə*). Suffice it here to present some frequently used examples: the comitative case particle *hako* 'and, with' (from the verb stem *ha* 'do' + the conjunctive suffix *-ko* 'and'), the dative case particle *poko* 'to' (from the verb stem *po* 'see' + the conjunctive suffix *-ko*), the delimiter particle *pak'e* 'except' (from the noun *pak'* 'outside' + the locative particle *e* 'at'), and the transferentive suffix *-taka* 'and then' (from the verb stem *tak* 'approach' + the infinitive suffix *-a*).

Many native words went out of use due to the continuous influx of a large number of Chinese words and the formation of new words based on Chinese characters. For instance, native words like *mø* (< *moj*) 'mountain', *kalam* (< *kolom*) 'river', and *azom* 'relative' were replaced by Sino-Korean words *san*, *kaŋ*, and *chinchək*, respectively. This happened throughout the Middle and Modern Korean periods. On the other hand, new Western cultural words began to be introduced into the Korean vocabulary in the Modern Korean period, largely due to the importation of a variety of books on science and religion as well as other cultural items, and through contacts with foreigners visiting or residing in Korea. For more discussions on lexical replacements, see chapter 5.

Regarding Contemporary Korean, twentieth century Korea has had an unprecedentedly complex history: the entry of missionaries, the collision between foreign powers in Korea, Japanese domination of Korea for thirty-five years, liberation from Japanese rule, division into North and South Korea, wide international contacts, the Korean War, rapid economic and technological growth, and social transformation in recent decades. All these events have had various effects on the Korean language.

During the Japanese occupation, patriotic grammarians and literary scholars endeavored to maintain and standardize the use of the Korean language. Monumental events include the Korean Language Society's development of a Unified Spelling System in 1933, codification of a standard vocabulary in 1936, and compilation of a Korean language dictionary, entitled *Khun Sacen* 'The Great Dictionary' (six volumes with 164,125 entries) that was initiated in 1929 and first published in 1947.

The description of Contemporary Korean is the main concern of the rest of this volume.

4

Dialects

This chapter surveys the dialectal divisions of Korean, salient phonological isoglosses, typical features of each dialect, and the phenomena of linguistic divergence between South and North Korea. All Korean expressions including linguistic examples and proper names are transcribed in Yale romanization. Thus, for instance, the southernmost island province of Korea is spelled as Ceycwu instead of the widely used McCune–Reischauer-based romanization Cheju.

4.1   Dialectal zones

The Korean language is relatively homogeneous, with good mutual intelligibility among the speakers from different areas. There are, however, minor but rather distinct geographically based dialectal differences. The Korean peninsula, including both North and South Korea, may be divided into seven dialectal zones which correspond by and large to administrative districts as described in (1) (e.g., H.K. Kim 1972, 1982). Although Seoul is a separate administrative unit, in the following it will be regarded as part of Kyengki Province, in view of its being surrounded by the province.

(1)   a. Hamkyeng Zone (northeast): North Hamkyeng Province, South Hamkyeng Province extending to the north of Cengphyeng, and Hwuchang in North Phyengan Province

             b. Phyengan Zone (northwest): North and South Phyengan Provinces (excluding Hwuchang)

             c. Central Zone: Kyengki Province, Kangwen Province, Hwanghay Province, and South Hamkyeng Province extending to Yenghung to the north

             d. Chwungcheng Zone (southcentral): North and South Chwungcheng Provinces, and Kumsan and Mucwu in North Cenla Province

             e. Kyengsang Zone (southeast): North and South Kyengsang Provinces

f. Cenla Zone (southwest): North and South Cenla Provinces (except for Kumsan and Mucwu)

g. Ceycwu Zone: Ceycwu Province (the island of Ceycwu)

The seven dialectal zones are roughly indicated in the following map.

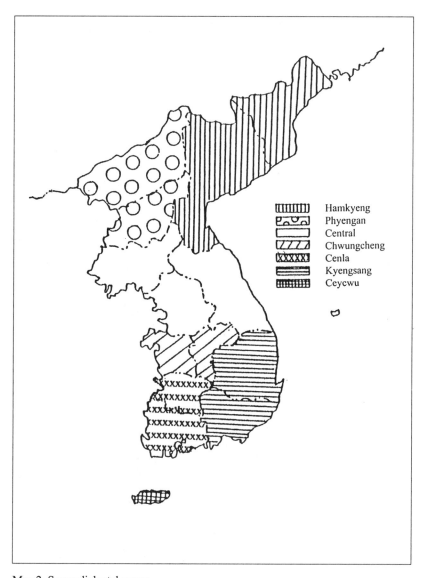

Map 2 Seven dialectal zones

The dialect used by the Korean community in the Yanbian Autonomous Prefecture of China in Manchuria can be included in the Hamkyeng Zone because it has evolved as part of the Hamkyeng dialect due to the early immigration of Hamkyeng people to that area and their subsequent linguistic contacts. The dialects spoken by Koreans in the other areas of China and other countries around the globe also reflect the seven dialectal zones, depending on where the speakers originally migrated from.

The major cause of the formation of the dialectal zones has been geographic, but historical and political factors have also played important roles. For instance, the characteristics of the Ceycwu dialect have been formed largely due to its isolation from the mainland. Also, the two neighbouring areas, Kyengsang and Cenla, manifest great differences since, in the past, there was no major transportation network connecting the two zones. Historically, too, these two zones were under two different dynasties, Kyengsang being the Sinla kingdom and Cenla, the Paykcey kingdom. Another historical factor explains the demarcation between the Hamkyeng dialect and the Central dialect, where there is no natural barrier. During the Kolye (918–1392 AD) and Cosen (1392–1910 AD) dynasties, the area between Cengphyeng in the Hamkyeng zone and Yenghung in the Central zone was a place of constant battle between the Manchu tribes called Yecin (Jurchen or Nuchen) in the north and the Koreans in the south. After the Manchu tribes were driven away to the north during the Cosen dynasty, Phyengan Province was inhabited by people from the neighbouring Hwanghay Province, and Hamkyeng Province was settled mainly by people from Kyengsang Province in the south. This is the reason for the similarity between the Phyengan dialect and the Central dialect on one hand, and between the Hamkyeng dialect and the Kyengsang dialect on the other. While influencing each other, the two northern dialects have constantly been influenced by foreign languages, such as Chinese, Tungus, Yecin, and Russian, a fact responsible for the maturation of the Phyengan and Hamkyeng dialects.

One of the major political factors contributing to dialectal differences is the post-1945 division into North and South Korea, which has concomitantly made the two Koreas linguistically divergent to a great extent. The different language policies implemented in the two Koreas are also responsible in large measure for the divergence, as we shall see in 4.10.

When a group of leading Korean linguists regulated the Unified Spelling System in 1933, they defined the 'standard' Korean as the Seoul speech (in the Central zone) spoken, in general, by the middle class. In South Korea's *Phyocwun.e Kyuceng* (Regulations on Standard Language) issued in 1988, the government stated that Standard Korean is, in principle, the current Seoul speech being used by educated people. In South Korea, books, public and private letters, government documents, mass communication, etc. are based essentially on the standard language as defined above. North Korea, however, has gradually deviated in actual language use from the above notion of standard language, and has originated and used, since 1966, the so-called Cultured Language that is based on the Phyengyang speech.

One of the basic methods most dialectologists of Korean follow is to identify the isoglosses of certain phonological features and selected vocabulary. Another common practice is to relate different dialectal forms to the corresponding Middle Korean forms to explicate the historical development of certain phonological features. From the distribution of isoglosses, one can establish many dialectal subzones, while admitting that two or more dialectal zones may overlap in certain particular features.

Ogura 1944 represents earlier and pioneering studies of Korean dialects. More recent works include S.N. Lee, et al. 1971; H.K. Choy 1974; Y.T. Kim 1975; Y.B. Kim 1977, 1992; Ramsey 1978; H.K. Kim 1982; AKS 1986–94; King 1991; NAS 1993; and I.S. Lee, et al. 1997, among other works. There are also numerous studies on the tones of the Kyengsang dialect, as we shall see in 7.5.3.

4.2   Representative isoglosses

Korean dialects are distinguished by the isoglosses of representative phonological, morphological, lexical, syntactic, and discoursal features. Of particular interest are the following phonological features.

4.2.1   *Prosodemes: tones and vowel length*

While Middle Korean was a tone language with high, rising, and low tones, tonemes have since disappeared in the Central (standard) and other dialects, except mainly in the Kyengsang and Hamkyeng dialectal zones. Instead, the Central and other dialects retain vowel length in the places where a rising tone occurred, except in the Ceycwu and some other dialects where neither tones nor vowel length occur. Thus, Contemporary Korean is divided into three dialectal groups in terms of prosodemes: (a) the dialects having tone as a distinctive feature, (b) the dialects having vowel length as a distinctive feature, and (c) the dialects having neither vowel length nor tones. The following regions have tones (NAS 1993).

(2)   a. South and North Kyengsang Provinces
            b. Samchek, Myengcwu, Yengwel in Kangwen Province
            c. eastern Hwuchang in North Phyengan Province
            d. South and North Hamkyeng Provinces except Cengphyeng

The area having neither tone nor vowel length includes the following regions.

(3)   a. Ceycwu Province

             b. Hoyyang, Ichen, Yangkwu, Hwachen in Kangwen Province

             c. Pongsan, Caylyeng, western Hwuchang, Chosan, Sakcwu, Wunsan,
                Thaychen in North Phyengan Province

             d. Yengwen, Maysan, Swunchen, Phyengwen, Yongkang, Kangse,
                Cwunghwa in South Phyengan Province

The remaining regions have vowel length as a phoneme, although vowel length is
distinctive only in word-initial syllables and younger generation speakers tend to have
difficulty in distinguishing the length. NAS (ibid.:E1) provides the following dialectal
map based on the prosodemes.

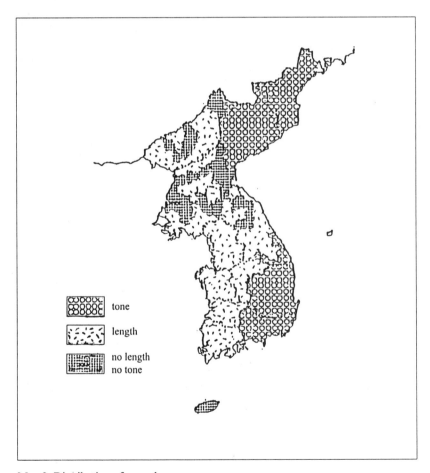

Map 3 Distribution of prosodemes

Tonal patterns are not the same in all tone dialects (NAS ibid.:3). For instance, there are four types of patterns with regard to monosyllabic nouns: (a) regions having only high tone (H) (Wulcwu, Ham.yang, Sancheng, Hatong in South Kyengsang Province); (b) regions with low tone (L) and H (the remainder of South Kyengsang Province; most of South and North Hamkyeng Province); (c) regions with H and rising tone (R) (entire North Kyengsang Province; Yengwel in Kangwen Province); and (d) regions with L, H, and R (Kilcwu, Hakseng in North Hamkyeng Province; Tanchen in South Hamkyeng Province; Samchek, Mucwu in Kangwen Province). Thus, the forms of *mal* have the following distributions.

(4)   (a) regions: *mal* (H)   'horse, measuring unit, word'
           (b) regions: *mal* (L)   'word'
                               mal (H)   'horse, measuring unit'
           (c) regions: *mal* (H)   'horse, measuring unit'
                               mal (R)   'word'
           (d) regions: *mal* (L)   'horse'
                               mal (H)   'measuring unit'
                               mal (R)   'word'

Different tonal patterns are also manifested in combinations of words. NAS (ibid.) sets up three areas of isoglosses as illustrated by the two-syllable phrase *mal-i* (word-NOM) in the sense of only 'word' (nominative). The word *mal* 'word' had a rising tone and the nominative particle *i* had a high tone in the Central dialect of Middle Korean. The three areas are: Area I (RH) (North Kyengsang Province and some regions in Hamkyeng Provinces), Area II (LH) (most of South Kyengsang Province), and Area III (HL) (some regions of South Kyengsang and most of Hamkyeng Provinces).

4.2.2   *Reflexes of Middle Korean ɔ*

The Middle Korean vowel ɔ is reflected in four different shapes in Contemporary Korean: (a) as *a*, (b) as *u*, (c) as *o*, and (d) as unchanged ɔ. As discussed in 3.5, the first three shapes exist in all dialectal zones except in the Ceycwu dialect where it is retained unchanged as shown in (5). Standard forms are given in parentheses (cf. I.S. Lee, et al. 1997:323).

(5)   *tɔl*   (*tal*)   'moon'
           tɔli   (*tali*)   'bridge'
           sɔl   (*sal*)   'skin'

hɔ	(*ha*)	'do'
hɔk	(*hulk*)	'soil'

While Middle Korean (MK) word-initial ɔ is generally reflected as *a*, it has become *o* after a bilabial consonant only in Kyengsang and Cenla Provinces and the Yukcin area in Hamkyeng Province, as illlustrated in (6).

(6)   *mol*   (*mal* < MK *mɔl*)   'horse'
               mosil   (*maul* < MK *mɔzɔl*)   'village'
               molu   (*malu* < MK *mɔlɔ*)   'dry'
               phol   (*phal* < MK *phɔl*)   'arm'
               pholi   (*phali* < MK *phɔli*)   'house fly'
               phol   (*phal* < MK *phɔl*)   'sell'

4.2.3   Other vowel alternations

There are some other patterns of vowel alternations. For instance, *wu/i* alternation is observed in standard *kalwu* 'powder' and *nolwu* 'roe deer'. Thus, 'powder' is *kali* (most of Cenla, Kyengsang), *kalli* (Kyengsang), *kalki* (Hamkyeng), *kallwu* (Hwanghay), and *kalwu* (elsewhere). Alternation between *o* and *wu* is observed in words like standard *songkos* 'a drill', as in *songkwus* (Cenla, Ceycwu, Kyengsang, South Chwungcheng, part of North Chwungcheng) and *songkos* (elsewhere).

There is no phonemic distinction between *e* and *u* in the Kyengsang dialect, both sounding like *e*, as in *cengmyeng* (*cungmyeng*) 'identification' and *nel* (*nul*) 'always'. In the Kyengsang and Cenla dialects, *ay* and *ey* are not distinctive in speech. Thus, standard *Paykcey* 'Paykcey dynasty' is pronounced as *Peykcey* [pek.c'e] in these dialects. The two front round vowels *wi* and *oy* are pronounced respectively as monophthongs [y] and [ø] in Chwungcheng, Cenla, Hwanghay, and Kangwen, as monophthongs [i] and [e] in Kyengsang, and as diphthongs [wi] and [we] in the remaining dialects including the standard speech.

4.2.4   Reflexes of Middle Korean z

The Middle Korean consonant *z* has been completely deleted in all words in the Central and Phyengan zones, whereas it remains as *s* in many dialects. The following examples are from S.N. Lee, et al. (ibid.:74–81). Each variant form is followed by the provinces where the form is used.

(7)   **muu** (standard) 'turnip' (< MK *muzwu*)
               musu: Cenla, Chwungcheng, Kangwen, South Hamkyeng

> *musi*:   Cenla, Kyengsang
> *mu*:   South Chwungcheng, Kangwen, Kyengki, Hwanghay,
>   Phyengan, South Hamkyeng
> *mui*:   Kangwen, Hwanghay
> *mu.yu*:   Kyengki, Hwanghay

Similar examples are *kasay/kasikay* (*kawi*) 'scissors', *yesi/yasi/yeswu* (*yewu*) 'fox', *kasil/kasul* (*kaul*) 'autumn', and *masil/masul/mosil* (*maul*) 'village'. For more examples, see H.K.Kim (1982:II, 48–59). Standard irregular verbs such as *is* 'connect', *ces* 'stir', *cis* 'build, make', and *nas* 'recover' are regular in Kyengsang, Cenla, Chwungcheng, and Hamkyeng Provinces, as in *is-umyen* (*i-umyen*) 'if (he) connects', *ces-ela* (*ce-ela*) 'stir!', and *nas-ase* (*na-ase*) 'as (he) has recovered'.

4.2.5   Reflexes of Middle Korean β

The Middle Korean voiced bilabial fricative consonant β occurred in intervocalic positions. This consonant has changed to *w* in the Central and many other dialects and to *p* in Kyengsang and Hamkyeng Provinces and some areas of Cenla and Chwungcheng Provinces. For instance, The Middle Korean word *saβ* 'shrimp' is reflected variously as *saywu* (Central, Hwanghay, Kyengki, Kangwen, South and North Phyengan), *sayo* and *saypi/syaypi* (South and North Hamkyeng, South and North Cenla, South and North Kyengsang), *saypayngi* (South and North Chwungcheng, southern Kyengki), etc. (KAS 1993:4). Similarly, S.N. Lee, et al. (ibid.) present the following examples.

(8)   ***awuk*** (standard) 'marshmallow'
> *apuk*:   Hamkyeng, Kyengsang
> *apok*:   South Hamkyeng, North Kyengsang
> *awuk*:   Kyengki, Chwungcheng, Kangwen, Phyongan, Hwanghay,
>   part of Kyengsang
> *aok* :   Kangwen, Hwanghay, Kyengki, Cenla, Chwungcheng,
>   part of Kyengsang

An extensive list of similar examples is in H.K. Kim (ibid. II, 28–48). Standard irregular adjectives such as *chwup* 'cold', *tep* 'hot', *kop* 'pretty', *musep* 'scary', and *mip* 'hateful' are regular in *p*-carrying dialects, as in *chwup-ela* (*chwuw-ela*) 'It's cold' and *kop-ase* (*kow-ase*) 'as (it) is pretty'.

4.2.6   Word-medial k

Numerous words manifest alternation between the presence and absence of *k* in word-medial positions depending on different dialects (cf. S.N. Lee, et al. ibid.).

(9)   *pawi* (standard) 'rock'
          pakwu: Kyengsang, South Cenla
          pangkwu:Kyengsang, North Chwungcheng, Kangwen, Hwanghay
          pawu: Cenla, Kyengsang, Chwungcheng, Kangwen, Hwanghay
          pawi: South Chwungcheng, Kyengki, Kangwen, Hwanghay
          pai: part of Kyengsang

Other similar examples are *kaykol/kaykwul/kaykwul* (*kaywul*) 'brook', *olkay* (*olhay*) 'this year', *tolkaci/tolkay* (*tolaci*) 'Chinese bellflower', *silkeng/sikeng* (*sileng*) 'wall shelf, rack', *naykwuli/naykwul/nay(ng)kal* (*nay*) 'smoke', and *nangkwu/nangki* (*namu*) 'tree' (cf. H.K. Kim ibid.:II, 1–24 for more examples). As for the presence or absence of the word-medial *k*, it is not clear whether the original form of the consonant was a voiced velar fricative *ɣ*, a voiced glottal fricative *ɦ*, or *k* (cf. K.M. Lee 1976:129). In any case, this historical word-medial *k* appears in Kyengsang, Hamkyeng, and part of Cenla, while it has been mostly dropped in the Central zone, Chwungcheng, Phyengan, and part of Cenla.

4.2.7   Word-initial l and n

Northern dialectal zones including the provinces of Phyengan and Hamkyeng retain the pronunciation of initial *l* in Sino-Korean words, whereas the rest of the dialectal zones have either lost it (before *i* or *y*) or replaced it with *n* (elsewhere). This *l* is often replaced by *n* before *i* or *y* in the Phyengan zone, as illustrated in *lipal/nipal* (*ipal*) 'haircut', *lyeksa/neksa* (*yeksa*) 'history', *lyoli/noli* (*yoli*) 'cooking', *lyangsim/nangsim* (*yangsim*) 'conscience', and *lotong* (*notong*) 'labor'.

The Phyengan zone and the Yukcin dialect of North Hamkyeng Province also retain the pronunciation of initial *n* before *i* or *y*, whereas the other dialects have lost it, as in *nyeca/neca* (*yeca*) 'female', *nelum* (*yelum*) 'summer', *nima* (*ima*) 'forehead', *ni* (*i*) 'tooth', *nilkwup* (*ilkop*) 'seven', and *nwu-wel* (*yu-wel*) 'June'. For more discussion, see 4.10.3.

4.2.8   Palatalization

While no palatalization existed in Middle Korean, it is observed in certain dialects in Contemporary Korean. There are three dialectal groups in regard to palatalization: (a) dialects with no palatalization, (b) dialects with palatalization from alveo-dental to palatal consonants; i.e., *t*, *th*, *tt* > *c*, *ch*, *cc* before *i* and *y* [j], and (c) dialects with palatalization from alveo-dental and velar to palatal consonants, i.e., *t/k*, *th/kh*, *tt/kk* > *c*, *ch*, *cc* before *i* and *y* [j]. In the (c) dialects, palatalization of the glottal fricative *h* to *s* is also observed, i.e., *h* > *s* [ʃ] before *i* or *y* [j].

The Phyengan dialectal zone and the Yukcin area of North Hamkyeng Province belong to (a), as observed in *tel* (*cel*) 'Buddhist temple', *tengketang* (*cengkecang*) 'railroad station', *te kes* (*ce kes*) 'that thing', *temsim* (*cemsim*) 'lunch', *totha* (*cohta*) '(It) is good', *ttilunta* (*ccilunta*) 'porks', and *kath-i* [ka.thi] (*kath-i* [ka.chi]) 'in the same way'. As noticed in the parenthesized standard forms in these examples, the Central dialectal zone belongs to (b). The (c) dialectal zones include Kyengsang, Cenla, Hamkyeng, Chwungcheng, Ceycwu, and Kangwen Provinces. Examples include *cim* (*kim*) 'seaweed', *cilum* (*kilum*) 'oil', *cil* (*kil*) 'road', *ceth* (*kyeth*) 'side', *chi* (*khi*) 'winnow', *cciwuta/ccingkwuta* (*kkiwu*) 'insert', *sim* (*him*) 'strength', *seng* (*hyeng*) 'older brother', *sey* (*hye*) 'tongue', and *swung-nyen* (*hyung-nyen*) 'lean year'.

Many characteristics are quite unique either to each dialectal zone or to only a few zones. The general intonation patterns, utterance tempo, and sound qualities are quite different from one dialect to another. Sound patterns, vocabulary, morphology, and syntax are all slightly dissimilar. Typical features of each dialectal zone are summarized below, based essentially on the descriptions made in S.N. Lee, et al. 1971; H.K. Kim 1982, II:331–428; Y.B. Kim 1992; and I.S. Lee, et al. 1997 with occasional reference to some other written and spoken data. Notice that many of the phonological features are already discussed above. Standard forms are given in parentheses for comparison.

4.3   Hamkyeng zone

Several representative phonological features characteristic of the Hamkyeng dialect are (a) retention of phonemic tones; (b) pronunciation of Sino-Korean word-initial *l*; as in *lotong* (*notong*) 'labour' and *lyensup* (*yensup*) 'practice'; (c) frequent vowel fronting, as in *soysik* (*sosik*) 'news', *imay* (*ima*) 'forehead', and *kamcay* (*kamca*) 'potato'; (d) frequent palatalization, as in *sim* (*him*) 'strength' and *ciwa* (*kiwa*) 'roof tile'; and (e) retention of the historical word-medial or intervocalic *β*, *z*, and *k*, as *p*, *s*, and *k*, respectively, as in *nwupey* (*nwuey*) 'silkworm', *hapulaypi* (*holapi*) 'widower', *kasay* (*kawi*) 'scissors', *mosi* (*moi*) 'feed (for chickens)', *molkay* (*molay*) 'sand', and *nolki* (*nolwu*) 'roe deer'.

Morphological features include (a) the prevalence of fossilized nominal suffixes such as *-ki*, *-ngi*, *-aci*, and *-i*, as in *ipswulki* (*ipswul*) 'lip', *tomayki* (*toma*) 'cutting board', *phayngi* (*pha*) 'onion', *kesangi* (*kewi*) 'goose', *cokaci* (*cokay*) 'shell', and *peyli* (*pyel*) 'star', and (b) the extensive use of characteristic sentence enders, as illustrated in (10) with the verb *hata* 'do'.

(10)   *declarative*
            plain level: *ha-n-ta-ya* (*ha-n-ta*)
            intimate, familiar, blunt levels: *ha-m-mey, ha-m-ney, ha-p-cipi,*
                                                               ha-way (*hay, ha-ney, ha-o*)
            polite, deferential levels: *ha-ota, ha-wuta, ha-weyta, ha-o-ita,*
                                                               ha-op-cipi, ha-m-mey-ta
                                                               (*hey-yo, ha-p-ni-ta*)

            interrogative
            plain level: *ha-wa?, ha-m?* (*ha-ni?, ha-nu-nya?*)
            intimate, familiar, blunt levels: *ha-wu?, ha-m-mey?, ha-cipi?,*
                                                               ha-m-nungka?, ha-m-twu(ng)?
                                                               (*hay?, ha-na?, ha-o?*)
            polite, deferential levels: *ha-sswu-ta?, ha-m-mengi?,*
                                                               ha-p-syo?, ha-p-mi-kka?
                                                               (*hay-yo?, ha-p-ni-kka?*)

            imperative and propositive
            plain level: *ha-la-kwu, ha-lema, ha-llemuna,*
                                                               ha-lyey (*ha-la, ha-lyemuna*)
            intimate, familiar, blunt levels: *ha-langi, ha-p-sey, ha-p-so, ha-cipi*
                                                               (*hay, ha-key, ha-sey, ha-o*)
            polite, deferential levels: *ha-sosey, ha-ota, ha-wuta,*
                                                               ha-si-p-so, ha-op-sey, ha-op-ci,
                                                               ha-op-cipi (*hay-yo, ha-si-p-si-o,*
                                                               ha-(si)-p-si-ta)

Examples of predicates that end in some of these endings are *chayk i-ta.ya* (*chayk i-ta*) '(It) is a book', *chayk i-m-mey* (*chayk i-ney*) '(It) is a book', *ka-m-mey* (*ka-ney*) '(He) goes', *ka-p-cipi* (*ka-o*) '(He) goes', *iss-ota* (*iss-up-ni-ta*) '(He) stays', *ka-m?* (*ka-ni?*) 'Does (he) go?', *ka-wu?* (*ka-na?*) 'Does (he) go?', *ka-m-twung?* (*ka-o?*) 'Does (he) go?', *ka-m-mengi?, ka-p-syo?* (*ka-p-ni-kka?*) 'Does (he) go?', *ka-la-kwu* (*ka-la*) 'Please go!', *ip-wuta* (*yepo-sey-yo*) 'hello', *ka-ota* (*ka-sey-yo*) 'Please go!', *ka-p-sey* (*ka-p-si-ta*) 'Let's go', and *ka-op-cipi* (*ka-si-p-si-o*) 'Please go!'.

There are many words not shared by the standard speech. Some of them are putative old forms. These include the indirect question word *twu/twung* (*ci, ka*) 'whether', the accusative case particle *u/lu* (*ul/lul*), *solay* (*tayya*) 'wash basin', *meykwuli* (*kaykwuli*) 'frog', *ankkan* (*anay*) 'wife', *haym* (*panchan*) 'side dishes', *yel* (*moi*) 'feed', *halki* (*hulk*) 'soil', *kayngkay* (*kamca*) 'potato', *phusungkay* (*hepha*) 'lung', *peyli* (*pyel*) 'star', *nwuli* (*wupak*) 'hail', *twuley* (*tul*) 'field', *misikkan* (*oyyangkan*) 'stable', *naco* (*cenyek*) 'evening', *polti* (*acwu*) 'very', *esi* (*epei*) 'parent', and *kasieypi* (*cangin*) '(male's) father-in-law'. Some loan words from Manchu and Russian are used, as in Manchu *than* (*olkaymi*) 'noose, trap', *sinacwungi* (*sanay*) 'boy', *eymina* (*kyeycip.ay*) 'girl', and *wuthi* (*os*) 'clothes'; and Russian *keluman* (*hocwumeni*) 'pocket', *picikkay* (*sengnyang*) 'matches', and *meytuley* (*yangtongi*) 'bucket'. Relevant sentence examples are given in (11) (I.S. Lee, et al. 1997:337–8).

(11)　　a. *poli-pap   pokwu-sa   nas-cipi.*
　　　　　barley-rice than-EM   better-SUP
　　　　　(*poli-pap pota-ya nas-ci.*)
　　　　　'It is certainly better than barley rice.'

　　　　b. *tep-un-tey kule-ng ke   ip-hiwu-ci   ma-wuta.*
　　　　　hot-RL-as that-RL thing wear-CAS-NOM stop-IM
　　　　　(*tew-un-tey kule-n kes ip-hi-ci ma-si-p-si-o.*)
　　　　　'Don't make him wear such a thing as it is hot.'

4.4　　Phyengan zone

The Phyengan dialect may be characterized by the following phonological features: (a) pronunciation of Sino-Korean word-initial *l*; (b) pronunciation of *c*, *ch*, and *cc* more or less as dental, i.e., as [ts], [ths], and [t's], respectively; (c) retention of some historical diphthongs in vowel sequences in certain words, as in *oi* (*oy*) 'cucumber', *kei* (*key*) 'crab', and *kai* (*kay*) 'dog'; (d) umlaut and vowel fronting, as in *meynwuli* (*myenuli*) 'daughter-in-law' and *songayci* (*songaci*) 'calf'; (e) resistance to palatalization probably due to the influence of Chinese, as in *tiph* (*ciph*) 'straw' and *tengketang* (*cengkecang*) 'railroad station'; (f) loss of the glide *y* after a consonant, as in *pho* (*phyo*) 'ticket' and *nengkam* (*yengkam*) 'old man'; (g) occurrence of *n* before *i* and *y* in the word-initial position, as in *ni* (*i*) 'tooth' and *niwus* (*iwus*) 'neighbor'; and (h) retention of the historical intervocalic *k*, as in *silkeng* (*sileng*) 'wall shelf', *naykwuli* (*nay*) 'smoke', and *molkay* (*molay*) 'sand'.

Morpho-lexical characteristics of this dialect are represented by (a) certain fossilized suffixes such as *-ngi*, *-ki*, *-akwu*, and *-ci*, as in *phangi* (*pha*) 'onion', *kkolangi* (*kkoli*) 'tail', *tomayki* (*toma*) 'cutting board', *motakwu* (*mos*) 'nail', *pelkeci* (*pellay*) 'worm', and *nolkaci* (*nolwu*) 'roe deer'; (b) some unique words such as *sepsepi (hepha)* 'lung', *yel (ssulkay)* 'gallbladder', *mulwu (wupak)* 'hail', *wuteng (ilpule)* 'on purpose', *omani (emeni)* 'mother', *eyminey (anay, yeca)* 'wife, female', and *talwuki (sin)* 'shoes'; and (c) many idiosyncratic sentence enders which are partly shared by the Hamkyeng dialect: the declarative *-ta-ya (-ta)*, *-(u)m-ney/mey*, *-(u)wey (-e, -ney, -(u)o)*, *-swu-ta*, *-(su)p-ney-ta*, *-(su)p-mey-ta*, *-(u)wa-yo*, *-(u)p-ti*, *-(u)wey-ta (-e.yo, -(su)p-ni-ta)*; the interrogative *-(u)m-ma?*, *-(u)wa? (-ni?, -(n)u-nya?)*; *-(u)m-mey?*, *-wu?*, *-kan? (-e?, -na?, -(u)o?)*, *-(u)op-ni-kka?*, *-(su)p-ney-kka?*, *-(su)p-mey-kka? (-(su)p-ni-kka?)*; and the imperative *-(u)lema*, *-(u)lyem (-ela, -(u)lyemuna* [obsolete])*, *-(u)si-tana*, *-(u)m-mey (-key, -sey, -(u)o)*, *-(u)si-la-yo*, *-(u)si-kyo*, *-(u)si-p-syo (-(u)sey-yo, -(u)si-p-si-o)*. Sentence examples are given in (12).

(12) a. *nay ley   ka-tulays-ti   yo.*
          I   NM   go-PST-PST-SUP   POL
          (nay ka ka-ss-ess-ci yo.)
          'I had gone (there).'

      b. *etum   ey   ka-si-p-ney-kka?*
          where to   go-SH-AH-IN-Q
          (eti ey ka-si-p-ni-kka?)
          'Where are you going?'

      c. *na ampulla an   ka-mun   ekha-kan?*
          I   even   not go-if   how do-Q
          (na cocha an ka-myen etheh-key ha-keyss-na?)
          'If even I don't go, what could we do?'

      d. *onel ka-ss-ta   o-kas-swu-ta.*
          today go-PST-and   come-will-AH-DC
          (onul ka-ss-ta o-keyss-sup-ni-ta.)
          'I will go there and come back today.'

4.5   Central zone

With Seoul as its geographical centre, the Central dialect contains the standard speech of Korean as a subset. Since the synchronic description of the standard speech of Korean is the main concern of this book, its characterization here would be redundant. Suffice it here to make a few salient phonological points.

First, the historical sound sequence *uy* (still spelled as such) has three divergent pronunciations: [e] (when used as a possessive case particle), as in *na uy* (pronounced as [na.e]) 'my', [ɨ] (word-initially), as in *uysa* [ɨ.sa] 'doctor', and [i] (elsewhere), as in *sanguy* [sa.ŋi] 'consultation'.

Second, in colloquial speech, the vowel *o* is frequently raised to *wu* in final syllables of certain native morphemes, especially when it occurs as part of a suffix, as in *kuli-ko/kuli-kwu* 'and', *mek-eto/mek-etwu* 'eat but', *na to/na twu* 'I also', *sikol/sikwul* 'countryside', and *ka-ss-o?/ka-ss-wu?* 'Has (he) gone?'

Third, palatalization is not as prevalent as in the southern dialects, but not as weak as in the Phyengan dialect. Thus, 'road' is *kil* as compared with the southern *cil* and 'strength' is *him* as compared with the southern *sim*, whereas 'heaven and earth' is *chenci* [chən.ɟi] as compared with the Phyengan dialect counterpart *thyenti* [thjən.di].

Finally, the historical word-medial (or intervocalic) β, *z*, and *k* are deleted completely or weakened as in β to *w*, while some other dialects (e.g., southern dialects) retain them as *p*, *s*, and *k*, respectively.

(13)	Central dialect	Some other dialects	
	seywu	*seypi*	'shrimp'
	kawuli	*kapuli*	'stingray'
	tali	*talpi*	'false lock of hair'
	moi	*mosi*	'feed'
	muu	*muswu, musi*	'turnip'
	kaywul	*keykwul*	'brook'
	sileng	*silkeng*	'shelf'
	melwu	*melkwu*	'wild grapes'

4.6   Chwungcheng zone

In many respects, the southern variant of this dialect is similar to the Cenla dialect, while the northern variant is close to the Central dialect. Some relatively idiosyncratic aspects of the Chwungcheng dialect are: (a) slow tempo of speech; (b) general retention of the historical intervocalic *z* as *s*, as in *masil (maul)* 'village', *asi (awu)* 'younger brother', *is-e (i-e)* 'connect and', and *muswu (muu)* 'turnip'; (c) extensive palatalization, as in *ce (kye)* 'chaff', *cil (kil)* 'road', *chi (khi)* 'winnow', *sim (him)* 'strength', and *sey (hye)* 'tongue'; (d) extensive tensification, as in *ttol (tolang)* 'ditch', *kkompo (kompo)* 'pockmarked person', *ssalip-mun (salip-mun)* 'a gate made of twigs', *sswuswu (swuswu)* 'broomcorn', and *ppes (pes)* 'cherry'; and (e) maintenance of historical diphthongs in vowel sequences, as in *moi (moy)* 'mountain', *oi (oy)* 'cucumber', and *sei (seys)* 'three'.

Although the northern areas of the Chwungcheng dialect share many sentence enders with the Central dialect and its southern areas with the Cenla dialect, some idiosyncratic sentence enders occur, as in the declarative *-ta-ya* (*-ta*), *-swu* (*-so*), *-e.yu* (*-e.yo*); the interrogative *-wu?* (*-o?*), *-e.yu?* (*-e.yo?*), *-sup-ni-kkya?* (*-sup-ni-kka?*); and the imperative/propositive *-keyna* (*-key*), *-wu* (*-o*), *-e.yu* (*-e.yo*). The following dialogue between an adult (A) and a child (B) illustrates discourse forms in this dialect.

(14)   A: *ni   pap   mek-ess-nya?*↑ or ↓
              you   meal   eat-PST-Q
              (*ne pap mek-ess-ni?*↑)
              'Did you have your meal?'

      B: *aniyu,*↑ *an mek-ess-iyu.*↓
              no   not eat-PST-POL
              (*anio,*↑ *an mek-ess-eyo.*↓)
              'No, (I) didn't.'

4.7   Kyengsang zone

This dialect has undergone many simplifications in the course of its evolution. First, it has a six-vowel (*i* [i], *ey* [e], *wu* [u], *e* [ə], *a* [a], *o* [o]) system compared to the overall ten-vowel system of the standard speech. This simple vowel system was caused by the neutralization between *u* [ɨ] and *e* [ə] and between *ey* [e] and *ay* [ɛ], and the lack of the two rounded monophthongs *wi* [y] and *oy* [ø], the former usually being pronounced as *i* [i] and the latter as *ey* [e]. Second, unlike in the other dialects, *s* and *ss* are not phonemically distinct, with *s* being preferred, as in *sal* (*ssal*) 'rice' and *sawum* (*ssawum*) 'fighting'. Third, as stated earlier, distinctive tones or pitch accents (low, mid, high) are retained (see 7.5.3). For instance, the noun *son* means 'grandchild, loss' with a low tone, 'hand' with a mid tone, and 'guest' with a high tone in South Kyengsang Province (W. Huh 1985:20). Similarly, *wenswu* 'enemy' and *wenswu* 'head of a country' are different only in tones, the former having high–mid tones and the latter mid–high tones. Fourth, semivowels tend to disappear after a consonant, as in *pho* (*phyo*) 'ticket', *saka* (*sakwa*) 'apple', *ki* (*kwi*) 'ear', *haksilhi* (*hwaksilhi*) 'surely', and *munha* (*munhwa*) 'culture'. Fifth, extensive contractions occur in colloquial speech. Some sentence examples are *eps-sim-te* [əp.s'im.də] (*eps-sup-ni-ta*) '(I) don't have (it)', *Tongteymun kha-ni* [toŋ.de.mun.kha.ni] (*Tongtaymun i-la ko ha-nikka*) 'I told you that (I am going to) the East Gate', *me-la kha-no?*

[mə.ɾa.kha.no] (*mwes i-la ko ha-ni?*) 'What are you talking about?', and *wa ikha-no?*
[wa.i.kha.no] (*way ileh-key ha-ni?*) 'Why do you do this way?'

This dialect also has its own characteristic set of sentence enders. The polite ender
-e/a.yey (*-e.yo/a.yo*) is used by both genders, but more predominantly by female
speakers, as observed in *acik an mu-ss-eyey* (*acik an mek-ess-eyo*) '(I) didn't eat yet.'
The deferential enders deviate from standard forms, as in the declarative *-(si)m-te*, *-si-
te*, and *-ni-te* (*-(su)p-ni-ta*), the interrogative *-neng-kyo?* (*-nun-ka-yo?*) and *-((si)p)-ni-
kk(y)e?* (*-(su)p-ni-kka?*), the imperative *-si-i-so* (*-si-p-si-o*), and the propositive *-ip-si-
te* (*-si-p-si-ta*).

Reflecting a similar distinction in Middle Korean, the non-honorific interrogative
sentence enders in this dialect are *-no* and *-ko* (after a copula) in question word
questions and *-na* and *-ka* (after a copula) in yes/no questions, as in *ni etey ka-ss-no?*
'Where did you go?', *i ke nwu chayk i-ko?* 'Whose book is this?', *pap mun-na?* 'Did
you eat?', and *kuk i ni chayk i-ka?* 'Is that your book?' Yes/no questions are usually
asked with a falling intonation. Rising intonation is possible, but only with the pitch
level 3 as against the standard pitch level 4.

The plain, intimate, and familiar levels are generally neutralized and not
distinguished in forms. Thus, the interrogative enders *-no/-na* and *-ko/-ka* may
correspond to the standard forms *-ni/-(n)unya*, *-na*, *-e*, etc. Similarly, the ender *-ceyi*
which corresponds to *-ela*, *-ca*, *-key*, *-sey*, *-e*, etc. in the standard speech is used for the
imperative and propositive, covering the same three speech levels. The following
examples are from I.S. Lee, et al. ibid.:339.

(15)   a. *cip   ey iss-nu-n   twung eps-nu-n   twung mol-si-te.*
            home at be-IN-RL if   be not-IN-RL if   not know-AH-DC
            (*cip ey iss-nu-n ci eps-nu-n ci molu-keyss-sup-ni-ta.*)
            'I don't know whether (he) is at home or not.'

         b. *phettek   o-si-i-so.*
            quickly   come-SH-AH-POL
            (*ppalli o-si-p-si-o.*)
            'Please come quickly.'

         c. *ni   khang nay khang   talm-ess-cey?*
            you and   I   and   resemble-PST-SUP
            (*ne lang na lang talm-ass-ci?*)
            'You and I are alike, aren't we?'

4.8 Cenla zone

Salient phonological features characterizing the Cenla dialect include (a) merging of the vowel *ay* into *ey* in speech, as in *key* (*kay*) 'dog' and *Peykcey* (*Paykcey*) 'Paykcey kingdom'; (b) existence of the phonemic monophthongs *wi* [y] and *oy* [ø], as in *kwi* [ky] (*kwi* [kwi]) 'ear' and *soy* [sø] (*soy* [swe]) 'metal'; (c) extensive palatalization, as in *cimchi* (*kimchi*) 'kimchee', *cil* (*kil*) 'road', *cim* (*kim*) 'steam, seaweed', *cesil* (*kyewul*) 'winter', *cce-anta* (*kkye-anta*) 'hug', *cicip* (*kyeycip*) 'girl', *ce* (*kye*) 'chaff', *sey* (*hye*) 'tongue', and *seng* (*hyeng*) 'older brother'; (d) vowel fronting or raising, as in *kusil* (*kusul*) 'bead', *kasim* (*kasum*) 'chest', *mesim* (*mesum*) 'farm servant', *cali* (*calwu*) 'handle', *kali* (*kalwu*) 'powder', *musi* (*muu*) 'turnip', *yesi* (*yewu*) 'fox', *kochi* (*kochwu*) 'red pepper', *tomey* (*toma*) 'cutting board', *chimey* (*chima*) 'skirt', *khoy* (*kho*) 'nose', *ki* (*key*) 'crab', *pita* (*peyta*) 'cut', *pikey lul pita* (*peykay lul peyta*) 'rest one's head on a pillow', and *peyley ppul-ela* (*pely-e pely-ela*) 'Throw (it) away!'; (e) extensive monophthongization of standard diphthongs, as in *ppey* (*ppye*) 'bone', *ppam* (*ppyam*) 'cheek', *sengnang* (*sengnyang*) 'matches', *kalkhwu* (*kalkhwi*) 'rake', *kwusin* (*kwisin*) 'ghost', *kapopta* (*kapyepta*) 'light' (weight), *talkal* (*talkyal*) 'egg', *cia* (*kiwa*) 'roof tile', *pakhwu* (*pakhwi*) 'wheel', *peyl* (*pyel*) 'star', *pey* (*pye*) 'unhusked rice', *meylchi* (*myelchi*) 'anchovy', and *kkamakwu* (*kamakwi*) 'crow'; (f) high vowel backing, as in *congwu* (*congi*) 'paper', *kemu* (*kemi*) 'spider', *meymul* (*meymil*) 'buckwheat', and *cokwu* (*coki*) 'yellow corvina', (g) extensive tensification of word-initial lax consonants, as in *ttwupu* (*twupu*) 'tofu', *ppitwulkwu* (*pitwulki*) 'pigeon', *ccange* (*cange*) 'eel', *kkeykwulakci* (*kaykwuli*) 'frog', and *ssonayki* (*sonaki*) 'rain shower', (h) retention of the historical word-medial *z* and *k* as *s* and *k*, respectively, in many words, as in *kasey* or *kasikey* (*kawi*) 'scissors', *kasim* (*kam*) 'material', *pusak* 'fuel hole' (*puekh*) 'kitchen', *musi* (*muu*) 'turnip', *kasil* 'autumn harvest' (*kaul*) 'autumn', *masil* (*maul*) 'village', *tolkaci* (*tolaci*) 'Chinese bellflower', *pakwu* (*pawi*) 'rock', *tok* (*tol*) 'stone', *nangkwu* (*namu*) 'tree', *akop* (*ahop*) 'nine', *pelkeci* (*peleci*, *pelley*) 'worm', *melkwu* (*melwu*) 'wild grapes', and *silkeng* (*sileng*) 'wall shelf'. Even the historical word-initial *s* is retained in such words as *sitong* (*ttong*) 'excrement used for manure'.

This dialect has many diminutive or derogatory nominal suffixes. Frequently used ones are *-eyki*, *-kci*, *-eyngi*, *-angkwu*, *-ali*, *-phak*, *-t(t)eyki*, *-t(t)eyngi*, and *-t(t)akwu*. Word examples with such suffixes are *congceyki* (*congci*) 'small cup', *mikkwulakci* (*mikkwulaci*) 'loach', *kellekci* (*kelley*) 'floor rag', *kkoleyngi*, *kkolangkwu*, or *kkolangteyngi* (*kkoli*) 'tail', *homeyngi* (*homi*) 'weeding hoe', *peyaci* (*pay*) 'stomach', *theykaci* (*thek*) 'chin, jaw', *momttwungali* (*momttwungi*) 'body', *mothwungali* (*mothwungi*) 'corner', *muluphphak* (*muluph*) 'knee', *tolphak* (*tol*) 'stone', *kwutteyki* (*kwi*) 'ear', *kamanitteyki* (*kamani*) 'straw bag', *phalmokteyngi* (*phalmok*) 'wrist', *ppamttakwu* (*ppyam*) 'cheek', and *ppeytakwu* (*ppye*) 'bone'. Words like *nayngkal* (*yenki*, *nay*) 'smoke', *toyptay* (*tolie*) 'on the contrary', *koytayki* (*koyangi*) 'cat', *koypi* (*hocwumeni*) 'pocket', *cengcay* (*puekh*) 'kitchen', *nucakwu* (*canglayseng*) 'hope', *hosupta* (*kipun cohta*) 'feel good', and *photo(p)si* (*kyewu*) 'barely' are unique to this dialect.

Sentence enders unique to this dialect include the plain-level declarative -*eya* (-*ta*) and interrogative and *eya?*, *nya?*(-*ni*, -*(n)u-nya?*) and the polite-level declarative and interrogative -*elawu* (-*e.yo*) and -*elawu?* (-*eyo?*), the familiar-level copula declarative -*si* (-*ney*) and intimate-level copula declarative -*ye* (-*ya*), the deferential-level interrogative -*(su)p-ni-kkye?* (-*(su)p-ni-kka?*), the familiar-level imperative -*so* (-*key*). Conjunctive suffixes somewhat unique to this dialect include -*(u)ngkkey* (-*(u)nikka*) 'because' as in *ka-ngkkey* (*ka-nikka*) 'because (he) goes' and *kule-ngkkey* or *ku-ngkkey* (*kule-nikka*) 'thus, therefore', -*(u)msilong* (-*(u)myense*) 'while doing/being' as in *coh-umsilong* 'while (he) feels happy', and *ttamsi* (*ttaymun-ey*) 'because' as in *ni ttamsi* 'because of you'. The sentence-final particle *ing* indicates a connotation of assurance, intimacy, or concern. Idiosyncratic vocative forms in the sense of 'hello' include *ai* (plain), *ei* (familiar), and *yey* (polite). The following dialogue between an adult (A) and a child (B) illustrates the discourse forms of this dialect.

(16)   A: *ni   pap   muk-ess-nya?*↑ or ↓
              you   meal   eat-PST-Q
              (*ne pap mek-ess-ni?*↑)
              'Did you have your meal?'

         B: *ani-lawu,*↑ *an   muk-ess-elawu.*↓
              no   not   eat-PST-POL
              (*anio,*↑ *an mek-ess-eyo.*↓)
              'No, (I) didn't.'

4.9   Ceycwu zone

The dialect spoken on the island of Ceycwu, off the southern tip of the Korean peninsula, is of great linguistic value in that it has evolved independently without frequent contact with the mainland dialects. While sharing many features with the Cenla and Kyengsang dialects, this dialect retains many interesting old forms.

Some of the phonological features that characterize the dialect include (a) general reflection of the historical fricative *z* as *s*, as in *mɔsil* (*maul*) 'village', *kɔsil* (*kaul*) 'autumn', and *mɔsim* (*maum*) 'mind'; (b) extensive palatalization (as in the Cenla dialect), as in *swung-nyen* (*hyung-nyen*) 'year of bad harvest', *seng* (*hyeng*) 'older brother', *soca* (*hyoca*) 'filial son', *sey* (*hye*) 'tongue', and *chin* (*kkun*) 'string'; (c) retention of old lax consonants, as in *kocang* (*kkoch*) 'flower', *kanchi* (*kkachi*) 'magpie', *sis* (*ssis*) 'wash', *cɔlita* (*ccalpta*) 'short', *kekkta* (*kkekkta*) 'break', and *sekta* (*ssekta*) 'rot'; (d) widespread aspiration phenomena, as in *phenkay* (*penkay*) 'lightening', *pho* (*po*) 'wrapping cloth', *challi* (*calwu*) 'sack', *chey* (*kye*) 'chaff', and *chak* (*ccak*) 'pair'; and (e) retention of the old vowel ɔ, as in *mɔsil* (*maul*) 'village', which is completely lost in the mainland dialects.

Some fossilized suffixes are -*ang*, -*(ay)ngi*, and -*ayki*, as observed in *patang* (*pata*) 'sea', *halwupang* (*halapeci*) 'grandfather, old man', *halamang* (*halmeni*) 'grandmother, old woman', *apang* (*apeci*) 'father', *kocang* (*kkoch*) 'flower', *sayngi* (*say*) 'bird', *cwungi* (*cwi*) 'rat', *keyngi* (*key*) 'crab', *kɔlkayngi* (*homi*) 'weeding hoe', *kangsayngi* (*kangaci*) 'puppy', *mangsayngi* (*mangaci*) 'foal', *cineyayngi* (*ciney*) 'centipede', *cokayngi* (*cokay*) 'shell', *tɔksayki* (*talkyal*) 'egg', *songayki* (*songaci*) 'calf', and *paksayki* (*pakaci*) 'gourd dipper'. Notice that the suffix -*ayki* corresponds to the standard -*aci*, both of which may have been derived from *aki* 'child'.

There are numerous sentence enders unique to this dialect. Declarative enders include -*(u)khiye*, -*em-ce*, -*em-se*, -*em-chwu*, -*khwu-ta* (-*ta*, -*e*, -*ney*, -*(u)o*), -*em-swu-ta*, -*(s)wu-ta* (-*eyo*, -*(su)p-ni-ta*). Interrogative enders are also varied, as shown in -*em-ti(ya)?*, -*em-sini?*, -*esinya?* (-*ni?*, -*(n)u-nya?*), -*m-kka?*, -*m-kko?*, -*em-se?*, -*em-singa?* (-*e?*, -*na?*, -*(u)o?*), -*em-swu-kkwa?*, -*(wu)-kkwa?*, (-*e.yo?*, -*(su)p-ni-kka?*). Imperative and propositive enders include -*(u)p-se*, -*(u)p-ce*, -*(u)sim*, -*cwu* (imperative -*ela*, -*key*, -*e*, -*o*, -*eyo*, -*(u)si-p-si-o*; propositive -*ca*, -*sey*, -*e*, -*eyo*, -*(u)si-p-si-ta*). Sentence examples are as follows (I.S. Lee, et al. ibid.:342–3).

(17)   a. *etu   ley   ka-m-swu-kkwa?*
             where   to   go-IN-AH-Q
             (*eti lo ka-si-p-ni-kka?*)
             'Where are you going, sir?'

         b. *ka-tang   mul-eng   ka-khwu-ta.*
             go-while   ask-and   go-will-DC
             (*ka-taka mul-ese ka-keyss-o.*)
             'I will go asking around.'

         c. *na-yeng   hɔnti   sala-m-ce.*
             I-with   together   live-IN-DC
             (*na-lang hamkkey sal-ko iss-ta.*)
             '(He) is living with me.'

The Ceycwu vocabulary contains many old forms, some unique and some shared by mainland dialects. Examples include *tulu* (*tul*) 'field', *olim* (*san*) 'mountain', *puay* (*hepha*) 'lung', *kwulmay* (*kulimca*) 'shadow', *keyyemci* (*kaymi*) 'ant', *taysani* (*manul*) 'garlic', *cisay* (*kiwa*) 'roof tile', *wuley* (*wulthali*) 'fence', *pulwu* (*sangchi*) 'lettuce', *cengcey* (*puekh*) 'kitchen', *tochi* (*tokki*) 'ax', *palul* (*pata*) 'sea', *tongnangpachi* (*keci*) 'beggar', *katal* (*kalangi*) 'crotch', *pomi* (*tungkye*) 'rice chaff', *sek* (*koppi*) 'reins', *kokoli* (*isak*) 'ear of grain', *-kok* (*-ko*) 'and', and *meythos* (*meystwayci*) 'wild boar'. In addition, there are many words whose etymology is unclear. These include, among many others, *pipali* (*kyeycip.ay*) 'girl', *simpang* (*mutang*) 'shaman', *nɔmphi* (*muu*) 'turnip', *kkwang* (*ppye*) 'bone', *pukpuki* (*hepha*) 'lung', *taychwuk* (*swuswu*) 'Indian millet', *montok* (*menci*) 'dust', *cakci* (*cakal*) 'gravel', *pappuli* (*camcali*) 'dragonfly', and *kongcwungi* (*kwittwulami*) 'cricket'.

4.10   Linguistic divergence in South and North Korea

In addition to the geographically based dialectal differences discussed thus far, there is a superordinate politico-social dialectal bifurcation between North and South Korea. Linguistic divergence between the two Koreas since 1945 has been accelerated mainly by three interrelated factors: (a) complete physical insulation for over fifty years, (b) polarized political, ideological, and social distinctions (with socialism in the North and capitalism in the South), and (c) the different language policies implemented by the two governments, culminating in North Korea's institution of the Phyengyang-based 'Cultured Language' (*munhwa-e*) as their standard speech as against the traditional Seoul-based 'Standard Language' of South Korea (*phyocwun-mal*). Linguistic divergence appears, to varying degrees, in the lexicon, phonology, morphology, grammar, usage, and orthography, with the lexicon being affected most. A brief survey is made below covering the different language policies involved and the range of linguistic divergence effected.

The years following the end of the Second World War saw Koreans in both Koreas demanding a national language that is independent of foreign elements such as Chinese characters and Japanese expressions. Both Koreas launched extensive crusades against illiteracy based on Hankul. In South Korea, the Korean Language Society took the lead for this campaign, whereas in North Korea, Premier Kim Il Song's Teachings (*kyosi*) on the purge of Japanese remnants in education and the fight against illiteracy kindled a widespread movement. Both Koreas have launched respective language purification movements, with essentially the same spirit but with extremely different results. The two Koreas have carried out many other significant policies which are divergent.

4.10.1   South Korean policies

Noteworthy is the evolvement of the policies towards Chinese characters in South Korea. Due to the forceful movement of the Korean Language Society to eliminate Chinese characters, the National Assembly passed a law to enforce the exclusive use of Hankul in 1948. While schools observed the law, society did not. Presidential decrees for the exclusive use of Hankul in 1956 and 1957 achieved only limited success, such as the Hankul-only practice in government documents and in street signboards, but the general public and newspapers kept using characters. Thus, in 1964 the Ministry of Education (MOE) conceded to allow 1,300 common Chinese characters to be taught at elementary (600), intermediate (400), and high (300) schools.

Urged by Hankul scholars, however, the MOE again enforced a Hankul-only policy in January 1970, allowing no characters in documents and textbooks in elementary and secondary schools. The ensuing situation that even high school graduates would be unable to read newspapers led the MOE (with the support of the Korea Research Association of Language Education, the Korean Academy of Sciences, and the press) to decide in 1972 to reinstate character education and chose 1,800 basic characters to be taught at secondary schools, but not at elementary schools. As a result, from 1975, secondary school textbooks were revised to include Chinese characters side by side with Hankul. This practice still obtains at present, although the 1,800 characters do not have a binding force on South Korean society.

As for romanization, the major issue is what symbols are to be used for individual sounds, and how to spell them. This had been a long standing issue in South Korea, until 1984 when the MOE drastically revised its 1959 system and announced a new system largely based on the McCune–Reischauer system. How to spell loan words in Hankul had also been a controversial issue until 1986 when the MOE announced the current Loan Word Spelling Conventions. From 1970 the MOE and scholars made efforts to revise the 1936 version of Standard Language and the 1933 Hankul Spelling Conventions. As a result, the MOE announced the current Revised Standard Language Regulations and Hankul Spelling Conventions in January 1988.

As a free democratic nation, South Korea has achieved only limited success in the area of language purification, despite the continued efforts of the government, scholars, and Korean language associations. Thus, in addition to the existing Sino-Korean words which already occupy more than half of the entire Korean vocabulary, numerous new ones are coined or being introduced from Sino-Japanese as needs arise. Moreover, the Korean lexicon is inundated with thousands of recent English-based loan words (5.5).

4.10.2   *North Korean policies*

North Korea has launched two stages of language policy with complete success: (a) the policy to prohibit the use of Chinese characters and a Hankul-based literacy movement in order to popularize the doctrine of socialism by eliminating illiteracy (1945–64), and (b) the policy of Cultured Language (*munhwa-e*) to standardize Korean essentially based on the Phyengyang dialect and Kim Il Song's self-reliance or *cwuchey* ideology (1964–present). Success of the first stage policies was due to Kim's 1946 Teachings on the Hankul-only policy and the North Korean government's initiation in 1949 of compulsory elementary education.

The second stage policies have been implemented according to Kim Il Song's two sets of language-related Teachings (via dialogues with linguists), one in 1964 and the other in 1966 (e.g., H.M. Sohn 1991). The former presented the basic directions and the latter substantiated them. In the former, Kim issued eight directives: (a) any attempt at script reform be deferred until after the two Koreas are reunified and science and technology become sufficiently advanced; (b) coinage of new words and recovery of old words be based on native elements; (c) use of loan words be limited, and spellings of proper-noun loan words be faithful to their original pronunciations; (d) Chinese characters be abolished in writing but taught for reading purposes only in order to understand South Korean publications; (e) words be spaced properly; (f) unnecessary Sino-Korean words be removed from dictionaries, and local agencies be tightly controlled for the correct use of words; (g) a nationwide campaign be undertaken for the correct use of the language; and (h) Korean language education be improved and strengthened at all levels of education.

In the 1966 Teachings, Kim elaborated upon detailed procedures of refining vocabulary, while directing the linguists to preserve and develop the national characteristics of the Korean language based on the speech of Phyengyang. This is the notion of Kim's Cultured Language. Kim denounced Seoul-based Standard Language as having lost its legitimacy as a national language because 'it is deprived of national characteristics and popular elements and has become the speech of bourgeoisie, a jumble filled with Western, Japanese, and Chinese elements due to American imperialists and their followers' national language erasure policy'. Kim's specific directives on vocabulary refinement procedures in the Teachings are: (a) eliminate from dictionaries those Sino-Korean words which form synonyms with native words; (b) introduce fine dialectal words into the Cultured Language lexicon; (c) introduce native words for place names if necessary; (d) coin new native words based on native elements; (e) change, as far as possible, Sino-Korean terms for fruits, grains, etc. to native terms; (f) try to give native names to newborn babies; (g) change new loan words to native words, except technical terms; (h) preserve native-like Sino-Korean words; and (i) have the Korean Language Assessment Committee (*kwuk.e saceng wiwenhoy*) control new words. In the 1966 Teachings, Kim restated the need for limited Chinese character teaching to students; called for the training of more linguists to develop *cwuchey*-oriented Korean; encouraged research on script reform; and reemphasized the need for proper spacing among words in sentences, indicating that the existing practice allowed too many spaces.

Linguistic theory, policies, planning, and practices in North Korea are aimed at realizing Kim's two sets of Teachings. Dealing with linguistic phenomena and refining Korean had to be done taking Kim's *cwuchey* ideology into account. An unprecedented linguistic reform has thereby resulted.

Many studies are available on the language policies of Korea, especially those of North Korea, e.g., Martin (1968b), M.S. Kim (1972), Y. Hong (1977), H.B. Lee (1977), C.W. Kim (1978b), Sasse (1980), Chon and Choy (1989), CEH (1990), and H.M. Sohn (1991, 1997b). For a comprehensive survey of linguistic studies of Korean in North Korea, see M.S. Kim 1991.

4.10.3   Areas of major linguistic divergence

As stated above, North Korea takes Cultured Language (hereafter, CL) as standard both in pronunciation and spelling. CL is defined as 'the richly developed national language that is formed centering around the revolutionary capital under the leadership of the proletarian party that holds the sovereignty during the socialism-constructing period, and that all people hold as a standard, because it has been refined revolutionarily and polished culturally to fit the proletariat's goals and lifestyle' (CMS 1973). South Korea's Standard Language (hereafter, SL), on the other hand, is defined as 'the contemporary Seoul speech used by educated people' (MOE 1988b), a version modified from the definition in KLA (1933) and KLA (1936) which read 'the contemporary Seoul speech used by middle-class people'. The major areas of linguistic disparity at present between CL and SL comprise the following.

4.10.3.1   Pronunciations

There are many words which manifest phonological divergence. In many cases, these differences are reflected in their respective spellings. The most conspicuous phonological difference is related to the word-initial *l* in Sino-Korean words. In CL, *l* (pronounced as flap *r* [ɾ]) occurs freely in this position, whereas in SL it is omitted before *i* and *y* and replaced by *n* otherwise. Word-medial (but morpheme-initial) Sino-Korean *l* also frequently becomes silent before *i* and *y* only in SL, as observed in (18a). Another productive difference appears in the presence in CL and absence in SL of the word-initial *n* before *i* and *y*, as in (18b). Based on the Phyengyang dialect, CL takes the appearance of these sounds as standard in both speech and spelling.

(18)		South Korea (SL)	North Korea (CL)	
	a.	*i-lon*	*li-lon*	'theory'
		i-ssi	*li-ssi*	'Mr Lee'
		kyeng-cey-nan	*kyeng-cey-lan*	'economic hardship'
		nak-wen	*lak-wen*	'paradise'
		nay-il	*lay-il*	'tomorrow'
		nayng-swu	*layng-swu*	'cold water'
		nong-tam	*long-tam*	'joke'
		pi-yul	*pi-lyul*	'ratio'
		yek-i-yong	*yek-li-yong*	'reverse use'
		yek-sa	*lyek-sa*	'history'
		yey	*lyey*	'example'
	b.	*i*	*ni*	'tooth'
		ilkop	*nilkop*	'seven'
		imca	*nimca*	'you dear'
		i-than	*ni-than*	'peat'
		ye-seng	*nye-seng*	'female'
		yen-lyeng	*nyen-lyeng*	'age'
		yo-so	*nyo-so*	'urea'

Another regular phonological difference is found in vowel harmony. While vowel harmony is strictly observed in CL, there is slight deviation in SL. The deviation is in polysyllabic *p*-irregular predicates followed by an infinitive suffix *-e* or *-a*. Only in SL, *w* (from *p*) and the infinitive suffix are pronounced as *we*, regardless of the bright/dark quality of the preceding vowel, as in (19a). Monosyllabic *p*-irregular predicates in SL observe vowel harmony as in CL, as in (19b).

(19)		South Korea (SL)	North Korea (CL)	
	a.	*alumtaw-e*	*alumtaw-a*	'be beautiful and'
		komaw-e	*komaw-a*	'be thankful and'
		kakkaw-ese	*kakkaw-ase*	'be near, so'
		koylow-ess-ta	*koylow-ass-ta*	'was distressing'
	b.	*tow-a*	*tow-a*	'help and'
		kwuw-e	*kwuw-e*	'bake and'

Less productive phonological differences apply to limited sets of lexical items, which are all reflected in their respective spellings. First, *wi* [wi, y] and *oy* [we, ø] in SL correspond to *wu* [u] and *o* [o] respectively in some words in CL, as in (20a). Second, only CL has aspiration in words like those in (20b). Third, numerous other native or Sino-Korean words are pronounced and spelled differently, as in (20c).

(20)   South Korea (SL)   North Korea (CL)

        a. *ppyektakwi*   *ppyektakwu*   'bone'
            kwi-cel   *kwu-cel*   'paragraph'
            soy-koki   *so-koki*   'beef'
            oyyang-kan   *oyang-kan*   'stable'
            wi   *wu*   'the upper part'

        b. *swu-kom*   *swu-khom*   'male bear'
            kalchi   *khalchi*   'hair-tail'
            kattuk-i   *kattuk-hi*   'fully'
            chwuk-chwuk-i   *chwuk-chwuk-hi*   'moistly'
            ttokttok-ci anh-ta *ttokttok-chi anh-ta* 'be not smart'

        c. *wuloy*   *wuley*   'thunder'
            kulke-moa   *kule-moa*   'collecting'
            talkyal   *talk-al*   'egg'
            wenswu   *wensswu*   'enemy'
            hayp-ssal   *hays-ssal*   'new rice'
            khunak-say   *khullak-say*   'woodpecker'
            huy-no-ay-lak   *huy-lo-ay-lak*   'emotions'
            phay-lyem   *phay-yem*   'pneumonia'

Particularly noteworthy is the fact that although CL is essentially based on the Phyengyang dialect, it observes the spelling practice of SL as far as palatalization is concerned. For instance, 'heaven and earth' is pronounced as *thyenti* in the Phyengyang dialect. Yet, CL defines the palatalized SL pronunciation *chenci* as standard and requires it to be spelled as *chenci* as in the South.

Pronunciations and spellings of loan words are considerably different between SL and CL. The following examples are from Chon and Choy 1989:258–70.

(21)   South Korea (SL)   North Korea (CL)

        a. *payllensu*   *palansu*   'balance'
            khepe   *khapa*   'cover'

tilleyma	*cileynma*	'dilemma'
khep	*koppu*	'cup'
taynsu	*ttansu*	'dance'
mainesu	*minwusu*	'minus'
latio	*lacio*	'radio'
thayngkhu	*ttangkhu*	'tank'

b.
khongko	*kkongko*	'Congo'
hengkali	*weyngkulia*	'Hungary'
khailo	*kkahila*	'Cairo'
pathikhan	*pattikkano*	'Vatican'
suweyteyn	*suweyliyey*	'Sweden'
meyksikho	*meyhikko*	'Mexico'
khaynata	*khanata*	'Canada'

As observed in (21a), North Korean pronunciations of general-term loan words appear to be due to Russian or Japanese influence, whereas SL is more faithful to English pronunciations. As for place names (21b), CL follows the original pronunciations used in the respective countries, apparently in accordance with Kim Il Song's 1964 Teachings, which regulate the pronunciation and spelling of loan words. SL follows the English tradition.

4.10.3.2   Hankul spelling conventions

Considerable spelling disparities exist, as observed from a comparison of two currently used Hankul spelling systems stipulated in South Korea's *Hankul Macchwumpep* (Hankul Spelling Conventions, MOE 1988a) and North Korea's *Kaycenghan Cosenmal Kyupem-cip* (A Revised Collection of Korean Language Norms, KLAC 1988). The discussion on this subject will be deferred to 6.5 in chapter 6 (writing systems).

4.10.3.3   Lexicon

Divergence is particularly great in the lexicon mainly due to the ideological and social differences and the divergent language policies adopted. North Korea has enforced teleological and systematic policies to standardize the language in accordance with their communist ideologies. In North Korea, both the abolishment of the use of Chinese characters and the initiation of the CL policy have been tied to a strong language purification movement. Thus, North Korea has coined some 5,000 lexical items either by nativising Sino-Korean words or by creating new words based on native roots, affixes, obsolete forms, and dialectal elements, while maximally limiting the importation of new loan words. On the other hand, South Korea has been relatively generous in increasing the number of Sino-Korean words by either creating new ones or importing Sino-Japanese words. In addition, over 10,000 English-based loan words have been imported.

One lexical peculiarity of CL is that not many loan words have been newly introduced in the lexicon and many old ones have been eliminated, unless they are very familiar to the general public. The loan words which are still used in North Korea were introduced during the Japanese occupation and have become part of daily life, e.g., *ingkhi* 'ink', *seymeynthu* 'cement', *kapang* 'bag', *khisu* 'kiss', *suphochu* 'sports', *lacio* 'radio', *lokheythu* 'rocket', *pulucyoa* 'bourgeois', *olukang* 'organ', *canglu* 'genre', *ppalchisan* 'guerrilla', and *alkhol* 'alcohol'. CL has nativized many Sino-Korean words which are currently used in SL. In general, North Koreans prefer native to Sino-Korean words, and Sino-Korean to loan words, as alluded to in the following comparison.

(22)	South Korea (SL)	North Korea (CL)	
	Sino-Korean	*Native*	
	hwa-mul-sen	cim-pay	'cargo ship'
	kwu-e	ip-mal	'spoken language'
	cep-mi-sa	twi-puth-i	'suffix'
	cwu-wi	twuli	'surrounding'
	tay-noy	khun-kol	'the cerebrum'
	pha-ak-hata	thule-cwita	'grasp'
	hong-swu	khun-mul	'flood'
	tan-um-cel	hoth-mati	'monosyllable'
	tay-yang	han-pata	'ocean'
	Sino-Korean	*Native + Sino-Korean*	
	swu-ca-wen	pata-cawen	'marine resource'
	en-e-hak-ca	e-mun-il-kwun	'linguist'
	cep-chok-sen	mac-tah-i-sen	'contact line'
	cen-kwu	cen-ki-al	'electric bulb'
	yang-kok	al-kok	'grains'
	hoyng-tan-myen	kalo-calun-myen	'cross section'
	Loan	*Native or Sino-Korean*	
	heyl-ki	cik-sung-ki	'helicopter'
	hokhu	mac-tanchwu	'hook button'

khalle-thipi	*sayk-theyleypicyon*	'colour T.V.'
nokhu	*son-kichek*	'knock'
phama	*pokkum-meli*	'perm'
sulliphe	*kkul-sin*	'slippers'
ssekhesu	*kyo-yey-tan*	'circus'
taiethu	*sal-kka-ki*	'diet'

In many cases, different forms in the same lexical stock (native or Sino-Korean) are used to denote identical concepts or objects.

(23)	South Korea (SL)	North Korea (CL)	
	Native	*Native*	
	tosilak	*pap-kwak*	'lunch box'
	ttey-cwuk-um	*muli-cwuk-um*	'mass dying'
	cwuk	*cwuk-mul*	'gruel'
	ay-po-nun i	*ai-po-kay*	'babysitter'
	kkoch-tapal	*kkoch-mukk-um*	'bouquet'
	onthong	*mangthang*	'totally'
	sangchi	*pulwu*	'lettuce'
	catwu	*chwuli*	'plum'
	nalan-hi	*cwulen-i*	'in a line'
	palo	*incha*	'that is, soon'
	nwun-ka	*nwun-kup*	'edge of eyelid'
	calang-sulepta	*calang-chata*	'be boastful'
	cala-key hata	*calay-wuta*	'make grow, raise'
	cwungel-kelita	*cwechita*	'grumble'
	sichimi-tteyta	*anunposal-hata*	'feign indifference'
	Sino-Korean	*Sino-Korean*	
	han-kwuk	*co-sen*	'Korea'
	kwuk-min	*in-min*	'people'
	chin-kwu	*tong-mu*	'friend'
	chong-cay	*chong-pi-se*	'president'
	kwan-kyey	*lyen-kyey*	'connection'
	kun-wen	*lay-wen*	'origin, source'
	tha-to	*tha-sung*	'overthrowing'
	pay-tal-wen	*thong-sin-wen*	'mailman'
	tay-phung-nyen	*man-phung-nyen*	'year of abundance'
	kyel-uy-mun	*mayng-sey-mun*	'written resolutions'

sang-pan-ki	*sang-pan-nyen*	'first half of a year'
san-pha	*co-san-wen*	'midwife'
sang-ho	*ho-sang*	'each other, mutual'
kwuk-nay-oy	*hay-nay-oy*	'home and abroad'
chey-yuk	*kyo-yey*	'gymnastics'
kak	*may-kay*	'each'
po-co	*pang-co*	'assistance'
so-wi-wen-hoy	*so-co*	'division'
pul-pep-cek	*pi-pep-cek*	'unlawful'
sang-i	*pu-tong*	'difference'
sayng-san	*san-sayng*	'production'

One word innovated in North Korea is *wensswu* 'enemy' which was derived from the Sino-Korean word *wen-swu* 'enemy' (South Korean form) to avoid homonymic clash with the same form (with different Chinese characters) that refers to 'head of the nation'. Different phrasal forms are also observed, as illustrated below.

(24)

	South Korea (SL)	North Korea (CL)	
	-nun-tey tay-han	*-ul-tey tay-han*	'regarding'
	-nun tay-sin	*-ul tay-sin*	'instead of'
	yey lul tul-myen	*yey-ha-myen*	'for instance'
	him-cha-key ile-seta	*il-tte-seta*	'rise up firmly'
	twicip-e ssuy-wuta	*tul-ssuy-wuta*	'put (blame) on'
	cwuk-tolok	*cwuk-ul nayki lo*	'to the end'
	yekhal ul hata	*yekhal ul nolta*	'take a role'
	cak-yong ul hata	*cak-yong ul nolta*	'function'

In North Korea, many abbreviated forms are used.

(25)

	South Korea (SL)	North Korea (CL)	
	ku-li-ha-ye	*ha-ye*	'accordingly'
	lo in-ha-ye	*lo ha-ye*	'due to'
	sim-ci-e nun	*ci-e nun*	'what is more'
	han-phyeng-sayng	*han-sayng*	'one's lifetime'
	kyeng-kyey-sen	*kyey-sen*	'boundary'
	kang-uy-sil	*kang-sil*	'lecture room'
	sang-tay-pang	*tay-pang*	'the other party'
	chong-chey-cek	*chong-cek*	'overall'

4.10.3.4   Meanings and styles

While meanings and styles of words and phrases in South Korea are largely neutral, many expressions in North Korea have metaphorical connotations, orienting the people towards the 'socialistic revolutionary struggle'. Thus, denotational or connotational meaning differences have been developed in certain words of daily usage. For instance, *in-min* (person-people) 'people' in North Korea refers to all the people who take a positive role in the development of a socialist country. Due to such ideological connotation, South Korea does not use this term, but favours *kwuk-min* (country-people) 'people'. Similarly, *lo-tong* (CL)/*no-tong* (SL) 'labour' has a different meaning in North and South Korea. In the North, it denotes a purposive action by means of political or physical effort that is beneficial to the society, whereas in the South it simply refers to physical work. The word *il-kwun* (CL)/*il-kkwun* (SL) refers to a person who is engaged in either physical or mental work in the North, but refers in general to a person engaged in hard manual labour in the South. The word *tongmu* refers, in the North, to a person who shares socialistic ideology with the speaker, whereas it simply refers to a friend in the South where it is coming into disuse in favour of *chin-kwu* 'friend'. The word *pi-phan*, meaning 'criticism' in the South, has aquired in the North the sense of examining and analysing whether a conduct accords with ideological orientations. The word *pang-co-hata*, which means 'to assist' in a good sense in the North, has acquired a bad sense in the South, i.e., 'assist a person in criminal conduct'. Some other examples are given in (26).

(26)   South Korea (SL)   North Korea (CL)
         cek-kuk-cek   *cin-kong-cek*   'positive'
         positive   attacking
         phi na-nun   *phi tha-nun*   'very strenuous'
         blood appearing   blood burning
         kaul-keti/chwu-swu   *kaul-keti cen-thwu*   'harvest'
         fall-harvest/harvest   fall-harvest combat

A headline in the North Korean newspaper *Lotong Sinmun* reads as follows. Its South Korean equivalent is given in parentheses.

(27)   *1500 man thon uy   alkok koci lul cemlyenghal tey tay-han mokphyo*
         15 million ton GN grain hill AC occupying   regarding   goal
         (SL: *1500 man   thon   uy   yangkok   sayngsan   mokphyo*)
              15 million ton   GN grain   production   goal
         'the goal of achieving the production of 15,000,000 tons of grain'

5

Lexicon

This chapter presents the composition and general characteristics of the Korean lexicon and the salient features of each of the three lexical stocks (native, Sino-Korean, and loan) that constitute the Korean vocabulary. All Korean words and expressions appearing in this chapter are represented by the Yale system of romanization reflecting the South Korean Hankul spelling convention. In romanization, hyphens are used as needed to indicate affixal or compound boundaries.

5.1   Composition of the Korean lexicon

Due to her long and frequent historical contact with China and Japan as well as rapid modernization in all walks of life, Contemporary Korea is provided with a lexicon unprecedentedly enriched with new coinages and borrowings. Some 450,000 lexical items are entered in *Wulimal Khun Sacen* (A Great Dictionary of the Korean Language, 1991) compiled by the Korean Language Society.

The Contemporary Korean lexicon consists of approximately 35% of native, 60% of Sino-Korean (hereafter SK), and 5% of loan elements. Native elements (*ko-yu-e*) are the lexical items inherited from time immemorial, which express natural objects, basic actions and states, concrete concepts, and grammatical relations essential to basic human subsistence and Koreans' traditional agrarian culture. Both SK and loan words represent all kinds of cultural items and abstract concepts that traditional and modern civilizations have to offer. The number of SK and loan words is growing fast, while that of native words remains largely stagnant. Due to their historical anteriority and productivity in new word creation, SK words are perceived by Koreans as more native-like than loan words.

Traditionally borrowing was mainly from China. Although borrowings from Chinese ceased long ago, Chinese characters (also called Chinese logographs) and the morphemes they represent have been used expediently and productively to coin thousands of new words as needs arose. All Koreanized words based on Chinese-character morphemes, whether they are ancient borrowings directly from Chinese or reborrowings indirectly from Sino-Japanese, or coinages in Korea, are called SK words or *han-ca-e* 'Chinese character words'. The SK origin of more than half of the total Korean vocabulary can be attributed to two facts: (a) that Chinese culture and learning deeply permeated all facets of Korean life in the past, as historically Korea long subordinated herself to the political and cultural influence of China, and (b) that, due to the ideographic nature of the characters and the monosyllabic nature of the morphemes, Chinese-character morphemes facilitate new word formation, much more efficiently than native morphemes, to represent the new concepts and products that continuously appear as civilization progresses. Thus, nearly all technical terms in academic fields, politics, economics, law, society, and other cultural aspects, as well as personal, place, and institutional names, are SK words. The majority of technical terms have been coined in Japan as Sino-Japanese and then introduced to Korea, as well as to China, since Japan was the first nation in the East to import Western civilization and culture during the Meiji Restoration Period. The difference between Sino-Japanese and SK words is primarily in pronunciation.

Modern borrowing has been predominantly from scientifically and technologically advanced America and Europe. These non-SK borrowings are called loan words or *oy-lay-e* (literally 'words from abroad'). Before the Second World War, a majority of loan words were introduced into the Korean lexicon by way of Japanese. Japanese occupation of Korea (1910–45) also left many native Japanese words in the Korean lexicon. Since 1945 when Korea was liberated from Japan, few new loan words have come from Japanese, but many have entered from English, along with various technological concepts and cultural products. New loan words in many cases compete with SK coinages. For instance, the SK word *sung-kang-ki* (move up-move down-machine) has long been used to denote an elevator, but is gradually being replaced by the loan word *eyleypeythe*. Similarly, the loan word *khemphyuthe* is more frequently used than the SK *cen-san-ki* (electronic-calculate-machine) for a computer. The SK word *tha-ca-ki* (hit-letter-machine) and the loan word *thaiphulaithe* for a typewriter and the SK word *cen-cha* (war-vehicle) and the loan word *thayngkhu* 'tank' seem to be used with about equal frequency. Many SK words are still exclusively used, e.g., *sen-phung-ki* (fan-wind-machine) 'electric fan', *ca-tong-cha* (self-move-vehicle) 'car', *cen-hwa* (electric-talk) 'telephone', and *nayng-cang-ko* (cold-store-storehouse) 'refrigerator'.

The impact of non-native words on the Korean language is great. One effect is the proliferation of a large number of synonymous expressions. Frequently, synonymous words are associated with different shades of meaning and stylistic or social values, thus enriching the Korean vocabulary. When synonyms exist, native words usually represent unsophisticated traditional culture, whereas SK words convey more formality and tend to denote higher quality objects and more formal, abstract, and sometimes more socially prestigious concepts. Loan words are, in general, associated with modern and stylish objects and concepts. For instance, the native word *kalak* for 'rhythm' is usually used with reference to traditional Korean folk songs, the SK word *wun-yul* (rhyme-law) in formal or academic situations, and the loan word *litum* for some sort of Western flavour. The triplet *chwum* (native), *mu.yong* (SK), and *taynsu* (loan) for 'dance' have similar connotational differences. The native word *cip* is used when referring to one's own house or a house of a social inferior, but the SK word *tayk* is used when referring to a socially superior adult's house. While there is no native term for a hotel, the SK word *ye-kwan* (travel-house) refers to less expensive Korean-style hotels without beds, whereas the loan word *hotheyl* refers to expensive Western-style hotels with beds.

A second impact, which is extremely negative, is that many native words have been lost in the battle with SK and loan words and, as a result, disappeared from usage long ago, frequently irrecoverably. While Chinese characters in Japanese are read not only in Sino-Japanese pronunciation but also in the pronunciation of corresponding native morphemes, thereby contributing to the maintenance of native words, Chinese characters in Korea have been read only in SK pronunciation, which must have contributed to the disuse of native words. For instance, SK *san* 'mountain', *kang* 'river', *sangca* 'box', *wusan* 'umbrella', *payk* '100', and *chen* '1000' have completely replaced native *moy*, *kalam*, *tamsan*, *syulwup*, *on*, and *cumun*, respectively.

Third, while most SK and loan words have been adapted to the phonological patterns of native Korean, there are cases where the native sound patterns themselves have been affected by non-native words. For instance, fifteenth-century Korean (Middle Korean) had, and the Kyengsang and Hamkyeng dialects still have, lexical tones which may be due to the prolonged influx of Chinese words. Loan words where word-initial *l* appears, such as *lakheys* 'racket', *latio* 'radio', *laithe* 'lighter', *lostey hotheyl* 'Lotte Hotel', and *lenchi* 'lunch', have been disrupting the original sound pattern where no native words begin with an initial *l* sound, a typological characteristic shared by Altaic languages. Furthermore, SK words where vowel harmony is not observed have contributed to the disruption of vowel harmony in native words.

Fourth, non-native words in Korean also have had certain effects on the morphology of Korean. For instance, most SK compounds have internal morphology reflecting Chinese word or morpheme order. Thus, the SK-native compound verb *ke-twu-cel-mi-hata* (discard-head-cut-tail-do) 'give the gist; summarize' (lit. 'discard the head and lop off the tail') reflects the Chinese order in the SK word *ke-twu-cel-mi*, not the Korean order which would be the unacceptable **twu-ke-mi-cel-hata*.

Another morphological effect is the derivation of thousands of compound verbs and adjectives based mostly on SK but also on loan elements. When Chinese and other foreign verbs and adjectives are introduced into Korean as SK or loan words, they are frozen as so-called verbal or adjectival nouns, and never function as independent predicates in Korean. In order for them to function as predicates, they must be compounded with a native predicate (e.g., *hata* 'do, be', *toyta* 'become', *ita* 'be'). The native elements in such hybrid compounds are necessary for grammatical inflection. Examples include *kongpu-hata* (SK study-) 'study', *poksa-hata* (SK copy-) 'copy', *khaphi-hata* (copy-) 'copy', *suthulaikhu-hata* (strike-) 'strike', *teymo-hata* (demonstration-) 'demonstrate (against)', *thephu-hata* (tough-) 'be tough', *cheypho-toyta* (SK arrest-) 'be arrested', *khaynsul-toyta* (cancel-) 'be cancelled', *poksa-toyta* (SK copy-) 'be copied', *khaphi-toyta* (copy-) 'be copied', *yelsim-ita* (SK enthusiasm-) 'be enthusiastic', and *pi-kwahakcek-ita* (SK un-scientific-) 'be unscientific'.

Fifth, SK elements have added a sizable number of conjunctive and manner adverbs to the Korean lexicon, as shown in *cuk-si* (immediate-time) 'immediately', *tan* 'but', and *cem-cem* (gradual-gradual) 'gradually'. The monosyllabic SK element *cha* (next, second) 'as, when, in order to' functions as a conjunctive suffix when attached to an SK verbal noun, as in *mikwuk ul pangmun-cha hankwuk ul ttena-ss-ta* (America AC visit-*cha* Korea AC leave-PST-DC) '(He) left Korea in order to visit America.'

Finally, non-native words rarely function as particles or other functional words. Thus, there are an infinite number of coined phrases based only on SK words that do not contain any particle or other functor, a syntactic process not shared by native elements. Notice that the following phrase consists only of SK words.

(1)   *Kwuk-cey   yen-hap   kyo-yuk   kwa-hak   mun-hwa ki-kwu*
         internation union   education science   culture   organization
         'United Nations Educational, Scientific, and Cultural Organization
         (UNESCO)'

Both SK and loan words are an integral part of the Korean lexicon, and they are not foreign words. First of all, these non-native words are assimilated to the phonological patterns of Korean. Native elements do not have such fricative sounds as [f, v, θ, ð, z, x]. Neither voicing nor tone ever becomes phonemic in standard Korean. Therefore, SK and loan words are Koreanized in pronunciation, as in *pang-wi* 'direction' (SK) and *phawul* 'foul (in baseball)' (loan), whose source languages have the initial *f*. Furthermore, native Korean does not allow word-initial *l*. SK initial *l* also gets deleted (before *i* and *y*) or changed to *n* (elsewhere) in the word-initial position in South Korean (but not in North Korean) speech, a phenomenon not found in Chinese and Sino-Japanese. Thus, in SK *i-lon* 'theory' and *non-li* 'logic', occurrence of the allomorphs *i/li* 'reason' and *lon/non* 'discussion' is due to their following the native sound pattern. Some loan words are subject to this rule, as in *nasa* (from Portuguese *raxa*) 'woollen cloth'. Even 'radio' and 'racket' used to be rendered as *nacio* and *nakheythu*, respectively, although the current forms are *latio* and *lakheys*. Similarly, the rule changing *n* to *l* before or after *l* applies to both native and non-native words, e.g., *sel-nal* [səl.lal] 'New Year's Day' (native), *sin-la* [sil.la] 'the Sinla dynasty' (SK), and *sseyil nothu* [s'e.il.lo.thɨ] 'notebooks on sale' (loan). Palatalization has also applied to both native and non-native words, as in native *cita* (< *tita*) 'to lose a game' and SK *chenci* (< *thyenti*) 'heaven and earth'.

Like native words, SK and loan words are susceptible to semantic change independently of the source (foreign) words. The most common type of change is specialization. That is, only one sense, among many, of a source word is usually adopted. This can be observed abundantly in the loan words imported through Japanese (cf. Shibatani 1990:150–2). For instance, unlike the German word *Arbeit* 'work', its loan counterpart *alpaithu* refers only to a part-time job held by students. Similarly, *suthuleysu* from 'stress' refers only to the sense of mental tension, *teymo* from 'demonstration' only to a public diplay of group feelings against authorities, *ppol* from 'ball' only to a large-sized ball, *kkol* from 'goal' only to a goal in games, *mithing* from 'meeting' only to students' group dates, *sita* from Japanese *sida* 'underside, an assistant' only to the sense of an assistant in skilled labour, *p(p)othu* from 'boat' only to a small boat, and *matam* from 'madam' only to a head hostess in a restaurant or a bar.

Also, many non-native elements have undergone shifts in meaning. For instance, *apeykhu* from French *avec* 'with' only to a dating couple, and *ppoi* from 'boy' only to a hotel waiter. SK *ki-cha* (steam-vehicle) refers to a train, while the same word denotes an automobile in Chinese. SK *hak-wen* which means a private institute in Korean refers to a college in Chinese. SK *yang-pan* (two-classes) used to refer to the two highest social classes (civilian and military), but is now used roughly in the sense of 'a gentleman'. Similarly, SK *yeng-kam* (command-supervision) which used to denote a high ranking government official is now used to refer to any old man or one's aged husband. The loan word *notaci* from 'no touch' only denotes a bonanza, a rich vein, or, adverbially, 'always'. This loan word is said to have its origin in 1898 when an American named Morse who leased a Korean mine shouted 'no touch' to Korean miners when dynamite was exploded.

Like native words, SK and loan words are subject to local coinage or change in form. This is overwhelmingly productive in SK, but is also observable in loan words. In addition to hundreds of locally coined SK words based on Chinese characters, words like *pyelak* 'thunder', *kimchi* 'Korean pickle', *sellengthang* 'beef soup with rice', and *wensswu* 'enemy' (only in North Korea) are nativized forms of SK *pyek-lyek* (lightning-thunder), *chim-chay* (pickled-vegetable), *sel-nong-thang* (snow-thickness-soup), and *wen-swu* (hate-enemy), respectively. Loan words like *potey* 'body' (of car), *ppila* 'flyer', *tampay* 'tobacco', and *khaypineys* 'cabinet' are also locally changed forms. Words like *payk-mile* (from 'back' and 'mirror') 'a rear-view mirror' and *oltu missu* (from 'old' and 'miss') 'spinster, old maid' were created in Japanese and then introduced to Korean. More examples will be given in 5.2, 5.3, and 5.4.

As for the distribution of native and non-native words in daily written usage, statistics indicate that SK words are particularly predominant in science magazines and scholarly journals and books, as well as in the political, economic, and financial columns of newspapers, whereas native words prevail in novels and popular magazines as well as in the social columns of newspapers. Loan words are widespread in magazines and newspapers on sports, cooking, fashion, technology, and other aspects of recently imported culture.

5.2   Native words

Most native words have been either inherited or coined on the basis of the native stock. However, some SK words which were borrowed from either written or spoken Chinese in ancient times and have undergone radical change either in form alone or in both form and meaning are generally considered as native words by the general public. These nativized SK words are illustrated in (2). Corresponding SK source words and available Ancient Chinese (An-Chn) or reconstructed proto-Chinese forms are given in parentheses for comparison (cf. J. Shim 1983; K.M. Lee 1991; J.H. Jeon 1992; C.T. Kim 1993).

(2)   *cacwu*   'purple' (SK *ca-cek* 'purple')

      caycwu   'talent' (SK *cay-co* 'talent')

      cek   'time' (SK *si* 'time', proto-Chinese *dieg)

      cimsung   'beast' (SK *cwungsayng* 'living things')

      hwuchwu   'black pepper' (SK *ho-cho* 'Manchu-pepper')

      ka   'edge' (SK *kyey* 'edge', An-Chn *kai*)

      kaci   'eggplant' (SK *ka-ca* 'eggplant')

      kakey   'store' (SK *ka-ka* 'false house')

      kanan   'poverty' (SK *kan-nan* 'hardship')

      mek   'ink-stone' (SK *muk* 'ink-stone', An-Chn *mek*)

      mumyeng   'cotton' (SK *mok-myen* 'tree cotton')

      nwupi   'quilting' (SK *nap-uy* 'quilted clothes')

      paychwu   'Chinese cabbage' (SK *payk-chay* 'white vegetable')

      pey   'hemp cloth' (SK *pho* 'cloth', An-Chn *puo*)

popay	'treasure' (SK *po-phay* 'treasure shell')
pus	'calligraphy brush' (SK *phil* 'brush', An-Chn *piet*)
pye	'unhulled rice' (SK *phay*, An-Chn *pai*)
sal	'arrow' (SK *si*, proto-Chinese *sier*)
salang	'love' (SK *sa-lyang* 'consideration')
sam-cit/cil	'the third day' (SK *sam-il* 'the third day')
sangchwu	'lettuce' (SK *sang-chay* 'common vegetable')
sanyang	'hunting' (SK *san-hayng* 'mountain going')
sathang	'candy' (SK *sa-tang* 'sugar')
sayngchel	'sheet zinc' (SK *se-yang-chel* 'Western metal')
sengnyang	'matches' (SK *sek-lyu-hwang* 'sulphur')
si-wel	'October' (SK *sip-wel*)
sselmay	'sled' (SK *sel-ma* 'snow horse')
ssu	'write' (SK *se* 'write', An-Chn *siwo*)
thokki	'rabbit' (SK *tho* as in *ok-tho* 'white rabbit', proto-Chinese **thogs*)
yo	'sleeping mat' (SK *yok* as in *san-yok* 'childbirth quilt')

Some of the SK words from Sanskrit have also been nativized, e.g., *puche* 'Buddha' (SK *pul-tha*; Buddha), *kental* 'penniless rake' (SK *ken-tal*; *gandharva*), and *posal* 'Buddhist saint' (SK *po-sal; Bodhisattva*). Words of Manchu-Tungus origin are considered native, e.g., *homi* 'weeding hoe' (< *homin*), *swuswu* 'Indian millet' (< *syusyu*), *kewi* 'goose' (< *kalwu*), *pa* 'place', *kawi* 'scissors' (< *hasaa*), and *malwu* 'floor' (< *mulwu*).

Many native words have undergone changes, as illustrated in (3). Some changes are only semantic, while others are both semantic and formal.

(3)

Middle Korean		Contemporary Korean
eli 'origin, fountain'	>	*el* 'soul'
elita 'be stupid'	>	*elita* 'be very young'
e.yesputa 'be pitiful'	>	*yeypputa* 'be pretty, cute'
him 'muscles'	>	*him* 'strength, energy'
ipati 'feast'	>	*ipaci* 'contribution'
kolochita 'point, teach'	>	*kalikhita* 'point'; *kaluchita* 'teach'
komapta 'be noble'	>	*komapta* 'be thankful'
kwuwisil 'government post'	>	*kwusil* 'function, role'
kyeyota 'be unable to win'	>	*keywuta* 'vomit'
namta 'go over'	>	*namta* 'remain'
nolɔs 'play'	>	*nolus* 'role'

nulta 'win, excel'	>	*nulta* 'increase, get better'	
nyelum 'fruit, summer'	>	*yelum* 'summer'	

Native words include not only the vocabulary essential to the maintenance of basic human life but other items that are unique to the time-honoured culture of traditional Korea. Thus, not only body parts, natural objects, flora and fauna, basic actions, physical and psychological states, but also terms for agriculture and fishery, low-level numerals, kinship terms, honorific expressions, all kinds of basic grammatical functions, and extensive sound symbolism are represented by native words.

Thus, for instance, rice is the major staple food and is represented by many different native words: *mo* 'rice seedling', *pye/nalak* 'rice plant, unhusked rice', *ssal* 'husked rice', *ssal-aki* 'broken bits of husked rice', *pap* 'cooked rice', *nwi* 'unhusked rice in husked rice', *ol-pye* 'early ripening rice plant or its unhusked rice', *ip-ssal* 'white husked rice', *chap-ssal* 'sticky husked rice', *meyp-ssal* 'non-glutinous husked rice'. Another aspect of traditional culture is reflected in the verbs of 'wearing' and 'carrying' which are differentiated depending on what parts of the body are involved. These include *chata* 'wear (a watch, a sword, a decoration)', *cita* 'carry an inanimate object on the back', *epta* 'carry an animate object on the back', *ita* 'carry on the head', *ipta* 'wear (a dress)', *twuluta* 'wear (a shawl)', *kelchita* 'throw on', *kkita* 'wear (gloves, a ring, glasses)', *mayta* 'wear (a tie)', *meyta* 'carry on the shoulder', *sinta* 'wear (footwear)', *ssuta* 'wear (headgear, an umbrella, glasses)', and *talta* 'wear (a decoration, a nametag)'.

Native terms for numbers go up to ninety-nine in Contemporary Korean, the higher numbers being taken over by either SK numerals as in *payk-i-sip-il* (SK 100-2-10-1) '121' or SK-native compounds as in *payk-sumul-hana* (SK 100-native 20-1) '121'.

(4)								
	hana, han	'1'	*twul, twu*	'2'	*seys, sey*	'3'		
	neys, ney	'4'	*tases*	'5'	*yeses*	'6'		
	ilkop	'7'	*yetelp*	'8'	*ahop*	'9'		
	yel	'10'	*sumul*	'20'	*selhun*	'30'		
	mahun	'40'	*swin*	'50'	*yeyswun*	'60'		
	ilhum	'70'	*yetun*	'80'	*ahun*	'90'		
	yel-han(a)	'11'	*sumul-sey(s)*	'23'	*ahun-ahop*	'99'		

Native numeral counters are well developed. Counters follow the numeral in a numerative construction, as in *cip twu chay* (house 2 counter for houses) 'two houses', There are also a number of SK and a small number of loan counters (e.g., *khilo* 'kilogram, kilometer', *phulo* 'per cent', *thasu* 'dozen'), which generally cover products of contemporary civilization. Counters are either for classification, representing the general quality of the items being counted, or for measurement in accordance with legal systems such as weights, measures, time fractions, and currency. Native counters are illustrated in (5) and (6), while SK examples will be given in 5.4.

(5)   Classificatory counter   Members (examples)

       calwu   'long slender things'   pencils, brooms

       khyelley 'pairs'   shoes, socks, gloves

       kulwu   'tree stocks'   trees of all kinds

       maciki   'patches of fields'   rice fields (*non*), dry fields (*path*)

       mali   'animate objects'   animals of all sorts

       mo   'angles'   bean-curd (*twupu*), jelly (*muk*)

       pel   'sets'   clothes, vessels (*kulus*)

       phoki   'roots, heads'   cabbages, grasses

       songi   'bunches'   all species of flowers, grapes

(6)   Measurement counters

    a. *sem* = SK *sek*   47.6 U.S. gallons; 2 straw sacks of grains

        mal = SK *twu*   1/10 *sem* or 10 *toy* or approx. 4 gallons

        toy = SK *sung*   1/10 *mal* or 10 *hop*

    b. *ca* = SK *chek*   10/33 meter

        chi = SK *chon*   1/10 *ca*

    c. *nyang*   1.325 ounce

        ton   0.1325 ounce = 3.7565 grammes

    d. *hay* = SK *nyen*   'years' (for counting)

        tal = SK *kay-wel*   'months' (for counting)

Like numerals, kinship and colour terms of the native stock are very limited (SK words in these classes are predominant). Native kinship terms cover two generations up and one generation down, as well as ego's siblings, as in *apeci* 'father', *emeni* 'mother', *halapeci* 'grandfather', *halmeni* 'grandmother', *acessi* 'uncle', *acwumeni* 'aunt', *oppa*, *olapeni* 'older brother' (of a female), *nwuna* 'older sister' (of a male), *enni* 'older sister' (of a female), *awu* 'younger sibling' (of the same sex), *nwui* 'sister', *atul* 'son', *ttal* 'daughter', *cokha* 'nephew, niece', *sawi* 'son-in-law', and *myenuli* 'daughter-in-law'. Colour terms include the nouns *kemceng* 'black', *nolang* 'yellow', *phalang* 'blue, green', *pola* 'purple', and *ppalkang* 'red'; adjectives *huyta*, *ha.yahta* 'be white', *kemta*, *kkamahta* 'be black', *nolahta*, *nwulehta* 'be yellow', *phuluta*, *phalahta* 'be blue, green', and *pulkta*, *ppalkahta* 'be red'; and extended adjective forms such as *kemuteytey-hata*, *kemusulum-hata*, *kemucwukcwuk-hata*, *kemus-hata* 'be darkish', *nwulusulum-hata* 'be yellowish', *pulkusuley-hata* 'be reddish', *say-phalahta, si-phelehta* 'be deep blue', and *say-ppalkahta, si-ppelkehta* 'be dark red'.

As will be observed in great detail in chapter 9 (9.14), the Korean native lexicon has a rich variety of native hierarchical honorific expressions, which encompass address–reference terms, personal pronouns, nouns, verbs, adjectives, adverbs, case particles, and suffixes. In addition, as will be discussed in chapters 8 and 9, Korean has numerous particles that indicate case relations (e.g., nominative *ka/i*, accusative *(l)ul*) or function as delimiters (e.g. *(n)un* 'as for', *to* 'also', *man* 'only') and hundreds of inflectional and derivational suffixes (e.g., interrogative ender *-kka*, conjunctive *-ko* 'and', and passive and causative suffixes). Almost all such particles and suffixes are native. Also, so-called auxiliary predicates are all native. Having developed from regular or 'main' predicates with change in meaning, auxiliary predicates occur after a main predicate, as in *mek-e pota* 'try eating', where the verb *mekta* 'eat' is a main verb, *-e* an infinitive suffix, and *pota* 'try' (derived from the main verb *pota* 'see') an auxiliary verb. Furthermore, all demonstrative elements are native and display deictic-anaphoric forms that are differentiated in four ways: *i* 'this' (close to speaker), *ku* 'that' (close to hearer; known to both speaker and hearer), *ce* 'that over there' (away from speaker and hearer), and *enu* 'which'.

Finally, the Korean lexicon is characterized by the proliferation of sound symbolic words in the native stratum. Since sound symbolism is particularly pervasive in Korean, it is discussed in a separate section (5.3) below. For more on lexical classes, see H.M. Sohn 1994.

5.3   Sound symbolism

The Korean lexicon contains several thousands of sound symbolic (or ideophonic) words, most of which belong to the native stock. Such words have delicate Sprachgefühls as well as connotational nuances, and not only give vividness, expressiveness, and vitality to daily human interactions but are widely employed for their effect in literary works of all genres. Many ideophonic words appear in two or more shapes, as in *phatak* vs. *phetek* 'flapping, flopping, splashing', *nol-ahta* vs. *nwul-ehta* 'be yellow', *koso-hata* vs. *kwuswu-hata* 'taste or smell like sesame or rice tea', *kolita* vs. *kwulita* 'be stinking', *tongkul-ahta* vs. *twungkul-ehta* 'be round', *panccak* vs. *penccek* vs. *ppanccak* vs. *ppenccek* 'glittering', and *callang* vs. *challang* vs. *ccallang* 'jingling'.

As observed in the above examples, sound symbolism is reflected in both vowels and consonants. As for vowels, 'bright' (Yang) vowels **a, ɛ, o** tend to connote brightness, sharpness, lightness, smallness, thinness, and quickness, whereas 'dark' (Ying) vowels **e, u, ə** indicate darkness, heaviness, dullness, slowness, deepness, and thickness. For instance, in pairs such as *phatak* vs. *phetek*, *nol-ahta* vs. *nwul-ehta*, *hwanhata* vs. *hwenhata* 'be bright, clear', and *ppo.yahta* vs. *ppu.yehta* 'be misty, pearly', the first word contains a bright vowel *a* or *o* while the second has a dark vowel *e* or *wu*, showing 'bright' and 'dark' connotational differences.

As for consonants, sound symbolic words show differences among plain, aspirate, and tense consonants. A plain consonant tends to connote slowness, gentleness, heaviness, and bigness, an aspirate consonant flexibility, elasticity, crispness, and swiftness, and a tense consonant compactness, tightness, hardness, smallness, and extra swiftness. Thus, aspirate and tense consonants are related to more intensity, compared with lax consonants, as in *pelttek* 'pitapat' (relatively slow and deep) vs. *phelttek* 'pitapat' (faster and agile) vs. *ppelttek* 'pitapat' (fastest and violent), and also in *seyta* 'strong' vs. *sseyta* 'very strong'. Similarly, the geminate *ll* tends to be more intensive than a single *l*, as in *cwuleng-cwuleng* vs. *cwulleng-cwulleng* 'in clusters'. In some alternating variants, the difference is no longer connotational, but instead has evolved as denotational, as illustrated in (7).

(7)

atuk.hata	'be far off'	*etwuk.hata*	'be a bit dark'
cakta	'small' (in size)	*cekta*	'small' (in quantity)
kacwuk	'skin, hide'	*kecwuk*	'surface'
kkakkta	'cut'	*kkekkta*	'break'
kopta	'be winding'	*kwupta*	'be bent'
kot.ta	'be straight'	*kwut.ta*	'be hard'
malkta	'be clean'	*mulkta*	'be watery, thin'
mali	(counter for animals)	*meli*	'head'
mas	'taste' (of food)	*mes*	'taste' (of manner)
nalkta	'be old' (things)	*nulkta*	'be old' (animates)
namta	'remain'	*nemta*	'go over'
ta	'all'	*te*	'more'
tahata	'exhaust'	*tehata*	'add'

Many ideophonic words appear in reduplicated forms, as reduplication is associated with temporal or spatial repetition or continuation, as in *phatak-phatak* 'flapping' and *kemus-kemus* 'dotted with black' (*kemus* 'black'). Variety is often expressed by deleting the initial consonant in the first member in reduplication, as in *allok-tallok*, *ellwuk-tellwuk* 'mottled', *wulkus-pulkus* 'multi-coloured', and *along-talong* 'spotted'. To indicate slowness of action, a meaningless syllable is often added to a word, as in *huntuleng-huntuleng* (cf. *huntul-huntul*) 'swinging, swaying', *komcilak-komcilak* (cf. *komcak-komcak*) 'budging', *kkwupultheng* (cf. *kkwupul*) 'winding, twisting', *ttayngkulang* (cf. *ttayngkul*) 'tinkling', and *kwumulek-kwumulek* (cf. *kwumul-kwumul*) 'sluggish'.

Onomatopoeic words constitute the most productive subset of the sound symbolic vocabulary. Notice the difficulty in translating them into English in the following sentence. The three mutually related onomatopoeic words give us different feelings, the most salient feature being the different relative degrees of wind speed, *sal-sal* the slowest and *swul-swul* the fastest.

(8)   *palam-i*   **sal-sal/sol-sol/swul-swul**   *pul-e.yo.*
         wind-NM   softly   blow-POL
         'The wind blows *softly.*'

The broad category of onomatopoeia in Korean may be subclassified as phonomimes (mimicking of natural sounds), phenomimes (depicting manners of the external world), and psychomimes (depicting mental conditions or states). In the following, however, the latter two sets are combined under the rublic of *uy-thay-e* 'phenomimes, mimeses' (lit. 'manner-imitating words') as against *uy-seng-e* 'phonomimes' (lit. 'sound-imitating words'), a practice commonly adopted by Korean linguists. Phonomimes refer primarily to the impressions of sounds and mimeses to the impressions of sight, smell, taste, touch, or mental condition or state. Onomatopoeic words are typically of one or two syllables and are used very often as reduplicated forms. A broad semantic classification is given in (9) and (10).

(9)   *Uyseng-e* (Phonomimes)
         a. animate-related forms
             ang-ang, eng-eng, ung-ung 'bawling, squalling' (in a cry)
             ccik-ccik, ccayk-ccayk 'tweeting, chirp' (of a bird or rat)
             kaykwul-kaykwul 'croaking' (of a frog)
             kkal-kkal, kkel-kkel 'ha-ha, haw-haw'
             kkawuk-kkawuk 'caw-caw' (of a crow)
             kkokkyo 'cock-a-doodle-doo'
             kkwul-kkwul 'oink-oink' (of a pig)
             maym-maym 'chirping' (of a locust)
             meng-meng 'bow-wow'
             ppekkwuk-ppekkwuk 'cuckooing'
             pueng-pueng 'hooting' (of an owl)
             sokon-sokon, swukun-swukun 'whispering'
             ummey 'moo'
             yaong 'meow'

b. solid-related forms
ccalk(k)ak, ccalkhak, ccalkhatak, ccalkhatang, chalk(h)ak,
 chelk(h)ek, chelkheteng 'with a click, snap'
callang, celleng, ccallang, ccelleng 'clink, jingle'
khwang, kkwang, khwung, kkwung 'with a boom, bang, thud'
phak, phayk, phik, phuk, phek, phok 'with a thud, hiss'
talka, telkek, ttalkak, ttelkek, talkatak, ttelketek 'rattling'
tong-tong, twung-twung, ttang-ttang, thang-thang, teng-teng,
 theng-theng, tteng-tteng 'drumming, tum-tum, banging'
ttwuk-ttwuk, thwuk-thwuk, ttok-ttok, thok-thok,ttwuk-ttak,
 thwuk-thak 'dripping, knocking, with snaps'

c. liquid-related forms
challang-challang, chwulleng-chwulleng, ccwulleng-ccwulleng,
 chelleng-chelleng, chilleng-chilleng 'lapping, slopping'
chalpatak, chelpetek 'splashing, slopping, dabbling'
col-col, ccol-ccol, cwul-cwul, ccwul-ccwul, cayl-cayl, ccayl-ccayl,
 cal-cal, ccal-ccal, cel-cel, ccel-ccel 'tricklingly, murmuringly'
cwulwuk, cwulwulwuk, ccwulwulwuk 'in sudden downpours'
kkwulleng-kkwulleng 'slushing (splashing) around inside'
pokul-pokul, ppokul-ppokul, pakul-pakul, ppakul-ppakul,
 pukul-pukul, ppukul-ppukul 'boiling, bubbling'

c. air-related forms
phallang-phallang, phelleng-phelleng, phallak-phallak,
 phellek-phellek 'fluttering, flapping, waving'
phik, phik-phik 'hissing' (as in air escaping from a tyre)
ssayng-ssayng, ssing-ssing 'hissing' (of wind)
wayng-wayng, weyng-weyng, wing-wing 'hissing' (of wind)

(10)   *Uythay-e* (Phenomimes)
a. animates: manner of action or movement
acang-acang, eceng-eceng 'toddlingly'
allang-allang 'cunningly, with flattery'
c(c)ellwuk-c(c)ellwuk, celttwuk-celttwuk 'limping, hobbling'
engkum-engkum, engkhum-engkhum 'with long strides'
hetwung-citwung 'all flustered'
kkampak, kkamppak, kkempek, kkemppek 'momentarily'
malttong-malttong, melttwung-melttwung 'with wide fixed eyes'

putul-putul, patul-patul, pal-pal 'quivering, trembling'
salccak, sulccek 'stealthily'
salkum-salkum, sulkum-sulkum 'surreptitiously, stealthily'
saphun-saphun 'with a soft step, lightly'
singkul-pengkul 'smilingly'
watul-watul, wutul-wutul 'shivering' (from cold)
wuc(c)wul-wuc(c)wul 'with a swinging motion, pompously'
wumul-ccwumul 'vaguely, hesitantly'

b. animates: state, appearance, feeling
accil-accil, eccil-eccil, ecil-ecil 'giddy'
alttul-salttul 'frugally'
maysuk-maysuk 'nauseated'
nalssin, nulssin 'slender, slim'
photong-photong, phutwung-phutwung 'chubby, plump'
singswung-sayngswung 'distracted'
swulleng-swulleng 'disturbedly, uneasily'
thong-thong, ttwung-ttwung 'plump'

c. inanimates: manner of action or movement
ikul-ikul '(burning) lively'
kkwak, kkok 'tightly, surely'
ping-ping, phing-phing, pping-pping, payng-payng
    'round and round (spinning, whirling, turning)'
pingkul-pingkul, ppingkul-ppingkul, phingkul-phingkul,
    payngkul-payngkul, ppayngkul-ppayngkul
    'around and around (skating, dancing, gliding)'
sal-sal, sel-sel, sol-sol, swul-swul 'gently, softly, lightly'
taykwul-taykwul, ttaykwul-ttaykwul 'rolling, rumbling'

d. inanimates: shape, appearance, property
alssong-talssong, elsswung-telsswung 'jumbled, obscure'
cintuk-cintuk, ccintuk-ccintuk 'gluey, sticky'
cwuleng-cwuleng, cwulleng-cwulleng 'in clusters'
kketul-kketul, kkotul-kkotul, kkwutul-kkwutul 'dry and hard'
kkong-kkong '(frozen) hard'
mallang, mollang, mulleng, malkhang, molkhang, mulkheng
    'all soft' (as potatoes)
maykkun, mikkun, maykkull, mikkul, mikkul 'smoothly, slippery'

> *omok-comok* 'sunk here and there'
> *potul-potul, putul-putul* 'all soft'
> *panccak, penccek, ppanccak, ppenccek* 'sparkling, twinkling'
> *phuk-phuk, phok-phok* 'throbbing, piercing repeatedly'
> *twungkul, tongkul, ttongkul, ttwungkul* 'in a round shape'
> *wukul-ccwukul, okul-ccokul* 'crumpled, rumpled, wrinkled'
> *wulthwung-pulthwung* 'uneven, bumpy'

As observed in the above examples, onomatopoeic words are either used singly, when the action takes place only once or, more frequently, in reduplicated forms to indicate a continuing or repeated action. Some words are partially reduplicated, as shown in *cwulwulwuk* (cf. *cwulwuk, cwulwuk-cwulwuk*) 'in sudden downpours' and *ttaykwulwulwu* (cf. *ttaykwul, ttaykwul-ttaykwul*) 'rolling, rumbling'.

Almost all onomatopoeic words function syntactically as adverbs, as in *kay ka meng-meng cic-nun-ta* 'A dog barks bowwow' and *palam i sol-sol pu-n-ta* 'The wind blows gently.' In addition, many of these words combine with the suffix *-kelita* 'keep doing' to form a verb indicating a continuing action, as in *tel-tel-kelita* 'keep rattling' (but not **meng-meng-kelita* 'keep barking'). If a reduplicated form consists of polysyllabic words, however, only one member (the first one if the two members are different) combines with *-kelita*, as in *pithul-kelita* '(walk) staggering', *telketek-kelita* 'keep rattling', and *ellwuk-kelita* 'appear mottled' (but not **ellwuk-tellwuk-kelita* or **tellwuk-kelita*). Another combination into which many, but not all, onomatopoeic words enter is the attachment of *hata* 'do, be' to form a compound verb or adjective, as in *khwang-hata* 'make a banging noise', *ellwuk-tellwuk-hata* 'be mottled', *mikkul-mikkul-hata* 'be slippery', and *twungkulehta* (from *twungkul-hata*) 'be round'.

Onomatopoeic words are often used, either as they are or more frequently with the nominalizing suffix *-i*, to denote the object that produces that sound or manner. Examples include *cing* 'gong', *holccwuk-i* 'lanky person' (from *holccwuk-hata* 'be thin'), *kaykwul-i* 'frog' (from *kaykwul-kaykwul*), *maym-i* 'cicada' (from *maym-maym*), *nwutek-i* 'rags' (from *nwutek-nwutek* 'in patches'), *ppekkwuk-i* 'cuckoo' (from *ppekkwuk-ppekkwuk*), *puk* 'drum', and *ttwungttwung-i* 'fat person' (from *ttwungttwung-hata* 'be fat')

Sound qualities are correlated to a certain degree with synaesthetic effects. In general, forms ending in a stop consonant tend to symbolize sudden cessation or intermittence of action or tightness (e.g., *chelssek* 'with a thud or slap', *kkwak* 'tightly', *kkwul-kkek* 'at a gulp', *ppak-ppak* 'dry and hard', *ttalkak-ttalkak* 'rattling'); those ending in a nasal sound indicate prolonged resonance, flexibility, roundness, or openness (e.g., *khwung-khwung* 'banging, pounding', *mulleng-mulleng* 'all soft', *ping-ping* 'round and round'); and those that end in a liquid sound symbolize the flowing of liquid or smoothness of action (e.g., *col-col* 'trickling', *mikkul-mikkul* 'slippery', *posul-posul* 'in a drizzle'). Rarely, vowels participate as the last sound of a reduplicated form. Two examples are *sswa-sswa* 'briskly, whistling' and *swi-swi-hata* 'hush up'.

In the examples given in (9) and (10), it is not easy to render correct English translations to the members of each horizontal set. The difference is not in semantic content but in what Trubetzkoy called 'phonostylistique', or in the expression of emotional colouring. For instance, *cwul-cwul*, *chwul-chwul*, and *ccwul-ccwul* 'trickling, flowing persistently' denote, among other things, an increasingly smaller quantity of liquid but faster action. In *pancak-pancak*, *panccak-panccak*, *ppancak-ppancak*, and *ppanccak-ppanccak* 'twinkling', the light they denote is increasingly intense but the volume of the light is felt to be decreasingly lower. Similarly, in *ping-ping*, *phing-phing*, and *pping-pping* 'round and round (spinning, turning, whirling)', the manner of turning is gradually faster. Thus, a plane whirls in the sky in a *ping-ping* manner, a top turns in a *phing-phing* manner, and a rotary press spins in a *pping-pping* manner.

When the words with the same denotative meaning have several shapes with different vowels, the different vowel qualities also give different Sprachgefühls or phonostylistic effects. This general tendency applies not only to onomatopoeic words, as in *panccak-panccak* (e.g., stars' twinkling) vs. *penccek-penccek* (e.g., flash of light), but also to other types of sound symbolic words such as *yalpta*, *yelpta* 'be thin', *nolahta*, *nwulehta* 'be yellow', *yawita*, *yewita* 'lose weight', *yamchi*, *yemchi* 'sense of honour', and *i kes*, *yo kes* 'this thing'. Thus, for instance, *yalpta* is more frequently used for the thinness of clothes, paper, etc., whereas *yelpta* is more appropriate for thinness in density. While *nolahta* means neutrally 'be yellow', *nwulehta* gives the feeling of being quite yellow or golden yellow.

For details of phonological phenomena such as vowel harmony, see chapter 7 (7.4). An extensive wordlist of Korean ideophonic words is provided in H.M. Sohn 1994. A special publication of the National Academy of the Korean Language journal *Say Kwuk.e Saynghwal* (New National Language Life, vol. III, no. 2, 1993) is devoted entirely to the discussion of sound symbolic words in Korean, ranging over their basic concepts, syntax, semantics, phonology, morphology, history, lexicography, and poetic function. A detailed semantic classification of both phonomimes and phenomimes is attempted in Yenpyen En.e Yenkwuso 1981.

5.4   Sino-Korean words

The question of when Chinese words and characters were first introduced into Korea remains unanswered due to the lack of historical data. The only deduction we can make, however, is that Chinese words and characters must have been used in Korea as early as the first century BC, when Han China colonized the western and northern parts of the Korean peninsula and established its four commanderies there. Historical records show that a Paykchey.an named Wang In went to Japan with many Chinese books around 400 AD, suggesting that Chinese culture and writing had achieved considerable popularity during the Three Kingdoms period. With the unification of the Korean peninsula by the Sinla dynasty in 677 AD, the use of Chinese writing and characters in Korea gained more popularity since Sinla's unification was achieved with Tang China's military support and subsequently contact between the two countries became very frequent. Earlier, the name of the country and the title of the king were changed from native terms to Sino-Korean (SK) terms in the fourth year of King Cicung (503 AD) of Sinla. In the second year of King Sinmun (682 AD) of Unified Sinla, Kwukhak (lit. 'national studies'), a government organization in charge of national education, was established and many Chinese classics began to be taught. In the sixteenth year of King Kyengtek (757 AD), native place names were changed to two-character SK, and in his eighteenth year, all official titles were also Sino-Koreanized. Personal names of the nobility also began to be Sino-Koreanized during the Sinla period.

SK words began to be predominant in the Kolye dynasty. This was particularly the case after King Kwangco adopted, in 958 AD, the Chinese system of the civil service examinations based on Chinese classics. In this period, government officials and the nobility, as well as scholars and literary men, used native words in speaking but SK words in writing. The Cosen dynasty observed the all-out infiltration of SK words into every facet of Korean culture and society, chiefly because of the dynasty's adoption of Confucianism as a national religion and, as a result, the popular admiration of everything Chinese. For a long time SK words and characters remained primary instruments for recording official documents and for scholarly writing and written communication in upper-class society, before they gradually penetrated everyday language.

In regard to the origin of SK sounds, it is generally assumed that the pronunciations of Chinese characters used in the northern part of China during the Swu and Tang dynasties around the seventh and eighth century constituted the basis of SK sounds. This was during the Unified Sinla period when many written materials on Chinese civilization were imported from China. Thus, pronunciations of contemporary Chinese-character words in Korean are similar to those of Middle Chinese, although some independent vowel and consonant changes as well as the loss of tones have occurred in Korea. See chapter 6 (6.1.2) for further discussion.

There are three layers of SK words, (a) those introduced from China, (b) those introduced from Sino-Japanese, and (c) those coined in Korea. These are illustrated respectively in (11).

(11)   a. SK words from Chinese

ca-yen 'nature'   *cep-tay* 'reception'
chen-ci 'heaven and earth'   *cil-mun* 'question'
cwun-pi 'preparation'   *hak-kyo* 'school'
hak-sayng 'student'   *hyo-ca* 'filial son'
no-lyek 'effort'   *pang-hyang* 'direction'
phung-nyen 'rich year'   *pu-mo* 'parents'
pyen-hwa 'change'   *sayng-myeng* 'life'
sin-chey 'body'   *thay-yang* 'sun'
uy-pok 'clothes'   *yey-cel* 'manners'

     b. SK words from Sino-Japanese

can-ko 'deposit balance'   *cen-sen* 'electric cord'
chel-hak 'philosophy'   *cwa-tam* 'table-talk'
cwung-kong-ep 'heavy industry' *ip-kwu* 'entrance'
kwa-hak 'science'   *mun-pep* 'grammar'
sang-tam 'consultation'   *sik-mul-hak* 'botany'
swu-sok 'procedure'   *wen-ca* 'atom'
yak-sok 'promise'   *yek-hal* 'role'

     c. SK words coined in Korea

cen-tap (rice field-dry field) 'paddies and dry fields'
chong-kak (all-horn) 'bachelor'
il-ki (day-energy) 'weather'
oy-sang (outside-upperside) 'on credit'
pok-tek-pang (blessing-virtue-room) 'real estate agency'
phyen-ci (comfortable paper) 'letter'
sa-cwu (four-pillar) 'one's destiny' ('four pillars': year, month,
   date, and hour of a person's birth)
sam-chon (three-inch) 'uncle'
si-ka (husband's side-home) 'family of one's husband'
sik-kwu (eating-mouth) 'family, members of a family'
yuk-chon (six-inches) 'second cousin'

The first of the three layers has the largest number of members, to which may be added words that came from Chinese but have subsequently undergone semantic change in Korea, e.g., *oy-myen* 'looking away from' (from 'the outside'), *nay-oy* 'husband and wife' (from 'inside and outside'), and *sam-si* 'three meals' (from 'three times'). The SK words in this layer were introduced mainly through Confucian classics, history and literary books, and Chinese works written in colloquial Chinese. Sino-Japanese coinages abound in Korean. Words like *pi-hayng-ki* (fly-go-machine) 'airplane', *yeng-hwa* (shine-picture) 'movie', *kong-cang* (work-place) 'factory', *chwuk-kwu* (kick-ball) 'soccer', *wun-cen-sa* (move-roll-engineer) 'driver', *pul* (shape of $) 'dollar', and many other words coined by Japanese are used only in Japan and Korea, not in China.

Due to the influx of Chinese borrowings and coinage of new character words, the phenomenon of synonyms is widespread, especially in non-scientific and non-academic areas, as illustrated in (12).

(12)	Native	Sino-Korean	
	anay, manwula	*che, pu-in*	'wife'
	apeci	*pu-chin*	'father'
	chan-mul	*nayng-swu*	'cold water'
	kelum	*pi-lyo*	'fertilizer'
	kil	*to-lo*	'road'
	koluta	*sen-thayk-(hata)*	'choose'
	kos	*cang-so*	'place'
	mat-ttal	*cang-nye*	'oldest daughter'
	non-path	*cen-tap*	'paddy and dry fields'
	os	*uy-pok*	'clothes'
	pes, tongmu	*chin-kwu*	'friend'
	salam	*in-kan*	'human'
	sek-tal	*sam-kay-wel*	'three months'
	son-pal	*swu-cok*	'hands and feet'
	susung	*sen-sayng*	'teacher'
	swum-swita	*ho-hup-(hata)*	'breathe'
	talkyal	*kyey-lan*	'egg'
	ttus	*uy-mi*	'meaning'

The two members of each doublet set may not mean exactly the same thing and frequently have different syntactic or pragmatic usages. Even when they share the same meaning, SK words tend to be more formal and abstract (being detached from vivid reality), and thus occasionally sound more prestigious and sometimes even pedantic. Native words generally belong to more colloquial speech, while their SK counterparts tend to be found in the literary language, academic vocabulary, and formal speech. For instance, the native word *nala* 'country' manifests more emotional attachment than its SK counterpart *kwuk-ka* (country-house). Thus, *wuli nala*, not *wuli kwuk-ka*, is used to refer to 'our country'. The native word *il-cali* (lit. 'work-place') refers usually to a low-waged job such as blue-collar work, whereas *cik-cang* (job-place) implies a white-collar job. Similarly, *kakey* (derived from SK *ka-ka* (false-house)) usually refers to a small store and *sang-cem* (business-shop) to a larger one. SK counterparts are also frequently used for deferential objects, as observed in the following pairs.

(13)

	Native (plain)	Sino-Korean (deferential)
wife	*anay*	*pu-in*
mother	*emeni*	*mo-chin*
house	*cip*	*tayk*
tooth	*i*	*chi-a*
age	*nai*	*yen-sey*
name	*ilum*	*seng-ham*

As already indicated, many native words have ceased to survive the doublet status, being either completely wiped out by SK words or passed into obsolete status at best. Some of these unfortunate native words that were of common use in the writings of the Cosen dynasty period are given in (14), together with the SK culprits.

(14)

Native	Sino-Korean	
aam	*chin-chek*	'relative'
ay	*cang*	'intestines'
cas	*seng*	'castle'
ceca	*si-cang*	'market'
ciapi	*nam-phyen*	'husband'
ciemi	*che*	'wife'
cumun	*chen*	'thousand'
cwulyen	*(son)swu-ken*	'handkerchief'
epei	*pu-mo, yang-chin*	'parents'
kalam	*kang*	'river'
moy	*san*	'mountain'
muth	*yuk-ci*	'land'
nwuli	*sey-sang*	'world'
on	*payk*	'hundred'

palam	*pyek*	'wall'
pua	*phyey*	'lung'
syulwup	*wu-san*	'umbrella'
yang	*wi*	'stomach'

Morphologically, SK words are more analytic and thus semantically more transparent than native words. SK words are composed, by and large, of two or more morphemes, with each morpheme consisting of a single syllable, as in *hak-kyo* (study-house) 'school', *kyo-hoy* (teaching-meeting) 'church', *in-kan* (human-relation) 'human being', *sen-sayng* (preceding-birth) 'teacher', and *tay-hak-kyo* (big-study-house) 'university'. The last morpheme in a SK word frequently indicates a semantic class. For instance, the terms for different branches of learning all contain the morpheme *hak* 'study'.

(15)   *ceng-chi-hak* (administer-control-study)   'political science'
        chen-mun-hak (sky-letters-study)   'astronomy'
        han-kwuk-hak (Korea-country-study)   'Korean studies'
        in-lyu-hak (man-kind-study)   'anthropology'
        kong-hak (engineering-study)   'engineering'
        mun-hak (letters-study)   'literature'
        sa-hoy-hak (society-gathering-study)   'sociology'
        sayng-mul-hak (live-thing-study)   'biology'
        sik-mul-hak (plant-thing-study)   'botany'
        swu-hak (number-study)   'mathematics'
        tong-mul-hak (move-thing-study)   'zoology'
        uy-hak (medicine-study)   'medical science'

In general, a SK morpheme is a free word if there is no native word denoting the same sense, otherwise bound. For instance, *pang* 'room', *chayk* 'book', *cha* 'car', *cha* 'tea', *hyeng* 'older brother', *chang* 'window', *sang* 'table', *mun* 'door, gate', *tung* 'lamp', *pyeng* 'bottle', *pyeng* 'illness', *cho* 'vinegar', *cong* 'bell', and *cwuk* 'porridge' are free single-morpheme words for which there are no corresponding native words. On the other hand, most bound morphemes, such as *chen* 'heaven' (native *hanul*), *ci* 'earth' (native *ttang*), *ka* 'house' (native *cip*), *il* 'sun' (native *hay*), *pu* 'father' (native *apeci*), *ca* 'son' (native *atul*), *um* 'sound' (native *soli*), *in* 'human' (native *salam*), *pi* 'flying' (native *nal*), *hayng* 'going' (native *ka*), and *ki* 'machine' (native *thul*), do not occur by themselves, but must combine with other morphemes to form free words, as in *chen-ci* 'heaven and earth', *in-ka* 'human house', and *pi-hayng-ki* 'airplane'.

SK words have phonological characteristics too. First, the three tense consonants *pp*, *tt*, and *cc* do not occur in any SK morphemes, and even *kk* and *ss* are limited to only one or two morphemes, as in *kkik* 'smoke, drink', *ssang* 'pair', and *ssi* 'Mr, Mrs, Miss'. Second, *ph*, *t*, *th*, *c*, *ch*, *s*, and *kh*, as well as all tense consonants, do not occur in the syllable-final position. Third, no consonant clusters (e.g., *ps*) occur in SK morphemes. Fourth, the most productive diphthong *ye* follows the widest variety of consonants, as in *yen* 'research', *pyeng* 'bottle', *lyel* 'row', *phyen* 'side', *kyen* 'see', *nye* 'female', and *hyeng* 'older brother'. Fifth, phonological contraction is very rare in SK words. Examples of contraction are *ko.yangmi* 'rice offering to Buddha' (< *kong-yang-mi* (provide-raise-rice)), and *co.yong* 'quietness' which developed from *cong-yong* (follow-accept) 'obedience' with a slight change in meaning.

Unlike Chinese characters in Japanese which have multiple readings, each Chinese character in Korean is associated, in principle, with a single pronunciation. Exceptionally, there are characters which are read in two (or rarely three) ways. One type of such characters with multiple reading does not involve any meaning difference, as illustrated in (16a). Another type includes characters in which difference of meaning goes with the difference in reading, as in (16b). For more characters with multiple readings, see Martin 1992:116-22.

(16)   a. *cha/ke* 'vehicle':   *ca-tong-cha* (self-move-car)   'automobile'
                                    ca-cen-ke (self-roll-car)   'bicycle'
             cha/ta 'tea':   *hong-cha* (red-tea)   'black tea'
                                    ta-pang (tea-room)   'teahouse'
             mok/mo 'tree':   *mok-ma* (tree-horse)   'wooden horse'
                                    mo-kwa (wood-fruit)   'Chinese quince'
             phal/pha 'eight':   *phal-wel* (8-moon)   'August'
                                    cho-pha-il (first-8-day)   'April 4: Buddha's
                                                                   birthday'
             pul/pu 'not, un-':   *pul-ka-nung* (not-may-able)   'impossibility'
                                    pu-tang (not-right)   'injustice'
             sip/si 'ten':   *sip-cho* (10-second)   'ten seconds'
                                    si-wel (10-moon)   'October'
             thayk/tayk 'house': *cwu-thayk* (live-house)   'residence'
                                    si-tayk (husband side-house) 'husband's house'
             yuk/yu 'six':   *yuk-il* (6-day)   'six days'
                                    yu-wel (6-moon)   'June'

         b. *ak* 'bad', *o* 'hate':   *sen-ak* (good-bad)   'good and bad'
                                       cung-o (hate-hate)   'hatred'

hap 'join', *hop* (measure):

hoy-hap (meet-join)	'meeting'
il-hop (1-*hop*)	'1/3 pint'

kum 'gold', *kim* (surname):

hwang-kum (yellow-gold)	'gold'
Kim-yang (Kim-Miss)	'Miss Kim'

pu 'again', *pok* 'recover':

pu-hwal (again-active)	'resurrection'
hoy-pok (return-recover)	'recovering'

puk 'north', *pay* 'suffer defeat':

nam-puk (south-north)	'North and South'
phay-pay (lose-defeat)	'defeat'

pun 'divide', *phun* 'farthing':

pun-swu (divide-number)	'fraction'
il-phun (1-farthing)	'one farthing'

sal 'kill', *sway* 'scatter, attack':

sal-in (kill-person)	'manslaughter'
sway-to (scatter-arrive)	'onslaught'

Syntactically, SK words, phrases, and even clauses all function essentially as nouns in Korean sentences. Only some of them function as adverbs, as already indicated (e.g., *cuk-si* 'immediately', *e-cha-phi* 'anyhow', *sim-ci-e* 'even'). Thus, SK constructions like *il-ke-yang-tuk* (one-raise-two-get) 'killing two birds with one stone' and *a-cen-in-swu* (my-field-draw-water) 'seeking one's own interest' are clauses in SK, but function as nouns in Korean syntax.

Representative semantic classes are as follows. First, all Contemporary Korean surnames and most given names are in SK. There are 284 surnames in current use (e.g., Martin 1992:366–7), most of which consist of one Chinese character, the exceptions including *Tok-ko, Sen-wu, Sa-kong, Tong-pang, Cey-kal, Nam-kwung, Hwang-po*, and *Se-mun*, which have 2 characters. The 10 most common surnames, which occupy 65.4% of the whole population, are *Kim, I* (usually romanized as *Lee* or *Yi*), *Pak (Park), Choy (Choe), Ceng (Chung), Kang, Co (Cho), Yun (Yoon), Cang (Chang)*, and *Im (Lim)*, in that order of frequency. The 3 surnames *Kim, I*, and *Pak* occupy 45% of the population, with *Kim* alone being 21.7%. The usual form of a given name consists of 2 characters, although single-character names are also used. Given names follow the surname, as in *I Swun-sin, Kim Swuk-huy, Son A-lan, Pak In, Nam-kwung Ok-pun*, and *Sen-wu Hwi*.

Most place names, including names of administrative districts, lakes, mountains, rivers, oceans, scenic or historical places, countries, and continents, are in SK. One exception is the name of the capital city *Sewul* 'Seoul', which is a native word. Even the title of South Korea is SK *Tay-han-min-kwuk* (big-Korea-people-country) 'Republic of Korea' or its contraction *Han-kwuk* 'Korea'. Many foreign proper names are in SK, e.g., *Thay-phyeng-yang* (big-peace-ocean) 'the Pacific Ocean', *Il-pon* (sun-origin) 'Japan', *Mi-kwuk* (beauty-country) 'America', *Yeng-kwuk* (flower corolla-country) 'England', *Cwung-kwuk* (centre-country) 'China', and *Ho-cwu* (moat-continent) 'Australia'. Names of institutions, firms, restaurants, stores, hotels, teahouses, books, newspapers, transportational means, etc., are all in SK, e.g., *I-hwa tay-hak* (pear-blossom-big-study) 'Ewha Woman's University', *un-hayng* (silver-store) 'bank', *kwuk-hoy* (nation-meeting) 'National Assembly', *pep-wen* (law-house) 'court', *pyeng-wen* (sickness-house) 'hospital', *Ho-pan sik-tang* (lake-side dining-hall) 'Hopan Restaurant', *Chwun-hyang-cen* (spring-fragrance-legend) 'Story of Chwunhyang', and *Tong-a il-po* (East-Asia day-report) 'Tonga Daily'.

Most academic, technical, and occupational terms are in SK, as in *chel-hak* (enlightening-study) 'philosophy', *mu-yong* (dance-jump) 'dance', *pem-cwu* (frame-group) 'category', *um-wun-lon* (sound-rhythm-theory) 'phonology', *swu-swul* (hand-skill) 'surgical operation', *kwan-hyen-ak* (tube-string-music) 'orchestra', *san-ep* (produce-business) 'industry', *kyo-swu* (teach-give) 'professor', *uy-sa* (medicine-teacher) 'medical doctor', *pak-sa* (broad-scholar) 'Ph.D.', *thay-thong-lyeng* (big-control-command) 'the President', and *uy-cang* (discussion-head) 'chairman'.

There is an open class of SK names for various cultural products and concepts. Some examples are *cen-cha* (war-car) 'tank', *chayk* 'book', *kwa-ca* (sweets-thing) 'cookies', *sel-thang* (snow-candy) 'sugar', *seng* 'castle', *uy-ca* (chair-thing) 'chair', *chim-sil* (sleep-room) 'bedroom', *cang-hwa* (long-shoe) 'boots', *cen-hwa* (electric-talk) 'telephone', *sin-mun* (new-hearing) 'newspaper', *ken-mul* (build-thing) 'building', *man-nyen-phil* (10,000-year-pen) 'fountain pen', *twu-noy* (head-brain) 'brains', *sim-cang* (mind-intestine) 'heart', and *wu-yu* (cow-milk) 'milk'.

Days of the week, as given in (17), major folk festivals (by the lunar calendar), national holidays (by the solar calendar), and seasonal divisions are expressed mostly in SK.

(17)		
	il-yo-il (sun-weekday)	'Sunday'
	wel-yo-il (moon-weekday)	'Monday'
	hwa-yo-il (fire-weekday)	'Tuesday'
	swu-yo-il (water-weekday)	'Wednesday'
	mok-yo-il (wood/tree-weekday)	'Thursday'
	kum-yo-il (gold/metal-weekday)	'Friday'
	tho-yo-il (earth-weekday)	'Saturday'

SK numerals are extensively used since native ones are not available for the numbers of 100 and above. In writing, Arabic numerals are commonly used with SK pronunciations.

(18)   a. *il* '1'   *i* '2'   *sam* '3'   *sa* '4'

            o '5'   *yuk* '6'   *chil* '7'   *phal* '8'

            kwu '9'   *sip* '10'   *payk* '100'   *chen* '1,000'

            man '10,000' *ek* '100 million' *co* 'trillion'

    b. *sam-sip-chil* '37'   *kwu-payk-sa-sip-kwu* '949'

        o-sip-i-man '520,000'   *sam-payk-man* '3,000,000'

        phal-chen-man '80,000,000'   *kwu-chen-i-sip-sam* '9,023'

        yuk-ek-i-chen-man '620,000,000' *sam-payk-ek* '30,000,000,000'

        chil-chen-ek '700,000,000,000' *i-sip-co* '20,000,000,000,000'

There are many SK numeral counters that either coexist with synonymous native counterparts or are complementary to the native stock, as illustrated in (19).

(19)   Classificatory counters   Members (examples)

cang	'sheets'	paper, bricks
cey	'20-pack sets'	herb medicine
kap	'cases'	cigarettes, matches
kay	'items'	desks, stones, clocks, watches
kwen	'volumes'	books, notebooks
myeng	'persons'	any category of person
ssang	'pairs'	any animate couples
tay	'machines'	cars, typewriters, pianos, TV sets

(20)   Measurement counters

a.	*ceng*	60 *kan* or 109 metres
	kan	6 *chek* or 180 cm
	chek	10/33 metres
b.	*ceng-po*	10 *tan* or 3,000 *phyeng*
	tan	300 *phyeng*
	phyeng	6 square *chek*
c.	*kwan*	3.75 kg
	kun	601.04 g
d.	*to*	degree
	pu	1/10 *to*

e. *wen*	unit of Korean currency
cen	1/100 *wen*
f. *nyen*	year
wel	month
il	day
si	o'clock'
pun	minute
cho	second

Colour terms are finely segmented by combining different basic colour-term morphemes. Examples of basic terms and compounds include *hong* 'red', *pun-hong* (powder-red) 'pink', *yen-pun-hong* (light-powder-red) 'light pink', *cwu-hong* (red-red) 'reddish orange colour', *cin-hong* (real-red) 'crimson', *hwang* 'yellow', *cwu-hwang* (red-yellow) 'orange colour', *huk* 'black', *cek* 'red', *cek-huk* (red-black) 'reddish black', *cheng* 'blue', *nam* 'indigo, dark blue', *nok* 'green', *cheng-nok* (blue-green) 'bluish green', *kal* 'brown', *cek-kal* (red-brown) 'reddish brown', *ca* 'purple', and *ca-cwu* (purple-red) 'maroon'.

The system of SK kinship terms is very complex. Important semantic components are [lineal/collateral], [ascending/descending], [male/female], [consanguineous/in-law], [mother's side/father's side], and [elder/younger]. The pattern of combining the morphemes that represent various semantic components is very systematic, as illustrated in (21). The hyphen (-) following a single-syllable form indicates that the form cannot occur by itself.

(21) a. lineal ascendants and descendants

     pu- 'father'; *mo-* 'mother'; *pu-mo* 'parents'

     co-pu/mo (ancestor-father/mother) 'grandfather/grandmother'

     cung-co-pu/mo (early-ancestor-father/mother)

      'great grandfather/grandmother'

     ca- 'son'; *nye-* 'daughter'; *ca-nye* 'children'

     son-ca/nye (grandchild-son/daughter) 'grandson/granddaughter'

     cung-son-ca/nye 'great grandson/granddaughter'

   b. collateral ascendants: father's side

     payk-pu (oldest-father) 'father's older brother'

     payk-mo 'father's older brother's wife'

     swuk-pu (uncle-father), *sam-chon* (three-inch)

      'father's younger brother'

     ko-mo (paternal aunt-mother) 'father's sister'

> *ko-mo-pu* (-husband), *ko-swuk* 'father's sister's husband'
> *cong-co-pu* (subordinate-) 'grandfather's brother'
> *tay-ko-mo* (big-) 'grandfather's sister'

c. collateral ascendants: mother's side
> *oy-swuk-pu* (outside-uncle-father), *oy-sam-chon* 'mother's brother'
> *oy-swuk-mo* 'mother's brother's wife'
> *i-mo* (maternal aunt-mother) 'mother's sister'
> *i-mo-pu*, *i-swuk* 'mother's sister's husband'
> *oy-co-pu/mo* 'mother's father/mother'

d. collateral descendants
> *cil-* (nephew) 'brother's son'
> *cil-nye* (niece-female) 'brother's daughter'
> *sayng-cil* (sister's child-nephew) 'sister's son'
> *sayng-cil-nye* 'sister's daughter'
> *cong-son* (secondary-grandson) 'brother's grandson'
> *cong-son-nye* 'brother's granddaughter'

e. lineal and collateral siblings
> *hyeng* '(male's) older brother, (rarely female's) older sister'
> *cey-* '(male's) younger brother, (rarely female's) younger sister'
> *ca-* 'older sister'; *may-* 'younger sister'; *ca-may* 'sisters'
> *tong-sayng* (same-birth) 'younger brother/sister'
> *cong-hyeng* (subordinate-older brother), *sa-chon* (four-inch) *hyeng*
>   '(male's) older male first cousin'
> *cay-cong-hyeng* (second-), *yuk-chon* (six-inch) *hyeng* '(male's)
>   'older male second cousin' (grandfather's brother's grandson)
> *ko-cong-hyeng* (father's sister-), *ko-cong sa-chon hyeng*
>   '(male's) older male first cousin' (father's sister's son)
> *oy-cong-hyeng*, *oy sa-chon hyeng*
>   '(male's) older male first cousin' (mother's brother's son)
> *i-cong-hyeng*, *i-cong sa-chon hyeng*
>   '(male's) older male first cousin' (mother's sister's son)

f. ascendant and descendant in-laws
> *si-pu/mo* (husband's side-father/mother)
>   '(female's) father/mother-in-law'
> *si-swuk* (husband's side-uncle) 'husband's older brother'

ping-pu/*mo* (invite-father/mother), *cang-in*/*mo* (wife's side-person/mother) '(male's) father/mother-in-law'
ca-pu (son-wife) 'daughter-in-law'
ye-se (daughter-son-in-law) 'son-in-law'

g. siblings in-law
hyeng-swu (older sibling-sister-in-law)
  '(male's) older brother's wife'
cey-swu (younger sibling-sister-in-law)
  '(male's) younger brother's wife'
ca-hyeng (older sister-older brother)
  '(male's) older sister's husband'
may-cey (younger sister-younger brother)
  '(male's) younger sister's husband'
hyeng-pu (older sibling-husband)
  '(female's) older sister's husband'
cey-nang (younger sibling-husband)
  'younger sister's husband'
che-nam (wife-male) 'wife's brother'
che-nam-pu (wife-male-husband) 'wife's brother's wife'
che-hyeng 'wife's elder sister'
che-cey 'wife's younger sister'
tong-se (same-son-in-law) 'wife's sister's husband'

Notice that most single morpheme terms are bound and must occur with other morphemes to form free words, as in *pu-mo* (father-mother) 'parents', *pu-chin* (father-parent) 'father' (deferential), and *ca-nye* 'sons and daughters'. Only *che* 'wife' and *hyeng* '(male's) older brother, (rarely) female's older sister' are used as free words. The three homonyms *pu* 'husband', *pu* 'wife', and *pu* 'father' are written differently in SK, e.g., *pu-pu* 'husband and wife' and *pu-mo* (father-mother) 'parents'.

In regard to SK kinship terms, *chon* 'inch' indicates the relational distance between an ego and the person referred to. The relation between an ego and a parent is *il-chon* 'one inch'. Thus, one's lineal siblings are *i-chon* 'two inches' because his distance to his parents is *il-chon* 'one inch' and the distance between his parents and his siblings is also *il-chon* 'one inch' (thus, 1+1=2). One's father's brother (i.e., uncle) is called *sam-chon* 'three-inches' and one's father's cousin is called *o-chon* 'five-inches'. Similarly, one's first cousin is termed *sa-chon* 'four-inches', second-cousin *yuk-chon* 'six-inches', and third cousin *phal-chon* 'eight-inches'.

In addition to the nominal categories illustrated thus far, thousands of SK verbal and adjectival nouns combine with a native verb or adjective (e.g., *hata* 'do, be'), as in the verb *an-sim-hata* (peace-mind-do) 'feel at ease' and the adjective *hayng-pok-hata* (happy-blessing-be) 'be happy'. SK adverbs include pure SK words such as *cem-cha* (gradual-order) 'gradually' and *cuk-si* (straight-time) 'immediately' and SK-native compounds such as *cen-hye* (all-AD) 'utterly' and *khway-hi* (pleasant-AD) 'gladly'.

5.5   Loan words

Until 1945 when Korea was liberated from thirty-five years of Japanese domination, loan words were introduced into the Korean lexicon exclusively through Japanese, with necessary spelling and pronunciation adjustments in accordance with Korean phonological patterns. Only since 1945 has direct importation (e.g., through books, magazines, news media, movies, language learning, importation of new commodities and other cultural items, and interactions with native speakers) been prevalent. Sometimes words borrowed before 1945 were reborrowed after 1945, from the same source or a different language, with a slightly different spelling and pronunciation. Compare the currently used spellings and pronunciations of some loan words with the corresponding Japanese versions in (22).

(22)

Loan word	Source language	Japanese version	
cokki	Port. *jaqueta*	*chokki*	'vest, waistcoat'
kipsu	Ger. *Gips*	*gibusu*	'plaster cast'
latio	Eng. *radio*	*razio*	'radio'
lamyen	Chn. *lao-mien*	*raamen*	'instant noodles'
linneylu	Fr. *linière*	*rinneru*	'linen'
matolosu	Dut. *matroos*	*madorosu*	'sailor'
mephulle	Eng. *muffler*	*mahura*	'muffler'
meyliyasu	Sp. *medias*	*meriyasu*	'knit undershirt'
nawang	Malaysian *lauan*	*rawang*	'lauan'
pangkallo	Indian *bangala*	*bangaroo*	'bungalow'
pinil	Eng. *vinyl*	*biniiru*	'vinyl'
petun	Port. *botão*	*botan*	'button'
puleyikhu	Eng. brake	*bureeki*	'brake'
teymppula	Port. temporo	*tenpura*	'deep-fried food'
teypwi	Fr. début	*debyuu*	'debut'
tasu	Eng. *dozen*	*dasu*	'dozen'
tones	Eng. *doughnut*	*doonatsu*	'doughnut'

Some salient structural features in the sound patterns of Korean bear on the phonology and spelling of loan words. For details of the Korean phonological patterns, see chapter 7. The MOE (1986) provides detailed regulations for the spelling of loan words.

(a) The syllable structure of Korean is of the form (C)(G)V(C), where C stands for a consonant, G a glide (semivowel), V a vowel, and parentheses the optionality of the occurrence. Thus, any consonant sequence in a syllable of the source word has to be broken by an intervening vowel *u*, the most neutral vowel in Korean, as in *kolphu* 'golf', *suthaymphu* 'stamp', *suthulaikhu* 'strike', and *khulisumasu* 'Christmas'. If the final consonant of a foreign word is a palatal consonant, the epenthetic vowel is the palatal *i*, instead of *u*, as in *lenchi* 'lunch', *oleynci* 'orange', *masaci* 'massage', *milaci* 'mirage', *phullaysi* 'flash', and *suwichi* 'switch'.

(b) Korean stops have three-way contrasts: lax, aspirated, and tensed. Word-initial stops are always voiceless, although word-medial lax phonemes are voiced. Thus, both foreign voiced and voiceless lax consonants are usually rendered as lax consonants, whereas foreign aspirated and tensed sounds generally remain the same in Korean. Thus, 'bus' is spelled as *pesu*, 'band' as *payntu*, 'dam' as *taym*, 'drama' as *tulama*, 'tyre' as *thaie*, 'jam' as *caym*, 'cheese' as *chicu*, 'game' as *keyim*, 'cake' as *kheyik*, 'sign' as *sain*, and 'sports' as *suphochu*. In casual speech, native speakers frequently pronounce *p*, *t*, *c*, and *k* as tensed [p', t', c', k'], respectively, before a vowel in foreign words, as in *pesu* [p'ə.su], *taym* [t'ɛm], *caym* [c'ɛm], *keyim* [k'e.im], and *sain* [s'a.in].

(c) There is systematic consonant neutralization in the syllable-final position due to unreleasing: *p*, *ph*, *pp* becoming [p] (e.g., *iph* [ip] 'leaf'); *t*, *th*, *tt*, *s*, *ss*, *c*, *ch*, *cc*, *h* all becoming [t] (e.g., *os* [ot] 'clothes'); and *k*, *kh*, *kk* becoming [k] (e.g., *puekh* [puək] 'kitchen'). Both the spelling and pronunciation of loan words are affected by this widespread neutralization pattern. For instance, epenthesis of the vowel *u* in loan words (see above) is motivated partly by the effort to block the neutralization of consonants. If 'Christmas' were spelled as *khlismas*, instead of *khulisumasu*, the pronunciation would turn out to be the unacceptable form [khɨ.ɾin.mat] due to the neutralization involved.

(d) When a final *t* in a foreign word is to be spelled without the epenthetic vowel *u* following, the *t* is spelled as *s*, as in *lakheys* 'racket', *lokheys* 'rocket', *haymlis* 'Hamlet', and *khaypineys* 'cabinet'. This is because these words are pronounced with a final *s*, instead of *t*, when they are followed by a vowel-initial particle, as in *lakheys ey* [ɾa.khe.se] 'on the racket'. Independently, however, these words are pronounced with a final [t] due to the syllable-final neutralization as stated in (c), as in *lakeys* [ɾa.khet].

(e) Korean does not have many fricative phonemes including [f, v, θ, ð, ʃ, tʃ, ʒ, dʒ, z]. Hence these sounds are spelled and pronounced with the corresponding stop or fricative sounds: *ph* for [f], *p* for [v], *s*/*t* for [θ, ð], *s* for [ʃ], *ch* for [tʃ], and *c* for [ʒ, dʒ, z], as in *phom* 'form', *phawul* 'foul', *s(y)opha* 'sofa', *khephi* 'coffee', *picen* 'vision', *paiollin* 'violin', *paylpu* 'valve', *sulil* 'thrill', *heylsu khullep* 'health club', *peyitu* 'bathe', *mammosu*/*maymetu* 'mammoth', *syophing* 'shopping', *phaysyen* 'fashion', *hichihaikhu* 'hitchhike', *lwucu* 'rouge', *pulici* 'bridge', *cikucayku* 'zigzag', *silicu* 'series', and *khwicu* 'quiz'.

(f) Although vowel length is phonemic in the word-initial position in native words, length in loan words as well as in native and SK words is ignored in spelling. Thus, many loan words lose their length in pronunciation, as in *mithing* [mi.thiŋ] 'students' group date', *sukhaphu* [sɨ.kha.phɨ] 'scarf', *sukhethu* [sɨ.khə.thɨ] 'skirt', and *suphochu* [sɨ.pho.chɨ] 'sports'.

Due to the recent influx of loan words, there have appeared many native/loan or SK/loan doublets or even native/SK/loan triplets, as illustrated in (23). Notice that many native counterparts are lacking.

(23)

	Native	Sino-Korean	Loan	
	—	ceng-kwu	theynisu	'tennis'
	—	cwu-cha	phakhing	'parking'
	—	pay-nang	lwuksayk	'rucksack'
	—	sa-cin-ki	khameyla	'camera'
	—	tha-ca-ki	thaiphulaithe	'typewriter'
	—	thak-ca	theyipul	'table'
	—	yang-san	phalasol	'parasol'
	—	yu-kyek-tay	ppalchisan	'guerrilla unit'
	tanchwu	—	pethun	'button'
	thwikim	—	hwulai	'frying, fried food'
	tosilak	—	peyntto	'lunch box'
	chwum	mu-yong	taynsu	'dance'
	kis	ey-li	khalla	'collar'
	pi-os	wu-uy	leyinkhothu	'raincoat'
	tehaki	ka-san	phullesu	'addition'

The following statistics are generated based on Y.S. Pae 1970.

(24)
Origin	Number of words	%
English	9,005	78.5
Japanese	749	6.5
German	535	4.7
French	363	3.2
Italian	268	2.3
Latin	78	0.7
Greek	76	0.7
Dutch	65	0.6
Portuguese	35	0.3
Spanish	31	0.3
Russian	29	0.3
Others	231	1.9
Total	11,465	100 %

The category 'others' includes borrowings from Chinese (some recent words such as names of foods), Sanskrit (mainly Buddhist terms like *sekkamoni* 'Buddha', *namu amithapul* 'save us, merciful Buddha'), Hebrew (Bible terms), Manchu, Indian, Arabic, Persian, Malaysian, Norwegian, Turkish, etc., as well as many words whose origins are not determinable. Since Pae was published, a large number of English words have been introduced as new loan words and many existing loan words from other languages have been replaced by English loans. As a result, the total number of current loan words is estimated at over 20,000, of which English occupies over 90%.

English loan words have been introduced into the Korean lexicon either through Japanese (before 1945) or directly (after 1945). In fact, most borrowings since 1945, especially in South Korea, are words from English which range over all aspects of life including clothing, food and drink, electricity and electronics, automobiles, sports, arts, education, social activities, politics, economy, and business transactions. Random examples are given in (25).

(25)
aisu-khulim 'ice-cream'	*allipai* 'alibi'
heytu-laithu 'headlight'	*heyting* 'heading' (in soccer)
hinthu 'hint'	*hiphu* 'hip'
inphulley 'inflation'	*khaymphesu* 'campus'
khisu 'kiss'	*kholla* 'Coke'
khuleytis khatu 'credit card'	*khwicu* 'quiz'
laithe 'lighter'	*leyncu* 'lense'
milkhu 'milk'	*misail* 'missile'
nyusu 'news'	*okheysuthula* 'orchestra'

phakhing 'parking'   *phillum* 'film'
pica 'visa'   *picen* 'vision'
puliphing 'briefing'   *pullawusu* 'blouse'
pulokhe 'broker'   *pultoce* 'bulldozer'
pum 'boom'   *sepisu* 'service'
suthail 'style, one's form'   *sutop* 'stop'
syophing 'shopping'   *s(y)uphe* 'supermarket'
teyithu 'date'   *thaol* 'towel'
thayksi 'taxi'   *thim* 'team'
tuleysu 'dress'   *tulaipu* 'drive'

Loan words from native Japanese are not many, despite long contact between the two countries. Due to anti-Japanese sentiment after the Second World War, many Japanese words have been expelled from the Korean lexicon. Examples of remaining Japanese words are *acinomoto* (*azinomoto*) 'a kind of seasoning', *angkko* (*anko*) 'red-bean paste', *hoccikkisu* (*hochikisu*) 'stapler', *ippai* (*ippai*) 'fully', *kala* (*kara*) 'empty, fake', *kapang* (*kaban*) 'bag', *kwutwu* (*kutsu*) 'leather shoes', *meykki* (*mekki*) 'welding', *mocci* (*mochi*) 'rice-made pastry', *sasimi* (*sashimi*) 'raw fish fillet', *sukkiyakki* (*sukiyaki*) 'beef dish with vegetables', *takkwang* (*takuan*) 'pickled dry turnips', *talai* (*tarai*) 'large washbasin', *tama* (*tama*) 'marble, electric bulb', *tansu* (*dansu*) 'chest', *wakkwu* (*waku*) 'frame', *wukki* (*uki*) 'float', *wutong* (*udon*) 'noodles', *yoci* (*yooji*) 'toothpick', and *yutoli* (*yudori*) 'flexibility'. For extensive studies on the linguistic influences of Japanese on Korean, see *Say Kwuk.e Saynghwal* 5.2 (1995).

German loan words in Korean are mostly related to medicine, philosophy, science, and sports: *aisupail* (*Eisbeil*) 'ice-digger', *alleyluki* (*Allergie*) 'alergy', *alupaithu* (*Arbeit*) 'student's part-time job', *cail* (*Seil*) 'rope', *heykeymoni* (*Hegemonie*) 'hegemony', *hisutheyli* (*Hysterie*) 'hysteria', *impho* (*Impotenz*) 'impotence', *iteyolloki* (*Ideologie*) 'ideology', *khalloli* (*Kalorie*) 'calorie', *khapheyin* (*Koffein*) 'caffeine', *lwuksayk* (*Rucksack*) 'rucksack', *lwumpheyn* (*Lumpen*) 'jobless person', *noilocey* (*Neurose*) 'neurosis', and *theyma* (*Thema*) 'theme'.

French borrowings abound in many areas: *angkheythu* (*enquête*) 'questionnaire', *angkhol* (*encore*) 'encore', *apeykku* (*avec*) 'dating' (lit. 'with'), *canglu* 'genre', *eyllithu* (*élite*) 'elite', *khaphey* (*café*) 'coffee house', *khongkhwul* (*concours*) 'music contest', *khuleyyong* 'crayon', *khwutheytha* 'coup d'état', *leysuthelang* 'restaurant', *mongthacu* 'montage', *nwiangsu* 'nuance', *pakhangsu* (*vacance*) 'vacation', *peytteylang* (*vétéran*) 'veteran', *phiangsey* 'fiancé(e)', *phulophil* (*profil*) 'profile', *pukhey* (*bouquet*) 'large flower bunch', *sapothaci* 'sabotage', *teypwi* 'début', *teysang* '(rough) sketch in art', and *tileksu* 'deluxe'.

Italian borrowings are mainly terms for music and food, as in *alia* 'aria', *alleykulo* 'allegro', *antanthey* 'andante', *khacino* 'casino', *makhaloni* 'macaroni', *matonna* 'madonna', *meyco* 'mezzo', *opheyleytha* 'operetta', *phiano* 'piano', *phica* 'pizza', *phinalley* 'finale', *sophulano* 'soprano', *sonatha* 'sonata', *suphakeythi* 'spaghetti', *theympho* 'tempo', and *tisukhu-cakhi* 'disk jockey'.

Words from Latin are mainly medical, scientific, and Christian terms, e.g., *eyteyn* 'Eden', *eytheylu* 'ether', *nathulyum* 'natrium', *oasisu* 'oasis', *olola* 'Aurora', *tisuthoma* 'distoma', *wulanyum* 'uranium', and *yanwusu* 'Janus'. Greek elements include *akaphey* 'an agape', *alpha* 'alpha', *ameyn* 'amen', *eylosu* 'Eros', *iteya* 'idea', *kamma* 'gamma', *khalisuma* 'charisma', *lokosu* 'logos', and *omeyka* 'omega'.

Dutch borrowings are related mainly to clothing, medicine, and science, as in *alkhol* (*alcohol*) 'alcohol', *ammonia* (*ammonia*) 'ammonia', *cokki* (*jak*) 'vest', *hokkwu* (*hoek*) 'hook-button', *hosu* (*hoos*) 'hose', *khininey* (*kinine*) 'quinine', *kholleyla* (*cholera*) 'cholera', *khompasu* (*kompas*) 'compass', *kipsu* (*gips*) 'plaster cast', *laymphu* (*lamp*) 'lamp', *leytheylu* (*letter*) 'trademark', *matolosu* (*matroos*) 'sailor', *phinthu* (*brandpunt*) 'focus', *phemphu* (*pomp*) 'pump', and *thiphusu* (*Typhus*) 'typhus'.

Portuguese words include *khasutheylla* (*castella*) 'sponge cake', *lakha* (*lacca*) 'lacquer', *localio* (*rosario*) 'rosary', *nasa* (*raxa*) 'woollen cloth', *phulo* (*procent*) 'percent', *pilotu* (*veludo*) 'velvet', *pethun* (*botão*) 'button', *panana* 'banana', *ppang* (*pão*) 'bun, bread', *salata* (*salada*) 'salad', *tampay* 'tobacco', and *teynppula* (*tempero*) 'deep-fried fish'. Spanish borrowings include *chachacha* (*chachacha*) 'chacha dance', *khey-sseyla-sseyla* (*que será será*) 'whatever will be will be', *lwumpa* (*rumba*) 'rumba dance', *mampo* (*mambo*) 'mambo dance', *meyliyasu* (*medias*) 'clothes made of fine cotton cloth', *peylanta* 'veranda', and *thoneyito* 'tornado'.

Finally, while there are many Russian loan words in North Korea, Russian borrowings are very few in South Korea. Examples are *lwupul* 'ruble', *potukha* 'vodka', *ppalchisan* (partizan) 'guerrilla unit', *thochikha* (*tochka*) 'fort', and *thwuntula* 'tundra'.

New words have been coined based on foreign words. This is particularly the case with English morphemes, as in *ayphuthe sepisu* (after-service) 'after-sales service', *eyku-phulai* (egg-fry) 'fried egg', *hom-tuleysu* (home-dress) 'Western-style home-wear', *khanning* (cunning) 'cheating on an exam', *khethu-lain* (cut-line) 'passing score on an exam', *kkol-in* (goal-in) 'kicking a goal in a game', *leyce-pum* (leisure-boom) 'boom for enjoying leisure', *lie-kha* (rear-car) 'two-wheeled pushing cart', *oltu-misu* (old-Miss) 'old maid', *ope-seynsu* (over-sense) (often contracted to *ope*) 'misunderstanding', *ophun-keyim* (open-game) 'game played before the main event', *payk-mile* (back-mirror) 'rear-view mirror', and *phaysu-misu* (pass-mistake) 'passing mistake in sports'.

6

Writing systems

This chapter surveys the writing systems that have been used for the graphic representation of Korean. At present, the Korean alphabet, called Hankul, is the main writing system used by all Koreans to represent native, Sino-Korean, and loan words, while Chinese characters are optionally used to represent only Sino-Korean words. The Itwu (lit. 'Clerk Reading') script which was derived from Chinese characters is a historical relic. Romanization systems are mainly for those who are not familiar with the Hankul system or for publications written in English.

6.1   Chinese characters

The Chinese script was created to represent (Classical) Chinese, a language which is not related to Korean either genetically or typologically. Genetically, Korean is viewed as belonging to the Altaic language family as discussed in chapter 2, whereas Chinese belongs to the Sino-Tibetan family, along with Tibetan and Burmese. Typologically, Korean is a language with agglutinative and inflectional morphology, Subject–Object–Verb syntax, and polysyllabic-word phonology, whereas Chinese is an isolating language with Subject–Verb–Object syntax, non-inflectional morphology, and monosyllabic-word phonology.

Moreover, the Chinese script was, and still is, an ideographic writing consisting of approximately 50,000 different characters, each being composed of one to thirty-two strokes. Basically there is one symbol per morpheme. Due to the virtual lack of grammatical affixes and nominal particles in Chinese, accordingly, there are no symbols to represent such grammatical concepts. Thus, the grammatical meanings carried by a wide variety of Korean affixes and particles cannot be represented by Chinese characters.

In short, Korean and Chinese are completely different, not only in sound patterns but also in morphological, syntactic, and semantic structure. This makes the ideographic Chinese script unfit to represent the sounds and structure of native Korean affixes, words, and sentences. Despite the structural disparities between Chinese and

Korean, Koreans have long been using Chinese characters. Although, at present, Chinese characters are used only to represent imported as well as coined Sino-Korean words, they were also employed as glossograms and phonograms to represent native words and affixes, as will be observed in 6.2.

6.1.1   Introduction of Chinese characters

Before the nineteenth century when Western cultures began to permeate East Asia, China had long been the centre of East Asian culture and civilization. Thus, Chinese culture and civilization were propagated to neighbouring countries mainly through written Chinese based on Chinese characters. As a result, the Chinese script has long been an integral part of the writing systems of Koreans, and was the only system before the creation of Hankul in 1446. Since Chinese characters were used mostly by upper-class people, commoners were devoid of any means of daily written communication before 1446.

It is not known exactly how and when Chinese characters were introduced into Korea. As stated in 5.4, practical knowledge of the Chinese script in Korea, however, is assumed to date back to the second century BC, when Wiman from Yen in China founded a primitive Korean state (the last state of Ancient Cosen) in the northwestern part of the peninsula in 194 BC. The establishment by China's Han dynasty of their four commanderies on the soil of Wiman's Ancient Cosen in 108 BC must have familiarized the resident Korean population with the Chinese script.

According to *Samkwuk Saki* (1145), the Kokwulye people had the Chinese script from the beginning of their existence as a state in 37 BC. One stele that was erected in 414 AD in honour of King Kwangkaytho of Kokwulye contains over 1,800 Chinese characters. This proves that the Kokwulye people were already using Chinese characters in the early fifth century. *Samkwuk Saki* also records that history books written in Chinese characters were compiled in the Paykcey dynasty in 375 AD and in the Sinla dynasty in 545 AD.

A large number of written Chinese words flooded into Middle Korean during the Kolye and early Cosen dynasty periods. These words came into Korea in the form of Chinese characters. During the Cosen dynasty, even after the creation of Hankul, laws, regulations, administrative decrees, official documents, petitions to government agencies, scholarly works, etc. were written solely in Chinese characters until 1894, when the government was reformed for modernization and adopted the policy of using primarily Hankul for all administrative purposes, including the enactment of laws and royal decrees. Since then, the status of Hankul has been enhanced, although Chinese characters have never been completely abandoned.

6.1.2 Sino-Korean pronunciation

Chinese characters currently used in Korea, which are termed Sino-Korean characters, are pronounced differently from the same Chinese characters used in contemporary China and Japan, as the sounds represented by identical characters have evolved independently in the three countries. First of all, Chinese lexical tones are no longer retained in Sino-Korean and Sino-Japanese. In an absolute majority of cases, the sounds of character words in the three East Asian countries are not the same. For instance, the words for Korea and college, written in Chinese characters as 韓國 and 大學, respectively, are pronounced differently in the three countries, as approximately transcribed in (1).

(1)		'Korea'	'college'
	Mandarin	[hán.k'wó]	[t'à.ɕyé]
	Korean	[han.guk]	[tɛ.hak]
	Japanese	[kan.k'o.k'u]	[da.i.ga.k'u]

Aside from the lack of tones, a relatively small number of Sino-Korean characters have essentially the same sounds as those of Mandarin Chinese, whereas the majority of Sino-Korean characters have sounds different from their Mandarin counterparts. For instance, 化 'change', 花 'flower', and 話 'speech' are pronounced as [hwa] in both Korean and Mandarin, but 和 'peace', 火 'fire', and 貨 'currency' are pronounced as [hwa] in Korean and [hwə] in Mandarin (cf. B. Huh 1994).

Scholars do not agree as to the detailed origins of Sino-Korean sounds. As briefly indicated in 5.4, however, Korean linguists generally agree that the pronunciations of Chinese characters used in the northern part of China during the Sui and Tang dynasties around the seventh and eighth centuries constituted the basis of Sino-Korean sounds. As a result, contemporary Sino-Korean sounds are quite similar to Middle Chinese, although some independent vowel and consonant changes as well as the loss of tones have been effected in Korea. Thus, for instance, compare the following Sino-Korean pronunciations with their corresponding sounds in Early Middle Chinese (as given in Pulleyblank 1991) and Contemporary Mandarin.

(2)	Character		Sino-Korean	Middle Chinese	Mandarin
	一	'one'	[il]	[ʔjit]	[ji]
	百	'hundred'	[pɛk]	[paɨjk]	[p'ǎj]
	國	'country'	[kuk]	[kwək]	[k'wó]
	七	'seven'	[chil]	[tshit]	[tɕɕi]

兵	'soldier'	[pjəŋ]	[piajŋ]	[p'īŋ]
不	'not'	[pul]	[put]	[p'ù]
冊	'book'	[chɛk]	[tshɛːjk]	[tɕə̀]
答	'answer'	[tap]	[tap]	[t'ā]
立	'stand'	[ɾip]	[lip]	[lì]
葉	'leaf'	[jəp]	[jiap]	[jè]
店	'shop'	[cəm]	[tɛmh]	[t'jàn]
見	'see'	[kjən]	[kɛnh]	[tʃ'jàn]
江	'river'	[kaŋ]	[kaɨwŋ]	[tʃ'jāŋ]

Notice that Middle Chinese morpheme-final stop sounds are reflected in Sino-Korean, but deleted in Mandarin. Notice further that Middle Chinese morpheme-final [t] has changed to [l] in Korean. It is notable that some southern dialects of Chinese still retain the syllable-final *p*, *t*, *k*, and *m* as in Korean.

6.2   The Itwu (Clerk Reading) script

In the past, the ruling class of Korea devoted their entire lives to the study of Classical Chinese, written in characters, because it was the main goal of education, the official means of government affairs, and the medium of civil service examinations. Chinese characters were used for documenting public and private records. Children of the ruling-class started learning written Chinese around the age of five, whereas most common people remained completely illiterate.

In an effort to improve this predicament, early scholars devised writing systems using Chinese characters for the pronunciation and transcription of native Korean affixes, words, and sentences. A few varieties of this writing, to be discussed below, were often subsumed under the term Itwu (lit. Clerk Reading), and were used during all three ancient kingdoms of Korea (Sinla, Paykcey, and Kokwulye), and also later during the Kolye and early Cosen dynasties. The Itwu script allowed people to record personal names, place names, and vernacular songs and poems. This writing was also used to clarify government documents and other books written in Chinese. The stele for King Kwangkaytho of Kokwulye contains many phonetic transcriptions written in the Itwu script, as do early Sinla inscriptions. Also, a number of Chinese characters used in the Itwu script are found in *Samkwuk Saki* and *Samkwuk Yusa*.

The Itwu script was used to record Korean expressions by means of (a) Chinese characters borrowed in their Chinese meaning but read as the corresponding Korean morphemes (glossograms), or (b) Chinese characters borrowed in their Chinese sounds only (phonograms). These two means are illustrated in (3).

(3) a. Glossograms

明	*pɔl* 'bright'	月	*tɔl* 'moon'	夜	*pam* 'night'
爲	*hɔ* 'do'	是	*i* 'be'	以	*lo* 'with'

b. Phonograms

阿	*a*	伊	*i*	加	*ka*	古	*ko*
仇	*kwu*	只	*ki*	奈	*na*	奴	*no*
多	*ta*	知	*ti*	羅	*la*	馬	*ma*
未	*mi*	時	*si*	也	*ya*	音	*m*
隱	*n*	邑	*p*	乙	*l*		

Thus, in 明期月 *pɔl-kuy-tɔl* 'bright moon', the first and third characters are glossograms, while the second character, a suffix in Korean, is a phonogram. Similarly, in 加于 *te-wuk* 'all the more', 必只 *pantɔ-ki* 'necessarily', 爲去乙 *hɔ-ke-nul* 'since/as/because (he) does', and 是去乃 *i-ke-na* 'whether (he) is', the first character in each is a glossogram and the rest phonograms.

More specifically, the Itwu script comprises three mutually related variants or subtypes: Hyangchal, Itwu proper, and Tho or Kwukyel (cf. H.K. Kim 1972:173–8; I.S. Lee, et al. 1997:65–71). The term Hyangchal (lit. vernacular letters) first appeared in Monk Kyun.ye's (917–73) biography at the end of the Sinla dynasty. Hyangchal was used mainly to transcribe *hyangka* (vernacular poetry). Currently, only twenty-five such vernacular poems are in existence. In this system, the basic words in the text were mostly native Korean, the word order was completely Korean, and each syllable tended to be transcribed with a single graph. Hyangchal covered not only functional items such as particles, suffixes, and auxiliary verbs, but also content words such as nouns, verbs, adjectives, and adverbs. This system continued to be used during the Kolye dynasty for the transcription of native poems. *The Song of Che.yong* (a shamanist song written by Che.yong during King Henkang's reign of the Sinla dynasty) is presented below as an illustration of the use of Hyangchal. Approximate romanized transcriptions are provided, along with translations based on Ogura 1929; C. Yang 1957; Ledyard 1966:38; H.K. Kim 1972; and Gim 1993:429–62, among many other works.

(4) 東京　明期　月良
　　si-sepɔl pɔl-kuy tɔl-ey
　　In the bright moonlight in the east capital,

夜入伊　　遊行如可
pam-tul-i　no-ni-ta-ka
Having caroused far into the night,

入良沙　　寢矣見昆
tul-e-sa　cal-i-po-kon
I entered my house, and beheld the bed,

脚烏伊　　四是良羅
kal-ɔl-i　nek-i-e-la
There were four legs!

二兮隱　　吾下於叱古
twu-hul-un　na-hay-e-s-ko
Two were mine,

二兮隱　　誰支下焉古
twu-hul-un　nwu-i-hay-en-ko
Whose were the other two?!

本矣　　吾下　　是如馬於隱
mot-i　na-hay　i-ta-mal-ɔ-n
She was mine of origin,

奪叱良乙　　何如爲理古
asa-s-e-nul　es-ta-hɔ-lis-ko
She was now taken away, what could I do?!

The term Itwu (written variously as 吏讀, 吏頭, 吏吐, 吏道, 吏套) first appeared in the *Taymyengyul Cik.hay* (the Korean translation of the Chinese Ming dynasty penal code *Ta Ming Liw*), which was compiled in 1395 during the time of the first king of the Cosen dynasty. Unlike Hyangchal, which was used to transcribe native poems, Itwu proper was used mainly as a bureaucratic instrument to clarify, for Korean readers, government documents written in Chinese. In this system, the basic words in the text were Chinese, Korean word order was generally followed, and each text was marked by extensive insertion of Korean grammatical elements (written in Itwu characters arranged in Korean word order). Itwu proper was limited mainly to grammatical relationals (particles, suffixes, auxiliaries) and adverbs. The following excerpts from the *Taymyengyul Cik.hay* illustrates Itwu proper. The Itwu forms (underlined) are followed by romanized transcriptions in parentheses.

(5)   a. 他人<u>矣</u> (uy)   四支<u>乙</u> (lul)   截割<u>爲旀</u> (hɔ-mye)
          other person-'*s*   four limbs-*AC*   mutilate-*do-and*
          'mutilating other persons' limbs'

      b. 自<u>以</u> (lo)   省覺現告<u>爲在乙良</u> (hɔ-kye-nul-lang)
          self-*with*   realize-report-*do-if*
          'if one realizes (his own error), and voluntarily reports (it)'

      c. 必于 (pilok)   七出<u>乙</u> (ul)   犯<u>爲去乃</u> (hɔ-ke-na}
          although   7-expel-*AC*   violate-*do-but*
          三不出<u>有去乙</u> (is-ke-nul)   黜送<u>爲去乙良</u> (hɔ-ke-nul-lang)
          3-not-expel-exist-*therefore*   expel-*do-if*
          減二等<u>遣</u> (ko)   婦女還本夫<u>齊</u> (cey)
          reduce-2-grades-*and*   woman-return-original-husband-*DC*

      'Even though a woman breaks the law of the seven valid reasons for divorce, there exist three exceptions. If one expels his wife despite the exceptional cases, he will be demoted by two grades and his wife will be sent to her husband.'

In addition to various official documents, certificates, contracts, receipts, personal memoirs, etc., this script was widely used in the teaching of Chinese, especially during the Kolye period, when Neo-Confucianism was being introduced into Korea. This system lasted as long as Chinese documents lasted, that is, to the end of the nineteenth century or the end of the Cosen dynasty.

The third subtype was Tho 'particle' (also called Kwukyel 'oral formulae' and Hyentho 'hanging particle'), a term coined when Chinese classics such as *Sase Samkyeng* (Four Books of Confucianism and Three Chinese Classic Books) were studied during the Cosen dynasty. The term Tho first appeared in a footnote of the King Seycong Annals. While teaching Chinese and reading Chinese classics, people came to adopt a system in which Chinese texts retained their original form and word order, and in order to clarify the Chinese words and phrases, Itwu characters were inserted to represent Korean particles, verbal suffixes, and basic verbs that did not appear in the Chinese texts. The characters used in this way are called Tho. Unlike the other types, Tho characters were frequently used in simplified forms, as in 厂 (厓) *ay* 'at', ア (隱) *nun* 'as for' (topic particle), 夕 (多) *ta*, ヤ or ㄱ (也) *ya*, 스 (羅) *la* (declarative sentence enders), 丶 (是) *i* 'be' or subject particle, ㅏ (臥) *wa* 'and, with',

口 (古) *ko* 'and', ㅅ (爲) *hɔ* 'do, be', and ㅌ (尼) *ni* 'because'. For instance, the first sentence of *Tongmong Sensup* (a children's primer on moral rules, written by Pak Seymu in 1670) reads as follows. Simplified Tho characters and their romanized transcriptions are given in parentheses (cf. Ledyard 1966:46–8; H.K. Kim 1972:175). Notice that without the Tho particles, the text is nothing more than standard Chinese.

(6)   天地之間萬物之衆匡(厂 *ay*) 唯人是(㇏ *i*) 最貴爲尼(㇗ㅌ *hɔ-ni*)
        所貴乎人者隱(ㄆ *nun*) 以其有五倫是羅(㇏ ㇗ *i-la*)

   '*Of* all the things under the sun, only man [*subject particle*] *is* the most
   noble; what is noble in man [*topic particle*] *is* his possession of the Five
   Cardinal Articles of Morality.'

Incidentally, the Itwu script was thus used frequently as a tool of teaching Chinese classics as well as the Neo-Confucian teachings of Sung philosophy which had been introduced into Korea in the later years of the Kolye period.

The slight differences among the three interrelated subtypes of the Itwu script may be recapitulated as follows (H.K. Kim ibid.:177–8). First, as for the coverage of Korean elements, Hyangchal covers not only relationals such as particles, suffixes, and auxiliary verbs, but also contentives such as adverbs, nouns, and verbs; Itwu proper is limited mainly to grammatical elements and adverbs; and Tho is limited to grammatical elements. Second, as for the word order in texts, Hyangchal follows Korean word order because there are no Chinese words involved. The same can be said of the texts in Itwu proper although nouns and verbs are in Chinese. The main texts in Tho are written according to Chinese word order. Third, as for the time of usage, Hyangchal was used mostly during the Sinla dynasty, although there were some Hyangchal writings found from the Kolye dynasty. Itwu proper, on the other hand, flourished mostly during the Kolye era and the early part of the Cosen dynasty. Tho started to be used at the end of the Kolye era, but the peak of its use was in the early and middle part of the Cosen dynasty when the philosophical study of imported Chinese classical works was at its height. Fourth, as for the forms of Chinese characters, Hyangchal and Itwu proper used only full character forms, whereas Tho was based on both full and simplified forms.

Evidently, all three varieties of the Itwu script, which consisted only of Chinese characters and their abbreviated forms, were extremely inadequate as a means of written communication, in addition to the difficulty of learning them. It was under these circumstances that Hankul was created, a phonetic writing system that was completely disengaged from the Chinese script.

6.3 Hankul: the Korean alphabet

6.3.1 Creation of Hankul

The indigenous phonetic writing system Koreans currently use is called Hankul, which means 'the Great Writing'. This alphabet was named Hankul by Cwu Sikyeng (1876–1914), a pioneer linguist of Korean. Before, it was popularly called Enmun 'vernacular writing, vulgar script'. Hankul, including its early sound values, has long been an object of study in many works such as Pang 1946; K.M. Hong 1947; M.S. Kim 1957; H.P. Choy 1961; C.D. Yu 1962; Ledyard 1966; W.J. Kim 1971; C.H. Lee 1972; K.M. Lee 1976; *Say Kwuk.e Saynghwal* 6.2 (1996); Kim-Renaud 1997; and Kim-Cho 1999. Ledyard provides a well-organized picture of the origin, cultural background, and early history of Hankul. The following discussions owe greatly to Ledyard's monumental work and rely heavily on his meticulous translations of the original documents on Hankul.

Hankul is one of the most remarkable writing systems ever devised in the world. It is an alphabet which follows a rigorous phonological analysis of Korean sound patterns. Observing the letter compositions of Hankul, Sampson (1985:120–44) terms Hankul a unique 'featural' writing system in that the strokes constituting letters represent phonological distinctive features such as aspiration and tenseness.

For the design of the Hankul alphabet, Seycong (1397–1450), the fourth king of the Cosen dynasty, and his scholars studied the rich Chinese linguistic tradition, such as the concepts of consonants, syllables, and tones, as well as their underlying philosophical background. Yet the features of Hankul are original and unique in its represention of the Korean language. Seycong assigned the phonological research, of which Hankul was a direct result, to members of his academy called Cip.hyencen (Hall of Assembled Sages). The king took keen interest in all activities of the academy.

The orthographical design of Hankul was completed in 1443. To test the new writing system, the king ordered his subjects (Kwen Cey, et al.) to write the voluminous *Yongpi Echenka* (Songs of Flying Dragons, published in 1447) in Hankul with translations in Chinese characters. A canto of the Songs will be cited in 6.3.2.

King Seycong promulgated Hankul to the public on October 9, 1446, in the name of *Hwunmin Cengum* (The Correct Sounds to Instruct the People). *Hwunmin Cengum* (written by Seycong himself) was accompanied by *Hwunmin Cengum Haylyey* (Explanations and Examples of the *Hwunmin Cengum*), which was compiled by a group of scholars (headed by Ceng Inci) commissioned by Seycong. These two documents were written in Chinese characters and originally published as a single book.

The text of *Hwunmin Cengum* consists of three parts: preface, explanations of the pronunciation of the twenty-eight letters, and rules regarding the use of the letters and other symbols. The preface briefly summarizes Seycong's motives for inventing Hankul as follows.

(7)   國之語音，異乎中國，與文字不相流通，故愚民，
        有所慾言而終不得伸其情者多矣，予，爲此憫然，新制二十八字，
        欲使人人易習，便於日用耳

> 'The speech sounds of Korea are distinct from those of China and thus are not communicable with Chinese characters. Hence, many people having something to put into words are unable to express their feelings. To overcome such distressing circumstances, I have newly devised twenty-eight letters that everyone can learn with ease and use with convenience in daily life.'

In the second part, the sounds of the twenty-eight letters are explained in reference to the pronunciations of relevant Chinese characters, as shown in the English translations in (8). Note that the phonetic terms given do not necessarily conform to the terms used in contemporary linguistics. As will be discussed shortly, the short horizontal or vertical stroke in current vowel and diphthong letters such as ㅏ, ㅗ, and ㅘ was originally a round dot.

(8)   ㄱ   molar sound, like the initial sound of the Chinese character *kwun* 'king'; as the diplogram (ㄲ), like the initial sound of the Chinese character *kkyu* 'tadpole'

        ㅋ   molar sound, like the initial sound of the Chinese character *khwai* 'cheerful'

        ㆁ   molar sound, like the initial sound of the Chinese character *ngep* 'job'

        ㄷ   lingual sound, like the initial sound of the Chinese character *twu* 'measure'; as the diplogram (ㄸ), like the initial sound of the Chinese character *ttam* 'deep'

        ㅌ   lingual sound, like the initial sound of the Chinese character *thɔn* 'swallow'

        ㄴ   lingual sound, like the initial sound of the Chinese character *na* 'how'

        ㅂ   labial sound, like the initial sound of the Chinese character *pyel* 'rough'; as the diplogram (ㅃ), like the initial sound of the Chinese character *ppo* 'walking'

ㅍ	labial sound, like the initial sound of the Chinese character *phyo* 'float'
ㅁ	labial sound, like the initial sound of the Chinese character *mi* 'broad'
ㅈ	dental sound, like the initial sound of the Chinese character *cuk* 'immediate'; as the diplogram (ㅉ), like the initial sound of the Chinese character *cco* 'love'
ㅊ	dental sound, like the initial sound of the Chinese character *chim* 'invade'
ㅅ	dental sound, like the initial sound of the Chinese character *syul* 'dog'; as the diplogram (ㅆ), like the initial sound of the Chinese character *ssya* 'sly'
ㆆ	glottal sound, like the initial sound of the Chinese character *ʔup* 'bail out'
ㅎ	glottal sound, like the initial sound of the Chinese character *he* 'empty'; as the diplogram (ㆅ), like the initial sound of the Chinese character *hhong* 'wide'
ㅇ	glottal sound, like the initial sound of the Chinese character *(ɦ)yok* 'desire'
ㄹ	semi-lingual sound, like the initial sound of the Chinese character *lye* 'village entrance'
ㅿ	semi-dental sound, like the initial sound of the Chinese character *zyang* 'planting'

·	like the medial sound of the Chinese character *thɔn* 'swallow'
ㅡ	like the medial sound of the Chinese character *cuk* 'immediate'
ㅣ	like the medial sound of the Chinese character *chim* 'invade'
ㅗ	like the medial sound of the Chinese character *hhong* 'wide'
ㅏ	like the medial sound of the Chinese character *ttam* 'deep'
ㅜ	like the medial sound of the Chinese character *kwun* 'king'
ㅓ	like the medial sound of the Chinese character *ngep* 'job'
ㅛ	like the medial sound of the Chinese character *(ɦ)yok* 'desire'
ㅑ	like the medial sound of the Chinese character *zyang* 'planting'
ㅠ	like the medial sound of the Chinese character *syul* 'dog'
ㅕ	like the medial sound of the Chinese character *pyel* 'rough'

Hwunmin Cengum identifies the sound of the letter ㅇ with the intial sound of *(ɦ)yok*. Its sound quality at the time of Seycong is still controversial. While a widely held view is that it was a null sound quality as it is today, a few scholars including

K.M. Lee (1976:128–9) argue that it represented the voiced glottal fricative [ɦ].

The third part of *Hwunmin Cengum* presents rules regarding the use of the Hankul letters and other symbols in syllable blocks. Such rules include the following.

(a) Letters representing syllable-initial consonants are also used as letters representing syllable-final consonants (e.g., 싯 *sis*).

(b) When a small circle ㅇ is written immediately below a labial sound, it indicates that the labial sound is light (e.g., 병 [β], 퐁 [ɸ], 뼝 [β']).

(c) Syllable-initial sound clusters are written side by side (e.g., 쓸 *spul* 'horn'). The same applies to syllable-final sound clusters (e.g., 홁 *hɔlk* 'soil').

(d) One dot (ˊ) added to the left of a syllable indicates a high tone; two dots (:) indicate a rising tone; and the absence of a dot means a level (low) tone (e.g., ˊ사, :사, and 사).

Hwunmin Cengum Haylyey explains and illustrates the contents of *Hwunmin Cengum*. It consists of seven parts: design of the letters (6.3.1.1), syllable-initial sounds (6.3.1.2), syllable-medial sounds (6.3.1.3), syllable-final sounds (6.3.1.4), combination of the letters (6.3.1.5), examples of the use of the letters (6.3.1.6), and postface by Ceng Inci (6.3.1.7). The main points are summarized below based essentially on Ledyard 1966:123–260 and C.H. Lee 1972:35–60. Some notes and examples are added as appropriate.

6.3.1.1   Design of the letters

(a) The universe is governed by the principle of Yin 'dark' and Yang 'bright' and the rotation of the Five Elements (water, wood, fire, metal, and earth). Human speech sounds are also based on the same cosmological principles, i.e., the patterns of Yin–Yang and the Five Elements. So are the speech sounds of Korean.

(b) The seventeen consonant letters were designed to depict the shapes of the speech organs. The symbol ㄱ *k* depicts the shape of the root of the tongue blocking the throat; ㄴ *n*, the shape of the tongue touching the alveo-dental area; ㅁ *m*, the shape of the mouth (i.e., lips); ㅅ *s*, the shape of an incisor; and ㅇ (*ɦ*), the shape of the throat. Other consonants were made by adding strokes to the above basic symbols. For instance, ㅋ *kh* is pronounced using the same oral position (soft palate) as ㄱ *k*, but it has an added stroke because its articulation is more 'severe' or aspirated than that of ㄱ *k*. The sounds represented by ㄴ *n*, ㄷ *t*, ㅌ *th*, and ㄹ *l* are all pronounced using the same oral place of articulation (the alveo-dental area), but compared with ㄴ *n*, ㄷ *t* has an added stroke, symbolizing the blockage of the passage leading to the nasal cavity, whereas ㅌ *th* has one more

stroke by virtue of its aspiration, and ㄹ *l* one more by virtue of its sound quality
of trill or flap liquid. In the same way, ㅂ *p*, ㅍ *ph*, and ㅁ *m* are all bilabial
sounds, but the first two have some added strokes in view of their respective
manners of articulation. Similarly, the fricative sounds ㅿ *z*, ㅈ *c*, and ㅊ *ch* are
written parallel to ㅅ *s*, and the letters for the velar nasal ㆁ *ng*, glottal stop ㆆ *ʔ*,
and glottal fricative ㅎ *h* are modelled after ㅇ (*ɦ*).

(c) The articulatory organs are related to the Five Elements. The throat is water
because it is deep and moist; the molar is wood because it is uneven and
extended; the tongue is fire because it is pointed and moving; the incisor is metal
because it is hard and cutting; and the lips are earth because they are squarish and
yet joined. Just as water is the source of life and fire is the operation that perfects
things, so are the throat and the tongue sounds primary, in that the throat is the
articulator and the tongue the differentiator of speech sounds.

(d) The consonants ㄱ *k*, ㄷ *t*, ㅂ *p*, ㅈ *c*, ㅅ *s*, and ㆆ *ʔ* are wholly clear; the
consonants ㅋ *kh*, ㅌ *th*, ㅍ *ph*, ㅊ *ch*, and ㅎ *h* are partly clear; the consonants ㄲ
kk, ㄸ *tt*, ㅃ *pp*, ㅉ *cc*, ㅆ *ss*, and ㆅ *hh* are wholly cloudy; and the consonants ㆁ
ng, ㄴ *n*, ㅁ *m*, ㅇ (*ɦ*), ㄹ *l*, and ㅿ *z* are neither clear nor cloudy.

(e) Eleven letters make up the syllable-medial (peak) sounds: three cardinal vowels
· *ɔ* [ɔ], ㅡ *u* [ɨ], and ㅣ *i* [i]; four derived vowels ㅗ *o* [o], ㅏ *a* [a], ㅜ *wu* [u],
and ㅓ *e* [ə]; and four yodized vowels ㅛ *yo* [jo], ㅑ *ya* [ja], ㅠ *yu* [ju], and ㅕ *ye*
[jə]. For · *ɔ*, the tongue retracts and its sound is deep; the roundness of its shape
is a depiction of Heaven. For ㅡ *u*, the tongue retracts a little, and its sound is
neither deep nor shallow; the flatness of its shape is a depiction of Earth. For ㅣ *i*,
the tongue does not retract, and its sound is shallow; the uprightness of its shape
is a depiction of Man. Thus, the basic vowel symbols are based on the trinity of
Heaven, Earth, and Man. The other eight vowel and diphthong letters are
combinations of the three cardinal vowel letters as in (9). Recall that the currently
used short horizontal or vertical stroke was originally the cardinal vowel letter ·
ɔ. (The cosmological explanations given to all these letter combinations are
omitted here.)

(9) ㅗ *o* same as · *ɔ* except that the mouth is contracted.
ㅏ *a* same as · *ɔ* except that the mouth is spread.
ㅜ *wu* same as ㅡ *u* except that the mouth is contracted.
ㅓ *e* same as ㅡ *u* except that the mouth is spread.
ㅛ *yo* same as ㅗ *o* except that it arises from ㅣ *i*.
ㅑ *ya* same as ㅏ *a* except that it arises from ㅣ *i*.
ㅠ *yu* same as ㅜ *u* except that it arises from ㅣ *i*.
ㅕ *ye* same as ㅓ *e* except that it arises from ㅣ *i*.

(f) In ㅗ *o*, ㅏ *a*, ㅑ *ya*, and ㅛ *yo*, the round dot (Heaven), i.e., a short stroke in the
current system, is located above and on the outside, hence they are called Yang
'bright' sounds. In ㅜ *wu*, ㅓ *e*, ㅠ *yu*, and ㅕ *ye*, the round dot is located below
and on the inside, hence they are called Yin 'dark' sounds. (The distinction
between Yang and Yin sounds is relevant to sound alternations such as vowel
harmony as discussed in chapter 7.)

6.3.1.2   Syllable-initial sounds

There are twenty-three letters which are used as syllable-initial consonant letters: (i)
molar ㄱ, ㅋ, ㄲ, ㆁ; (ii) lingual ㄷ, ㅌ, ㄸ, ㄴ; (iii) labial ㅂ, ㅍ, ㅃ, ㅁ; (iv) dental
ㅈ, ㅊ, ㅉ, ㅅ, ㅆ; (v) glottal ㆆ, ㅎ, ㆅ, ㅇ; (vi) semi-lingual ㄹ; and (vii) semi-dental
ㅿ. For instance, the initial sound of the Chinese character *kkyu* is ㄲ *kk*. This initial
sound and the medial sound ㅠ *yu* make ㆠ *kkyu*.

6.3.1.3   Syllable-medial sounds

(a) The syllable-medial sounds are located in the middle of the syllabic rhyme,
combining with the initial and final sounds to complete the articulation. For
instance, the medial sound of the Chinese character *chim* 'invade' is ㅣ *i*, which
is located between the initial ㅊ *ch* and the final ㅁ *m*, forming the articulation 침
chim.

(b) Diphthongs and triphthongs are formed as shown in the following examples.

(10) | ㅗ | *o* | + | ㅏ | *a* | = | ㅘ | *wa* |
ㅜ	*wu*	+	ㅓ	*e*	=	ㅝ	*we*
·	*ɔ*	+	ㅣ	*i*	=	·ㅣ	*ɔy*
ㅡ	*u*	+	ㅣ	*i*	=	ㅢ	*uy*
ㅗ	*o*	+	ㅣ	*i*	=	ㅚ	*oy*
ㅏ	*a*	+	ㅣ	*i*	=	ㅐ	*ay*
ㅓ	*e*	+	ㅣ	*i*	=	ㅔ	*ey*
ㅑ	*ya*	+	ㅣ	*i*	=	ㅒ	*yay*
ㅕ	*ye*	+	ㅣ	*i*	=	ㅖ	*yey*

ㅗ *o* + ㅏ *a* + ㅣ *i* = ㅙ *way*
ㅜ *wu* + ㅓ *e* + ㅣ *i* = ㅞ *wey*

6.3.1.4   Syllable-final sounds

(a) The syllable-final sounds follow the initial and medial sounds, completing the
syllable rhyme. Thus, for instance, ㅇ *ng* is located below ㆅㅗ *hho* and completes

the syllable 뽕 *hhong*.

(b) The eight letters ㄱ *k*, ㆁ *ng*, ㄷ *t*, ㄴ *n*, ㅂ *p*, ㅁ *m*, ㅅ *s*, and ㄹ *l* are sufficient for the final sounds.

(c) The sound ㅇ is insipid and empty and need not be written in syllable-final positions. In this case, the medial sound completes the syllable.

6.3.1.5 Combination of letters

(a) When the initial, medial, and final sounds combine to complete a syllable, the round and horizontal medials (· *o*, ㅡ *u*, ㅗ *o*, ㅛ *yo*, ㅠ *yu*) are placed below the initial sound, as in 즉 *cuk*; and the vertical ones (ㅣ *i*, ㅏ *a*, ㅑ *ya*, ㅓ *e*, ㅕ *ye*) are placed to the right, as in 침. The final sounds are placed below the initial and medial, as in 군 *kun* and 깊 *kiph*.

(b) When two or three letters are used for the initial sounds, they are written side by side from left to right, as in 짝 *pcak* 'one of a pair'. Two or three letters may be used for the medial sounds, written left to right, as in 홰 *hway*. Two or three letters used for the final sounds are written side by side from left to right, as shown in 돐ᄲᆌ *tolks pstay* 'hours of the cock (5–7 p.m.)'.

(c) The nominative case particle ㅣ *i* is added directly to the preceding noun if the noun ends in a vowel, as in 조 *co* + ㅣ *i* = 죄 *coy*. If the noun is a Chinese character or character compound, ㅣ *i* is written separately, as in 孔子 ㅣ 'Confucius (nominative)'.

(d) In the semi-lingual sound ㄹ *l*, there are two sound varieties, light ㄹ [ɾ] (syllable-initial position) and dark ㄹ [l] (syllable-final position). Examples are 여름 *yelum* [jə.ɾɨm] 'fruit' and 불 *pul* [pul] 'fire'.

6.3.1.6 Examples of the use of letters

Consisting of a list of approximately ninety words, this section illustrates occurrences of various sounds in syllable-initial, -medial, and -final positions, with examples such as 우ㆍ케 *(fi)wu·khey* 'unhusked rice', :뫼 *:moy* 'mountain', and :밀 *:mil* 'honey'. (Notice that the words are tone-marked.)

6.3.1.7 Postface by Ceng Inci

The key points of the postface are as follows: Just as there are sounds natural to Heaven and Earth, there must also be writings natural to Heaven and Earth. Just as the winds and soils of the Four Quarters are not the same, so are the speech sounds and breaths of different languages different. Chinese characters are inadequate for the needs of Koreans. People are troubled by the difficulty of understanding the meanings of the texts written in Chinese characters. In the winter of the year 1443–4, our King originated and designed the twenty-eight letters of the Correct Sounds. The letters are simple and fine and very easy to learn; their shifts and changes in function are endless; and there are no sounds that cannot be written. Commanded by the King, the royal subjects in charge have attentively written all the explanations and examples of the letters so that the framework and structure may be easily understood by readers without the help of a teacher.

6.3.2   *Early literature in Hankul*

It was indicated in 6.3.1 that King Seycong ordered his royal scholars to test the validity of Hankul by writing *Yongpi Echenka* (Songs of Flying Dragons). The Songs is a eulogy cycle in 125 cantos comprising 248 poems, composed to celebrate the founding of the Cosen dynasty and praise the achievements of Seycong's predecessors. As an elaborate product of linguists and literary scholars, it is not only the first experimental use of Hankul, but also an important statement of the Confucianism-oriented policies of the new dynasty. Comprising heroic tales, foundation myths, folk beliefs, and prophecies, it also marks the birth of a national vernacular literature. The second canto of the Songs is cited below as an illustration. Romanized transcriptions are provided along with glosses and an English translation given in P. H. Lee 1975.

(11)   불·휘   기·픈   남ㄹ
        pul·hwi ki·phun   namkɔn
        root   deep-RL   tree-TC
        The tree that strikes deep root

        ㅂㄹ·매   아·니 :뮐·쎠,
        pɔlɔ·may   a·ni   :muyl·ssɔy
        wind-to   not   move-as
        Is firm amidst the winds.

        곳   :됴코
        koc   :tyokho
        flower good-and
        Its flowers are good,

        여름   ·하ㄴ·니
        yelum   ·hanɔ·ni
        fruit   abundant-DC
        Its fruits abundant.

:싀·미　기·픈　·므·른
:soy·mi　ki·phun　·mu·lun
stream-NM　deep-RL　water-TC
The stream whose source is deep

·ᄀᄆ·래　아·니　그·츨·쎠,
·komo·lay　a·ni　ku·chul·ssoy
drought-at　not　stop-as
Gushes forth even in a drought.

:내·히　이·러
:nay·hi　i·le
river　form-and then
It forms a river

바·ᄅ·래　·가ᄂ·니
pa·lo·lay　·kano·ni
sea-to　go-DC
And gains the sea.

King Seycong ordered Prince Swu.yang in 1446 to write a book in Hankul entitled *Sekpo Sangcel* (Episodes from the Life of Buddha) as a tribute to Seycong's late Queen Sohen. This book was published in 1449 in the first metal Hankul type. In the same metal type were published in 1449 three volumes of Seycong's *Wel.in Chenkang-ci Kok* (Songs of the Moon's Reflection on a Thousand Rivers) which included over five hundred poems. None of these volumes are extant. Another early Hankul-related book, written on King Seycong's instruction, is Sin Swukcwu, et al.'s *Tongkwuk Cengwun* (Correct Rhymes of the Eastern Nation, published in 1448), which is a dictionary of Hankul-based standard pronunciations of Chinese characters.

6.3.3　Hankul in current use

The Hankul letters, originated as discussed thus far, have undergone considerable modifications, due partly to the sound changes that have since taken place in Korean and partly to the research conducted by many Hankul scholars. Moreover, as indicated in H.K. Kim (1972:187–90), the main goal of designing Hankul letters is assumed to have been to transcribe the sounds of the Chinese characters as well as Korean expressions. Thus, certain Hankul letter clusters must have been relevant only to Chinese character words, as in the spellings represented by *ssyelʔ* (舌) 'tongue' and *hhong* (洪) 'wide' where ᄙ *lʔ* and ᅘ *hh* appear to be non-Korean. The following changes are noteworthy.

(a) The two consonant letters ㅿ *z* and ㆆ *ʔ* have been abolished because the former sound disappeared from the Korean language and the latter sound turned out to be insignificant in distinguishing the meanings of Korean words.

(b) The consonant letter ㆁ which formerly represented the velar nasal sound [ŋ] is no longer in use. Instead, ㅇ which has lost the assumed original sound quality of voiced glottal fricative [ɦ] and turned out to be silent, takes dual functions, assuming ZERO sound quality in the syllable-initial (i.e., onset) position and [ŋ] quality in the syllable-final (i.e., coda) position, as in 앙 *ang* [aŋ].

(c) The vowel sound that the basic letter ㆍ *ɔ* represented has since disappeared from the language (except perhaps in some parts of Ceycwu Island). Thus, the letter is no longer used to represent an independent vowel, but is used only in combination with another basic vowel letter (ㅣ or ㅡ) to represent other vowel or semivowel sounds. Furthermore, as already stated, the letter has been changed to a short vertical stroke when combined with ㅡ and to a short horizontal stroke when combined with ㅣ, as in ㅛ instead of ᆢ and ㅑ instead of ㅣ:.

(d) Bilabial fricative symbols such as ㅸ and ㅹ have been abolished because the associated sounds became extinct.

(e) All complex consonant letters in the syllable-initial position such as ㅄ and ㅵ have been abolished, as no contemporary syllable has a consonant cluster in that position. A maximum of two syllable-final consonant letters are used in Contemporary Korean. Thus, *tɔlks pstay* 'hours of the cock (5–7 p.m.)' is now spelled as 닭때 *talk ttay*.

(f) Tones have disappeared from most dialects of Korean. Accordingly, tone markers have been completely abolished.

Individual Hankul letters were not given names in *Hwunmin Cengum*. In 1527, during the reign of King Cwungcong (the eleventh king of the Cosen dynasty), Choy Seycin wrote *Hwunmong Cahoy* (Explanations of Chinese Characters with Hankul), a primer to teach characters a total of 3,360 Chinese characters. In this book, the sounds and meanings of the Chinese characters are written in Hankul. The author gave names to Hankul letters and rearranged the letters in an order very similar to the current practice, as follows.

(12) a. Consonant letters occurring in syllable-initial and -final positions

ㄱ	其役	*ki-yek*	ㄴ	尼隱	*ni-un*	ㄷ	池末	*ti-kut*
ㄹ	梨乙	*li-ul*	ㅁ	眉音	*mi-um*	ㅂ	非邑	*pi-up*
ㅅ	時衣	*si-os*	ㅇ	異凝	*i-ung*			

b. Consonant letters occurring only in the syllable-initial position

ヨ	箕	*khi*	ㅍ	皮	*phi*	ㅈ	之	*ci*	ㅊ	齒	*chi*
△	而	*zi*	ㅇ	伊	*(ɦ)i*	ㅎ	屎	*hi*			

c. Vowels and diphthongs

ㅏ	阿	*a*	ㅑ	也	*ya*	ㅓ	於	*e*
ㅕ	余	*ye*	ㅗ	吾	*o*	ㅛ	要	*yo*
ㅜ	牛	*wu*	ㅠ	由	*yu*	ー	應	*ung* (without *ng*)
ㅣ	伊	*(ɦ)i* (without *(ɦ)*)				·	思	*sɔ* (without *s*)

In (12a) the names of the Hankul letters are designed to represent both syllable-
initial (onset) and syllable-final (coda) consonants. Notice the phonetic irregularities in
the names, however. Obviously, this irregularity was caused by the lack of appropriate
Chinese characters to regularize the names. Notice that the three Chinese characters 末
(*kut* 'end'), 衣 (*os* 'clothes'), and 箕 (*khi* 'winnow') are used as glossograms as
against all the other phonograms. The same irregular names are still used in South
Korea, whereas in North Korea the names have been regularized as in ㄱ *ki-uk*, ㄷ *tiut*, and ㅅ *si-us*.

The current Hankul letters are arranged in (13) in the order taught in schools,
together with the basic sounds they represent. The names of the letters used in South
Korea are given in Hankul, romanized spellings, and IPA transcriptions of the
pronunciations in parentheses, dots [.] standing for syllable boundaries. Notice that
vowels are simply termed as they are pronounced.

(13)

	Letter	Roman	Sound	Name of letter	

Simple consonant letters

	Letter	Roman	Sound		Name of letter	IPA
	ㄱ	*k*	[k, g]	기역	*ki-yek*	[ki.jək]
	ㄴ	*n*	[n]	니은	*ni-un*	[ni.ɨn]
	ㄷ	*t*	[t, d]	디귿	*ti-kut*	[ti.kɨt]
	ㄹ	*l*	[l, ɾ]	리을	*li-ul*	[ɾi.ɨl]
	ㅁ	*m*	[m]	미음	*mi-um*	[mi.ɨm]
	ㅂ	*p*	[p, b]	비읍	*pi-up*	[pi.ɨp]
	ㅅ	*s*	[s, ʃ]	시옷	*si-os*	[ʃi.ot]
	ㅇ	*ng*	[ŋ]	이응	*i-ung*	[i.ɨŋ]
	ㅈ	*c*	[c, ɟ]	지읒	*ci-uc*	[ci.ɨt]
	ㅊ	*ch*	[ch]	치읓	*chi-uch*	[chi.ɨt]

ㅋ	*kh*	[kh]	키읔	*khi-ukh*	[khi.ɨk]
ㅌ	*th*	[th]	티읕	*thi-uth*	[thi.ɨt]
ㅍ	*ph*	[ph]	피읖	*phi-uph*	[phi.ɨp]
ㅎ	*h*	[h]	히읗	*hi-uh*	[hi.ɨt]

Twin (ssang) consonant letters

ㄲ	*kk*	[k']	쌍기역	*ssang ki-yek*	[s'aŋ.gi.jək]
ㄸ	*tt*	[t']	쌍디귿	*ssang ti-kut*	[s'aŋ.di.gɨt]
ㅃ	*pp*	[p']	쌍비읍	*ssang pi-up*	[s'aŋ.bi.ɨp]
ㅆ	*ss*	[s', ʃ']	쌍시옷	*ssang si-os*	[s'aŋ.ʃi.ot]
ㅉ	*cc*	[c']	쌍지읒	*ssang ci-uc*	[s'aŋ.ɟi.ɨt]

Consonant clusters

ㄳ	*ks*	[ks]	기역시옷	*ki-yek si-os*	[ki.jək.si.ot]
ㄵ	*nc*	[nɟ]	니은지읒	*ni-un ci-uc*	[ni.ɨn.ɟi.ɨt]
ㄶ	*nh*	[nh]	니은히읗	*ni-un hi-uh*	[ni.ɨn.hi.ɨt]
ㄺ	*lk*	[lg]	리을기역	*li-ul ki-yek*	[ɾi.ɨl.gi.jək]
ㄻ	*lm*	[lm]	리을미음	*li-ul mi-um*	[ɾi.ɨl.mi.ɨm]
ㄼ	*lp*	[lb]	리을비읍	*li-ul pi-up*	[ɾi.ɨl.bi.ɨp]
ㄽ	*ls*	[ls, lʃ]	리을시옷	*li-ul si-os*	[ɾi.ɨl.ʃi.ot]
ㄾ	*lth*	[lth]	리을티읕	*li-ul thi-uth*	[ɾi.ɨl.thi.ɨt]
ㄿ	*lph*	[lph]	리을피읖	*li-ul phi-uph*	[ɾi.ɨl.phi.ɨp]
ㅀ	*lh*	[lh]	리을히읗	*li-ul hi-uh*	[ɾi.ɨl.hi.ɨt]
ㅄ	*ps*	[ps, pʃ]	비읍시옷	*pi-up si-os*	[pi.ɨp.ʃi.ot]

Vowels and diphthongs

ㅏ	*a*	[a]	아	*a*	[aː]
ㅑ	*ya*	[ja]	야	*ya*	[jaː]
ㅓ	*e*	[ə]	어	*e*	[əː]
ㅕ	*ye*	[jə]	여	*ye*	[jəː]
ㅗ	*o*	[o]	오	*o*	[oː]
ㅛ	*yo*	[jo]	요	*yo*	[joː]
ㅜ	*wu*	[u]	우	*wu*	[uː]
ㅠ	*yu*	[ju]	유	*yu*	[juː]
ㅡ	*u*	[ɨ]	으	*u*	[ɨː]
ㅣ	*i*	[i]	이	*i*	[iː]
ㅐ	*ay*	[ɛ]	애	*ay*	[ɛː]
ㅒ	*yay*	[jɛ]	얘	*yay*	[jɛː]
ㅔ	*ey*	[e]	에	*ey*	[eː]

ㅖ	*yey*	[je]	예	*yey*	[je:]
ㅚ	*oy*	[ø, we]	외	*oy*	[ø:, we:]
ㅟ	*wi*	[y, wi]	위	*wi*	[y:, wi:]
ㅘ	*wa*	[wa]	와	*wa*	[wa:]
ㅝ	*we*	[wə]	워	*we*	[wə:]
ㅙ	*way*	[wɛ]	왜	*way*	[wɛ:]
ㅞ	*wey*	[we]	웨	*wey*	[we:]
ㅢ	*uy*	[ɨ, i, ɨj, e]	의	*uy*	[ɨj]

6.3.4   *Spelling conventions*

Spelling conventions include two aspects: how the letters representing individual sounds may be grouped as written units, and how they are spelled to represent morphemes, words, and sentences.

6.3.4.1   Writing in syllable blocks

Hankul letters are combined into syllable blocks, each block with a squarish shape similar to a Chinese character. The current rules of building syllable blocks are essentially the same as those stated in *Hwunmin Cengum Haylyey*. That is, a written syllable is composed of three positions, i.e., initial, medial, and final, to be written in that order. The initial position is written with a consonant letter including the ZERO consonant ㅇ (null sound quality in Contemporary Korean), as ㅅ *s* in 서 *se* [sə] and ㅇ in 울 *wul* [ul] in the word 서울 *Se.wul* 'Seoul'. The medial position is written with a vowel or diphthong letter, as ㅓ *e* [ə] in 서 *se* and ㅝ *we* [wə] in 궐 *kwel*. The final position is either filled with one or two consonant letters, or left empty, as in 물 *mul*, 울 *wul*, 밖 *pakk*, 닭 *talk*, and 서 *se*. The arrangements of the three positions in the syllable block are as follows:

(a)   A vowel or diphthong letter which has its longer stroke standing upright has the initial consonant letter to the left, as in 가 *ka*, 갸 *kya*, 꺼 *kke*, 지 *ci*, 때 *ttay*, and 예 *yey*.

(b)   A vowel or diphthong letter which has its longer stroke lying horizontally has the initial consonant letter on top, as in 고 *ko*, 누 *nwu*, 흐 *hu*, 요 *yo*, and 슈 *syu*. In this pattern, a vertical short stroke placed under a long horizontal stroke is written relatively long (e.g., 누 *nwu* and 슈 *syu*). This is often attributed to the 'principle' that Hankul syllable blocks be written with the same general appearance as Chinese characters, which do not allow any short vertical strokes at the bottom.

(c)   When a diphthong letter has both a vertical and a horizontal longer stroke, the initial consonant is placed to the left of the vertical and on top of the horizontal stroke, as in 취 *chwi*, 콰 *kkwa*, and 희 *huy*.

(d) The syllable-final simple consonant or cluster letters are written below the blocks, as in 땀 *ttam*, 삯 *saks*, 얹 *enc*, 춹 *chwul*, 굶 *kwulm*, 휄 *hwel*, and 봤 *pwass*.

Notice in the above that the shapes of the Hankul letters are altered slightly depending on the positions in which they occur. This is due to the effort to arrange different numbers of letters within equal-sized squares.

6.3.4.2   Direction of writing

Hankul syllable blocks are written either horizontally or vertically in a running text. In general, horizontal writing is preferred in contemporary Korea. When horizontal, the rows are written from top to bottom, each row moving from left to right; when vertical, the columns are written from right to left, each column moving from top to bottom. These are illustrated with the first stanza of the folk song *Alilang*.

(14)   a.   Horizontal writing

   i.   아리랑 아리랑 아라리요
         a.li.lang a.li.lang a.la.li.yo
   ii.   아리랑 고개를 넘어 간다.
         a.li.lang ko.kay.lul nem.e kan.ta
   iii. 나를 버리고 가시는 님은
         na.lul pe.li.ko ka.si.nun nim.un
   iv.   십리도 못가서 발병 난다.
         sip.li.to mos ka.se pal.pyeng nan.ta

   b.   Vertical writing

iv.		iii.		ii.		i.	
발	십	가	나	넘	아	아	아
병	리	시	를	어	리	라	리
	도		는		랑	리	랑
난			버	간		요	
다	못	님	리	다	고		아
	가	은	고	개			리
	서			를			랑

i.   'Arirang, Arirang, Arariyo,
ii. We now go over the Arirang Hill;
iii. He who deserts me and goes away
iv. Will have sore feet within a mile.'

6.3.4.3   Morphophonemic spelling

When Hankul was created, the letters were combined into blocks consisting essentially of spoken (phonetic) syllables. The current practice, especially since Korean linguists' enactment of the Unified Spelling System (1933), is the binding of letters into morpheme-based (morphophonemic) syllables. Thus, for instance, the previous spelling 기픈 *ki.phun* 'being deep' is now changed to 깊은 *kiph.un*, because, although it is pronounced as [ki.phɨn], the meaning 'deep' is represented by the morpheme 깊 *kiph* and the meaning 'being' by the morpheme 은 *un*. Similarly, 한국인 *han.kwuk.in* 'Koreans', although pronounced as 한구긴 [han.gu.gin], consists of three morphemes, 한 *han* 'Korea', 국 *kwuk* 'country', and 인 *in* 'person', each morpheme consisting of one syllable. 나무 *na.mu* [na.mu] 'tree' is a single morpheme consisting of two syllables, and is written as pronounced. 값 *kaps* 'price', although pronounced as 갑 [kap] when no vowel-initial morpheme follows, is spelled as such because it is pronounced as 값 *kaps* when followed by a vowel, as in 값이 *kaps.i* [kap.ʃ'i] with the nominative case particle 이 *i*.

Forms like 깊 *kiph*, 은 *un*, 한 *han*, 국 *kwuk*, 인 *in*, 나무 *namu*, 값 *kaps*, and 이 *i* are morphemic or morphophonemic forms because all the different surface (phonetic) forms are derived from them, conditioned by various sound environments. For instance, the morphemic form 깊 *kiph* is realized phonetically as 깁 [kip] before a non-nasal consonant, as in 깁고 [kip.k'o] 'deep and', as 김 [kim] before a nasal consonant, as in 김니 [kim.ni] 'is it deep?', and as it is before a vowel, as in 기피 [ki.phi] 'depth' (lit. 'deep-ness'). Since the current spelling convention allows only 깊 *kiph*, disregarding the other sound variations, as in 깊고 *kiph-ko* 'deep and', 깊니 *kiph-ni* 'is it deep?', and 깊이 *kiph-i* 'depth', the Hankul spelling can be called morphemic or morphophonemic. For a detailed discussion of the rules involved in deriving phonetic forms from morphophonemic representations, see chapter 7 (sound patterns).

Single spelling blocks may contain two morphemes as in 갔 *kass* 'went', 볼 *pol* 'to see', and 않 *anh* 'not do/be', which consist of 가 *ka* 'go' and ㅆ *ss* (past tense suffix), 보 *po* 'see' and ㄹ *l* (prospective suffix), and 안 *an* 'not' and ㅎ *h* 'do/be', respectively. That is, if a morpheme does not contain a vowel, it is attached to the preceding syllable block in the syllable-final position.

6.3.4.4   Spacing and marks

In running texts, space is placed before all nouns, including compound or bound nouns as well as pronouns. There is no space between the elements within a compound. As for the other word classes, space is placed only before each free word. Thus, all suffixes are attached to the respective stems, and all particles to the heads.

(15)   나는 나미가 공부하는 줄 알았다.
Na-nun na.mi-ka   kong.pu-ha-nu-n cwul   al-ass-ta.
I-TC   Nami-NM study-do-IN-RL   that   think-PST-DC
'I thought Nami was studying.'

Commas, periods, question or interjection marks, quotation marks, etc. are used essentially in the same way as they are used in English. No hyphen is used to identify morphemes or for any other purposes, except in morpheme entries in dictionaries to indicate boundness. For detailed regulations of the current spelling conventions observed in South and North Korea, see MOE (1988a) and KLAC (1988). For a brief comparison of the systems of the two Koreas, see 6.6.

6.4   Mixed use of Hankul and Chinese characters

Its scientificity and facility in use notwithstanding, Hankul underwent several major ordeals in the course of its diffusion in the face of the long tradition of the use of Chinese characters by the nobility and government officials. Although King Seycong's invention of Hankul was a great cultural achievement, a group of scholar-officials led by Choy Manli, then Associate Academician of Cip.hyencen, vehemently opposed the king's promulgation of Hankul to the public. They presented an anti-Hankul appeal to the Throne in 1444, their main argument being that Korea had long emulated Chinese ideas and institutions and that adoption of Korea's own writing system would make it impossible to identify Korean civilization with that of China but rather identify Korea with 'barbarians' such as Mongolians, Tanguts, Jurchen, Japanese, and Tibetans who had their own scripts. This appeal had little effect on Seycong's determination.

After the death of Seycong, the opposition to Hankul was resumed and continued until Seyco, the seventh king of the Cosen dynasty, propagated Hankul with Buddhism. Still, Hankul was not widely used for official purposes for a long time during the Cosen dynasty. Classical Chinese and Itwu were predominant while Hankul served as an aid for the study of Classical Chinese and was used mostly by women. This state continued until the so-called Enlightenment Period around the nineteenth century. Not until the Kap.o Reform was implemented by the government as a modernization movement in 1894 did Hankul come to be used in official documents.

King Kocong's royal decree issued on 21 November 1894 stipulated that all regulations and royal decrees be written in Hankul. However, exclusive use of Hankul in government documents was rather exceptional and a host of government regulations were written in Hankul mixed with Chinese characters. As for the newpapers published during the Enlightenment Period, B.H. An (1992) indicates that the *Toklip Sinmun* (the Independence Newspaper, 1896) and the *Ceykwuk Sinmun* (the Imperial Newspaper, 1898) were published exclusively in Hankul, while other newspapers such as the *Hwangseng Sinmun* (the Imperial City (Seoul) Newspaper, 1898) and the *Tayhan Mayil Sinpo* (the Korea Daily, 1905) were written in the Hankul–Chinese mixed scripts. Mixed use of the two scripts became a common practice among the general public.

During the Japanese occupation of Korea (1910–45), the use of Korean, including Hankul, was suppressed and the Korean people were forced to use Japanese as the sole means of communication. By 1942, Korean was phased out as a subject in school curricula. Nevertheless, Hankul was preserved and refined by patriotic scholars. When Korea was liberated from Japan in 1945, use of the Korean language including Hankul was restored and became a symbol of liberation and independence. Indeed, use of Hankul marked the reawakening of Korean national consciousness, its independence from China and Japan, its sense of national solidarity, and democratization of all walks of Korean life. South Koreans celebrate October 9 as Hankul Day, which is the day Hankul was promulgated by King Seycong in 1446.

North Korea abolished the daily use of Chinese characters in 1949 to expedite their 'revolutionary tasks', although they have subsequently reintroduced teaching of characters at schools only for reading purposes so that people can read South Korean publications. On the other hand, the tradition of the mixed use of Hankul with Chinese characters continues to be observed by the general public in South Korea, Hankul to represent native, Sino-Korean, and loan words and Chinese characters to represent Sino-Korean words.

In South Korea, pros and cons have been raised among linguists and government officials regarding the exclusive use of Hankul, and the policies of the government have not always been consistent, once instructing all the textbooks for elementary and secondary schools to be written only in Hankul, but now allowing 1,800 selected Chinese characters to be taught in secondary schools. Newspapers and scholarly books often go beyond this government-regulated set of characters. However, a distinct tendency is that use of Chinese characters is less favoured by younger generation Koreans who use Hankul predominantly in social functions. B.H. An (1992) provides an extensive review of the South Korean government's post-liberation policy changes regarding the issue of the mixed use of Hankul and Chinese characters.

6.5   Orthographic divergence in South and North Korea

Since the division of Korea into South and North in 1945, linguistic divergence is found not only in the lexicon, phonology, grammar, and usage, but also in orthography, as reflected in MOE (1988a) in South and in KLAC (1988) in North Korea. Both MOE and KLAC evolved from KLA 1993 through independent revisions. However, the sharing of the source system (KLA) and the two basic spelling principles stipulated in KLA (i.e., morphophonemic spelling and word-based spacing) have prevented extreme diversification.

The existing differences have been created by three partly interrelated causes: (i) the emergence of two standards of speech, i.e., South Korea's *phyocwun.e* (Standard Language) and North Korea's *munhwa.e* (Cultured Language), (ii) different linguistic analyses of similarly or identically pronounced compounds, words, and suffixes, and (iii) different conventions followed in breaking with tradition for the sake of regularization. The major areas of disparities are summarized as follows (for details, see H.M. Sohn 1997b).

(a)   In regard to the direction of writing, South Korea follows the tradition allowing both horizontal and vertical writing, as already illustrated, whereas North Korea stipulates that only horizontal writing be used in principle.

(b)   The names of three consonant letters and geminate letters have been changed in North Korea. Thus, South Korea's *kiyek* (ㄱ), *tikut* (ㄷ), and *sios* (ㅅ) correspond to North Korea's more regularized *kiuk*, *tiut*, and *sius*, respectively, and South Korea's *ssang kiyek* (ㄲ), *ssang piup* (ㅃ), etc. to North Korea's *toyn kiuk, toyn piup*, etc. where *ssang* means 'twin' and *toyn*, 'tensed'.

(c)   The alphabetic orders used for dictionary entries and other purposes do not agree. (In the following, SK stands for South Korea and NK for North Korea.)

(16)   a. Syllable-onset consonants
SK: ㄱ ㄲ ㄴ ㄷ ㄸ ㄹ ㅁ ㅂ ㅃ ㅅ ㅆ ㅇ ㅈ ㅉ ㅊ ㅋ ㅌ ㅍ ㅎ
NK: ㄱ ㄴ ㄷ ㄹ ㅁ ㅂ ㅅ ㅇ ㅈ ㅊ ㅋ ㅌ ㅍ ㅎ ㄲ ㄸ ㅃ ㅆ ㅉ

b. Syllable-nuclear vowels and diphthongs
SK: ㅏ ㅐ ㅑ ㅒ ㅓ ㅔ ㅕ ㅖ ㅗ ㅘ ㅙ ㅚ ㅛ ㅜ ㅝ ㅞ ㅟ ㅠ ㅡ ㅢ ㅣ
NK: ㅏ ㅑ ㅓ ㅕ ㅗ ㅛ ㅜ ㅠ ㅡ ㅣ ㅐ ㅒ ㅔ ㅖ ㅚ ㅟ ㅢ ㅘ ㅝ ㅙ ㅞ

c. Syllable-coda consonants

SK: ㄱ ㄲ ㄳ ㄴ ㄵ ㄶ ㄷ ㄹ ㄺ ㄻ ㄼ ㄽ ㄾ ㄿ ㅀ ㅁ ㅂ
ㅄ ㅅ ㅆ ㅇ ㅈ ㅊ ㅋ ㅌ ㅍ ㅎ

NK: ㄱ ㄳ ㄴ ㄵ ㄶ ㄷ ㄹ ㄺ ㄻ ㄼ ㄽ ㄾ ㄿ ㅀ ㅁ ㅂ ㅄ
ㅅ ㅇ ㅈ ㅊ ㅋ ㅌ ㅍ ㅎ ㄲ ㅆ

(d) In South Korea, Sino-Korean word-initial ㄹ is not pronounced before the vowel [i] and the semivowel [j] and pronounced as [n] elsewhere, and thus is spelled as such (e.g., 역사 *yeksa* 'history', 노동 *notong* 'labour'). In North Korea, it is pronounced as [ɾ] and spelled as such (e.g., 력사 *lyeksa* 'history', 로동 *lotong* 'labour').

(e) In South Korea, Sino-Korean word-initial ㄴ becomes silent before [i] and [j] and thus is not spelled (e.g., 여성 *yeseng* 'woman', 이탄 *ithan* 'peat'). North Korea requires it to be pronounced and spelled (e.g., 녀성 *nyeseng* 'woman', 니탄 *nithan* 'peat').

(f) Vowel harmony is strictly observed in North Korea, whereas there is some deviation in South Korea when a polysyllabic ㅂ irregular predicate is followed by an infinitive suffix. Thus, South Korean 고마워 *komawe* 'be thankful' corresponds to North Korean 고마와 *komawa*.

(g) Spellings of loan words are considerably different in the two Koreas. North Korea's spellings of terms for general objects are influenced by Russian and Japanese, whereas South Korea's spellings reflect English pronunciations.

(17)

	SK:	딜레마	댄스	마이너스	컵	스튜디오
		til.ley.ma	*tayn.su*	*ma.i.ne.su*	*khep*	*su.thyu.ti.o*
	NK:	지렌마	딴스	미누스	고뿌	스타지오
		ci.leyn.ma	*ttan.su*	*mi.nwu.su*	*ko.ppu*	*su.tha.ci.o*
		'dilemma'	'dance'	'minus'	'cup'	'studio'

(h) In regard to loan word place names, North Korean spellings follow the pronunciations used in the respective countries, whereas South Korean spellings follow English convention.

(18)

	SK:	바티칸	멕시코	스웨덴	헝가리
		pa.thi.khan	*mek.si.kho*	*su.wey.teyn*	*heng.ka.li*
	NK:	바띠까노	메히꼬	스웨리에	왱그리아
		pa.tti.kka.no	*mey.hi.kko*	*su.wey.li.ey*	*wayng.ku.li.a*
		'Vatican'	'Mexico'	'Sweden'	'Hungary'

(i) Some sentence enders are spelled differently, as in South Korean sentence enders -을까 *ul.kka* 'will it?, shall we?' vs. North Korean -을가 *-ul.ka*.

(j) Different etymological considerations are given to many compounds. In some cases, South Korea is more faithful to etymology, as in South Korean 넓적코 *nelp.cek.kho* 'flat nose' (넓 *nelp* 'wide') and 더욱이 *te.wuk.i* 'moreover' (더욱 *te.wuk* 'more', 이 *i* (adverbializer)) vs. North Korean 넙적코 *nep.cek.kho* and 더우기 *te.wu.ki*. In other cases, North Korea is more faithful to etymology, as in South Korean 손뼉 *son.ppyek* 'palm' and 일꾼 *il.kkwun* 'worker' vs. North Korean 손벽 *son.pyek* (손 *son* 'hand', 벽 *pyek* 'wall') and 일군 *il.kwun* (일 *il* 'work', 군 *kwun* 'group').

(k) The so-called epenthetic ㅅ *s* in compound nouns is spelled in South Korea only when the preceding noun root ends in a vowel, otherwise it is left out, as in 냇가 *nays.ka* 'river-side' (내 *nay* 'river', 가 *ka* 'side'), 길가 *kil.ka* 'road-side' (길 *kil* 'road', 가 *ka* 'side'), and 샛별 *says.pyel* 'the morning star' (새 *say* 'new, newness', 별 *pyel* 'star'). In North Korea (since 1966), it is left out everywhere, except when the preceding root is interpreted as a prefix, as in 내가 nay.ka 'river-side', 길가 kil.ka 'road-side', and 샛별 *says.pyel* 'the morning star'. In North Korea, 샛 *says* 'new' is considered a prefix.

(l) Sporadic lexical disparities are abundant, as illustrated below:

(19)

SK:	지푸러기	쇠고기	아내	가뜩이	달걀
	ci.phu.le.ki	*soy.ko.ki*	*a.nay*	*ka.ttuk.i*	*tal.kyal*
NK:	지푸레기	소고기	안해	가뜩히	닭알
	ci.phu.ley.ki	*so.ko.ki*	*an.hay*	*ka.ttuk.hi*	*talk.al*
	'straw'	'beef'	'wife'	'fully'	'egg'
SK:	원수	곤란	폐렴	퍽이나	아니오
	wen.swu	*kon.lan*	*phyey.lyem*	*phek.i.na*	*a.ni.o*
NK:	원쑤	곤난	패염	퍼그나	아니요
	wen.sswu	*kon.nan*	*phay.yem*	*phe.ku.na*	*a.ni.yo*
	'enemy'	'trouble'	'pneumonia'	'very'	'no'

(m) Although both Koreas observe the principle of word-based spacing, North Korea's convention is, in many cases, to spell two or more words without spacing, giving them compound-word status, while South Korea observes the principle rather narrowly. Thus, for instance, South Korea's phrases 아는 이 *a.nun i* 'an aquaintance' (lit. 'a person whom (one) knows'), 놀 수 *nol swu* 'able to play' (lit. 'a way of playing'), 학교 앞 *hak.kyo aph* 'front of the school', and 하늘 높이 *ha.nul noph.i* 'high in the sky' correspond to North Korea's 아는이

a.nun.i, 놀수 *nol.swu*, 학교앞 *hak.kyo.aph*, and 하늘높이 *ha.nul.noph.i*, respectively.

6.6   Romanization

Over twenty romanization systems have appeared in print and the most widely used are the McCune–Reischauer (hereafter M–R in this section) system, the South Korean Ministry of Education (MOE) system, and the Yale system (e.g., Martin, et al. 1967, Klein 1979, Austerlitz, et al. 1980, H.M. Sohn 1986). Being phonetic, the M–R system (designed in 1939) best suits non-Koreans in that its purpose is to romanize Korean for use by a wide variety of scholars, including historians, geographers, political scientists, sociologists, economists, philosophers, musicians, and natural scientists, as well as by Korean language learners, tourists, and general readers.

In 1988, the South Korean Government revised its previous MOE system (used from 1969 to 1988) and adopted a system which is closer to the M–R system. The Yale system has been used by linguists involved in the structural analysis of the language, such as for dictionaries, grammars, and linguistic papers. This system is strictly morphophonemic like Hankul and thus deviates considerably from the actual pronunciation. Retaining all relevant morphemic information in words, this system closely adheres to the Hankul spelling. While the M–R practices use diacritics to differentiate sounds that are not available in English, the Yale system does not employ any diacritics. A comparison between the Yale system and the M–R system *vis-à-vis* the Hankul letters and pronunications in IPA symbols was provided in chapter 1 (1.1).

Recall that in M–R, the lax consonants of Hankul (ㅂ, ㄷ, ㅈ, ㄱ) are spelled in two ways one voiceless and the other voiced. The voiced counterparts occur between two voiced sounds, the voiceless forms occurring elsewhere, as in 부부 *pu.pu* [pubu] 'husband and wife' being spelled as *pu.bu*. Similarly, the liquid sound ㄹ *l* is spelled in two ways following its pronunciations, r [ɾ] between two vowels and *l* [l] elsewhere. In addition to the differences in the symbols used, the spelling conventions are quite different in that the M–R system is mainly phonetic whereas the Yale system is morphophonemic. Thus, for instance, 앞문 [am.mun] 'front door' is spelled as *ammun* in M–R and *aphmun* in Yale. Similarly, compare the two systems below in romanizing the given Hankul words. Note that the M–R forms represent the sounds in which the words are actually pronounced, whereas the Yale forms represent the basic sounds of each word, just as the Hankul spelling does.

(20)	Hankul	Gloss	Sound	Yale	M–R
	부엌	'kitchen'	[pu.ək]	*puekh*	*puŏk*
	닭	'chicken'	[tak]	*talk*	*tak*

바보	'fool'	[pa.bo]	*papo*	*pabo*
선생	'teacher'	[sən.sɛŋ]	*sensayng*	*sŏnsaeng*
쪽	'page'	[c'ok]	*ccok*	*tchok*
법률	'law'	[pəm.ɲul]	*peplyul*	*pŏmnyul*
금강	'Kum River'	[kɨm.gaŋ]	*Kumkang*	*Kŭmgang*
술집	'tavern'	[sul.c'ip]	*swulcip*	*sulchip*

As already stated, all Korean expressions including words, phrases, sentences, and proper names appearing in this book, except for the already individualized spellings of personal names, are transcribed following the Yale system, unless indicated otherwise.

7

Sound patterns

This chapter presents the speech sounds of Korean, their patterns of combination and alternation, and their rhythmic patterns. The sound patterns discussed in this chapter are mostly based on contemporary standard speech. Occasional reference is made to other dialects as needed (e.g., tones in the Kyengsang dialect). Throughout this chapter, romanized spellings of Korean forms are followed by the corresponding phonological transcriptions in IPA symbols.

7.1   Introduction

Two levels of phonological representation (morphophonemic and phonetic) are taken into account. The morphophonemic representation, often called the morphemic representation or underlying or systematic phonemic representation, concerns the invariable phonemic shape of each morpheme (minimal meaningful unit) wherever it occurs. For instance, the morphophonemic representation of the romanized spelling *toklipmun* 'the Independence Gate' is **tok+lip+mun**, in that it represents the invariable phonemic forms of the three morphemes **tok** 'independent', **lip** 'standing', and **mun** 'gate', regardless of the actual pronunciation of the word. The + symbol stands for a compound boundary, i.e., a boundary between the roots or stems that form a compound word. The phonetic representation concerns the actual pronunciation of each morpheme resulting from its sound environment. Thus, the phonetic representation of **tok+lip+mun** is [toŋ.ɲim.mun], where [ɲ] represents the sound quality of the palatalized [n]. How the morphophonemic form **tok+lip+mun** is realized systematically as the phonetic form [toŋ.ɲim.mun] will be made clear as we proceed.

   Morphophonemic representation is important in Korean, because contemporary spelling conventions with Hankul (the Korean alphabet) in both South and North Korea are essentially based on that level, as alluded to in the romanized spelling *toklipmun* vis-a-vis **tok+lip+mun**. As will be observed in (Hankul-based) romanized spellings, however, some discrepancies appear between Hankul spellings and the corresponding morphophonemic representations. For instance, vowel length is not represented in Hankul spellings; morphophonemically significant word-initial l and **n** are not represented in South Korean orthography; and the so-called epenthetic **s** is not consistently represented in Hankul in either South or North Korea.

In this chapter, romanized spellings are italicized, morphophonemic forms are bold-faced, and phonetic forms are bracketed, as shown in (1).

(1)   Romanized spelling: *toklipmun*
        Morphophonemic representation: **tok+lip+mun**
        Phonetic representation: [toŋ.ɲim.mun]

Many words, especially single-morpheme words, have the same form in both the romanized spelling and the morphophonemic representation. For instance, *salam* 'person' is represented as *salam*, **salam**, and [sa.ɾam], where [ɾ] is a flap *r*. Many other words have the same forms in all three representations, as in *kil*, **kil**, and [kil] 'road'. Predictable representations are often omitted in the following discussions.

In the IPA transcriptions of morphophonemic forms, word or phrase boundaries are marked by a space, compound boundaries by +, and affixal boundaries by -. Syllable boundaries in phonetic transcriptions are marked by dots, as in [toŋ.ɲim.mun], phonetic juncture by [#], and vowel length by a colon [:]. In phonological rules, # stands for a word boundary.

Synchronic studies of various aspects of the Korean sound patterns are numerous, exhibiting a wide variety of theoretical and methodological sophistication. Works before the first half of the 1960s are based on traditional or taxonomic phonological approaches, while later works are mostly generative studies. As will be noticed in the appended bibliography, descriptive frameworks employed by generative phonologists are varied, including linear phonology, lexical phonology, prosodic phonology, theory of underspecification, and optimality theory. Numerous spectrographic or acoustic analyses of Korean are also available.

The following survey of Korean phonology is essentially descriptive, with a minimum of theoretical argumentation. For a wide variety of theoretical discussions and conflicting proposals on various topics, readers are referred to relevant works cited in the bibliography.

7.2   Speech sounds

There are altogether nineteen consonant, ten vowel, and two semivowel phonemes in Korean. Some dialectal zones lack a few of the consonants and/or vowels that appear in the overall inventory.

7.2.1   **Consonants**

The nineteen consonant phonemes can be arranged according to the places and manners of their articulation, as shown in (2).

(2)

place of articulation / articulatory manner			Bi-labial	Alveo-dental	Palatal	Velar	Glottal
stop	lax	voiceless or voiced	p	t	c	k	
	aspirated	voiceless	ph	th	ch	kh	
	tensed	voiceless	p'	t'	c'	k'	
fricative	aspirated	voiceless		s			h
	tensed	voiceless		s'			
nasal		voiced	m	n		ŋ	
liquid	lateral or flap	voiced		l			

There are a few salient articulatory features in Korean that are not shared by English. For one thing, the alveo-dental consonants are produced with the top (not the tip) of the tongue touching or approaching the back of the upper teeth and the gum-ridge area with the tongue tip touching the back of the lower teeth. Second, the palatal series and the alveo-dental fricatives are produced with the lips flattened, unless they are followed by a round vowel. Unlike English affricates such as [tʃ] and [dʒ], Korean palatals are monotonous stops without the fricative quality such as [ʃ] or [ʒ]. Third, all stop and fricative consonants are voiceless, except the lax stops that become lightly voiced between voiced sounds. Fourth, no Korean consonant is released in the syllable-final (coda) position. In pronouncing the word *aph* 'front', for instance, the lips are closed for *ph* and the resultant sound is [ap] despite the fact that its morphophonemic form is **aph**. Because of this rule of unrelease (called *coda neutralization*), only a limited number of consonants may occur in the syllable-final position in pronunciation, as we shall see in detail in 7.4.2 (Rule 2). Other properties of the consonants will be discussed as we proceed.

The lax stops **p, t, c, k** are basically voiceless, with only a minor degree of aspiration and no tenseness. As stated above, they become lightly voiced between voiced sounds, as in *papo* **papo** [pa.bo] 'fool', *kalpi* **kalpi** [kal.bi] 'spare ribs', *totwuk* **totuk** [to.duk] 'thief', *sam-to* **sam+to** [sam.do] 'three degrees', *cinci* **cinci** [cin.ɟi] 'meal' (honorific form), *panci* **panci** [pan.ɟi] 'ring', *koki* **koki** [ko.gi] 'meat', and *hankul* **han+kɨl** [han.gɨl] 'the Korean alphabet'.

The aspirated stops **ph, th, ch, kh** are never voiced, and are pronounced with a strong puff of air. The tensed stops **p', t', c', k'** are not voiced but produced with the glottis constricted and by building up air pressure behind the closed place of articulation and instantaneously releasing the closure while pushing the air forward without any aspiration. Both aspirated and tensed stops are constant in sound quality, with a minimum of allophonic variation. While the phonetic quality of the lax stops is not shared by English, the aspirated stops are similar to English voiceless stressed stops occurring in the word-initial position, as in *pill, till, chilly,* and *kill*. The tensed quality is comparable to that of the English voiceless stops that occur after *s*, as in *speak, strong,* and *ski,* and that of *j* in such an utterance as 'Please sit, John'. The sound quality of the Korean **p'** is very close to *pp* in English *happy*. The following minimal trios illustrate the contrast among lax, aspirated, and tensed stops.

(3)   a.   *pul*   'fire'   **pul**   [pul]
               phul   'grass'   **phul**   [phul]
               ppul   'horn'   **p'ul**   [p'ul]

    b.   *telta*   'reduce'   **tə:l-ta**   [tə:l.da]
               thelta   'shake off'   **thə:l-ta**   [thə:l.da]
               ttelta   'tremble'   **t'ə:l-ta**   [t'ə:l.da]

    c.   *cata*   'sleep'   **ca-ta**   [ca.da]
               chata   'kick'   **cha-ta**   [cha.da]
               ccata   'be salty'   **c'a-ta**   [c'a.da]

    d.   *kun*   'a pound'   **kɨn**   [kɨn]
               khun   'big'   **khɨn**   [khɨn]
               kkun   'string'   **k'ɨn**   [k'ɨn]

The fricative series consist of the lax–tense pair **s** and **s'** and the glottal **h**. Produced with the top (not the tip) of the tongue approaching the gum-ridge and palatal area, **s** has a certain degree of aspiration, sounding somewhat like *s* in *strong* in English, whereas **s'** does not contain any aspiration, sounding like *s* in *sun* in English.

Some minimal pairs include *sal* **sal** [sal] 'flesh' vs. *ssal* **s'al** [s'al] 'rice' and, dialectally, *seng* **səŋ** [səŋ] 'castle' vs. *sseng* **s'əŋ** [s'əŋ] 'anger'. Unlike lax stops, **s** does not become voiced between voiced sounds. When **s** and **s'** occur before **i** or **y**, they become strongly palatalized, as in *sikyey* **si+kje** [ʃige] 'watch, clock' and *swita* **sy:-ta** [ʃy:.da] 'rest'. When **s** and **s'** are followed by **j**, they merge and become [ʃ] and [ʃ'], respectively, as in *syechu* **sjəchɨ** [ʃə.chɨ] 'undershirt' and *akassi* **akas'i** [a.ga.ʃ'i] 'young lady'. In the Kyengsang dialect, no phonemic distinction is made between **s** and **s'**, which are free variants although **s** is more predominantly used.

Although **h** is basically glottal, it is vulnerable to the influence of the following vowel or semivowel. That is, before a high vowel or a semivowel, the friction for **h** is made at the oral place where the respective vowel or semivowel is produced, as in *him* **him** [çim] 'energy' and *hwuchwu* **hu+chu** [ɸu.chu] 'black pepper'.

While **m** and **ŋ** are relatively stable in sound quality, **n** is usually palatalized before **i** and **j**. Thus, *enni* **ən.ni** is pronounced as [əɲ.ɲi] '(female's) older sister' and *emeni* **əməni** as [ə.mə.ɲi] 'mother'. The combination of **nj** becomes [ɲ] as in *mun-yey* **mun+je** [mu.ɲe] 'literature and art' and *o nyen* **o: njən** [o:.ɲən] 'five years'. Palatalization does not occur in recently coined words and loan words, as in *ni* **ni** [ni] (derived from *ney* [ne:]) 'you', *nisu* **nisɨ** [ni.sɨ] 'varnish', *nikhothin* **nikhothin** [ni.kho.thin] 'nicotine', and *niksun* **niksɨn** [nik.s'ɨn] 'Nixon'.

The liquid **l** has two distinctly different allophones: the lateral [l], which is always 'light' (the tongue top touching the alveo-dental area), and the flap [ɾ] (like the Japanese and Spanish *r*). The former appears in the syllable-final position, i.e., before a pause or another consonant (except **h**), or in the neighbourhood of another **l**, as in (4a). The latter occurs elsewhere, i.e., after a pause, between two vowels, or between a vowel and a semivowel, as in (4b).

(4) a. *kwul*   'tunnel'   **ku:l**   [ku:l]
        pal-mok 'ankle'   **pal+mok** [pal.mok]
        cinli   'truth'   **cin+li**   [cil.li]

    b. *latio*   'radio'   **latio**   [ɾa.di.o]
        meli   'head'   **məli**   [mə.ɾi]
        kwul i 'tunnel (subj.)' **ku:l-i** [ku:.ɾi]
        il-wen 'one *won*'   **il+wən** [i.ɾwən]

When a sequence of two [l]'s is followed by **i** or **j**, the second [l] may be palatalized in casual speech, as in *cinli* **cin+li** [cil.ʎi] 'truth', *melli* **mə:li** [mə:l.ʎi] 'far away', and *mul-yak* **mul+jak** [mul.ʎak] 'liquid medicine'. When **l** is followed by **h** in a word, it is usually pronounced as [ɾ], whether the **h** is pronounced or omitted, as in *ilhun* **ilhɨn** [i.ɾ(h)ɨn] 'seventy' and *kyelhon* **kjəl+hon** [kjə.ɾ(h)on] 'wedding'.

7.2.2   Vowels

The ten vowel phonemes may be arranged in terms of the oral place of articulation, lip shape, and tongue height, as shown in the following table.

(5)

place / lips / tongue	front		back	
	unround	round	unround	round
high	i	y	ɨ	u
mid	e	ø	ə	o
low	ε		a	

All ten of the simple vowels are orthographically distinguished throughout the country. However, some vowels are not distinct in certain dialects. For instance, there is no phonemic distinction between **e** and **ε** in southern dialects, both existing merely as allophonic or free variants. The two vowels **ɨ** and **ə** are neutralized into the latter in the Kyengsang dialect. The two vowels **y** and **ø** are pronounced as on-glide diphthongs [wi] and [we], respectively, by many speakers of the Central and some other dialects. Thus, for instance, *wi* [y; wi] 'upside, stomach', *cwi* [cy; cwi] 'rat', *kwi* [ky; kwi] 'ear', *halkhwita* [hal.khy.da; hal.khwi.da] 'scratch', *twi* [ty; twi] 'back', *moy* [mø:; mwe:] (obsolete) 'mountain', *coyin* [cø:.in; cwe:.in] 'criminal', *cham-oy* [cha.mø; cha.mwe] 'melon', *soykoki* [sø.go.gi; swe.go.gi] 'beef', and *koymul* [kø:.mul; kwe:.mul] 'monster' have two ways of pronunciation, the choice of which depends largely on dialects, and also on idiolects.

All vowels are voiced monotones and quite consistent in sound quality, with a minimum of allophonic variation. In casual speech, however, simple high vowels tend to be voiceless after an aspirated consonant, as in *phili* **phili** [phI.ɾi] 'flute' and *theyle* **thelə** [thE.ɾə] 'terrorism' where capitalized letters indicate voicelessness. In whispering, only voiceless sounds occur throughout the utterance. When expressed with much emotion or admiration, vowels often get devoiced in the initial syllable of a word, as in *cham* **cha:m** [chA:m] 'indeed!', *melli* **mə:l-li** [MƎ:l.li] 'far away', and *acwu kiph-kwun* **a:cu kiph-kun** [A:.cu.kip.k'un] '(It)'s very deep!'

In the speech of older generation Koreans (approximately fifty and older as of 2000), vowel length remains significant in differentiating meanings. Corresponding to the ten short vowels are ten long vowels, which are pronounced about twice as long while retaining the same monotone quality. As already stated, despite its phonemic status, vowel length is not indicated in Hankul orthography nor in the romanized spellings in this volume, as in *cong* **coŋ** 'bell' vs. *cong* **co:ŋ** 'servant', *i* **i** 'this' vs. *i* **i:** 'louse', *mal* **mal** 'horse' vs. *mal* **ma:l** 'language', *nwun* **nun** 'eye' vs. *nwun* **nu:n** 'snow', and *pay* **pɛ** 'ship/pear/stomach' vs. *pay* **pɛ:** 'double'.

Long vowels occur only in phrase-initial syllables. When a syllable with a long vowel is preceded by another syllable in either a prefix or a word, the long vowel becomes shortened. Thus, *huyn nwun* 'white snow' is **hɨjn nu:n** [hin.nun] and *i i* 'this louse' is **i i:** [i.i]. Unable to distinguish phonemic vowel length, younger generation speakers tend to pronounce phonemically long syllables short and utilize vowel length for stress or rhythmic purposes.

In addition to long vowels, there are double vowels, which are produced when one element of a word ends in a vowel and another element begins with the same vowel. In this case, there is usually a slight pause (i.e., hiatus) between the two vowels. In orthography, the two vowels are spelled in sequence in two different syllable blocks. Unlike long vowels, double vowels do not get shortened in any environment (except in the case of historical mergers).

(6)   Long vowels   Double vowels

     il 'work' **i:l**   [i:l]   *i il* 'two days' **i il**   [i.il]

     ca 'well!' **ca:** [ca:]   *caa* 'one's self' **ca+a** [ca.a]

     kil 'long' **ki:l** [ki:l]   *kiil* 'due date' **ki+il** [ki.il]

The phonetic values of the ten short and ten long vowels are roughly indicated in (7) with reference to the IPA Cardinal Vowel scale (cf. H.B. Lee 1989).

(7)
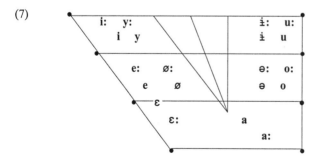

The vowel qualities can be described in comparison with English vowel sounds of the British 'Received Pronunciation' (cf. H.B. Lee ibid.). That is, **i:** (as in *il* **i:l** 'work')

is similar to the English vowel occurring in *meat, sea,* etc., while **i** (as in *il* **il** 'one') is pronounced with a lower and more retracted tongue position. The lip-rounded vowels **y:** (as in *kwi* **ky:** 'your') and **y** (as in *kwi* **ky** 'ear') are pronounced with a slightly more retracted tongue position than for **i:** and **i**, respectively. The vowel **e:** (as in *ney* **ne:** 'yes') is similar to the lengthened form of the English vowel occurring in *bet, set,* etc., while **e** (as in *ney* **ne** 'you') is pronounced with a lower and more retracted tongue position. The lip-rounded **ø:** (as in *noy* **nø:** 'repeat') and **ø** (as in *noy* **nø** 'brain') are pronounced with a slightly more retracted tongue position than for **e:** and **e**, respectively. The vowel **ɛ:** (as in *ay* **ɛ:** 'baby') is similar to the English vowel in words such as *bad* and *sad*, while its short form **ɛ** (as in *ay* **ɛ** 'effort') is pronounced with a higher tongue position than for **ɛ:**.

The high back vowel **u:** is similar to the English vowel in *pool, boot,* etc., while its short form **u** is pronounced with a slightly lower and more advanced tongue position and slightly weaker lip-rounding, as in *pul* **pu:l** 'blow' vs. *pul* **pul** 'fire'. The vowel **o:** is similar to the English vowel in *all, call,* etc., while the short **o** is pronounced with a lower tongue position and weaker lip-rounding than for its longer counterpart, as in *moca* **mo:-ca** 'mother and son' vs. *moca* **mo-ca** 'cap, hat'. The vowels **ɨ:** and **ɨ** combine the high tongue position of **u(:)** and the flat lip shape of **i(:)**, as in *tul* **tɨ:l** 'field' vs. *tul* **tɨl** 'hold up'. The short **ɨ** is similar to the English vowel in *put, book,* etc. Compare the four high vowels in *ki* **ki** 'flag', *kwi* **ky** 'ear', *ku* **kɨ** 'that', and *kwu* **ku** 'nine'. The vowel **ə:** is similar to the English vowel in *fir* or *girl*, but pronounced with the back of the tongue approaching the back part of the soft palate, while the short form **ə** is pronounced with a lower tongue position, as in *pyeng* **pjə:ŋ** 'illness' vs. *pyeng* **pjəŋ** 'bottle'. The rounded counterparts of these vowels are **o:** and **o**. The **ə(:)–o(:)** minimal pairs include *mek* **mək** [mək] 'ink-stick' vs. *mok* **mok** [mok] 'neck', *kelum* **kəl-ɨm** [kə.ɾɨm] 'manure' vs. *kolum* **kolɨm** [ko.ɾɨm] 'pus', and *tep* **tə:p** [tə:p] 'hot' vs. *top* **to:p** [to:p] 'help'. The most frequently occurring vowel is **a(:)**, which is the most audible of all the sounds in Korean, due to its having the largest resonance chamber in the mouth. The long vowel **a:** is like the English vowel in *park, car,* etc., while its shorter counterpart **a** is similar to the English vowel in *but, cut,* etc., as in *pam* **pa:m** 'chestnut' vs. *pam* **pam** 'night'.

7.2.3   *Semivowels (glides)*

The semivowels **w** and **j** have sound qualities similar to **u** and **i**, respectively. They function like both vowels and consonants. Like vowels, they neither block a speech organ nor produce any friction; and they may follow a consonant, as in *kwak* **kwak** 'box' and *pyek* **pjək** 'wall'. Like consonants, they occur in the syllable-initial position before a vowel as in *wang* **waŋ** 'king' and *yang* **jaŋ** 'sheep' (cf. *kang* **kaŋ** 'river'), and they cannot have length. They are glides, in that the tongue starts at the position for **u** or **i** and then 'glides' into the position for the immediately following vowel.

As shown in (8), the semivowels of Contemporary Korean are always on-glides, which always precede a vowel, and never off-glides, which follow a vowel. In Middle Korean, however, **j** was used not only as an on-glide but also as an off-glide, as we have already observed in chapter 3.

(8)	*wenchik*	'principle'	**wən+chik**	[wən.chik]
	kwail	'fruit'	**kwa:il**	[kwa:.il]
	kwenlyek	'power'	**kwən +ljək**	[kwəl.ljək]
	yelum	'summer'	**jəlɨm**	[jə.ɾɨm]
	myoci	'graveyard'	**mjo:+ci**	[mjo:.ʥi]
	kohyang	'hometown'	**ko+hjaŋ**	[ko.hjaŋ]

7.3 Sound combination

Thus far, Korean speech sounds have been observed from the perspective of the paradigmatic relations they have with one another in a system. Speech utterances, however, are produced and perceived successively in time, one sound following another. Thus, it is these syntagmatic relations that concern us in this and the following section.

7.3.1 Syllable structure

One of the basic units in the syntagmatic relation of sounds is the syllable, which is the rhythmic unit correlated with the chest pulse in speech. A syllable consists of one obligatory vowel and one or more optional consonants or semivowels (glides). In Korean, there is a structural difference between syllables in the morphophonemic level and those in the phonetic level, in that the former allow consonant clusters to occur in the syllable-final position while the latter do not allow more than one consonant in that position, as observed in *kaps* **kaps** [kap] 'price' and *talk* **talk** [tak] 'chicken'. That is, in pronunciation, either one of the coda consonants in the morphophonemic representation must drop before a word-boundary or before a syllable that begins with a consonant (e.g., **kaps** [kap] 'price' and **kaps-kwa** [kap.k'wa] 'price and'), or else the second consonant in the cluster is carried over to the onset position of the following syllable when this syllable begins with a vowel (e.g., **kaps-i** [kap.s'i] 'price (subject)'). The syllables associated with speech utterances, i.e., those in phonetic representations, are the main concern in this section.

Korean phonetic syllables have a relatively simple internal structure. One and only one vowel (simple or long) must be present as the peak or nucleus of a syllable. It may be preceded by a consonant, a semivowel (glide), or both, and may be followed by a consonant. This is formulated in (9).

(9)   Korean syllable structure: [.(C)(G)V(:)(C).]

> where . is a syllable boundary, C a consonant, G a glide or semivowel, V a vowel, and : vowel length, and parentheses indicate optionality in occurrence.

Thus, a syllable boundary in Korean is placed between two vowels (V(:).V(:)), between two consonants (C.C), between a vowel and a consonant if the latter is followed by a vowel, whether a semivowel intervenes or not (V.C(G)V), and between a vowel and a semivowel if the latter is followed by a vowel (V.GV). Some lexical items illustrating the above phonetic syllable structure are given in (10).

(10)	V(:)	*i*	[i]	'this'	*wuli*	[u.ɾi]	'we'
		i	[i:]	'louse'	*aytul*	[ɛ:.dɨl]	'children'
	GV(:)	*yo*	[jo]	'blanket'	*yuli*	[ju.ɾi]	'glass'
		way	[wɛ]	'why'	*oykyo*	[we:.gjo]	'diplomacy'
	CV(:)	*na*	[na]	'I'	*heli*	[hə.ɾi]	'waist'
		pa	[pa:]	'bar'	*keli*	[kə:.ɾi]	'distance'
	CGV(:)	*hye*	[hjə]	'tongue'	*kyo.yuk*	[kjo:.juk]	'education'
		hwa	[hwa:]	'anger'	*hwatan*	[hwa.dan]	'flower-bed'
	V(:)C	*ip*	[ip]	'mouth'	*elta*	[ə:l.da]	'freeze'
		il	[i:l]	'work'	*angsim*	[aŋ.ʃim]	'grudge'
	GV(:)C	*yel*	[jəl]	'fever'	*yensel*	[jə:n.səl]	'oration'
		wang	[wa:ŋ]	'king'	*wi*	[wi]	'stomach'
	CV(:)C	*cip*	[cip]	'house'	*cilmun*	[cil.mun]	'question'
		pel	[pə:l]	'bee'	*cenhwa*	[cə:n.hwa]	'telephone'
	CGV(:)C	*pyeng*	[pjəŋ]	'bottle'	*kyul*	[kju:l]	'tangerine'
		kwan	[kwan]	'pipe'	*kwankay*	[kwa:n.gɛ]	'irrigation'

In addition to the above productive syllable types, two minor types **V(:)lC** and **lhV** may be set up to accommodate some native speakers' pronunciation of the [lC] coda as in *palp-ko* [palp.k'o] 'step on and' and *palk-ta* [palk.t'a] 'is bright', and the [ɾh] onset as in *ilhun* [i.ɾhɨn] '70'.

As we saw at the outset of this subsection, phonetic syllable structure plays an important role in sound alternations, because the function of certain phonological rules is to preserve the syllable structure. Furthermore, the sequence CV is preferred to VC in Korean as is the case with many other languages. For instance, if a word has a morphemic structure of the form **CVC-V**, it is realized as **CV.CV** in its phonetic representations, as in *kkoch i* **k'och-i** [k'o.chi] 'flower (subject)'. Such sound alternations will be discussed in great detail in 7.4.

7.3.2   *Sequential constraints*

In the cooccurrence of phonemes in speech utterances, there are certain restrictions caused partly by the tendency to economize physical and mental energy in the speech production process and partly by linguistic habits that have been established over a long period of time. In Korean, any vowel may precede or follow any other vowel or consonant quite freely. Restrictions exist mostly in the combinations of a semivowel with a vowel or of a semivowel with a consonant, in consonant sequences, and in word-initial or word-final consonants.

As observed in the previous subsection (7.3.1), the current syllable structure does not allow a semivowel (glide) to follow a vowel within a syllable. Off-glides are historical remnants reflected only in Hankul spellings (and in Yale-romanized spellings for that matter), except perhaps for **ɨj**, which is generally pronounced as [ɨ] (in a word-initial position), [i] (elsewhere), or [e] (as a genitive case particle), but which some young speakers pronounce as [ɨj] probably due to spelling pronunciation. For instance, *uysa* 'doctor', which is morphophonemically represented as **ɨj+sa** (medicine-teacher), is pronounced as [ɨ(j).sa]. Despite this exception, Korean diphthongs may be said to be of the on-glide type, consisting of a semivowel followed by a vowel. The following twelve diphthongs, of which **wi(ː)** alternates with **y** and **ɨj** with **ɨ** and **i**, are all that are available in Contemporary Korean.

(11)   a. On-glide diphthongs: jV(ː)   = je(ː), jɛ(ː), jə(ː), ja(ː), ju(ː), jo(ː)
                              wV(ː) = wi(ː), we(ː), wɛ(ː), wə(ː), wa(ː)

            b. Off-glide diphthong: Vj = ɨj (used only by some young speakers)

Notice that out of the ten Korean vowels, only six can form diphthongs by following **j**, and only five can follow **w**. There are no diphthongs of the forms **ji, jy, jɨ, jø, wu, wø, wɨ, wy**, and **wo**. The diphthong **wi** occurs in the speech of those (such as Central dialect speakers) who use it instead of **y**. In Central and some other dialects, *oy* is realized as **we(ː)**, rather than as **ø(ː)**, merging into the original *we* **we(ː)**.

Of the nineteen consonants, only **p, t, k, s, m, n, ŋ**, and **l** can occur in the syllable-final (i.e., coda) position in pronunciation, with the occurrence of **s** being limited to the position before another **s** or **s'** (e.g., *os sok* [o(s).s'ok] 'inside of clothes'). This syllable-final constraint is due to the principle that no consonant in Contemporary Korean is released in this position except **s** before another **s** or **s'**. This process of unreleasing or coda neutralization will be discussed shortly in regard to sound alternations (7.4.2).

While all consonants can occur in the syllable-initial position, ŋ does not occur in the word-initial position. Thus, even though *kangaci* **kaŋaci** [ka.ŋa.ɟi] 'puppy' is possible, no words begin with ŋ. The liquid **l** [l/ɾ] is not pronounced in the initial position of native words. It occurs in the initial position of North Korean Sino-Korean words, as in *lotong* **lo+toŋ** [ɾo.doŋ] 'labour' and *lilon* **li:+lon** [ɾi:.ɾon] 'theory', but not in South Korean Sino-Korean words, as in *notong* **lo+toŋ** [no.doŋ] 'labour' and *ilon* **li:+lon** [i:.ɾon] 'theory'. It did not occur in the initial position of loan words in the past, as attested to in the obsolete form *nacio* **nacio** [na.ɟi.o] 'radio'. Due to the recent massive influx of loan words, however, it now appears freely in the word-initial position, as observed in the contemporary form *latio* **latio** [ɾa.di.o] 'radio'. Another word-initial constraint applicable only in South Korea is associated with **n**, which is not pronounced before **i** or **j**, as shown in *i* **ni** [i] 'tooth' vs. *aph-ni* **aph+ni** [am.ɲi] 'front tooth' and *ye-nam* **njə+nam** [jə.nam] 'female and male' vs. *nam-nye* **nam+njə** [nam.ɲə] 'male and female'. One execption is the second person pronoun *ni* **ni** [ni] 'you' which has recently developed, as an allomorph, from *ney* **ne** [ne] 'you', apparently to avoid possible clash with the phonetically close *nay* **nɛ** [nɛ] 'I'.

Aside from the above-mentioned constraints in the syllable-final and word-initial positions, there are several other specific constraints on cooccurrence between a consonant and a vowel or a diphthong, or between consonants. First, the bilabial consonants **p, ph, p'**, and **m** are seldom followed by **y** or **w**, since two labial sounds tend to avoid combination. The same bilabial consonants are not followed by **ɨ** in Contemporary Korean, because historically the latter vowel has changed to **u** in assimilation with the bilabial consonants in terms of lip-rounding. Second, all consonants are rarely followed by [je] or [jɛ]. Third, the alveo-dental stops **t, th, t'**, palatal stops **c, ch, c'**, and alveo-dental fricatives **s, s'** are not followed by the diphthong **jə, ja, ju**, or **jo** in either native or Sino-Korean words. This is partly due to the tendency to avoid homorganic combination, in that the consonants involved and **j** are all 'coronal' sounds. In loan words, however, the combination of an alveo-dental consonant and **j** in a syllable is frequently observed, as in *thyupu* **thjupɨ** [thju.bɨ] 'tube' and *syechu* **sjəchɨ** [ʃə.chɨ] 'shirt'. Fourth, no syllable-final consonant is followed by the syllable-initial velar nasal ŋ. Fifth, no syllable-final consonant other than **l** is followed by [l] or [ɾ] at the phonetic level. Finally, no syllable-final consonant other than a nasal is followed by [m] or [n] at the phonetic level, except that **l** is followed by [m]. Some of these constraints are correlated with sound alternations to be discussed below.

7.4   Sound alternations

7.4.1   Automatic vs. non-automatic alternation

Just as allophones of a phoneme alternate in different sound environments without any difference in meaning, so do different phonemes alternate in different environments without changing meanings. For instance, **ch** in the morphophonemic form **k'och** of *kkoch* 'flower' shows the following phonetic alternations: [ch] as in **k'och-i** [k'o.chi] 'flower (subject)' (i.e., before a vowel), [t] as in **k'och** [k'ot] 'flower' and **k'och-to** [k'ot.t'o] 'flower also' (i.e., pronounced independently or before a non-nasal consonant), [n] as in **k'och-namu** [k'on.na.mu] 'flower tree' (i.e., before an alveo-dental nasal), [m] as in **k'och-munɨj** [k'om.mu.ni] 'floral design' (i.e., before a bilabial nasal), [s] as in **k'och-soɲi** [k'o(s).s'o.ɲi] 'blossom' (i.e., before an alveo-dental fricative), [p] as in **k'och-pjəŋ** [k'op.p'jəŋ] 'flower vase' (i.e., before a bilabial stop), and [k] as in **k'och-kalu** [k'ok.k'a.ɾu] 'pollen' (i.e., before a velar stop). Notice that the phonemes alternate in the above examples without changing the meaning 'flower'. In this chapter, sound alternations of the above type, i.e., those which are predictable from sound environments alone, are called automatic.

Certain sound alternations cannot be predicted by sound environments alone. Both sound environments and the lexical or grammatical meaning of the morphemes are involved. For instance, **kwa** and **wa** alternate, the former occurring after a consonant and the latter after a vowel, only when they have the meaning 'and, with', as in *mul kwa* **mul-kwa** [mul.gwa] 'water and' and *cha wa* **cha-wa** [cha.wa] 'car and'. Alternations of this type are called non-automatic.

While in the case of automatic alternations only a single morphophonemic form is entered in a dictionary, the alternating allomorphs which are not automatic are usually entered separately although there is no meaning difference among them. Automatic alternations in Korean will be addressed in 7.4.2 and non-automatic ones in 7.4.3. Although all sound alternations are dichotomized in this way, there are borderline cases. Some of the alternations that are regarded here as non-automatic are claimed to be automatic or regular by some phonologists. Such claims are often possible only by postulating abstract morphophonemic forms, certain arbitrary boundaries, intricate rule formulation, or strict rule ordering.

7.4.2   Automatic sound alternations

As mentioned earlier, Hankul spellings represent only morphophonemic forms, not the alternating forms which are automatic variants. It is essential, therefore, for Korean language learners to become well-versed with automatic sound alternation rules in order to produce correct pronunciations. In this section are discussed the major processes of automatic sound alternation that appear in Korean. The alternation rules are presented partly, but not necessarily, in the order they apply. It will be noted that strict ordering is required among certain rules.

Note in the examples given below that the word (space), phrase (space), compound (+), and affixal (-) boundaries are phonological, and do not always agree with syntactic boundaries. For instance, the boundary between a noun and a particle (e.g., *i* (subject), *ul* (object), *un* (topic)) or between a noun and the copula *i* is regarded as a word boundary in syntax, but should be treated as an affixal boundary in phonology, in that certain phonological rules such as coda neutralization (Rule 2) and [n, l] epenthesis (Rule 5), which are sensitive to a word or compound boundary, do not apply in these boundaries. Thus, for instance, no major sound change is observed, except resyllabification (Rule 1), in **k'och-i** [k'o.chi] 'flower (subject)' and **k'och-ita** [k'o.chi.da] '(It) is a flower', as compared to **k'och aph** [k'o.dap] 'in front of the flower' and **k'och+iph** [k'oɲ.ɲip] '(flower) petal'.

Since allophonic variations such as the intervocalic voicing of lax stops (**p, t, c, k** [b, d, ɟ, g]), palatalization (**s** [ʃ] and **n** [ɲ]), and delateralization (**l** [ɾ]) have already been discussed, the following rules deal only with syllabic and phonemic alternations.

Rule 1   Resyllabification

$$\textbf{V(C)C.(G/h)V} \Rightarrow \textbf{V(C).C(G/h)V}$$

When a syllable-final (coda) consonant is followed, without pause, by a vowel, a glide + a vowel, or **h** + a vowel in the following syllable, that consonant is carried over to the following syllable as its onset, as in (12a). The following syllable may be part of a suffix, a root, or a word. When the coda of the preceding syllable is a cluster of two consonants, only the second consonant is resyllabified as the onset of the following syllable, as in (12b).

(12)	a.	*chayk i*	'book (subj.)'	**chɛk-i**	[chɛ.gi]
		iss-e.yo	'exists'	**is'-ejo**	[i.s'ə.jo]
		cik.wen	'staff'	**cik+wen**	[ci.gwən]
		kyelhon	'marriage'	**kjəl+hon**	[kjə.ɾ(h)on]
		yak.hon	'engagement'	**yak+hon**	[ya.khon]
	b.	*ilk-e.yo*	'reads'	**ilk-ejo**	[il.gə.jo]
		anc-ass-ta	'sat'	**anc-as'-ta**	[an.ɟat.t'a]
		kaps ul	'price (obj.)'	**kaps-il**	[kap.s'ɨl]
		palp-a.yo	'steps on'	**palp-ajo**	[pal.ba.jo]

Rule 2   Coda neutralization

p, ph, (p')   ⇒   [p]
t, th, (t'), s, s', c, ch, (c'), h   ⇒   [t]
k, kh, k'   ⇒   [k]
when unreleased (i.e., in the environment of ___ C, #, +)

Before a consonant, a word boundary, or a compound boundary, consonants are not released, except in sibilation (Rule 4). Since many sound distinctions are made only when they are released, unrelease causes many sound interdistinctions to be blocked, resulting in coda neutralization phenomena of the following kinds.

First, the bilabial stops **p** and **ph** are neutralized to [p]. No Korean word has a **p'** before a consonant or a word boundary, but if any word were to have it, it too would become [p] in the given environments.

(13)	*ip*	'mouth'	**ip**	[ip]
	iph	'leaf'	**iph**	[ip]
	aph-cip	'front house'	**aph+cip**	[ap.c'ip]

Second, alveo-dental and palatal stops and fricatives **t, th, s, s', c, ch,** and **h** are all neutralized to [t]. Korean lacks words with **t'** and **c'** before a consonant or a word boundary, but these consonants would also become [t] if they existed. One exception to this process is **h** which aspirates a following lax stop (see Rule 3 h-aspiration).

(14)	*nat*	'cereal grains'	**nat**	[nat]
	nath	'piece, unit'	**nath**	[nat]
	nas	'sickle'	**nas**	[nat]
	nac	'daytime'	**nac**	[nat]
	nach	'face'	**nach**	[nat]
	hi-uh	'the letter *h*'	**hiɨh**	[hi.ɨt]
	path-kali	'field plowing'	**path+kal-i**	[pat.k'a.ɾi]
	os-an	'garment lining'	**os+an**	[o.dan]
	wus-os	'upper garment'	**us+os**	[u.dot]
	ka-ss-ta	'went'	**ka-s'-ta**	[kat.t'a]
	ic-ta	'forget'	**ic-ta**	[it.t'a]
	pich-kkal	'colour'	**pich-k'al**	[pit.k'al]

Third, velar stops **k, kh,** and **k'** are neutralized to [k], as illustrated in (15).

(15)	*cenyek*	'evening'	**cǝnjǝk**	[cǝ.ɲǝk]
	nakksi	'fish hook'	**nak'-si**	[nak.ʃ'i]
	pakk	'outside'	**pak'**	[pak]
	puekh-pi	'kitchen broom'	**puǝkh+pi**	[pu.ǝk.p'i]

When a neutralized form is followed by a vowel that begins a following word, the neutralized form, instead of the morphophonemic form, is released.

(16)	*kaps-echi*	'value'	**kaps+ǝchi**	[ka.bǝ.chi]
	phath-al	'red-bean grains'	**phath+al**	[pha.dal]
	puekh aph	'kitchen front'	**puǝkh aph**	[pu.ǝ.gap]

Rule 3   h-aspiration (mirror image)

lax stop + h   ⇒   aspirated stop

When the initial or final lax stop of a morpheme and the initial or final **h** of another morpheme become contiguous, they merge into an aspirated stop. This is a mirror image rule as it applies whether the lax stop precedes or follows **h**. This rule must apply before Rule 2. Otherwise, the coda neutralization rule would 'bleed' Rule 3 by changing the morpheme-final **h** to [t].

(17)	a.	*coh-ta*	'is good'	**coh-ta**	[co.tha]
		manh-key	'in abundance'	**manh-ke**	[man.khe]
		olh-ci	'That's right.'	**olh-ci**	[ol.chi]
	b.	*cik.hayng*	'going straight'	**cik+hɛŋ**	[ci.khɛŋ]
		pap-hata	'cook rice'	**pap+ha-ta**	[pa.pha.da]
		pat-hita	'supply'	**pat-hi-ta**	[pa.chi.da]

Rule 4   Sibilation

t   ⇒   [s]   in the environ. of ___ s, s'

Alveo-dental and palatal stops and fricatives become [t] according to Rule 2 (coda neutralization). This [t] becomes [s] before **s** or **s'**. This rule applies across a word boundary. The sibilated consonant may often be deleted in pronunciation due to Rule 14 (pre-tense/aspirate reduction).

(18)
pich-sal	'rays of light'	**pich+sal**	[pi(s).s'al]
cec-so	'milking cow'	**cəc+so**	[cə(s).s'o]
coh-so	'That's good!'	**coh-so**	[co(s).s'o]
mos ssu-n-ta	'is bad'	**mos s'ɨn-ta**	[mo(s).s'ɨn.da]
tah-soli	'consonant'	**tah-soli**	[ta(s).s'o.ɾi]

Rule 5   [n, l] epenthesis

    i. **ZERO** ⇒ [ɲ]   in the environ. of C (other than l) +, # ___ **i, j**
    ii. **ZERO** ⇒ [l] or [ʎ]   in the environ. of l +, # ___ **i, j**

An epenthetic [ɲ] is prefixed to a word or stem that begins with **i** or **j**, if the word or stem is preceded by another word or stem that ends in a consonant other than **l**.

(19)
cis-ikita	'knead to a mash'	**cis+iki-ta**	[ciɲ.ɲi.gi.da]
hoth-ipul	'sheet'	**hoth+ipul**	[hoɲ.ɲi.bul]
khong-yes	'bean candy'	**khoŋ+jəs**	[khoŋ.ɲət]
kkoch ilum	'flower name'	**k'och ilɨm**	[k'oɲ.ɲi.ɾɨm]
os ip-ko	'get dressed and'	**os ip-ko**	[oɲ.ɲip.k'o]
Taycen-yek	'Taejon Station'	**tɛcən+jək**	[tɛ.ɟən.ɲək]
us-i	'upper tooth'	**us+i**	[uɲ.ɲi]

An [l] (optionally [ʎ]) is prefixed to a word or stem that begins with **i** or **j**, if the word or stem is preceded by another word or stem that ends in **l**. Rule 5 could be simplified so that only [n] is epenthesized before **i** or **j**, and this epenthetic [n] changes to [l] after **l** by way of Rule 6 (liquidization). In this case, Rule 5 would be reduced to a rule dealing only with [n] epenthesis: **ZERO** ⇒ [n] in the environ. of **C** +, # ___ **i, j**.

(20)
mul-yak	'liquid medicine'	**mul+jak**	[mul.ljak]
ppayl i	'tooth to extract'	**p'ɛ:l i**	[p'ɛ:l.li]
Sewul-yek	'Seoul Station'	**səul+jək**	[sə.ul.ljək]
tul-il	'field work'	**tɨ:l+i:l**	[tɨ:l.lil]

Rule 5 does not apply if a compound word consists of two Sino-Korean morphemes, as in *Phyengyang* **phjəŋ+jaŋ** [phjə.ŋjaŋ] 'Phyengyang City', *yuk il lyuk+il* [yu.gil] 'six days', *ingye* **iŋ+yə** [i.ŋjə] 'surplus', *tok.yak* **tok+jak** [to.gjak] 'poisonous drug', *yangyak* **ljaŋ+jak** [ja.ŋjak] 'good medicine', *man.il* **man+il** [ma.nil] 'if', and *sal.in* **sal+in** [sa.ɾin] 'manslaughter'. Nor does it apply when the word in question is a particle or a copula, as in *salang i* **salaŋ-i** [sa.ɾa.ŋi] 'love (subject)', *sikol ita* **sikol-i-ta** [ʃi.go.ɾi.da] '(It) is the countryside', and *sikol ina* **sikol-ina** [ʃi.go.ɾi.na] 'countryside or something'.

Rule 6   Liquidization

      i. **n** ⇒ [l]   in the neighbourhood of **l**
      ii. **n-n** ⇒ [ll]   (optionally applicable only to older
                                generation speakers)

Liquidization (also called lateralization) is a mirror-image process in that **n** changes to [l] either before or after **l**. Two subtypes are involved in (i): **n-l** changes to [ll] across a compound boundary within a word, as in (21a), and **l-n** changes to [ll] across a word boundary (i.e., within an utterance) as well as within a word, as in (21b). As indicated in (ii), only in the speech of some older generation speakers, **n-n** optionally changes to [ll] if there is a compound boundary between the two **n**'s and the second **n** is followed by **j**, as in (21c).

(21)   a. *Cenla-to*   'Cenla province' **cen+la+to** [cəl.la.do]
        cinli   'truth'   **ci:n+li:** [ci:l.li]
        Cinlo   'Cinlo liquor' **cin+lo** [ci:l.lo]
        man-li '10,000 miles' **man+li** [mal.li]
        Sinla   'Sinla dynasty' **sin+la** [ʃil.la]

    b. *chil-nyen* 'seven years' **chil+njən** [chil.ljən]
        chwulpal nal 'departure day' **chul+pal nal** [chul.bal.lal]
        cim ul nayly-e 'Unload!' **cim-il nɛli-e** [ci.mɨl.lɛ.ɾjə]
        sel-nal 'New Year's Day' **se:l+nal** [sə:l.lal]
        sil-nay 'inside the room' **sil+nɛ** [ʃil.lɛ]
        tal nala 'the moon world' **tal nala** [tal.la.ɾa]

    c. *chen-nyen* '1,000 years' **chen+njən** [chəɲ.ɲən; chəl.ljən]
        sinnyem 'conviction' **si:n+njəm** [ʃi:ɲ.ɲəm; ʃi:l.ljəm]

If **n** is followed by **l** across a word boundary, it does not change to [l], as in *kipon ilon* **ki+pon li:+lon** → ki+pon i:+lon (by Rule 7) [ki.boɲ.ɲi(:).ɾon] (by Rule 5) 'basic theory' and *kin notong* **ki:-n lo+toŋ** [ki:n.no.doŋ] (by Rule 7) 'long labour'. This is because the **l** has already changed to [n] word-initially.

Rule 7 **n/l** shifting (in South Korean speech only)

    i. **n, l** ⇒ **ZERO** in the environ. of # ___ **i, j**
    ii. **l** ⇒ [n]   a. in the environ. of # ___ **V** (other than **i, j**)
                  b. in the environ. of **C** (other than **l, n**) + ___

Except in loan words, the nasal **n** and the liquid **l** drop word-initially if they are followed by either **i** or **j** (in South Korean dialects only), as in (22a) and (22b). Exceptions occur in some native words too, as in *ni* **ni** [ni] (derived recently from **ne**) 'you', *nyesek* **njəsək** [jə.sək; ɲə.sək] 'fellow, chap', and *im* **nim** [(n)im] (obsolete) 'lord, sweetheart'. In the word-initial position, **l** changes to [n] if it is not followed by **i** or **j**, as in (22c). After a consonant other than **l** and **n** and a compound boundary, **l** changes to [n] regardless of the nature of the following sound, as in (22d). Change of **l** to [n] or ZERO is often referred to as delateralization.

(22) a. *ipul*   'quilt'   **nipul**   [i.bul]
        (cf. *hoth-ipul* 'sheet'   **hoth-nipul** [hoɲ.ɲi.bul])
        yenam   'female and male' **njə+nam** [jə.nam]
        (cf. *namnye* 'male and female' **nam+njə** [nam.ɲə])
        yensey   'age'   **njən+se** [jən.se]
        (cf. *haknyen* 'academic year' **hak+njən** [haŋ.ɲən])

    b. *I ssi*   'Mr. Lee'   **li:+s'i** [i:.ʃ'i]
        (cf. *misuthe Li* 'Mr. Lee' **misɨthə+li** [mi.sɨ.thə.ɾi])
        ilon   'theory'   **li:+lon** [i:.ɾon]
        (cf. *nonli* 'logic'   **lon+li:** [nol.li])
        yeksa   'history'   **ljək+sa** [jək.s'a]
        (cf. *ilyek* 'personal history' **li+ljək** [i.ɾjək])

    c. *noksayk* 'green colour' **lok+sɛk** [nok.s'ɛk]
        (cf. *cholok* 'grass-green' **cho+lok** [cho.ɾok])
        nonli   'logic'   **lon+li:** [nol.li]
        (cf. *ilon* 'theory'   **li:+lon** [i:.ɾon])
        notong 'labour'   **lo+toŋ** [no.doŋ]
        (cf. *philo* 'fatigue'   **phi+lo** [phi.ɾo])

    d. *caplok* 'miscellany' **cap+lok** [cam.nok]
        (cf. *kilok* 'recording' **ki+lok** [ki.ɾok])
        Aplokkang 'the Yalu River' **ap+lok+kaŋ** [am.nok.k'aŋ]

(cf. *cholok*   'grass-green'   **cho+lok**   [cho.ɾok])

toklipmun   'Independence Gate'   **tok+lip+mun**   [toŋ.nim.mun]

(cf. *kilip*   'standing up'   **ki+lip**   [ki.ɾip])

Loan words and North Korean dialects are free from these so-called *Twuum Pepchik* 'Initial Sound Constraints'. Loan words used to be subject to this rule to a considerable extent, but have recently been exempted from it due to the on-going influx of a large quantity of loan words from English. This fact is observed in the following examples.

(23)   *nyusu*   'news'   **njusɨ**   [nju.sɨ], formerly [ju.sɨ]

nikheyl   'nickel'   **nikhel**   [ni.khel]

lakheys   'racket'   **lakhet**   [ɾa.khet], formerly [na.khet]

lamyen   'instant noodles'   **lamjən**   [ɾa.mjən], also [na.mjən]

leyncu   'lens'   **lencɨ**   [ren.ɟɨ]

lotheli   'rotary'   **lotheli**   [ɾo.thə.ɾi], also [no.tha.ɾi]

Rule 8   Consonant cluster simplification

CC ⇒ C   in the environ. of ___ C, +, #

This is a process in which a morpheme-final consonant cluster is reduced to a single consonant if both consonants occur in the syllable-final position, i.e., before another consonant or a word or compound boundary.

Many Korean morphemes end in two consonants. For instance, *kaps* **kaps** 'price' is a single-syllable morpheme with two consonants in the coda position. As we have seen, the syllable structure of contemporary spoken Korean does not allow a consonant cluster to occur within a phonetic syllable. Thus, **kaps** is realized as [kap] when it occurs alone, before a word or compound boundary, or before a consonant, as in *kaps-echi* **kaps+əchi** [ka.bə.chi] 'value' (lit. 'price-worth') and *kaps kwa* **kaps-kwa** [kap.k'wa] 'price and'. This so-called stray erasure does not occur if a cluster is followed by a vowel within a word, hence **kaps** is fully realized before a vowel. In this case, as we have already observed under Rule 1, **s** in **kaps** is resyllabified as the onset of the following syllable, as in **kaps-ɨl** [kap.s'ɨl] 'price (object)'.

The consonant clusters that occur in the syllable-final position of morphophonemic forms are **ps, ks, lp, lph, lth, lk, ls, lh, lm, mh, nc,** and **nh**, as illustrated respectively in *kaps* **kaps** 'price', *saks* **saks** 'wage', *palp* **pa:lp** 'step on', *ulph* **ɨlph** 'recite', *halth* **halth** 'lick', *ilk* **ilk** 'read', *kols* **kols** 'blind lane', *kkulh* **k'ɨlh** 'boil', *kolm* **ko:lm** 'form pus', *am-* **amh-** 'female (animal)', *anc* **anc** 'sit', and *manh* **ma:nh** 'many'. In

addition, there are clusters consisting of a nasal or liquid consonant followed by an
epenthetic **s** (7.4.3), as in *cam-cali* **cam-s+cali** [cam.c'a.ɾi] 'sleeping (**cam**) place
(**cali**)' and *mul-ka* **mul-s+ka** [mul.k'a] 'water (**mul**) edge (**ka**)'.

The consonant which remains is the first one, except in **lph** and **lm** where **l** drops
and in **lk** and **lp** where **l** or the following consonant (**k** or **p**) drops depending on the
phonological environment, the kind of words involved, dialects, and/or idiolects.
When **lh**, **mh**, and **nh** are followed by a lax stop (**p, t, c, k**), **h** aspirates the lax stop as
per Rule 3 before it is deleted. (24a) illustrates words with first consonant deletion,
(24b) words with second consonant deletion, (24c) and (24d) irregular ones, and (24e)
words involving **h**-aspiration. The pronunciations in these examples are based on Y.
Chon (1992).

(24)   a. *eps-ta*   'does not exist'   **ə:ps-ta**   [ə:p.t'a]

             neks   'soul'   **nəks**   [nək]

             halth-nun-ta   'licks'   **halth-nɨn-ta**   [hal.lɨn.da]

             anc-nun-ta   'sits'   **anc-nɨn-ta**   [an.nɨn.da]

         b. *salm*   'life'   **sa:lm**   [sa:m]

             kwulm-nun-ta   'starves'   **ku:lm-nɨn-ta**   [ku:m.nɨn.da]

             ulph-nun-ta   'recites'   **ɨlph-nɨn-ta**   [ɨm.nɨn.da]

         c. *talk*   'chicken'   **talk**   [tak]

             nulk   'be old, get old'   **nɨlk**   [nɨk; nɨl] as in:

             nulk-ko   'be old and'   **nɨlk-ko**   [nɨl.k'o]

             nulk-ki   'being old'   **nɨlk-ki**   [nɨl.k'i]

             nulk-nun-ta   'gets old'   **nɨlk-nɨn-ta**   [nɨŋ.nɨn.da]

             nulk-sup-nita   'gets old'   **nɨlk-sɨp-ni-ta**   [nɨk.sɨm.ni.da]

             nulk-tali   'old animal'   **nɨlk-tali**   [nɨk.t'a.ɾi]

             nulk-ciman   'be old but'   **nɨlk-ciman**   [nɨk.c'i.man]

         d. *ccalp*   'short'   **c'alp**   [c'al]
                                                                         [c'ap] (dialect)

             yetelp   'eight'   **jətəlp**   [jə.dəl]
                                                                         [jə.dəp] (dialect)

             palp   'step on'   **pa:lp**   [pa:p; pa:l]

         e. *anhta*   'be not'   **anh-ta**   [an.tha]

             ilh-ko   'lose and'   **ilh-ko**   [il.kho]

manh-ciman	'be many but'	**ma:nh-ciman**	[ma:n.chi.man]
silh-ki	'disliking'	**silh-ki**	[ʃil.khi]

Notice in (24c) that in verbs and adjectives, **l** remains and **k** drops before **k** to prevent the geminate **k-k** from occurring; **k** remains elsewhere. In (24d), **l** is preferred in a short syllable and both **l** and **p** are acceptable in a long syllable. Young speakers frequently pronounce both **l** and the following **k** or **p(h)**, as in **palk-ta** [palk.t'a] 'is bright', **ɨlph-ko** [ɨlp.k'o] 'recites and', and **pa:lp-taka** [pa:lp.t'a.ga] 'while stepping on'.

As noticed in (24c) and (25a), the stop consonant in the second position of a cluster tensifies the following lax consonant as per Rule 10 (tensification) before it is deleted. In consonant clusters formed with an epenthetic **s**, the epenthetic **s** is always deleted after tensifying the following lax consonant, as shown in (25b).

(25) a. *anc-ko*   'sits and'   **anc-ko**   [an.k'o]
          ccalp-ta 'is short'   **c'alp-ta**   [c'al.t'a]
          halth-taka 'while licking'   **halth-taka** [hal.t'a.ga]

       b. *mul-ka*   'water-side'   **mul-s+ka**   [mul.k'a]
          mul-ka   'price of things' **mul-s+ka**   [mul.k'a]
          pam-keli 'night street'   **pam-s+kəli** [pam.k'ə.ɾi]

Rule 9   Nasalization

C other than **l** ⇒ **nasal**   in the environ. of ___ [+**nasal**]

All non-nasal consonants other than **l** become nasal before a nasal consonant. The rule of coda neutralization (Rule 2) changes all bilabial stops to [p], all alveo-dental and palatal stops and fricatives to [t], and all velar stops to [k]. Before a nasal consonant, all these consonants become [m], [n], and [ŋ], respectively. Nasalization occurs across an affixal, compound, or word boundary.

(26) *cip-mun*   'house gate'   **cip+mun**   [cim.mun]
      kiph-ni   'Is (it) deep?'   **kiph-ni**   [kim.ni]
      tut-nun-ta 'hears'   **tɨt-nɨn-ta** [tɨn.nɨn.da]
      os-nong   'clothes chest'   **os+noŋ**   [on.noŋ]
      cec naymsay 'milk smell'   **cəc nɛmsɛ**   [cən.nɛm.sɛ]
      kkoch-namu 'flower tree'   **k'och+namu** [k'on.na.mu]
      coh-ni   'Is (it) good?'   **co:h-ni**   [co:ɲ.ɲi]

| *hakmun* | 'learning' | **hak+mun** | [haŋ.mun] |
| *puekh mun* | 'kitchen door' | **puəkh mun** | [pu.əŋ.mun] |

The nasalization rule also applies to the outputs of **l** shifting (Rule 7), [n] epenthesis (Rule 5), and cluster-simplification (Rule 8), as illustrated in (27a), (27b), and (27c), respectively.

(27) a. *aplyek* 'pressure' **ap+ljək** → ap+njək [am.ɲək]

    caplok 'miscellany' **cap+lok** → cap+nok [cam.nok]

    phoklak 'slump' **phok+lak** → phok+nak [phoŋ.nak]

  b. *path il* 'field work' **path il** → path nil [paɲ.ɲil]

    os ipta 'get dressed' **os ip-ta** → ot nip-ta [oɲ.ɲip.t'a]

    kkoch-yes 'flower candy' **k'och+jəs** → k'ot+njət [k'oɲ.ɲət]

  c. *kaps man* 'price only' **kaps-man** → kap-man [kam.man]

    palp-ney 'steps on' **palp-ne** → pap-ne [pam.ne]

    ilk-nun-ta 'reads' **ilk-nɨn-ta** → ik-nɨn-ta [iŋ.nɨn.da]

Rule 10 Tensification

    lax C ⇒ tensed C in the environ. of [p, t, k] ___

The lax stops **p, t, c, k** and the fricative **s** change to their respective tensed counterparts [p'], [t'], [c'], [k'], and [s'], when they appear after [p], [t], or [k], including those stops that have resulted from Rule 2 (coda neutralization). The cause of this so-called post-obstruent tensification appears to be the air pressure built up due to the unrelease of these stops for a fraction of a second.

(28) *capci* 'magazine' **cap+ci** [cap.c'i]

    coh-so 'is good' **co:h-so** [co:(s).s'o]

    kaps-i 'price (subject)' **kaps-i** [kap.s'i]

    kiph-ta 'is deep' **kiph-ta** [kip.t'a]

    kwukswu 'noodles' **kuksu** [kuk.s'u]

    myech pen 'several times' **mjəch pən** [mjət.p'ən]

    mith-patak 'bottom' **mith+patak** [mit.p'a.dak]

    nac swul 'daytime liquor' **nac sul** [na(s).s'ul]

    nuc-key 'late (adverb)' **nɨc-ke** [nɨt.k'e]

    talk-koki 'chicken meat' **talk+koki** [tak.k'o.gi]

Although it is essentially a word-level rule, post-obstruent tensification occurs even across a word boundary if this boundary is not accompanied by a phonetic juncture (pause) within an intonational phrase. For instance, *kkoch pwa-la* 'Look at the flowers!' is [k'op.p'(w)a.ɾa] in casual speech, i.e., when it is pronounced without a juncture between *kkoch* 'flower' and *pwa-la* 'look at!'.

Furthermore, as we shall see in 7.4.3, one main reason for postulating an epenthetic **s** is to account for the occurrence of tensification. After it tensifies the following lax consonant, this **s** is deleted, optionally when its presence does not violate the syllable structure and obligatorily as in cluster simplification (Rule 8). For instance, *cho* 'candle' and *pul* 'light' are combined as **cho-s+pul** [cho(t).p'ul] and *san* 'mountain' and *pul* 'fire' as **san-s+pul** [san.p'ul]. Observe more examples in (29).

(29)	*an-ta*	'hug'	**an-s-ta**	[an.t'a]
	hays-pich	'sunlight'	**hɛ-s+pich**	[hɛ(t).p'it]
	kalcung	'thirst'	**kal-s+cɨŋ**	[kal.c'ɨŋ]
	kang-ka	'riverside'	**kaŋ-s+ka**	[kaŋ.k'a]
	swul-cip	'bar, tavern'	**sul-s+cip**	[sul.c'ip]

Rule 11   Palatalization

$$t \Rightarrow [c]$$
th $\Rightarrow$ [ch]   in the environ. of __ - (h)i, (h)j

Alveo-dental stops become palatal stops before **i**, **hi**, or **hj**, if there is an intervening affixal boundary (-). For the non-phonemic palatalization of **s** and **n**, see 7.2.1.

(30)	*hay-toti*	'sunrise'	**hɛ-tot-i**	[hɛ.do.ʥi]
	kath-i	'together'	**kath-i**	[ka.chi]
	kut-i	'positively'	**kut-i**	[ku.ʥi]
	mitat-i	'sliding door'	**mi+tat-i**	[mi.da.ʥi]
	nath-nath-i	'one by one'	**nath+nath-i**	[nan.na.chi]
	pat-hye-yo	'is butted'	**pat-hjə-jo**	[pa.chə.jo]
	path i	'dry field (subj.)'	**path-i**	[pa.chi]
	tat-hita	'be closed'	**tat-hi-ta**	[ta.chi.da]

If there is no affixal boundary or if there is a word or compound boundary instead, palatalization does not occur.

(31)   *titita*   'step on'   **titi-ta**   [ti.di.da]

        keth him   'outside strength'   **kət him**   [kə.thim]

        path-ilang   'plowed row'   **path+ilaŋ**→ pat+nilaŋ [paɲ.ɲi.ɾaŋ]

Rule 12   Decoronization (optional)

        t ⇒ [p]   in the environ. of ___ [+**bilabial**]

            [k]   in the environ. of ___ [+**velar**]

In casual speech, alveo-dental and palatal consonants (which are neutralized as [t])
are optionally changed to the bilabial consonant [p] before a bilabial consonant, and to
the velar consonant [k] before a velar consonant, irrespective of the kind of boundary.
These assimilation processes are called decoronization because the coronal sounds
(alveo-dental and palatal consonants) are moved to the [–coronal] positions in the
mouth.

(32)   *kkoch-path*   'flower garden'   **k'och+path**   [k'ot.p'at; k'op.p'at]

        sinmun   'newspaper'   **sin+mun**   [ʃin.mun; ʃim.mun]

        kas kkun   'hat string'   **kas k'ɨn**   [kat.k'ɨn; kak.k'ɨn]

        son-kum   'palm lines'   **son-s+kɨm**   [son.k'ɨm; soŋ.k'ɨm]

Rule 13   **h** weakening (optional)

        h ⇒ **ZERO**   in the environ. of [+**voice**] ___ [+**voice**]

In casual speech, **h** is weakened in pronunciation and usually becomes silent
between voiced sounds, even across a word or compound boundary.

(33)   *ahop*   'nine'   **ahop**   [a.(h)op]

        cenhwa   'telephone'   **cə:n-hwa**   [cə:n.hwa; cə:.nwa]

        il-hanta 'work'   **il ha-n-ta** [il.han.da; i.ɾan.da]

        kihwu   'weather'   **ki-hu**   [ki.(h)u]

        kyelhon   'marriage'   **kjəl-hon**   [kjə.ɾ(h)on]

Rule 14   Pre-tense/aspirate reduction (optional)

        p, t, k, s ⇒ **ZERO**   in the environ. of ___ homorganic **C', Ch**

In casual speech, an alveo-dental, palatal, or velar stop or a fricative may be
deleted when it is followed by a homorganic tensed (**C'**) or aspirated consonant (**Ch**)
unless emphasis is intended. For instance, **hak+pi** [hak.p'i] is not reduced to [ha.p'i]
because **k** and **p** are not homorganic. Note that the alveo-dental **t** and the palatal
consonant **c'** or **ch** are homorganic in view of their being coronal sounds.

(34)   *appak*   'pressure'   **ap+pak**   [a(p).p'ak]

         cec-so   'milk-cow'   **cəc+so** → cət.so   [cə(s).s'o]

         hakkyo   'school'   **hak+kjo:**   [ha(k).k'jo]

         kkoch-cip   'flower shop'   **k'och+cip**   [k'o(t).c'ip]

         sip-phal   '18'   **sip+phal**   [ʃi(p).phal]

An epenthetic **s** may also be reduced in the same way, as in *chos-pul* **cho-s+pul**
[chot.p'ul; cho(p).p'ul] 'candle light', *hays-pich* **hɛ-s+pich** [hɛt.p'it; hɛ(p).p'it]
'sunlight', and *seys-cip* **se:-s+cip** [se:(t).c'ip] 'house for rent'.

Rule 15   Vowel shortening

    V: ⇒ **V**   in a non-phrase-initial syllable

Long vowels are shortened, if the syllable in which it occurs does not take a
phrase-initial position. That is, a long vowel becomes neutralized into its
corresponding short vowel in a position other than the first syllable of a phonological
phrase. Korean orthography does not indicate vowel length despite its phonemic status
in older generation speakers.

(35)   a. *nun*   'snow'   **nu:n**   [nu:n]

             huyn nun   'white snow'   **hɨj-n nu:n**   [hin.nun]

         b. *salam*   'person'   **sa:lam**   [sa:.ɾam]

             khun salam   'tall person'   **khɨn sa:lam**   [khɨn.sa.ɾam]

         c. *nol-ko*   'play and'   **no:l-ko**   [no:l.go]

             ttwinol-ko   'skip about and' **t'wi+no:l-ko**   [t'wi.nol.go]

Rule 16   **ɨj** monophthongization

    ɨj ⇒ [ɨ(j)]   in the environ. of # ___

           [i]   elsewhere

The only partly surviving off-glide diphthong **ɨj** is pronounced as [ɨ(j)] in the word-initial position when it is not preceded by a consonat. Otherwise, it is [i]. While older generation speakers use [ɨ] in the word-initial position, younger generation speakers prefer [ɨj], as indicated earlier. When the written form **ɨj** represents the genitive case particle meaning 'of', its form is [e]. But this change is a case of historical restructuring, and its morphophonemic form should be **e** rather than **ɨj**.

(36)	a.	*uychi*	'false tooth'	**ɨj+chi**	[ɨ(j).chi]
		uymi	'meaning'	**ɨj+mi**	[ɨ(j).mi]
		uymun	'question'	**ɨj+mun**	[ɨ(j).mun]
		uykyen	'opinion'	**ɨj+kjən**	[ɨ(j).gjən]
		uysa	'medical doctor'	**ɨj+sa**	[ɨ(j).sa]
	b.	*hoy.uy*	'meeting'	**hwe:+ ɨj**	[hwe:.i]
		huymang	'hope'	**hɨj+maŋ**	[hi.maŋ]
		sanguy	'upper garment'	**saŋ+ɨj**	[sa.ɲi]
		tonguy	'agreement'	**toŋ+ɨj**	[to.ɲi]
		uyuy	'significance'	**ɨj+ɨj**	[ɨ(j).i]

Rule 17   **je** monophthongization (optional)

je ⇒ [e]   in the environ. of **C** ___

In casual speech, **je** is usually pronounced as [e] when it is preceded by a consonant. This monophthongization is optional in initial syllables, but it is generally obligatory in non-initial syllables. Examples include *hyeythayk* **hje:+thɛk** [h(j)e.thɛk] 'favour', *kyeysan* **kje:+san** [k(j)e:.san] 'calculation', *phyey* **phje:** [ph(j)e:] 'lung', *sikyey* **sikje:** [ʃi.ge] 'watch, clock', and *chelphyey* **chəl+phje:** [chəl.phe] 'abolition'. This reduction does not occur (except in dialects) when **je** is not preceded by a consonant, as in *yeyswul* **je:+sul** [je:.sul] 'art'.

7.4.3   *Non-automatic sound alternations*

The alternations to be discussed in this subsection are conditioned not only by the sound environments in which the morphemes involved occur but also by the lexico-grammatical information of the morphemes. Such alternations have been historically fossilized. Such morphologically or lexically conditioned allomorphs are represented usually as separate morphophonemic forms (e.g., **kwa** and **wa** 'and'). Some important types of non-automatic alternations are given below.

Rule A   Epenthetic **s**

The so-called epenthetic **s** (Bindungs-s or *sai sios*) frequently appears between the morphemes that compose a word or compound. This **s** (or **t** by a few more recent phonologists) behaves exactly the same way as any other **s** (or **t**) in reinforcing the following consonant. That is, it tensifies the following lax consonant. It also becomes a nasal before a nasal sound. For instance, compare *pi* 'rain' followed by the epenthetic **s**, with *pis* 'comb' in (37a) and notice the phonological parallelism. Observe in (37b) that the epenthetic **s** follows the regular sound alternations discussed in 7.4.2.

(37)   a. *pis-sok*   'the midst of rain' **pi-s+sok**   [pi(s).s'ok]
                 pis-sok   'inside of a comb'   **pis+sok**   [pi(s).s'ok]

             b. *pis-mul*   'rain water'   **pi-s+mul**   [pin.mul; pim.mul]
                 pis-cwulki   'sheets of rain'   **pi-s+culki**   [pi(t).c'ul.gi]
                 pis-pangwul   'rain drops'   **pi-s+paŋul**   [pi(t/p).p'a.ŋul]

The epenthetic **s** usually does not occur before a vowel-initial element in a compound except in two cases. First, it occurs when the first root of a compound is *wi* or *wu* 'upper', as in *wis-elun* **wi-s+əlɨn** [wi.də.ɾɨn] 'senior person' and *wus-os* **u-s+os** [u.dot] 'upper garment'. Second, it occurs when the second root begins with the vowel **i**, as in *namus-iph* **namu-s+iph** [na.muɲ.ɲip] 'tree leaf' and *alays-ipswul* **alɛ-s+ip-sul** [a.lɛɲ.ɲip.s'ul] 'lower lip'.

The epenthetic **s** occurs not only after a vowel but also after a nasal or liquid. When it occurs after a vowel, its phonetic form is obligatory (e.g., as [n] or [m]) before a nasal and optional (e.g., as [t], [p], [k], or [s]) before a non-nasal consonant, as shown in the above examples. When it occurs after a consonant, on the other hand, it is completely deleted after tensifying the following lax consonant. This deletion of **s** is due to cluster simplification (Rule 8), as already discussed in 7.4.2, and further illustrated below.

(38)   a. *an-pang*   'inner room'   **an-s+paŋ**   [an.p'aŋ]
                 i-chung-cip   'two-storey house'   **i-chɨŋ-s+cip** [i.chɨŋ.c'ip]
                 palam-soli   'sound of wind'   **palam-s+soli** [pa.ɾam.s'o.ɾi]
                 pom-pi   'spring rain'   **pom-s+pi**   [pom.p'i]
                 san-pul   'mountain fire'   **san-s+pul**   [san.p'ul]

             b. *kil-patak*   'road surface'   **kil-s+patak**   [kil.p'a.dak]

kaul-palam	'autumn wind'	**kaɨl-s+palam**	[ka.ɨl.p'a.ɾam]
mil-kalwu	'wheat flour'	**mil-s+kalu**	[mil.k'a.ɾu]
mul-soli	'sound of water'	**mul-s+soli**	[mul.s'o.ɾi]

The epenthetic **s** is significant in that it keeps the meanings of words apart. For instance, *kang-ka* **kaŋ-s+ka** [kaŋ.k'a] 'river-bank' differs from *kang-ka* **kaŋ-ka** [kaŋ.ga] 'surname Kang' because of the presence of the epenthetic **s** in the former. The same is true with such pairs as *cey sam-kwa* **ce:+sam+kwa** [ce:.sam.gwa] 'lesson three, third division' vs. *cey sam-kwa* **ce:+sam-s+kwa** [ce:.sam.k'wa] 'the third department', *pang-pi* **paŋ-s+pi** [paŋ.p'i] 'room broom' vs. *pangpi* **paŋ+pi** [paŋ.bi] 'defence', *pam pap* **pam-s+pap** [pam.p'ap] 'night-time meal' vs. *pam-pap* **pa:m+pap** [pa:m.bap] 'rice mixed with chestnut', *il-to* **il-s+to** [il.t'o] 'one degree' vs. *il-to* **il-to** [il.do] 'one also', *kong-pang* **koŋ-s+paŋ** [koŋ.p'aŋ] 'free room' vs. *kongpang* **koŋ+paŋ** [koŋ.baŋ] 'empty room', *kam-ca* **kam-s-ca** [kam.c'a] 'Let's wind (it)' vs. *kamca* **kamca** [kam.ɟa] 'potato', *cam-cali* **cam-s+cali** [cam.c'a.ɾi] 'bedding' vs. *camcali* **camcali** [cam.ɟa.ɾi] 'dragon-fly', *kam-ki* **ka:m-s-ki** [ka:m.k'i] 'winding' vs. *kamki* **ka:m+ki** [ka:m.gi] 'flu', *pal-pyeng* **pal-s+pjəŋ** [pal.p'jəŋ] 'foot trouble' vs. *palpyeng* **pal+pjəŋ** [pal.bjəŋ] 'attack of a disease', and *henpep* **hən-s+pəp** [hən.p'əp] 'constitutional law' vs. *he-n pep* **hə:-n pəp** [hə:n.bəp] 'old law'.

There have been a number of proposals regarding the predictability of the epenthetic **s**, that is, whether it is an active automatic process of insertion or whether it is a historical result. One general rule is that **s** usually appears after the first of two noun roots or stems in a compound noun of the subcompounding structure (a modifier followed by a head) as illustrated in (37) and (38), whereas it rarely occurs in a co-compounding structure (two heads) as in *non-path* **non+path** [non.bat] 'rice field and dry field', *ma-so* **ma+so** [ma.so] 'horse and cow', and *phal-tali* **phal+tali** [phal.da.ɾi] 'arms and legs'. However, that is not always the case, since many nominal subcompounds do not have an epenthetic **s,** as illustrated in (39a). Furthermore, all Sino-Korean examples in (39b) and (39c) have a compound boundary (+), but only those in (39b) have an epenthetic **s.**

(39)	a.	*isul-pi*	'drizzle (dew-rain)'	**isɨl+pi**	[i.sɨl.bi]
		kay-tali	'dog's leg'	**kɛ:+tali**	[kɛ:.da.ɾi]
		khong-pap	'bean-mixed rice'	**khoŋ+pap**	[khoŋ.bap]
		kol-pang	'back room'	**ko:l+paŋ**	[ko:l.baŋ]
		pay-path	'pear orchard'	**pɛ+path**	[pɛ.bat]
		son-capi	'handle'	**son+cap-i**	[son.ɟa.bi]
	b.	*chwulsan*	'childbirth'	**chul-s+san**	[chul.s'an]

coken	'condition'	**co:-s+kən**	[co:(t).k'ən]
inkyek	'integrity'	**in-s+-kjək**	[in.k'jək]
kyelceng	'decision'	**kjəl-s+cəŋ**	[kjəl.c'əŋ]
phyeypyeng	'lung disease'	**phje:-s+pjəŋ**	[ph(j)e:.p'jəŋ]
phal-to	'eight degrees'	**phal-s+to**	[phal.t'o]
saken	'incident'	**sa:-s+kən**	[sa:(t).k'ən]
tayka	'price'	**tɛ:-s+ka**	[tɛ:(t).k'a]

c.

chwulpyeng	'dispatch of troops'	**chul+pjəŋ**	[chul.bjəŋ]
henpyeng	'military police'	**hə:n+pjəŋ**	[hə:n.bjəŋ]
hwaki	'heat of fire'	**hwa:+ki**	[hwa:.gi]
il-kwa	'lesson one'	**il+kwa**	[il.gwa]
in-kwu	'population'	**in+ku**	[in.gu]
kakyek	'price'	**ka+kjək**	[ka.gjək]
kongki	'air'	**koŋ+ki**	[koŋ.gi]
sam-to	'three degrees'	**sam+to**	[sam.do]

Note that all Sino-Korean morphemes ending in l get an epenthetic s before a Sino-Korean morpheme beginning with a coronal consonant such as t, c, or s, as alluded to in (39b). In order to account for the non-occurrence of the epenthetic s in words like those in (39a, c), one must have recourse to the morpho-syntactic or semantic information of the compounds or idiosyncratic lexical conditioning (e.g., S.C. Ahn 1985; H.Y. Kim 1990; Shi 1997). This leads to the conclusion that the appearance of s is the result of at least a semihistorical or on-going restructuring process.

Another type of s insertion that is both phonologically and grammatically conditioned occurs when a verb stem ending in a nasal is immediately followed by a verbal suffix beginning with a lax consonant (p, t, c, k, s), as illustrated in (40).

(40)   *an-sup-nita*   'hugs'   **an-s-sɨp-ni-ta**   [an.s'ɨm.ni.da]
         (-*sup* (addressee honorific suffix), -*nita* (deferential sentence ender))
         kam-ki   'winding'   **kam-s-ki**   [kam.k'i]
         (-*ki* (nominalizer suffix))
         kem-ta   'is black'   **kə:m-s-ta**   [kə:m.t'a]
         (*kem* 'black', -*ta* (plain declarative ender))
         sim-ko   'plant and' **si:m-s-ko**   [ʃi:m.k'o]
         (*sim* 'plant', -*ko* 'and' (conjunctive suffix))
         sim-taka   'while planting' **sim-s-taka**   [ʃim.t'a.ga]
         (-*taka* 'while, and then' (conjunctive suffix))

The epenthetic **s** also appears after the 'prospective' modifier ender -(ɨ)l, as in (41). These appearances of **s** are not automatic because they are conditioned by the existence of grammatical information such as 'verb stem' and 'verbal suffix'.

(41)   *ka-l kil*   'road to take'   **ka-l-s kil**   [kal.k'il]

                po-l kes   'thing to see'   **po-l-s kəs**   [pol.k'ət]

                no-l ci   'whether to play'   **no:-l-s ci**   [no:l.c'i]

A variety of conventions have been adopted so far in both North and South Korea for the orthographic representation of the epenthetic **s**. The current practice in the South is to include the Hankul letter for **s** after a vowel, while leaving it out after a consonant, as in *pis-sok* **pi-s+sok** [pi(s).s'ok] 'the midst of rain' and *kang-ka* **kaŋ-s+ka** [kaŋ.k'a] 'river-bank'. In the North, on the other hand, the present practice is to leave it out altogether regardless of the sound environments, as in *pi-sok* and *kang-ka*.

Rule B   Vowel harmony

Vowel harmony is an assimilatory phenomenon in which one vowel becomes harmonious with another one in the neighbouring syllable. Korean used to have much more stringent and regular vowel harmony rules than it has now. At present, harmony exists only (a) in the ə/a alternation in verbal suffixes, which is often called suffixal vowel harmony; (b) in onomatopoeic and mimetic expressions, including colour terms, which is often called sound symbolic or lexical vowel harmony; and (c) in some prefixal alternations. Vowel harmony in Contemporary Korean is not automatic in that not only is grammatical or lexical information required for the rule of vowel harmony to apply but many exceptions also exist.

Korean vowel harmony operates in terms of 'bright' or Yang vowels and 'dark' or Yin vowels. In suffixal vowel harmony, in Contemporary Korean, only **a** and **o** are considered Yang vowels and the rest Yin vowels. That is, the so-called infinitive suffix -ə/-a (e.g., **kuw-ə cu-ta** 'bake for' vs. **tow-a cu-ta** 'help for'), the past tense suffix -əs'/-as', the intimate sentence ender -ə/-a, the polite sentence ender -əjo/-ajo, the plain imperative ender -əla/-ala, the concessive verbal suffix -əto/-ato, etc. all have two allomorphs, in which ə and **a** alternate. This alternation is conditioned by the vowel in the preceding syllable, as illustrated in (42). That is, the Yang (bright) vowel **a** appears only when the preceding vowel is also a Yang vowel (**a** or **o**), otherwise the Yin (dark) vowel ə is used.

(42)   a. *cwuk-essta*   'died'   **cuk-əs'-ta**   [cu.gə(t).t'a]

               nol-assta   'played'   **nol-as'-ta**   [no.ɾa(t).t'a]

b. *ttwi-ela*   'Jump!'   **t'wi-əla**   [t'wi.ə.ɾa]
   cap-ala   'Catch (it)!'   **cap-ala**   [ca.ba.ɾa]

c. *cwu-eto*   'though (he) gives' **cu-əto**   [cu.ə.do]
   po-ato   'though (he) sees'   **po-ato**   [po.a.do]

There are a number of irregularities in the -ə/-a alternation, although, compared to ideophonic processes (see below), this suffixal vowel harmony is an active and synchronic process to a considerable extent. First, the verb stem *ha* **ha** 'do, make' still retains its old form **haj** before suffixes that begin with -ə. Thus, we have forms such as *ha-ye* **haj-ə** [ha.jə] or its contraction *hay* **hɛ** [hɛ] (infinitive form), *ha-yess* **haj-əs'** [ha.jət] or its contraction *hay-ss* **hɛ-s'** [hɛt] (past form), *hay-yo* **hɛ-jo** [hɛ.jo] (polite-level form derived from **haj-əyo**), *ha-yela* **haj-əla** [ha.jə.ɾa] or its contraction *hay-la* **hɛ-la** [hɛ.ɾa] (plain-level imperative form), etc.

Second, superficial dissimilation is observable in places where **a** would otherwise occur. That is, the past tense suffix retains ə after another past tense suffix with **a**, as in *coh-ass-ess-ta* **coh-as'-əs'-ta** [co.a.s'ə(t).t'a] 'had been good'. Thus, vowel harmony occurs only between a stem (e.g., **coh** 'good') and the immediately following suffix (-**as'** in this example). Similarly, *coh-ass-e* **coh-as'-ə** [co.a.s'ə] (not **coh-as'-a*) '(it) was good' and *noph-ass-e.yo* **noph-as'-əjo** [no.pha.s'ə.jo] (not **noph-as'-ajo*) '(it) was high' show such apparent dissimilation. A historical explanation will account for this deviation. The past tense suffix *-ess/-ass* **-əs'/-as'** has derived from the infinitive suffix -ə/-a + the 'existential' predicate *isi* **isi** (> *iss* **is'**). Notice that **isi** ends in a syllable with a Yin vowel (**i**). Thus, vowel harmony requires the infinitive suffix following **isi** to be ə. Although -ə/-a + **isi** has been restructured as a past tense suffix, the infinitive vowel following this restructured past tense suffix remains as -ə; hence, for instance, we have **coh-as'-əs'-əjo** [co.a.s'ə.s'ə.jo] 'had been good', and not **coh-as'-as'-ajo* [co.a.s'a.s'a.jo].

Third, **a** optionally changes to ə if the preceding syllable has the vowel **a** followed by a consonant or a consonant cluster. For instance, *anc-ass* **anc-as'** [an.ɟat] and *anc-ess* **anc-əs'** [an.ɟət] 'sat' are free variants, whereas only *nol-ass* **nol-as'** [no.ɾat] 'played' is allowed and **nol-ess* **nol-əs'** [no.ɾət] is not. Similarly, *cap-a.yo* **cap-ajo** [ca.ba.jo] and *cap-e.yo* **cap-əjo** [ca.bə.jo] '(he) catches' are both possible, while **cop-e.yo* **cop-əjo** [co.bə.jo] '(it) is narrow' is not. The optional shift from **a** to ə is more lenient in polysyllabic adjectives ending in **w**, as in *komaw-a.yo* **komaw-ajo** [ko.ma.wa.jo] vs. *komaw-e.yo* **komaw-əjo** [ko.ma.wə.jo] 'thank you!', and *koylow-a.yo* **kølow-ajo** [kø.ɾo.wa.jo] vs. *koylow-e.yo* **kølow-əjo** [kø.ɾo.wə.jo] '(it) is distressing.' Notice here that the shift to ə is allowed even after a syllable with **o**. This shift does not occur in monosyllabic adjectives, as shown in *kow-a.yo* **kow-ajo**

[ko.wa.jo] '(it) is pretty' vs. its unacceptable counterpart **kow-e.yo* **kow-əjo**
[ko.wə.jo].

Fourth, after the copula adjective stem *i*, the sentence-final infinitive suffix that
indicates the intimate speech level is not the expected **-ə** but **-a**, as in *chayk i-ya*
chɛk-i-a [chɛ.gi.(j)a] '(it) is a book' and *na y-a* **na-i-a** [na.ja] '(it) is I'. When the
copula is followed by other kinds of suffixes with **ə/a**, it manifests regular vowel
harmony alternation, as in *chayk i-ess-ta* **chɛk-i-əs'-ta** [chɛ.gi.ə(t).t'a] '(it) was a
book'.

Finally, there are minor phonological adjustments that involve **ə/a**, such as vowel
shortening, diphthongization, and fusion. Vowel shortening will be discussed under
Rule I and diphthongization under Rule J. Fusion is illustrated below. Notice that the
subject honorific suffix *-(u)si* **-(ɨ)si** is optionally fused with the following vowel **ə** in
the polite sentence ender *-e.yo* **-əjo** to form *-(u)sey* **-(ɨ)se.**

(43)   *an-usi-e.yo; an-useyyo* '(He) hugs.'   **an-ɨsi-əjo**   [a.nɨ.ʃə.jo]
                                            → **an-ɨsejo**   [a.nɨ.se.jo]
          ka-si-e.yo; ka-seyyo   '(He) goes.'   **ka-si-əjo**   [ka.ʃə.jo]
                                            → **ka-se-jo**   [ka.se.jo]

Vowel harmony occurs extensively in ideophonic words such as onomatopoeic,
mimetic, and colour expressions in Korean, although many exceptions are also
observed. In general, other things being equal, 'bright' or Yang vowels tend to
connote relative brightness, sharpness, lightness, smallness, thinness and quickness,
whereas the corresponding 'dark' or Yin vowels indicate relative darkness, heaviness,
dullness, slowness, deepness, and thickness.

Unlike in suffixal vowel harmony, **ɛ** and **ø** behave as Yang vowels in sound
symbolic (lexical) vowel harmony. Obviously, this is because the current **ɛ** and **ø**
were off-glide diphthongs **aj** and **oj**, respectively in Middle Korean, in which the
Yang vowels **a** and **o** appeared. This attests to the fact that lexical vowel harmony
stopped being active before **aj** and **oj** were monophthongized, whereas suffixal vowel
harmony continued to be active even after the monophthongization.

There are three harmony groups regarding sound symbolism: (i) **a, ɛ, o, ø** (Yang
or bright vowels), (ii) **u, ə, e, y** (Yin or dark vowels), and (iii) **ɨ, i** (neutral vowels).
Harmony occurs among the members of each group (i, ii, or iii). In addition, the
members of (iii) may occur with those of (i) or (ii).

(44)   a.   *ccayl-ccayl*   'trickling'   **c'ɛ:l+c'ɛ:l**   [c'ɛ:l.c'ɛl]
            khoykhoy-hata   'stinking'   **khøkhø+ha-ta**   [khø.khø.ha.da]
            kkopak   'noddingly'   **k'opak**   [k'o.bak]

	sol-sol	'smoothly'	**so:l+so:l**	[so:l.sol]
	taykak-taykak	'snapping'	**tɛkak+tɛkak**	[tɛ.gak.t'ɛ.gak]
	toylok-toylok	'waddling'	**tølok+tølok**	[tø.ɾok.t'ø.ɾok]

b.	*cwul-cwul*	'swiftly'	**cu:l+cu:l**	[cu:l.ɟul]
	khwikhwi-hata	'stinking'	**khykhy+ha-ta**	[khy.khy.ha.da]
	kkwupek	'noddingly'	**k'upək**	[k'u.bək]
	swul-swul	'smoothly'	**su:l+su:l**	[su:l.sul]
	teykek-teykek	'snapping'	**tekək+tekək**	[te.gək.t'e.gək]
	twilwuk-twilwuk	'waddling'	**tyluk+tyluk**	[ty.ɾuk.t'y.ɾuk]

c.	*cikkun*	'snappingly'	**cik'ɨn**	[ci.k'ɨn]
	ping-ping	'in a circle'	**piŋ+piŋ**	[piŋ.biŋ]
	pingkul	'smilingly'	**piŋkɨl**	[piŋ.gɨl]
	tul-tul	'rummaging'	**tɨ:l-tɨ:l**	[tɨ:l.dɨl]

d.	*ccokul*	'crumpled'	**c'okɨl**	[c'o.gɨl]
	ccwukul	'crumpled'	**c'ukɨl**	[c'u.gɨl]
	mongsi	'plump'	**moŋsil**	[moŋ.ʃil]
	mungsil	'plump'	**muŋsil**	[muŋ.ʃil]
	namsil-namsil	'overflowing'	**namsil+namsil**	[nam.ʃil.lam.ʃil]
	nemsil-nemsil	'overflowing'	**nəmsil-nəmsil**	[nəm.ʃil.ləm.ʃil]

Due to vowel harmony, forms like **kkopek-kkopek* **k'opək+k'opək** and **kkwupak-kkwupak* **k'upak+k'upak** are not allowed for the meaning of 'noddingly', while forms such as *kkopak-kkopak* **k'opak+k'opak** and *kkwupek-kkwupek* **k'upək+k'upək** are.

There are many exceptions to the above generalizations. For instance, *ttaykwul* **t'ɛkul** is used along with the regular *tteykwul* **t'ekul** 'rolling', *haycwuk-haycwuk* **hɛcuk+hɛcuk** is used along with the regular *hicwuk-hicwuk* **hicuk+hicuk** '(smile) sweetly', *malttung-malttun* **malt'uŋ+malt'uŋ** is used along with the regular *melttwung-melttwung* **məlt'uŋ+məlt'uŋ** and *malttong-malttong* **malt'oŋ+malt'oŋ** 'blankly', and *kkangchwung-kkangchwung* **k'aŋchuŋ+k'aŋchuŋ** is used along with the regular *kkangchong-kkangchong* **k'aŋchoŋ+k'aŋchoŋ** and *kkengchwung-kkengchwung* **k'əŋchuŋ+k'əŋchuŋ** 'lanky'.

Prefixal vowel harmony includes (i) the alternation between the prefix *say-* **sɛ-** 'vivid, deep, intense' and its allomorph *si-* **si-** in relation to sound symbolically paired colour terms and (ii) the alternation between the prefix *hay-* **hɛ-** 'whitish' and its allomorph *huy-* **hɨj-** in relation to a few paired words. The prefixes *say-* **sɛ-** and *hay-*

hɛ- go with words with a Yang vowel, while *si-* **si-** and *huy-* **hɨj-** occur with words with a Yin vowel.

(45)   a. *sayha.yahta* 'pure white'   **sɛ-hajah-ta**   [sɛ.ha.ja.tha]

              sihe.yehta   'pure white'   **si-həjəh-ta**   [ʃi.hə.jə.tha]

              saykkamahta 'deep black'   **sɛ-k'amah-ta**   [sɛ.k'a.ma.tha]

              sikkemehta   'deep black'   **si-k'əməh-ta**   [ʃi.k'ə.mə.tha]

              saynolahta   'vivid yellow'   **sɛ-nolah-ta**   [sɛ.no.ɾa.tha]

              sinwulehta   'vivid yellow'   **si-nuləh-ta**   [ʃi.nu.ɾə.tha]

      b. *haymalkahta*   'glossy white'   **hɛ-malkah-ta**   [hɛ.mal.ga.tha]

              huymelkehta   'glossy white'   **hɨj-məlkəh-ta**   [hi.məl.gə.tha]

              haymalsswuk- 'clean and fair'   **hɛ-mals'uk**   [hɛ.mal.s'uk]

              huymelsswuk- 'clean and fair'   **hɨj-məls'uk**   [hi.məl.s'uk]

For a recent study on Korean vowel harmony, see M.H. Cho 1994.

Rule C   l deletion

While **ɨ** is considered the weakest vowel in Korean, l (togehter with **h**) is considered a weak consonant, in that it is easily deleted in certain morphologically conditioned sound environments. The most salient case is that predicate stems ending in l lose the l before a suffix that begins with -s, -n, -p, -m, -l, or -o. Thus, for instance, stem-final l is deleted before the honorific suffix *-(u)si* -(ɨ)**si**, the addressee-honorific suffix *-(su)p* -(sɨ)**p**, the familiar-level propositive sentence ender *-sey* -**se**, the blunt-level sentence ender *-(s)o* -(**s**)**o**, the adnominal modifier suffixes -((n)ɨ)n, the familiar-level declarative sentence ender *-ney* -**ne**, the plain-level interrogative sentence enders *-ni* -**ni** and *-nunya* -**nɨnja**, the conjunctive suffix *-(u)nikka* -(ɨ)**nik'a** 'because', the nominalizer suffix *-(u)m* -(ɨ)**m**, and the prospective suffix *-(u)l* -(ɨ)**l**.

One may wonder why l is deleted before such heterogeneous sounds which do not constitute any apparent natural class. One possible answer may be that the deletion of the coronal consonant l is due to the coronality of the immediately following consonant. This assumption will account for the deletion before s, n, and l. Furthermore, the addressee honorific -p has an allomorph -**sɨp** which occurs after a stem-final consonant. It may be the case that l drops before -**sɨp** due to the coronality of s and then -**sɨp** is replaced by -p because the latter allomorph must appear after a stem-final vowel. The blunt level suffix -o has an allomorph -**so** which occurs after a consonant. Thus, the deletion of l before the suffix -o may be due to the coronal consonant s in -**so** as in the case of the addressee honorific -(**sɨ**)**p**. The deletion of l before the nominalizer -(ɨ)m, as in *no-m* **no:-m** 'playing' (*nol* **no:l** 'play'), seems to have gone through the following processes: **no:l-ɨm** → **no:l-m** (via ɨ deletion (cf. Rule F)) → **no:-m** [no:m] (via consonant cluster simplification (Rule 8)). Thus, the ɨ deletion 'feeds' the deletion of the l in the consonant cluster **lm** in the same way as *kwulm* **ku:lm** ' starve' is reduced to [ku:m].

Then, we may generalize l deletion in such a way that a stem-final l, which is a coronal consonant, is deleted before a suffix beginning with the coronal consonant **s** or **n** due to homorganic weakening and before the monoconsonant morpheme **m** due to cluster simplification. These generalizations are illustrated in (46) with the verb stem *nol* **no:l** ' play'. For the deletion of ɨ in some examples, see Rule F.

(46)   *no-nun kos*   'place where (he) plays'   **no:l-nɨn kos** → **no:-nɨn kos**
                                                                    [no:.nɨn.got]

        no-nta   '(He) plays.' (PLN)   **no:l-nɨn-ta** → **no:-nɨn-ta**
                                            → **no:-n-ta**   [no:n.da]

        no-ni?   'Does (he) play?' (PLN)   **no:l-ni** → **no:-ni** [no:.ni]

        no-nikka   'because (he) plays'   **no:l-ɨnik'a** → **no:-nik'a**
                                            [no:.ni.k'a]

        no-si-nta   '(He) plays.' (PLN)   **no:l-ɨsi-n-ta** → **no:l-si-n-ta**
                                            → **no:-si-n-ta**   [no:.ʃin.da]

        no-p-nita   '(He) plays.' (DEF)   **no:l-sɨp-ni-ta** → **no:-sɨp-ni-ta**
                                            → **no:-p-ni-ta**   [no:m.ni.da]

        no-p-sita   'Let's play (DEF)   **no:l-ɨp-si-ta** → **no:-p-si-ta**
                                            [no:p.ʃ'i.da]

        no-se   'Let's play.' (FML)   **no:l-se** → **no:-se** [no:.se]
                                        ([no:l-se] is marginally acceptable.)

        no-o   '(He) plays.' (BLN)   **no:l-so** → **no:-o** [no:.o]

        no-m   'playing'   **no:l-ɨm** → no:l-m → **no:-m**
                                            [no:m]

        no-l sikan   'time to play'   **no:l-ɨl sikan** → **no:ll sikan**
                                        → **no:l sikan**   [no:l.ʃ'i.gan]

Before suffixes such as *-myen* **-mjən** 'if' and *-myense* **-mjənsə** 'while', stem-final ls are not deleted because the suffix-initial consonant is not a coronal sound, as in (47a). When a stem-final l occurs before a suffix whose initial syllable does not begin with **n** or **s**, the l remains, as in (47b).

(47)   a.   *nol-myen*   'if (he) plays'   **no:l-mjən**   [no:l.mjən]
              nol-myense   'while playing'   **no:l-mjənsə**   [no:l.mjən.sə]

b. *nol-taka* 'while playing' **no:l-taka** [no:.l.da.ga]

   nol-key 'Play!' (FML) **no:l-ke** [no:l.ge]

   nol-ato 'although (he) plays' **nol-ato** [no.ɾa.do]

There is still another type of l deletion. A relatively small set of noun stems that end in l lose the l when they form a compound with another noun stem that begins with a coronal consonant such as t, s, n, or c. Notice that these consonants are generally homorganic with l.

(48)   *na-nal-i* 'day by day' **nal+nal-i → na+nal-i** [na.na.ɾi]

       panu-cil 'needlework' **panɨl-cil → panɨ-cil** [pa.nɨ.ɟil]

       pu-cok 'shortage' **pul+cok → pu+cok** [pu.ɟok]

       pu-tong 'inequality' **pul+toŋ → pu+toŋ** [pu.doŋ]

       pu-sap 'iron fire-spade' **pul+sap → pu+sap** [pu.sap]

       tta-nim 'daughter' (hon.) **t'al-nim → t'a-nim** [t'a.nim]

Similarly to (48), in casual speech, the adjective stem *mel* **məːl** 'be far' tends to lose its l even before the negative nominalizer suffix *-ci*, as in *me(l)-ci anh-a.yo* **məː(l)-ci an-h-ajo** '(it) is not far' and *me(l)-ci anh-a* **məː(l)-ci an-h-a** 'before long' (lit. 'not far').

The fact that l deletion of the kind illustrated in (48) is not automatic is evidenced by the existence of examples like *pal-tal* **pal+tal** 'development', *pul-sengsil* **pul+səng+sil** 'insincerity', *kil-son* **kil+son** 'traveller', *pul-chi* **pul+chi** 'incurability', *pul-sin* **pul+sin** 'discredit', *ssal-cip* **s'al+cip** 'rice store', and *mil-ciph* **mil+ciph** 'wheat straw'.

Another rare type of l deletion is observable in the casual speech of some speakers. That is, the l in the prospective suffix *-(u)l* is deleted optionally before a tensed velar stop that begins several sentence enders.

(49)   *kal-key* '(I) will surely go.' **ka-l-k'e** [ka(l).k'e]

      mek-ul-kka-yo 'Shall (we) eat?' **mək-ɨl k'a-jo** [mə.gɨ(l).k'a.jo]

Rule D   Consonant weakening in irregular verbs

In the stem-final position of irregular verbs and adjectives, when followed by a vowel, p becomes w, t becomes l, s becomes ZERO, and h becomes ZERO. There are many regular verbs that do not undergo this process of weakening in the same sound environment. There are also dialects that do not have one or more of these consonant weakenings. For instance, the Kyengsang dialect does not have the p-to-w process.

Neither the Kyengsang nor the Cenla dialect has the **s**-to-ZERO process. Hence there are no **p**-irregular (**p**-to-**w**) or **s**-irregular (**s**-to-ZERO) verbs in these dialects.

Conjugations of the **p**-irregular verbs in Standard Korean are illustrated in (50). To this irregular class belong other examples such as *chwup* **chup** 'be cold', *kop* **ko:p** 'be pretty', *kwup* **ku:p** 'roast', *mip* **mip** 'be hateful', *swip* **swi:p** 'be easy', *mayp* **mεp** 'be hot (in taste)', *nwup* **nu:p** 'lie down', *alumtap* **alɨmtap** 'be beautiful', *ttukep* **t'ɨkəp** 'be hot (in temperature)', *mukep* **mukəp** 'be heavy', *komap* **komap** 'be thankful', *twukkep* **tuk'əp** 'be thick', and *sikkulep* **sik'ɨləp** 'be noisy'.

(50)   *tep-ta*   'is hot'   **tə:p-ta**   [tə:p.t'a]

    tew-ese   'as (it) is hot'   **tə:p-əsə → təw-əsə**   [tə.wə.sə]

    tew-i   'heat'   **tə:p-i → təw-i**   [tə.wi]

    tew-uni   'as (it) is hot'   **tə:p-ɨni → təw-ɨni**   [tə.u.ni]

Stem vowel shortening as in (50) will be discussed shortly under Rule I. Regular verb stems include *cop* **cop** 'be narrow', *cip* **cip** 'pick up', *kwup* **kup** 'be bent', *cap* **cap** 'hold', and *ip* **ip** 'wear', among many others, as shown in *cop-ase* **cop-asə** [co.ba.sə] 'as (it) is narrow', *cip-ela* **cip-əla** [ci.bə.ɾa] 'Pick (it) up!', *kwup-ess-ta* **kup-əs'-ta** [ku.bət.t'a] 'was bent', *cap-umyen* **cap-ɨmjən** [ca.bɨ.mjən] 'if (he) holds', and *ip-uni* **ip-ɨni** [i.bɨ.ni] 'since (he) gets dressed'.

The **t**-irregular stems include *tut* **tɨt** 'hear', *mut* **mu:t** 'ask', *ket* **kə:t** 'walk', *nwut* **nu:t** 'scorch', *kkaytat* **k'εtat** 'realize', and *ilkhet* **ilkhət** 'entitle'.

(51)   *tut-ko*   'hear and'   **tɨt-ko**   [tɨt.k'o]

    tul-ess-ta   'heard'   **tɨt-əs'-ta → tɨl-əs'-ta**   [tɨ.ɾə(t).t'a]

    tul-uni   'as (he) hears'   **tɨt-ɨni → tɨl-ɨni**   [tɨ.ɾɨ.ni]

    tul-ela   'Listen!'   **tɨt -əla → tɨl-əla**   [tɨ.ɾə.ɾa]

    tul-ese   'by listening'   **tɨt-əsə → tɨl-əsə**   [tɨ.ɾə.sə]

Regular stems include *mut* **mu:t** 'bury', *ket* **kət** 'roll up', *pat* **pat** 'receive', *tat* **tat** 'close', and *mit* **mit** 'believe', as shown in *mut-ela* **mu:t-əla** [mu.də.ɾa] 'Bury (it)!', *ket-imyen* **kət-ɨmjən** [kə.dɨ.mjən] 'if (he) rolls (it) up', *pat-ase* **pat-asə** [pa.da.sə] 'by receiving', *tat-imyen* **tat-ɨmjən** [ta.dɨ.mjən] 'if (he) closes', and *mit-ese* **mit-əsə** [mi.də.sə] 'by believing'.

The **s**-irregular stems include *is* **i:s** 'join, connect', *nas* **na:s** 'get well', *.ces* **cə:s** 'stir', and *cis* **ci:s** 'build, make'. The irregular behavior may be illustrated with the verb *ista* 'connect' in (52).

(52)   *is-ko*   'joins (them) and'   **i:s-ko**   [i:t.k'o]

    i-ela   'Join (them)!'   **i:s-əla → i-əla**   [i.ə.ɾa]

| *i-uni* | 'as (he) joins (them)' | **i:s-ɨni → i-ɨni** | [i.ɨ.ni] |
| *i-ese* | 'as (he) joins (them)' | **i:s-ǝsǝ → i-ǝsǝ** | [i.ǝ.sǝ] |

Regular stems include *wus* **u:s** [u:t] 'laugh', *ssis* **s'is** [ʃ'it] 'wash', and *pis* **pis** [pit] 'comb', as in *wus-uni* **us-ɨni** [u.sɨ.ni] 'since (he) laughs', *ssis-ela* **s'is-ǝla** [ʃ'i.sǝ.ɾa] 'Wash!', and *pis-uni* **pis-ɨni** [pi.sɨ.ni] 'as (he) combs'.

The **h**-irregular stems are mostly colour indicating terms such as *nolah* **no:lah** 'be yellow', *phalah* **pha:lah** 'be blue, green', *ppalkah* **p'a:lkah** 'be red', *ha.yah* **ha:jah** 'be white', and *kkamah* **k'a:mah** 'be black'.

(53)	*nolahta*	'is yellow'	**no:lah-ta**	[no:.ɾa.tha]
	nolayse	'as (it) is yellow'	**no:lah-asǝ → no:lɛ-sǝ**	[no:.ɾɛ.sǝ]
	nola-ni	'as (it) is yellow'	**no:lah-ɨni → no:la-ni**	[no:.ɾa.ni]

Regular stems, such as *coh* **coh** 'be good', follow the normal **h** weakening, as discussed in 7.4.2, as in *coh-uni* **coh-ɨni** [co.(h)ɨ.ni] 'as (it) is good' and *coh-umyen* **coh-ɨmjǝn** [co.(h)ɨ.mjǝn] 'if (it) is good'.

Rule E   Aspirated stop reduction

In casual speech, aspirated bilabial and velar stops are optionally reduced to their corresponding lax stops, as in (54a). Aspirated alveo-dental and palatal stops tend to be reduced to the alveo-dental lax fricative **s**, as in (54b).

(54)	a.	*i nuph ey*	'in this swamp'	**i nɨph-e**	[i.nɨ.phe; i.nɨ.be]
		pwuekh i	'kitchen' (sub.)	**puǝkh-i**	[pu.ǝ.khi; pu.ǝ.gi]
		pwuekh ey	'in the kitchen'	**puǝkh-e**	[pu.ǝ.khe; pu.ǝ.ge]
	b.	*soth ey*	'in the kettle'	**soth-e**	[so.the; so.se]
		phath ulo	'with red beans'	**phath-ɨlo**	[pha.thɨ.ɾo; pha.sɨ.ɾo]
		pyeth i	'sunshine' (sub.)	**pjǝth-i**	[pjǝ.chi; pjǝ.ʃi]

There are, however, many words which resist the above reduction, i.e., *aph ulo* **aph-ɨlo** [a.phɨ.ɾo] (not *[a.bɨ.ɾo]) 'to the front' and *kyeth ey* **kjǝth-e** [kjǝ.the] (not *[kjǝ.se]) 'by the side'.

Incidentally, the **th-to-s** conversion is obligatory in multi-syllabic loan words with a final aspirated *t* [th]. Such loan words are spelled with a final **s** in Hankul because the original aspirated *t* in a loan word behaves like **s** in Korean pronunciation. Thus, for instance, English *racket* inflects as *lakheys* **lakhes** [ɾakhet], *lakheys i* **lakhes-i** [ɾa.khe.ʃi] (subject), *lakheys ul* **lakhes-ɨl** [ɾa.khe.sɨl] (object), *lakheys ulo* **lakhes-ɨlo** [ɾa.khe.sɨ.ɾo] 'with a racket', *lakheys to* **lakhes-to** [ɾa.khe(t).t'o] 'also a racket', *lakheys un* **lakhes-ɨn** [ɾa.khe.sɨn] 'as for a racket', etc. The shift from aspirated *t* [th] to **s** in loan words is not a synchronic rule internal to Korean, but rather a convention for nativizing loan words.

Rule F   ɨ deletion

The vowel ɨ, which is the least sonorant among the Korean vowels, is deleted when it comes into contact with another vowel in a neighbouring morpheme or occurs between certain consonants. As will be seen in Rule G, this vowel is frequently epenthesized in loan words, to maintain the Korean syllable structure. The vulnerability of ɨ is comparable to that of **l** and **h** in consonants.

A morpheme-initial ɨ, which is retained after a consonant, is omitted after another vowel that ends the preceding morpheme, as illustrated in (55). This non-occurrence or deletion of ɨ after a vowel is viewed as due to its relative weakness in the neighborhood of a more sonorous vowel.

(55)   a. *cip ulo*   'to a house'   **cip-ɨlo**   [ci.bɨ.ɾo]
              cha lo   'to the car'   **cha-ɨlo** → **cha-lo**   [cha.ɾo]

         b. *ilk-usi-nta*   '(He) reads.'   **ilk-ɨsi-n-ta**   [il.gɨ.ʃin.da]
              po-si-nta   '(He) sees.'   **po-ɨsi-n-ta** → **po-si-n-ta** [po.ʃin.da]

         c. *mek-umyen*   'if (he) eats'   **mək-ɨmjən**   [mə.gɨ.mjən]
              ka-myen   'if (he) goes'   **ka-ɨmjən** → **ka-mjən**   [ka.mjən]

         d. *mek-ul kes*   'thing to eat'   **mək-ɨl kəs**   [mə.gɨl.k'ət]
              po-l kes   'thing to see' **po-ɨl kəs** → **po-l kəs**   [pol.k'ət]

The vowel ɨ is not deleted after an s-irregular verb stem, whose final **s** is deleted before the ɨ. Thus, for instance, ɨ remains in *ci-umyen* **ci-ɨmjən** [ci.ɨ.mjən] (from **ci:s-ɨmjən**) 'if (he) builds' and *ce-unikka* **cə:-ɨnik'a** [cə.ɨ.ni.k'a] (from **cə:s-ɨnik'a**) 'because (he) stirs'.

The liquid **l** behaves like a vowel in ɨ deletion. Thus, a morpheme-initial ɨ is deleted after **l**, as shown in *mal lo* **mal-ɨlo** → **mal-lo** [mal.lo] 'in words' and *pil-myen* **pi:l-ɨmjən** → **pi:l-mjən** [pi:l.mjən] 'if (he) prays'. However, the **l** derived from **t** in t-irregular verb stems does not behave like a vowel in ɨ deletion. Thus, *tul-umyen*

tɨt-ɨmjən 'if (he) hears' is realized as **tɨl-ɨmjən** [tɨ.ɾɨ.mjən] and not as *__tɨl-mjən__ [tɨl.mjən]. The irregular verb stem *mut* **mut** 'ask' also behaves this way. A stem-final **ɨ** is deleted if it is followed by a vowel that begins a suffix.

(56)   a. *kipputa* 'be happy'   **kip'ɨ-ta**   [ki.p'ɨ.da]

             kipp-ese 'as (he) is happy' **kip'ɨ-əsə → kip'-əsə** [ki.p'ə.sə]

        b. *khu-ko* 'is big and'   **khɨ-ko**   [khɨ.go]

             kh-essta 'was big, grew'   **khɨ-əs'-ta → kh-əs'-ta** [khə(t).t'a]

             khiwuta 'make (it) grow' **khɨ-iu-ta → kh-iu-ta**   [khi.u.da]

        c. *camkuta* 'lock'   **camkɨ-ta**   [cam.gɨ.da]

             camkita 'be locked'   **camkɨ-i-ta → camk-i-ta** [cam.gi.da]

In passive formation as in (56c), monosyllabic stems such as *ssu* **s'ɨ** 'use, write, wear' and *thu* **thɨ** 'open, break' lose **ɨ** only optionally when they occur before a passive suffix -i, as in *ssu-ita* **s'ɨ-i-ta** [s'ɨ.i.da; s'i:.da] and *thu-ita* **thɨ-i-ta** [thɨ.i.da; thi:.da].

In s-irregular verb stems, as stated above, **ɨ** is normally not deleted even if the **ɨ** preceding the deleted **s** meets with another vowel. Thus, *ku-ela* **kɨ:-əla** [kɨ.ə.ɾa] (from **kɨ:s-əla**) 'Draw (a line)!' does not further contract to **k-ə:la** in formal speech. Only in casual speech does it optionally become [kə:.ɾa]. Furthermore, **ɨ** remains when the morphemes involved are nouns. This is particularly noticeable in Sino-Korean words, as in *kium* **kɨ+ɨm** [ki.ɨm] 'aspirated sound', but also occurs in native and loan constructions, such as *ku eykey* **kɨ-eke** [kɨ.e.ge] 'to him'; and *ingkhu ey* **iŋkhɨ-e** [iŋ.khɨ.e] 'in the ink'.

Within a morpheme, **ɨ** may optionally be replaced by a lengthening of the preceding vowel in casual speech, as in *maum* **maɨm** [ma.ɨm; ma:m] 'mind' and *maul* **maɨl** [ma.ɨl; ma:l] 'village'. To this type may belong such s-irregular constructions as *ku-essta* **kɨ:-əs'-ta** 'drew (a line)' which is realized as either [kɨ.ə(t). t'a] or [kə:(t).t'a] in casual speech.

Rule G   ɨ/i insertion in loan words

When foreign words are introduced into the Korean lexicon as loan words, the Korean sound pattern including the canonical syllable structure (CGVC) forces the high vowel **ɨ** or **i** to be inserted in the foreign words to break consonant clusters or, especially in the word-final position, to keep unwanted Korean sound alternation rules from applying. In general, only when a foreign word is restructured following the Korean sound pattern is it considered a loan word. Insertion of such a vowel is regarded, therefore, as a device to create new morphophonemic loan-word forms from foreign words, rather than as a phonological process that produces phonetic forms from morphophonemic forms. Other devices include changing foreign sounds to available Korean sounds, as in English *valve* to *paylpu* **pɛlpɨ** [pɛl.bɨ], English *feet* to *phithu* **phithɨ** [phi.thɨ], and English *design* to *ticain* **ticain** [ti.ʒa.in].

The structural pressure of the Korean sound pattern requires the vowel ɨ to be inserted in various places, as in (57a), except after a palatal consonant in which case the vowel i occurs, as in (57b).

(57)   a. *aisukulim*   'ice cream'   **aisɨ+kɨlim**   [a.i.sɨ.kɨ.ɾim]
             khulisumasu   'Christmas'   **khɨlisɨmasɨ**   [khɨ.ɾi.sɨ.ma.sɨ]
             suthulaikhu   'strike'   **sɨthɨlaikhɨ**   [sɨ.thɨ.ɾa.i.khɨ]
             tulaipu   'drive'   **tɨlaipɨ**   [tɨ.ɾa.i.bɨ]

         b. *lenchi*   'lunch'   **lənchi**   [ɾən.chi]
             oleynci   'orange'   **olenci**   [o.ɾen.ʒi]
             sapothaci   'sabotage'   **sapothaci**   [sa.bo.tha.ʒi]
             suphenci   'sponge'   **sɨphənci**   [sɨ.phən.ʒi]

In loan words like *suphochu* **sɨpho:chɨ** [sɨ.pho.chɨ] 'sports' and *syechu* **sjəchɨ** [ʃə.chɨ] 'shirt(s)', the vowel ɨ is epenthesized after the palatal **ch** because the original consonants are dental [ts].

Rule H   Compensatory l doubling

As a result of the deletion of the stem-final *u* ɨ before a vowel, the stems that end in lɨ have the now morpheme-final l doubled before ə/a in verbal suffixes, as illustrated in (58b). This l doubling may be regarded as compensatory for the loss of the ɨ vowel. Examples of such stems are *caluta* 'cut', *huluta* 'flow', *kaluta* 'part', *kiluta* 'raise, grow', *maluta* 'dry', *moluta* 'be unaware', *naluta* 'carry', *nwuluta* 'press', *paluta* 'paste', and *ppaluta* 'be fast'.

(58)   a. *malu-n-ta*   'dries'   **malɨ-n-ta**   [ma.ɾɨn.da]
             malu-na   'dries but'   **malɨ-na**   [ma.ɾɨ.na

         b. *mall-ass-ta*   'dried'   **malɨ-əss-ta** → **mall-ass-ta**   [mal.la(t).t'a]
             mall-a.yo   'dries'   **malɨ-əjo** → **mall-ajo**   [mal.la.jo]
             mall-ase   'dry so'   **malɨ-əsə** → **mall-asə**   [mal.la.sə]

One exception to this regularity is the stem *chilu* **chilɨ** 'pay', which loses **ɨ** but does not undergo **l** doubling, as in **chil-ela** [chi.ɾə.ɾa] 'Pay!' (not *chill-ela [chil.lə.ɾa]).

Rule I   Vowel shortening

A long vowel in the stem-final syllable of a verb stem becomes shortened before a vowel in the immediately following suffix, as shown in (59a), and before a causative or passive suffix, as shown in (59b).

(59)   a.   *mel-ese*   'as (it) is far'   **me:l-ese → mel-ese**   [me.ɾə.se]

kwulm-e 'by starving'   **ku:lm-e → kulm-e**   [kul.me]

ce-uni 'as (he) stirs'   **cə:s-ɨni → cə:-ɨni → cə-ɨni**   [cə.ɨ.ni]

tewi 'heat'   **tə:p-i → tə:w-i → təw-i**   [tə.wi]

kel-uni 'as (he) walks'   **kə:t-ɨni → kə:l-ɨni → kəl-ɨni**   [kə.ɾɨ.ni]

b.   *cwulita*   'reduce'   **cu:l-i-ta → cul-i-ta**   [cu.ɾi.da]

kellita 'walk (him)'   **kə:l-li-ta → kəl-li-ta**   [kəl.li.da]

allita 'inform'   **a:l-li-ta → al-li-ta**   [al.li.da]

millita 'be pushed'   **mi:l-li-ta → mil-li-ta**   [mil.li.da]

kamkita 'be wound'   **ka:m-ki-ta → kam-ki-ta**   [kam.gi.da]

Another type of vowel shortening is the simplification of two adjacent vowels. This shortening occurs when a stem-final vowel such as **a**, **ɛ**, **ə**, or **e** is followed by the vowel **a** or **ə** that begins a verbal suffix, as in (60).

(60)   *ka-ss-ta*   'went'   **ka-as'-ta → ka-s'-ta**   [ka(t).t'a]

ponay-la 'Send (it)!'   **ponɛ-ela → ponɛ-la**   [po.nɛ.ɾa]

se-se 'by standing'   **sə-əsə → s-əsə**   [sə.sə]

pey-la 'Cut it!'   **pe:-ela → pe:-la**   [pe:.ɾa]

Rule J   Glide formation

Verbal stems with the stem-final syllable of the **C + i**, **o**, **u** type undergo glide formation when immediately followed by a suffix beginning with **ə/a**. Some glide formations are optional as in (61a) while others are obligatory as in (61b).

(61)   a.   *ki-ela*   'Crawl!'   **ki-əla**   [ki.ə.ɾa; kjə:.ɾa]

noh-a.yo 'puts down'   **noh-ajo → no-ajo**   [no.a.jo; nwa:.jo]

po-a.yo	'sees'	**po-ajo**	[po.a.jo; pwa:jo]
cwu-ese	'by giving'	**cu-əsə**	[cu.ə.sə; cwə:.sə]
pu-e.yo	'pours'	**pu-əjo**	[pu.ə.jo; pwə:.jo]

b. *cy-ess-ta* 'lost in game' **ci-əs'-ta → cj-əs'-ta** [cə(t).t'a]
   iky-ela 'Win!' **iki-əla → ikj-əla** [i.gjə.ɾa]
   w-ass-ta 'came' **o-as'-ta → w-as'-ta** [wa(t).t'a]

Glide formation manifests various degrees of fossilization as observed above. It does not occur when the boundary between the stem-final syllable and the following element is not a suffixal boundary. Thus, *uahata* 'be elegant' is **u+a+ha-ta** [u.a.ha.da] and not *[wa:.ha.da]. For glide formation from the copula *i* , see Rule M below.

Rule K   Umlaut

Umlaut in Korean is a type of word-level assimilation in which a vowel is fronted when followed by the high front vowel **i**. As observed in (62), both umlauted and regular forms may be used, although in casual speech preference is for umlauted forms.

(62)   *aki/ayki*   'child'   **aki**   [a.gi]   →   **ɛki**   [ɛ.gi]
        cami/caymi   'interest'   **cami**   [ca.mi]   →   **cɛmi**   [cɛ.mi]
        emi/eymi   'mother'   **əmi**   [ə.mi]   →   **emi**   [e.mi]
        naki/nayki   'person'   **naki**   [na.gi]   →   **nɛki**   [nɛ.gi]
        nampi/naympi   'kettle'   **nampi**   [nam.bi]→   **nɛmpi**   [nɛm.bi]

Umlaut is more widespread in southern dialects such as the Kyengsang and Cenla dialects than in standard speech. For instance, **mek-i-ta** (standard: **mək-i-ta**) 'feed', **paŋmeŋi** (standard: **paŋmaŋi**) 'bat', **peli-ta** (standard: **pəli-ta**) 'spoil, throw away', **poceki** (standard: **pocaki**) 'wrapping cloth', **soneki** (standard: **sonaki**) '(sudden) shower', **son-cep-i** (standard: **son-cap-i**) 'handle', and **teli-ta** (standard: **tali-ta**) 'iron' are obligatory forms in these dialects, while in Seoul they are acceptable only in casual speech.

Umlaut does not occur (i) between two roots nor between a prefix and a root, (ii) when a geminate consonant (e.g., **kk**) intervenes between a vowel and the umlaut-causing **i,** (iii) when the vowel preceding **i** is inherently long, and (iv) when the intervening consonant is coronal (i.e., palatal or alveo-dental) (cf. S.H. Shin 1997). Thus, for instance, **kalaŋ+pi** (small-rain) 'drizzle', **salaŋ-i-ta** '(it) is love', **mak-ki** 'blocking', **kwa:-hi** 'overly', **al-li-ta** 'inform', **tachi-ta** 'get hurt', **əməni** 'mother', and **masi-ta** 'drink' do not undergo umlaut. Umlaut tends to occur in a root if the following suffix is the nominalizer -*i* or passive/causative -*(h)i*, but not if the suffix is not one of these. Thus, for instance, **son+cap-i** (hand-hold-NOM) 'handle' may be umlauted as **son-cɛp-i** [son.ɟɛ.bi] and **cap-hi-ta** as **cɛp-hi-ta** [cɛ.phi.da] 'be caught'.

Rule L   Initial consonant deletion

Korean has many nominal particles and verbal suffixes that have two forms, whose occurrence is conditioned by phonological environments. One form of a particle or a suffix begins with a consonant and the other without that consonant. This has been observed in connection with ɨ deletion where ɨ is deleted after a stem ending in a vowel, as in *cip ulo* **cip-ɨlo** 'to the house' vs. *cha lo* **cha-lo** 'to the car' and *coh-un* **coh-ɨn** 'good' vs. *ki-n* **ki-n** 'long'. As in the case of ɨ deletion, the initial consonant in certain morphemes is deleted after a vowel, as shown in (63a). In certain other morphemes, the consonant is deleted after a consonant, as in (63b). The morphemes in question include the comitative particle *(k)wa* 'and, with', the blunt level sentence ender -*(s)o*, the addressee honorific suffix -*(su)p*, the topic-contrast particle *(n)un*, and the accusative particle *(l)ul*. In the addressee honorific suffix -*(su)p* -**(sɨ)p**, the vowel ɨ also gets deleted, due to the ɨ deletion discussed under Rule F.

(63)	a.	*salang kwa*	'love and'	**salaŋ-kwa**	[sa.ɾaŋ.gwa]
		chinkwu wa	'friend and'	**chinku-wa**	[chin.gu.wa]
		mek-so	'(He) eats.'	**mək-so**	[mək-s'o]
		ca-o	'(He) sleeps.'	**ca-o**	[ca-o]
		mek-sup-nita	'(He) eats.'	**mək-sɨp-ni-ta**	[mək.s'ɨm.ni.da]
		ka-p-nita	'(He) goes.'	**ka-p-ni-ta**	[kam.ni.da]
	b.	*kay nun*	'as for a dog'	**kɛ:-nɨn**	[kɛ:.nɨn]
		cip un	'as for a house'	**cip-ɨn**	[ci.bɨn]
		kay lul	'dog (object)'	**kɛ:-lɨl**	[kɛ:.ɾɨl]
		cip ul	'house (object)'	**cip-ɨl**	[ci.bɨl]

The alternation in the subject (or nominative case) particle *ka*/*i* manifests a pattern somewhat similar to (63b), although it is not a case of initial consonant deletion in one and the same morpheme: *cha ka* **cha-ka** 'car (subject)' vs. *san i* **san-i** 'mountain (subject)'.

Rule M   Copula **i** reduction

The copula *i* 'be' is reduced to ZERO between V and C, changes obligatorily to the glide **j** between V and V, and remains unchanged between C and C.

(64)   a. *Mia ta*   'is Mia'   **mia-ita → mia-ta**   [mi.a.da]
             cha ta   'is a car'   **cha-ita → cha-ta**   [cha.da]

         b. *ku y-ess-ta*   'was him'   **kɨ-i-əs'-ta → kɨ-jəs'-ta**   [kɨ.jə(t).t'a]
             cha y-eyyo   'is a car'   **cha-i-əjo → cha-je-jo**   [cha.je.jo]

         c. *pheyn i-ta*   'is a pen'   **phen-i-ta**   [phe.ni.da]
             pul i-ess-ta 'was fire'   **pul-i-əs'-ta →** pul-i-jəs'-ta   [pu.ɾi.jə(t).t'a]

7.5   Rhythmic patterns

7.5.1   *Length, stress, pitch*

As already mentioned in 7.2.2, there is phonemic vowel length in the speech of older Koreans that differentiates lexical items, as in *say* sɛ 'new' vs. *say* sɛː 'bird', *pal* **pal** 'foot' vs. *pal* **paːl** 'screen', *pay* pɛ 'pear' vs. *pay* pɛː 'double', *swul* **sul** 'wine' vs. *swul* **suːl** 'tassel', and *kol* **kol** 'marrow' vs. *kol* **koːl** 'valley'.

In addition, vowels (sometimes even consonants) may be lengthened for emphatic or connotative purposes. While a lexical long vowel is usually twice the length of a simple vowel, emphatic or connotative length is usually longer and varies depending on the speaker's emotional intensity, and thus may be represented as ꞉꞉. For emphatic purposes, length is attached to the first syllable of a word to be emphasized, even to an already long vowel.

(65)   a. *ceki*   **cə-ki**   [cə.gi]   'over there'
                         cə꞉꞉-ki   [cə꞉꞉.gi]   'way over there'

         b. *kkok*   **k'ok**   [k'ok]   'for sure'
                         k'o꞉꞉k   [k'o꞉꞉k]   'by all means'

         c. *noph-a.yo* **noph-ajo**   [no.pha.jo]   '(It) is high.'
                         no꞉꞉ph-ajo   [no꞉꞉.pha.jo] '(It) is very high!'

Length adds to part or all of an utterance various connotative meanings representing the speaker's delicate feelings or presuppositions (e.g., surprise, apology, humility, and attention-drawing). Connotative length, usually occurring together with certain characteristic pitch levels, occurs on the vowel or nasal or lateral consonant of the last syllable of a major nominal phrase or an utterance. In (66), **t'o::** has an emphatic length, while **-əjo::** has a connotative length, conveying a presupposition such as 'contrary to my expectation'. A recent tendency in conversations is that young females use extra connotative lengthening on phrase-final syllables.

(66)   *ku salam   i   tto   w-ass-e.yo?*
         the person   NM   again   come-PST-POL
         'Are you saying that he came again?! Incredible!'
         (lit. 'Did he come again?')

kɨ salam-i t'o:: w-as'-əjo::?
[kɨ.sa.ɾa.mi.t'o::.wa.s'ə.jo::~]

Lexical stress is not significant in Korean, because it does not contribute to meaning differentiation. Feeble as it may be, non-phonemic stress normally occurs on the first syllable of an intonational phrase, especially when that syllable ends in a consonant, as in **hakca-nɨn** [hak.c'a.nɨn] 'as for scholars'. The initial syllable is known as the locus of intonational prominence in Korean (H.S. Koo 1986). Thus, phonemic long vowels, which are allowed only in phrase-initial syllables, receive stress. If the phrase-initial syllable ends in a simple vowel and the second syllable has an onset (e.g., CV(C)), the second syllable tends to receive stress, as in **onɨl-to** [o.nɨl.do] 'today also'. On the other hand, a speaker may put stress on any word which he thinks is relatively important or needs to be emphasized or focused. Except for these occurrences, stress is distributed more or less evenly.

Significant lexical pitches (or tones) existed in Middle Korean. These were musical tones accompanying vowels in words in an utterance, but they have since disappeared, except in the Kyengsang and Hamkyeng dialects (see 4.2.1 and 7.5.3). Thus, Contemporary Korean pitches in all other dialects and standard speech are related to the intonation contours of utterances, and not to lexical items.

7.5.2   *Intonation contours*

Intonation (the chain of pitches in an utterance) plays an essential role in expressing a speaker's emotions and attitudes as well as intended sentence types. In Korean standard speech, distinctive pitches are associated essentially with the intonation of utterances, and not with lexical items. Four distinct pitch levels may be recognized, ignoring minor variations in each level: 1 (low), 2 (mid), 3 (high), and 4 (highest).

These four pitch levels are distributed over various intonation (or pitch) contours (which are also called speech melodies), each of which overlays a phrase stretching between two pauses. The most important pause is the terminal one, because the contour before this pause not only determines the sentence type, but also shows the speaker's modality toward the utterance and/or the hearer. Also the speaker may or may not insert one or more non-terminal pauses after certain phrases within an utterance, and different contours can occur before these non-terminal pauses, resulting in shades of meaning.

A phrase with an intonation contour is called an intonational phrase, which is enclosed by #. . .# in the examples below. A sentence may have one or more intonational phrases. For instance, the sentence in (67) has three intonational phrases when uttered at a normal speed.

(67)   *ecey   hakkyo ey an   ka-ss-e.*
         yesterday school to not go-PST-INT
         '(I) didn't go to school yesterday.'

         əce hakk'jo-e an ka-s'-ə:
         [#ə.ɟe#ha.k'jo.e#an.ga.s'ə:#]
          2 3 2   23 2 2   31

Each intonational phrase has one most prominent syllable called the nucleus, and it is in this syllable that a major pitch level change occurs. This is the final syllable of each intonational phrase. Notice in the three intonational phrases in (67) that the pitch level changes in phrase-final syllables.

The three most frequently used types of intonation contours are #2—2.3#, #2—2.31#, and #2—2.4# where 2—2 indicates one or more 2 levels and . a syllable boundary appearing immediately before the nucleus. The #2—2.3# contour is typically associated with non-final intonational phrases, while the other two types are for utterance-final phrases. As illustrated in the declarative sentence in (67), the #2—2.31# contour typically occurs in the last intonational phrases of all sentence types (declaratives, interrogatives formed with a question word, imperatives, propositives, vocatives, etc.) except for interrogatives not formed with a question word. This pattern also includes words, phrases, or names uttered in isolation. For instance, (68a) is an interrogative formed with a question word and (68b) an imperative sentence.

(68)   a. *eti   ka-sey-yo?*
            where   go-SH-POL
            'Where are (you) going?'

əti ka-se-jo:
[#ə.di.ga.se.jo:#]
2 2 2 2 31

b. *kuman   nol-ko   kongpuhay-la.*
that much play-and   study-IM
'Quit playing and study!'

kɨman nol-ko koŋpuhɛ-la
[#kɨ.man.nol.go#koŋ.bu.hɛ.ɾa#]
  2 2 2 3 2 2 2 31

If a phonological phrase consists of only one syllable, so-called kinetic tones such as #23#, #32#, #24#, or #231# occur on that syllable. In [#nan#] in (69), #23# is either concentrated on the vowel [a] alone or stretched over [an] with #3# falling on [n]. A kinetic tone such as #31# occurs on the last syllable of an utterance.

(69)   *nan   mom   i   aph-a!*
           I-TC body NM sick-INT
           'I am sick.'

nan mom-i aph-a
[#nan# mo.mi.a.pha#]
 23   2 2 2 31

The #2—2.4# pattern is characteristic of yes/no questions. Rhetorical and echo questions also follow this pattern.

(70)   a. *ecey   hakkyo ey   an   ka-ss-e?*
              yesterday school to   not go-PST-INT
              'Didn't (you) go to school yesterday?'

əce hakk'jo-e an ka-s'-ə
[#ə.ɟe#ha.k'jo.e#an.ga.s'ə#]
 2 3 2 2 3 2 2 4

b. *hay ka   seccok   eyse   ttu-keyss-ni?*
   sun NM west   from rise-may-Q
   'Do you think the sun rises in the west? (No way!)'

hɛ-ka səc'ok-esə t'ɨ-kes'-ni
[#hɛ.ga#sə.c'o.ge.sə.t'ɨ.geɲ.ɲi#]
　2　3　2　2　2　2　2　2　　4

c. *Pak-sensayng-nim　　i　　　tol-a-ka-sy-ess-ta-ko?*
　　Park-teacher-HT　　NM　　pass away-SH-PST-DC-QT
　　'(Are you saying) that Professor Park passed away?'

pak-sənsɛŋ-nim-i tolaka-sj-əs'-ta-ko
[#pak.sən.sɛŋ.ni.mi#to.ɾa.ga.ʃə(t).t'a.go#]
　2　　2　　2　　2　3　2　2　2　2　　2　4

The three basic intonation patterns are subject to modifications, depending not only on the speaker's insertion or deletion of non-terminal pauses but also on his instillation of emphasis, contrast, emotion, conjecture, or presupposition (cf. S. Park 1991; H.M. Sohn 1994).

7.5.3　　Tones in the Kyengsang dialect

Lexical tones, which do not exist in standard speech, occur in the Kyengsang and Hamkyeng dialects as a reflex of Middle Korean, a tonal language. The Hamkyeng dialect has lexical tones due to the massive migration of speakers of the Kyengsang dialect to that province during the early Cosen dynasty period (in the fifteenth century). Studies on the tones of Kyengsang and/or Hamkyeng dialects, sometimes in comparison with Middle Korean include Y.M. Kim 1966, 1972; Y.C. Jeong 1968, 1985; C.K. Kim 1970, 1973; Hashimoto 1973; W.J. Kim 1973; Ramsey 1975; S.O. Lee 1978; W. Huh 1985; G. Kim 1988; Y.H. Chung 1991; and N.J. Kim 1994, 1996.

According to Huh (1985), three tonal levels exist in the South Kyengsang dialect: low (L), mid (M), and high (H). Huh proposes that tonological units consist either of a noun optionally followed by one or more particles, or of a verbal stem followed by one or more suffixes. Huh further indicates that nouns tend to have fixed tones while tones of verbs and adjectives generally fluctuate depending on their cooccurring suffixes, and that there are no changes of more than one step in the tones of adjacent syllables, rendering HL and LH unacceptable. The phonemic status of tones is attested to in the following minimal trios.

(71)　　　　　　H　　　　　　M　　　　　　L
　　　　ki　　ki 'flag'　　ki 'ear, air'　　ki 'crab'
　　　　mal　mal 'horse'　mal 'measuring unit'　mal 'word'

| pay | pɛ 'pear' | pɛ 'ship, belly, cloth' | pɛ 'double' |
| *son* | **son** 'guest' | **son** 'hand' | **son** 'loss, grandson' |

As Huh and others point out, while older generation speakers of the Seoul and some other dialects are sensitive to the length of vowels, Kyengsang and other tone dialect (e.g., Hamkyeng) speakers are more sensitive to tones than to vowel length. For related discussions on dialectal variations, see chapter 4 (4.2.1 prosodemes: tones and vowel length).

Tones in the Kyengsang dialect occur on all vowels. Some monosyllabic examples of nouns are: *cip* [cip] (H) 'house', *kkoch* [k'ot] (H) 'flower', *mok* [mok] (H) 'neck', *kkwum* [k'um] (M) 'dream', *khal* [khal] (M) 'knife', *cil* [cil] (M) 'road', *tol* [tol] (L) 'stone', *say* [sɛ] (L) 'bird', and *ton* [ton] (L) 'money'. Bisyllabic nouns are of four tonal types and trisyllabic nouns are of five tonal types., as illustrated in (72) and (73), respectively.

(72)
	MH	*cimseng*	'beast'	**cimseŋ**	[cim.seŋ]
	HM	*atel*	'son'	**atəl**	[a.dəl]
	HH	*eymi*	'mother'	**emi**	[e.mi]
	LM	*salam*	'person	**salam**	[sa.ɾam]

(73)
	MHM	*kkamakwu*	'crow'	**k'amaku**	[k'a.ma.gu]
	HMM	*meyneli*	'daughter-in-law'	**menəli**	[me.nə.ɾi]
	HHH	*haleypi*	'gradfather'	**halepi**	[ha.ɾe.bi]
	LMM	*kwumpingi*	'white grub'	**kumpiŋi**	[kum.bi.ŋi]
	MHH	*seytali*	'ladder'	**setali**	[se.da.ɾi]

Tones alternate in some nouns due to the immediately following particles or verbals. For instance, certain M-toned monosyllabic nouns, such as *cil* 'road', *nac* 'daytime', and *nwun* 'eye', change their M to H when followed by an M-tone initial particle, such as *ey* 'at, to', *eyto* 'also at, to', or *eyse* 'at, on, in'. Other M-toned monosyllabic nouns, such as *mul* 'water', *pul* 'fire', *ttey* 'time', and *pha* 'scallion', do not undergo this alternation even in the same environment. Another example is that the M-tone of monosyllabic nouns shifts to H, and the H-tone to M, before the particles *cocha* 'even', *kkaci* 'until', *puthe* 'from', and *manen* 'only', or before verbs that form compounds with such nouns. For instance, *cho* means 'vinegar' with an H-tone and 'candle' with an M-tone. When they are followed by the verb *santa* (HM) 'buys', the tones reverse, as in *cho-santa* (MHM) 'buys vinegar' and *cho-santa* (HHM) 'buys a candle'.

The tones of predicate stems are of several types depending on the kind of suffixes with which they occur. For instance, the tones of the stems *cap* 'catch', *swum* 'hide', and *wus* 'laugh' fluctuate differently in relation to the following suffixes.

(74)   a. *cap-ca* (HM)   'Let's catch (it).'
             cap-nen-ta (MHM)   'catches (it)'

         b. *swum-ca* (MM)   'Let's hide.'
             swum-nen-ta (HHM)   'hides'

         c. *wus-ca* (LM)   'Let's laugh.'
             wus-nen-ta (LMM)   'laughs'

For a detailed classification of tonal types of predicates, see Huh ibid.

8

Word structure

This chapter discusses how Korean words are classified into significant lexical-functional categories (word classes); how words are formed via derivation, compounding, abbreviation, and grammaticalization; and how words inflect for various syntactic and semantic functions. Typically agglutinative, the morphological structure of Korean words has been investigated extensively and productively by Korean linguists, from both synchronic and diachronic perspectives. Selected works are included in the appended bibliography. This chapter serves as a basis for the discussion of grammatical phenomena in chapter 9.

8.1   Word categories

8.1.1   Classification

The Korean lexicon becomes richer, due not only to extensive borrowings but also to productive coinages of new words through derivational processes such as affixation, compounding, abbreviation, and contraction. In addition, Korean predicates (verbs and adjectives) conjugate productively by means of a wide variety of inflectional suffixes.

In order to examine the word structure and word-formational processes in Korean, it is essential to determine what kinds of significant lexical-functional categories of words are to be recognized. Linguists disagree on this issue. H.P. Choy (1971) proposes ten categories, North Korean grammar books eight, and some others more or less. For instance, Choy (ibid.:198) establishes ten categories based on form, function, and meaning: noun, pronoun, numeral, verb, adjective, copula, determiner, adverb, interjection, and particle. To Choy's scheme, W. Huh (1984:193) adds the category of conjunctor which includes fossilized compounds such as *kuliko* 'and', *kulena* 'but', and *kulemulo* 'therefore', which are assigned to the category of adverb in Choy. On the other hand, North Korean grammars (e.g., Kwahak.wen 1960) establish eight categories: noun, numeral, pronoun, verb, adjective, article, adverb, and interjection. In H.M. Sohn (1994), seven categories are proposed: noun, pronoun, verb, adjective, determiner, adverb, and particle. It is common practice among Korean linguists and lexicographers to set up an independent numeral category, and so in this volume, the following eight categories and their subcategories are established based on morphosyntactic and semantic properties.

(1) a. NOUN: Proper, Counter, Defective, Verbal, Adjectival, Common
     b. PRONOUN: Personal, Reflexive, Reciprocal, Interrogative-Indefinite, Demonstrative
     c. NUMERAL: Native, Sino-Korean, Loan
     d. VERB: Main/Auxiliary, Transitive/Intransitive
     e. ADJECTIVE: Copula, Existential, Sensory, Descriptive
     f. DETERMINER: Demonstrative, Qualifier, Quantifier
     g. ADVERB: Negative, Attributive, Modal, Conjunctive, Discoursal
     h. PARTICLE: Case, Delimiter, Conjunctive

In this volume, the term nominal is used to encompass noun, pronoun, and numeral and the term predicate to encompass verb and adjective in view of their shared grammatical properties.

8.1.2   *Nouns*

Nouns may follow determiners and precede particles in a sentence. They can also be modified by a preceding genitive or a relative clause. The noun category contains the largest number of members, encompassing a majority of the native vocabulary and most Sino-Korean (SK) and loan words. SK and loan words, except for a small number of adverbs (e.g., SK *cem-cem* 'gradually', loan (Japanese) *ippai* 'fully'), are nouns in Korean regardless of the word categories they belong to in the source languages. For instance, SK *mincwu-cwuuy-cek* 'being democratic', SK *ye-hayng* 'travel', SK *hayngpok* 'happiness', loan *khaphi* 'making copies', loan *khawunthu* 'counting', loan *apeykhu* (from French *avec* 'with') 'dating', and loan *thephu* 'being tough' all function as nouns in Korean.

Nouns may be subclassified into proper nouns, (numeral) counters, defective nouns, verbal nouns, adjectival nouns, and common nouns. Proper nouns include names of persons, places, books, institutions, countries, continents, and other objects of unique reference, e.g., *I Swunsin* 'I Swunsin', *Hankwuk* 'Korea', *Chwunhyang-cen* 'Chwunhyang Legend', *Pulkwuk-sa* 'Pulkwuk Temple', *Han-kang* 'Han River', *Phal-phal-ollimphik* (8-8-Olympic) '1988 Seoul Olympic', and *Sewul* 'Seoul'. Noteworthy is a fact that, in casual speech, children's consonant-final given names such as *Milan* and *Tongsik* are followed by the vowel *i* before a particle other than a vocative, as in *Milan.i ka* 'Milan' (nominative), *Tonsik.i nun* 'as for Tongsik', *Milan.i eykey* 'to Milan', *Tongsik.i lo puthe* 'from Tongsik'. This vowel does not occur when the given name is followed by a title suffix or a vocative particle, as in *Milan-ssi* 'Miss Milan' and *Milan a* 'Milan!' It does not occur after a foreign name, as in *Con un* 'as for John' but not **Con.i nun*.

Numeral counters, which occur after a numeral, have classificatory or measurement functions (see 5.2; 5.4). They consist of native, SK, and a few loan words, which are by and large complementary: e.g., native *mali* (animals), *chay* (houses), *calwu* (long slender objects), and *khyelley* (pairs of shoes, stockings, gloves); SK *myeng* (people), *kwen* (book volumes), *kay* (items), *tong* (buildings), and *cang* (flat objects such as sheets of paper); and loan *tasu* 'dozen' (pencils) and *kulaym* 'gramme'. Counters are usually used as bound nouns, either preceded by a numeral or followed by some other element, as in *twu mali* 'two animals', *tases kwen* 'five volumes', *yel tasu* 'ten dozens' (pencils), *mali swu* 'number of animals', and *kwen tang* 'per volume'. Nouns like *salam* 'person', *pyeng* 'bottle', and *kap* 'case' are used as both common nouns and counters. For instance, *salam* 'person' is a common noun in *salam i manh-ta* 'there are many people' and a counter in *han salam* 'one person'. A numeral followed by a counter may be called a numeral compound, in which the numeral functions as a determiner (see 8.1.4; 9.7.3).

Korean, especially the native stock, abounds in defective nouns, i.e., bound nouns which do not occur without being preceded by a demonstrative, a clause, or another noun. Defective nouns include *ccok* 'direction', *ccum* 'approximation', *cek* 'time, experience, occasion', *cuum* 'occasion, time', *chay* 'intact, as it is', *chek* 'false show, pretence', *cwul* 'assumed fact, probability, method', *i* 'person', *ka/kka/ci* 'whether, if, assumed fact', *kes* 'fact, thing, event', *kim* 'chance, occasion', *kos* 'place', *li* 'reason', *mal* 'the end', *man* 'size, extent, worth', *mankhum* 'as much as, much', *mulyep* 'around the time when', *nalum* 'dependence, style', *nawi* 'necessity', *nyekh* 'toward', *nolus* 'role, the verge', *pa* 'way, method, point', *ppen* 'the verge, coming near', *ppun* 'alone, only', *pun* 'person', *seng* 'appearance, impression', *seym* 'thinking, plan', *swu* 'way', *tey* 'place, feature', *thek* 'reason, degree', *tongan* 'during', *ttalum* 'nothing but', *ttaymun* 'reason, because of', *tul* 'etc.', *tung* 'etc.', and *tus* 'likelihood'. Many of these defective nouns are functionally limited. For instance, while *ccok* and *kes* can be preceded by a demonstrative, a clause, or a noun and function as all cases, *cwul* is preceded only by a clause and occurs only as an object of a cognitive verb (e.g., *alta* 'know', *moluta* 'do not know'); *swu* can be preceded only by a clause and occurs only as a subject of an existential predicate (*issta* 'exist', *epsta* 'do not exist'); and *ttaymun* 'reason' occurs only with a preceding nominal and never as the subject of a sentence.

In the following sentence, defective nouns are bold-faced.

(2)   *ku-i nun kenkang **ttaymun** ey o-l   **swu** eps-ul   **kes** i-ta.*
       he TC health   reason   for come-PRS way lack-PRS fact be-DC
       'He will be unable to come due to his health.'

Verbal nouns denote activity and, combined with a native verb such as *hata* 'do, make' or *toyta* 'become, get', they become either transitive or intransitive verbs depending on the nature of the activities they denote and the cooccurring native verb. Examples of transitive verbs are native *salang-hanta* (love-do) 'loves' and *seym-hanta* (counting-do) 'counts'; SK *kongpu-hanta* (study-do) 'studies' and *kwukyeng-hanta* (sightseeing-do) 'sightsees'; and loan *puliphing-hanta* (briefing-do) 'briefs' and *nothu-hanta* (taking notes-do) 'takes notes'. Examples of intransitive verbs are native *ssilum-hanta* (wrestling-do) 'wrestles' and *cilal-hanta* (epileptic fit-do) 'goes crazy'; SK *mang-hanta* (perishing-do) 'perishes' and *kunmu-hanta* (working-do) 'works'; and loan *teyithu-hanta* (dating-do) 'dates' and *alupaithu-hanta* (work-do) '(student) works on a part-time basis'.

Adjectival nouns indicate stativity. They can combine with a native adjective such as *hata* 'be (in the state of)' or *(i)ta* 'be' (copula). Examples of native nouns (mostly bound) include *cilwu-hata* (boredom-be) 'is boring', *ttak-hata* (pity-be) 'is pitiful', *ttattus-hata* (warmth-be) 'is warm', and *kattuk-ita* (fullness-be) 'is full'. SK adjectival nouns (free except single-syllable words which are bound) include *hayngpok-hata* (happiness-be) 'is happy', *yak-hata* (weakness-be) 'is weak', *philyo-hata* (necessity-be) 'is necessary', *yelsim-ita* (diligence-be) 'is diligent', *tahayng-ita* (much luck-be) 'is lucky', *choyko-ta* (best-be) 'is the best', *kyelsek-ita* (absence-be) 'is absent', and *kwahak-cek-ita* (being scientific-be) 'is scientific'. Examples of loan words are *ceynthul-hata* 'is gentle', *haynsem-hata* 'is handsome', *sumathu-hata* 'is smart', *theykhunikal-hata* 'is technical', and *ippai-ta* (fully-be) 'is full'.

The common noun subclass is a waste basket, so to speak, to which all the other types of nouns may be assigned. Many subsets can be distinguished according to semantic features such as [+/–concrete], [+/–countable], [+/–animate], [+/–human], [+/–locational], and [+/–compound]. Suffice it here to give some examples to illustrate the diversity of this catch-all subclass: *aitie* 'idea', *alay* 'the bottom', *aykyo* 'charms', *cangkwun* 'general', *cellumpal-i* 'lame person', *cengpu* 'government', *chayk* 'book', *haksayng* 'student', *halapeci* 'grandfather', *hay* 'sun', *ilum* 'name', *kang-ka* 'riverside', *kay* 'dog', *mincwu-cwuuy* 'democracy', *molay* 'sand', *mul* 'water', *nam-nye-no-so* (male-female-old-young) 'people of all ages', *namu* 'tree', *nwun* 'eye', *onul* 'today', *ppalkang* 'red', *ppang* 'bread', *san* 'mountain', *salang* love', *uymu* 'duty', and *uy-sik-cwu* 'food, clothing, and shelter'.

8.1.3   *Pronouns*

Pronouns may be subclassified into personal, reflexive, reciprocal, interrogative-indefinite, and demonstrative pronouns. Personal, reflexive, and reciprocal pronouns are given in (3).

(3)		Singular	Plural
First person			
	Plain	*na*	*wuli(-tul)*
	Humble	*ce*	*ce-huy(-tul)*
Second person			
	Plain	*ne*	*ne-huy(-tul)*
	Familiar	*caney*	*caney-tul*
	Intimate	*caki*	*caki-tul*
	Blunt	*tangsin*	*tangsin-tul*
		ku tay (obsolete)	*kutay-tul* (obsolete)
		tayk	*tayk-tul*
	Deferential	*elusin* (rare)	*elusin-tul* (rare)

Third person (*D* stands for a definite demonstrative)

	Singular	Plural
Thing	*D-kes*	*D-kes-tul*
Child	*D-ay*	*D-ay-tul*
Adult-familiar	*D-salam*	*D-salam-tul*
Adult-blunt	*D-i*	*D-i-tul*
Adult-polite	*D-pun*	*D-pun-tul*

Reflexive pronouns 'self'

	Singular	Plural
Plain	*ce(-casin)*	*ce(-casin)-tul*
Neutral	*caki(-casin)*	*caki(-casin)-tul*
Deferential	*tangsin(-casin)*	*tangsin(-casin)-tul*

Reciprocal pronouns   *selo* 'each other, one another'
phicha 'each other, both sides'
sangho (*hosang* in N. Korea)
'mutual(ity), reciprocal(ity)'

Notice that the personal and reflexive pronouns reflect relative social hierarchy between the speaker and the addressee or third-person referent. However, no deferential second-person pronoun is currently used except the rare form *elusin* which refers exclusively to a respected male of over sixty years of age. As a result, reference terms such as *apeci* 'father', *sensayng-nim* 'teacher', and *sacang-nim* 'company president' are employed as pronominal subsitutes, as in *apeci nun an ka-sey-yo?* 'Aren't you going, father?' Notice further that the derivational suffix *-huy* (plurality) occurs only with plain form *ne* 'you' and humble form *ce* 'I' and can be followed redundantly by the plural suffix *-tul*.

Also notice that several SK words are used as pronouns: *tangsin* (that-body) 'you, self', *caki* (self-body) 'you, self', *tayk* (respected house) 'you', *phicha* (that-this) 'each other', and *sangho* (mutual-together) 'mutual(ity)'. The SK *tangsin* and *caki* are used as both second-person pronouns and reflexive pronouns. In particular, *caki* as a second person is a recent innovation used to one's spouse or girl- or boyfriend. Thus, *caki-tul* as a second person usually refers to 'you (spouse, girl- or boyfriend) and your friends'. Reciprocal pronouns are also used as adverbs.

Interrogative-indefinite pronouns such as *nwukwu* (*nwu* before the nominative particle *ka*) 'who, someone', *amu* 'anyone', *mues* 'what, something', *eti* 'where, somewhere', *encey* 'when, some time', *elma* 'how much, some amount', and the compounds *enu-ay/salam/pun* 'who, someone' are all native words. Demonstratives are used as pronouns in phrases like *i hwu* 'after this', *ku ilay* 'since that (time)', and *ce kath-i* 'like that'. The compounds *yeki* (< *i* 'this' + *eki* 'place') 'here', *keki* (< *ku* 'that (near you)' + *eki*) 'there (near you)', and *ceki* (< *ce* 'that over there' + *eki*) 'over there' are locational demonstrative pronouns.

8.1.4   Numerals

Numerals are from the native, SK, and English loan stocks, as in the native–SK–loan trios *hana/il/wen* '1', *twul/i/thwu* '2', *yel/sip/theyn* '10'. Loan words are rarely used for numerals over ten, hence only the native–SK pairs are available as in *yel-twul/sip-i* '12' and *ahun-twul/kwu-sip-i* '92'. Both the native and SK numerals are based on the decimal system. As indicated in 5.2, in Contemporary Korean, numbers 100 and above are not available in native words, but only in SK, as in *payk* '100', *i-chen* '2,000', *i-payk-man* (2-100-10000) '2 million', and *i-ek* '200 million'. In colloquial speech, native numerals can follow SK digits of 100 and above, as in SK *payk-kwu-sip-i* (formal) vs. SK–native *payk-ahun-twul* (informal) '192'.

Bare numerals are used for enumeration, as in *yeses/yuk kop-ha-ki seys/sam* '6 x 3' and *hana, twul, seys, neys, . . .* 'one, two, three, four, . . .'. In counting items, a native or SK numeral is usually followed by a counter, as in native *yel myeng*, SK *sip myeng* '10 people' and native *selun mali*, SK *sam-sip mali* '30 animals', where *myeng* and *mali* are counters (see 5.2, 5.3, and 8.1.2 for counters). When followed by a counter, five native numerals *hana* '1', *twul* '2', *seys* '3', *neys* '4', and *sumul* '20' are contracted to *han, twu, sey, ney,* and *sumu,* respectively, as in *han/twu/sey/ney/sumu kwen* '1/2/3/4/20 volume(s)'. In writing, Arabic numerals are commonly used, as in 1999 *nyen* (pronounced as *chen-kwu-payk-kwu-sip-kwu nyen*) 'the year 1999' and *12 si* (pronounced usually as *yel-twu si*) 'twelve o'clock'.

8.1.5 Verbs

Predicates (verbs and adjectives) are different from all other categories in that they must inflect. Unlike in English, an adjective inflects in the same way as a verb without the help of a copula, as in *tew-ess-ta* 'was hot' (adjective) and *mek-ess-ta* 'ate' (verb). As will be seen shortly, however, there are morphological, syntactic, and semantic differences to warrant two separate categories – verbs and adjectives (cf. 9.2.2).

The category of verbs, the second largest in terms of members, may be subclassified broadly as in (4) (see 9.2.3 for further subclassification).

(4)   a. Main verbs: i. transitive   ii. intransitive
        b. Auxiliary verbs: i. transitive   ii. intransitive

Verbs are either main or auxiliary, the former being by far the majority. A verb which may occur alone is a main verb, while a verb which requires a preceding verb is an auxiliary verb. Examples are: (ai) main transitive *mekta* 'eat', *pista* 'comb', and *alta* 'know'; (aii) main intransitive *tallita* 'run', *nolta* 'play', and *palcen-hata* 'develop'; (bi) auxiliary transitive *pelita* 'finish up' (e.g., *mek-e pelita* 'finish eating') and *cwuta* 'do (something) for (someone)' (e.g., *tow-a cwuta* 'help someone'); and (bii) auxiliary intransitive *nata* 'come from' (e.g., *thay-e nata* 'be born'), *cita* 'become' (e.g., *phul-e cita* 'get to be untied'), and *poita* 'appear, look' (e.g., *coh-a poita* 'look good').

Verbs may also be subclassified variously depending on their syntactic behaviour (cf. chapter 9). One such classification may be: locomotive (e.g., *kata* 'go', *ota* 'come'), processive (e.g., *nata* 'happen', *tulta* 'enter'), inchoative (e.g., *toyta* 'become', *cita* 'get, become'), cognitive (e.g., *sayngkak-hata* 'think', *mitta* 'believe', *alta* 'know'), emotive (e.g., *coha-hata* 'like', *sulphe-hata* 'feel sad'), causative (e.g., *mek-ita* 'feed'), passive (e.g., *mek-hita* 'be eaten'), and common (e.g., *cata* 'sleep', *nolta* 'play', *cwukta* 'die', *mekta* 'eat', *ilkta* 'read', *ttaylita* 'hit').

8.1.6 Adjectives

Adjectives denote stativity. There are a few morphosyntactic criteria by which an adjective can be distinguished from a verb, the most clear-cut one being to test what non-past indicative form the stem in question takes. If the stem takes the suffix -*nun* (after a stem ending in a consonant) or -*n* (after a stem ending in a vowel), it is a verb. If the stem has a ZERO non-past indicative form, it is an adjective.

(5)   Verbs   Adjectives

        *mek-**nun**-ta*   'eats'   *musep-ta*   'is scary'

        *talli-**n**-ta*   'runs'   *sulphu-ta*   '(I am) sad'

From this test, the copula *ita* 'be' is an adjective. Words like *issta* 'stay, exist', *hata* 'do, be', *khuta* 'grow, be tall', *kamsahata* 'thank, be thankful', *kyeysita* 'stay' (honorific), and *palkta* 'become bright, be bright' are both verbs and adjectives, as in *iss-nun-ta* 'is staying' vs. *iss-ta* 'stays, exists', *ha-n-ta* 'does' vs. *ha-ta* 'is (in the state of)' (e.g., *kongpu-ha-n-ta* 'studies' vs. *hayngpok-ha-ta* 'is happy'), *khu-n-ta* 'grows' vs. *khu-ta* 'is big', *kamsaha-n-ta* 'thanks' vs. *kamsaha-ta* 'is thankful', *kyeysi-n-ta* 'is staying' vs. *kyeysi-ta* 'stays', and *palk-nun-ta* 'gets bright' vs. *palk-ta* 'is bright'.

Adjectives may be classified into the copula (*ita* 'be', *anita* 'not be'), existential (e.g., *issta* 'exist, stay, have', *epsta* 'not exist, not stay, lack'), sensory (e.g., *sulputa* 'be sad', *pulepta* 'be envious', *tepta* 'be hot'), and descriptive (e.g., *ppalkahta* 'be red', *celmta* 'be young', *kenkang-hata* 'be healthy'), as will be discussed in 9.2.4.

8.1.7   Determiners

Determiners may also be termed pre-nouns or unconjugated adjectives, in that they do not inflect and they modify nouns in a pre-noun position. This small class may be subclassified as in (6). Although qualifiers and quantifiers have less determinative property than demonstratives, they are grouped together in view of their similar syntactic behaviour.

(6)   a. Demonstrative: definite, indefinite

        b. Qualifier

        c. Quantifier

Demonstratives show a four-way distinction: definite *i* 'this', *ku* 'that (close to hearer or known to both speaker and hearer)', and *ce* 'that over there', and indefinite *enu* 'which, any, a certain', as in *i salam* 'this person', *ku chayk* 'that book (near you); the book (we are talking about)', *ce cha* 'that car over there', and *enu nal* 'which day, one certain day'. Demonstratives are used very frequently and go into a wide variety of compounds. They are also used as demonstrative pronouns, as mentioned in 8.1.3.

Qualifiers are those pre-noun words which qualitatively modify the head noun, as in *say* 'new' in *say cha* 'a new car'. Other examples are *hen* 'used', *hyen* 'current', *musun* 'what kind of, some kind of', *talun* 'another', *olun* 'right-hand side of', *oyn* 'left-hand side of', *pyel-pyel* 'all kinds of', *ttan* 'different', *weyn* 'what manner/sort of, some manner/sort of', *yenu* 'ordinary', *etten* 'what kind of, some kind of', *yeys* 'old', and *yo-kkacis* 'this much of'.

Quantifiers modify the head noun quantitatively, as in *may* 'every' in *may hakki* 'every semester'. Other examples are *cen* 'whole', *ches* 'first', *cho* 'beginning', *kak* 'each', *kun* 'approximately', *motun* 'all, every', *myech* 'how many, several', *on* 'entire, full', *yak* 'approximately', *yele* 'many', and *yenam.un* 'some ten odd, a dozen'. All numerals that occur before a numeral counter behave as quantifiers, as in *han kwen* 'one (book, notebook)'. Thus, numerals are (quantifier) determiners when used as part of a numeral compound.

8.1.8   *Adverbs*

Adverbs modify a verb, an adjective, another adverb, a clause, or a nominal phrase in terms of negation, time, place, manner, degree, modality, conjunction, or discoursal purposes. An adverb must always occur before the element it modifies in a sentence or discourse. Adverbs in Korean may be grouped into the following heterogeneous subclasses.

(7)   a. Negative
          b. Attributive: time, place, manner, degree
          c. Modal
          d. Conjunctive
          e. Discoursal

The class of negative adverbs is very small, the typical members being the native words *an(i)* 'not' and *mos* 'not possibly, cannot, unable'.

Attributive (or property) adverbs constitute the largest class. They modify an attribute or property of the action or state of a predicate in terms of time, place, manner, or degree. Typical time adverbs include *acik* 'still, yet', *akka* 'a while ago', *camsi* 'for a while', *cha-cha* 'by and by', *cuksi* 'immediately', *hangsang* 'always', *imi* 'already', *ittaka* 'after a while', *kot* 'soon', *pangkum* 'just now', *pelsse* 'already', *nul* 'always', *pilose* 'for the first time', and *yeng-yeng* 'forever'. Place adverbs form a small class, including *ili* 'this way', *kuli* 'that way' (towards hearer's direction), *celi* 'that way over there', *cel(i)lo* 'towards that direction', *eti* 'where, somewhere', *kakkai* 'near', *koskos.i* 'everywhere', *melli* 'far way', and *yeki* 'here'. Notice that some of these words such as *eti* and *yeki* are pronouns as well as adverbs. Manner adverbs constitute a large class, which includes *cal* 'well', *ese* 'quickly', *himkkes* 'with all one's might', *khukey* 'large', *kiph.i* 'deeply', *kulek-celek* 'somehow', *noph.i* 'highly', *kkok* 'surely', *manhi* 'a lot', *phyenhi* 'comfortably', *ppalli* 'fast', and *pyello* '(not) particularly'. Several thousands of onomatopoeic adverbs (phonomimes and phenomimes) are manner adverbs (e.g., *ttayng-ttayng* 'clangingly', *swul-swul* 'smoothly'), as observed in chapter 5 (5.3). Degree adverbs include *acwu* 'very', *cemcem* 'gradually', *cikuk.hi* 'extremely', *cokum* 'a little', *hwelssin* 'by far', *kacang* 'the most', *keuy* 'almost', *kuli* '(not) so much', *maywu* 'very', *phek* 'very', *taytan.hi* 'very', *tewuk* 'all the more', *yak.kan* 'slightly', and *yekan* '(not) ordinarily'.

Modal adverbs refer to the speaker's modality, while usually taking a sentence as their domain of modification. Sometimes, the one and the same adverb can be both attributive and modal. For instance, *palo* is a time adverb in the sense of 'immediately', a manner adverb in the sense of 'straightly, directly', and a modal adverb in the sense of 'rightly, the very'. Some frequently used modal adverbs include *ama* 'perhaps', *cengmal* 'indeed', *ceypal* 'please', *hoksi* 'by any chance', *kwa.yen* 'truly', *man.il* 'if', *mullon* 'of course', *pilok* 'although', *puti* 'by all means', *sasilsang* 'in fact', *selma* 'on no account', *tahaynghi* 'fortunately', and *totaychey* 'in the world'.

Conjunctive adverbs include *cuk* 'that is', *hamulmye* 'much more, much less', *hok.un* 'or', *kolo* 'therefore', *kulayse* 'therefore', *kulena* 'but', *kulentey* 'by the way', *kuliko* 'and', *kulehciman* 'however', *ohilye* 'rather', *tekwuna* 'moreover', *tolie* 'rather', and *ttalase* 'accordingly'.

Finally, discoursal adverbs are so termed not only because they occur outside the boundary of a sentence but also because they are conditioned by discourse contexts or speech situations. They usually occur alone, or precede a sentence, as in a yes/no response, a term of address, or an interjection. Adverbs of yes/no response include *onya* 'yes' (plain), *kulem* 'certainly' (intimate), *ung* 'yes' (intimate), *yey/ney* 'yes' (polite), *ani(y)o* 'no' (polite), and *kulay-yo* 'that's right' (polite). Adverbs of address include *ya* (plain), *yey* (plain), *ipwa* (intimate), *yepokey* (familiar), *yepo*, *yeposio* (blunt), *yeposeyyo* (polite), and *yeposipsio* (deferential) 'hello', and many nouns used for addressing, such as *appa* 'daddy!' and *papo-ya* 'idiot!'. Adverbs of interjection, which denote speaker's sensation, emotion, or wish, include *aiko* 'oh!', *ani* 'good heavens!', *ca* 'well!', *celen* 'o my!', *ceykilal* 'shucks!, damn it!', *emena* 'oh my!', and *ikhu* 'gosh!'. For an extensive syntactic discussion of adverbs, see 9.12.

8.1.9   Particles

Particles are postpositional function words that either indicate the syntactic relation of the cooccurring element with other constituents of the sentence, delimit the meaning of the element to which they are attached, or perform some other function such as plurality, conjunction, quotation, or politeness. As postpositions, particles follow a nominal (noun, pronoun, or numeral), a nominal phrase or nominalized clause, an adverb or adverbialized clause, or a sentence.

There are some phonological grounds for particles to be equated with suffixes. No phonological word boundary exists before a particle but only an affixal boundary, as observed in *os* [ot] 'clothes' vs. *os i* [o.si] 'clothes (subject)', where *i* is a nominative case particle. Notice that *s* in *os* is not changed to [t] before the particle *i*, unlike the case in *os an* [o.tan] 'inside of the clothes' where *s* is changed to [t] before the word boundary. Indeed, the class of particles borders between a word category and a suffixal category in its phonological and morphosyntactic behaviour. However, we will follow tradition and give particles a separate word category status. One syntactic reason in favour of treating them as words is that they occur not only after a nominal but also after a verb, an adverb, a clause, or even a full-fledged sentence. In *cwuk-nu-nya sa-nu-nya **ka** muncey ta* 'To die or live is the problem', *tul-e o-sey-yo **tul*** 'Come in, you all', and *pi o-n-ta **ko** malhay-ss-ta* 'He said it was raining', the nominative particle *ka*, the plural particle *tul*, and the quotative particle *ko* occur after a sentence.

Korean particles may be grouped into three types: (i) case particles, which mark the syntactic relation of a nominal element with its coocurring predicate or with another nominal (as in genitive or connective constructions) or the discourse relation of a nominal element (denoting the addressee) with a main sentence (as in vocative constructions); (ii) delimiters, which delimit the meanings of the cooccurring elements; and (iii) conjunctive particles, which conjoin two or more clauses. These three types are illustrated in the sentence in (8).

(8) *apeci **ka** ne   **hako** na   **man** nol-la   **ko**   ha-si-ess-e.*
      father NM you   and   I   only play-IM   QT   say-SH-PST-INF
        (i)   (i)   (ii)   (iii)
      'Father said that only you and I can play.'

Case particles are of the kinds given in (9). Of the slashed pair, the form before the slash occurs after a vowel, and the one following the slash, after a consonant. (AN) stands for animates only, (IN) for inanimates only, and (hon.) for honorific.

(9) Nominative: *ka/i, kkeyse* (AN, hon.; functions only as subject)
     Accusative: *lul/ul*
     Genitive: *uy* 'of, 's'
     Dative: *ey* (IN), *eykey* (AN), *hanthey* (AN), *kkey* (AN, hon.) 'to'
     Goal: *ey* (IN), *eykey* (AN), *hanthey* (AN), *kkey* (AN,

	hon.) 'to'; *tele* (AN), *poko* (AN) '(tell, ask) to'
Locative-static:	*ey* (IN), *eykey* (AN), *hanthey* (AN), *kkey* (AN, hon.) 'on, at, in'
Locative-dynamic:	*eyse* (IN), *eykeyse* (AN), *hantheyse* (AN) 'on, at, in'
Source:	*eyse* (IN), *eykeyse* (AN), *hantheyse* (AN), *kkeyse* (AN, hon.; rarely used) 'from'
Ablative:	*puthe* 'starting from'
Allative (Directional):	*lo/ulo* 'towards'
Instrument:	*lo/ulo(-sse)* 'with'
Capacity:	*lo/ulo(-se)* 'as'
Comitative:	*wa/kwa, hako, lang/ilang* 'with'
Connective:	*ey(ta(ka))* 'in addition to'; *mye/imye, hamye, hako, lang/ilang, wa/kwa* 'and'; *na/ina* 'or'
Comparative:	*pota* 'than'
Equative:	*chelem* 'as, like'; *kathi* 'like'; *mankhum* 'as much as'
Vocative:	*ya/a* (plain), ZERO/*i* (familiar/intimate), *i(si)e* (hyper-deferential)

Notice that identical forms are used for dative, goal, and static locative particles on the one hand, and for dynamic locative and source particles on the other. Allative, instrument, and capacity particles also partially share identical forms. For the syntax of case particles, see 9.3 and 9.5.

Delimiters are attached to a word, a phrase, a clause, or even a sentence. Examples are given in (10). For the syntax of delimiter particles, see 9.6.

(10)	Topic-contrast:	*nun/un* 'as for'
	Inclusion:	*to* 'also, too, indeed'
	Limitation:	*man* 'only, solely'
	Toleration:	*ya/iya* 'only if it be, as only for, finally'
	Concession:	*lato/ilato* 'even, for lack of anything better'
	Inception:	*puthe* 'beginning with'
	Bounds:	*kkaci* 'as far as, even, up to'
	Comprehensiveness:	*mata* 'each, every'
	Addition:	*cocha* 'even, as well'
	Exhaustion:	*mace* 'so far as, even'
	Dissatisfaction:	*nama/inama* 'in spite of'
	Alternative:	*na/ina* 'rather, or something'

Contrariness:	*khenyeng* 'far from, on the contrary'
Exclusiveness:	*pakkey* '(not) except for, other than'
Illustration:	*sekken* 'and so on, and others'
Goal focus:	*ta(ka)* (only in transitive sentences)
Plurality:	*tul* (e.g., *ese o-sey-yo tul* 'Welcome, you all.')
Politeness:	*yo* (e.g., *al-ko-mal-ko yo* 'Of course I know.')
Confirmation:	*kulye* 'indeed, I confirm' (sentence-final)

Conjunctive particles are clause-final, and include *man(un)* 'but' (e.g., *komap-sup-ni-ta man(un) sa.yangha-keyss-e.yo* 'Thank you but I will decline' and *ko* 'that' (quotative). See 9.4.2 and 9.4.6 for relevant syntactic discussions.

8.2   Affixation

8.2.1   *Affixes, stems, and roots*

Words may carry one or more affixes. A typical agglutinative language, Korean has over 600 affixes (prefixes and suffixes). Among the eight word classes presented in 8.1, nouns, verbs, and adjectives participate in affixation most productively. For instance, the adjectival expression *an-nyeng-ha-sey-yo?* 'How are (you)?' is one word consisting of five morphemes: SK *an* 'peace', SK *nyeng* 'safety', native *ha* 'be', native *-sey* (subject honorific), and native *-yo* (polite sentence ender). The two suffixes *-sey* and *-yo* are 'inflectional' suffixes in that they do not contribute to forming a new word but simply indicate the respective grammatical categories. The part *an-nyeng-ha* 'be peaceful' is an adjective stem. Following tradition, the stem of a predicate is defined as that part to which an inflectional suffix is attached. A non-affix part of a predicate which cannot take an inflectional suffix is called a root. The part *an-nyeng* in the stem *an-nyeng-ha* is a compound root which in turn consists of two simple roots *an* and *nyeng*.

Aside from verbs and adjectives, all other word categories do not inflect in principle (see 8.1.4 for the plural suffix), although they may take one or more 'derivational' affixes as will be observed in great detail in subsequent sections. Therefore, the notion of stem is irrelevant to these categories, although the notion of root is still applicable. For instance, single-syllable or multi-syllable free SK nouns like *pang* 'room', *chayk* 'book', *chang* 'window', *hak-kyo* 'school', *en-e* 'language', and *pu-mo* 'parents' are words. However, *hak* 'study' and *kyo* 'house' in *hak-kyo*, *en* 'speech' and *e* 'word' in *en-e*, and *pu* 'father' and *mo* 'mother' in *pu-mo* may be called roots. Similarly, the native adverb *kkaykkus-i* 'cleanly' contains the root *kkaykkus* 'cleanness' and the SK adverb *cuk-si* 'immediately' consists of two roots *cuk* 'immediate' and *si* 'time'.

The stems of all Korean predicates are bound in that they do not occur without one or more clause- or sentence-final inflectional suffixes which are termed a clause or sentence ender. Thus, for instance, the verb stem *ka* 'go' and the adjective stem *coh* 'be good' cannot stand alone. They become free words only with an ender, as in *ka-n-ta* 'goes' (plain level), *ka-myen* 'if (he) goes', *ka-yo* '(he) goes' (polite level), and *ka-p-ni-kka?* 'does (he) go?' (deferential level); and *coh-a.yo* 'is good' (polite level), *coh-ko* 'is good and', and *coh-ni?* 'is (it) good?' (plain level) where the bold-faced elements are enders. Even in citation form (dictionary entry form), bare stems like *ka* 'go' and *coh* 'good' are not used; instead, they must be followed by the citation suffix (ender) *-ta*, as in *kata* and *cohta*.

8.2.2   Derivation and inflection

It is necessary to draw a line between derivation and inflection in the discussion of affixation, although there are some borderline cases. Treated as derivational in this volume, passive and causative suffixes are somewhat on the border between derivation and inflection.

There are several criteria by which one can distinguish derivation from inflection. First, derivational affixes tend to be more meaning-oriented, while inflectional ones are by and large syntax-oriented and their meanings are more functional than lexical. Second, derivational affixes are of 'inner-formation', while inflectional ones are of 'outer-formation', as in [*kkay-ttuli*]*-ess-e.yo* '(He) crushed (it)' where the derivational suffix *-ttuli* (emphatic) is located close to the root *kkay* 'break', hence inside, and the inflectional suffixes *-ess* (past) and *-e.yo* (polite) are distant from the root, hence outside. Third, derivational affixes coin new words, while inflectional ones do not contribute to word formation. Fourth, derivational affixes can occur only with specific roots, while inflectional ones are lexically free in combination, occurring widely with all the words belonging to a certain word class or subclass.

In accordance with these criteria, all prefixes in Korean are derivational while suffixes may be either derivational or inflectional. Prefixes and inflectional suffixes do not change the original word category, whereas many derivational suffixes cause category change, as summarized in (11) where CC stands for category change.

(11)   Affixes   a. Derivational   i. Prefixal [–CC]
                                             ii. Suffixal [+/–CC]
                     b. Inflectional   Suffixal [–CC]

A derivational affix is attached to a simple or compound root. For instance, in the verb stem [*cis-*[*palp*]]*-hi* 'be overrun', the verb root *palp* 'step on' is preceded by the derivational prefix *cis-* 'randomly' and the prefixed root *cis-palp* 'overrun' is followed by the derivational passive suffix *-hi*. Similarly, in the verb stem *pis-[na-ka]* 'go astray', the derivational prefix *pis-* 'aslant' is attached to the compound verb root consisting of *na* 'move out' and *ka* 'go'. In both examples, the verb status is not changed by the affixation (i.e., [–CC]), although in the former case the transitive verb *cis-palpta* 'overrun' is subcategorially changed to an intransitive verb *cis-palp-hita* 'be overrun' due to the attachment of the passive suffix *-hi*. An example of category change is the noun *po-ki* 'example' which is derived from the verb root *po* 'see' and the derivational nominalizer suffix *-ki*.

An inflectional affix is attached to a stem. For instance, in *[cis-palp-hi]-si-ess-ta* '(a respectable person) was stepped on', the inflectional suffixes *-si* (subject honorific), *-ess* (past), and *-ta* (declarative sentence ender) are attached to the verb stem. Notice that the lexical category of the verb has not been affected, hence [–CC].

8.2.3   Native and Sino-Korean affixes

While inflectional suffixes are exclusively native, derivational prefixes and suffixes are from both the native and SK stocks. No loan affixes exist.

One vexing problem in Korean morphology is whether a native or SK bound element is a word or an affix (e.g., Y.G. Ko 1989; Martin 1992; W. Huh 1995; C.S. Kim 1996; K.G. Kim 1996; *Say Kwuk.e Saynghwal* 8.1 (1998); *Hyengthaylon* 1.1 (1999)). For instance, Korean linguists do not agree on whether the native ordinalizer *ccay* '-th' (e.g., *seys-ccay* 'the third') and the native honorific title *nim* 'esteemed' (e.g., *sensayng-nim* 'esteemed teacher') are suffixes or nouns, and whether the native predicate formative *ha(ta)* 'do, be' in *kongpu-hata* 'study', *hayngpok-hata* 'be happy', etc. is a suffix, a root, or a stem (a verb or adjective word). This problem is particularly serious with SK words, which normally consist of two or more morphemes. For instance, SK *min-cwu-cek* 'democratic' consists of a free noun *min-cwu* (people-head) 'democracy' and the bound element *cek* '-ic', while *no-tong-ca* 'labourer' consists of the free noun *no-tong* (toilsome-move) 'labour' and the bound element *ca* 'person'. It is not agreed on whether *cek* and *ca* in these SK words are roots or suffixes. In a majority of recent dictionaries published in Korea, however, all the above questionable elements (i.e., *ccay*, *nim*, *hata*, *cek*, and *ca*) are entered as derivational suffixes. Martin, et al. (1967) and Martin (1992), on the other hand, categorize *ccay* and *nim* as postnouns, *cek* and *ca* as postnouns or Chinese suffixes, and *hata* as a postnominal verb or adjective.

Indeed, numerous affixes have developed from formerly full-fledged words and this kind of grammaticalization process is still going on, making the boundary between word or stem and root and between root and affix quite opaque (see 8.7).

Thus, making some arbitrary decisions based on the semantic, syntactic, and phonological behaviour of the morphemes involved appears inevitable. While considering the native *-ccay* and *-nim* as suffixes is acceptable, treating the native element *ha* following a verbal or adjectival noun as a suffix seems to be premature. If *ha* is to be regarded as a suffix in compounds like *kongpu-hata* 'study' and *hayngpok-hata* 'be happy', how could we account for the insertion of a particle or an adverb before it in constructions like *kongpu man ha-n-ta* 'only studies', *kongpu an ha-n-ta* 'does not study', and *hayngpok to ha-ta* 'is happy too'? In this volume, therefore, *hata* is treated as a verb or adjective root that is compounded with other roots such as the verbal noun *kongpu* and the adjectival noun *hayngpok* (see 8.5.5; 8.5.6). The compounds *kongpu-hata* 'study', *hayngpok-hata*, etc. function as stems. SK *cek* '-ic, characteristics of' and *ca* 'person' may be viewed as either suffixes or roots with impunity. In this volume, both are treated as derivational suffixes.

In general, a native affix occurs with a native root or stem, and rarely with an SK root or stem, and vice versa. There are many exceptions, however, as illustrated in (12) where affixes are bold-faced.

(12)   ***kwun**-umsik* (native 'extra' + SK 'food') 'snack'
        ***amh**-saca* (native 'female' + SK 'lion') 'lioness'
        ***sin**-nayki* (SK 'new' + native 'person') 'new person'
        *sayk-**kkal*** (SK 'colour' + native intensifier) 'colour'
        *kan-kan-**i*** (SK space-space + native adverbializer) 'at times'
        *sa-nyen-**ccay*** (SK '4-year' + native '-th') 'the fourth year'
        *Sewul-**sik*** (native 'Seoul' + SK 'style') 'Seoul style'

8.3   Derivational morphology

There are several hundred derivational affixes, including some 270 prefixes (cf. C.S. Kim 1998; B.G. Ku 1988). Derivational affixes occur mainly in nouns and predicates, providing them with additional lexical meanings. Some prefixes are attached to both nouns and predicates, as in the noun *hes-soli* (false-sound) 'talking nonsense' vs. the verb *hes-titita* (false-step on) 'make a false step' and the noun *tes-sin* (added-shoe) 'overshoes' vs. the verb *tes-sinta* (added-wear) 'wear (something) over one's shoes'.

In addition to affixal derivations, vowel and consonant gradations derive new words, as in sound symbolic words (5.3; 7.4.3). For instance, the demonstratives *i* 'this', *ku* 'that (near you)', and *ce* 'that over there' alternate with *yo*, *ko*, and *co*, respectively, the latter set having diminutive connotation. Similarly, through the alternation between Yang and Yin vowels, many sound symbolic words have been derived with connotational differences. As indicated in 5.3, Yang vowels are generally associated with brightness, sharpness, lightness, etc. and Yin vowels with darkness, heaviness, dullness, etc., as in *phongtang/phungteng* 'with a splash', *say-ha.yahta/si-he.yehta* 'be very white', and *molak-molak/mulek-mulek* 'rapidly (grow)'. Sound symbolic words are also derived by gradation between plain, aspirated, and tensed consonants with connotational differences. In general, plain consonants are associated with slowness, gentleness, and heaviness, aspirated ones with flexibility, elasticity, crispiness, and swiftness, and tense ones with compactness, tightness, hardness, smallness, and extra swiftness, as in *kamahta* vs. *kkamahta* 'be black', *panccak* vs. *ppanccak* 'glitteringly', and *palttak/pelttek* vs. *phalttak/phelttek* vs. *ppalttak/ppelttek* 'suddenly, with a jerk'.

In the following subsections, only affixal derivations of nouns, verbs, adjectives, adverbs, and determiners will be discussed. Pronouns, numerals, and particles are diachronically so fossilized in both form and meaning that it will be of little synchronic use to attempt to analyse them in terms of derivation (see 8.7 for diachronic derivations of certain particles and other words).

8.3.1 Noun derivation

Frequently used prefixes that derive a noun from another noun and relevant examples of the derived nouns are presented in (13). Recall that no prefix changes the lexical category of the source word.

(13)   a. Native Korean prefixes

al- 'naked, tiny, true':	*al-mom* 'naked body'
	al-kaymi 'very small ant'
	al-puca 'truly rich person'
am(h)- 'female (animal)':	*am-nom* 'female animal'
	am-khay 'female dog' (*kay* 'dog')
cham- 'true, real':	*cham-kilum* (true-oil) 'sesame oil'
	cham-mal 'true remark, truth'
es- 'crooked':	*es-kakey* 'slant-roofed stall'
	es-kyel 'cross-grain' (of timber)
han- 'big, peak':	*han-kil* 'main street'
	han-swum (-breath) 'sigh'
hol- 'single':	*hol-api* (-father) 'widower'
	hol-mom (-body) 'unmarried person'
kalang- 'small, dead':	*kalang-iph* 'dead leaf'
	kalang-pi (-rain) 'drizzle'
kwun- 'extra' :	*kwun-sal* 'superfluous flesh'

	kwun-umsik (-food) 'snack'
mat- 'first':	*mat-atul* 'the eldest son'
	mat-mul 'the first cut' (of vegetables)
mayn- 'bare':	*mayn-pal* 'barefoot'
	mayn-pap (-rice) 'boiled rice served without any side dishes'
nal- 'raw':	*nal-koki* 'raw meat'
	nal-kyeylan 'uncooked egg'
nath- 'each, small':	*nath-kaypi* 'each split piece of wood'
	nath-ton 'odd money, small change'
ol- 'early':	*ol-pye* 'early ripening rice plant'
	ol-khong 'early beans'
oy- 'only':	*oy-atul* 'only son'
	oy-kil 'single path'
phus- 'premature':	*phus-salang* 'puppy love'
	pus-kochwu 'unripe red pepper'
pis- 'aslant':	*pis-kum* 'deviant crease'
	pis-cang 'cross bar'
swuh- 'male animal':	*swuh-kay* 'male dog'
	swuh-nom 'male animal'
swus- 'pure, innocent':	*swus-chongkak* 'innocent bachelor'
	swus-salam 'simple person'
tes- 'added':	*tes-sin* 'overshoes'
	tes-mun 'outer door'

b. Sino-Korean prefixes

cen- 'entire':	*cen-seykey* 'the whole world'
cen- 'former':	*cen-sacang* 'former president'
cwung- 'heavy':	*cwung-kongep* 'heavy industry'
cin- 'dark, thick':	*cin-pola* 'dark purple'
ka- 'temporary':	*ka-kenmul* 'temporary building'
kwa- 'excessive':	*kwa-sopi* 'excessive spending'
kwu- 'old':	*kwu-sitay* 'old age'
kyeng- 'light':	*kyeng-kongep* 'light industry'
oy- 'mother's side':	*oy-halmeni* 'maternal grandmother'
phi- 'receiving':	*phi-pohem-ca* 'the insured'
sayng- 'living':	*sayng-ciok* 'living hell'
si- 'husband's family':	*si-emeni* 'mother-in-law'
sin- 'new':	*sin-yeseng* 'modern girl'

ta- 'multi-':   ta-mokcek 'multi-purpose'
tay- 'great':   tay-kacok 'big family'

SK nouns are negated by SK negative prefixes such as pi-, pul-, pu-, mu-, mol-, and mi- that are comparable to English affixes im-, in-, dis-, un-, non-, de-, ir-, -less, etc. Cooccurrence between a negative prefix and a noun is not predictable.

(14)   pi- 'un-, anti-, non-':   pi-kongkay 'not open to the public'
          pul- 'non-, in-, un-, ir-':   pul-kanung 'impossibility'
          pu- 'non-, in-, un-, ir-':   pu-tongsan 'immovable property'
          mu- 'no-, -less, ir-':   mu-chaykim 'irresponsibility'
          mol- 'non-, -less, no':   mol-sangsik 'senselessness'
          mi-'not yet, un-, in-':   mi-wanseng 'incompleteness'

Derivational suffixes deriving a noun from another noun are illustrated in (15).

(15)   a.   Native Korean
               -aci (diminutive):   kang-aci (dog-) 'puppy'
                                            mok-aci 'neck' (derogatory)
               -cang (intensifier):   kkuth-cang (end-) 'the very end'
                                            phal-cang (arm-) 'arms'
               -cayngi 'practitioner':   cem-cayngi 'fortune-teller'
                                            mes-cayngi 'dandy'
               -cil 'activity':   kelley-cil (mop-) 'mopping'
                                            sepang-cil (husband-) 'cuckolding'
               -i 'person':   cellum-pal-i 'cripple'
                                            aykkwu-nwun-i 'one-eyed person'
               -i (endearment; occurs only after a final consonant of a given name):
                                            Alan-i 'Little Alan'
                                            Pktong-i 'Little Poktong'
               -kkal (intensifier):   pich-kkal/sayk-kkal 'colour'
                                            nwun-kkal 'eye' (vulgar)
               -kkwuleki 'overindulger':   cam-kkwuleki 'late riser'
                                            malsseng-kkwuleki 'burden'
               -kkwun 'doer':   il-kkwun 'labourer'
                                            cangsa-kkwun 'merchant'
               -meli (vulgarizer):   cwupyen-meli 'adaptability'
                                            cincel-meli 'disgust'
               -nay 'all the way'   il-nyen-nay 'through the whole year'

	yelum-nay 'all summer'
-ney 'group, family':	*Mia-ney* 'Mia's family'
	puin-ney 'group of wives'
-po 'thing, person':	*maum-po* (mind-) 'temper'
(derogatory)	*thel-po* (hair-) 'hairy person'
-ssi 'mode':	*mal-ssi* (speech-) 'mode of expression'
	nal-ssi (day-) 'weather'
-thwungi 'person, thing':	*cam-thwungi* (sleep-) 'sleepyhead'
	mo-thwungi (angle-) 'corner'
	nwun-thwungi (eye-) 'bags under eyes'

b. Sino-Korean

-ca 'person':	*kwahak-ca* (science-) 'scientist'
-cang 'chief':	*wiwen-cang* 'committee chair'
-cang 'place':	*wuntong-cang* 'athletics field'
-cek '-ic':	*pi-kwahak-cek* 'unscientific(ity)'
-hak 'study':	*en.e-hak* (language-) 'linguistics'
-hwa '-ization':	*pi-kwunsa-hwa* 'demilitarization'
-hoy 'meeting':	*tongchang-hoy* 'alumni association'
-ki 'machine':	*pi-hayng-ki* (fly-go-machine) 'airplane'
-kwu 'exit, mouth':	*pisang-kwu* (unusual-) 'fire exit'
-kyeng 'around':	*sip-sa-il-kyeng* 'around the 14th'
-sa 'person':	*ipal-sa* 'barber'
-sang 'in':	*yeksa-sang* 'in history'
-seng 'nature':	*centhong-seng* 'traditionalism'
-sik 'style, method':	*hankwuk-sik* 'Korean style'
-tay 'age, generation':	*phalsip-nyen-tay* (80-year-) '1980s'
-ye 'excess':	*sam-sip-ye* 'over 30'

Occasionally native (NT) or loan words are followed by an SK suffix, as in *kul-ca* (NT writing-SK letter) 'letter', *mul-ki* (NT water-SK nature) 'moisture', *ssa-cen* (NT rice-SK store) 'rice store', *silh-cung* (NT hate-SK symptom) 'boredom', *ceythu-ki* (jet-SK plane) 'jet plane', *heyl-ki* (heli-SK plane) 'helicopter', *peyici-sayk* (beige-SK colour) 'beige colour'.

Nouns are also derived from verbs or adjectives by native nominalizer suffixes, usually with slightly changed meanings, as illustrated in (16). SK words, however, are not derived in this way. Notice in (16c) that the nominalizers are also attached to clausal constructions where a verb and an argument occur.

(16)   a. Nouns from verbs
            -i 'act, thing':   *mek-i* (eat-) 'animal food'
                                                pel-i (earn-) 'money making, job'
            -(k)ay, key '-er':   *cip-key* (pick up-) 'tweezers'
                                                mak-ay (stop-) 'stopper'
                                                nal-kay (fly-) 'wing'
            -ki 'act, thing':   *po-ki* (see-) 'example'
                                                ppay-ki (subtract-) 'subtraction'
            -po 'thing, person':   *ccay-po* (tear-) 'hare-lipped person'
                                                wul-po (cry-) 'cry-baby'
            -(u)m/-em 'fact, thing':   *chwu-m* 'dance'
                                                cwuk-em (die-) 'corpse, death'
                                                el-um (freeze-) 'ice'
                                                ilu-m (tell-) 'name'

         b. Nouns from adjectives
            -ang/-eng (subject to vowel harmony) 'quality' (in colour terms):
                                                kem-eng 'black'
                                                nol-ang 'yellow'
            -i 'quality':   *chwuw-i* (cold-) 'coldness'
                                                kil-i (long-) 'length'
                                                kh-i (< *khu-i* 'big-') 'stature, height'
            -ki 'quality':   *khu-ki* (big-) 'size'
                                                sey-ki (strong-) 'strength'
            -po 'person':   *yak-po* (shrewd-) 'shrewd person'
            -twungi 'one, guy':   *cilki-twungi* 'tough fellow'
                                                kem-twungi 'black guy'
            -(u)m 'fact, thing':   *kel-um* (fertile-) 'fertilizer'
                                                kippu-m 'happiness'

         c. Nouns from verbal clauses
            -i 'act, thing':   *kwi-kel-i* (ear-hang-) 'earring'
                                                hay-tot-i (sun-rise-) 'sunrise'
                                                path-kal-i (field-plough-) 'ploughing'
                                                kaul-ket-i (autumn-collect-) 'harvest'
            -ki 'act, thing':   *hay-pala-ki* (sun-gaze-) 'sunflower'
                                                swullay-cap-ki (hoodman-catch-) 'tag'

Notice that derivational nominalizers are usually fossilized with their cooccurring stems. However, *-(u)m* and *-ki* are used as both derivational and inflectional suffixes. As inflectional suffixes, they occur with any verb or adjective without change in the original meaning of the stem. There may be a slight formal difference in derivational and inflectional uses in certain forms, as in *el-um* 'ice' (derivation) vs. *e-m* 'freezing' (inflection), *cwuk-em* 'corpse, death' (derivation) vs. *cwuk-um* 'dying' (inflection), and *mut-em* 'grave' (derivation) vs. *mut-um* 'burying' (inflection).

As discussed in chapter 5 (5.3), certain nouns are derived from sound-symbolic adverbs by means of the nominalizer *-i*, as in *kaykwul-i* (croaking-) 'frog', *kkaktwuk-i* (slicing unevenly-) 'radish pickles', *kkwulkkwul-i* (grunting-) 'pig, greedy person', *maym-i* (chirping-) 'locust', *ppicwuk-i* (poutingly-) 'habitually pouting person', and *ttwungttwung-i* (fatty-) 'fat person'.

8.3.2   Verb derivation

Some commonly used verbal prefixes are given in (17). As indicated earlier, no prefix can change word categories. Verbal prefixes have adverbial meaning, in that they modify the meaning of the cooccurring verb roots. Note that SK words do not participate in verbal derivation.

(17)	*ch(y)e-* 'recklessly':	*che-mekta* 'eat greedily'
		chye-nehta (-put in) 'push in'
	cis- 'randomly, hard':	*cis-palpta* (-step) 'overrun'
		cis-ikita (-kneed) 'mesh'
	es- 'crookedly':	*es-kata* 'go awry'
		es-kelta (-hang) 'stack'
	nay- 'outwardly'	*nay-nohta* 'put out'
		nay-tencita 'throw out'
	nuc- 'late':	*nuc-toyta* (-become) 'ripe/grow late'
		nuc-panhata 'belatedly fall in love'
	pi- 'twisted':	*pi-wusta* 'scorn'
		pi-thulta 'contort'
	pis- 'aslant':	*pis-nakata* (-go out) 'go astray'
		pis-seta (-stand) 'stand a bit sidewise'
	sel- 'insufficiently':	*sel-cwukta* (-die) 'be half-alive'
		sel-ikta (-ripe) 'be half-cooked or ripe'
	tes- 'additionally':	*tes-kelta* 'hang (something) on top'
		tes-nata 'grow extra'
	yes- 'stealthily':	*yes-pota* 'spy on'
		yes-tutta 'eavesdrop'

Derivational suffixes which do not change the verb category are illustrated in (18a) and those which do change the category in (18b, c, d).

(18)   a. Verbs from verbs

        -chi (intensifier):   *tat-chita* (close-) 'close'

                                teph-chita (cover-) 'attack'

        -i, -hi, -li, -ki, etc. (causative and passive suffixes):

                                po-ita (see-) 'show, be seen'

                                mek-ita (eat-) 'feed'

                                mek-hita (eat-) 'be eaten'

                                mal-lita (stop-) 'dissuade'

                                math-kita (take charge-) 'entrust'

                                kam-kita (wind-) 'be wound'

        -cilu (intensifier):   *kwuki-ciluta* (wrinkle it-) 'wrinkle up'

        -coli 'gently':   *ulph-colita* 'recite gently'

        -kkali (intensifier):   *noy-kkalita* 'repeat'

        -m (intensifier):   *phu-mta* (dip out-) 'pump'

        -ttul (intensifier):   *ppay-ttulta* (take out-) 'grab'

        -ttuli (intensifier):   *kkay-ttulita* (break-) 'smash'

    b. Verbs from nouns

        -ci 'get characterized by': *kunul-cita* (shade-) 'get shaded'

                                mith-cita (bottom-) 'suffer a loss'

                                swum-cita (breath-) 'die'

        ZERO verbalizer: *payta* (*pay* 'belly') 'conceive'

                                pista (*pis* 'comb') 'comb (hair)'

                                sinta (*sin* 'shoes') 'wear shoes'

                                ttita (*tti* 'belt') 'tie a belt'

    c. Verbs from adjectives

        -i, -hi, -chwu, -iwu, etc. (causative suffixes):

                                noph-ita (high-) 'heighten'

                                cop-hita (narrow-) 'make narrow'

                                nac-chwuta (low-) 'lower'

    d. Verbs from adverbs

        -ci 'get characterized by': *along-cita* 'get mottled'

                                ellwuk-cita 'become stained'

        -i 'be doing':   *kkutek-ita* 'nod'

	pentuk-ita 'shine'
	soksak-ita 'whisper'
-keli 'keep doing':	*cwungel-kelita* 'keep muttering'
	panccak-kelita 'keep twinkling'
-tay 'do repeatedly':	*cwungel-tayta* 'mutter repeatedly'
	ppikek-tayta 'creak repeatedly'

Note that causative and passive suffixes change only the subcategories of verbs from intransitive to transitive in causatives and vice versa in passives. When adjectives are causativized, however, word categories are changed. Both causative and passive suffixes have many phonologically or morphologically conditioned variants. Only a limited number of intransitive and transitive verbs are causativized with a causative suffix, and only a limited number of transitive verbs are passivized with a passive suffix. That is, not all verbs participate in causativization and passivization. Causative and passive suffixes cannot cooccur. These facts suggest that passive suffixes may have developed from causative suffixes by way of functional shift (H.M. Sohn 1996). Causative suffixes include *-y*, *-i*, *-hi*, *-li*, *-ki*, *-khi*, *-(i)wu*, *-chwu*, *-kwu*, and *-ay*.

(19)

Stem		Stem + Causative suffix + *ta*	
na	'come out'	*nayta* (< *na-ita*)	'take out'
mek	'eat'	*mek-ita*	'feed'
cap	'hold'	*cap-hita*	'give as security'
nelp	'be wide'	*nelp-hita*	'widen'
nol	'play'	*nol-lita*	'have (him) play'
wul	'cry'	*wul-lita*	'cause (him) cry'
wus	'laugh'	*wus-kita*	'make (him) laugh'
ha	'do'	*si-khita*	'cause (him) to do'
mil	'push'	*mil-wuta* (push-)	'postpone'
ca	'sleep'	*caywuta* (< *ca-iwuta*)	'make (him) sleep'
ssu	'put on'	*ssiwuta* (< *ssu-iwuta*)	'make (him) put on'
khu	'be big'	*khiwuta* (< *khu-iwuta*)	'enlarge, raise'
nuc	'be late'	*nuc-chwuta*	'delay, loosen'
tot	'rise'	*tot-kwuta*	'raise'
eps	'not exist'	*eps-ayta*	'eliminate'
		(< *eps-i hata* 'make it not exist')	

The causative form of *hata* 'do' is *si-khita*, suggesting a historical connection between *ha-* and *si-* 'do'. There are some unique causative suffixes, as in *kwup-wulita* 'bend' (*kwup* 'be bent'), *al-oyta* 'let (a deferential person) know' (*al* 'know'), *tol-*

ikhita 'turn (something) around' (*tol* 'turn around'), and *il-ukhita* 'raise' (*il* 'rise').

Passive suffixes can be added only to certain transitive verbs. Commonly used variants of the passive suffix are *-i*, *-hi*, *-ki*, and *-li*.

(20)

Stem		Stem + Passive suffix + *ta*	
mukk	'bind'	*mukk-ita*	'be bound'
ssah	'pile'	*ssah-ita*	'be piled'
ket	'lift'	*ket-hita*	'be lifted'
palp	'step on'	*palp-hita*	'be stepped on'
ccoch	'chase'	*ccoch-kita*	'be chased'
ttut	'tear out'	*ttut-kita*	'be torn out'
mil-	'push'	*mil-lita*	'be pushed'
tut	'hear'	*tul-lita*	'be heard'

Due to some overlappings of causative and passive suffix forms, many homonymic words have resulted, as in *po-ita* 'show, be seen', *kkakk-ita* 'make someone trim, be trimmed', *cap-hita* 'cause someone to catch, be caught', *mul-lita* 'cause someone to bite, be bitten', and *an-kita* 'cause someone to hug, throw oneself in someone's arms'. For the syntactic constructions of causative and passive verbs, see 9.9.

8.3.3 Adjective derivation

Adjectives are derived mostly from other adjectives, nouns, and verbs. When they are derived by prefixation, they are necessarily from adjectives because no prefix changes a word category. The prefixes have adverbial meaning.

(21)   *es-* 'obliquely, about': *es-kwuswuhata* (-tasty) 'be rather tasty'
es-pisushata (-similar) 'be similar'
es-pittwulumhata (-crooked) 'be a bit crooked'
ol- 'early, all': *ol-chata* (-filled) 'be substantial, sturdy'
ol-kotta (-straight) 'be upright'
say-/si- 'ideep, vivid': *say-kkamahta/si-kkemehta* 'be deep black'
say-nolahta/si-nwulehta 'be vivid yellow'
tu- 'very': *tu-nophta* (-high) 'be very high'
tu-seyta (-strong) 'be very strong'
yal- 'peevishly': *yal-mipta* (-hateful) 'be mean and nasty'
yal-kwucta (-bad) 'be perverse'

Adjective-deriving suffixes are mostly attached to either other adjectives as in

(22a) and or nouns as in (22b). A few rare suffixes that derive adjectives from verbs are fossilized, as shown in (22c). The forms on both sides of a slash are subject to vowel harmony.

(22)   a. Adjectives from adjectives
                -ah/-eh 'give the impression' (in colour or shape):
                            kkam-ahta/kkem-ehta 'be black'
                            nol-ahta/nwul-ehta 'be yellow'
                            tongkul-ahta/twungkul-ehta 'be round'
                -c(c)ik.ha 'rather, sort of':
                            muk-cik.hata (heavy-) 'be rather heavy'
                            nel-ccik.hata (wide-) 'be rather wide'
                            yal-ccik.hata (thin-) 'be a bit thin'
                -kap/-ep 'give the feeling of':
                            tal-kapta (sweet-) 'be satisfying'
                            muk-epta (heavy-) 'be heavy'
                -talah 'rather, sort of':
                            kil-talahta 'be rather long'
                            kop-talahta 'be rather pretty'
                            noph-talahta 'be rather high'
                -(u)cwukcwukha/-(u)cokcokha '-ish, slightly':
                            pulk-ucwukcwuk.hata (red-) 'be reddish'
                            kkam-ucokcok.hata (black-) 'be blackish'
                -(u)sulumha, -(us)uleyha '-ish, slightly':
                            kanu-sulumhata (thin-) 'be rather thin'
                            pulk-usuleyhata (red-) 'be reddish'

        b. Adjectives from nouns
                -ci 'be characterized by':
                            entek-cita (hill-) 'be hilly'
                            kaps-cita (price-) 'be expensive'
                            kilum-cita (oil-) 'be fertile'
                -kyep 'be full':   *nwunmul-kyepta* (tears-) 'be touching'
                          him-kyepta (strength-) 'be strenuous'
                          hung-kyepta 'be full of fun'
                -lop 'be characterized by':
                          ca.yu-lopta (freedom-) 'be free'
                          hay-lopta (harm-) 'be harmful'
                          hyangki-lopta (aroma-) 'be fragrant'

-*mac* 'give the impression of':

        iksal-macta (humour-) 'be humourous'

        nungcheng-macta (guile-) 'be deceitful'

        pangceng-macta (rashness-) 'be rash'

-*sulep* 'be suggestive of, seeming':

        salang-sulepta (love-) 'be adorable'

        pok-sulepta (blessing-) 'be happy-looking'

        swuta-sulepta (many-) 'be talkative'

-*tap* 'be like, worthy of':

        ceng-tapta (affection-) 'be affectionate'

        hakca-tapta (scholar-) 'be scholarly'

        sanay-tapta (man-) 'be manly'

-*(y)ep* 'be in the state of':

        kwi-yepta (value-) 'be cute'

        no-yepta (anger-) 'be offended'

c. Adjectives from verbs

   -*(e)p*/-*up* 'able, in the state of':

        kuli-pta (long for-) 'be missing'

        nolla-pta (get surprised-) 'be surprising'

        mul-epta (bite-) 'be itchy'

        wus-upta (laugh-) 'be funny'

   -*pu* 'in the state of':

        a-phuta (*alh-* 'sick') 'be sick, painful'

        mip-puta (*mit-* 'trust') 'be trustworthy'

        kotal-phuta (*kotalh-* 'get tired') 'be tired'

8.3.4 *Adverb derivation*

Most adverbs are derived from other adverbs, nouns, verbs, adjectives, or determiners by means of suffixes. Only a few adverbs are derived through prefixation.

(23)   a. Adverbs from adverbs

       -*(h)i* (AD):   *ilccik-i* (early-) 'earlier'

                  katuk-hi (full-) 'fully'

       -*cang* (intensifier): *kot-cang* (directly-/soon-) 'straightaway'

       -*kkum* (intensifier after the adverbializer -*key*):

                  coh-key-kkum (good-AD-) 'to be good'

       -*nay* 'finally':   *machim-nay* (just in time-) 'at last'

b. Adverbs from nouns

-(h)ye (AD; occurs after a monosyllabic adjectival noun root):

> *cen-hye* (SK totality-) 'totally, utterly'
> *hayng-ye* (SK luck-) 'by chance'

-i (AD; occurs after a reduplicated noun):

> *na-nal-i* (days-) 'day by day'
> *nath-nath-i* (units-) 'one by one'
> *sath-sath-i* (crotches-) 'all over'

-kkes 'to the utmost':

> *him-kkes* (force-) 'with all one's might'
> *maum-kkes* (mind-) 'with all devotion'

-nay 'all the way': *kyewu(l)-nay* (winter-) 'all winter'

> *machim-nay* (finishing-) 'finally'

c. Adverbs from native or SK adjectival nouns

-(h)i (AD):   *hwaksil-hi* (SK certainty-) 'surely'

> *sok-hi* (SK speed-) 'quickly'
> *kkaykkus-i* (cleanness-) 'cleanly'

d. Adverbs from adjectives

-i/-li (AD):   *kath-i* (same-) 'like, together'

> *saylo-i* (*saylop* 'new-') 'newly'
> *mel-li* (far-) 'far away'

-key (AD):   *caymi-iss-key* (*interesting-*) 'with fun'

> *ha.yah-key (white-)* 'white'
> *kup.ha-key* (SK hurried-) 'hurriedly'

e. Adverbs from determiners

-li 'direction':   *i-li* 'this way'

> *ce-li* 'that way over there'

-man 'only':   *ku-man* 'to that extent only, that much'

> *i-man* 'to this extent only, this much'

-tholok 'extent':   *i-tholok* 'to this extent' (< *i-li-ha-tolok* 'to the
> extent that it is so')
> *ku-tholok* 'to that extent'

The suffix *-(h)i* is a productive adverbializer (AD), as observed in examples such as *katuk-hi* 'fully', *hwaksil-hi* 'surely', *sok-hi* 'quickly', and *kkaykkus-i* 'cleanly'. It seems that the *h* in *-hi* is a contraction of the adjective root *ha* and the original AD is simply *-i*. Thus, *katuk-hi*, *hwaksil-hi*, *sok-hi*, and *kkaykkus-i* may be analyzed as having developed from *katuk-ha* 'be full' + AD *-i*, *hwaksil-ha* 'be certain' + AD *-i*, *sok-ha* 'be fast' + AD *-i*, and *kkaykkus-ha* 'be clean' + AD *-i*, respectively. In *kkaykkus-i*, *h* is further reduced to ZERO because it is not pronounceable after *s*. In the same vein, *cen-hye* 'totally' may be viewed as having derived from the obsolete *ceh-ha* 'be total' + conjunctive suffix *-ye* 'and so'.

Fossilized suffixes like *-o/-wu* have turned verbs into adverbs, as in *nem-wu* (go over-) 'overly', *tol-o* (turn-) 'back', and *cac-wu* (frequent-) 'frequently'.

8.3.5   Determiner derivation

Some verbs and adjectives have been fossilized into determiners with the relativizer (RL) suffix *-(u)n*. This suffix is basically an inflectional one, but functions as a derivational suffix in the formation of determiners.

(24)	*ol-un*	'right-hand side'	(*olhta* 'be correct')
	oy-n	'left'	(< *oy-i-n* (outside-be-RL))
	kac-un	'all kinds of'	(*kacta* 'be well furnished, have all sorts')
	motu-n	'all'	(*motwuta* 'gather').
	mus-un	'what kind of'	(< *mues-i-n* (what-be-RL))
	wey-n	'what kind of'	(< *way-i-n* (why-be-RL))

8.4   Inflectional morphology

8.4.1   Inflectional categories

The agglutinative nature of Korean is distinctly reflected in its abounding in inflectional suffixes that are attached to predicate stems. Nominal case particles behave like inflectional suffixes, but they are regarded as words in this volume, as they are more word-like than suffix-like. That is, they are frequently omittable, loosely associated with nominals, and can occur after a clause as in [*nwu ka ka-nu-nya*] **ka** *muncey i-ta* 'Who is going, that is the problem' where the bold-faced nominative case particle takes the whole preceding clause as its domain. Thus, case particles will be discussed in the chapter on syntax (9.5).

The only suffix which may be considered inflectional in nouns is the plural *-tul*, although it also functions as a defective noun (e.g., *so, mal, kay, tul* 'cows, horses, dogs, **etc.**'; 8.1.2) and a particle (see below; 8.1.9). As a suffix, as in *haksayng-tul* 'students', it has various inflectional properties. It carries the grammatical meaning of plurality, does not change the word category of the cooccurring noun, does not contribute to word formation, is used productively after nouns and pronouns, and is of 'outer-formation'. For instance, in the noun *nol-um-kkwun-tul* 'gamblers', the verb root *nol* 'play' and the derivational suffix *-um* (nominalizer) form a noun root *nol-um* 'gambling', to which another derivational suffix *-kkwun* 'person' is attached. The suffix *-tul* is attached to the whole noun *nol-um-kkwun*. More examples follow.

(25)   a. Nouns: *kacok-tul* 'family members'
                            kilum-tul 'different kinds of oil'
                            kyoswu-nim-tul (professor-HT-PL) 'professors'

          b. Pronouns: *wuli-tul* (we-PL) 'we' (plain)
                            ce-huy-tul (I-group-PL) 'we' (humble)
                            tangsin-tul 'you' (blunt)

The words belonging to the categories of numerals, determiners, adverbs, and particles do not inflect even in plurality. Although *ku-tul* 'they' consists of the demonstrative determiner and the plural suffix, this *ku* functions as a third person pronoun. Similarly, although the adverb construction *ppalli tul* 'quickly' is acceptable, the plural *tul* in this case is a particle (not a suffix) denoting the plurality of the understood subject, as in *ppalli tul o-sey-yo* 'Please come quickly, you all!'

In verbs and adjectives, on the other hand, there are scores of inflectional suffixes. Inflectional suffixes follow derivational ones in morphological constructions, as in *cap-hi-si-ess-sup-ni-ta* '(a respectable person) was caught', where *cap-hi* 'be caught' is the stem consisting of the transitive verb root *cap-* 'catch' and the passive derivational suffix *-hi*, and the rest are all inflectional suffixes: *-si* (subject honorific SH), *-ess* (past/perfect PST), *-sup* (addressee honorific AH), *-ni* (indicative mood IN), and *-ta* (declarative suffix DC).

As for the inflectional suffixes for verbs and adjectives, it is necessary to distinguish between enders and non-terminal suffixes, in that enders such as sentence enders (e.g., plain interrogative ender *-ni?*, deferential declarative ender *-sup-ni-ta*), conjunctive enders (e.g., *-ko* 'and', *-myense* 'while'), and adnominal (relative clause) enders (e.g., non-past indicative *-nu-n*) occur at the end of a sentence or a clause and must be present in order for a verb or adjective to stand independently. Thus, for instance, the verb stem *mek* 'eat' is never used alone in utterances. It must be followed by an ender, as in *mek-sup-ni-ta*, *mek-nun-ta*, *mek-ko*, *mek-nu-n*, etc. Furthermore, enders take the syntactic role of relating the whole preceding clause either to the main clause (when they occur in subordinate clauses) or to the discourse (when they occur in main clauses).

Non-terminal inflectional suffixes lack these features, being optional in occurrence in positions before the enders. They are, however, distinguished from derivational suffixes in that, like enders, they (i) always follow derivational suffixes, if any, in a predicate construction, (ii) carry grammatical meanings, such as honorific, tense/aspect, and modal, (iii) occur with all types of verbs and adjectives, without changing the word category of the stem, and (iv) do not participate in new word formation. The sequential morphological structure of non-terminal suffixes and enders may be summarized as follows. Optional non-terminal elements occur strictly in the order given, following the stem which may have one or more derivational suffixes.

(26)   (Predicate stem) + Inflectional suffixes

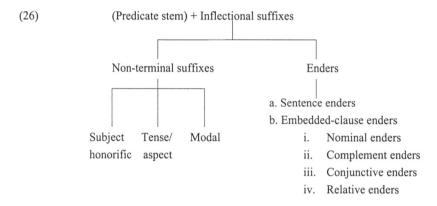

Non-terminal suffixes   Enders

                                                    a. Sentence enders
                                                    b. Embedded-clause enders

Subject   Tense/   Modal   i.   Nominal enders
honorific   aspect   ii.   Complement enders
                                                   iii. Conjunctive enders
                                                   iv.   Relative enders

8.4.2   *Non-terminal suffixes*

The forms of non-terminal inflectional suffixes are as follows.

(27)   a. Subject honorific (SH)   *-si/-sy* (after a vowel)
                                                   -usi/-usy (after a consonant)

          b. Tense/aspect
              past/present perfect (PST):   *-ass* (after a syllable with *a, o*)
                                                -ess (elsewhere)
              past past/past perfect: *-ass-ess* (after a syllable with *a, o*)
                                                -ess-ess (elsewhere)

          c. Modal
              intention or conjecture: *-keyss*
              prospective (PRS):   *-l(i)* (after a vowel)
                                                -ul(i) (after a consonant)

The subject honorific suffix *-(u)si* optionally merges with the vowel *-e* in the polite sentence ender *-e.yo* to become *-(u)sey*, as in *ka-sy-e.yo/ka-sey-yo* '(He) goes.' The tense/aspect forms are subject to vowel harmony, a Yang (bright) vowel occurring with a Yang vowel and a Yin (dark) vowel with a Yin vowel. After *a* or *e* the suffixes are contracted to *-ss*, as in *ka-ss-ta* 'went' and *se-ss-ta* 'stood'. The modal suffix *-(u)li* occurs in a main clause, as in *ka-li-la* 'will go' and *mek-uli-la* 'will eat', while the shortened form *-(u)l* occurs in a relative clause, as in *ka-l salam* 'the person who will go', *mek-ul salam* 'the person who will eat', and *ka-l-nu-n ci* 'whether (he) might go'.

While non-terminal suffixes freely occur in main clauses, there are restrictions on the occurrence of tense/aspect and modal suffixes in embedded clauses. For instance, the past/perfect *-ess/-ass* and the modal *-keyss* cannot occur in various embedded clauses, as in *ka(*-ss)-key* 'so that (he) would go', *ka(*-keyss)-key* 'so that he may go', *ka(*-ss)-ese* 'went and', *ka(*-keyss)-ese* 'may go and', *ka(*-ss)-un* '(someone) who went', and *ka(*-keyss)-un* '(someone) who may go'.

8.4.3   Sentence enders

Sentence (main clause) enders consist of three suffix categories: addressee honorific, mood, and sentence (S)-type. These categories occur in that order, although frequently mood and S-type suffixes have coalesced into single-syllable units, as will be seen shortly. Each category has one or more members, as schematized in (28). In the mood and S-type categories, only the major ones are given. For relevant syntactic discussions, see 9.8.

(28)

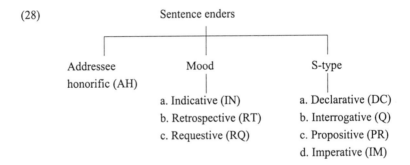

Sentence enders are used in six different speech levels that reflect the speaker's relationship with the addressee: plain (PLN), intimate (INT), familiar (FML), blunt (BLN), polite (POL), and deferential (DEF). For instance, the speaker uses the plain- or intimate-level enders to children, familiar- or intimate-level enders to one's adult students or one's son-in-law, blunt- (rarely) or polite-level enders to one's junior members in a company or to one's spouse, and polite- or deferential-level enders to one's distant adult equals or superiors.

Thus, a sentence ender, consisting of one or more suffixes, denotes not only one of the four sentence (S-) types (e.g., declarative, interrogative) but also one of the six speech levels (e.g., plain, deferential), as well as one of the three moods (e.g., indicative). The most elaborate forms are used for deferential-level enders. For instance, the addressee honorific (AH) suffix appears only in deferential-level utterances. The AH suffix is *-sup* after a consonant and *-p* after a vowel, as in *mek-sup-ni-ta* 'eats' and *ka-p-ni-ta* 'goes'. In blunt-level constructions, however, *-sup* is reduced to *-up* while *-p* remains the same, as in *mek-**up**-si-ta* (not **mek-sup-si-ta*) 'Let's eat' and *ka-**p**-si-ta* 'Let's go.'

The mood category has several subcategories. The indicative suffix (denoting an act or state as an objective fact) occurs only in declarative and interrogative sentences among the four sentence types. It also occurs in embedded clauses, as will be seen in 8.4.4. Its contemporary form is *-ni* in deferential-level constructions as in *ka-p-**ni**-kka?* 'Does (he) go?', *-nun*, (after a consonant) or *-n* (after a vowel) in plain-level verbal declarative sentences as in *mek-**nun**-ta* 'eats' and *ka-**n**-ta* 'goes', *-nu* in plain- and familiar-level verbal interrogative sentences (as well as in relative clauses) as in *ka-**nu**-nya* 'Does (he) go?' and *mek-**nu**-nka(-yo)* 'Does (he) eat?', and ZERO in all polite-level expressions as in *mek-e.yo* 'eats', plain-level adjective constructions as in *coh-ta* 'is good', and predicates with a past/perfect or modal suffix as in *ka-ss-ta* '(He) went' and *ka-keyss-ta* '(He) may go.' Furthermore, the indicative suffix has diachronically merged with the following S-type suffix in the plain-level interrogative ender *-ni* (e.g., *ka-ni?* 'Does (he) go?') and the familiar-level declarative ender *-ney* (e.g., *ka-ney* '(He) goes').

The retrospective mood suffix (denoting an act or state as the speaker's past observation or experience) occurs only in declarative and interrogative sentences. Its contemporary form is *-ti* in the deferential-level expressions as in *ka-p-**ti**-ta* 'went (I observed)' and *-te* in most other cases including the plain-level declarative *ka-te-la*. The retrospective suffix has merged with the following S-type suffix in the plain-level interrogative ender *-ti* (e.g., *ka-ti?* 'Did you see (him) go?') and the familiar-level declarative ender *-tey* (e.g., as *ka-**tey*** 'I saw (him) go').

The requestive mood suffix *-si* occurs only in the blunt-level propositive and the deferential-level propositive and imperative, otherwise ZERO, as in *ka-p-si-ta* 'Let's go' (blunt), *ka(-si)-p-**si**-ta* 'Let's go' (deferential), *ka-si-p-**si**-o* 'Please go' (deferential), and *ka-ca* 'Let's go' (plain). The familiar-level propositive ender *-sey* (e.g., *ka-sey* 'Let's go') incorporates a requestive mood element which may be related to *-si*. The fossilized imperative mood suffix *-ke* appears optionally after certain verbs in plain-level imperative expressions, as in *ka(-ke)-la* 'Go!' and *mek-(k)e-la* 'Eat!', and obligatorily in the familiar-level imperative ender *-key*.

The forms of S-type suffixes are extremely varied, reflecting six different speech levels. Some suffixes have allomorphic alternations (e.g., plain-level declarative *-ta* becomes *-la* in retrospective), while others are merged with mood suffixes. As discussed above, the single-syllable interrogative enders *-ni* (indicative) and *-ti* (retrospective) and the familiar-level enders *-ney* (declarative indicative), *-tey* (declarative retrospective), *-sey* (propositive), and *-key* (imperative) incorporate both mood and S-type suffixes. These enders can be analyzed as *-n-i*, *-t-i, -ne-y*, *-te-y*, *-se-y*, and *-ke-y*, respectively, where *-n(e)* (indicative), *-t(e)* (retrospective), *-se* (suggestive requestive), and *-ke* (instructive requestive) represent respective moods, *-i* is an allomorph of the plain-level interrogative S-type suffix, and *-y* is the familiar-level S-type suffix covering declarative, propositive, and imperative. The familiar-level interrogative enders *-nu-nka* (indicative), *-na* (indicative), and *-te-nka* (retrospective) have developed via grammaticalization from the corresponding indirect question constructions *-nu-n ka* (IN-RL whether) 'whether . . .', *-na* (whether) 'whether . . .', and *-te-n ka* (RT-RL whether) 'whether (it) did/was . . .', respectively. All these diachronic phenomena have contributed to the heterogeneity and irregularity of S-type suffixes.

The table in (29) shows how the verbs *mek* 'eat' (consonant-final) and *ka* 'go' (vowel-final) and the adjectives *coh* 'good' (consonant-final) and *khu* 'big' (vowel-final) inflect in sentence-ender suffixes according to the four major sentence types and the six speech levels. Notice that no contemporary retrospective enders are available at the intimate and blunt levels. Adjectives cannot usually be used in propositive and imperative constructions.

(29)

	DECLARATIVE		INTERROGATIVE	
	Indicative	Retrospective	Indicative	Retrospective
PLN:	*mek-nun-ta*	*mek-te-la*	*mek-nu-nya*	*mek-te-n(ya)*
			mek-n-i	*mek-t-i*
	ka-n-ta	*ka-te-la*	*ka-nu-nya*	*ka-te-n(ya)*
			ka-n-i	*ka-t-i*
	coh-ta	*coh-te-la*	*coh-unya*	*coh-te-n(ya)*
			coh-n-i	*coh-t-i*
	khu-ta	*khu-te-la*	*khu-nya*	*khu-te-n(ya)*
			khu-n-i	*khu-t-i*
INT:	*mek-e*	—	*mek-e*	—
	ka	—	*ka*	—
	coh-a	—	*coh-a*	—
	kh-e	—	*kh-e*	—

FML: *mek-ne-y*   *mek-te-y*   *mek-nu-nka*   *mek-te-nka*
                                            mek-na

        ka-ne-y   *ka-te-y*   *ka-nu-nka*   *ka-te-nka*
                                            ka-na

        coh-ne-y   *coh-te-y*   *coh-unka*   *coh-te-nka*
                                            coh-na

        khu-ne-y   *khu-te-y*   *khu-nka*   *khu-te-nka*
                                            khu-na

BLN: *mek-so/-uo* —   *mek-so/-uo*   —

        ka-o   —   *ka-o*   —

        coh-so   —   *coh-so*   —

        khu-o   —   *khu-o*   —

POL: *mek-e.yo* *mek-te-yyo*   *mek-e.yo*   *mek-te-nka-yo*

        ka-yo   *ka-te-yyo*   *ka-yo*   *ka-te-nka-yo*

        coh-a.yo   *coh-te-yyo*   *coh-a.yo*   *coh-te-nka-yo*

        kh-e.yo   *khu-te-yyo*   *kh-e.yo*   *khu-te-nka-yo*

DEF: *mek-sup-ni-ta* *mek-sup-ti-ta* *mek-sup-ni-kka* *mek-sup-ti-kka*

        ka-p-ni-ta   *ka-p-ti-ta*   *ka-p-ni-kka*   *ka-p-ti-ta*

        coh-sup-ni-ta *coh-sup-ti-ta* *coh-sup-ni-kka* *coh-sup-ti-kka*

        khu-p-ni-ta   *khu-p-ti-ta*   *khu-p-ni-kka*   *khu-p-ti-ta*

(30)   PROPOSITIVE   IMPERATIVE

PLN: *mek-ca*   *mek-ela*

        ka-ca   *ka-la*

INT: *mek-e*   *mek-e*

       ka   *ka*

FML: *mek-se-y*   *mek-ke-y*

        ka-se-y   *ka-ke-y*

BLN: *mek-up-si-ta*   *mek-uo*

        ka-p-si-ta   *ka-o*

POL: *mek-e.yo*   *mek-e.yo*

        ka-yo   *ka-yo*

DEF: *capswu-si-p-si-ta*   *capswu-si-p-si-o* (*capswu*: hon.)
　　　ka-si-p-si-ta   *ka-si-p-si-o*

Thus, for instance, the morphological structure of *mek-nun-ta* '(Someone) eats' is eat-IN-DC, that of *mek-te-nya* 'Did you see (him) eating?' is eat-RT-Q, that of *mek-ela* 'Eat!' is eat-IM, that of *mek-up-si-ta* 'Let's eat' is eat-AH-RQ-PR, and that of *capswu-si-p-si-o* 'Please eat' is eat-SH-AH-RQ-IM.

Sentence enders also include the following minor ones. For the syntactic behaviour of these enders, see 9.2.1.

(31)　　*-kwun(-yo)*   (apperceptive)
　　　　-ney(-yo)   (apperceptive)
　　　　-ci(-yo)   (suppositive)
　　　　-(u)llay(-yo)   (intentive)
　　　　-(u)lla   (admonitive)
　　　　-ela/-ala   (exclamatory)
　　　　-(u)msey, *-(u)ma*, *-(u)lkey(-yo)*   (promissive/assurance)

Some of these suffixes have derived diachronically from complex constructions (cf. 8.7). The intentive suffix *-(u)llay* has obviously developed from *-(u)lye-ko-hay* (intending-and-do) 'intends to do', the admonitive (warning) suffix *-(u)lla* from *-(u)li-la* (PRS-DC) 'will/may', and the promissive/assurance suffix *-(u)lkkey* from *-(u)l kes i-e* (PRS fact be-INT) 'will do/be' (prediction).

8.4.4   *Embedded-clause enders*

Four embedded clause types, i.e., nominal, complement, conjunctive, and relative clauses, take clause ender suffixes called nominalizers, complementizers, conjunctors, and relativizers (or adnominalizers), respectively. Although all of these suffixes may be preceded by the subject honorific suffix and some of them by the past/perfect, the prospective, and/or an indicative or retrospective mood suffix, none of them occur with the addressee honorific suffix in contemporary spoken Korean. For syntactic behaviours of these and other inflectional suffixes, see 9.4.

The nominalizers in current use are *-m* (after a vowel)/*-um* (after a consonant) '(do/be)ing', as in *ka-m* (go-NOM) 'going' and *ka-ss-um* (go-PST-NOM) 'having gone'; *-ki* (before a non-negative predicate)/*-ci* (before a negative predicate) 'to . . .', as in *ka-ki sicakha-n-ta* (go-NOM begin-IN-DC) 'begins to go' and *ka-ci mos ha-n-ta* (go-NOM unable do-IN-DC) 'is unable to go'; and *-ko* (before the desiderative adjective *siphta* 'want'), as in *ka-ko siph-ess-ta* (go-NOM wishful-PST-DC) 'wanted to go'. A nominalizer may be preceded by the subject honorific suffix -*(u)si* and the past/perfect -*ess*/-*ass*. Rarely, -*ki* may also be preceded by the modal -*keyss*, as in *ka-si-ess-keyss-ki ey* (go-SH-PST-may-NOM at) 'as (he) may have gone'.

The class of complementizers includes the so-called infinitive (INF) suffix -*e*/-*a*, as in *cwuk-e ka-n-ta* (die-INF go-IN-DC) 'is in the process of dying' and *malk-a ci-n-ta* (clear-INF get-IN-DC) 'becomes (to be) clear'; the adverbializer (AD) -*key* 'so that', as in *ka-key hay-ss-ta* (go-AD cause-PST-DC) 'caused (someone) to go'; and the adverbializer -*tolok* 'so that, to the point where', as in *ka-tolok hay-ss-ta* (go-AD do-PST-DC) 'arranged (someone) to go'. Before a complementizer, no inflectional suffix other than the subject honorific suffix may appear.

Conjunctors are numerous. While all conjunctors allow the subject honorific suffix to cooccur with them, only a small portion of them allow the past/perfect suffix to precede them, as indicated in (32). Cooccurrence with the modal suffix -*keyss* is even rarer. No other inflectional suffixes are permitted to cooccur.

(32)	-*ci-man*	'but, although' (suppositive -*ci* 'supposedly' + particle *man* 'only') [+PST, +*keyss*]
	-*e(-se)*/-*a(-se)*	'and then, so' (INF -*e*/-*a* + -*se* 'then') [–PST, –*keyss*]
	-*ketun*	'provided that, if' (provisional) [+PST, +*keyss*]
	-*key*	'(in a way) so that' [–PST, –*keyss*]
	-*ko*	'and (also)' [+PST, +*keyss*]
	-*ko(-se)*	'and then, after (doing) [–PST, –*keyss*]
	-*nula(-ko)*	'as a result of . . .' [–PST, –*keyss*]
	-*nula-myen*	'while doing, what with doing' [–PST, –*keyss*]
	-*nu-n-tey*	'given that, and, but' (background information provider) (-IN-RL-place) [+PST, +*keyss*]
	-*taka*	'and then, while' (transferentive) [+PST, +*keyss*]
	-*e-taka*	'and then' (with shift of location) [–PST, –*keyss*]
	-*te-la-to*	'even though' (RT-DC-although) [+PST, –*keyss*]
	-*eto*	'although, but' [+PST, –*keyss*]
	-*tolok*	'so that, to the point where, until' [–PST, –*keyss*]
	-*tu-n-ci*	'whether, or' (RT-RL-whether) [+PST, –*keyss*]
	-*(u)le*	'in order to, for the purpose of' (occurs with the locomotive verb *ota* or *kata*) [–PST, –*keyss*]
	-*(u)lyeko*	'intending' (intentive) [–PST, –*keyss*]
	-*(u)myen*	'if, when' (conditional) [+PST, +*keyss*]
	-*(u)myen-se*	'while . . . at the same time' [–PST, –*keyss*]
		'while . . . yet' [+PST, +*keyss*]
	-*(u)na*	'but, though' (adversative) [+PST, +*keyss*]

-(u)ni	'since, as, so' [+PST, +*keyss*]
-(u)ni-kka	'when, as, because' [+PST, +*keyss*]

The relativizer connects a relative (adnominal) clause to a nominal in the main clause. Its forms are *-(u)n* and ZERO (after a prospective suffix). It may be preceded by a tense/aspect and/or a mood suffix, with which it constitutes a relative clause ender such as non-past indicative *-nu-n* (after verb) and *-(u)n* (after adjective), past/perfect *-un* (after consonant) and *-n* (after vowel), prospective *-(u)l*, past prospective *-ess-ul/-ass-ul*, non-past retrospective *-te-n*, and past retrospective *-ess-te-n/-ass-te-n*. Verbs and adjectives have slightly different forms of enders, as illustrated in (33) with the verb stems *mek* 'eat' and *ka* 'go' and the adjective stems *coh* 'be good' and *khu* 'be big'.

(33)

		Verb	Adjectve
non-past		*mek-nu-n*	*coh-un*
		ka-nu-n	*khu-n*
past		*mek-un*	—
		ka-n	—
prospective		*mek-ul*	*coh-ul*
		ka-l	*khu-l*
past prospective		*mek-ess-ul*	*coh-ass-ul*
		ka-ss-ul	*kh-ess-ul*
retrospective		*mek-te-n*	*coh-te-n*
		ka-te-n	*khu-te-n*
past retrospective		*mek-ess-te-n*	*coh-ass-te-n*
		ka-ss-te-n	*kh-ess-te-n*

Notice that the past/perfect ender is simply *-(u)n* in standard Korean. In the Kyengsang dialect, the equivalent form is *-ess-nu-n/-ass-nu-n*, as in *mek-ess-nu-n* and *ka-ss-nu-n*. Thus, the standard *mek-un ai* 'a child who ate' is rendered as *mek-ess-nu-n ai* in that dialect. This may suggest that the standard past/perfect ender has developed from the regular *-ess-nu-n/-ass-nu-n* with the deletion of the tense/aspect suffix and the indicative mood suffix *-nu*, while retaining the semantic contents of the deleted elements. Existence of fossilized constructions in standard Korean such as the conjunctor *-nu-n tey* (IN-RL place) 'given that, but' as in *mek-ess-nu-n tey* 'ate but' and the indirect question form *nu-n ci* (IN-RL whether) 'whether . . .' as in *ka-ss-nu-n ci* 'whether (he) went' may also provide evidence that the past/perfect relative clause ender *-(u)n* after a verb stem has derived from *-ess-nu-n/-ass-nu-n* with the deletion of *-ess-nu/-ass-nu*.

8.4.5   *Irregular predicates*

As discussed in chapter 7 (7.4.3), there are predicates that change their final sound before an inflectional suffix that begins with a certain sound. These predicates are commonly called irregular and are of seven types, as shown below.

(a)   *t*-irregular predicates are those whose stem-final *t* becomes *l* before a vowel, as in *ket-nun-ta* 'walks' vs. *kel-ess-ta* 'walked', *mut-nun-ta* 'asks' vs. *mul-ess-ta* 'asked', and *tut-nun-ta* 'hears' vs. *tul-ess-ta* 'heard' (cf. *pat-nun-ta* 'receives' vs. *pat-ass-ta* 'received').

(b)   *l*-irregular predicates are those whose stem-final *l* is deleted before *n*, *p*, *s*, and *o*, as in *mil-ess-ta* 'pushed' vs. *mi-n-ta* 'pushes', *al-ass-ta* 'knew' vs. *a-p-ni-ta* 'knows' (deferential), *nol-ass-ta* 'played' vs. *no-si-n-ta* 'plays' (subject honorific), *phal-ass-ta* 'sold' vs. *pha-o* 'sells' (blunt)'. Strictly speaking, they are not irregular predicates as all *l*-final predicates share this property.

(c)   *lu*-irregular predicates are those whose final *lu* becomes *ll* before a suffix beginning with *e* or *a*, as in *nalu-n-ta* 'carries' vs. *nall-a* 'by carrying', *molu-n-ta* 'doesn't know' vs. *moll-a.yo* (polite) 'does not know', and *kilu-ko* 'raise and' vs. *kill-ese* 'by raising'. All *lu*-final predicates share this property.

(d)   *p*-irregular predicates are those whose final *p* sound becomes *w* before a vowel, as in *chwup-ta* 'is cold' vs. *chwuw-ela* '(I) feel cold!', *mayp-ta* 'is hot' (taste) vs. *mayw-ese* 'as it is hot', *elyep-ta* 'is difficult' vs. *elyew-eyo* (polite) 'is difficult', and *top-nun-ta* 'helps' vs. *tow-ala* 'Help!' (cf. *cip-nun-ta* 'picks up' vs. *cip-ela* 'Pick (it) up!').

(e)   *s*-irregular predicates are those whose final *s* is deleted before a vowel, as in *ces-nun-ta* 'stirs' vs. *ce-ela* 'Stir!', *ces-nun-ta* 'builds' vs. *ci-uni* 'as (he) builds', and *nas-nun-ta* 'gets well' vs. *na-ase* 'as (he) gets well' (cf. *pes-nun-ta* 'puts off' vs. *pes-uni* 'as (he) puts off').

(f)   *u*-irregular predicates are those whose final *u* is deleted before another vowel. All *u*-final predicates follow this pattern, as in *khu-ta* 'is big' vs. *kh-ese* 'as (it) is big', *ssu-n-ta* 'uses, writes, wears' vs. *ss-ela* 'Use!, Write!, Wear!', and *pappu-ta* 'is busy' vs. *papp-a.yo* 'is busy' (polite).

(g)   *h*-irregular predicates are those whose final *h* is deleted before a nasal consonant and a vowel. They may undergo further phonological change with the following vowel, as in *ppalkah-ta* 'is red' vs. *ppalka-n* 'red' vs. *ppalkay-se* (< *ppalka-ase*) 'as (it) is red', *nolah-ta* 'is yellow' vs. *nola-ni* 'because (it) is yellow' vs. *nolay-yo* (< *nola.yo*) 'is yellow' (polite), and *kuleh-ta* 'is so' vs. *kule-myen* 'if (it) is so' vs. *kulay-se* (< *kule-ese*) 'therefore' (cf. *coh-ko* 'is good and' vs. *coh-ni* 'Is (it) good?' vs. *coh-ase* 'as (it) is good').

8.5 Compounding

8.5.1 General properties

Compounding is overwhelmingly the most common process of creating new words. A compound consists of two or more roots whose meanings are idiomatized to varying degrees from complete fusion such as native *nwun-cis* (eye-behaviour) 'wink' and *ttang-kemi* (earth-black) 'dusk', and SK *ke-lay* (go-come) 'transaction' and *phung-wel* (wind-moon) 'poetry' to relatively transparent association such as native *pam-nac* 'day and night', *ma-so* 'horses and oxen', and *cip-cip* 'houses', and SK *hyo-ca* (filial piety-son) 'filial son' and *mi-in* (pretty-person) 'pretty woman'. Structurally, compound words are of three general types:

(a) subcompounding (modifier + head) as in native *muk-path* 'fallow field', *pom-pi* 'spring rain', *nuc-cam* 'late-sleep', *cha-n mul* 'cold water', SK *mul-ka* (thing-price) 'prices of things', *hak-sayng* (study-person) 'students', *kyo-sil* (teach-room) 'classroom', SK–native *kang-ka* 'river-side', and native–SK *say-sinlang* (new-bridegroom) 'bridegroom'.

(b) co-compounding (or apposition) as in native *pam-nac* 'day and night', *cip-cip* 'houses', *na-nal* 'day after day' and SK *chwun-chwu* (spring-autumn) 'age', *myel-mang* (destroy-perish) 'collapse', *sey-wel* (year-month) 'time and tide', *mo-swun* (shield-spear) 'contradiction', *chwun-ha-chwu-tong* 'spring, summer, autumn, and winter'.

(c) argument-predication as in native *hay-tot-i* (sun-rise-NOM) 'sunrise', *son-capta* (hand-hold) 'grasp another person's hand', *mal-tetum-i* (speech-grope-person) 'stammerer', SK *ak-swu* (grasp-hand) 'shake-hands', *kwu-kyeng* (seek-scenery) 'sightseeing', *il-chwul* (sun-rise) 'sun-rise', and SK–native *cheka-sal-i* (wife's house-live-NOM) 'living at one's wife's family's house'.

These three types of compounding may be mixed in a compound, as in SK *tong-se-yang* (east-west-ocean) 'East and West' where *tong* and *se* are co-compounded and *tong-se* and *yang* are subcompounded. Furthermore, compounds may be hierarchically embedded within a word and may be preceded or followed by affixation. For instance, SK *pi-min-cwu-cwu-uy-cek* 'undemocratic' embeds a series of hierarchically structured compounds with the prefix *pi-* 'un-' and the suffix *-cek* 'ic' as in [*pi*-[[[*min-cwu*]-[*cwu-uy*]]-*cek*]] where *min* is 'people', *cwu* 'head, main', and *uy* 'righteousness'. Note that *min* and *cwu* are in a noun–predicate relation, whereas *cwu* and *uy*, *min-cwu* and *cwu-uy*, *min-cwu-cwu-uy* and *cek*, and *pi* and *min-cwu-cwu-uy-cek* are all in a modifier–head relation.

As alluded to in the foregoing examples, although there are many exceptions (e.g., native–SK *son-swuken* 'handkerchief' and *mul-kwisin* 'water demon'), a general rule is that the stems of the same vocabulary stock combine among themselves (e.g., native with native and SK with SK), as shown in native *sek-tal* and SK *sam-kay-wel* both meaning 'three months'.

Compounds are formed not only from two or more roots, but also, in the case of native compounds, from those roots or stems which have derivational or inflectional affixes. For instance, *ca-n soli* (small-voice) 'scolding, grumbling' consists of the relative (or adnominal) clause *ca-n* (< adjective stem *cal* 'be small' + relativizer *-n*) and the head noun *soli* 'voice'. On the other hand, affixes are attached to compound roots, as in *mi-tat-i* 'sliding door' where the nominalizer suffix *-i* is attached to the compound root *mi-tat* (< *mil-tat* 'push-close').

The order among the roots in native and SK compounds generally reflects the normal word order of native Korean and Chinese, respectively. Both these languages manifest an order of modifier–head, which is also true of the order of elements in compounds, as in native *chel-say* (season-bird) 'migration bird', *mul-kephum* (water-foam) 'bubble', *nuc-tewi* (late-heat) 'lingering summer heat', and *pus kulssi* (brush-letter) 'calligraphy', and SK *sel-kyeng* (snow-scape) 'snowscape', *ta-hayng* (much-blessing) 'luck', *nak-yep* (fall-leaf) 'fallen leaf', *ay-in* (love-person) 'lover', and [*kong-cwung*]-[*nwu-kak*] (air-middle-attic-house) 'castle in the air'. In compounds with an intransitive root, the same order of elements is generally shared by native and SK forms, as in native *hay-tot-i* (sun-rise-NOM) 'sunrise', *pam-nol-i* (night-play-NOM) 'night amusement', *nuc-toyta* (late-become) 'ripen late', *mos-nata* (badly-appear) 'be stupid', etc. vs. SK *il-chwul* (sun-rise) 'sunrise', *ya-yu* (night-play) 'night amusement', *kup-hayng* (rapid-go) 'going fast, express', *sil-cay* (actually-exist) 'actually existing', *tok-lip* (alone-stand) 'independence', etc.

The major difference in the order of roots appears in compounds with a transitive root, being reminiscent of the basic SOV order of Korean and SVO order of Chinese. Native compounds have the OV order, as in *mo-nay-ki* (seedling-take-out-NOM) 'rice-planting', *nel-ttwi-ki* (board-jump-NOM) 'seesawing', *path-kal-i* (field-plough-NOM) 'cultivation', *kul-cis-ki* (sentence-make-NOM) 'composition', and *mal-tetum* (word-stammer) 'stammering'. SK compounds, on the other hand, have the VO order, as in *ay-kwuk* (love-country) 'patriotism', *cak-mun* (make-sentence) 'composition', *kyeng-ci* (plough-land) 'cultivation', *um-cwu* (drink-wine) 'wine drinking', [*ke-twu*]-[*cel-mi*] (eliminate-head-cut-tail) 'summarization', [*cho-hon*]-*ka* (invite-soul-song) 'soul-inviting-song', and [*e*]-[*pul-seng-sel*] (words-not-form-theory) 'lack of logic'.

As for the transitive predicate–adverb relation, native compounds are always of the adverb–predicate form, as in *aph-seywuta* (front-make stand) 'make (him) go ahead', *palo-capta* (correctly-hold) 'straighten up', and *tule-nayta* (upholding-put out) 'distinguish'. In SK compounds, a root with an adverbial meaning frequently follows a transitive root, as in *si-ceng* (correct-right) 'correction', *yen-cang* (stretch-long) 'extension', *kak-ha* (reject-below) 'rejection', and *hwak-tay* (enlarge-big) 'enlargement'.

Some phonological aspects of compounds are worth mentioning (see 7.4). A boundary between roots constituting a compound is similar to a word boundary, but the following points are characteristic of compound boundaries. First, root-final *l* disappears before a homorganic consonant of the following root in many compounds, e.g., *atu-nim* 'esteemed son' (*atul* 'son'), *hwa-sal* 'arrow' (*hwal* 'bow'), *ma-so* 'horses and oxen' (*mal* 'horse'), *na-nal-i* 'day by day' (*nal* 'day'), and *panu-cil* 'needlework' (*panul* 'needle'). Stem-final *l* is deleted before an epenthetic *t* (< *s*) in certain compounds, e.g., *set-tal* 'December' (*sel* 'the New Year' + epenthetic *t* + *tal* 'month') and *swut-kalak* 'spoon' (*swul* 'spoon' + epenthetic *t* + *kalak* 'fork').

Second, an epenthetic nasal *n* [ɲ] is prefixed to the stem-initial *i* or *y* [j] in a compound if the stem is preceded by another stem ending in a consonant, e.g., *cip-il* (house-work) [cim.ɲil] 'housework', *kkoch-iph* (flower-leaf) [k'oɲ.ɲip] 'flower petal', *tam-yo* (fur-blanket) [tam.ɲjo] 'blanket', and *wu-s-i* (upper-tooth) [uɲ.ɲi] 'upper-tooth'. Notice that the final consonant of the preceding stem assimilates to the epenthetic *n*. In examples like *mul-yak* (water-medicine) [mul.ljak] 'liquid medicine' and *sol-iph* (pine-leaf) [sol.lip] 'pine leaf', the epenthetic *n* assimilates to the preceding *l*, a general rule in Korean.

Third, an epenthetic *s* (or *t*) is inserted between nouns in many compounds of the subcompounding (modifier–head) type. This *s* tensifies (or reinforces) the following consonant, as in *cho-s-pul* (candle-fire) [cho.p'ul] 'candle-light', *kang-s-ka* (river-edge) [kaŋ.k'a] 'riverside', *mul-s-koki* (water-meat) [mul.k'o.gi] 'fish', and *sey-s-pang* (rent-room) [se.p'aŋ] 'rented room', where **s** is not spelled in Hankul orthography. Many other subcompounds such as *kkwul-pel* (honey-bee) [k'ul.bəl] 'honeybee', *mun-pakk* (door-outside) [mun.bak] 'outside the door', *pul-koki* (fire-meat) 'barbecued meat', and *kiwa-cip* (tile-house) [ki.wa.ɟip] 'tile-roofed house' do not have an epenthetic *s*. An epenthetic *s* does not occur, in general, in compound nouns of the argument-predication type, as in *hay-tot-i* (sun-rise-NOM) [hɛ.do.ɟi] 'sun-rise' and *son-cap-i* (hand-hold-thing) [son.ɟa.bi] 'handle'.

Fourth, a historical *h* or *p* is inserted between roots in certain compounds, e.g., *am-khay* (< *amh* 'female' + *kay* 'dog') 'female dog' and *cop-ssal* (< *co* 'millet' + *pssal* 'husked rice') 'husked millet'. Finally, sporadic phonological reduction occurs, as in *ec-cenyek* (< *ecey* 'yesterday'-night) 'last night', *engteng-chwum* (< *engtengi* 'hips'-dance) 'hip dance, hula', and *kac-sin* (< *kacwuk* 'leather'-shoe) 'leather shoes'. Let us observe compound constructions by different word categories, and under each category, by different vocabulary stocks (native, SK, loan, and hybrid).

8.5.2   Compound nouns

Of all types of compounds, compound nouns are the most numerous and varied. The component roots may be fused in both meaning and form, as in *hal-apeci* 'grandfather' (< *han-api* 'big father'), *hwang-so* 'bull' (< *han-so* 'big cow'), and *kalang-pi* 'drizzle' (< *kalwu-pi* 'powder rain') (cf. J. Shim 1983:197-200). More frequently, however, change occurs only in meaning, as in *mok-swum* (neck-breath) 'life', *sin-pal* (shoe-foot) 'shoes', *son-wi* (hand-upper) 'senior (in age)', *son-mok* (hand-neck) 'wrist', *o-l hay* (come-PRS year) 'this year', and *na-tul-i* (go out-enter-NOM) 'outing'.

8.5.2.1   Native compounds

The first and most productive type of compound nouns is the noun–noun combination of the subcompounding type, in which the first root modifies the second. Long compounds such as [*ssal-aki*] *nwun* (husked rice-baby snow) 'fine snow' are doubly subcompounded. Notice in (34) that some compounds have an epenthetic *s*.

(34)	*cham-kilum*	(true-oil)	'sesame oil'
	chel-s-say	(season-bird)	'migratory bird'
	isul-pi	(dew-rain)	'drizzle'
	kho-s-mul	(nose-water)	'nasal mucus'
	mul-s-kay	(water-dog)	'seal'
	nwun-mul	(eye-water)	'tears'
	polum-s-tal	(half a lunar month-moon)	'full moon'
	ssal-aki	(husked rice-baby)	'broken bits of rice'

There are many noun–noun combinations of the co-compounding (appositive) type too, as in *pi-palam* (rain-wind) 'rainstorm'. A predominant subset of these consists of dvandva compounds, as illustrated in (35). Notice the fixed ordering of elements, the more culturally 'important' one usually coming first.

(35)	*an-phakk*	(inside-outside)	'inside and outside'
	aph-twi	(front-rear)	'front and rear'
	non-path	(rice field-dry field)	'farm'
	o-nwui	(brother-sister)	'brother and sister'
	pam-nac	(night-day)	'day and night'
	son-pal	(hand-foot)	'hand and foot'
	wi-alay	(up-down)	'upper and lower'

A second type of native noun compounds is adverb (mostly onomatopoeic) + noun/adverb. The adverb + noun pattern is illustrated in (36).

(36)
ellwuk-so	(mottles-cow)	'brindled cow'
kopsul-meli	(curly-hair)	'curly hair'
omok-nwun	(concave-eye)	'sunken-in eye'
ppekkwuk-say	(cuckooing-bird)	'cuckoo'
pueng-say	(hoot-bird)	'owl'
santul-palam	(gentle-wind)	'gentle breeze'
ttokttak-tanchwu	(snapping-button)	'snap button'

The adverb + adverb pattern is rare. Examples are *cal-mos* (well-unable) 'mistake' and *i-man-ce-man* (this much-that much) 'no small quantities'.

A third type is noun + predicate + nominalizer (e.g., *-i*, *-ki*, *-(u)m*). In this pattern, the noun and predicate frequently do not constitute a compound predicate. For instance, we have *pay-s-nol-i* (boat-play-NOM) 'boating' and *nol-i* 'game, playing', but not the compound verb **pay-s-nolta*.

(37)
cec-mek-i	(milk-eat-er)	'baby'
mok-kel-i	(neck-hang-thing)	'necklace'
pap-pel-i	(meal-earn-NOM)	'job'
pon-po-ki	(example-see-NOM)	'model'
somay-chi-ki	(sleeve-hit-NOM)	'pickpocket'
swulley-cap-ki	(tagger-catch-NOM)	'hide and seek'
nac-ca-m	(day-sleep-NOM)	'nap'
nwun-wus-um	(eye-laugh-NOM)	'smile'
saywu-ca-m	(lobster-sleep-NOM)	'sleeping all curled up'

A fourth type which is less productive is nominalized predicate + noun, as in *pipi-m-pap* (mix-NOM-rice) 'cooked rice mixed with vegetables, sliced beef, and hot pepper sauce', *kelli-m-tol* (be caught-NOM-stone) 'obstacle', and *kalli-m-kil* (be divided-NOM road) 'forked road'.

A fifth type is predicate + noun. The examples in (38a) contain a verb, and those in (38b) an adjective.

(38)
a.	*cep-khal*	(fold-knife)	'pocketknife'
	kkek-soy	(break-iron)	'clamp'
	muk-path	(get stale-field)	'fallow field'
	nwupi-os	(quilt-clothes)	'quilted clothes'

    b. *kot-elum/kotulum* (straight-ice)   'icicle'
        nuc-cam   (late-sleeping)   'late rising'
        nuc-pye   (late-unhusked rice)   'late-ripening rice'

A sixth type is determiner + noun.

(39)   *ce-sung*   (that-world)   'the world of the dead'
            enu-tes   (some-short space of time)   'before one knows'
            i-sung   (this-world)   'this world'
            ku-cen   (that-front)   'former days'
            on-tal   (full-moon)   'full moon'
            oyn-son   (left-hand)   'left hand'
            say-tal   (new-month)   'next month'

A seventh type is relative clause + noun. Despite the relative clause structure, the forms of this type are considered compound nouns in view of their idiomatic nature.

(40)   *cha-n mul*   (cold water)   'cold water'
            mi-l chang   (pushing window)   'sliding door'
            mos-na-n i   (badly-shaped person)   'stupid person'
            teyli-l sawi   (invited son-in-law)   'son-in-law living with one'

An eighth type is predicate + predicate + nominalizer suffix. Some predicate sequences function as compound verbs (e.g., *po-salphita* 'look after'), while many others do not (e.g., **mi-tatta* 'push and close' is not acceptable).

(41)   *mi-tat-i*   (push-close-thing)   'sliding door'
            noph-nac-i   (high-low-ness)   'relative height'
            po-salphi-m   (see-look about-NOM)   'looking after'
            tot-po-ki   (raise-see-thing)   'long-distance glasses'
            twulwu-mal-i (surround-roll-NOM)   'rolled stationary'

8.5.2.2   Sino-Korean compounds

Recall that about sixty percent of all Korean vocabulary items are SK, that SK morphemes are monosyllabic, that an absolute majority of SK words are compounds consisting of two or more roots, and that most SK words are nouns, while only a small number are adverbs. Although native morphemes are employed to form new compounds, by far the more productive way is making use of SK roots, which are shorter in form and thus more economical, more varied, and are more readily available (cf. chapter 5). For instance, the following long SK compound noun is hardly translatable into native words, due to the lack of available morphemes in the native stock.

(42)   *kong-mwu-wen chwi-cik   si-hem il-ca pyenkyeng kong-ko*
        public worker employment exam date change   announcement
        'announcement of the change in the dates of the employment exam for
        prospective government employees'

There are numerous SK compounds whose component roots are semantically fused. In many cases, the derived meanings are metaphorically associated with the original meanings, as in *nay-oy* (inside-outside) 'husband and wife', *phi-an* (that-shore) 'better world, life after death', *tha-kyey* (other-world) 'death', *san-swu* (mountain-water) 'scenery', and *sam-chen-li kang-san* (three-thousand-mile river-mountain) 'Korea'.

SK compounds abound in subcompounding constructions, the usual order being the modifier preceding the head. There are several subtypes. First, one noun root may modify another noun root, always preceding the latter, as in *chwun-mong* 'spring dreams', *chayk-sang* (book-table) 'desk', and *mul-ka* (thing-price) 'price'. Second, one verb root modifies a noun root, always preceding the latter, as in *hak-kyo* (study-house) 'school' and *ip-kwu* (enter-mouth) 'entrance'. Third, one adjective root may modify a noun root, always preceding the latter, as in *ta-hayng* (much-luck) 'good luck' and *cap-ci* (miscellaneous-paper) 'magazine'. Fourth, one verb root may be preceded or followed by a modifying adverb root, as in *thuk-phil* (specially-write) 'writing specially', *tay-se* (instead-write) 'writing for a person', *hwak-tay* (expand-large) 'enlargement', and *kam-so* (deduct-small) 'reduction'. These subtypes form larger compound constructions, as in *ca-tong-cha* (self-move-car) 'automobile' where *ca-tong*, an adverb–verb relation, modifies the head *cha* 'car' in a verb–noun relation. In *pin-min-kwul* 'slum', *pin-min* 'poor people' is in an adjective–noun relation, which modifies the head *kwul* 'cave' in a noun–noun relation.

There are many SK words whose component roots are in a co-compounding relation. One of the common appositive patterns is that of dvandva compounds, as illustrated in (43). To this set may be added multi-syllabic words such as *huy-lo-ay-lak* (happiness-anger-sadness-pleasure) 'feelings, emotions', *nam-nye-no-so* (male-female-old-young) 'people of all ages', *tong-se-nam-puk* (east-west-south-north) 'four directions', and *uy-sik-cwu* (clothing-food-shelter) 'food, clothing, and shelter'.

(43)   *cen-tap*   (dry field-paddy field)   'paddies and dry fields'
        chen-ci   (heaven-earth)   'universe'

cwa-wu	(left-right)	'right and left'
cwu-ya	(day-night)	'day and night'
i-hay	(advantage-damage)	'advantages and disadvantages'
nam-may	(brother-sister)	'brothers and sisters'
pu-mo	(father-mother)	'parents'
sayng-sa	(live-die)	'life and death'

Other co-compounds include the constructions whose constituent roots have similar meanings, as in *wu-cwu* (house-house) 'universe', *san-ho* (coral-coral) 'coral', *pep-lyul* (law-regulation) 'laws and regulations', *hayng-pok* (luck-luck) 'happiness', and *pho-to* (grape-grape) 'grapes', the constructions whose constituent roots have the same or similar verbal or adjectival meanings, as in *mok-yok* (bathe-bathe) 'bath, bathing', *sal-hay* (kill-harm) 'murder', *chwul-pal* (come out-come out) 'departure', *pha-myen* (finish-avoid) 'dismissal from a job', *pu-phay* (rot-fail) 'rotting, spoiling', *hayng-tong* (go-move) 'behaviour', *pu-ka* (attach-add) 'imposition', *so-pak* (simple-simple) 'simplicity', and *yu-yen* (soft-soft) 'softness', and the constructions that contain a meaningless root in the second syllable, as in *uy-ca* (chair-son) 'chair', *mo-ca* (hat-son) 'hat, cap', *sang-ca* (box-son) 'box', *cong-ca* (seed-son) 'seeds', *i-ca* (interest-son) 'interest', and *ka-twu* (street-head) 'street'.

The SK compounds that are of the argument–predication type are numerous. The constituent roots manifest various functional relations such as subject–predicate, object–predicate, oblique–predicate, or adjunct–predicate. For instance, subject–predicate relations are observed in *il-mol* (sun-set) 'sunset', *i-myeng* (ear-ring) 'ringing in the ears', *twu-thong* (head-ache) 'headache', and *yu-myeng* (exist-name) 'being famous', object–predicate relations in *wi-pep* (violate-law) 'violation of law', *kyel-sek* (vacate-seat) 'absence', and *pak-swu* (clap-hand) 'hand clapping' oblique–predicate relations in *cay-mi* (stay-America) 'residence in America', *chwul-cen* (come out-war) 'going to the war', and *chey-hem* (body-experience) 'personal experience', and adjunct–predicate relations in *wan-hayng* (slow-go) 'going slow', *sen-cem* (ahead-occupy) 'prior occupation', and *chwuk-so* (reduce-small) 'reduction'.

8.5.2.3   Loan and hybrid compounds

Loan-word based compounds are illustrated in (44). Some of such compounds were coined in Korea, while some others were coined in Japan and imported into Korea.

(44)	*aisu-thi*	(ice-tea)	'iced tea'
	ophun-keyim	(open-game)	'match before the main event'
	payk-mile	(back-mirror)	'rearview mirror'

pol-pheyn	(ball-pen)	'ball-point pen'
saylleli-mayn	(salary-man)	'salaried man'
kao-matam	(Jpn face-Fr Madame)	'head hostess at a restaurant'
pinil-kapang	(vinyl-Jpn bag)	'vinyl bag'

Many compounds consist of forms from different vocabulary stocks, the most productive pattern being SK + native (NT) ones.

(45)   a. SK noun + NT noun

chang-sal	(window-strips)	'lattice'
chosayng-tal	(newborn-moon)	'crescent'
hankwuk-mal	(Korea-language)	'the Korean language'
mun-ccak	(door-one of a pair)	'a door'
tong-ccok	(east-side)	'eastern direction'
yak-pap	(medicine-rice)	'flavored glutinous rice'

b. NT noun + SK noun

kong-pang	(free-room)	'free room'
mal-taytap	(word-answer)	'back talk'
mul-mantwu	(water-dumpling)	'water-boiled dumpling'
pal-pyeng	(foot-illness)	'foot trouble'
pap-sang	(rice-table)	'dining table'

c. Loan/SK/NT noun compounding

am-ttalla	(SK dark-dollar)	'black market dollars'
ciphu-cha	(jeep-SK vehicle)	'jeep'
cang-thiphwusu	(SK intestines-)	'intestine-typhus'
kosok-theminal	(SK high speed-)	'express-bus terminal'
kyeylan-hwulai	(SK egg-)	'fried egg'
thongkun-pesu	(SK commuting-)	'commuting bus'
yang-tampay	(SK ocean-tobacco)	'American cigarettes'

d. NT/SK determiner + SK/NT noun

cho-halwu	(SK first-NT one day)	'first day (of the month)'
cho-yelum	(SK first-NT summer)	'early summer'
may-tal	(SK every-NT month)	'every month'
oyn-phyen	(NT left-SK side)	'the left side'
yeys-chinkwu	(NT old-SK friend)	'old friend'

e. NT verb + SK noun

kel-sang	(hang-table)	'chair'
puth-cang	(attach-chest)	'built-in cupboard'

f. NT relative clause construction + SK noun

mi-l-chang	(push-window)	'sliding window'
toy-n-cang	(thick-soy)	'soybean paste'
toy-n-sepang	(hard-husband)	'hard husband'
tu-l-chang	(raise-window)	'push-up window'

g. SK noun + NT verb + Nominalizer suffix

chayk-kkoc-i	(book-insert-thing)	'bookshelf'
kwutwu-takk-i	(shoe-polish-person)	'shoeshine boy'
sicip-sal-i	(husband's home-living)	'living with one's husband's family'

8.5.3   Compound pronouns

All third-person pronouns are demonstrative + noun compounds (8.1.3). Some SK second-person, reflexive, and reciprocal pronouns are composed of two roots: *tang-sin* (self-body) 'you, himself (hon.)', *ca-ki* (self-body) 'self, oneself', *ca-sin* (self-body) 'one's self', *sang-ho* (mutually-mutually) 'each other', and *phi-cha* (that-this) 'both, each other'. A native-SK pronoun is *ku-nye* (that-woman) 'she'. Native pronouns consisting of a demonstrative (D) and a defective noun are illustrated in (46).

(46)			
	D-*i*	(D-adult person)	'D person'
	D-*kes*	(D-thing)	'D thing'
	i-cey	(this-time)	'now'
	ce-ki	(that-place)	'that place over there'
	e-ti	(which-place)	'where'

8.5.4   Compound numerals

Numerals above ten are compounded systematically on the basis of native or SK numerals from 1 to 10, native numerals for multiples of 10 (20 to 90), and SK *payk* '100', *chen* '1,000', *man* '10,000', *ek* '100 million', and *co* '1 trillion'. Thus, 11 is either native *yel-hana* (10-1) or SK *sip-il* (10-1). 55 is either native *swin-tases* (50-5), SK *o-sip-o* (5-10-5), or SK–native *o-sip-tases* (5-10-5), but not native–SK *swin-o (50-5). 361 is either SK *sam-payk-yuk-sip-il* (3-100-6-10-1), SK–native *sam-payk-yeyswun-hana* (3-100-60-1), or SK–native *sam-payk-yuk-sip-hana* (3-100-6-10-1). 30

million is *SK sam-chen-man* (3-1000-10000). Approximate numerals are native *han-twu(l)* '1 or 2', *twu-sey(s)* '2 or 3', *se-ne(s)* '3 or 4', *ne-tays* '4 or 5', *tay-yeses* '5 or 6', etc. and SK *il-i* '1 or 2', *i-sam* '2 or 3', *sam-sa* '3 or 4', *sa-o* '4 or 5', etc.

Native terms for multiples of ten, i.e., *sumul* '20', *selhun* '30', *mahun* '40', *swin* '50', *yeysun* '60', *ilhun* '70', *yetun* '80', and *ahun* '90', appear to have consisted of two morphemes in the past, but they are not neatly traceable. The form *(h)un* seems to have something to do with '10'. Similarly, native terms for days from one to ten may be analysed as consisting of two roots although again they are opaque: *halwu* '1 day, 1st day', *ithul* '2 days, 2nd day', *sahul* '3 days, 3rd day', *nahul* '4 days, 4th day', *tas.say* '5 days, 5th day', *yes.say* '6 days, 6th day', *iley* '7 days, 7th day', *yetuley* '8 days, 8th day', *ahuley* '9 days, 9th day', and *yelhul* '10 days, 10th day'.

8.5.5   *Compound verbs*

The most frequently occurring pattern is the noun–verb combination, where the noun and the verb may be compounds or derivatives. Since SK or loan words can function as verbs only when they are compounded with a native verb, such compound verbs will be discussed under SK/loan–native compounds.

8.5.5.1   Native compounds

One type is noun + intransitive verb. The verbs involved usually denote process, rather than activity. In general, the noun and verb can be split by inserting a nominative particle after the noun. When split, they no longer constitute a compound, but function as a subject and a predicate, respectively. Thus, *cam-tulta* (sleep-set in) 'fall asleep' is a compound, but *cam i tulta* (sleep NM set in) 'fall asleep' is not. In rare cases, a locative or directional particle may occur, as in *aph-seta* (front-stand) vs. *aph ey seta* (front at stand) 'stand ahead' and *kewul-samta* (mirror-take) vs. *kewul lo samta* (mirror as take) 'take as a model'. The following examples all allow a nominative particle to be inserted after the noun.

(47)			
	kep-nata	(fear-come out)	'be scared'
	kil-tulta	(road-enter)	'get used to'
	kum-kata	(line-go)	'crack, split'
	sal-ccita	(flesh-grow fat)	'gain weight'
	sin-nata	(excitement-occur)	'get excited'
	swum-cita	(breath-fall)	'breathe one's last breath'

A second type is noun + transitive verb. This type usually allows an accusative particle to be inserted after the noun if the noun can be used independently, as in *cam-*

cata (sleep-sleep) vs. *cam ul cata* (sleep AC sleep) 'sleep (a sleep)'. Although the compounds of this type contain a transitive verb root, they themselves are not necessarily transitive verbs. For instance, *cam-cata* 'sleep' is an intransitive verb, whereas *mal-hata* (word-do) 'speak' is a transitive verb in clauses such as *yenge lul mal-hata* 'speak English'. The following examples all allow an accusative particle to be inserted after the noun.

(48)   *aph-mos-pota*   (front-unable-see)   'be blind'
           ay-ssuta   (effort-use)   'make efforts'
           him-ipta   (power-wear)   'owe, be indebted to'
           maum-mekta   (mind-eat)   'intend, plan'
           pap-hata   (rice-do)   'cook rice'
           salang-hata   (love-do)   'love'
           sin-sinta   (shoe-wear)   'wear shoes'
           sok-thaywuta   (inside-burn)   'worry oneself'
           son-pota   (hand-see)   'fix'

Another major native type is verb + complementizer + verb. The most common complementizer is the infinitive suffix *-e/-a*. Some other suffixes such as the transferentive *-eta/-ata* 'and then' and the conjunctive *-ko* 'and' are also used.

(49)   a. Infinitive
               al-a-tutta   (know-hear)   'understand'
               eps-e-cita   (not exist-become)   'disappear'
               hay-nayta   (do-let out)   'finish up' (*hay* < *hay-e*)
               il-e-nata   (rise-come out)   'rise up'
               pil-e-mekta   (beg/pray-eat)   'live as a beggar'
               po-a-cwuta   (see-give)   'give a favor to, look after'
               sumy-e-tulta   (soak-enter)   'soak in'

           b. Transferentive
               chy-eta-pota   (raise-see)   'look up'
               nayly-eta-pota   (lower-see)   'look down'
               pala-ta-pota   (gaze-see)   'gaze at' (*-ta* < *-ata*)
               tuly-eta-pota   (put in-see)   'look in'

           c. Conjunctive
               cca-ko-tulta   (organize-enter)   'plot'
               mul-ko-nulecita   (bite-hang)   'hang on tenaciously'

pha-ko-tulta	(dig-enter)	'look into'
tul-ko-nata	(enter-exit)	'interfere'

Juxtaposition of verbs is another pattern of verbal compounding.

(50)	*kkwey-mayta*	(pierce-bind)	'sew'
	kwulm-cwulita	(starve-hungry)	'go hungry'
	may-talta	(tie-suspend)	'bind up, hang'
	olu-naylita	(ascend-descend)	'go up and down'
	po-salphita	(see-look about)	'look after'
	puth-capta	(stick to-hold)	'grasp'
	ttwi-nolta	(jump-play)	'skip about'
	tu-na-tulta	(enter-go out-enter)	'frequent'

Another compound verb type is adverb + verb. Frequently, reduplicated sound symbolic adverbs combine with the verb *hata* 'do'.

(51)	*cal-hata*	(well-do)	'do habitually'
	kalo-makta	(across-block)	'obstruct, interrupt'
	kuman-twuta	(that much-put down)	'stop doing'
	palo-capta	(correctly-hold)	'straighten up'
	pithul-pithul-hata	(staggeringly-do)	'stagger'
	sokon-sokon-hata	(in whispers-do)	'whisper'
	te-hata	(more-do)	'add'

8.5.5.2   SK–native and loan–native compounds

A large number of SK nouns and a small number of loan nouns combine with a native verb (e.g., *hata* 'do') to form hybrid compound verbs. The compounds may be intransitive (52a) or transitive (52b). Loan-native compounds are illustrated in (52c).

(52)	a.	*kan-thata*	(liver-burn)	'be anxious'
		ki-makhita	(vitality-blocked)	'suffocate, feel choked'
		mang-hata	(ruin-do)	'go to ruin'
	b.	*hon-nayta*	(soul-take out)	'give a good scolding'
		kongpu-hata	(studying-do)	'study'
		pel-cwuta	(punishment-give)	'punish'

	c.	*khophi-toyta*	(copy-become)	'get copied'
		litu-hata	(lead-do)	'lead'
		teymo-hata	(demonstration-do)	'demonstrate (against)'

8.5.6 Compound adjectives

8.5.6.1 Native compounds

Typical native compounds consist of a noun and an adjective. The noun is either a free (e.g., *hemul* 'fault', *kaps* 'price') or a bound noun (e.g., *kkaykkus-* 'cleanness', *ttattus-* 'warmth'), as illustrated in (53a) and (53b), respectively. In general, the component roots of the bound noun type cannot be separated by a case particle. The most frequently used adjective in the bound type is *hata* 'be (in the state of)'.

(53)	a.	*hemul-epsta*	(fault-lack)	'be on friendly terms'
		kaps-ssata	(price-cheap)	'be cheap'
		nwun-melta	(eye-far)	'be blind'
		pay-puluta	(belly-bulgy)	'be full, satisfied'
		pay-taluta	(belly-different)	'be of a different mother'
	b.	*chak-hata*	(niceness-be)	'be nice, virtuous'
		kenpang-cita	(conceit-exist)	'be overbearing'
		neknek-hata	(sufficiency-be)	'be enough'
		ttattus-hata	(warmth-be)	'be warm'
		tumppuk-ita	(full-be)	'be full'

There are compounds consisting of an adjective/adverb + an adjective. The adverb is often an onomatopoeic word.

(54)	*kem-phuluta*	(black-blue)	'be blue-black'
	kkun-kkun-hata	(sticky-be)	'be sticky'
	kwut-seyta	(solid-strong)	'be firm and strong'
	mikkul-mikkul-hata	(slippery)	'be slippery'
	mos-hata	(bad-be)	'be inferior'

Adjectives are reduplicated with the insertion of the emphasizer *-ti* 'and, very'.

(55)	*celm-ti-celmta*	'be very young'
	chakha-ti-chakhata	'be very gentle and good'
	ssu-ti-ssuta	'be very bitter'

8.5.6.2   SK–native and loan–native compounds

Compound adjectives of the SK noun + native adjective type are numerous (56a). The majority of the SK nouns are adjectival nouns, and the most common native verb is *hata* 'be (in the state of)'. A loan noun may also be followed by a native adjective (56b). In general, no case particle can be inserted between the noun and the adjective.

(56)   a. *hayngpok-hata*   (happiness-be)   'be happy'
             kwahak-cek-ita   (scientific-be)   'be scientific'
             maksang-makha-ita (equal-be)   'be equally matched'
             sen-hata   (good-be)   'be good'
             tahayng-ita   (good luck-be)   'be lucky'
             yelsim-ita   (diligence-be)   'be diligent'

         b. *motan-hata*   (modern-be)   'be modern'
             sumathu-hata   (smart-be)   'be smart'
             thephu-hata   (tough-be)   'be tough'
             theykhunikhal-hata (technical-be)   'be technical'

8.5.7   *Compound determiners*

Compound determiners are rare and may include native demonstratives such as *etten* (< *e-tte-ha-n* (which-kind-be-RL)) 'what kind of, some kind of', *i-kkacis* (< *i kaci* (this kind)) 'this much of', and *ku-len* (< *ku-le-ha-n* (that-kind-be-RL)) 'that kind of', and native compound qualifiers and quantifiers such as *amu-amu* 'such and such', *musun* (< *mues-i-n* (what-be-RL)) 'what kind of', *myech-myech* 'several', *motun* (< *motwu-n* (collect-RL)) 'all', *on-kac* 'all kinds of', and *weyn* (< *way-i-n* (why-be-RL)) 'what sort of', and SK determiners such as *pyel(-uy)-pyel* 'various kinds of' where *pyel* means 'speciality'. The emphasizer affix *-na* 'and, very, extremely' is infixed between two reduplicated forms of a few adjectives in relative clauses, as in *khu-na-khu-n* 'very big' (*khuta* 'be big'), *me-na-me-n* 'very far' (*melta* 'be far'), and *ki-na-ki-n* 'very long' (*kilta* 'be long'). These forms are used only as compound determiners.

8.5.8   *Compound adverbs*

8.5.8.1   Native compounds

Compound adverbs are of several types, most of which are not very productive:

(a) noun + noun, e.g., *onul-nal* (today-day) 'nowadays', *pam-nac* (night-day) 'day and night', *yeki-ceki* (here-there) 'here and there', *chalyey-chalyey* (order-order) 'one by one';

(b) reduplicated noun + adverbializer suffix (AD), e.g., *aph-aph-i* (front-front-AD) 'in front of one another', *kan-kan-i* (space-space-AD) 'at times', *na-nal-i* (day-day-AD) 'day by day', *ta-tal-i* (month-month-AD) 'every month';

(c) compound predicate (mostly adjective) + adverbializer suffix, e.g., *i-le-k ce-le-k* (this-way-AD that-way-AD) 'somehow or other' (*-k* < *-key*), *i-le-na ce-le-na* (this-way-whether that-way-whether) 'at any rate', *i-le-khwung ce-le-khwung* (this-way-AD that-way-AD) 'this or that', *i-leh-key* (this-way-AD) 'in this way', *kkomcccak-eps-i* (budging-lack-AD) 'helplessly', *ku-le-na* (that-way-but) 'but', *ku-li-ko* (that-way-and) 'and', *thullim-eps-i* (mistake-lack-AD) 'surely', *twu-mal-eps-i* (two-words-lack-AD) 'without any complaint';

(d) determiner + bound noun, e.g., *ku-nyang* 'as it is', *ku-taylo* 'like that', *i-li* 'this way', *i-taci* 'to this extent', *weyn-kel* (what-thing) 'why no!', *weyn-mankhum* (some-extent) 'to a certain degree', *han-chung* (one-floor) 'all the more', *han-pathang* (one-ground) 'for a spell', *ilu-n-pa* (saying-RL-thing) 'so to speak', *on-thong* (all-state) 'entirely, totally', *yo-cuum* (this-time) 'nowadays, these days';

(e) reduplicated onomatopoeic or other adverbial forms, e.g., *huci-puci* 'hushing up', *hunucek-hunucek* 'loosely', *katuk-katuk* 'fully', *kil.i-kil.i* 'for a long time', *kkok-kkok* 'for sure', *kol(wu)-kolwu* 'evenly', *nemu-nemu* 'very, extremely', *olay-olay* 'for a long time', *tumun-tumun* 'occasionally', *tulsswuk-nalsswuk* 'jagged', *ttuyem-ttuyem* 'sparsely', *wumcik-wumcik* 'moving slightly';

(f) adverb + adverb, e.g., *cal-mos* (well-unable) 'in a wrong way', *com-te* 'a little more', *i-li ce-li* 'here and there', *kot-cal* (straightaway-well) 'readily', *kot-palo* (straightaway-directly) 'at once', *te-tewuk* 'all the more'; and

(g) other sporadic combinations, e.g., *cwul-kot* (line-straightaway) 'all the time', *ku-tholok* (< *ku-le ha-tolok*) (that-way do-until) 'to such an extent', *ye-po* (here-look) 'hello, say'.

As observed in the above, in forming compound adverbs, reduplication is used to denote temporal or spatial repetition, continuation of action, state or manner, or emphasis of the action or state involved. Thus, not only are many onomatopoeic words reduplicated for temporal extension, but other words are also reduplicated, as in *nath-nath-i* 'one by one, entirely' (*nath* 'unit'), *kulus-kulus-i* 'all plates' (*kulus* 'plate'), *kemus-kemus* 'dotted with black' (*kemus* 'black'), and *kelum-kelum* 'every step' (*kelum* 'step'). Variety is often expressed by deleting an initial consonant of the first element in reduplication as in *allok-tallok*, *ellwuk-tellwuk* 'mottled', *wulkus-pulkus* 'multi-coloured', and *along-talong* 'spotted' or differentiating the initial syllables of the two components as in *ancel-pucel* 'restlessly', *oksin-kaksin* 'wrangling', *singkul-pengkul* 'with a broad smile', and *kalphang-cilphang* 'at a loss,

going this way and that'. Partial reduplication also occurs. Notice in (57) that only CV
or CVC in a two syllable base is usually reduplicated. The reduplicated part may
come from the initial or final syllable. Further notice that, in the three-syllable base
elssikwu, the last two syllables are reduplicated.

(57)			
	asasak	(< *asak*)	'crunching, crisping'
	ccilulung	(< *ccilung*)	'ringing'
	cwululu	(< *cwulu*)	'trickling, dribbling'
	cwulwulwuk	(< *cwulwuk*)	'pouring hard'
	elssikwussikwu	(< *elssikwu*)	'Hurrah!, Whoopee!'
	khwungcakcak	(< *khwungcak*)	(a rhythmic pattern)
	taykwulwulwu	(< *taykwul*)	'rolling'
	ttaykttaykwul	(< *ttaykwul*)	'rolling'
	twutwungtwung	(< *twung*)	'tee-dum-dum'
	twutwungsil	(< *twungsil*)	'floating gently'

8.5.8.2   Sino-Korean compounds

A relatively small set of SK adverbs are available as illustrated in (58). Some of these
may be used as nouns as well.

(58)			
	cem-cem	(gradually-)	'gradually'
	cha-cha	(order-)	'by and by'
	cuk-kak	(immediate-time)	'immediately, at once'
	e-cha-phi	(at-this-that)	'anyhow, after all'
	hang-sang	(always-usual)	'always'
	ka-lyeng	(false-command)	'supposing (that)'
	ka-pu-kan	(right-wrong-between)	'at any rate'
	man-il	(ten thousands-one)	'by any chance, if'
	sel-sa	(establish-use)	'even if'
	ta-so	(much-less)	'more or less'
	tan-ci	(only-only)	'merely, however'

8.5.9   Compound particles

Compound particles consist mainly of sequences of case, delimiter, and/or conjunctive
particles. Many of these compounds are syntactic rather than lexical, as noticed in the
following examples, where N stands for a nominal element (a noun, a pronoun, a
numeral, or a noun phrase).

(59) a *N ey-se*   (at-from)   'from, at N'
         N ey-se-kkaci-to   (at-from-even-also)   'even at N'
         N hako-man-uy   (with-only-of)   'only with N'
         N man-i   (only-NM)   'only N (subject)'
         N ulo-man-un   (with-only-as for)   'only with N'
         N ulo-puthe-man-uy   (direction-from-only-of)   'only from N'

      b. *Hankwuk*   *ulo-puthe-man-uy*   *sosik*
         Korea   DR-from-only-GN   news
         'news only from Korea'

As will be discussed in 8.7, many particles, especially delimiters, have developed historically from complex constructions where more than one morpheme is involved.

8.6   Abbreviation

Probably due to Chinese tradition, the majority of SK words consist of two syllables, i.e., two morphemes. SK words of one syllable such as *chayk* 'book', *pyek* 'wall', *pyeng* 'sickness', *mun* 'door, gate', *san* 'mountain', *kang* 'river', *cil* 'quality', *pang* 'room', *tayk* 'house, you', *wi* 'stomach', *kan* 'liver', *sang* 'table', and *sang* 'prize' are rather rare. Some SK words are even composed of two nearly synonymous morphemes to conform with the bisyllabic structure, as in *cel-tan* (cut-sever) 'sever', *chim-lyak* (invade-invade) 'invasion', *wu-cwu* (house-house) 'universe', and *ay-ceng* (love-love) 'love'. On the other hand, native words usually have one or two syllables, as in *son* 'hand', *pal* 'foot', *ima* 'forehead', and *muluph* 'knee'.

Native word abbreviations are rather sporadic. Words like *achim* for *achim pap* (morning-meal) 'breakfast', *cenyek* for *cenyek pap* (evening-meal) 'dinner', *pul-payk* for *pulkoki-paykpan* (roast beef-white rice) 'rice and roast beef dish', *kho* for *khos mul* (nose-water) 'snivel', *meli* for *meli thel* (head-hair) 'hair', etc. are some frequently used examples. There are many argots that are formed through abbreviation. For instance, the student argot *ccong-thi* 'semester-end party' is an abbreviation of the SK–loan compound *congkang-pathi* (end of lecture-party) and *a-te-mey-chi* is an abbreviated form of the native expression *anikkop-ko telep-ko meysukkep-ko chisaha-ta* 'disgusting, dirty, nauseating, and shameful'.

Abbreviations are observed most extensively in SK compounds, especially in non-human proper nouns. The overwhelmingly preferred pattern is to reduce a four-syllable form to a two-syllable one, taking the first and third syllables, as illustrated in (60). Notice that the first and third syllables are, in fact, the first root of each compound word.

(60)   han-kwuk un-hayng   →   han-un   'Bank of Korea'

        i-hwa tay-hak   →   i-tay   'Ewha Womans University'

        kwuk-cey yen-hap   →   kwuk-lyen   'United Nations'

        no-tong co-hap   →   no-co   'labour union'

        yeng-kwuk mi-kwuk   →   yeng-mi   'England and America'

The above pattern is extended to include phrases with more than four syllables.

(61)   ca-tong-phan-may-ki   →   ca-phan-ki   'vending machine'

        ceng-sin pak-yak a-tong →   ceng-pak-a   'mentally retarded child'

        e-hak yen-kwu-so   →   e-yen   'Language Research Institute'

        no-tong-ca sa-yong-ca   →   no-sa   'labour and management'

        pyen-ho-sa hyep-hoy   →   pyen-hyep   'the Bar Association'

        tay-hak ip-hak si-hem   →   tay-ip-si   'college entrance exam'

Some irregularities are also observed, as shown in (62). These may be due to semantic or other reasons (e.g., homonymic clash or semantic weight).

(62)   cen-ca kyey-san   →   cen-san   'electronic calculation'

        il-pon-sik   →   il-sik   'Japanese style (dish)'

        pi-mil phan-may   →   mil-may   'illicit sale'

        pul-lan-se-e   →   pul-e   'French'

        seng-kong sil-phay   →   seng-phay   'success or failure'

        se-yang-sik   →   yang-sik   'Western-style (dish)'

        tay-han min-kwuk   →   han-kwuk   'Republic of Korea'

In addition, there are SK abbreviations that have been fossilized. For instance, *sin-mun* 'newspaper' is from *sin-mun-ci* (new-hearing-paper), *in-co* 'artificial silk' is from *in-co-kyen-sa* (man-made-silk-weaving), *chang-cak* 'creative work' (novel, etc.) is from *chang-cak-phum* (creative-make-work), *ko-huy* 'seventy years of age' is from *in-sayng-chilsip-ko-lay-huy* (human-life-seventy-ancient times-from-rare), and *thay-twu* 'authority, expert' is from *thay-san-puk-twu* (big-mountain-Great-Bear).

Abbreviation also occurs quite extensively in loan words.

(63)   aphathu   'apartment'

        eyekhon   'air-conditioner'

        eykkisu   'extract'

        heyl-ki   'helicopter' (SK *ki* 'plane')

        khillo   'kilometre, kilogramme'

kholla	'Coca-Cola'
inphulley	'inflation'
ope	'overly sensitive'
pihwukkasu	'beef cutlets'
pol-pheyn	'ball-point pen'
phengkhu	'puncture (flat tyre)'
sutheyng	'stainless'
s(y)uphe	'supermarket'
teymo	'demonstration'
tasu	'dozen'
thi	'T-shirts'

In loan words, the most productive pattern is to clip everything after the first two or three syllables. This practice has created some homonyms such as *khillo* which means both 'kilometre' and 'kilogramme' and *phulo* which means 'per cent', 'program', and 'professional'. A less common pattern is the clipping of other parts, as noticed in some examples above.

There are many loan-based acronyms of wide use that are either direct borrowings or are coined in Korea: e.g., GI (*ci-ai*) 'American soldier' (lit. 'Government Issue'), IQ (*ai-khyu*), KO (*kheyi-o*) 'knockout', KAL (*khal*) 'Korean Airline', KBS (*kheyi-pi-eysu*) 'Korean Broadcasting Station', MP (*eym-phi*) 'Military Police', NATO (*na-tho*), PR (*phi-al*) 'Public Relations', PX (*phi-eyksu*) 'American Post Exchange', UN (*yu-eyn*), UNESCO (*yu-ney-su-kho*), USA (*yu-eysu-eyi*), and YMCA (*wai-eym-si-eyi*).

8.7   Grammaticalization

Many words and affixes have developed from other words or larger constructions through a long period of evolution. It has been widely observed that living languages constantly change unidirectionally from larger to smaller units. Korean is no exception. Many syntactic constructions have evolved into lexical items; and many words in a major category (nouns, verbs, and adjectives) have developed into minor category elements such as adverbs, particles, and affixes. For instance, the adjective *kwaynchanhta* 'be fine, good' has developed from the complex verbal construction *kwan-kyey-ha-ci ani hata* (relate-relate-do-NOM not do) 'do not get involved' through syntactic reduction, semantic shift, and phonological attrition. The conjunctive adverbs *kuliko* 'and' and *kulena* 'but' are from *ku-li ha-ko* (that-way do-and) 'does so and' and *ku-le ha-na* (that-way do/be-but) 'does/is so but', respectively. Similarly, the adverb *tepule* 'together' is from *tepul-e* (accompany-and) 'by accompanying'; the vocative adverb *imma* 'you!' is from *i nom-a* (this-fellow-VOC) 'this guy!', the sentence-initial adverb *isscanh-a.yo* 'hey, by the way' is from *iss-ci ani hay-yo* (exist-NOM not be-POL) 'isn't there (something)?', the time adverb *encey* 'when' is from *enu cey* (which time) 'which time'; the determiner *musun* 'what kind of' is from *mues i-n* (what is-RL) 'being what', and the determiner *yo-kkacis* 'this much of' is from *i kaci (uy)* (this kind (of)) 'of this kind'.

All auxiliary verbs have developed from the corresponding main verbs through syntactic and semantic changes. For instance, the auxiliary *pota* 'try' is from the main *pota* 'see, look', the auxiliary *pelita* 'finish up' is from the main *pelita* 'throw away', and the auxiliary *cwuta* 'do for' is from the main *cwuta* 'give'.

Numerous particles (case, delimiter, and conjunctive) have developed from complex predicate or nominal constructions. Notice in (64) that some of them are completely fossilized, others are premature, and still others are at the incipient stage of grammaticalization.

(64)　　*cocha* 'even'　　　　　　< *coch-a* (follow-and) 'by following'

eytaka 'in addition to' < *ey tak-a* (at approach/hold-and) 'approaches and, by holding onto'

hako 'with, and'　　　< *ha-ko* 'do/be and'

(i)lan 'as for'　　　　< *(i)-la ko ha-nu-n kes un* (copula-DC QT say-IN-RL thing TC) 'the thing which is called'

(i)lato 'even'　　　　< *(i)-la ko hay-to* (copula-DC QT say-but) 'even if (someone) says that . . .'

(i)na 'or something'　< *(i)-na* (copula-whether) 'whether it be'

(i)nama 'in spite of'　< *(i) nam-a* (NM remain-and) 'as (it) remains'

kaciko 'with'　　　　< *kaci-ko* (carry-and) 'by carrying'

kkaci 'till, as far as'　< *s kac(ang)* (of edge) 'the edge of'

kkey (humble dative)　< *s kuy* (of place) 'the place of'

kkey 'around (a time)' < *ke kuy* (that place) 'that place'

ko (quotative)　　　　< *ha-ko* (say-and) 'saying that . . .'

mace 'so far as'　　　< *mach-a* (finish-and) 'by finishing'

poko 'to'　　　　　　< *po-ko* (look at-and) 'by looking at'

puthe 'from'　　　　< *puth-e* (stick to-and) 'by sticking to'

pakkey 'except'　　　< *pakk ey* (outside at) 'outside of'

tele 'to'　　　　　　< *tali-e* (accompany-and) 'by accompanying'

(u)losse 'with'　　　< *(u)l/lo ssu-e* (AC/with use-and) 'by using'

Many inflectional suffixes have developed from content words or complex syntactic constructions. For instance, the past/perfect suffix *-ess/-ass* has evolved from the resultative existential construction *-el-a isi* (INF exist) 'be in the state of doing/being'; the modal suffix *-keyss* 'may' from the past periphrastic (long-form) causative construction *-key ha.y-ess* (AD cause-PST) 'caused (someone/something) to do/be'; and the addressee honorific suffix *-(su)p* from the verb *s ɔlp* 'tell (a senior)'. Similarly, many conjunctive suffixes have derived from complex constructions. For instance, *-koca* 'intending to' is from *-ko cap-a* (NOM intend-and) 'wishes to do and so'; *-cako* 'intending to' is from *-ca ko ha-ko* (PR QT say-and) 'says 'let's . . .' and then', *-esel-ase* 'and then, and so' is from *-el-a isi-e* (INF exist-and) 'be in the state of doing/being . . . and so', and *-ultheyntey* 'supposedly' is from *-ul the i-n tey ey* (PRS site/situation be-RL place at) 'in the circumstance which will be the case that . . .'.

New sentence enders have been created by contracting various complex constructions (cf. 8.4.3). For instance, *-(u)llay* 'I intend to' is from *-(u)lye-ko-hay* 'intends to do', *-(u)lla* 'I warn you that . . .' is from *-(u)li-la* 'will/may', *-canh.a* 'you see!' is from *-ci ani hay?* 'Isn't it the case that . . .?', *-ulkey* 'I assure you that . . .' is from *-ul kes i-e* (PRS case/thing be-INT) 'it will be the case that . . .', *-ul kes kath-ta* 'it seems that . . .' is from *-ul kes kwa kath-ta* 'is the same as', and *-napota* 'it appears that . . .' is from *-na po-n-ta* (whether see-IN-DC) 'see whether . . .'. Numerous other sentence enders have developed from conjunctive, nominal, or other constructions by way of main clause deletion (see 9.14.3; H.M. Sohn 1990a). For instance, *-ulkkel* 'I wish/suppose that . . .' is from *-ul kes ul* (PRS fact/thing AC), *-tanikka* 'I told you that . . .' is from *-ta ko ha-nikka* (DC QT say-because), and *-tamyense* 'I heard that . . . is it true?' is from *-ta ko ha-myense* (DC QT say-while), all by way of main clause deletion. As discussed in 8.4.3, the familiar-level interrogative enders *-nu-nka* (e.g., *ka-nu-nka?* 'Does (he) go?), *-na* (e.g., *ka-na?* 'Does (he) go?'), and *-te-nka* (e.g., *ka-te-nka?* 'Did you see (him) go?') have developed via main clause deletion from the indirect question constructions *-nu-n ka* (IN-RL whether) 'whether . . .', *-na* (whether) 'whether . . .', and *-te-n ka* (RT-RL whether) 'whether (it) did/was . . .', respectively.

It may be assumed that most derivational prefixes and suffixes have developed from full words or complex constructions through grammaticalization. While there are many recently grammaticalized affixes whose source words are either transparent or readily recoverable, there are many other fossilized affixes whose sources are vague and thus not easily identifiable. For instance, the adjectival prefix *cham-* 'true, real, genuine' as in *cham-kilum* 'sesame oil', *cham-kkay* 'sesame seeds', *cham-mal* (-word) 'true remark, truth', *cham-namu* (-tree) 'a kind of oak', *cham-say* (-bird) 'sparrow', and *cham-ttus* (-intention) 'sincere intention' can easily be associated with the noun *cham* 'truth, reality' and the adverb *cham* 'really, trully'. Similarly, the adjectival prefix *tul-* 'wild, of low quality' as in *tul-kilum* (-oil) 'perilla oil' (lit. 'wild oil'), *tul-kkay* (-sesame) 'perilla seeds', and *tul-kwuk.hwa* (-chrysanthemum) 'wild camomile' must have developed from the noun *tul* 'field'. The adjectivizer suffix *-tap* 'be like' as in *yeca-tapta* 'be womanly, woman-like' and *sanay-tapta* 'manly, man-like' can be related to the obsolete adjective *tapta* (standard: *kathta*) 'be like' which is still used only in the Ceycwu dialect.

On the other hand, lexical sources of many fossilized and unproductive suffixes such as the nominalizer suffix *-ang/-eng* 'quality' as in *kem-eng* (black-) 'black colour' and *nol-ang* (yellow-) 'yellow colour', the adjectiviser suffix *-(y)ep* 'be in the state of' as in *kwi-yepta* (value-) 'be cute' and *no-yepta* (anger-) 'be offended', and the adjectivizer suffix *-(e)p/-up* 'able, in the state of' as in *kuli-pta* (long for-) 'be missing', *mul-epta* (bite-) 'be itchy', and *wus-upta* (laugh-) 'be funny' are opaque.

As briefly noted in 8.3.2, the passive derivational suffixes in Korean seem to have diverged from causative suffixes by way of functional or semantic shift. First of all, the passive suffix forms (*-i*, *-hi*, *-li*, and *-ki*) constitute a subset of the causative suffix forms (*-i*, *-hi*, *-li*, *-ki*, *-wu*, *-kwu*, *-chwu*, etc.). Thus, numerous passive and causative verbs have the same forms (e.g., *po-ita* 'show, be seen', *an-kita* 'cause (one) to hug, be hugged'). Second, both passive suffixes and causative suffixes are allomorphic variants in each set whose forms are phonologically and lexically conditioned. Third, only a limited number of verbs participate in causative or passive suffixation. Fourth, causative and passive suffixes share a single mophological slot in predicates. Thus, a causative suffix and a passive suffix cannot occur together in a sentence, that is, they are mutually exclusive in syntactic usage (see 9.9). Fifth, functional or semantic shift from causative to passive may have been facilitated by the necessary implicational relation between causing (causative) and undergoing (passive) an event. For more discussion, see 9.9. Then, where did the causative suffixes come from? Without any concrete historical evidence, one can only speculate from a grammaticalization perspective that they might have diverged from the ancient form of the periphrastic causative *-key ha* 'cause (someone/something) to do/be' via contraction, in a way somewhat similar to the historical derivation of the modal suffix *-keyss* from the past causative construction *-key ha.y-ess* (H.M. Sohn 1996). One recent innovation in support of this hypothesis is the frequent use of the form *nolla-khita* 'surprise (someone)' which has obviously diverged from the periphrasitic causative *nolla-key hata* 'make (someone) surprise'.

There are many interesting studies on grammaticalization phenomena in Korean, from which many of the above examples are quoted. Representative works include W. Huh 1972, 1984; K.M. Lee 1976; H.M. Sohn 1990b, 1996, 1998; J.I. Kwon 1992; H.S. Lee 1992; Martin 1992; Kawanishi and S.O. Sohn 1993; J.H. Ahn 1994, 1996; J.W. Park 1994; Shibatani 1994; Y.W. Kim 1995; J. Lee 1996; S. Rhee 1996; S.O. Sohn 1996, 1998; S.H. You 1996; Bak 1997; S. Oh 1998; and D.J. Choe 1999.

9

Grammatical structure

This chapter surveys the syntactic and semantic characteristics of contemporary standard Korean. The discussions proceed in the order of structural essentials (9.1), sentence types (9.2), syntactic relations (9.3), embedded clauses (9.4), case marking (9.5), delimiter constructions (9.6), numeral constructions (9.7), modality and tense-aspect (9.8), passive and causative constructions (9.9), complex predicate constructions (9.10), negation (9.11), adverbial constructions (9.12), reduction phenomena (9.13), and honorifics and politeness strategies (9.14). For further descriptive and theoretical studies, see the works cited in the appended bibliography.

9.1   Structural essentials

Korean is predicate-final, sharing the typical properties of predicate-final languages, such as Japanese, and very different from languages like English and Chinese. Thus, the predicate (verb or adjective) expression always comes at the end of a clause, whether the clause is a main (matrix) or embedded one.

Korean is also a head-final language and so dependent elements usually precede their heads. All modifiers, whether they are adjectives, adverbs, numerals, relative or complement clauses, subordinate or coordinate clauses, determiners, or genitive constructions, must *precede* the element they modify.

Case, conjunctive, and delimiter particles are all postpositional; titles follow names; an 'auxiliary' predicate follows the 'main' predicate; tense-aspect and modality elements follow the verbal stem in the form of inflectional suffixes; and various sentence or clause types are expressed by a sentence or clause ender which is suffixed to the predicate. The comparative expression takes the order: standard + comparative particle + degree adverb + adjective/adverb as in *Mia pota te yeyppu-n/yeyppu-key* 'prettier than Mia'.

Like many other predicate-final languages, there are no articles or relative pronouns, and there is no movement of a *wh*-element or inversion of any kind in question sentences. Sentence (1) illustrates many of these structural characteristics.

(1)   [*cey ka   pangkum cap-un*]   [*khu-n*]   *koki lul   po-sy-ess-e.yo?*
        I   NM just now catch-RL   big-RL   fish AC   see-SH-PST-POL
        'Did (you) see the big fish I caught just now?'

Notice in (1) that in both the embedded (bracketed) and main (unbracketed) clauses, the verb stem *cap* 'catch', the adjective stem *khu* 'be big', and the verb stem *po* 'see' appear at the end of their respective clauses; the tense-aspect and modality suffixes *-(u)n* (past relativizer in verbs and non-past relativizer in adjectives), *-sy* (subject honorific), *-ess* (past/perfect), and *-e.yo* (polite ender) are attached to their respective predicate stems; the two bracketed relative clauses are placed before the head noun *koki* 'fish'; the time adverb *pangkum* 'just now' precedes the head verb stem *cap* 'catch'; both the nominative and accusative case particles *ka* and *lul* are postpositional; and no article or relative pronoun appears in the sentence.

Due to the predicate-final requirement, the omission or 'gapping' of repeated predicates in conjunctive constructions takes place in the backward direction, as opposed to English, which allows gapping only in forward direction.

(2)   *emma nun   insam (tu-si-ko),   appa nun nok.yong   tu-sey-yo.*
        mom TC   ginseng take-SH-and   dad   TC dear-antler take-SH-POL
        'Mom takes ginseng tonic and dad (takes) dear-antler tonic.'
        (lit. 'Mom (takes) ginseng tonic and dad takes dear-antler tonic.')

Korean has a large number of postpositional case and delimiter particles and predicate suffixes that are responsible for a wide variety of syntactic and semantic functions. Sentences (1) and (2) illustrate that various particles and predicate suffixes are agglutinated to their head words to perform relevant syntactic functions. In particular, conjunctive, relative, and complement clauses, as well as honorification, tense-aspect, modality, and sentence types, are expressed by means of inflectional suffixes.

Korean allows reordering or 'scrambling' among pre-predicate nominal elements only with slight connotative differences in terms of topicality or focus. That is, probably due to the productive use of case particles, nominal elements indicating grammatical functions such as time, subject, direct and indirect object, location, source, goal, instrument, and direction may be scrambled rather freely in syntactic ordering. This will be discussed in 9.2.8. Scrambling also occurs among pre-nominal elements such as relative clauses, genitive phrases, and determiners (9.3).

Korean allows sentential elements that are predictable from the discourse context or situation to be omitted. That is, any nominal construction that is contextually or situationally recoverable is usually not expressed at all, unless it is to be particularly delimited, focused, or topicalized. There are no dummy elements that are comparable to the English deontic *it* or *there* whose sole purpose is to show grammatical functions. In sentence (1), for instance, the subject of the main clause that refers to the addressee 'you' is left out because it is recoverable from the speech situation. Moreover, antecedents of an anaphor such as *ce* 'self' (plain), *caki* 'self' (neutral), *tangsin* 'self' (deferential), or a ZERO pronoun are frequently found in the discourse context, rather than in actual text, as illustrated in (3).

(3)   A: *hal.ape-nim   i   kuli-sy-ess-e.yo?*
           grandfather-HT   NM   draw-SH-PST-POL
           'Did grandfather draw (it)?'

        B: *kulay,   tangsin   i   cikcep   kuli-sy-ess-e.*
           right   self   NM in person draw-SH-PST-INT
           'Yes, (he) drew (it) himself.'

Proliferation of multiple topic constructions is another salient property. One such construction, which is called a multiple subject, multiple nominative, or multiple topic construction is illustrated in (4) (see also 9.2.6).

(4)   *nay yangmal i   patak   i   kwumeng   i   sayngky-ess-e.*
        my sock   NM   bottom NM   hole   NM   appear-PST-INT
        'The bottom of my sock has a hole.'

Korean is characterized by the boundness of predicates. While most nouns are free, all verbs and adjectives are bound and unable to function without a clause or sentence ender. For this reason, the dummy suffix *-ta* is attached to a stem for citation or dictionary entry, as is done in this volume. For instance, the verb stem *mek* 'eat' and the adjective stem *coh* 'be good' are entered in the dictionary as *mekta* and *cohta*, respectively.

Proliferation of predicate compounding is also noteworthy. Serial–verb and auxiliary–verb constructions are abundant. Events tend to be sliced into minute pieces for verbal expressions in Korean. In (5a), the action of 'crawling into' is expressed by serializing three verbs, *kita* 'crawl', *tulta* 'enter', and *ota* 'come'. In (5b), the event is expressed by using two auxiliary verbs, *pelita* and *malta*.

(5)   a. *ai   ka   pang ey   ki-e   tul-e   w-ass-ta.*
           child   NM   room to   crawl-INF   enter-INF   come-PST-DC
           'The child crawled into the room.'

b. *cip*   *i*   ***mun-e***   *cy-e*   ***peli-ko***   ***mal-ass-e.***
   house   NM   fall-INF   become-INF   end-and   stop-PST-INT
   'The house finally collapsed.'

Finally, Korean is well known for its honorific pattern. The speaker–addressee perspective and the speaker–referent perspective are systematically manifested in the sentence structure, as illustrated in (6), where the speaker shows his deference towards the subject referent (Professor Kim) by using the honorific forms *-nim, kkeyse, cinci, capswu-,* and *-si,* and towards the addressee by means of the addressee honorific suffixes *-sup, -ni,* and *-kka.*

(6)   *Kim-sensayng-nim   kkeyse   cinci   capswu-sy-ess-sup-ni-kka?*
     Kim-prof.-HT(H)   NM(H)   meal(H)   eat(H)-SH-PST-AH-IN-Q
     'Did Professor Kim eat?'

Korean has many other characteristic syntactic features. These and the elaboration of the above-mentioned major properties will be the concern of the rest of this chapter.

9.2   Sentence types

Korean sentences are either complex or simplex, depending on whether an embedded clause appears in them. A simplex sentence has essentially the same structure as the main clause of a complex sentence. Thus, all Korean clauses may be dichotomized into main or embedded clauses, in that the latter lack certain adverbials such as vocatives, address terms, and exclamatory words as well as sentence ender elements such as speech-level and sentence-type suffixes. This section deals with main clauses, while embedded clauses will be discussed in 9.4.

Main clauses or simplex sentences may be classified variously in terms of the clause-internal structure: sentence-types, speech levels, and types of predicates. Sentence-types such as declarative, interrogative, propositive, and imperative form the most basic classification of sentences. Speech levels such as plain, intimate, familiar, blunt, polite, deferential, and neutral also constitute an important dimension, since all sentences in Korean must belong to one of these speech levels. As we observed in 8.4, sentence-types and speech levels, however, are fused into sentence enders. Hence, the two dimensions will be discussed together in 9.2.1.

Based on the type of their predicates, Korean sentences are divided into verb and adjective types, each being subclassified into smaller types. The types of verbs and adjectives and case marking are interrelated to a large extent, in that the majority of case marking patterns are dependent on the predicate types. They will be discussed separately, however, the former in this section and the latter under the rubric of syntactic relations in 9.4 because the two dimensions are different in perspective. Multiple topic constructions, subjectless sentences, and word-order scrambling will be discussed in this section.

9.2.1 Declarative, interrogative, propositive, and imperative

A simplex sentence or the main clause of a complex sentence belongs to one of four basic sentence types: declarative (making a statement), interrogative (asking a question), propositive (making a proposal), and imperative (making a command). These four sentence types are marked by sentence enders each of which consists of one or more inflectional suffixes (8.4.3). Superimposed on the four sentence types are six speech levels, plain, intimate, familiar, blunt, polite, and deferential, plus the neutral level which will be discussed shortly. Observe the four different sentence types as they are inflected in the seven levels in (7).

(7)   a. Declarative

pi	*ka*	*o-n-ta.*	[plain]
rain	NM	come-IN-DC	
pi	*ka*	*w-a.*	[intimate]
		come-INT	
pi	*ka*	*o-ney.*	[familiar]
		come-FML	
pi	*ka*	*o-o.*	[blunt]
		come-BLN	
pi	*ka*	*w-a.yo.*	[polite]
		come-POL	
pi	*ka*	*o-p-ni-ta.*	[deferential]
		come-AH-IN-DC	
pi	*ka*	*o-n-ta.*	[neutral]
		come-IN-DC	

'It is raining.'

    b. Interrogative

pi	*ka*	*o-ni?/o-(nu)-nya?*	[plain]
rain	NM	come-Q/come-IN-Q	
pi	*ka*	*w-a?*	[intimate]
		come-INT	

pi	*ka*	*o-na?/o-nu-nka?*	[familiar]
		come-Q/come-IN-Q	
pi	*ka*	*o-o?*	[blunt]
		come-BLN	
pi	*ka*	*w-a.yo?*	[polite]
		come-POL	
pi	*ka*	*o-p-ni-kka?*	[deferential]
		come-AH-IN-Q	
pi	*ka*	*o(-nu)-nya.*	[neutral]
		come-IN-Q	

'Is it raining?'

c. Propositive

yeki	*tto*	*o-ca.*	[plain]
here	again	come-PR	
yeki	*tto*	*w-a.*	[intimate]
		come-INT	
yeki	*tto*	*o-sey.*	[familiar]
		come-PR	
yeki	*tto*	*o-p-si-ta.*	[blunt]
		come-AH-RQ-PR	
yeki	*tto*	*w-a.yo.*	[polite]
		come-POL	
yeki	*tto*	*o-si-p-si-ta.*	[deferential]
		come-SH-AH-RQ-PR	
yeki	*tto*	*o-ca.*	[neutral]
		come-PR	

'Let's come here again.'

d. Imperative

yeki	*tto*	*w-ala.*	[plain]
here	again	come-IM	
yeki	*tto*	*w-a.*	[intimate]
		come-INT	
yeki	*tto*	*o-key.*	[familiar]
		come-IM	
yeki	*tto*	*o-o.*	[blunt]
		come-BLN	

yeki	*tto*	*w-a.yo.*	[polite]
		come-POL	
yeki	*tto*	*o-si-p-si-o.*	[deferential]
		come-SH-AH-RQ-IM	
yeki	*tto*	*o-la.*	[neutral]
		come-IM	

'Come here again!'

The plain speech level, which is the lowest level, is used, in general, by any speaker to any child, to one's own younger sibling, child, or grandchild regardless of age, and to one's daughter-in-law, and also between intimate adult friends whose friendship began in childhood. The intimate level, also called the half-talk style, is used by a child of pre-school age to his or her family members including parents, and between close friends whose friendship began in childhood or adolescence. It may also be used to one's adult or adolescent student, or to one's son-in-law. This level is frequently intermixed with the plain level or the familiar level in the same discourse with the same person. The familiar level is slightly more formal than the intimate level, typically used by a male adult to an adolescent such as a high school or college student or to one's son-in-law, or between two close adult friends whose friendship began in adolescence. The remaining three levels are used only to adult addressees. The blunt level, which is gradually disappearing from daily usage probably due to its authoritative connotation, is sometimes used by a boss to his subordinates or by an old generation husband to his wife.

The most popularly used level is the polite one, which is the informal counterpart of the deferential level. In daily conversations with distant equals or superiors, male speakers usually intermix the deferential and polite levels in the same discourse, while female speakers tend to use only the polite level. Between close adults, however, the polite level alone is usually used by both sexes. In verbal news reports and formal announcements, the deferential level is exclusively used by both sexes.

While the enders of all six speech levels are used in conversation, neutral-level enders are used only in an embedded clause of a quotative construction, in writing to a general audience as in books, articles, and newspapers, and in written exam instructions. The neutral-level forms are the same as the plain-level forms except in interrogatives and imperatives. In interrogatives, the neutral-level ender is only *(-nu)-nya*, and not *-ni*; and in imperatives, the ender is *-(u)la*, and not *-(e/a)la*.

(8) a. *pi   ka   o-nu-nya/*o-ni   ko   mut-sup-ni-ta.*
rain   NM   come-IN-Q/come-Q   QT   ask-AH-IN-DC
'(He) asks if it is raining.'

b. *yeki   tto   o-la/*w-ala   ko   hay-yo.*
here   again   come-IM/come-IM   QT   say-POL
'(They) tell me to come back here again.'

c. *taum   kul   ul   ilk-ko   cilmun   ey tap.ha-la/*tap.ha.y-ela.*
next   writing AC read-and question to answer-IM/answer-IM
'Read the following sentences, and answer the questions.'

In addition to the six interactive speech levels, there is a superpolite level which is no longer used in spoken Korean. This level has the enders *-na-i-ta* (declarative), *-na-i-kka* (interrogative), and *-(si-op)-sose* (imperative), and appears only in religious prayers, poems, and in extremely formal and deferential letters. In both this and the blunt levels, no inherent propositive form is available. It seems that, in the former, the addressee is so vastly superior that the speaker could not propose to share an action, whereas, in the latter, the deferential propositive form *-p-si-ta* (without the subject honorific suffix *-(u)si*) fills the slot pragmatically, as illustrated by *yeki tto o-p-si-ta* 'Let's come here again' in (7c).

Declarative sentences include not only descriptive, assertive, or reporting sentences, but also so-called apperceptive sentences such as (9a, b), suppositive sentences such as (9c), promissive-assurance sentences such as (9d), admonitive (warning) sentences such as (9e), elliptical sentences such as (9f, g), and rhetorical sentences such as (9h).

(9)   a. *pi   ka   o-nun-kwun!*
rain   NM   come-IN-APP
'Oh, it's raining!' (discovery and confirmation)

b. *pi   ka   o-ney!*
rain   NM   come-APP
'Oh, it's raining!' (counterexpectation)

c. *na   nun   ka-ci.*
I   TC   go-SUP
'I think I had better go.'

d. *na   nun   ka-ma!*
I   TC   go-PRM
'I promise that I will go.'

e. *nwun   i   o-l-la.*
   rain   NM   come-PRS-ADM
   'It may snow, I warn you.'

f. *pi   ka   o-nun   **tey!***
   rain   NM   come-IN circumstance
   'It's raining, (what shall we do?)'

g. *Mia   nun   o-l   ke-l yo!*
   Mia   TC   come-PRS   that-AC POL
   'I suspect Mia will come.'

h. *Nami   ka   o-keyss-ta! ~*
   Nami   NM   come-may-DC
   'I DON'T think Nami will come.'

Interrogative sentences, whose basic meaning is asking or requesting information, also represent indirect requests (10a), indirect suggestions (10b), and offers (10c), as well as rhetorical questions (10d, e).

(10)   a. *way   an   ca-ni?*
        why   not   sleep-Q
        'Why don't you sleep? (Go to sleep.)'

       b. *wuli   nun   ka-ci?!~*
        we   TC   go-SUP
        'How about us going?'

       c. *wuli   ttena-l-kka?*
        we   depart-PRS-Q
        'Shall we leave?'

       d. *nwu   ka   molu-ni?*
        anybody   NM   not know-Q
        'Is anybody unaware of it? (Everybody knows.)'

       e. *pul   na-ss-ci   an-h-a.yo?! ~*
        fire   occur-PST-NOM   not-be-POL
        'Isn't it the case that fire broke out?! (It is!)'

Propositive and imperative sentences are largely equivalent to English *let's* constructions and imperative sentences, respectively, although there are some interesting syntactic and semantic differences. Unlike in English, most adjectives in Korean cannot be made into propositive and imperative constructions (see 9.2.2). Thus, English sentences like 'Let's be quiet' or 'Be quiet!' cannot be expressed with the adjective *co.yonghata* 'be quiet', unless it is changed to a verb phrase like *co.yong-hi hata* (lit. 'do quietly'), as in *co.yong-hi ha-ca* 'Let's be quiet' and *co.yong-hi hay-la!* 'Be quiet!' Propositive sentences may be used not only for suggesting both the speaker and the hearer's joint action but also the speaker's or the hearer's action alone.

(11)   a. *nay ka   ka-ca.*
         I   NM   go-PR
         'I propose that I go.'

         b. *co.yong-hi   ha-p-si-ta.*
         quiet-AD   do-AH-RQ-PR
         'You guys, be quiet!'

Notice in (11a) that the suffix *-ca* may relinquish the participation of the hearer while retaining the proposal meaning. Similarly, when one wants to get off a crowded bus, he or she usually says *nayli-p-si-ta* (get off-AH-RQ-PR) 'Let me get off!' (lit. 'Let's get off.').

The forces of command in imperative sentences may be of different degrees, including order, demand, permission, request, advice, warning, plea, and even welcome, as illustrated in (12) with the plain sentence ender.

(12)   a. *cenhwa   pat-ala.*
         phone   receive-IM
         'Answer the phone.'

         b. *cal   ca-la.*
         well   sleep-IM
         'Goodnight.' (lit. 'Sleep well.')

         c. *ney ka   ka-pw-ala.*
         you NM   go-try-IM
         'Why don't you go?' (lit. 'You try going!')

d. *ese   w-ala.*
   quickly   come-IM
   'Welcome.' (lit. 'Come quickly.')

e. *say-hay   pok   manhi   pat-ala.*
   new-year   blessing much   receive-IM
   'Happy New Year' (lit. 'Receive many blessings in the New Year.')

9.2.2   Verbs and adjectives

Korean has two classes of predicates: verbs (denoting activity and process) and adjectives (denoting stativity). Korean adjectives do not appear after a copula (which is an adjective in its own right), but instead inflect for honorifics, tense-aspect, and modality, just as verbs do. Thus, for instance, there is no syntactic difference between the verb *cwuk-ess-ta* (die-PST-DC) 'died' and the adjective *sulph-ess-ta* (be sad-PST-DC) 'was sad'.

The main difference between verbs and adjectives is morphological, in that different inflectional allomorphs are attached to them (8.1.5; 8.1.6; 8.4). Thus, the plain-level indicative form is *-(nu)n* for verbs, as in *ilk-nun-ta* 'reads' and *ka-n-ta* 'goes', and ZERO for adjectives, as in *sulphu-ta* 'is sad' and *khu-ta* 'is big'. Adnominal indicative forms are also different: *-nu* in verbs and ZERO in adjectives as in *ilk-nu-n* 'reading', *ka-nu-n* 'going' vs. *sulphu-n*, *khu-n* 'big'. The lack of past/perfect adnominal forms in adjectives is another difference. Thus, there are no past/perfect adjective forms comparable to verb constructions such as *ilk-un salam* 'a person who read' and *ca-n salam* 'a person who slept'.

There are syntactic differences too. First, adjectives are limited mostly to declarative and interrogative sentences, whereas verbs occur in propositive and imperative sentences as well. Adjective constructions in propositive or imperative sound unnatural. There are many exceptions, however, as shown in adjective constructions such as *kenkangha-p-si-ta* (healthy-AH-RQ-PR) 'Let's be healthy!', *hayngpokha-sey-yo!* (happy-SH-POL) 'Be happy!', *solcikha-ca!* 'Let's be frank', and *pucilenhay-la!* (diligent-IM) 'Be diligent!'

Second, only verbs are allowed to be made progressive with the progressive-forming construction *-ko iss-ta* (and exist-DC) 'be ~ing', as in (13).

(13)   a. *nay   ka   al-ko   iss-ta.*   (verb)
             I   NM   know-and   exist-DC
             'I am aware of it.' (Lit. 'I am knowing it.')

b. **Nami ka   **kenkangha-**ko   iss-ta.*   (adjective)
   Nami NM   healthy-and   stay-DC
   'Nami is being healthy.'

Third, only verbs occur with 'intentive' and 'purposive' conjunctive suffixes such as *-(u)lyeko* 'intending to' and the conjunctive phrase *-ki wiha-ye* (NOM do for-and) 'in order to, with a view to'. Notice that adjectives are not permitted in (14).

(14)   a. *Inho ka   **al-lyeko**   ayssu-n-ta.*
            Inho NM   know-to   try hard-IN-DC
            'Inho tries hard to find out.'

        a'. **Inho ka   **kippu-lyeko**   ayssu-n-ta.*
            Inho NM   happy-to   try hard-IN-DC
            'Inho tries hard to be happy.'

        b. *tongmul   un   **mek-ki**   **wiha-ye**   sa-n-ta.*
            animal   TC   eat-NOM   do for-to   live-IN-DC
            'Animals live to eat.'

        b'. **inkan   un   **kippu-ki**   **wiha-ye**   sa-n-ta.*
            human   TC   happy-NOM do for-to   live-IN-DC
            'People live to be happy.'

Fourth, while the sentence-ender *-(a/e)la* is imperative with a verb as in (15a), it is exclamatory with an adjective, as in (15b).

(15)   a. *mek-**ela**.*   (verb)
            eat-IM
            'Please eat.'

        b. *chwuw-**ela**.*   (adjective)
            cold-EX
            'I am cold!'

Fifth, the object (or patient) of a transitive verb takes the accusative particle *(l)ul* as in (16a) whereas the object (or patient) of a 'transitive adjective' takes the nominative particle *ka/i* as in (16b).

(16)   a. *Mia   ka   sosel   ul   ilk-ess-e.yo.*
          Mia   NM   novel   AC   read-PST-POL
          'Mia read a novel.'

       b. *Nami   ka   Mia   ka   pulew-ess-e.yo.*
          Nami   NM   Mia   NM   envy-PST-POL
          'Nami envied Mia.'

There are other more specific syntactic differences, which will be touched on here and there in the subsections that follow. A few words function as both verbs and adjectives with corresponding meaning differences: *ha-* 'do (verb); be in the state of (adjective)', *iss-* 'be staying (verb); stay, exist, have (adjective)', *khu-* 'grow (verb); be big, tall (adjective)', *nuc-* 'get late (verb); be late (adjective)', *kamsahata* 'thank (verb); be thankful (adjective)', etc.

9.2.3   Verb sentences

The simplest form of verb sentences is an intransitive type consisting of a subject in the nominative case and a verb, optionally accompanied by one or more modifiers or adjuncts.

(17)   a. *appa ka   emma hako caknyen ilpon ey pay lo ka-sy-ess-e.yo.*
          dad NM mom with last year Japan to ship by go-SH-PST-POL
          'My dad went to Japan with my mom by boat last year.'

       b. *Inho nun   kamki   ttaymun   ey   cip   eyse   swi-e.yo.*
          Inho TC   cold   due   to   home   at   rest-POL
          'Inho is resting at home due to a cold.'

Another intransitive type comprises simple sentences with two nominative cases. One such subtype includes inchoative (change of state) sentences where a subject and a complement, both in the nominative case, occur with the inchoative verb *toyta* 'become' as in (18a). Another subtype consists of experiencer–theme sentences as in (18b). Verbs in this category include *tulta* 'suffer from' (lit. 'enter') and *nata* 'appear'. Both the experiencer noun (subject) and the theme noun are in the nominative case.

(18)   a. *Kim-kwun i   mikwuk eyse kyoswu   ka toy-ess-e.*
          Kim-Mr   NM America in   professor NM become-PST-INT
          'Mr Kim became a professor in America.'

b. *hal.apeci   ka   kamki   ka   tu-sy-ess-e.yo.*
   grandpa   NM   flu   NM   enter-SH-PST-POL
   'Grandpa caught a cold.'

A third intransitive type contains a verb that denotes reciprocity and a nominal marked by the comitative particle *(k)wa/hako* 'and, with'. When the comitative-marked nominal follows the nominative-marked subject, only the 'with' interpretation is possible as in (19a); otherwise both 'with' and 'and' interpretations are possible as in (19b).

(19)   a. *Nami   ka   enni   wa   ssaw-ess-e.yo.*
          Nami   NM   sister with   fight-PST-POL
          'Nami fought with her older sister.'

       b. *nwuna   hako   ku   uysa   ka   khisuhay-ss-e.yo.*
          sister   and   the   doctor NM   kiss-PST-POL
          'My older sister and the doctor kissed.' or
          'The doctor kissed my older sister.'

A fourth intransitive type consists of passive sentences where a passive or pseudo-passive verb occurs with a 'patient' subject in the nominative case and an 'agent' nominal in the locative case marked by *eykey* or *hanthey* in the sense of 'by'. If the action denoted by a passive verb affects only a part of the patient's body or a thing belonging to the patient, that body part or thing can be expressed as an object in the accusative case.

(20)   a. *totwuk   i   swunkyeng   eykey   (phal ul) cap-hi-ess-ta.*
          thief   NM   police   by   arm AC catch-PAS-PST-DC
          'The thief was caught by a policeman (by the arm).'

       b. *Mia   nun   totwuk   hanthey   cikap   ul   ppayas-ky-ess-ta.*
          Mia   TC   thief   by   wallet AC   rob-PAS-PST-DC
          'Mia was robbed of her wallet by a thief.'

       c. *nay   chinkwu nun   caki   apeci   hanthey   mac-ass-e.*
          my   friend   TC   self   father by   get hit-PST-INT
          'My friend was spanked by his father.'

A fifth intransitive type is that of nominative–dative/locative, where verbs like *tulta* 'enter, appeal', *nata* 'appear, happen, occur', *kellita* 'hang, be caught, suffer from', *ceng-tulta* 'become fond of', *insa-hata* 'greet', *kamsa-hata* 'thank', *maytallita* 'cling to', and *uyci-hata* 'depend on' occur.

(21)   a. *ce*   *kulim* *i*   *maum* *ey* *tul-e.yo.*
             that picture NM mind to appeal-POL
             'That picture appeals to my taste.'

     b. *nay* *chinkwu* *ka* *pyeng* *ey* *kelly-ess-e.*
             my friend   NM sickness to suffer-PST-INT
             'My friend has fallen ill.'

Several types of transitive verb sentences exist, allowing adjuncts and modifiers to occur optionally. The most productive type consists of a subject and an object in the nominative and accusative cases, respectively.

(22)   *hyeng* *i* *kukcang* *eyse* *nay* *chinkwu* *lul*   *manna-ss-e.*
           brother NM theatre   in my friend   AC meet-PST-INT
           'My older brother met my friend at the theatre.'

Korean transitive verbs normally do not allow a subject to be an inanimate noun. In writings such as literary works, however, nouns like *pihayngki* 'airplane', *hwacay* 'fire', *hongswu* 'flood', *kanan* 'poverty', and *cencayng* 'war' are often used as the subject. Even then, such words carry a metaphorical sense of personification.

Another transitive type consists of verbs that occur with nominals in the nominative, accusative, and source cases. This includes not only receiving verbs such as *pat.ta* 'receive' and *tang-hata* 'undergo' but also certain passive verbs like *cap-hita* 'be caught' and *palp-hita* 'be stepped on'. The agentive source particle is *eykey(se)/hanthey(se)* for verbs of receiving as in (23a), but *eykey/hanthey* for passive verbs as in (23b).

(23)   a. *na nun ce* *cemwen* *eykey(se)* *changphi lul* *tanghay-ss-e.yo.*
             I TC that clerk   from   disgrace AC undergo-PST-POL
             'I was humiliated by that clerk over there.'

     b. *Nami nun nam* *haksayng* *hanthey* *pal* *ul*   *palp-hy-ess-e.*
             Nami TC male student   by   foot AC step-PAS-PST-INT
             'Nami got her foot stepped on by a male student.'

A third transitive type involves ditransitive verbs such as *cwuta* 'give' (plain), *tulita* 'give' (humble), *kaluchita* 'teach', *cisihata* 'direct', and *ceysihata* 'show'. This type has direct and indirect objects. Here also belong ditransitive causative verbs like *po-ita* 'show', *ip-hita* 'dress (someone)', and *mek-ita* 'feed (someone)'.

(24)   a. *apeci nun halmeni eykey ton   ul   tuli-sy-ess-e.yo.*
            father TC grandma to   money AC give-SH-PST-POL
            'Father gave money to grandma.'

      b. *Nami nun Inho hanthey caki sacin ul   po-y-ess-ta.*
            Nami TC Inho to   self picture AC see-CAS-PST-DC
            'Nami showed a picture of herself to Inho.'

Another ditransitive type is characterized by double accusative cases.

(25)   a. *hyeng   i   kay lul   kkoli lul   cap-ass-e.*
            brother NM dog AC   tail   AC   catch-PST-INT
            'My older brother caught the dog by its tail.'

      b. *Milan.i nun uyhak   ul   kongpu lul   hay-yo.*
            Milan   TC medicine AC study   AC   do-POL
            'Milan studies medicine.'

      c. *apeci nun halmeni lul   ton   ul   tuli-sy-ess-e.yo.*
            father TC grandma AC money AC give-SH-PST-POL
            'Father gave money to grandmar.'

(25a) is a case of macro–micro (*kay* vs. *kkoli*) relation. (25b) is a case of separating a verbal noun from *hata*. As for (25c), when occurring with a donatory verb such as *cwuta* or *tulita* 'give', a dative nominal with *eykey/hanthey* (neutral) or *kkey* (honorific) 'to' can be accusativized for focus, resulting in two accusative particles in that sentence or clause.

Notice in (25b) that consonant-final given names such as *Milan* are followed by the vowel *i*. This was discussed in 8.1.2.

9.2.4 *Adjective sentences*

Adjective sentences describe states and may be divided into two main groups: those expressing an objectively observable state or nature of an object or event and those expressing one's internal psychological state. The former may be called objective adjectives, and can be subclassified into the copula, descriptive adjectives, and locational adjectives, whereas the latter may be termed sensory (subjective or psycho-emotive) adjectives.

9.2.4.1   Copular sentences

The copula is *ita* 'be' which is an adjective because it inflects in the same way as other adjectives do. Its usual meaning is equational, definitional, identificational, or descriptive, and never existential. In casual speech, the copula stem *i* is pronounced as ZERO between a vowel and a consonant and *y* between vowels, as in *na ta* '(It) is me' (plain level), *na y-a* '(It) is me' (intimate level), and *na y-ess-ta* '(It) was me.' Being an adjective in its own right, unlike in English (e.g., 'He is happy'), it never occurs before or after another adjective. The negative counterpart is *anita* 'be not', which is analysable either as *ani* 'not' and ZERO copula or, as in this book, as *an* 'not' and *ita* copula. Like other adjectives, *ita* cannot be preceded by the negative adverb *mos* 'cannot', hence **mos ita* 'cannot be' is ungrammatical.

Copular sentences take a complement in the nominative case, and copulative complements are usually nominals (nouns, pronouns, numerals, noun phrases, etc.).

(26)   *ce   ay   nun **chencay** (i)-ciman Mia nun **chencay** ka   an   i-ta.*
          that child TC   genius   be-but   Mia TC   genius   NM not be-DC
          'That child is a genius but Mia is not.'

Notice in (26) that the nominal complement takes the nominative case and is overtly marked with *ka* in negative sentences. It is covert or unmarked in positive sentences. Thus, copular sentences are double nominative constructions. The subject and its complement in a copular sentence must occur in that order.

Although the complements of the following copular sentences are nominals, they are descriptive, not definitional, equational, or identificational. Together with a nominal complement, the copula indicates the state that the nominal denotes.

(27)   a. *wuli   tongsayng   un   **yelsim**   i-eyyo.*
              our   brother   TC   diligence   be-POL
              'My younger brother is diligent.'

          b. *ce   nun   wuli   ai   ka   **kekceng**   i-eyyo.*
              I   TC   our   child NM   worry   be-POL
              'As for me, my child worries me.'

    c. *Milan.i   nun   nemu   **kamsangcek**   i-a.*
       Milan   TC   too   sentimental   be-INT
       'Milan is too sentimental.'

The complements in (28) are composed of a head noun (bold-faced) preceded by a relative clause (bracketed). Note that the head noun of each complement and the copula are so cohesive that they function like descriptive adjectives.

(28)   a. *na   nun   [kot   ilpon   ey   ka-l]   **kyeyhoyk**   i-ta.*
       I   TC   soon   Japan   to   go-PRS   plan   be-DC
       'I plan to go to Japan soon.'

    b. *Kim   kyoswu-nim   un   [kkok   o-si-l]   **kes**   i-ney.*
       Kim   professor-HT   TC   surely   come-SH-PRS   fact   be-FML
       'Professor Kim will surely come.'

The complement of a copular sentence is usually a nominal, but may occasionally be a postpositional phrase (29a), a conjunctive clause (29b), a sentence (29c), or an adverb (29d).

(29)   a. *wuli   hakkyo   nun **ce   keli   tong-ccok ulo puthe** ZERO-ta.*
       our   school   TC   that   street   east-side   DR   from   be-DC
       'Our school is from the east side of that street.'

    b. ***ton   i   eps-ese** ka   an   i-eyyo.*
       money   NM   lack-so   NM   not   be-POL
       'It is not that (I) don't have money.'

    c. *muncey   nun   **cwuk-nu-nya   sa-nu-nya**   y-a.*
       question   TC   die-IN-Q   live-IN-Q   be-INT
       'To live or die, that is the question.'

    d. *i   swul-cip   un   **pyello**   y-eyyo.*
       this   wine-house   TC   (not) specially   be-POL
       'This bar is not especially good.'

Since understood elements may be deleted rather freely, the following kind of sentence may result.

(30)   *ce   nun   khephi   ZERO-p-ni-ta.*
        I   TC   coffee   be-AH-IN-DC
        'As for me, (what I would like) is coffee.'

The adjective *hata* or its contracted form *hta* 'be in the state of' behaves like a copula. Its semantic function is limited to being descriptive, which is comparable to the function of the copula *ita* in constructions like *yelsim i-ta* 'be diligent' and *kekceng i-ta* 'be worrisome'. This *hata* occurs productively after adjectival nouns as in *kenkang to ha-ta* '(He) is also healthy', but also after other types of complements such as a nominalized clause (31a), a defective head noun with a relative clause (31b), and a sound symbolic adverb (31c).

(31)   a. *sacang-nim   cha   ka   coh-ci   ka   an-h-ta.*
           president-HT   car   NM   good-NOM   NM   not-be-DC
           'Our (company) president's car is not good.'

        b. *nwun   i   o-l   tus   ha-ta.*
           snow   NM   come-PRS   seeming   be-DC
           'It seems that it will snow.'

        c. *kil   i   mikkul-mikkul   ha-ta.*
           road   NM   slippery   be-DC
           'The road is slippery.'

9.2.4.2   Descriptive adjective sentences

Constituting the largest subclass, descriptive adjectives denote both quality and quantity and are intransitive. Examples include *alumtapta* 'be beautiful', *celmta* 'be young', *ttokttok-hata* 'be smart', *hyenmyeng-hata* 'be wise', *sumathu-hata* 'be smart', *chata* 'be cold', *hayngpok-hata* 'be happy', *huyta* 'be white', *hwenhata* 'be bright', *kanan-hata* 'be poor', *khuta* 'be big', *kkaykkushata* 'be clean', *kilta* 'be long', *mukepta* 'be heavy', *nelpta* 'be wide', *nulita* 'be slow', *nophta* 'be high', *ttattushata* 'be warm', and *twungkulta* 'be round'. The typical patterns of adjective sentences are illustrated in (32).

(32)   a. *wuli   halmeni   nun   acik   celm-usy-e.yo.*
           our   grandma   TC   still   young-SH-POL
           'My grandma is still young.'

b. *Payktwu-san   un   Hanla-san   pota   te   **noph-ta.***
   Payktwu-Mt   TC   Hanla-Mt   than   more   high-DC
   'Mt Paektu is higher than Mt Halla.'

c. *ce   namca   nun   akma   (wa)   **kath-ta.***
   that   man   TC   devil   with   same-DC
   'That man over there is like a devil.'

Together with the defective noun *kes* 'thing, fact', the adjective *kathta* 'be same, like' has been grammaticalized to mean 'it seems/feels like' in constructions like *nay ka cwuk-ul kes kath-a.yo* 'I feel like I'm dying' and *nalssi ka coh-un kes kath-a.yo* 'The weather seems to be good.' In these constructions, a comitative particle cannot occur after *kes* (cf. 8.7).

9.2.4.3   Locational adjectives

There are adjectives that require, in addition to a subject, an overt or covert nominal in the locative case marked by the particles *eykey/hanthey/kkey* 'at, to (an animate)' or *ey* 'at, to (an inanimate)'. One subset comprises the adjectives which denote not only existence and location but also possession, e.g. *issta* 'be, stay, have', *kyeysita* 'be, stay' (honorific), *epsta* 'be not, not stay, do not have', *manhta* 'be much, many, have a lot', and *cekta* 'be little, few, do not have a lot'.

(33)   a. *hal.apeci   kkey   chayk   i   **manh-a.yo.***
        grandpa   at   book   NM   many-POL
        (lit. 'There are many books with my grandpa.')

       b. *na   eykey   coh-un   sayngkak   i   **iss-e.***
         I   at   good-RL   idea   NM   exist-INT
        (lit. 'There is a good idea with me.')

When possession is intended, the locative nominal denoting an animate is shifted to the nominative case functioning as the subject of the sentence. Then, the original nominative subject (*chayk*, *sayngkak* in (33)) functions as the object, although its nominative particle remains intact.

(34)   a. *hal.apeci   ka/nun   chayk   i   **manh-usy-e.yo.***
        grandpa   NM/TC   book   NM   many-SH-POL
        'My grandpa has many books.'

b. *na(y)* *ka/nun* *coh-un* *sayngkak* *i* ***iss-e.***
I   NM/TC   good-RL   idea   NM   exist-INT
'I have a good idea.'

Adjectives that refer to necessity may constitute another subset.

(35)   *Mia*   *eykey/ka*   *ton*   *i*   ***philyohay-yo.***
Mia   to/NM   money   NM   necessary-POL
'Mia needs money.'

9.2.4.4   Sensory sentences

Sensory adjectives which denote emotion or sensation constitute a relatively large subclass of adjectives. As a sensory adjective, some words such as *pulepta* 'be envious, envy', *mipta* 'be hateful, hate', and *silhta* 'be disagreeable, dislike' are always used as transitive, as in *na nun ney ka **pulew-e*** 'I envy you'. Some other words such as *simsimhata* 'be bored' and *kamsa-hata* 'be thankful' are usually used as intransitive, as in *(yele-pun eykey) **kamsa-ha-p-ni-ta*** 'Thank you; I am thankful (to all of you).' Still other sensory words, such as *sulphuta* 'be sad, feel sad', *komapta* 'be thankful, thank', and *musepta* 'be scared, fear', are used both intransitively as in (36a) and transitively as in (36b).

(36)   a. *ne*   *nun*   ***musep-ni?***
     you   TC   scary-Q
     'Are you scared?'

       b. *ne*   *nun*   *ce*   *kay*   *ka*   ***musep-ni?***
     you   TC   that   dog   NM   fear-Q
     'Do you fear that dog?'

Some sensory adjectives are compounds derived originally from a phrase with an existential adjective, as in *caymi issta* 'be interesting' (lit. 'interest exists'), *maum ey epsta* 'dislike' (lit. 'do not exist in mind'), and *kekceng epsta* 'do not worry' (lit. 'worry does not exist').

Certain adjectives are both sensory and descriptive depending on whether the subject is a human or non-human. For instance, *chwupta* is descriptive in *nalssi ka chwup-ta* 'The weather is cold', but sensory in *na nun chwup-ta* 'I am cold'; *cohta* is descriptive in *i kulim i coh-ta* 'This picture is good', but sensory in *na nun i kulim i coh-ta* 'I like this picture.' To this group belong adjectives such as *caymi issta* 'be interesting', *ipputa* 'be pretty', *musepta* 'be scary', and *oylopta* 'be lonely'. For instance, compare *ce kay ka musep-ta* 'That dog over there is scary' with the two sensory sentences in (36). On the other hand, many other sensory adjectives such as *pulepta* 'envy' and *koylopta* 'be distressed' cannot be used in this way since they cannot take non-human subjects.

Sensory adjectives denote only an unobservable internal state of mind. Therefore, they are used only with the first person subject in declaratives and with the second person subject in interrogatives when they occur in the present indicative mood; otherwise they are unnatural.

(37)   a. *na   nun   simsimha-ta.*
             I   TC   bored-DC
             'I am bored.'

         b. *ne   nun   simsimha-ni?*
             you   TC   bored-Q
             'Are you bored?'

         c. *?ne   nun   simsimha-ta.*
             you   TC   bored-DC
             'You are bored.'

Sentences like (37c) may be acceptable only when the speaker is in a position to know the subject referent's feeling or sensation. When they occur in the past tense or with a modal suffix, however, there is no such restriction, as observed in (38). This may be because, in the case of past tense, the speaker may have heard about the subject referent's internal feeling or sensation and, in the case of a modal, the speaker can make a guess or inference.

(38)   a. *halmeni   nun   ecey   simsimha-sy-ess-e.*
             grandma   TC   yesterday   bored-SH-PST-INT
             'My grandma felt bored yesterday.'

         b. *hal.apeci   nun   nayil   kippu-si-keyss-e.yo.*
             grandpa   TC   tomorrow   happy-SH-may-POL
             'My grandma may be happy tomorrow.'

Similarly, attachment of complex evidential forms like *-(u)n mo.yang i-ta* 'appear to be' or *-(u)l kes i-ta* 'will be/do', or the indicatory verb *hata* 'do, show signs of being' renders otherwise unnatural sentences acceptable, as in (39). Notice in (39b) that the sentence is no longer an adjective but a verb construction, in that it has a compound verb (i.e., *kipp-e hata*) of which a sensory adjective stem is a part.

(39) a. *ne   nun   cikum   sulphu-n   mo.yang   i-kwun.*
          you   TC   now   sad-RL   appearance   are-APP
          'You appear to be sad now!'

     b. *Inho   nun   cikum   acwu   kipp-e   hay-yo.*
          Inho   TC   now   very   happy-INF   do-POL
          'Inho is very happy now.'

The desiderative adjective *siphta* 'be desirable, wish' is a special transitive sensory adjective. It is a bound adjective and is used only when preceded by a verb clause that ends in the nominalizer suffix *-ko*.

(40) *na   nun   ku   chinkwu   ka   po-ko   siph-e.*
         I   TC   the   friend   NM   see-to   wishful-INT
         'I wish to see that friend.'

9.2.5   Transitivity

The dichotomy between transitive and intransitive has less syntactic motivation in Korean than in some other languages. Passivization, for instance, does not provide any conclusive evidence because only a limited subset of transitive verbs can be turned into passive forms, as in *mekta* 'eat' vs. *mek-hita* 'be eaten' and *mit.ta* 'believe' vs. *mit-kita* 'be believed', but *ttaylita* 'hit' vs. *?* 'be hit' and *cwuta* 'give' vs. *?* 'be given'. It is often claimed that the accusative particle *(l)ul* is the direct object marker and a verb preceded by a noun with this particle is transitive. It is true that all clearly transitive verbs have an object with this particle. If we follow this criterion, however, there would be very few verbs which are not transitive. For instance, the obviously intransitive verb *wulta* 'cry' can occur with a duration noun followed by *(l)ul*, as in *twu si-kan ul wu-n-ta* '(He) has been crying for two hours', the intransitive verb *kata* 'go' occurs with *(l)ul* in constructions such as *hakkyo lul ka-n-ta* '(He) goes to school' and *kwukyeng ul ka-n-ta* '(He) goes sightseeing.' Despite the lack of absolute criteria, it is useful to talk about (in)transitivity. For instance, we can say that so-called middle verbs like *wumcikita* 'move (something), move by itself' and *pulta* 'blow (something), blow by itself' are used both transitively and intransitively to correspond to the two meanings that each verb carries, and that *pota* 'see' and *cwuk-ita* 'kill' are transitives whose intransitive counterparts are *po-ita* 'be seen' and *cwukta* 'die', respectively.

Semantically, transitivity is traditionally understood as carry-over or transference of an action from one participant (e.g., an agent) to another (e.g., a patient). Needless to say, transitivity is a matter of degree, i.e., some sentences are more transitive than others depending on the kind of predicates involved, agency of the subject, affectedness of the object, etc. For instance, the sentences in (41), all of which are assumed to be transitive since at least one direct object appears, show semantic transitivity in decreasing order.

(41)   a. *Inho   nun   Nami   eykey   sakwa   lul   cwu-ess-e.yo.*
           Inho   TC   Nami   to   apple   AC   gave-PST-POL
           'Inho gave an apple to Nami.'

    b. *ku   swunkyeng   i   totwuk   ul   cap-ass-e.yo.*
           the   police   NM   thief   AC   caught-PST-POL
           'That policeman caught a thief.'

    c. *Inho   nun   pam-kil   ul   kel-ess-e.yo.*
           Inho   TC   night-road   AC   walk-PST-POL
           'Inho walked (along) the night road.'

    d. *hal.apeci   nun   ku sosik   ul   tul-usy-ess-e.yo.*
           grandpa   TC   the news   AC   hear-SH-PST-POL
           'Grandpa heard the news.'

    e. *na   nun   kay   ka   musew-e.yo.*
           I   TC   dog   NM   afraid of-POL
           'I am afraid of dogs.'

    f. *Mia   ka   cha   ka   iss-e.yo.*
           Mia   NM   car   NM   exist-POL
           'Mia has a car.'

As alluded to in the examples in (41), the traditional definition of transitive verbs is slightly modified for the description of Korean in this volume such that any predicate in a sentence with an agent or experiencer as the subject and a patient or a theme as the object is defined as transitive. Thus, the subject of a transitive sentence is not necessarily an agent but could also be an experiencer as in (41d, e, f), and an adjective can also be transitive if it occurs with a patient as in (41e, f). The objects of transitive verbs are marked with an accusative particle, while those of transitive adjectives are marked with a nominative particle due to their low transitivity. The predicates which do not satisfy the above conditions are intransitive.

9.2.6   Topic-stacking sentences

Along with single-subject or single-object sentences, Korean abounds in simple sentences where more than one 'subject' or 'object' appear. These sentences are frequently called multiple-subject (or multiple-nominative) and multiple-object (or multiple-accusative) constructions, respectively. Multiple-subject constructions are much more prevalent. H.M. Sohn (1986) places these constructions under the rubric of multiple-topic constructions.

(42)   a. **Mia**   *ka/nun/to*   **nwun**   *i/un/to*   **hana**   *ka*   *khu-ta.*
                 Mia   NM/TC/also eye   NM/TC/also one   NM   big-DC
                 'Mia (also) has one big eye.'

            b. *na nun*   **cwi** *lul*   **han**   **mali** *lul*   **kkoli**   *lul*   *call-ass-ta.*
                 I   TC   rat   AC   1   CN   AC   tail   AC   cut-PST-DC
                 'I cut the tail of one rat.'

Korean has a constituent structure rule of the form S → NP S (9.3) to account for productive multiple nominative constructions such as (42a). The NP in this case cannot be a subject of a predicate verb or adjective even though it is in the nominative case, but takes the following sentence as a whole as its predicate. This NP may be called a sentential topic or a sentential subject. Thus, in (42a), *Mia* is the sentential topic or subject of the following sentence in which *nwun* is the sentential topic or subject of the remaining sentence.

Korean also has a phrase structure rule of the form V' → NP V' (9.3) to account for multiple object constructions such as (42b). Notice that *cwi* 'rat' is not the object of the verb *caluta* 'cut' because the thing that is cut is not the rat but its tail. Thus, *cwi* may be regarded as the topic of the following verb phrase, and *han mali* is the topic of the rest of the verb phrase. These topics may be termed verb phrase objects since they are in the accusative case.

A wide variety of nominal constructions in sentences can be topicalized as sentential subjects. Whether a given topic sentence is acceptable or not depends by and large on the relationship between the topic and the rest of the sentence. In general, the syntactic and semantic relations between a topic nominal and the following nominative-marked nominal is anaphoric as in (43a), possessive as in (43b), class-member as in (43c), static location as in (43d), stage-setting as in (43e), and quantification as in (43f). Sentence (43g) illustrates stacking of nominals in different syntactic relations, involving multiple possession and static location.

(43)   a. ***Mia***   *nun*   *caki*   *ka*   *ka-ss-ta.*
        Mia   TC   self   NM   go-PST-DC
        '(As for) Mia, (she) herself went.'

    b. ***Waikhikhi*** *ka*   *kyengchi*   *ka*   *coh-ta.*
        Waikiki   NM   scenery   NM   good-DC
        'Waikiki has nice scenery.'

    c. ***kkoch***   *un*   *cangmi*   *ka*   *alumtap-ta.*
        flower   TC   rose   NM   beautiful-DC
        '(As for) flowers, roses are beautiful.'

    d. ***nyu.yok***   *i*   *pemcoy*   *ka*   *manh-ta.*
        New York NM   crime   NM   many-DC
        'New York has much crime.'

    e. ***nalssi***   *ka*   *pi*   *ka*   *o-keyss-ta.*
        weather   NM   rain   NM   come-may-DC
        'The weather, it may rain.'

    f. ***na nun mom*** *i*   ***mukey*** *ka* *200-phawuntu* *ka*   *naka-n-ta.*
        I   TC   body   NM   weight NM   200-pound   NM   weigh-IN-DC
        'I weigh 200 pounds.'

    g. ***i***   *cip*   *i*   *cipung* *i*   ***wi*** *ka kwumeng* *i*   *na-ss-ta.*
        this   house NM   roof   NM   top NM   hole   NM   appear-PST-DC
        'The top of the roof of this house has a hole.'

In a sentence like (44), *Mia* is considered a scrambled object of the verb since it is still in the accusative case. Thus, it is not a multiple-topic construction.

(44)   *Mia*   *nun/*ka/lul*   *nay*   *ka*   *po-ass-ta.*
        Mia   TC/NM/AC   I   NM   see-PST-DC
        'As for Mia, I saw her.'

Multiple-topic constructions are viewed as basic, and not derived from other constructions, although there are certain syntactic relationships between topic sentences and some other non-topic sentences in a considerably regular manner. Noticing such regularity, however, some linguists claim that multiple-topic sentences are derived from subject–predicate types. According to this claim, the sentence in (43g), for instance, is to be viewed as derived from the sentence in (45).

(45)   *i   cip   uy   cipung wi   ey   kwumeng   i   na-ss-ta.*
          this house GN   roof   top at   hole   NM   appear-PST-DC
          'There is a hole on the top of the roof of this house.'

There are, however, obvious semantic differences between the two sentences. For instance, (43g) is a description of the house, whereas (45) is a description of the top of the roof of the house. Furthermore, some topic sentences indicate a class-member relation or stage-setting which do not have a clearcut non-topic source.

(46)   a. *sayngsen   un   tomi   ka   mas   i   iss-ta.*
             fish   TC   red snapper NM   taste NM   exist-DC
             '(As for) fish, red snappers taste good.'

          b. *onul   nalssi   ka   nwun   i   nayli-keyss-ta.*
             Today   weather   NM   snow   NM   come down-may-DC
             'Today's weather, it may snow.'

Since these sentences contain an underived topic, no descriptive consistency can be attained by deriving only a partial set of multiple-topic sentences from other sentences (cf. I.S. Yang 1972; C. Youn 1989; K.S. Lee 1991; and J.O. Choi 1992).

9.2.7   *Subjectless sentences*

Omission of situationally or contextually understood elements is a widespread phenomenon in Korean to the extent that Korean may be called a situation or discourse oriented language. This is particularly true with noun phrases in various grammatical cases, the most frequent ones being the subject referring to the speaker in declarative sentences and to the hearer in interrogative sentences.

(47)   A: *eti   ka-sey-yo?*
             where   go-SH-POL
             'Where are (you) going?'

B: *pyengwen   ey   com   ka-yo.*
    hospital   to   just   go-POL
    '(I) am going to the hospital.'

Expressive (phatic or aknowledgement) speech acts such as apology, thanking, greeting, and congratulation are typically used without a subject, as in *sillyeyha-p-ni-ta* 'Excuse (me)', *mianha-p-ni-ta* '(I) am sorry', *coysongha-p-ni-ta* '(I) am very sorry' (lit. '(I) feel guilty'), *komap-sup-ni-ta* 'Thank (you)', *kamsaha-p-ni-ta* '(I) appreciate (it)', *annyengha-sey-yo?* 'How are (you)?', and *chwukhaha-p-ni-ta* 'Congratulations!' Using the subject renders these expressions either awkward or unacceptable. For instance, **cey ka komap-sup-ni-ta* 'I thank you' is unacceptable.

Aside from such subjectless sentences where the subject is omitted but imaginable, real subjectless sentences are rare in Korean. Some possible candidates are presented in (48).

(48)   a. [*sensayng-nim   i   o-si-n*]   *kes   **kath**-ta.*
              teacher-HT   NM   come-SH-RL   fact   same-DC
              'It seems that the teacher has come.'

          b. [*wuli   apeci   nun   ilpon   ulo   ttena-si-l*]   *ke   **y-eyyo**.*
              our   father   TC   Japan   to   leave-SH-PRS   fact   be-POL
              'My father will leave for Japan.'

          c. [*hal.apeci   ka   hayngpokha-si-n*]   *ka   **po**-a.yo.*
              grandpa   NM   happy-SH-RL   whether   seem-POL
              'Grandpa appears to be happy.'

          d. [*halmeni   ka   tolaka-si-n*]   *tus   **ha**-ta.*
              grandma   NM   die-SH-RL   as if   appear-DC
              'It appears that grandma has passed away.'

Notice in (48) that the adjectives *kathta* 'be same', *ita* 'be', *pota* 'seem', and *hata* 'appear' lack a corresponding subject. This is evidenced by the fact that the subject honorific suffix *-(u)si* occurs only in the embedded clause predicates whose subjects also appear in the embedded clauses. The sentences in (48) suggest that the bold-faced predicates have become so grammaticalized with the preceding elements that they have lost their ability to carry their own subject.

9.2.8 *Word order*

As an SOV language, Korean has the basic and neutral word order of subject, object, and verb/adjective. This order holds in both main and embedded clauses. Due to the basic SOV order, all modifiers including determiners, genitive constructions, relative and complement clauses, and conjunctive clauses precede their head elements. Case and delimiter particles always follow the nominals they are associated with. These orders are fixed and do not allow any variation. Among noun phrases that carry various cases, however, there seems to be a preferred or neutral word order. Roughly, the order in (49) appears to obtain. Note that case markers are optionally or obligatorily deleted in certain syntactic collocations.

(49)

	Order of cases	*Case marking particles*
a.	Time	*ey*
b.	Place	*ey* (static), *eyse* (dynamic)
c.	Subject	*kali, kkeyse*
d.	Comitative	*(k)wa, hako*
e.	Instrument	*(u)lo*
f.	Source; Ablative	*eyse, (lo)puthe*
g.	Goal/Dative; Directional	*ey, eykey, hanthey, kkey; (u)lo*
h.	Object; Complement	*(l)ul; i/ka*

In actual utterances, a speaker tends to place an animate, definite and/or specific noun phrase before the other noun phrases. Furthermore, due to the well-developed case-marking system, word order among the major constituents in a sentence is relatively free as long as the predicate-final constraint is maintained. Thus, all the following sentences are natural, only with slight connotative differences in terms of topicality or focus.

(50)   a. *na nun ecey   san   eyse kkweng ul   cap-ass-e.yo.*
        I   TC   yesterday   mountain   on   pheasant AC catch-PST-POL
        'I caught a pheasant on the mountain yesterday.'

    b. *ecey na nun san eyse kkweng ul cap-ass-e.yo.*
    c. *kkweng ul na nun ecey san eyse cap-ass-e.yo.*
    d. *san eyse na nun ecey kkweng ul cap-ass-e.yo.*
    e. *na nun kkweng ul san eyse ecey cap-ass-e.yo.*
    f. *san eyse ecey kkweng ul na nun cap-ass-e.yo.*

In principle, pre-predicate scrambling occurs among the major constituents within the sentence or clause, provided that reordering that would cause semantic anomaly or ambiguity is usually blocked (cf. J.H. Cho 1994). In general, a topicalized or focused nominal is placed at the beginning of a sentence. The subject must always occur before the complement of a copula and the verb *toyta* 'become' and before the object of a transitive adjective. This restriction may be due to the basicness of subject-initial order. Thus, the second nominative elements in the sentences in (51) must be interpreted as the complement or object.

(51)   a. *Minho   nun   haksayng   i-ta.*
            Minho   TC   student   be-DC
            'Minho is a student.'
            → **haksayng un Minho i-ta.*

         b. *emeni   ka   Mia   ka   phil.yoha-si-ta.*
            mother   NM   Mia   NM   need-SH-DC
            'Mother needs Mia.'
            → **Mia ka emeni ka phil.yoha-si-ta.*

Sentential adverbials are scrambled with clause-mate nominals relatively freely as in (52a), whereas constituent adverbials are, in general, restricted to the position before the element they modify as in (52b).

(52)   a. *tahaynghi   Milan.i   nun   sihem   ey   hapkyek.hay-ss-e.*
            fortunately   Milan   TC   exam   to   pass-PST-INT
            'Fortunately, Milan passed the exam.'
            → *Milan.i nun tahaynghi sihem ey hapkyek.hay-ss-e.*
            → *Milan.i nun sihem ey tahaynghi hapkyek.hay-ss-e.*

         b. *Tongmin.i   nun   ppalli   malhay-yo.*
            Tongmin   TC   fast   speak-POL
            'Tongmin speaks fast.'
            → **ppalli Tongmin.i nun malhay-yo.*

In multiple topic constructions, a nominal denoting possessor or 'class' precedes the one denoting the possessed or 'member'. Reversing the order renders the sentence ungrammatical or unnatural as in (53a). Similarly, the object of a verbal noun must precede the verbal noun as in (53b).

(53)   a. *kkoch   un   cangmi   ka   yeyppu-ta.*
             flower   TC   rose   NM   pretty-DC
             'As for flowers, roses are pretty.'
             → **cangmi ka kkoch un yeyppu-ta.*

          b. *Minho   ka   sinmun   ul   paytal   ul   ha-n-ta.*
             Minho   NM   paper   AC   deliver AC   do-IN-DC
             'Minho delivers newspapers.'
             → **Minho ka paytal ul sinmun ul ha-n-ta.*

There are cases where it is possible to move a constituent in a subordinate clause to
the sentence-initial position if no ambiguity is thereby caused and if the scrambled
embedded clause element is not the subject. Thus, while (54b') is allowed, (54a') is
not because the embedded subject (*ku umsik*) is scrambled with a matrix element
(*Kiho*).

(54)   a. *Kiho ka   [ku   umsik   i   sangha-key]   hay-ss-e.*
             Kiho NM   the   food   NM   spoil-AD   do-PST-INT
             'Kiho let the food get spoiled.'
             a'. → **ku umsik i Kiho ka sangha-key hay-ss-e.*

          b. *na   nun   [Nami   ka   ku   umsik ul   mek-key]   hay-ss-e.*
             I   TC   Nami   NM   the   food   AC   eat-AD   do-PST-INT
             'I caused Nami to eat that food.'
             b'. → *ku umsik ul na nun Nami ka mek-key hay-ss-e.*

For the same reason, all the following sentences are acceptable.

(55)   *Mia   nun   [na hanthey swuhak ul   paywu]-ko siph-e   ha-n-ta.*
          Mia   TC   me from   math   AC   learn-that want-INF do-IN-DC
          'Mia wants to learn math from me.'
          → *na hanthey Mia nun swuhak ul paywu-ko siph-e ha-n-ta.*
          → *swuhak ul Mia nun na hanthey paywu-ko siph-e ha-n-ta.*

In colloquial speech, the predicate-final constraint is often relaxed, with some non-
predicate elements being uttered after the predicate for 'after-thought' clarification,
amplification of information, or emphasis. Notice in (56a) that the sentence-final
intonation is retained on the non-final predicates.

(56)   a. *ne   ku   cikyew-un   sihem   kkuthna-ss-ni?*↑
           you   that   terrible-RL   exam   end-PST-Q
           'Did you finish that terrible exam?'
           → *ne sihem kkuthna-ss-ni?*↑ *ku cikyew-un sihem.*↓
           'Did you finish the exam, that terrible exam?'

        b. *oy-cey   mulphum   mullichi-ca!*
           foreign-made goods   reject-PR
           'Let's not buy foreign goods!'
           → *mullichi-ca, oy-cey mulphum!*
              'Let's not buy (them), foreign goods!'

As for the pre-nominal position, a demonstrative, a possessive, and a relative clause may be scrambled among themselves, as in (57). If a relative or possessive construction is 'heavy', it is usually placed first. Note that 'after-thought' scrambling is not possible at all between pre-nominal elements and their head.

(57)   a. *ku   [sal   i   cci-n]   twu-mali uy   mal*
           the   flesh NM   grow fat-RL 2-CL   GN   horse
           'those two fat horses'

        b. *ku twu-mali uy [sal i cci-n] mal*
        c. *[sal i cci-n] ku twu-mali uy mal*
        d. *[sal i cci-n] twu-mali uy ku mal*
        e. *twu-mali uy ku [sal i cci-n] mal*
        f. *twu-mali uy [sal i cci-n] ku mal*

So-called quantifier floating includes extraction and scrambling. All the sentences in (58) are thus grammatical.

(58)   a. *haksayng twu myeng i   yek   ey   w-ass-ta.*
           student   2   person NM station to   come-PST-DC
           'Two students came to the railway station.'
           → *haksayng i twu myeng i yek ey w-ass-ta.*
           → *haksayng i yek ey twu myeng i w-ass-ta.*

        b. *na nun haksayng twu myeng ul   yek   eyse po-ass-ta.*
           I TC   student   2   person AC   station at   see-PST-DC
           'I saw two students at the railway station.'

→ *na nun haksayng ul twu myeng ul yek eyse po-ass-ta.*
→ *na nun haksayng ul yek eyse twu myeng ul po-ass-ta.*

Clefting, which is used as a device to focus new information, changes word order. Korean clefting lacks a dummy element such as *it* in English.

(59)   *hyeng   un   Mia hako   kukcang   ey   ka-ss-e.yo.*
                 brother TC   Mia with   theatre   to   go-PST-POL
                 'My older brother went to the movies with Mia.'

         → *Mia hako kukcang ey ka-n   kes/salam   un   hyeng   i-ess-e.yo.*
            Mia with   theatre   to   go-RL that/person TC   brother be-PST-POL
            'It was my older brother who went to the movies with Mia.'

         → *hyeng   i   kukcang ey ka-n   kes un   Mia hako y-ess-e.yo.*
            brother NM theatre   to   go-RL that TC   Mia   with   be-PST-POL
            'It was with Mia that my older brother went to the movies.'

         → *hyeng   i   Mia hako ka-n   kes/kos   un   kukcang i-ess-e.yo.*
            brother NM Mia with   go-RL that/place TC   theatre   be-PST-POL
            'It was to the movies that my older brother went with Mia.'

Note that the pronominal *kes* 'fact, thing, that' is widely used for clefting and the verb is always the copula.

9.3   Syntactic relations

Syntactic relations among various constituents in simplex and complex sentences may be observed in terms of the overall syntactic structure. The relations between an embedded clause and its head are expressed by various clause enders, each of which consists of one or more inflectional suffixes, and certain connective particles (e.g., quotative particle *ko*), while the relations among nominals or between a nominal and its clause-mate predicate (verb or adjective) are represented by particles that carry various case functions (e.g., nominative, accusative, dative, locative, ablative, source, goal, instrument, and directional). Clause embedding will be discussed in 9.4, and case relations in 9.5. The syntactic structure of Korean may be represented in terms of traditional grammatical categories as in the following set of constituent structure rules. These rules are not exhaustive, but they do cover most of the essential constituents of Korean sentences.

(60)   a. DS → (ADV*) S   (DEL*)

b. S   → $\begin{cases} \text{(NP) (S-CNJ) S} \\ \text{NP VP} \end{cases}$

c. VP → (NP*) V'

d. V' → $\begin{cases} \text{NP V'} \\ \text{(CC) (ADV*) V SUF*} \end{cases}$

e. CC → S $\begin{cases} \text{CMP} \\ \text{QT} \end{cases}$ (DEL)

f. NP → $\begin{cases} \text{(RC*)(GNP*)(DET*) N (PL)} \\ \text{S   NOM} \end{cases}$ (CASE)(DEL*)(CASE)

g. GNP → NP   GN

h. RC → S   RL

where * = one or more occurrences
        ( ) = optionality of occurrence
        ADV = adverbial phrase or adverb
        CC = complement clause; CMP = complementizer suffix
        CNJ = conjunctive suffix; CON = connective particle
        CASE = case particle; CS = complement clause
        DEL = delimiter particle; DET = determiner
        DS = discoursal form of a sentence
        GN = genitive case particle; GNP = genitive phrase
        N = nominal (noun, pronoun, numeral)
        NP = noun phrase; PL = plural suffix
        QT = quotative particle
        RC = relative clause; RL = relativizer suffix
        S = sentence or clause within DS
        SUF = inflectional suffix
        V = verb, adjective
        V' = lower-level verb or adjective phrase
        VP = higher-level verb or adjective phrase

The above set of rules shows the basic syntactic structure underlying all grammatical utterances of Korean. It is simply a basic skeletal scheme. Needless to say, in order to generate actual sentences based on the above rules, a wide variety of morpho-syntactic, semantic, and pragmatic co-occurrence restrictions must be observed.

Rule (60a) states that a sentence in a discourse (DS) may optionally begin with one or more discourse-sensitive sentential adverbials (ADV) such as exclamations, time or place adverbials, address terms, and modal adverbials and end with one or more delimiters (DEL) such as the polite particle *yo*, the apperceptive particle *kulye* 'indeed', the sentence-final plural particle *tul*, and the conjunctive particle *man(un)* 'but'. Utterances like *aiko tahaynghi ipen ey nun Yongho ka sihem ey hapkyekhay-ss-sup-ni-ta yo!* 'Oh, fortunately Yongho passed the exam this time' illustrate Rule (60a).

The first expansion of Rule (60b) accounts for multiple nominative constructions as well as conjunctive sentence structure in Korean. It indicates that a sentence (S) may take one or more hierarchical noun phrases (NP) and/or one or more conjunctive clauses (S-CNJ) before the main clause (S). The recursiveness of topic nominals (sentential subjects) and conjunctive clauses is handled by embedding S within another S.

In the second expansion, Rule (60b) also shows that a sentence is minimally composed of one noun phrase which functions as the subject and one predicative verb phrase (VP). Despite some linguists' claims that Korean is a so-called non-configurational language where the nominal arguments of a sentence are equally related to the predicate and thus not hierarchical, the present study distinguishes the subject from the other nominal arguments. Notionally, the subject nominal is 'what is being talked about' or 'what the sentence is about' while the remaining arguments and their verb or adjective simply predicate the subject, denoting 'what is being said about the subject'. Syntactically, almost all Korean sentences must have an explicit or implicit subject while the other arguments and adjuncts are largely optional. Moreover, as observed in 9.2.8, constructions like copular, locational, and sensory sentences require the subject to appear in the sentence-initial position. Lastly, only the subject can trigger subject honorification, and reflexive pronouns usually agree only with the subject.

Rule (60c) expands a verb phrase into ZERO or more noun phrases (NP*) and a lower-level verb phrase (V'). Postulating NP*, all of which are related to the predicate (V') in terms of cases such as dative, goal, source, instrument, and accusative, implies that Korean has a flat syntactic structure of non-subject arguments. This flatness is particularly reflected in the allowance of free scrambling among pre-predicate constituents.

Rule (60d) is an expansion of a lower-level verb phrase. First, V' → NP V' accounts for the occurrence of multiple object constructions. The NP before V' is always accusative-marked, as in *Yongho ka so lul* [*kkoli* **lul** *cap-ass-ta*] 'Yongho seized the cow by the tail' and *na nun Allasukha lul* [*kwukyeng* **ul** *hay-ss-e*] 'I saw the sights of Alaska' where the first accusative particle *lul* is derived from Rule (60c) and the second *lul* from Rule (60d).

The second expansion of V ' accounts for the optional occurrence of a complement clause (CC), one or more constituent adverbials (ADV*) modifying the verb or adjective (V), and the obligatory occurrence of V and its one or more inflectional suffixes (SUF*). As discussed in 8.4, the sentence-ender and clause-ender suffixes are obligatory in occurrence, while pre-terminal suffixes are not.

Rule (60e) presents the structure of a complement clause. A complement clause, which may be followed by a delimiter (DEL), consists of a clause (S) and a complementizer (CMP) such as the infinitive *-e/-a* or the adverbializer *-key*, as in *emeni nun Mia eykey* [*sakwa lul sa-key man*] *hay-ss-ta* 'Mother caused Mia only to buy apples' where the adverbializer *-key* is a complementizer and the particle *man* is a delimiter. One unique subset of complement clause is the quotative construction, which is composed of a clause (S) and a quotative particle (QT). In *Yongho nun* [*nay ka haksayng i-nya*] *ko man mul-ess-e.yo* 'Yongho only asked whether I am a student', the bracketed part is S, *ko* is QT, and *man* is DEL. Recall that a clause before QT takes the form of a complete sentence in the neutral speech level.

Rule (60f) depicts the overall structure of Korean noun phrases (NP). Noun phrases are of two types. One consists of a noun stem (N), optionally preceded by one or more relative clauses (RC*), genitive phrases (GNP*), and/or determiners (DET*) and/or followed by a plural suffix (PL). Determiners include demonstratives (e.g., *i* 'this'), quantifiers (e.g., *twu* 'two') and qualifiers (e.g., *say* 'new'). The other noun phrase type involves nominalized clauses (S NOM). For instance, in *na nun* [*Mia ka ka-ss-um*] *ul al-ass-ta* 'I knew that Mia had gone', the bracketed part is a nominalized clause where *-um* is a nominalizer suffix. These two types of constructions are optionally followed by semantic and/or syntactic case particles, one or more delimiters (DEL*), as illustrated in (61a) and (61b).

(61)   a. [*maum i   chak.ha-n*] [*na uy*] [*ku*] [*twu*] [*say*] [*chinkwu*]
            heart NM kind-RL   I   GN the   two   new   friend
                RC   GNP DET DET   DET   N

[*tul*] [*hanthey*] [*man*] [*un*]   *ka-keyss-ta.*
PL   to   only   TC   go-will-DC
PL   CASE   DEL   DEL
'(I) will go only to those two kind-hearted new friends of mine.'

b. [[*nay ka po*]-*ki*]   [*ey*]   [*to*]   *Milan.i nun   pucilenha-ta.*
   I   NM see-NOM at   also Milan TC diligent-DC
   S   NOM CASE DEL
'In my observation also, Milan is diligent.'

The order among the pre-nominal modifiers given in Rule (60f) is a neutral one. Except for the qualifier determiners (e.g., *say* 'new', *oyn* 'left-side'), which must appear immediately before N, these pre-nominal modifiers can be scrambled rather freely, as discussed in 9.2.8. Post-nominal elements, on the other hand, have a relatively fixed order in the sequence of plural suffix, 'semantic' case particle, delimiter particle, and 'syntactic' case particle. For instance, in *haksayng-tul eykey* **man ul** *cwu-ess-ta* '(I) gave (them) only to students', *-tul* is a plural suffix, *eykey* 'to' is a dative (semantic) case particle, *man* 'only' is a delimiter particle, and *ul* is an accusative (syntactic) case particle.

More than one relative clause (RC*) or genitive construction (GNP*) may modify a head nominal, as illustrated in (62).

(62)   a. [*Milan.i ka   manna-n*] [*khi   ka   khu-n*]   *sinsa*
               Milan NM meet-RL height NM big-RL gentleman
               'a tall gentleman who Milan met'

      b. [*Tonghwan.i uy*] [*yel   kwen   uy*]   *chayk*
               Tonghwan GN 10 volume GN book
               'Tonghwan's ten books'

Rule (60g) is the expansion of a genitive phrase into a noun phrase (NP) and the genitive case particle *uy* (GN). Frequently, the genitive particle *uy* is omitted in utterances if no ambiguity or semantic anomaly is thereby caused, as in *ce salam (uy) nolay* 'that person's songs' and *Sewul (*uy) salam* 'a person living in Seoul'. It cannot, however, be omitted if the noun phrase has a particle, as in *na man uy sayngkak* (I only GN idea) 'only my idea'.

As noticed in [*Puk.kyeng ulo puthe man*] *uy phyenci* (Peking DR from only GN letter) 'letters only from (the direction of) Peking', one or more semantic case and delimiter particles may occur (as NP elements) before the genitive particle. No syntactic case particle (i.e., nominative *ka/i* and accusative *(l)ul*) may occur before the genitive particle which is also a syntactic case particle.

Since a genitive phrase may embed another genitive recursively, (60f) and (60g) accommodate recursiveness by allowing the NP in (60g) to reapply in (60f). This recursiveness may be demonstrated as in (63).

(63)

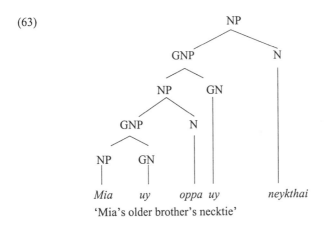

Mia   uy   oppa uy   neykthai
'Mia's older brother's necktie'

Rule (60h) states that a relative clause consists of a clause and a relativizer suffix
(RL) *-(u)n*, as in [*coh-un*] *salam* 'a good person'; [*khi ka khu-n*] *salam* 'a tall person'
(lit. 'a person (whose) height is big'); [*panana lul mek-nu-n*] *salam-tul* 'those people
who are eating bananas'; [*ttena-n*] *salam* 'a person who left', or ZERO, as in [*ka-l-
ZERO*] *salam* 'a person who will go'.

9.4   Embedded clauses

9.4.1   Types of embedding

Embedded clauses appear in complex sentences containing two or more predicates.
When two or more predicate stems are fossilized as an idiomatized compound
predicate, as in *nemeci* 'fall down' (derived from the verb stem *nem* 'cross over', the
infinitive suffix *-e*, and the verb stem *ci* 'become'), the sentence in which they occur
is regarded as simplex.

There are five basic types of embedded clauses, as shown in (64a). (64b) depicts
the syntactic structure underlying each embedded clause type. In all complex
sentences, the embedded clause precedes the main clause, and typically ends in an
inflectional clause-ender suffix such as CNJ (conjunctive suffix), RL (relativizer
suffix), CMP (complementizer suffix), or NOM (nominalizer suffix). In quotative
constructions, a quotative particle (QT), instead of an inflectional suffix, occurs after
the sentence ender of the quoted sentence.

(64)   a.   Embedded clauses

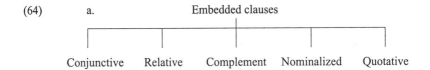

Conjunctive   Relative   Complement   Nominalized   Quotative

b.   Conjunctive Clause:

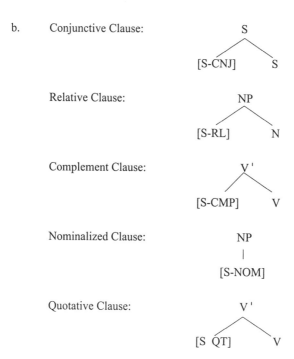

Relative Clause:

Complement Clause:

Nominalized Clause:

Quotative Clause:

Some suffixes may be used as both a conjunctive and a complement suffix. Examples are *-ko* 'and', *-(u)myen* 'if', *-key* 'so that', *-e.ya/-a.ya* 'only if', *-(u)lyeko* 'intending to', *-koca* 'wishing that', and *-tus* 'as if'. The distinction is made depending on which syntactic construction they appear in and on the concomitant minor meaning differences. (65a) illustrates the use of *-ko* as a conjunctive suffix, and (65b) its use as a verbal complementizer.

(65)   a. *Kiho   nun   pesu   lul   tha-**ko**   unhayng   ey   ka-ss-ta.*
             Kiho TC   bus   AC   ride-and   bank   to   go-PST-DC
             'Kiho took a bus and went to the bank.'

          b. *Nami   nun   ca-**ko**   iss-ta.*
             Nami   TC   sleep-and   stay-DC
             'Nami is sleeping.'

Notice that the clause-final suffixes that relate an embedded clause to another clause are typically attached to a predicate stem. On the other hand, the quotative particle *ko* and the concessive particle *man(un)* 'but' occur after a sentence ender, as in *na eykey [ppalli ka-la] ko hay-ss-ta* '(He) told me to go quickly.'

While conjunctive clauses may be either coordinative or subordinative, all other embedded clauses are essentially subordinative, in that they either modify the head noun (in relative constructions) or the main predicate (in complement and quotative constructions), or function as a nominal constituent in a clause or sentence (in nominalized constructions).

9.4.2   *Conjunctive constructions*

A sentence may contain two or more clauses that are conjoined either coordinately or subordinately. The distinction between coordination and subordination is not clear-cut and is a matter of degree. Although there may be some syntactic criteria, such as the permutability of conjuncts without change in meaning and the appearance or non-appearance of the tense suffix in the first conjunct, the absence or presence of semantic dependency is usually the most basic criterion.

There are various syntactic constraints associated with conjunctive suffixes. For instance, the suffix *-(u)myense* 'while' which connects two simultaneous events allows no tense suffix to appear before it because the tense of the main clause governs the tense of the *-(u)myense* clause. Notice in (66) that *na* 'I' is the subject of the two clauses, and that the *-umyense* clause is interpreted as past time even though *-umyense* is not preceded by the past tense suffix *-ess*.

(66)   *na   nun   pap   ul   mek-**umyense**   sinmun   ul   ilk-ess-e.*
        I   TC   meal AC   eat-while   newspaper AC read-PST-INT
        'While I was eating, I read the newspaper.'

9.4.2.1   Coordination

Coordination, consisting usually of *and*-coordination, *but*-coordination, and *or*-coordination, is realized by way of (i) a conjunctive suffix, (ii) repetition of a conjunctive suffix, (iii) the conjunctive particle *man(un)*, (iv) an idiomatized nominal form functioning as a verbal suffix, and (v) juxtaposition of clauses with appropriate intonation. The first pattern (use of a conjunctive suffix) is the most productive, for which the following suffixes are frequently used.

(67)   a.   simultaneity/sequentiality (*and*-coordination)
             -keniwa   'not only . . . but also, as well as'
             -ko   'and, and also, as well'
             -ko(se)   'and, and then'
             -(u)mye   'and, and on the other hand'
             -(u)myense   'while'

    b. contrastiveness (*but*/*or*-coordination)

-ciman(un)	'but, yet, nevertheless'
-kena	'or, or else, what- (when-, how-, etc.) ever'
-nuni	'rather, instead of doing'
-tunci	'or, or else, what- (when-, how-, etc.) ever'
-(u)na	'but, however'

The most typical and frequently used coordinative construction is formed with the suffix *-ko* 'and' as illustrated in (68).

(68)   a. *Kiho ka   ka-ci   an-h-**ko**   Nami ka   ka-ss-ni?*
                 Kiho NM go-NOM not-do-and Nami NM go-PST-Q
                 'Is it Nami who went, not Kiho?'

          b. *ce   salam un sensayng i   an i-**ko**   haksayng i-a.*
              that person TC teacher   NM not be-and student   be-INT
              'That person over there is not a teacher but a student.'

More formal counterparts of *-ko* are *-(u)mye* 'and' and *-yo* 'and', which may be used only in formal contexts or in writing. The latter conjoins only copular clauses.

(69)   a. *nam un kaypang-kwuk i-**mye**   puk un phyeysoy-kwuk i-ta.*
               south TC open-nation   be-and north TC closed-nation   be-DC
              'South Korea is an open and North Korea is a closed nation.'

          b. *ku   pun   un   cangkwan i-**yo**,   hakca ta.*
              that person TC   minister   be-and scholar be-DC
              'That person is a cabinet minister, and is a scholar.'

Disjunction is expressed by *-kena* or *-tunci*, and contrast by *-(u)na* or *-ciman(un)*. Each two suffixes are synonymous except that the former sounds more formal.

(70)   a. *Kiho ka   w-ass-**kena**/**tunci** Nami ka   w-ass-e.*
                 Kiho NM   come-PST-or   Nami NM   come-PST-INT
              'Either Kiho or Nami came.'

          b. *na nun keyulu-**na**/**ciman**   nay che   nun pucilenha-ney.*
              I   TC   lazy-but   my   wife TC   diligent-FML
              'I am lazy, but my wife is diligent.'

A second coordinative pattern is the repetition of paired conjunctive suffixes with a contrastive meaning. Paired forms include the synonymous *-kena . . . -kena* and *-tunci . . . -tunci* '(regardless) whether . . . or'.

(71)   *ku yenghwa ka   coh-**kena** nappu-**kena** na n   an   po-keyss-e.*
        the movie   NM   good-or   bad-or   I   TC not see-will-INT
        'Whether the movie is good or bad, I will not watch it.'

A third pattern of coordinative conjunction is the use of the conjunctive particle *man(un)* 'but' which occurs after a sentence ender.

(72)   a. *Mia nun ka-ss-up-ni-ta   **man(un)** ce nun an ka-keyss-e.yo.*
           Mia TC go-PST-AH-IN-DC but   I   TC not go-will-POL
           'Mia went, but I won't go.'

        b. *ka-po-sey-yo   **man(un)** pesu ka ttena-ss-ul   ke   yey-yo.*
           go-try-SH-POL   but   bus NM leave-PST-PRS fact be-POL
           'Please hurry, but the bus may have left.'

A fourth pattern is the use of fossilized forms such as *-nuntey* 'and, but, while' and the suppositive *-nunci* 'probably because, perhaps it does . . . so'. These forms consist of the indicative relative clause ender *-nu-n* (IN-RL) and a defective noun *tey* 'place, circumstance' or *ci* 'whether', suggesting that the earlier relative constructions (relative clause + head noun) have become grammaticalized as conjunctive suffixes.

(73)   a. *pom i   w-ass-**nuntey** nalssi ka   acik   chwup-ney.*
           spring NM come-PST-but   weather NM   still cold-APP
           'Spring is here, but it is still cold!'

        b. *ai-tul i   ca-**nunci**   cip i   co.yongha-kwun!*
           child-PL NM   sleep-perhaps house NM   quiet-APP
           'Perhaps the children are sleeping; the house is quiet.'

A final coordinative pattern is juxtaposition of two sentences. One subtype is the juxtaposition of two interrogative sentences including rhetorical ones for alternative questions, with rising intonation in the first conjunct and falling intonation in the second as in (74a). Another subtype is the juxtaposition of certain idiomatic declarative constructions as in (74b).

(74) a. *wuli ka   ka-l   kka-yo↑   Mia lul ponay-l   kka-yo?↓*
 we   NM go-PRS whether-POL Mia AC send-PRS whether-POL
 'Shall we go, or shall we send Mia?'

 b. *ne   nun   elkwul yeyppu-kes-ta,   ton   manh-kes-ta,*
 you TC   face   pretty-surely-DC   money   much-surely-DC
 mwe   ka   kekceng i-ni?
 what NM   worry   be-Q
 'You are certainly pretty and rich. What are you worried about?'

9.4.2.2   Subordination

A conjunctive clause can be subordinated to or dependent on another clause. Frequently used subordinative conjunctive suffixes are presented in (75).

(75)   cause-effect: *-e(se)/-a(se)* 'so, and then, as, so . . . that'
 -nulako 'while doing, as a result of'
 -(u)mulo 'because, due to'
 -(u)ni 'since, as, after'
 -(u)nikka 'as, since, because, when'
    conditional: *-e.ya/-a.ya* 'only if'
 -kentay 'when, if'
 -ketun 'if, when, provided that'
 -taka-nun 'if keep doing or being'
 -(u)myen(un) 'if, when'
    concessive: *-ca* 'even if' [occurs only with past tense.]
 -eto/-ato 'even though, although'
 -keniwa 'admitting that, even so'
 -kenman 'even though, while'
 -telato 'even though, granted that'
 -toy 'although, even though, yet'
 -(u)l-cienceng 'even if'
 -(u)l-cilato 'even though, regardless of'
 -(u)l-mangceng 'even though'
 -(u)nama 'even if'
 -(u)n-tul 'even if, granted that'
    intentive: *-(u)le* 'to, in order to, intending to' [occurs only with a locomotive verb, e.g., *kata* 'go'.]
 -(u)lye(ko) 'to, in order to, with the intention to'

	-koca 'wanting to, intending to'
resultative:	*-key(kkum)* 'so that'
	-tolok 'so that, to the extent that'
background:	*-tasiphi* 'as, in a way such that it is possible'
	-tus(i) 'like, as, as if'
	-(u)l swulok 'the more . . . the more'
temporal sequence:	*-ca (maca)* 'as soon as'
	-esel-ase-to 'even after'
	-ko(se) 'after, and then'
	-ta(ka) 'while doing, do and then'
	[transferentive or interruptive]
adverbializer:	*-i* '-ly'

Many of the above suffixes must have been grammaticalized from other constructions as indicated in 8.7. Thus, for instance, *-(u)mulo* must have developed from *-(u)m ulo* (NOM with), *-telato* from *-te-la ko hay-to* (RT-DC QT say-but) 'even if (someone) says that (he) observed . . .', *-(u)l-mangceng* from *-(u)l mangceng* (PRS fortune), *-koca* from *-ko cap-a* (NOM be wishful-and), *-tus.i* from *tus-i* (appearance-AD), *-(u)l swulok* from the prospective *-(u)l* and the defective noun *swulok* 'the more', and *-(u)ni* from *-(u)nikka* (after the retrospective suffix *-te*, only *-(u)ni*, not *-(u)nikka*, is allowed).

Sentences with representative subordinative suffixes are illustrated in (76).

(76) a. *Kiho   ka   ka-se   Nami ka   wul-ess-e.*
          Kiho   NM   go-and so   Nami NM   cry-PST-INT
          'As Kiho went away, Nami cried.'

      b. *Kiho   ka   ca-ya   Nami to   ca-p-ni-ta.*
          Kiho   NM   sleep-only if Nami also   sleep-AH-IN-DC
          'Nami sleeps only if Kiho sleeps.'

      c. *nay   ka   ka-to   Nami nun   an   ka-n-ta.*
          I   NM   go-though   Nami TC   not   go-IN-DC
          'Even though I go, Nami will not.'

      d. *apeci nun   ton   ul   pe-si-le   Pusan ey   ka-sy-ess-e.*
          father TC   money AC   earn-SH-to   Pusan to   go-SH-PST-INT
          'My father went to Pusan in order to earn money.'

e. *nay   ka   com   swi-key   motwu   co.yonghi-ha-sey-yo!*
   I   NM   just   rest-so that everybody quietly-do-SH-POL
   'Be quiet everybody, so that I can rest.'

f. *nwunmul   i   pi   o-tus(i)   ssot-a   cy-ess-ta.*
   tears   NM rain come-like   pour-INF   become-PST-DC
   'Tears poured down like rain.'

g. *nal   i   ka-l   swulok   na   nun   papp-a.yo.*
   day   NM go-PRS   the more   I   TC   busy-POL
   'As days go by, I get busier.'

h. *hal.apeci nun sinmun ul   po-si-taka   cam-tu-sy-ess-e.yo.*
   grandpa TC paper AC   see-SH-while   sleep-enter-SH-PST-POL
   'Grandpa fell asleep while reading the newspaper.'

i. *na   nun   malha-l   swu   eps-i   wun   i   napp-a.yo.*
   I   TC   say-PRS   way   lack-AD luck NM   bad-POL
   'I am unbelievably unlucky.'

As in coordination, repetition of suffixes is used for alternation.

(77)   *enni   nun   wus-taka   wul-taka   machimnay   cam-tul-ess-ta.*
          sister TC   laugh-ing cry-ing   finally   sleep-enter-PST-DC
          'After laughing and crying, my older sister finally fell asleep.'

9.4.3   *Relative clause constructions*

A clause modifying a head nominal in Korean is broadly called a relative or adnominal clause. While Korean has no relative pronouns that correspond to English relative pronouns like *who*, *whose*, *whom*, *which*, or *that*, relative clauses are connected to their head nominals by means of the relativizer suffix (RL) *-(u)n*. This relativizer is realized as ZERO after the prospective suffix *-(u)l* on the one hand, as in *ka-l salam* (go-PRS-RL person) 'a person who will go', and incorporates past tense after a verb stem on the other, as in *ka-n salam* (go-PST-RL person) 'a person who went'. Incorporation of past tense might have been caused by the historical deletion of the sequence of the past tense suffix and the indicative mood suffix (*-ess-nu/-ass-nu*) except in the Kyengsang dialect where *ka-ss-nu-n salam* is still used instead. Even in standard Korean, the undeleted form occurs in a limited number of grammaticalized constructions such as *ka-ss-nuntey* (< *nu-n tey*) 'while (he) went' and *ka-ss-nunci* (< *nu-n ci*) 'whether (he) went'. The regular relative clause enders are given in (78).

(78)   a. *Predicate* | | | *Indicative* | *Retrospective* | *Prospective*

			Indicative	Retrospective	Prospective
Verb	non-past:	*-nu-n*	*-te-n*	*-(u)l*
	past:	*-(u)n*	*-ess-/ass-te-n*	*-ess/ass-ul*
Adjective	non-past:	*-(u)n*	*-te-n*	*-(u)l*
	past:	—	*-ess/ass-te-n*	*-ess/ass-ul*

b. Examples (*pota* 'see', *mekta* 'eat'; *khuta* 'be big', *nophta* 'be high'):

Verb	non-past:	*po-nu-n*	*po-te-n*	*po-l*
		mek-nu-n	*mek-te-n*	*mek-ul*
	past:	*po-n*	*po-ass-te-n*	*po-ass-ul*
		mek-un	*mek-ess-te-n*	*mek-ess-ul*
Adjective	non-past:	*khu-n*	*khu-te-n*	*khu-l*
		noph-un	*noph-te-n*	*noph-ul*
	past:	—	*kh-ess-te-n*	*kh-ess-ul*
		—	*noph-ass-te-n*	*noph-ass-ul*

Notice that adjectives do not have any past indicative form and that the indicative past form of verbs and the indicative non-past form of adjectives are the same. Lack of the adjective past form is partly attributable to the continuity of the state over a certain time period that an adjective denotes, which is not the case with verbs which denote largely transient actions.

Four subtypes of relative clauses can be established depending on how a modifying clause and its head nominal are related: (i) relative clauses proper, (ii) fact-S type clauses, (iii) so-called headless relative clauses, and (iv) coreferent-opaque clauses. Relative clauses proper (traditional relative clauses) are those in which a relativized nominal (in the form of ZERO pronominal PRO) coreferential to the head nominal can be conceptually postulated within the relative clause. For instance, (79a) may be regarded as being derived from (79b) where the ZERO pronoun in the embedded clause is the object of the verb *mannata* 'meet' and refers to the head nominal *yeca* 'woman'.

(79)   a. *nay   ka   manna-n   **yeca***
          I   NM   meet-RL   woman
          'the woman whom I met'

b. [*nay ka* (*PRO lul*) *manna*]-*n* **yeca**
   I   NM   woman AC   meet-RL   woman

A majority of relative clauses are of this type. A PRO in a relative clause holds various grammatical relations such as subject, object, goal, locative, source, and adjunct. For instance, the PRO in (80a) is subject, that in (80b) is goal, that in (80c) is dative, that in (80d) is locative, that in (80e) is source, and that in (80f) is instrument.

(80)   a. (*PRO ka*)   *Nami* *lul* *manna-n* **Kiho**
          (Kiho NM)   Nami AC meet-RL Kiho
          'Kiho, who met Nami'

        b. *ney ka*   (*PRO ey*)   *ka-n*   **kukcang**
          you NM   (theatre to)   go-RL   theatre
          'the theatre you went to'

        c. *Kiho ka*   (*PRO   eykey*) *chayk ul*   *tuli-n*   **sensayng**
          Kiho NM   (teacher to)   book AC   give-RL teacher
          'the teacher to whom Kiho gave a book'

        d. *wuli tongsayng i*   (*PRO eyse*) *kongpuha-nu-n* **hak.kyo**
          our   brother   NM (school at)   study-IN-RL   school
          'the school at which my younger brother studies'

        e. *nay   ka*   (*PRO   eyse*) *na-o-n*   **kukcang**
          I   NM   (theatre from)   come out-RL theatre
          'the theatre from which I came'

       f. (*PRO   lo*) *celm-e*   *ci-nu-n*   **saym-mul**
          (well-water with) young-INF become-IN-RL well-water
          'the well-water by which one becomes young'

Notice that the nouns coreferential to the head noun are omitted together with the case particle, unlike in English where prepositions like *to* and *in* appear before a relative pronoun or at the end of the relative clause. It is often claimed that, in English, relativization involves the movement of a relativized noun to the front of the relative clause where it is then pronominalized or deleted. Movement and pronominalization are not involved in Korean, and only coreferential omission occurs. One possible exception to coreferential omission appears when the omission endangers the recoverability of the omitted nominal. In this case, a pronominal copy called a resumptive pronoun may be left behind with a relevant case particle.

(81)   *wuli ka* **keki eyse** *chwulpalhay-se hak.kyo-lo ka-n ku* **pyengwen**
         we NM there from depart-and   school-to go-RL the hospital
         'the hospital from which we departed and went to school'

Korean allows relativization out of multiply embedded clauses, as in (82).

(82)   [*(PRO ka)*   [*(PRO ka)*   [*ney ka*   *(PRO lul)*   *mek-un)*]
         (child NM)   (lady NM)   you NM   (apple AC)   eat-RL
         sakwa   *lul*   *sa-cwu-n*]   *acwuma*]   *lul*   *po-n*   *ai*
         apple   AC   buy-for-RL   lady   AC   see-RL   child
         'the child who saw the lady who bought the apples that you ate'

The fact-S type clause is so named because the head nominal is coreferential to or modified by the whole preceding clause as in the English construction 'the fact that …' No relativized nominal (i.e., PRO) coreferential to the head nominal can be conceptually postulated within the relative clause, as illustrated in (83).

(83)   a. [*nay ka   yeca   lul   manna*]-*n*   **sasil**
         I   NM   woman   AC   meet-RL   fact
         'the fact that I met a woman'

         b. [*enni   ka   casalha-keyss-ta   (ko   ha)-nu*]-*n*   **hyep.pak**
         sister   NM   suicide-will-DC   QT   say-IN-RL   threat
         'the threat that my older sister would commit suicide'

In addition to free nouns such as *sasil* 'the fact (that)', *sosik* 'the news (that)', *cungke* 'the evidence (that)', *kanungseng* 'the possibility (that)', and many others that can function as the head of the fact-S type relative clause, there are numerous defective nouns, such as *kes* 'fact, thing', *tus* 'as if', *cwul* 'how to, assumed fact', *chay* 'intact, just as it is', *chey/chek* 'pretence', *man* 'well worth (doing)', *pep* 'good reason', *li* 'good reason', *seng* 'seeming, appearance', *swu* 'method, possibility', *ci* 'since', *k(k)a* 'whether', and *ci* 'whether', which require this type of relative clause.

(84)   a. *ne   nun* [*nay   ka   Mikwuk   ka-nu*]-*n*   **kes** *ul sikihay-ss-e*.
         you TC I   NM America go-IN-RL fact AC jealous-PST-INT
         'You were jealous of my going to America.'

b. *Nami nun [phiano lul chi-l]* **cwul ul** *a-n-ta.*
Nami TC piano AC play-PRS way AC know-IN-DC
'Nami knows how to play the piano.'

c. *[Kiho ka encey ttena-nu]-n ci lul mul-e po-ala.*
Kiho NM when leave-IN-RL whether AC ask-INF try-IM
'Why don't you ask when Kiho is leaving?'

As illustrated in (83b), Korean has a set of head nominals (e.g., *hyep.pak* 'threat') that require quoting a statement. In such constructions, a quotative construction appears in the relative clause frequently with the deletion of the quotative particle *ko* and the saying verb *hata* 'say'. Head nouns of this type are numerous, which include *somun* 'rumour', *yaksok* 'promise', *sosik* 'news', *cwucang* 'claim', *ilon* 'theory', *poko* 'report', *cengpo* 'information', *myenglyeng* 'order', *kopayk* 'confession', *sayngkak* 'idea, thought', *uykyen* 'opinion', *chwuchik* 'speculation', and *nukkim* 'feeling'.

Relative clauses with the defective noun *kes* 'thing, fact, assumed fact' as the head often behave as if they do not have a head from a semantic point of view. Such constructions are often termed 'headless'. Examples follow.

(85)   a. *Minho nun [thayngkhu ka ka-nu]-n* **kes** *ul po-ass-e.*
Minho TC tank NM go-IN-RL fact AC see-PST-INT
'Minho saw a tank going.'

b. *ne-n [totwuk i unhayng eyse nao-nu]-n* **kes** *ul cap-ass-ni?*
you-TC thief NM bank from exit-IN-RL ? AC catch-PST-Q
'Did you catch the thief when he came out of the bank?'

b'. *ne-n [(PRO i) unhayng eyse nao-nu]-n* **totwuk** *ul cap-ass-ni?*
you-TC thief NM bank from exit-IN-RL thief AC catch-PST-Q
'Did you catch the thief coming out of the bank?'

Note in (85a), for instance, that syntactically *kes* is the head nominal of the relative clause and is coreferential with the whole relative clause meaning the tank's going. However, *kes* has nearly empty semantic content. Also, in (85b), *kes* does not refer to the whole preceding clause, i.e., the thief's coming out of the bank. Since the thief is the one who was caught, one might equate *kes* in this sentence with *totwuk* in the relative clause, suggesting that the nominal head is incorporated in the relative clause. In this interpretation, (85b) must be a variant of (85b') which is a relative clause proper. However, the intended meaning is that the police caught the thief when he came out of the bank, unlike (85b '). This intriguing issue requires further study.

The last relative clause type includes constructions where the relativized coreferent is opaque. As observed in (86), the relativized PRO cannot be easily identified within the relative clause.

(86)   *na nun   kapcaki   [koki kwup-nu]-n   **naymsay**   lul   math-ass-ta.*
            I   TC   suddenly meat bake-IN-RL   smell   AC   smell-PST-DC
            'I suddenly smelled the smell of (somebody) broiling meat.'

Similar examples are *[kicha ka ka-nu]-n soli* 'the sound of a train running' and *[ay ka wu-nu]-n soli* 'the sound of a baby crying'. In general, these are constructions with a head noun denoting one of the five senses or a trace (e.g., *huncek, palcachwi, cakwuk*). The head noun can be postulated in the relative clause not as a constituent PRO but a conjunctive clause something like *naymsay-lul phiwu-myense* 'while making a smell' or *soli-lul nay-myense* 'while making noise'.

A few additional remarks on Korean relativization are in order. In Korean, there is no distinction between a simple adjective expression (e.g., *a happy boy*) and a relative expression (e.g., *a boy who is happy*), nor between a participial construction (e.g., *a running boy*) and its relative counterpart (e.g., *a boy who is running*). Expressions like *hayngpok.ha-n ai* 'a happy child, a child who is happy' and *talli-nun ai* 'a running child, a child who is running' are all that there are. This is due to the word-order principle that all modifiers must precede their heads. Furthermore, as we have observed above, there is not much difference in syntactic behaviour between adjectives and verbs with regard to relative clause formation.

Both 'restrictive' (87a) and 'non-restrictive' (87b) relative clauses occur, but there is no overt linguistic marking distinguishing them.

(87)   a. *Yongho   ka   manna-n   yeca   nun   Kim   Nami   y-a.*
                Yongho   NM   meet-RL   woman TC   Kim   Nami   be-INT
                'The girl Yongho met is Kim Nami.'

            b. *nay ka   manna-n Kim   Nami nun nay chinkwu   tongsayng i-a.*
                I   NM meet-RL Kim   Nami TC my   friend   sister   be-INT
                'Kim Nami, whom I met, is my friend's younger sister.'

9.4.4   *Complement clause constructions*

A complement clause modifies or complements the verb or adjective of the matrix clause in which it is embedded, in terms of aspect, purpose, intent, obligation, wish, etc. A complement clause and its cooccurring main clause predicate are semantically cohesive to varying degrees. In some cases, they are so fossilized that they are considered single lexical items, as in *ilenata* 'get up' (< *il-e nata* (rise-INF come out)) and *phamutta* 'bury' (< *pha-a mutta* (dig-INF bury)).

There is a set of suffixes (i.e., complementizers) that relate a complement clause to the main predicate. Many of them are also used as conjunctive suffixes, as indicated in 9.4.1. Unlike in conjunctive constructions, however, complementizers occur only with a limited number of main clause predicates. Compare (88a), a conjunctive construction, with (88b), a complement construction.

(88) a. *na nun   kyohoy ey   ka-**lyeko**   ilccik   ilena-ss-e.*
        I   TC   church to   go-intending early   get up-PST-INT
        'Intending to go to church, I got up early.'

      b. *na nun   kyohoy ey   ilccik   ka-**lye(ko)**   hay-ss-e.*
        I   TC   church to   early   go-intending do-PST-INT
        'I intended to go to church early.'

Notice in (88a) that the two clauses *kyohoy ey ka-lyeko* and *ilccik ilena-ss-e* are conjoined conjunctively, being more or less independent of each other both syntactically and semantically. In this use, *-lyeko* cannot be contracted to *-lye*. In (88b), on the other hand, *kyohoy ey ilccik ka-lye(ko)* does not contain any conjunctive sense but complements the verb *hata*, which does not indicate the usual meaning 'do' but, together with the suffix *-lye(ko)*, means 'intend to'. In this use, *-lyeko* can be contracted to *-lye*.

Frequently used complementizers are given below, along with typical main clause predicates (mostly auxiliary verbs) that immediately follow these complementizers in a sentence. The most productively used complementizer is the infinitive suffix *-e/-a* with which a wide variety of main clause predicates cooccur. In the following, the predicate examples are given with the original meanings in parentheses from which their 'auxiliary' meanings are derived. Some grammatical terms used in Martin, et al. 1967 and elsewhere are given in square brackets.

(89) a. *-e/-a* 'to, in the state of being' [infinitive suffix]:
        cita   'get to be, become (< 'fall') [inchoative, passive]
        cwuta   'do for' (< 'give') [benefactive]
        hata   'show signs of being' (< 'do')
        issta   'be in the state of' (< 'exist, stay') [resultative]
        kata   'continue to' (< 'go') [persistentive]

nata	'have finished' (< 'appear, occur') [terminative]
nayta	'do all the way thoroughly' (< 'produce') [terminative]
nohta	'do for later' (< 'put down') [sustentive]
ota	'continue to' (< 'come') [persistentive]
pelita	'finish up, end up with, do completely' (< 'throw away') [terminative]
poita	'appear, seem' (< 'be seen')
pota	'try, experience (to see how it will be)' (< 'see, look at') [experiential, attemptive]
ppacita	'be extremely . . .' (< 'fall into')
ssahta	'continue to, do extremely' (< 'pile') [repetitive]
tayta	'(do) a lot' (< 'contact') [emphatic]
twuta	'get it done' (< 'place') [sustentive]

b. *-e.ya/-a.ya* 'only if, only to the extent that':

hata	'have to, must' (< 'do') [deontic]
toyta	'have to, get to be' (< 'become') [deontic]

c. *-keni* 'with confidence that; with assurance that':

hata	'think, assume' (< 'do')
sayngkakhata	'think, assume'

d. *-key, -keykkum* (emphatic) 'so that' [adverbial]:

hata	'cause, arrange, make' (< 'do') [causative]
mantulta	'cause, make' [causative]
toyta	'turn out, get to be, it is arranged (so that)' (< 'become') [inchoative, passive]

e. *-ko* 'with, and, in the state of doing' [gerundive]:

issta	'be ~ing' (< 'exist, stay') [progressive]
malta	'end up doing' (< 'stop (it)') [terminative]
nata	'just finish doing' (< 'appear, occur')
pota	'do and then realize' (< 'see')
siphta	'want, wish, desire' [desiderative]
tanita	'go around ~ing'

f. *-ko n(un)* 'habitually' (lit. 'and TC'):

hata	'habitually do' (< 'do') [habitual]

g. *-koca* 'wanting to, ready to, willing to':

   hata   'intend, wish' (< 'do') [desiderative]

h. *-tasiphi* 'in a way that tends to do, nearly':

   hata   'almost do, behave'

   toyta   'almost turn out, get to be'

i. *-tolok* 'so that, to the extent that' [extentive]:

   hata   'cause, arrange, make' [causative]

   toyta   'turn out, get to be, it is arranged (so that)'
                   [inchoative, passive]

j. *-(u)lye(ko)* 'intending to, ready to' [intentive]:

   hata   'intend to'

k. *-(u)lyeni* 'assuming that' [assumptive]:

   hata   'assume' (< 'do')

   sayngkak.hata 'assume'

l. *-(u)mcik* 'likely to, worth doing':

   hata   'be likely to, worth doing'

   sulepta   'be likely to, worth doing'

m. *-(u)myen* 'if' [conditional]:

   hata   'wish, desire, hope' [desiderative]

   siphta   'wish, desire' [desiderative]

There are two major complement constructions, serial and auxiliary, although there are many borderline cases. In a serial predicate construction, the meaning of the complement clause predicate and that of the main clause predicate are serialized or compounded, the former usually modifying the latter in terms of manner, as in *ki-e kata* (crawl-INF go) 'crawl away', *kkwulh-e ancta* (bend knees-INF sit) 'kneel down', *kapang ul tul-ko kata* (bag AC hold-and go) 'go holding a bag', *cwul ul cap-a tangkita* (rope AC hold-INF pull) 'pull the rope', *koki lul kwuw-e mekta* (meat AC broil-INF eat) 'broil and eat the meat', and *tol ul tul-e ollita* (rock AC hold-INF lift) 'hold the rocks up'. In serial constructions, as noticed in these examples, the main clause predicates generally retain their independent lexical meanings. Main clause predicates can be used independently without a complement clause, as in *hakkyo ey kata* 'go to school' and *tol ul ollita* 'lift the rocks'. While serial predicates can be treated as a subset of complement constructions (S.H. You 1996), they are also viewed as compound verbs of the V + V type (e.g., T. Chung 1993; J. Kim 1993). Under the latter view, only auxiliary constructions are of the complement clause type.

In auxiliary constructions, main clause predicates are popularly called 'auxiliary' predicates in that they cannot occur without a complement clause and their meaning is auxiliary to the complement clause predicate. They have been derived from corresponding regular verbs in the course of time with change in meaning as shown in (89). For instance, the inchoative auxiliary verb *cita* 'get to be' (e.g., *nac i kil-e ci-n-ta* 'Daytime is getting longer') is derived from the verb *cita* 'fall' (e.g., *hay ka ci-n-ta* 'The sun is setting'), the completive auxiliary verb *pelita* 'finish up' (e.g., *ton ul ta ss-e pely-ess-ta* '(He) used up all his money') is derived from the verb *pelita* 'throw away' (e.g., *ssuleyki lul pely-ess-ta* '(He) threw away the rubbish'), and the experiential auxiliary verb *pota* 'try' (e.g., *cenhwahay po-sey-yo* 'Try calling') is derived from the verb *pota* 'see, look' (e.g., *yeki lul po-sey-yo* 'Look here'). Together with the complementizers (e.g., *-e/-a*, *-ko*) they manifest various aspectual and modality meanings.

Notice that *hata* 'cause, think, show signs of, be in the state of' is widely used as a main clause predicate. In this function, *hata* does not retain its inherent meanings such as 'do' and 'make' but is compounded with the preceding predicate to derive another meaning, as in *silh-e hata* (hateful-INF do) 'dislike', *ka-ya hata* (go-only if do) 'must go', *o-lyeni hata* (come-assuming do) 'assume that (he) will come', *nol-key hata* (play-AD do) 'permit (him) to have fun', *ka-koca hata* (go-intending do) 'want to go', *ka-ko nun hata* (go-and TC do) 'go habitually', *ka-lyeko hata* (go-intending do) 'intend to go', *ka-mcik hata* (go-likely do) 'be likely to go', *kwulm-tasiphi hata* (starve-nearly do) 'almost starve', and *ka-ss-umyen hata* (go-PST-if do) 'wish to go'.

One property shared by many complement clause constructions is that no past/perfect suffix can be attached to the predicate preceding the complementizer. The event time of the complement clause is either the same as or after the time denoted by the predicate of the main clause.

(90)   a. *emeni   nun   tongsayng   ul   ca-(*ss)-key   ha-sy-ess-e.*
              mother   TC   brother   AC   sleep-so that   do-SH-PST-INT
              'Mother let my younger brother go to sleep.'

      b. *namu   ka   nemeci-(*ess)-e   iss-ess-ta.*
              tree   NM   fall-PST-INF   stay-PST-DC
              'A tree was in the state of falling.'

Among the suffixes listed in (89), *-e.ya/-a.ya*, *-keni*, *-(u)lyeni*, and *-(u)myen* constitute exceptions, taking a past/perfect suffix, as in *ka-ss-e.ya hay-ss-ta* '(He) should have gone' and *ka-ss-umyen hay-ss-ta* '(He) wished to go.'

Another characteristic of complement clauses is that they can be followed by the accusative particle *(l)ul*, as well as by delimiters, even if the following main predicate is intransitive. In this case, the accusative particle may be viewed as an emphatic delimiter.

(91) a. *Mia ka   ceki se panana   lul mek-ko (lul) iss-kwun-yo.*
          Mia NM there at banaana   AC eat-and AC stay-APP-POL
          'Mia is eating a banana over there!'

  b. *ku   sin ul   sin-e   (lul) po-sey-yo.*
       the shoe AC   wear-INF AC try-SH-POL
       'Try those shoes on.'

Since the predicate of a complement clause and its cooccurring main clause predicate function as a single grammatical unit in many types of construction (e.g., periphrastic causatives, indirect passives, and modal or aspectual constructions), complement constructions will be resumed from semantic perspectives in 9.10 (complex predicate constructions).

9.4.5   Nominalized constructions

Functioning syntactically as a nominal, a nominalized clause is embedded within the sentence to which it is subordinate. A nominalized clause is different from a relative clause in that it does not have a head noun but only a nominalizer suffix (NOM) and from a conjunctive or complement clause in that it functions as a grammatical case such as nominative, accusative, dative, locative, genitive, etc. There are several nominalizer suffixes. The suffix *-ki* 'the act of, the fact that' is the most frequently used one, and it occurs in many syntactic functions and combinations.

(92) a. *na nun [ku salam tasi   manna-ki] (ka) musew-ess-ta.*
          I   TC   the person again meet-NOM   NM afraid-PST-DC
          'I was afraid of seeing him again.'

  b. *pi   ka [o-ki]   sicak.hay-ss-ta.*
       rain NM come-NOM   start-PST-DC
       'It started raining.'

c. [*nwun   i   w-ass-ki*]   *ey sukhi tha-le ka-ss-e.*
   snow NM come-PST-NOM at skii ride-to go-PST-INT
   'Since it had snowed, (I) went skiing.'

d. [*palam i sey-ss-ki*]   *ttaymun ey cip ey iss-ess-ni?*
   wind NM strong-PST-NOM reason at home at stay-PST-Q
   'Did (you) stay home because the wind was strong?'

Notice in (92a, b) that the nominalized clauses cannot have the past/perfect suffix (PST) despite the past tense of the main clause predicate. This is because the events denoted by the nominalized clauses cannot precede the main clause events. No sequence of tense is applicable to Korean. In (92c, d), the event of the nominalized clause precedes the main clause event, and hence the past/perfect suffix appears.

A variant of the nominalizer *-ki* seems to be *-ko* which appears obligatorily before the desiderative adjective *siphta* 'be wishful'. Compare the two sentences below and observe the parallelism between *-ki* and *-ko*.

(93)   a. [*ku yeca lul tto manna-ki*]   *silh-e.yo.*
            the woman AC again meet-NOM   hateful-POL
            '(I) don't want to see her again.'

         b. [*ku yeca lul tto manna-ko*]   *siph-e.yo.*
            the woman AC again meet-NOM   wishful-POL
            '(I) want to see her again.'

The nominalizer *-ci* occurs before a negative adverb (*an* 'not', *mos* 'cannot') or the negative verb *malta* 'stop, don't do', as illustrated in (94). Occurrence of *-ci* only before a negative element has led some linguists to speculate that this suffix and *-ki* are allomorphic variants, the former occurring before a negative and the latter elsewhere.

(94)   a. *Nami nun [wul-ci]   an-h-ass-e.yo.*
            Nami TC cry-NOM   not-do-PST-POL
            'Nami didn't cry.'

         b. [*kukcang ey ka-ci*]   *mal-key.*
            theatre to go-NOM stop-IM
            'Don't go to the theatre.'

The nominalizer suffix -*(u)m* 'the act or fact of being/doing' is usually used before a 'cognitive' verb such as *alta* 'know', *moluta* 'not know', *kkaytat.ta* 'realize', *hwak.inhata* 'confirm', *palkyenhata* 'discover', *kiek.hata* 'remember', *cimcak.hata* 'guess', *nukkita* 'feel', *allita* 'inform', and *palk.hita* 'reveal'.

(95)   a. *ne-huy   nun   [haksayng   i-m]   ul   al-ala.*
            you-PL TC   student   be-NOM   AC know-IM
            'Keep in mind that you guys are students.'

          b. *[pem.in i   casalhay-ss-um]   i   palk.hy-e   cy-ess-ta.*
             criminal NM kill-self-PST-NOM NM found-INF get-PST-DC
             'The criminal was found to have committed suicide.'

The semantico-syntactic difference between -*ki* and -*(u)m* has been a controversial topic. In general, -*ki* clauses denote non-factivity to describe an event yet to be realized, whereas -*(u)m* clauses are more closely related to factivity to describe a factual event. Accordingly, they tend to cooccur with non-factive and factive main predicates, respectively, as shown in (96).

(96)   a. *na nun [hyeng i   sakitanghay-ss-um(/*-ki)] ul   al-ass-ta.*
            I TC   brother NM cheated-PST-NOM   AC know-PST-DC
            'I knew that my brother had been cheated.'

          b. *na nun [ku   yeca   lul po-ki(/*-m)] ka   silh-ess-e.*
             I TC   the   woman AC see-NOM   NM hateful-PST-INT
             'I didn't like seeing her.'

Many main clause predicates, including those indicating judgement, are neutral, occurring with both -*ki* and -*(u)m*. Notice in (97) that the verb *talli-ta* 'depend (on)' can occur with both nominalizers.

(97)   a. *sengkong   un [nolyek.ha-m]   ey   tally-e   iss-ta.*
            success   TC make effort-NOM on   depend-INF exist-DC
            'Success depends on one's making efforts.'

          b. *sengkong   un [nolyek.ha-ki]   ey   tally-e   iss-ta.*
            success   TC make effort-NOM on   depend-INF exist-DC
            'Success depends on how one makes efforts.'

In general, sentences with the suffix *-(u)m* sound rather formal. In casual speech, it is often replaced with a relative clause (the fact-S type) with the head noun *kes* 'fact, thing', as in *ney-huy nun haksayng i-n kes ul al-ala* 'Keep in mind that you guys are students.'

9.4.6   *Quotative constructions*

A quotative construction is similar to a verbal complement construction in that both are closely tied to the main predicate, complementing the latter. Notice the parallelism between (98a) which contains a quotative clause and (98b) which contains a verbal complement clause.

(98)   a. *emeni   nun   hyeng   eykey   [ppalli   ttena-la   **ko**]   hay-ss-ta.*
             mother TC   brother to   quickly leave-IM QT   do-PST-DC
             'My mother told my older brother to leave quickly.'

         b. *emeni   nun   hyeng   eykey   [ppalli   ttena-**key**]   hay-ss-ta.*
             mother TC   brother to   quickly leave-AD   do-PST-DC
             'My mother caused my older brother to leave quickly.'

As noticed in the above examples, one major difference is that a quotative construction ends in a predicate with a neutral-level sentence ender (e.g., declarative, interrogative, propositive or imperative), whereas a verbal complement ends in a clause ender. Thus, the former is followed by a quotative *particle*, whereas the latter is followed by a complementizer *suffix*. A second difference is that a quotative construction is more freely scrambled with other nominal elements, which is not generally possible in the case of a complement construction.

(99)   a. *[ppalli   ttena-la   **ko**]   emeni   nun   hyeng   eykey   malhay-ss-ta.*
             quickly leave-IM QT   mother TC   brother to   say-PST-DC
             'My mother told my older brother to leave quickly.'

         b. *?[ppalli   ttena-**key**]   emeni   nun   hyeng   eykey   hay-ss-ta.*
             quickly leave-AD   mother TC   brother to   do-PST-DC
             'My mother caused my older brother to leave quickly.'

A third difference is that, while quotative clauses allow tense suffixes to occur freely, complement clauses are subject to the control of the main predicate tense.

(100) a. *Kiho nun* [*Nami ka ttena-ss-ta* **ko**] *hay-ss-ta.*
     Kiho TC   Nami   NM   leave-PST-DC   QT   say-PST-DC
     'Kiho said that Nami had left.'

    b. *Kiho nun* [*Nami ka ttena(*-ss)-key*] *hay-ss-ta.*
     Kiho TC   Nami   NM   leave-PST-AD   do-PST-DC
     'Kiho caused Nami to leave.'

There are many other properties unique to quotative clauses, as described below, which warrant grouping them as a separate embedded clause type.

Quotative constructions primarily include reporting, saying, writing, asking, suggesting, ordering, and promising but secondarily hearing, thinking, and believing as well. For the sake of convenience, let us term all the predicates that are used to report, say, hear, think, and believe in quotative constructions as quoting verbs, which are of the following kinds.

(101) a. *cekta* 'write down'   *chinghata* 'call, term'
     cikkelita 'chatter'   *cwucanghata* 'insist, persist in'
     hata 'say, tell'   *kocip.hata* 'persist'
     malhata 'say'   *pokohata* 'report'
     puluta 'call, term'   *soksak.ita* 'whisper'
     solichita 'shout, yell'   *ssuta* 'write'
     woychita 'shout out, cry out'   *wukita* 'demand, persist, assert'

    b. *aywenhata* 'plead'   *ceyanhata* 'propose'
     kwenhata 'suggest'   *mut.ta* 'ask'
     myenglyenghata 'order'   *yaksok.hata* 'promise'
     yochenghata 'request'

    c. *hwaksinhata* 'firmly believe'   *mit.ta* 'believe'
     sayngkak.hata 'think'   *yekita* 'consider, regard'

    d. *tut.ta* 'hear'   *poko-pat.ta* 'be reported'

There are two ways to report what someone has stated, asked, commanded, suggested, or promised: a direct quotation, which reports the exact words spoken or written, and an indirect quotation, which reports only the content. All the examples given above are cases of indirect quotation. Direct quotation in Korean is used much less frequently than in English.

In direct quotation, the quoted expression (which contains the exact words spoken, written, conceived, or believed) is followed by the particle *hako* 'saying' (derived from the verb stem *ha* 'say' and the conjunctive suffix *ko* 'and') or *lako* 'saying' (derived probably from the copulative declarative *(i)la* and the contracted form of *hako*), and ends with a quoting verb. In general, *hako* sounds more colloquial than *lako*. After *hako*, the common quoting verb *hata* 'say' does not occur.

(102)　　 Mia nun ku ai   eykey 'ne nayil   i   kos ulo o-nela!'
　　　　　 Mia TC the kid to   you tomorrow this place to   come-IM
　　　　　 hako/lako　　 solichy-ess-ta.
　　　　　 QT　　　　　 shout-PST-DC
　　　　　 'Mia shouted to the kid, "Come here tomorrow!" '

Indirect quotation is distinct from its direct counterpart in many respects. First, the quotative particle that follows the indirectly quoted expression and precedes a quoting verb is typically *ko* '(saying) that'. Second, the clause ender of an indirectly quoted clause must be in the neutral speech level, regardless of the speech level that would appear in direct quotation.

(103)　　　 Declarative　　 Interrogative　　 Imperative　　 Propositive
　　　　　 -ta/-la　　　 *-nu-nya/-(u)nya*　 *-(u)la*　　　 *-ca*

The declarative ender *-la* occurs only after the copula *(ita)* and the retrospective suffix *-te*, otherwise *-ta*; the interrogative ender *-(u)nya* occurs after an adjective stem (*-unya* after a consonant and *-nya* after a vowel), otherwise *-nu-nya*; and the imperative ender *-la* occurs after a vowel and *-ula* after a consonant.

Third, deictic elements such as demonstratives, grammatical persons, time and place adverbials, and the subject honorific suffix *-(u)si* may be changed, when direct quotation becomes indirect. For instance, *i kes* 'this thing' may be changed to *ku kes* 'that thing', *ne* 'you' may be changed to *na* 'I', *ecey* 'yesterday' may be changed to *ku cen nal* 'the previous day', and the subject honorific *-(u)si* may be dropped or added depending on the social status the speaker has in relation to the subject of the quoted clause. Unlike in English, however, tense of the directly quoted clause will not be affected by indirect quotation.

Fourth, many elements cannot be expressed in indirect quotation, such as address terms, exclamatory words, certain sentence enders including the apperceptive *-kwun* and *-ney*, the suppositive *-ci*, the promissive *-(u)ma*, etc., and various incomplete sentences. Thus, the natural indirect quotation corresponding to the direct quotation in (102) is as follows.

(104)   Mia nun ku ai eykey [taum nal ku kos ulo o-la   ko]
          Mia TC the kid to   next day that place to come-IM QT
          solichy-ess-ta.
          shout-PST-DC
          'Mia shouted to the kid to go to that place the next day.'

When quoting verbs mean 'call, name, entitle, think, believe', etc. and the
quotative clause predicate is a copula, the quoting verbs may need a direct object.

(105)   ku ai   ka na lul/*ka sensayng-nim i-la   ko pull-ess-ta.
          the child NM me AC/NM   teacher-HT   be-DC QT call-PST-DC
          'That child called me teacher.'

          cf. Nami nun Inca lul/ka papo la   ko sayngkak.hay-ss-ta.
              Nami TC   Inca AC   fool be-DC QT think-PST-DC
              'Nami thought Inca to be a fool/was a fool .'

Quotative constructions are often contracted in colloquial speech. In direct
quotation, the quotative particle lako can be reduced to la, as in (106a). In indirect
quotation, the quotative particle ko can be omitted, especially so when the quoting
verb stem is ha 'say', and ko ha 'say that' can be deleted altogether almost anywhere,
as observed in (106b, c).

(106)   a. Nami nun   'ca-keyss-sup-ni-ta'   la(ko)   malhay-ess-ta.
              Nami TC   sleep-will-AH-IN-DC QT   say-PST-DC
              'Nami said, "I will go to sleep."'

          b. apeci nun   na hanthey [kongpuha-la]   (ko   ha)-sy-e.
              father TC   me to   study-IM   QT   say-SH-INT
              'My father tells me to study.'

          c. ni   ka   [an ka-n-ta]   (ko ha)-myen na to   an ka-keyss-e.
              you NM   not go-IN-DC   QT say-if   I also not go-will-INT
              'If you say you are not going, I am not going either.'

Due to the ko ha deletion, the 'orphaned' suffixes are attached to the quotative
clause. The omission of ko ha is so widespread that in some contexts, the omission
germinates a new meaning, in addition to the original meaning. This is observed in
declarative sentences, as in (107), where (a) is associated with both omitted and

unomitted constructions while (b), only with the omitted construction.

(107)   *Nami   nun   [ca-n-ta]   (ko   ha)-n-ta.*
          Nami   TC   sleep-IN-DC   QT   say-IN-DC
          a. '(They) say that Nami is sleeping.'
          b. '(I am saying that) Nami is sleeping.'

The omission may go beyond *ko ha* and more elements may be deleted. In some cases, unomitted expressions are less natural than their omitted counterparts. There is an order of omission among the optionally omitted elements: *ko* is the first to go, followed by the verb *ha*.

(108)   a. *na n   ['tayci'   la]   (((ko) ha)-nu)-n sosel ul sa-ss-e.*
              I   TC   Good Earth be-DC QT call-IN-RL novel AC buy-PST-INT
              'I bought a novel called "The Good Earth".'

          b. *[insayng i-la]   (((ko) ha)-nu-n   kes   u)n   hemuha-y.*
              life   be-DC   QT   call-IN-RL   thing   TC   vain-INT
              '(The thing that is called) life is vain.'

The repetitious quotative form *nuni . . . nuni* 'saying things like' may have been derived from *ko ha-nuni . . . ko ha-nuni* through *ko ha* deletion, but the original form is no longer used in Contemporary Korean.

(109)   *ka-keyss-ta-**nuni**   an   ka-keyss-ta-**nuni**   hay-ss-e.*
          go-will-DC-saying   not   go-will-DC-saying   say-PST-INT
          '(I) said one time that I would go and another time that I would not.'

Finally, for echo questions, the quotative particle *ko* is added to an indirect quotative clause to confirm what the other person has just said, as in *Milan.i ka ttena-ss-ta ko yo?* (Milan NM leave-PST-DC QT POL) 'Are you saying that Milan has left?' For partial echo questions with question words, expressions like *mue la ko yo?* (what be-DC POL) 'What did you say?' and *nwu ka ttena-ss-ta ko yo?* (who NM leave-PST-DC QT POL) 'Who did you say left?' can be used.

9.5   Case marking

A nominal expression (NP) takes a grammatical case in an utterance. Grammatical cases such as nominative, accusative, dative, static locative, dynamic locative, source, goal, instrument, and directional indicate the grammatical relation that a noun has *vis-à-vis* its predicate, another noun (in genitive, comitative, and connective cases), a clause (in multiple nominative constructions), or a discourse (in the vocative case). Cases are marked by case particles, which may often be omitted in various discourse contexts. Nominative, accusative, dative, static locative, goal, and genitive particles are frequently omitted in sentences, especially in colloquial speech, because these cases are most easily predictable from the syntactic structure, word order, and the nature of the predicate used. Thus, for instance, in *Mia enni hak.kyo ka-ss-ta* 'Mia's older sister went to school', *Mia* is still in the genitive case, *enni* in the nominative case, and *hak.kyo* in the goal case, despite their not being marked by any particle.

Cases may be divided into two groups: (i) those that mainly indicate syntactic functions of nominals, such as nominative (usually functioning as subject and complement), accusative (usually functioning as object), and genitive (usually functioning as possessive), and (ii) those that mainly express semantic functions of nominals such as dative, goal, locative, source, directional, instrument, and function. For instance, in *Alan.i ka hak.kyo eyse w-ass-e* 'Alan came from school', *Alan* plays the grammatical function of the subject of the sentence, whereas *hak.kyo*, marked by the source particle *eyse* 'from', has the semantic function of indicating the location from which *Alan* came. This dichotomy, however, does not preclude syntactic case particles from having some semantic functions as well and vice versa.

Among the particle slots of a noun phrase, nominative, accusative, and genitive particles occupy the last slot, whereas the semantic particles occur in an inner slot even before the delimiter slots, as in *na man i* (I only NM) 'only I' (subject), *ne hanthey man ul* (you to only AC) 'only to you' (object), and *ape-nim kkey man uy cinci* (father-HT to only GN meal) 'the meal only to father' (genitive).

9.5.1 Syntactic cases: nominative, accusative, and genitive

Nominative, accusative, and genitive cases, which may be termed syntactic (or structural) cases in Korean fulfil the most productive grammatical functions. Since they are, by and large, predictable from context, case particles are frequently omitted in colloquial speech if no emphasis, deference, or exclusiveness is intended. These three particles (*ka/i*, *(l)ul*, and *uy*) cannot cooccur with a delimiter denoting topicality such as *(n)un* 'as for', *(i)ya* 'as only for', and *to* 'also' because all of them occupy the last position in a noun phrase.

(110)   a. *Yongho ka/nun   Minca lul/to   manna-ss-ta.*
             Yongho NM/TC   Minca AC/also   meet-PST-DC
             '(As for) Yongho, (he) met Minca (also).'

b. *Minho   (man/*nun/*to)   **uy**   chayk*
   Minho   only/TC/also   GN   book
   '(only/as for/also) Minho's book'

The nominative case, whether ovetly marked by a particle or not, most frequently
functions as the subject of a predicate. Thus, few predicates can occur without the
nominative case. It also functions as the object of a transitive adjective, the
complement of the copula *ita* 'be' or *an ita* 'not be' and the verb *toyta* 'become', and
a sentential subject in multiple topic constructions, as illustrated in (111) with overt
case marking.

(111)   a. **Mia   ka**   *ceki   o-n-ta.*   (as subject)
             Mia   NM   there   come-IN-DC
             'Mia is coming over there.'

          b. *ne   **Mia   ka**   coh-ni?*   (as object of transitive adjective)
             you   Mia   NM   good-Q
             'Do you like Mia?'

          c. *na   nun   **haksayng**   **i**   an   i-a.*   (as complement of copula)
             I   TC   student   NM   not   be-INT
             'I am not a student.'

          d. *Minho   nun   **uysa   ka**   toy-ess-ta.*   (as complement of verb)
             Minho   TC   doctor   NM   become-PST-DC
             'Minho became a doctor.'

          e. **Milan.i   ka**   *nwun   i   khu-p-ni-ta.*   (as sentential subject)
             Milan   NM   eye   NM   big-AH-IN-DC
             'Milan has big eyes.'

The function of the nominative case as the subject of a predicate is ubiquitous. Its
function as the object of a transitive adjective includes not only emotive constructions
such as (111b) and *na nun **ney ka** kekceng i-ta* 'I am worried about you', but also
'possession' sentences such as *hal.apeci kkeyse **chayk i** manh-usey-yo* 'Grandpa has
many books', and 'necessity' sentences such as *Cihwan.i eykey/ka **ton i** philyohay-yo*
'Cihwan needs money', 'ease/difficulty' sentences such as *na nun **swuhak i** elyew-
e.yo* 'As for me math is difficult', and 'possibility' sentences such as *Mia nun **wuncen
i** kanunghay* 'It is possible for Mia to drive.' The function of the nominative case as a

complement can further be illustrated by sentences like *Yongho ka yelsim i-ta* 'Yongho is diligent', *wuli atul i yel sal i toy-ess-e.yo* 'My son has turned ten years of age', and *ku kes un mal i an toy-n-ta* 'That doesn't make sense.' Note that the nominative particle must be omitted when the complement appears immediately before the copula *ita*. Thus, **Yongho ka yelsim i i-ta* 'Yongho is diligent' is not acceptable. All hierarchical sentential subjects in a multiple-topic construction are in the nominative case, as illustrated in *halmeni ka os i somay ka han ccok i kkuth i ccic.eci-sy-ess-e.yo* 'The end of one sleeve of my grandma's clothes is torn.'

The honorific particle *kkeyse* is used to mark the subject, including the sentential subject of a multiple-topic construction. It has derived from the honorific source *kkeyse* (e.g., *apeci kkeyse pat-un ton* 'the money that I got from father') and cannot be used to mark a complement, as in *ape-nim kkeyse kyocang i(/*kkeyse) toy-sy-ess-e* 'My father became a principal', nor to mark an object of a transitive adjective, as in *na nun sensayng-nim i(/*kkeyse) coh-a* 'I like my teacher.'

The nominative particle *ka/i* and the deferential *kkeyse* are frequently used to introduce new information as a topic or subject into a discourse. Furthermore, *ka/i* (but not *kkeyse*) may indicate 'exclusiveness' of the referent of the cooccurring nominal. This exclusiveness meaning arises when the predicate is an adjective or a generic verb, or when the nominal and/or the particle are stressed. When the nominative particle is used to introduce new information or to convey the exclusiveness of the referent, it is never omitted, not even in casual speech.

(112)   a. ***nay ka***   *Mia ka   pulew-e.*   (adjective)
            I   NM   Mia NM enviable-INT
            'It is I who envies Mia.'

    b. ***inkan***   *i*   *cwuk-e.yo.*   (generic verb)
            human NM   die-POL
            'It is man that is mortal.'

    c. ***YONGHO KA***   *w-ass-ta.*   (stressed)
            Yongho   NM   come-PST-DC
            'It is Yongho who came.'

The accusative case, whether explicitly marked by a particle or not, functions not only as the direct object of a transitive verb (113a) but also as the direct object of a passive-transitive verb (113b), the purpose of an action denoted by a verb of movement (113c), the duration or distance covered by an action (113d), the object of a cognate verb (113e), the objects in multiple object constructions (113f), and a clausal object construction (113g).

(113)   a. *Tongmin.i   nun   Nami   eykey   **kkoch**   ul   ponay-ss-e.*
         Tongmin TC   Nami   to   flower   AC   send-PST-INT
         'Tongmin sent flowers to Nami.'

         b. *Milan.i   nun   Tongmin.i   eykey   **pal** ul   palp-hi-ess-ta.*
         Milan   TC   Tongmin   by   foot AC   step on-PAS-PST-DC
         'Milan got his foot stepped on by Tongmin.'

         c. *na   nun   nayil   **yenghwa-kwukyeng**   ul   ka-yo.*
         I   TC   tomorrow   movie-watching   AC   go-POL
         'I am going to the movies tomorrow.'

         d. *nwuna   nun   **yel   si-kan   ul**   ca-ss-e.yo.*
         sister   TC   10   hours   AC   sleep-PST-POL
         'My older sister slept ten hours.'

         e. *wuli   hyeng   un   Mia   hako   **chwum**   ul   chw-ess-ta.*
         our   brother   TC   Ma   with   dance   AC   dance-PST-DC
         'My older brother danced (a dance) with Mia.'

         f. *apeci nun   **cha** lul   Hyentay lul   **twu   tay** lul   sa-sy-ess-e.yo.*
         father TC   car   AC Hyundai AC   2   CL AC   buy-SH-PST-POL
         'My father bought two Hyundai cars.'

         g. *Tongmin.i   nun   **pap**   ul   **kwulm-ki**   lul   sicak.hay-ss-e.*
         Tongmin   TC   rice   AC   fast-NOM   AC   begin-PST-INT
         'Tongmin started fasting.'

The indirect object of a dative verb (e.g., *cwuta* 'give', *kaluchita* 'teach') and the goal of a locomotive verb (e.g., *kata* 'go') are usually marked by a static locative particle. If particular emphasis for exclusiveness is intended, however, it can be marked by an accusative particle as in (114a, b). Also, an accusative particle alternates with a directional particle *(u)lo* before certain transitive verbs as in (114c) (cf. 9.5.3).

(114)   a. *na   nun   ku   ton   ul   **hal.apeci** lul/kkey   tuly-ess-ta.*
         I   TC   the   money   AC   grandpa   AC/to   give-PST-DC
         'I gave the money to grandpa.'

b. *halmeni*   *nun*   **kyohoy**   *lul/ey*   *ka-sy-ess-e.yo.*
grandma   TC   church   AC/to   go-SH-PST-POL
'Grandma went to church.'

c. *sensayng-nim un ceyca lul* **myenuli** *lul/lo sam-usy-ess-e.yo.*
teacher-HT   TC student AC d.-in-law AC/as make-SH-PST-POL
'My professor made a student his daughter-in-law.'

The accusative particle alternates with the nominative particle in causative sentences (115a). The same alternation occurs in quotative sentences if the embedded predicate is a copula and the main clause verb is that of thinking, saying, or believing (115b). Desiderative sentences show similar alternation (115c).

(115)   a. *nay*   *ka*   **ku**   **say**   *lul/ka*   *cwuk-key*   *hay-ss-ta.*
         I   NM the   bird   AC/NM   die-so that   cause-PST-DC
         'I caused the bird to die.'

     b. *Yongho*   *nun*   **Mia**   *lul/ka*   *papo*   *la*   *ko*   *sayngkak.ha-y.*
         Yongho TC   Mia   AC/NM fool   is   QT   think-INT
         'Yongho thinks Mia is a fool.'

     c. *hyeng*   *un*   **tampay**   *lul/ka*   *phiwu-ko*   *siph-ess-e.yo.*
         brother TC   cigarette AC/NM   smoke-NOM   wish-PST-POL
         'My older brother wanted to smoke.'

The two constructions of (115a) can be bracketed as *nay ka ku say lul [cwuk-key] hay-ss-ta* and *nay ka [ku say ka cwuk-key] hay-ss-ta*. This dual bracketing is also true with (115b), as in *Yongho nun Mia lul [papo la] ko sayngkak.ha-y* and *Yongho nun [Mia ka papo la] ko sayngkak.ha-y*. In desiderative sentences, the accusative-marked nominal is associated with the transitive verb (e.g., *phiwuta* 'smoke'), whereas the nominative-marked nominal is related to the emotive adjective *siphta* 'wish', as in *hyeng un [tampay lul phiwu-ko] siph-ess-ta* and *hyeng un tampay ka [phiwu-ko] siph-ess-ta*, respectively.

The nominative or accusative particle may occur for emphasis after the nominalizer suffix *-ci* in negative sentences if the nominalized clause is an adjective or intransitive verb construction as in (116a, b). When the embedded clause of a negative construction has a transitive verb, only the accusative particle is optionally allowed, as in (116c, d).

(116) a. *na nun* [*enni ka pulep-ci*] *(ka/lul) an-h-ta.*
   I TC sister NM envy-NOM NM/AC not-be-DC
   'I don't envy my older sister.'

   b. *i cha ka* [*wumciki-ci*] *(ka/lul) an-h-nun-ta.*
   this car NM move-NOM NM/AC not-do-IN-DC
   'This car does not move.'

   c. *ce ko.yangi ka* [*pap ul mek-ci*] *(lul/*ka) an-h-ass-e.*
   that cat NM food AC eat-NOM AC/NM no-do-PST-INT
   'That cat did not eat.'

   d. *Yongho nun* [*Mia lul tow-a*] *(lul/*ka) cwu-ess-e.yo.*
   Yongho TC Mia AC help-to AC/NM give-PST-POL
   'Yongho helped Mia (for her).'

In a clause- or sentence-final position, the accusative particle and the preceding noun *kes* 'fact' are compounded to mark an antithetical clause, with senses such as 'I wish', 'I think', 'I should have done', and 'despite the fact that'. The compound *kes ul* or its contracted form *ke-l* may have developed from *kes ul kaciko* 'with the fact that', with the deletion of *kaciko* 'with' (< *kaci-ko* 'have-and'). This grammaticalized form of the accusative particle has nothing to do with a case or delimiter function.

(117) a. *na nun an ka-l ke-l.*↓
   I TC not go-PRS fact-AC
   'I wish I didn't go; I shouldn't have gone.'

   b. *palam i pu-l ke-l?!* ↑
   wind NM low-PRS fact-AC
   'I think the wind will blow.'

   c. *Milan.i ka silh-e-ha-nu-n kes ul, chac-a-ka-ss-ta.*
   Milan NM dislike-IN-RL fact AC visit-PST-DC
   'I visited Milan, despite the fact that she doesn't like it.'

The genitive case which connects one noun phrase to a head noun is marked by the particle *uy*, although the particle is frequently omitted. The genitive phrase has various semantic relations with regard to the head, including possession as in *Milan.i uy kwutwu* 'Milan's leather shoes'), relationship as in *ne uy oppa* 'your older brother', authorship as in *I Kwangswu uy Salang* 'Yi Kwangsu's book *Love*', classification as in *twu chay uy cip* (2 CL GN house) 'two houses', pertinence as in *tokse uy kyeycel* 'a season for reading', origin as in *Mikwuk uy soykoki* 'beef from America', location as in *Hocwu uy inkwu* 'the population of Australia', and reference as in *kaul uy nolay* 'a song of autumn'. In addition, when the head word is a verbal or adjectival noun, the relation is that of an argument and a predicate, as in *pesu uy chwulpal* 'the departure of the bus' [subject–verb], *Alan.i uy hayngpok* 'Alan's happiness' [subject–adjective], *Ilakhu uy phakoy* 'the destruction of Iraq' [subject–verb; verb–object], and *Nam Puk uy thongil* 'unification of South and North Korea' [subject–verb; verb–object]. The genitive particle in most of these constructions may be omitted in casual speech.

The genitive case may incorporate various thematic roles that the genitive nominal has in relation to the head nominal, as in *Mikwuk **uy** Ilpon kwa **uy** Thayphyengyang eyse **uy** cencayng* 'America's war against Japan in the Pacific Ocean' where *Mikwuk* 'America' functions as agent, *Ilpon* 'Japan', comitative, and *Thayphyengyang* 'the Pacific Ocean', dynamic locative in relation to the verbal noun *cencayng* 'war'. Notice that semantic case particles such as comitative and dynamic locative in this example are intact, cooccurring with *uy*. Only the other syntactic case particles (nominative and accusative) are obligatorily omitted before the genitive *uy*, hence *Mikwuk i uy and *Mikwuk ul uy are ungrammatical.

When a nominal in the genitive case contains case or delimiter particles, the genitive particle also must occur. Thus, in *Sewul lo puthe **uy** phyenci* (Seoul DR from GN) 'a letter from Seoul', *uy* must occur. Similarly, when a noun phrase in the genitive case consists of conjoined nominals as in *ne wa na uy chai-cem* 'differences between you and me' or a clause with a sentence ender as in *cwuk-nu-nya sa-nu-nya uy cencayng* 'a war of whether to live or die', *uy* cannot be deleted.

9.5.2   Dative, locative, goal, and source

Particles marking dative, locative, goal, and source cases are as follows.

(118)   a. Dative 'to':   *eykey* [formal, animate]
                            hanthey [informal, animate]
                            ey [inanimate]
                            kkey [deferential]

        b. Static locative 'at, in, on':   *eykey* [formal, animate]
                                            hanthey [informal, animate]
                                            ey [inanimate]
                                            kkey [deferential]

c. Dynamic locative 'at, in, on':   *eykeyse* [formal, animate]
hantheyse [informal, animate]
eyse [inanimate]
kkey [deferential]

d. Goal 'to':   *eykey* [formal, animate]
hanthey [informal, animate]
ey [inanimate]
kkey [deferential]

e. Source 'from':   *eykeyse* [formal, animate]
hantheyse [informal, animate]
eyse [inanimate]

Notice that dative, static locative, and goal cases on the one hand, and dynamic locative and source cases on the other, are marked by the same kinds of particles, except that the latter set contains the fossilized morpheme *-se*, whose meaning may be equated with 'inception' or 'dynamicity'. Needless to say, use of different case particles is correlated with the different predicates used, as illustrated in (119).

(119)   a. *Milan.i nun* **halmeni kkey** *ton   ul   tuly-ess-ta.*   (dative)
Milan   TC   grandma to   money AC   give-PST-DC
'Milan gave money to her grandma.'

b. ***Tongmin.i hanthey*** *chayk i   manh-a.*   (static locative)
Tongmin   at   book   NM   many-INT
'Tongmin has many books.' (lit. 'Many books are at Tongmin.')

c. *Alan.i   nun   **sensayng-nim   kkey** ka-ss-e.yo.*   (goal)
Alan   TC   teacher-HT   to   go-PST-POL
'Alan went to the teacher.'

As in (119a), the dative case occurs with ditransitive verbs that take both direct and indirect objects (e.g., *cwuta* 'give', *poita* 'show', *kaluchita* 'teach', *myenglyenghata* 'order', *pokohata* 'report', *allita* 'inform'). As in (119b), the static locative case occurs with existential, static, and passive predicates (e.g., *manhta* 'be much', *issta* 'exist, stay', *salta* 'live', *namta* 'remain', *kellita* 'get caught', *palphita* 'be stepped on'). The goal case occurs not only with movement verbs (e.g., *kata* 'go', *ota* 'come', *tanita* 'go to and from', *oluta* 'climb'), as in (119c), but also with non-dative transitive verbs (e.g., *ponayta* 'send', *nohta* 'put', *chilhata* 'paint', *ssuta* 'write', *moita* 'gather', *ancta* 'sit'). These three cases, represented by the same set of particles, share the semantic component [GOAL], in that a theme (in the nominative or accusative case) is oriented to the referent of a nominal. Therefore, these particles may be termed goal-oriented locative particles.

The distinction between dynamic location and source cases is made by the predicates used.

(120)   a. *Yongho nun **hak.kyo eyse** nol-ass-ta.*   (dynamic locative)
            Yongho TC   school   at   play-PST-DC
            'Yongho played at school.'

         b. *Cihwan.i nun **hak.kyo eyse** w-ass-ta.*   (source)
            Cihwan   TC   school   from come-PST-DC
            'Cihwan came from school.'

Notice that the dynamic locative case occurs with activity verbs (e.g., *nolta* 'play', *cata* 'sleep') and the source case with movement verbs (e.g., *kata* 'go', *ota* 'come', *pat.ta* 'receive'). These two cases, marked by the same set of particles, share the semantic component [SOURCE] in that a theme (in the nominative case) is originated from the referent of a nominal. They may be termed source-oriented locative particles. Thus, unlike in English, the difference between static locative and dynamic locative is more important than the distinction between dative/goal and locative.

Static locative particles are also used to denote the locations of time (e.g., *yel si ey cata* 'sleep at 10 o'clock'), age (e.g., *phal-sip sey ey tolaka-sita* 'die at the age of 80'), proportion (e.g., *chen wen ey twu kay* '2 items for 1,000 won'), reference (e.g., *kenkang ey cohta* 'be good for one's health'), agent (e.g., *kay hanthey mul-lita* 'be bitten by a dog'), cause (e.g., *kamki ey kel-lita* 'catch a cold'), and addition (e.g., *swul ey pap ey cal mekta* 'have a good meal with wine and rice'). All these are considered semantic extensions of the static locative case.

Many idiomatic phrases are formed with *ey*: *V-ki ey* 'as, because' (past event) (e.g., *pi ka o-ki ey* 'because it rained'), *N ttaymun ey* 'because' (e.g., *kongpu ttaymun ey* 'because of the study'), *N tekpun ey* 'thanks to' (e.g., *emeni tekpun ey* 'thanks to my mother'), *ey piha-ye* 'compared to' (e.g., *nolyek ey piha-ye* 'compared to his effort'), *ey tayha-ye* 'in regard to' (e.g., *kyengcey ey tayha-ye* 'in regard to the economy'), *ey ttal-a* 'per' (e.g., *ne uy yocheng ey ttal-a* 'per your request'), and *ey uyha-myen* 'according to' (e.g., *ilki yeypo ey uyha-myen* 'according to the weather forecast').

The goal-oriented particles can be followed by the 'transferentive' delimiter particle *ta(ka)* for emphasis, if the verb is a transitive one.

(121)   ***sensayng-nim kkey-(ta(ka))***   *ku   chayk   ul   ponay   tuly-ess-e.*
          teacher-HT   to   that   book   AC   send   give-PST-INT
          '(I) sent the book to the teacher.'

The dative case may be represented colloquially by the particles *tele* and *poko*
(derived from *po-ko* 'looking at'), in addition to *eykey* and *hanthey*, with a verb of
saying (stating and asking).

(122)   *na   nun   **Mia   eykey/hanthey/tele/poko**   ca-la   ko   hay-ss-ta.*
          I   TC   Mia   to   sleep-IM   QT   tell-PST-DC
          'I told Mia to sleep.'

The particle *eyse* can denote a temporal source, as in *han si eyse sey si kkaci* 'from
1 to 3 o'clock'. Due to its [SOURCE] component, it is also used as the subject when
the subject denotes a non-human collective agent, such as *hak.kyo* 'school' and *thim*
'team' (123a), and as the source of a superlative expression (123b).

(123)   a. ***wuli   thim   i/eyse   iky-ess-e.***
             our   team   NM/at   win-PST-INT
             'Our team won.'

          b. ***ku   pan   eyse***   *Milan.i   ka   ceyil   yeypp-e.*
             the   class   in   Milan   NM   most   pretty-INT
             'Milan is the prettiest in that class.'

There are verbs that can occur with both goal- and source-oriented locative
particles. Such verbs include *salta* 'live', *suta* 'stand', *cata* 'sleep', *nathanata*
'appear', *nata* 'occur', *phita* 'bloom', *issta* 'exist', and *epsta* 'not exist'. For instance,
in *Sewul ey/eyse salta* 'live in Seoul', there is hardly any semantic difference, except
for the nuance that *ey salta* gives the feeling of 'static' living and *eyse salta* that of
'dynamic' living. In *malwu ey/eyse seta*, the difference is clearer, the *ey seta*
indicating that the walking action ends on the floor, and the *eyse seta* indicating that
the standing action takes place on the floor. In the case of (124), the theme is a static
physical object (theatre) in (124a), but an event (movie) in (124b). Thus, we can
distinguish two meanings in *issta*, i.e., static and dynamic location.

(124)   a. ***ku   hak.kyo   ey***   *kukcang   i   iss-e.yo?*
             the   school   at   theatre   NM   exist-POL
             'Is there a theatre in that school?'

b. ***ku   hak.kyo eyse   yenghwa   ka   iss-e.yo?***
   the   school   at   movie   NM   exist-POL
   'Is there a movie in that school?'

Another phenomenon is the alternation, without much semantic variation, between *hanthey-se/eykey-se* 'from' and *hanthey/eykey*, as in (125a). This occurs when the nominal has a source meaning and the verb is transitive such as *paywuta* 'learn', *pillita* 'borrow', *pat.ta* 'receive', *tut.ta* 'hear', and *tanghata* 'undergo'. It seems that *hanthey/eykey* in such constructions are contracted forms of *hahthey-se/eykey-se*. When *hanthey/eykey* are used as agentive as in (125b), however, such alternation is not allowed.

(125)   a. *Mia   nun   **Cihwan.i   hanthey(-se)**   yenge   lul   paywu-n-ta.*
        Mia   TC   Cihwan   from   English AC   learn-IN-DC
        'Mia learns English from Cihwan.'

      b. *ku   totwuk   un   **kyengkwan   eykey(*-se)**   cap-hy-ess-e.yo.*
        the thief   TC police   by   catch-PAS-PST-POL
        'The thief was caught by the police.'

9.5.3   *Directional, instrumental, and function*

Direction in the sense of 'towards, to, for', instrument in the sense of 'with, of, by, in', and function in the sense of 'as, for, in the capacity of, in terms of' are marked by the same particle *(u)lo*. The instrument and function particles have emphatic counterparts *(u)losse* and *(u)lose*, respectively. Examples of directionals are given in (126).

(126)   a. *Milan.i   nun   **Yengkwuk   ulo**   ttena-ss-ta.*
        Milan   TC   England   DR   leave-PST-DC
        'Milan left for England.'

      b. *na nun   **an   ka-ki   lo**   hay-ss-e.*
        I TC   not   go-NOM DR   decide-PST-INT
        'I decided not to go.'

      c. *Alan.i   ka   **o-l**   cwul   **ul/lo**   al-ass-e.yo.*
        Alan   NM come-PRS likelihood AC/DR think-PST-POL
        '(I) thought Alan would come.'

d. *mwes   ul/ulo   tuli-l-kka   yo?*
   what   AC/DR   give-PRS-Q POL
   'What shall (I) give (you)?'

Notice that the directional particle *(u)lo* may be used as a substitute for the accusative particle. This is particularly common when the direct object is the result of a choice as in (126d). There is an idiomatic expression with the directional particle that is used as a temporal adverbial, i.e., *aph-ulo* 'in the future' (lit. 'towards the front').

The instrumental case is extremely polysemic as in *chong ulo(sse) capta* 'catch with a gun' (instrument), *pay lo kata* 'go by boat' (means), *yelsim ulo ilhata* 'work diligently' (manner), *namu lo(sse) cista* 'build with wood' (material), *am ulo cwukta* 'die of cancer' (cause, reason), *sanso wa swuso lo(sse) toyta* 'consist of hydrogen and oxygen' (constituency), and *ayssu-n tek ulo sengkonghata* 'succeed as a result of hard work' (consequence).

Many idiomatic expressions are formed with the instrumental particle as in the adverbials *hol-lo* (single-with) 'alone', *nal-lo* (day-with) 'by day', *ttay-ttay-lo* (time-time-with) 'once in a while', *sil-lo* (fact-with) 'in fact', *cengmal-lo* (truth-with) 'truly', *tay-tay-lo* (generation-generation-with) 'generation to generation', *pothong-ulo* (normality-with) 'usually', *tekthayk-ulo* (favour-with) 'thanks to', *cham-ulo* (truth-with) 'really', and *isang-ulosse* and conjunctive phrases such as *(u)lo inha-ye* 'due to' and *(u)lo malmiam-a* 'because of'.

The function case occurs in constructions like *taysa lo(se) kunmuhata* 'work as an ambassador', *mat ulo(-se) thayenata* 'be born eldest', and *cil lo(-se) na yang ulo(-se) na wuswuhata* 'be excellent in terms of both quality and quantity'.

9.5.4   Ablative

The ablative case is marked by the particle *puthe* 'from' or particle compounds such as *(u)lo puthe* (directional/instrumental + *puthe*) 'from the direction of, starting from, starting with', *eyse puthe* (source or dynamic locative + *puthe*) 'starting from the place of', and *kkeyse puthe* (honorific source or dynamic locative + *puthe*) 'from a respectable person'. The bare form *puthe* usually occurs with time nominals as in *nayil puthe* 'from tomorrow' and *akka puthe* 'from a while ago'. Directional, instrumental, and source (dynamic locative) ablatives are illustrated respectively in (127a, b, c).

(127)   a. *kicha   ka   **Pusan   ulo   puthe***   *tochak.hay-ss-e.yo.*
        train   NM   Pusan   DR   from   arrive-PST-POL
        'A train arrived from Pusan.'

b. *Hankwuk   yeksa   nun   **Tankwun   ulo puthe**   sicaktoy-n-ta.*
Korea   history TC   Tangun   with from   begin-IN-DC
'Korean history begins with Tangun.'

c. *Alan.i   nun   **hak.kyo   eyse   puthe** kel-e   w-ass-e.*
Alan   TC   school   at   from   walk-INF come-PST-INT
'Alan walked here from school.'

9.5.5   *Comitative and connective*

The comitative case, which is marked by the particles *wa* (after a vowel)/ *kwa* (after a consonant) [formal], *hako* [informal], and *lang* (after a vowel)/ *ilang* (after a consonant) [informal], has the function of connecting two nominals. With reciprocal verbs such as *kyelhonhata* 'marry', *talmta* 'resemble', *mannata* 'meet', *ssawuta* 'fight', *kathta* 'be same', and *taluta* 'be different', the comitative particle conveys a sense of reciprocity.

(128)   a. *enni   ka   **Mia   hako/lang/wa**   hamkkey   ttena-ss-ta.*
sister NM Mia   with   together   leave-PST-DC
'My sister left together with Mia.'

b. *Minca   ka   **Yongho   hako/lang/wa**   kyelhonhay-ss-e.yo.*
Minca   NM Yongho   with   marry-PST-POL
'Minca married Yongho.'

The connective case is represented by the same set of particles as those of the comitative case and the disjunctive particle *na* (after a vowel)/*ina* (after a consonant) 'or'. These particles connect nominals appositively with the coordinating meaning of 'and' or 'or'.

(129)   a. *[**enni   hako/lang/wa** Mia   (**hako**/*lang/*wa)]   ka   ttena-ss-e.*
sister and   Mia   and   NM leave-PST-INT
'My older sister and Mia left.'

b. *[**hyeng   ina   na   (na)**]   ka   ka-keyss-e.*
brother or   I   or   NM go-will-INT
'Either my older brother or I will go.'

Notice that the informal particle *hako* and the disjunctive particle *(i)na* may be repeated after the second nominal without any change in meaning.

9.5.6   *Comparative*

While there are no comparative or superlative affixes in Korean, there are particles associated with comparison: *pota* '(rather) than, (more/less) than', *mankhum* 'as much as, equal to', *chelem* 'like, the same as', and *kathi* 'like, the same as'. All of these may be immediately preceded by a demonstrative, as in *ku pota* 'more than that', *ce mankhum* 'as much as that', *i chelem* 'like this', and *i kathi* 'like this'. The form *mankhum* is also a defective noun which functions as the head of a relative clause, as in *ca-l mankhum ca-ss-ta* '(I) slept as much as (I) needed.'

The particle *pota* is used for comparison in the sense of '(more/less) than' and for selection in the sense of 'rather than'. If a sentence is clearly comparative, the adverb *te* 'more' is optional, because *pota* itself is often interpreted as 'more than'. The adverb *tel* 'less' is obligatory, however, if inferiority is intended. These adverbs always follow *pota* but precede the predicate. The adverb *chalali* 'rather' is often used in a construction where *pota* has a selectional meaning. A *pota*-nominal can be scrambled with other pre-predicate nominals. When *pota* occurs with other particles, it appears after certain delimiters such as *kkaci* 'until, as far as' and *man* 'only' and semantic cases such as *ey*, *eyse* 'at, on, in', *(u)lo* 'toward, with, as', *puthe* 'from', and *chelem* 'like', but before topic delimiters such as *nun* 'as for', *to* 'also', and *(i)ya* 'as only for'.

(130)   a. ***Milan.i pota*** *Mia* *nun*   ***te/tel***   *yeyppu-ta.*
        Milan   than   Mia   TC   more/less   pretty-DC
        'Milan is more/less pretty than Milan.'

    b. ***cengchika lose pota to***   *hakca* *lose* ***te***   *yumyenghay-yo.*
        politician   as   than even scholar as   more famous-POL
        '(He) is famous more as a scholar than as a politician.'

    c. ***ka-myense*** ***pota***   *o-myense*   ***te***   *wul-ess-ta.*
        go-while   than   come-while more   cry-PST-DC
        '(He) cried more while coming than while going.'

    d. *ca.yu*   *eps-i*   *sa-nu-n*   *kes pota chalali*   *cwuk-keyss-ta.*
        freedom without live-IN-RL fact than rather   die-will-DC
        'I would rather die than live without freedom.'

The superlative is expressed by the degree adverb *kacang* 'most' or *ceyil* 'most, the first', together with a locative noun phrase such as . . . *cwung eyse* (middle from) 'among', . . . *kawuntey eyse* (centre from) 'among', and . . . *eyse* 'at, in'.

(131) *Mia nun haksayng-tul kawuntey eyse kacang khu-ta.*
       Mia   TC   student-PL   middle   at   most   tall-DC
       'Mia is the tallest among the students.'

The equative particle *mankhum*, the analogy particle *chelem*, and the derived analogy particle *kathi* (*kath* 'same', -*i* (AD)) behave similarly, as in *Mia nun **Milan.i mankhum/chelem/kathi** khu-ta* 'Mia is as tall as Milan; Mia is tall like Milan.'

9.5.7 Vocative

Deferential address terms such as *sensayng-nim* 'Sir!, Madam!' (lit. 'esteemed teacher') which have the honorific title suffix -*nim* and plain address terms such as *Mia ya* 'Mia!' and *Milan a* 'Milan!' which consist of a given name and the vocative particle *(y)a* are functionally the same, in that they are used to draw the attention of the addressee in a discourse context, do not constitute an argument (such as the subject) of a sentence, and reflect the relationship between the speaker and addressee in terms of social status. Compare (132a) with (132b) and notice the status difference implied in the two utterances. In (132a), the speaker and addressee are most likely either in a child–child relationship or in an adult–child relationship, whereas in (132b), the addressee is an adult and the speaker is either an adult equal or inferior or a child.

(132)   a. ***Tongmin a,***   *ne   eti   ka-ni?*
            Milan   VOC   you   where   go-Q
            'Tongmin! Where are you going?'

         b. ***sensayng-nim,***   *eti   ka-sey-yo?*
            teacher-HT   where   go-SH-POL
            'Sir (lit. 'esteemed teacher')! Where are you going?'

Vocative particles are (i) *a* (after a consonant)/*ya* (after a vowel) [plain level], (ii) *i* (after a consonant)/ZERO (after a vowel) [intimate level], and (iii) *i(si)e* [hyper-deferential level] which appears to have developed from the copula *i*, the subject honorific suffix -*si*, and the obsolete vocative suffix -*e*. The hyper-deferential form without -*si* is contracted to *ye* after a vowel.

The plain-level vocative form *(y)a* following a given name is typically used to address a child by another child or an adult, but also an adult by his or her parents or by a friend whose friendship began in childhood. As in (132a), the plain vocative form agrees, in a sentence, with the plain personal pronoun *ne* 'you' and plain sentence enders such as *-ta* (declarative), *-ni* (interrogative), *-ca* (propositive), and *-la* (imperative).

The plain-level vocative particle is also attached to plural nominals, as in *haksayng-tul a* 'Students!' and *celm-un i-tul a* 'Youngsters!' and used in idiomatic expressions such as *papo ya* 'You fool!', *i kes a* 'You!' (lit. 'this thing!'), *pyengsin a* 'You idiot!', *apem a* 'Look here!' (lit.'(child's) father!', addressed to one's married son), *enni ya* 'Sis!', and *emma ya* 'Mommy!'.

(133)   ***emem a,***   *eti*   *ka-ss-ta(ka)*   *w-ass-ni?*
mom   VOC   where   go-PST-and   come-PST-Q
'Child's mom! Where have you been?'
(addressed to one's married daughter or daughter-in-law)

The intimate vocative particle *i/ZERO* is attached to personal names typically to address adolescent persons (generally males) by another adolescent or an adult. It is also used to address one's son-in-law or other inferior adult relatives. It agrees, in a sentence, with the intimate personal pronoun *caney* 'you' and the familiar sentence enders *-ney* (declarative), *-na/-nunka* (interrogative), *-sey* (propositive), and *-key* (imperative).

(134)   a. ***Tongmin i,***   *caney*   *ka*   *mence*   *ttena-key.*
Tongmin   VOC   you   NM   first   leave-IM
Tongmin! You leave first.'

b. ***Yongho,***   *wuli*   *hamkkey*   *ka-sey.*
Yongho   we   together   go-PR
'Yongho! Let's go together.'

The hyper-deferential vocative particle *i(si)e* is not used to address living people in face-to-face situations. God, Christ, or one's deceased lover (in a literary style) may be addressed with these particles, as in *cwu ye* 'lord!', *hananim isie* 'oh, God!', *im ie* 'oh, my beloved!'. This particle agrees with the obsolete hyper-deferential sentence enders *-naita* (declarative), *-naikka* (interrogative), and *-sose* (imperative), and blunt-level enders which used to be polite enders.

(135)   **cwu ye,**   *cehuy lul   posalphy-e*   *cwu-sose.*
          lord   VOC   us   AC   look after-INF   give-IM
          'Lord! Please look after us.'

The hyper-deferential particle *ye* is also used to address a group of people in writing, in which case the sentence enders may be either the plain- or blunt-level forms, as in *tongpho ye ilena-la/ilena-o* 'Brethren! Wake up!'

9.5.8   *Case-particle stacking*

A series of case particles may occur in sequence all associated with the same nominal, reflecting the agglutinative nature of Korean. However, not all of such stacked case particles perform active case functions in a given sentence as will be discussed shortly. In the sentences in (136), the particles performing an active case function are underlined.

(136)   a.   *yeki*   **eyse**   **puthe**   <u>**ka**</u>   *wuli*   *ttang*   *i-a.*
            here   at   starting-from   NM   our   land   is-INT
            'Our land starts from here.'

        b.   *Kim-sensayng*   **eykey**   <u>**lo**</u>   *man*   *ul*   *hoysin ul*   *ponay-ss-e.yo.*
            Kim-teacher   to   DR   only   AC   reply   AC   send-PST-POL
            '(I) sent a response only to Professor Kim.'

        c.   *paywu*   *ka*   [*Hankwuk* <u>**eyse**</u> <u>**wa/na**</u> *Ilpon*   *eyse*]   *w-ass-ta.*
            actor   NM   Korea   from and/or   Japan   from   come-PST-DC
            'The actors came from Korea and/or Japan.'

        d.   *Kim-sensayng*   **eykey**   <u>**lo**</u>   <u>**uy**</u>   *hoysin*
            Kim-teacher   to   DR   GN   reply
            'a reply to Professor Kim'

        e.   *Mikwuk*   *uy*   *Saiphan* <u>**eyse**</u> <u>**uy**</u>   *Ilpon*   <u>**kwa**</u> <u>**uy**</u>   *cencayng*
            America   GN   Saiphan   at   GN   Japan   with   GN   war
            'America's war against Japan in Saipan'

In (136a), three case particles occur in sequence. While the locative and ablative cases, marked respectively by *eyse* 'at, in' and *puthe* 'from', are inert in that they are not associated with the predicate (the copula in this case), only the nominative case, marked by the particle *ka*, is related to the copula as its subject. The two inert case particles simply contribute their semantic content to the subject noun phrase. In this respect they are like delimiters. In contrast to such inert cases, the case which maintains its syntactic relation with the predicate may be called the 'privileged' case. Thus, in (136a) the nominative case is the privileged case, while the locative and ablative case particles are privative.

In (136b), the three case particles *eykey*, *lo*, and *ul* are flanked by a delimiter (*man* 'only'). Here, the directional *lo* is the privileged case and is related to the predicate *ponayta* 'send', whereas the particle *eykey* 'to' and the accusative particle *ul* become privative and function as delimiters. In (136c), the source particle *eyse* and the connective particles *wa* 'and' and *na* 'or' all function as privileged, in that the former is related to the predicate and the latter two connect two noun phrases.

In genitive constructions such as (136d, e), the privileged syntactic case is always the genitive (marked by the particle *uy*) which relates the cooccurring nominal genitively to the head nominal. In addition, one or more semantic cases may also occur before the genitive case. In (136d), the privileged semantic case is the directional marked by *lo* which semantically relates its cooccurring nominal *Kim-sensayng eykey* to the head verbal noun *hoysin*. Here, the static locative case marked by *eykey* is privative. In (136e), the dynamic locative case marked by *eyse* and the comitative case marked by *kwa* are privileged.

Which one of a sequence of case particles becomes privileged depends on the argument structure (or thematic roles) of the predicate. For instance, the copula *ita* requires a theme subject, hence the nominative case in *yeki eyse puthe ka* must be privileged in (136a). Similarly, in (136b), the predicate *ponayta* 'send' requires a directional role, hence the directional case in *Kim sensayng eykey lo man ul* is privileged. Dependence on the argument structure of a predicate can be more clearly observed by comparing the two sentences in (137).

(137)   a. *tong-ccok* *ulo* *man* *ul* *ka-ss-ta.*
             east-side   DR   only   AC   go-PST-DC
             '(He) went only to the east side.'

         b. *tong-ccok* *ulo* *man* *ul* *po-ass-ta.*
             east-side   DR   only   AC   see-PST-DC
             '(He) looked only toward the east side.'

In a sequence of cases which are equally case-relatable to the predicate, the last one acquires priority in case privilege hierarchy over the preceding ones. Thus, in *Kim sensayng-nim eykey lo*, both *eykey* 'to/at' and *lo* 'towards' can be relatable to *ponayta* 'send', but *lo* is regarded as privileged and *eykey* is interpreted as a static human locative 'at'. As noticed in this example, there is a slight semantic difference in certain semantic case particles between when the particle is used as a privileged one and when it is used as a privative one. In a privative case, a goal particle (*kkey*, *eykey*, *ey*) in a privileged case loses its goal meaning and functions as a static locative, and the directional particle *(u)lo* also loses its directional meaning 'toward' and denotes a general direction, as in *hak.kyo lo puthe w-ass-ta* '(He) came from the direction of school.' The ablative *puthe* means 'from' in a privileged case as in *hak.kyo lo puthe w-ass-ta*, but 'starting from, beginning with' in a privative case as in (136a).

9.6 *Delimiter constructions*

While case particles mark syntactic relations among major constituents, delimiter particles delimit the meaning of the cooccurring element with little syntactic function. Many case particles including the nominative *ka/i*, accusative *(l)ul*, ablative *puthe*, and directional *(u)lo* behave like delimiters with their own semantic content, especially when they become privative case particles as observed in 9.5.8. Delimiters appear most productively in noun phrases but also with adverbs, complement clauses, and even main sentences. Due to their syntactic and semantic properties, delimiters can be classified into two types, constituent and sentential (or discoursal) delimiters, the former occurring in noun phrases (including nominalized clauses) and with adverbs and complement clauses, and the latter occurring at the end of a sentence and/or after any major constituent.

9.6.1 *Constituent delimiters*

Most of the important constituent delimiter particles were given in 8.1.9. The examples in (138) use delimiters in noun phrases.

(138) a. *ku   ai   nun   totwukcil   mace   ha-n-ta.*
          the child TC   theft   even   do-IN-DC
          'That child goes as far as committing theft.'

       b. *Mia nun emeni eykey na   ka-n   tus-i   kipp-ess-ta.*
          Mia TC   mother to   or so go-RL as if   happy-PST-DC
          'Mia was happy as if she had gone to her mother or something.'

The following sentences illustrate the occurrence of delimiters with adverbs (139a, b) and complement clauses (139c).

(139)   a. *Tongmin.i   nun   **phek   to***   *coh-a   hay-ss-e.*
         Tongmin   TC   very   indeed   good-INF   show sign-PST-INT
         'Tongmin indeed showed his happiness.'

         b. ***ppalli   man*** *ka-myen   toy-n-ta.*
         early   only   go-if   O.K.-IN-DC
         'It's okay only if (you) go early.'

         c. *na n   Mia eykey **nay sin ul   sin-key   kkaci nun** hay-ss-ta.*
         I   TC   Mia to   my   shoe AC   wear-AD   up to   TC   do-PST-DC
         'I did as much as letting Mia wear my shoes.'

Delimiters can occur with case particles in noun phrases, as shown in (138b) where the 'alternative' delimiter *na* 'rather, or something' occurs with the goal case particle *eykey*. Also, two or more delimiters may occur in sequence, in which case there are certain fixed orders among them.

I.S. Yang (1972) proposes that there are three sets of delimiters, that occur in the order of X, Y, and Z, where X includes *mace* 'even, also, so far as, on top of', *mata* 'each, every, all', *kkaci* 'till, up to, even, as far as', and *puthe* 'starting from'; Y includes *man* 'only, just', *cocha* 'even, as well', and *pakkey* 'except for, outside of'; and Z includes *(n)un* 'as for, regarding' (topic-contrast marker), *to* 'also, too, indeed', *(i)ya* 'as only for', *(i)na* 'or the like, or so, or something, about', *(i)lato* 'even, even if, as a last recourse', and *(i)yamallo* 'the very, no other than'. In addition, we have *khenyeng* 'far from doing or being, let alone' that occurs after *(n)un*. From each set, at most one member can occur within a noun phrase. Observe the following sentences that illustrate delimiter stacking and delimiter-case cooccurrence.

(140)   a. *sip   pen   **kkaci man un** ppop-ca.*
         10   no.   till   only TC   select-PR
         'Let's select only up to no. 10.'

         b. *Nami eykey **nun khenyeng** Mia eykey **cocha to**   an ka-ss-e.yo.*
         Nami to   TC far from   Mia to   even also   not go-PST-POL
         '(I) didn't even go to Mia, let alone to Nami.'

Z delimiters, all of which show a high degree of topicality, take the same slot as syntactic case particles such as the nominative, accusative, and genitive. Therefore, particles from both sets cannot cooccur. For instance, sequences like **ttek-un/to/iya-i/ul/uy* or **ttek-i/ul/uy-un/to/iya* 'as for/also/as only for rice cake' (nominative/

accusative/genitive) are ungrammatical.

Among the delimiters, the topic-contrast delimiter *(n)un* 'as for, concerning' has been most extensively discussed in the literature since its use is the most widespread and its meaning is not easy to determine. In particular, when it appears in the subject position with a topic sense (roughly 'as for'), its meaning can hardly be distinguished from the neutral (i.e., not exclusive) meaning of the nominative case particle *i/ka*.

(141)   *Milan.i* **ka/nun**   *nwun*   *i*   *kh-e.yo.*
         Milan   NM/TC   eye   NM   big-POL
         'Milan has big eyes.'

When the bold-faced particles in (141) are stressed, only then do the distinct meaning differences emerge. In this case, the meaning of the nominative particle is exclusiveness, as in 'It is Milan who . . .', whereas the meaning of the delimiter is contrastiveness, as in 'Milan (in contrast with other persons) . . .' or '(I don't know about other people, but) Milan . . .' In short, the topic-contrast particle provides the cooccurring noun phrase with either a topic meaning, usually when the noun phrase is unstressed and occurs in the sentence-initial position, or a contrast meaning, especially when the noun phrase is stressed or appears in a non-initial position. The dual meanings are clearer in a multiple topic construction, as illustrated in (142).

(142)   *Milan.i* **nun** *nwun* **un** *kh-e.yo.*
         Milan   TC   eye   TC   big-POL
         'As for Milan, her eyes are big (in contrast with other body parts).'

The first unstressed *(n)un*-marked element is interpreted as the topic of the sentence, whereas the second *(n)un*-marked element, whether stressed or not, indicates contrast. Since the first unstressed *(n)un*-marked element usually denotes the topic of the rest of the sentence, an embedded clause cannot have an unstressed *(n)un*-marked subject, as in *Mia ka/*nun tani-nu-n hak.kyo ka ceyil coh-ta* 'The school Mia attends is the best.'

The particle *(n)un* is not used when the subject noun phrase introduces new indefinite information to the hearer, in which case the nominative particle *i/ka* is used. Thus, in *akka enu keci ka/*nun w-ass-e.yo; ku keci ka/nun pap ul tal-la ko hay-ss-e.yo* 'A beggar came a while ago; he asked for food', *(n)un* cannot occur in the first sentence which introduces new indefinite information (*enu keci* 'certain beggar'), but it can occur in the second sentence because by then the information is already registered in the hearer's knowledge and is thus represented as a definite noun.

Constituent delimiters such as *(i)ya* 'only if, as only for, indeed', *(i)na* 'or the like, or something; approximately, as many/much as' (i.e., *emeni na manna-n tus-i kipp-ess-e* 'I was happy as if I had met my mother or something'), *(i)lato* 'even if, for lack of anything better' (e.g., *pay kophu-myen i kes i-lato mek-ela* 'If you are hungry, why don't you eat even this'), *(i)nama* 'lacking anything better, inconvenient though it is' (e.g., *may-wel cokum inama cechwuk.ha-ko siph-ta* 'I wish to save at least a little amount every month'), *(i)yamallo* 'indeed, precisely, none other than' (e.g., *Kumkang-san iyamallo cengmal alumtaw-e.yo* 'The Diamond Mountains are indeed beautiful'), appear to have developed from the copula *i* + a conjunctive suffix. As grammaticalized forms, they have various syntactic restrictions. For instance, *(i)ya* occurs only in declarative sentences, as in *ne ya ka-keyss-ci* 'I assume that you must be going' but **ne ya ka-keyss-ni?*, **ne ya ka-la*, and **ne hako na ya ka-ca.*

The constituent delimiters *kkaci* 'even, as far as, up to', *cocha* 'even, as well', and *mace* 'even, so far as, as a last alternative' are semantically so closely related to each other that they are more or less mutually interchangeable with only minute differences in meaning.

(143)   *Mia* **kkaci/cocha/mace**   *hoyuy*   *ey o-ci*   *an-h-ass-ta.*
          Mia even   meeting to come-NOM not-do-PST-DC
          'Even Mia did not come to the meeting.'

The delimiter *mata* 'every' behaves like a universal quantifier. It can be attached to a single nominal (e.g., *nala mata* 'every country'), a reduplicated nominal (e.g., *cip-cip mata* 'every house'), and a pluralized nominal (e.g., *salam-tul mata* 'every person'). The delimiter *sekken* is a colloquial counterpart of the Sino-Korean bound noun *tung* 'and so on, and the like, et cetera' as in *swul sekken ttek sekken manh-i mek-ess-e.yo* 'I had lots to eat and drink – cake, wines, and so on.'

9.6.2   *Sentential delimiters*

Sentential or discoursal delimiters do not delimit the constituent in which they occur, but affect the whole sentence in terms of the speaker's perception or modality in a discourse situation. Four representative delimiters of this type are the plural particle *tul*, the politeness particle *yo*, the obsolete 'apperceptive' sentence-final particle *kulye* 'indeed, I confirm', and the concessive particle *man(un)* 'but'. The first two can be attached, sometimes multiply, to any major constituent of a sentence and have corresponding inflectional suffixes *-tul* and *-e.yo/-a.yo*, respectively, while the latter two occur only in the sentence-final position and *man(un)* also functions as a particle connecting two sentences.

The particle *tul* and the suffix *-tul* have the same meaning but different functions.

Plurality in a nominal is marked by the suffix *-tul*, as in *ai-tul* 'children', *Yongho-ney-tul* 'Yongho's family members', *ne-huy-tul* 'you guys'. A plural suffix is frequently omitted as in *i san ey-nun namu(-tul) i manh-ta* 'There are many trees on this mountain.' It is generally required, however, when the cooccurring plural noun is preceded by a demonstrative, as in *ku salam-tul* 'those people'. On the other hand, the particle *tul* follows any word, phrase, clause, or sentence to indicate distributive plurality of the subject nominal, whether the subject is stated or implied. It can occur multiply after two or more constituents for emphasis.

(144)   a. *wuli   mek-e   **tul**   po-ca.*
             we   eat-INF   PL   try-PR
             'Let's try eating.'

         b. *sinmun   ul   ilk-umyense **tul** pap   ul   mek-nun-ta.*
             newspaper AC read-while PL meal AC eat-IN-DC
             '(They) are having their meals while reading newspapers.'

         c. *ppalli   **tul**   ttena-la   **tul**.*
             quickly PL   leave-IM PL
             'Everybody, leave quickly!'

Two *tul*'s may cooccur within the same noun phrase, the first one being suffixal and the second one sentential. Furthermore, a singular subject may be used with *tul* if the action of the subject referent is multiple towards a plural direct or indirect object in a transitive construction.

(145)   *na nun ku ai-**tul**   hanthey **tul**   chayk ul   cwu-ess-e.*
             I   TC   the child-PL to   PL   book AC   give-PST-INT
             'I gave books to the children individually.'

While the polite suffix *-e.yo/-a.yo* occurs in the sentence-final position, the polite particle *yo* can occur after any major constituent in a polite or deferential sentence with the effect of casual emphasis on the constituent concerned. It also makes an intimate sentence a polite one, as in the backgrounder *-nuntey (yo)*, apperceptive *-ney (yo)* and *-kwun (yo)*, promissive *-(u)l-key (yo)*, suppositive *-ci (yo)*, familiar interrogative *-na (yo)*, *-nu-n-ka (yo)*, and guessing *-(u)l-kel yo*. It can also follow deferential sentence enders, indicating intimacy and casualness, as shown in *-(su)p-ni-ta yo* (declarative) and *-(u)si-p-si-ta yo* (propositive).

(146)   *kulen-tey* **yo**, *ce nun* **yo** *mos   ka-keyss-sup-ni-ta* **yo**.
         by the way POL I TC POL unable go-may-AH-IN-DC POL
         'But, I am unable to go.'

The apperceptive particle *kulye* 'I realize, how about?' occurs after a complete declarative or propositive sentence, usually in the deferential or familiar level. The concessive particle *man(un)* is used as a hesitancy marker when placed at the end of a sentence. It mitigates the speaker's assertiveness of the proposition.

(147)   a. *icey   ka   po-p-si-ta   **kulye**.*
            now   go   try-AH-RQ-DC APP
            'How about leaving now?'

         b. *ce nun   an   ka-p-ni-ta   **man(un)**.*
            I   TC   not go-AH-IN-DC but
            '(I am sorry but) I am not going.'

9.7   Numeral constructions

Korean numerals, which consist of two sets, native and Sino-Korean, may be used by themselves when things are enumerated, but more frequently they compound with other nouns such as counters. Such numeral compounds are of several types.

9.7.1   *Time expressions*

The temporal counters *si* 'o'clock', *pun* 'minute', *cho* 'second', and *kan* (duration of time) follow numerals. For hours, native numerals are used with *si*, except in military affairs where Sino-Korean numerals are often employed. For minutes and seconds, only Sino-Korean numerals are used before *pun* or *cho*. For duration of time, Sino-Korean *kan* is placed at the end of time expressions, obligatorily after *si* and optionally after *pun* and *cho*. For a.m. and p.m., Sino-Korean *o-cen* (lit. 'noon-before') and *o-hwu* (lit. 'noon-after'), respectively, are placed before time expressions, except in military affairs where hours are extended to 24 o'clock, as in *i sip sam si* '23 o'clock'.

(148)   *o-cen yel han si*   '11:00 a.m.'
         myech si   'what time?'
         twu si pan = twu si sam sip pun   'two thirty' (*pan* 'half')
         sey si sa sip pun sip o cho   'three forty and 15 seconds'
         twu si kan   '2 hours'

i pun (kan)	'2 minutes'
sam sip pun (kan) = *pan si kan*	'30 minutes' = 'half an hour'
sey si kan pan	'3 and a half hours'
= *sey si kan sam sip pun*	'3 hours and 30 minutes'
myech si kan	'how many hours?'

Notice that *pan* 'half' may be used for thirty minutes, but not for thirty seconds, and that *kan* is placed immediately after hours if minutes and/or seconds follow.

Days of the month, months, and years are all expressed by Sino-Korean numerals followed by the Sino-Korean nouns *il* 'day', *wel* 'month', or *nyen* 'year', as in *il il* '1st', *i sip kwu il* '29th'; *il wel* 'January', *i wel* 'February', *sam wel* 'March', *sa wel* 'April', *o wel* 'May', *yu* (not *yuk*) *wel* 'June', *chil wel* 'July', *phal wel* 'August', *kwu wel* 'September', *si* (not *sip*) *wel* 'October', *sip il wel* 'November', *sip i wel* 'December'; and *chen kwu payk kwu sip phal nyen* 'year 1998'. The terms for days and years are also used to indicate duration of time, optionally followed by *kan* 'period', as in *sam sip il (kan)* 'thirty days' and *o nyen (kan)* 'five years'. For the duration of months, Sino-Korean numeral + *kay* + *wel (kan)* is used, where *kay* 'item' + *wel* refers to the number of months, as in *sam kay wel (kan)* 'three months'.

There is a native system too, which is declining in use especially among younger generation speakers. For the days of the month, the Sino-Korean term *cho* 'beginning' can be placed before the term for each date up to the tenth day, in which case the native term *nal* 'day' can be omitted, as in *cho halwu/halwus nal* '1st day'. Notice that *nal* is used for both the duration of days and for dates for twenty, thirty, forty, etc.

(149)	*halwu*	'1 day'	*halwus nal*	'1st day'
	ithul	'2 days'	*ithut nal*	'2nd day'
	tas.say	'5 days'	*tas.says nal*	'5th day'
	iley	'7 days'	*ileys nal*	'7th day'
	ahuley	'9 days'	*ahuleys nal*	'9th day'
	yelhul	'10 days'	*yelhul nal*	'10th day'
	yel halwu	'11 days'	*yel halwus nal*	'11th day'
	sumu nal	'20 days'	*sumu nal*	'20th day'
	sumu tas.say	'25 days'	*sumu tas.says nal*	'25th day'
	selhun nal	'30 days'	*selhun nal*	'30th day'

For months and years, native terms, i.e., a native numeral + *tal* 'month, moon' or *hay* 'year, sun', are only for duration, as in *han tal* '1 month', *ahop tal* '9 months', *ahun yetelp tal* '98 months'; *han hay* '1 year', *twu hay* '2 years', *yel hay* '10 years', *ahun yetelp hay* '98 years'.

9.7.2   *Ordinals, frequency, and number*

Native ordinals consist of native numeral + native ordinalizer *ccay*, as in *ches ccay*
'first' and *twul ccay* 'second'. Colloquially, the Sino-Korean defective noun *pen* 'turn,
time' may be placed after the numeral, as in *twu pen ccay* 'second time'. If *pen* is
used, Sino-Korean numerals are permitted to occur with *ccay*, as in *o pen ccay* 'fifth'
and *payk pen ccay* 'one hundredth'. The first numeral *han* 'one' is replaced by *ches*
'first'. Sino-Korean ordinals are formed by prefixing the Sino-Korean ordinalizer *cey*
to Sino-Korean numerals, as in *cey sip* 'tenth', and *cey payk sam-sip* '130th'.

Ordinals may occur as the possessor of a possessive construction usually without
the genitive particle, as in *twul ccay salam* 'the second person', *yel pen ccay (uy)
namca* 'the tenth man', *cey i kwa* 'lesson two', and *cey sam kwuk* 'the third country'.

Frequency is expressed by adding the Sino-Korean counter *pen* 'times' after either
native or Sino-Korean numerals. With Sino-Korean numerals, *pen* occurs only for
multiples of ten (from twenty) and above (without one to nine following), as in *i sip
pen* 'twenty times' and *payk pen* '100 times'. Thus, Sino-Korean *sip pen* 'ten times',
**sam sip il pen* 'thirty one times', **sam sip han pen* 'thirty one times' are not
normally acceptable, while native *han pen* 'once, one time', *twu pen* 'twice', *sumu
pen* 'twenty times', and *sumul twu pen* 'twenty-two times' are.

Numerical order is expressed by using the Sino-Korean counter *pen* 'number'
(generally for animates) or *ho* 'number' (generally for inanimates), as in *o pen* 'no.
five', *sam pen son-nim* 'guest no. 3', *i sip yuk ho sil* 'Room no. 26', *'Ene' sip kwu ho*
'Language 19', and *il ho yelcha* 'no. 1 train'. House numbers are expressed by *pen-ci*
(number-land), as in *Sewul si Conglo-kwu Myenglyun-tong 12 pen-ci* '12 Myenglyun
Street, Conglo Ward, Seoul'.

9.7.3   *Classifier constructions*

Classifier (or counter) constructions are made up of two types as in (150), the first
type being more natural than the second. NOUN in both constructions is any
countable noun. Some classifier constructions like time and frequency expressions
usually do not have NOUN, as we have seen above, but most others contain it,
whether expressed or understood.

(150)   Type 1: NOUN + [NUMERAL + COUNTER]

e.g.,   *chayk twu kwen*   'two books'
         haksayng sey myeng   'three students'
         noin tases pun   'five old people'
         kay yel mali   'ten dogs'
         soykoki han kun   'one pound of beef'

Type 2: [NUMERAL + COUNTER] + GENITIVE + NOUN

e.g.,	*twu kwen uy chayk*	'two books'
	sey myeng uy haksayng	'three students'
	tases pun uy noin	'five old people'
	yel mali uy kay	'ten dogs'
	han kun uy soykoki	'one pound of beef'

Numerals include not only pure numbers such as *han* 'one' and *yel twu* 'twelve' but quantifiers such as *yele* 'many, several', *yakkan* 'a few', and *myech* 'how many, several', as in *chayk yele kwen* and *yele kwen uy chak* 'several books'. NUMERAL + COUNTER in Type 1 may be replaced by non-numerical quantifiers such as *motwu* 'all', *ta* 'all', *taypupun* 'most', *cokum* 'a few, a little', *yeles* 'many, several', and *il-pu* 'part', as in *haksayng il-pu* and *il-pu uy haksayng* 'some of the students'. Numerals are often used without counters and the genitive particle, as in *haksayng twul* or *twu haksayng* 'two students' and *hyengcey seys* or *sey hyengcey* 'three brothers', but this usage is unnatural if non-human nouns are involved, especially when the number is above nine, as in *?cha sumul* or *?sumu cha* '20 cars'.

In Type 1, NOUN and [NUMERAL + COUNTER] are separable in a sentence, when the classifier construction is in the nominative or accusative case, as illustrated in (151a, b). This phenomenon is often called quantifier floating, and does not apply when the construction is neither nominative nor accusative, as shown in (151c).

(151) a. *haksayng   sey   myeng   i   ceki   o-n-ta.*
             student   3   person   NM   there   come-IN-DC
      → *haksayng i sey myeng i ceki o-n-ta.*
        haksayng i ceki sey meyng i o-n-ta.
      'Three students are coming over there.'

      b. *onul   say   twu   mali   lul   cap-ass-ta.*
             today   bird   2   animal   AC   catch-PST-DC
      → *onul say lul twu mali lul cap-ass-ta.*
        say lul onul twu mali lul cap-ass-ta.
      '(I) caught three birds today.'

      c. *onl   haksayng   twu myeng   eykey   chayk ul   cwu-ess-ta.*
          today   student   2   person   to   book   AC   give-PST-DC
      → **onul haksayng eykey twu myeng eykey chayk ul cwu-ess-ta.*
        *haksayng eykey onul twu myeng eykey chayk ul cwu-ess-ta.
      '(I) gave books to two students today.'

9.8   Modality and tense-aspect

The most important clausal or sentential constituent is the predicate (verb or adjective), which comes at the end of a clause or a sentence. The simplest form of a predicate construction consists of two obligatory elements: a predicate stem and a clause or sentence ender.

(152)   Clause/sentence type   Example (Stem + Ender)
          a. finitive   *coh-ta* '(it) is good'
          b. conjunctive   *coh-ko* '(it) is good, and'
          c. relative   *coh-un* 'good'
          d. complement   *coh-a* 'to be good'
          e. nominalized   *coh-ki* 'being good'

A predicate stem (STEM) consists of a single or compound root (ROOT), optionally accompanied by one or more derivational (Drv) affixes. A clause or sentence ender (CL-ENDER) consists of one or more suffixes representing addressee honorification (AH), mood (MD), and clause-type (CL-TYPE). Between a stem and a clause/sentence ender, several inflectional suffixes may occur, indicating subject honorification (SH), past/perfect tense (PST), and modal expressions (MDL), in that order. These non-final inflectional suffixes are called pre-finals (PRE-FINAL). The linear constituent structure of the predicate can be represented as in (153). Notice in the tree diagram and example in (154) that all the optional, as well as obligatory, elements are realized.

(153)   a. Predicate   →   STEM   (PRE-FINAL)   CL-ENDER
          b. STEM   →   (Drv-affix)   ROOT   (Drv-affix)
          c. PRE-FINAL   →   (SH)   (PST)   (PST)   (MDL)
          d. CL-ENDER   →   (AH)   (MD)   CL-TYPE

(154)

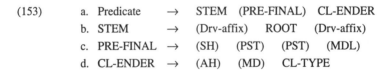
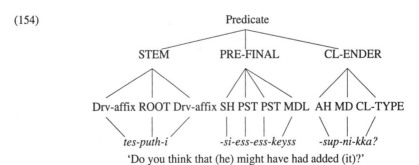

'Do you think that (he) might have had added (it)?'

Thus, for instance, in *sensayng-nim un ku malssum ul tes-puth-i-sy-ess-ess-keyss-sup-ni-kka?* 'Do you think that the professor might have added those words?', *tes-puth-i* (doubly-stick-CAS) 'add' is the stem consisting of a derivational prefix, a root, and a derivational suffix, -*sy* is the subject honorific suffix, -*ess-ess* (PST-PST) is past in the past or pluperfect, -*keyss* 'may' is a modal suffix denoting the speaker/hearer's conjecture, -*sup* is the addressee honorific suffix, -*ni* is an indicative mood suffix, and -*kka* is an interrogative sentence-type suffix. The sequence of the suffixes -*sup-ni-kka* is a deferential interrogative sentence ender.

While the suffixes -*ess* and -*ess-ess* are tense-aspect markers, the other inflectional suffixes are markers of the speaker/hearer's modality, such as the speaker's regard toward the subject referent (subject honorification), the speaker/hearer's conjecture or volition (modal expressions), the speaker's deference to the addressee (addressee honorification), the speaker/hearer's factual observation or request (indicative, retrospective, or requestive mood), and the speaker's performance of speech acts (clause or sentence types).

The inflectional morphology of predicate suffixes was discussed in 8.4. Clause-type enders were discussed briefly in 9.2 (sentence types) and 9.4 (embedded clauses). We will observe in the following subsections some additional aspects of sentence enders, mood and modal elements, and tense-aspect categories from syntactic and semantic perspectives. The two honorific categories SH (-*(u)si*) and AH (-*(su)p*) will be taken up in 9.14 under the rubric of honorifics.

9.8.1 Sentence enders

As observed above, sentence enders consist of three slots, addressee honorific, mood, and clause-type, although only the formal deferential level has all three slots filled, while one or two slots are left unfilled in the other speech levels, as in (155).

(155)		Declarative	Interrogative	Imperative	Propositive
	plain	-*(n)-ta*	-*ni?*/-*nu-nya?*	-*ela*/-*ala*	-*ca*
	intimate	-*e*/-*a*	-*e?*/-*a?*	-*e*/-*a*	-*e*/-*a*
	familiar	-*ne-y*	-*na?*/-*nu-nka?*	-*ke-y*	-*se-y*
	blunt	-*(s)o*	-*(s)o?*	-*(u)o*	-*(u)p-si-ta*
	polite	-*e.yo*/-*a.yo*	-*e.yo?*/-*a.yo?*	-*e.yo*/-*a.yo*	-*e.yo*/-*a.yo*
	deferential	-*(su)p-ni-ta*	-*(su)p-ni-kka*	-*(u)si-p-si-o*	-*(u)si-p-si-ta*
	neutral	-*(n)-ta*	-*nu-nya*	-*(u)la*	-*ca*

There are two minor declarative sentence ender types, apperceptive and promissive-assurance, which have their own paradigms, defective as they may be. The apperceptive type is represented by the suffix *-kwun* which typically denotes one's instantaneous perception of an event (e.g., *ceki o-nun-kwun* 'I see (him) coming over there!'). The suffix *-kwun* occurs only in three speech levels as in (156). Promissive-assurance is expressed in four speech levels with different forms.

(156)

	Apperceptive	Promissive-assurance
plain	*-kwun-a*	*-ma*
intimate	*-kwun*	*-l key*
familiar	—	*-(u)msey*
blunt	—	—
polite	*-kwun yo*	*-l key yo*
deferential	—	—

Examine the apperceptive sentences in (157) and notice that before *-kwun*, the present indicative suffix is ZERO with an adjective and *-nun* with a verb.

(157) a. *tal   i   palk-**kwun-a**.*
          moon   NM   bright-APP-PLN
          'The moon is bright!'

       b. *nwun   i   o-nun-**kwun**.*
          snow   NM   come-IN-APP
          'It is snowing!'

       c. *Mia   ka   ttena-ss-keyss-te-**kwun**   yo.*
          Mia   NM   leave-PST-may-RT-APP   POL
          'I noticed that Mia had presumably left!'

Promissive-assurance constructions are illustrated in (158).

(158) a. *nay   ka   ka-**ma**.*
          I   NM   go-PRM
          'I promise (and assure you) that I will go.'

       b. *cey   ka   ka-**l-key**   yo.*
          I   NM   go-PRS-PRM   POL
          'I promise (and assure you) that I will go.'

The promissive-assurance ender *-(u)l-key* appears to have developed, with semantic shift and phonological contraction, from *-(u)l kes i-e* (PRS fact be-INT) 'will be'.

There are many other idiosyncratic sentence enders that are used to tone down or boost the speaker's assertiveness in one way or another. Many of these enders have been grammaticalized from phrasal or clausal constructions, deletion of a main clause, or deletion of the quotative phrase *ko ha* 'say that . . .' (cf. 8.7). Enders of this kind include *-(u)lla* (admonitive) 'I warn you . . .', *-ney (yo)* (counterexpectation), *-tal/(nu) nya/ca/(u)la-nikka (yo)* (DC/Q/PR/IM-because POL) 'I told/asked you . . .', *-(n)untey (yo)* (background information provider) 'in the circumstance that . . . (what shall/ should/would I/you do?)', *-tal(nu)nya/ca/(u)la-ko/kwu (yo)* (DC/Q/PR/IM-QT POL) 'I am telling/asking . . .', *-te-la-ko/kwu (yo)* (RT-DC-QT POL) 'I saw/experienced/felt that . . ., indeed', *canh-a.(yo)* (< *-ci ani hay-yo* (NOM not do/be-POL)) 'You see; It's the case that . . .; Isn't it the case that . . .?', *-(u)l-ke ya* or *-(u)l-ke yey-yo* (< *-(u)l kes i-e.yo* (PRS fact be-POL)) 'will probably', *-(u)l kka (yo)* (PRS whether POL) 'shall we . . .?; I wonder whether . . .', *-na pw-a.(yo)/-nu-n ka pw-a.(yo)* (whether appear-POL) 'It seems that . . .', *-ketun (yo)* (if/as POL) 'indeed, by the way, you see', *-ta/-myense (yo)?* (DC-saying POL) 'I heard that . . . is that true?', *-(u)l-kel (yo)* (< *-(u)l kes ul yo* (PRS fact AC POL)) 'probably; should have done/been', *-(u)lyem(una)* (permissive, command) 'you may; you should', etc.

(159)   a. *pi   ka   o-lla!   wusan   kacy-e   ka-la.*
            rain NM come-ADM   umbrella take-INF go-IM
            'I warn you that it may rain. So, take an umbrella with you.'

    b. *na nun   an   ka-n-ta-nikka.*
        I   TC   not   go-IN-DC-I told you
        'I told you that I am not going.'

    c. *pi   ka   o-nuntey   yo.*
        rain NM come-what shall we do POL
        'It's raining. (What shall we do?)'

    d. *wuli   nun   ttena-l-kka   yo?*
        we   TC   leave-PRS-shall POL
        'Shall we leave?'

    e. *ai   ka   wul-canh-a.yo?*
        child NM   cry-you see-POL
        'You see, the child is crying.'

f. *Mia   nun   yelsim   i-te-la-ko   yo.*
   Mia   TC   diligence   be-RT-indeed   POL
   'Mia was indeed diligent! (I witnessed.)'

g. *na   nun   an   ka-n-ta-ko   yo.*
   I   TC   not   go-IN-I am telling   POL
   'I am saying that I am not going.'

h. *isaha-sy-ess-ta-myense   yo?*
   move-SH-PST-I heard   POL
   'I heard that you moved. Is that true?'

i. *Cihwan.i   nun   w-ass-ul-kel   yo.*
   Cihwan   TC   come-PST-probably   POL
   'Cihwan has probably come.'

Notice that many of the newly developed enders are due to main clause deletion. For instance, *-ta/(nu)nya/ca/(u)la-nikka*, *-(n)untey*, *-(u)l-kka*, *-te-la-ko/kwu*, *-ta/(nu)nya/ ca/(u)la-ko/kwu*, *-ta-myense*, *-ketun*, and *-(u)l-kel* have been grammaticalized as a result of main clause deletion. In addition to main clause deletion, *-ta/(nu)nya/ ca/(u)la-nikka* and *-ta-myense* have also undergone *ko ha* deletion, since they have developed from *-ta/(nu)nya/ca/(u)la ko **ha**-nikka* and *-ta ko **ha**-myense*, respectively.

9.8.2   *Mood: indicative, retrospective, requestive, and suppositive*

A sentence or clause ender has a morphological slot filled by a mood category: indicative, retrospective, requestive, or suppositive. This is illustrated in (160).

(160)   a. *ka-si-p-ni-ta.*   [declarative: indicative]
            go-SH-AH-IN-DC
            '(He) goes.'

         b. *ka-si-p-ti-kka?*   [interrogative: retrospective]
            go-SH-AH-RT-Q
            'Did you see (him) going?'

         c. *ka-si-p-si-ta.*   [propositive: requestive]
            go-SH-AH-RQ-DC
            'Let us go.'

d. *ka-si-**ci**-yo?*   [interrogative: suppositive]
go-SH-SUP-POL
'I suspect he is going, isn't he?'

Indicative mood is expressed by the suffix *-ni* in the deferential level, but also, in other speech levels, by *(nu)n* or *nu*, as in *mek-**nun**-ta* 'eats', *mek-**nu**-nya?* 'eats?', and *ca-**n**-ta* 'sleeps', or by ZERO, as in *coh-ta* 'is good', *coh-unya/coh-ni?* 'is good?', and *mek-ess-ta* 'ate'. The indicative mood is relevant only to declaratives and interrogatives.

Retrospective mood denotes a situation in which someone recalls a fact or an event he witnessed or experienced, and thus has meanings such as 'I saw, observed, experienced' in declaratives and 'did you see, observe, experience' in interrogatives. Retrospective mood forms inherently carry the past feature, along with the so-called retrospective meaning. This mood, like the indicative mood, occurs only in declarative and interrogative constructions. The retrospective suffixes are *-ti* in the plain interrogative and deferential levels, *-tey* in the polite level, and *-te* elsewhere, as shown in (161). There is no retrospective form in the intimate style.

(161)

	Declarative	Interrogative
plain	*-te-la*	*-ti*, *-te-nya*
intimate	—	—
familiar	*-te-y*	*-te-nka*
blunt	—	—
polite	*-tey-yo*	*-te-nka-yo*
deferential	*-(su)p-ti-ta*	*-(su)p-ti-kka*
neutral	*-te-la*	*-te-nya*

The plain level declarative suffix *-ta* changes to *-la* after a retrospective suffix. The vacant intimate and blunt declarative slots may be filled by the retrospective ender *-te-ntey* (background information provider) or *-te-la-ko* (see 9.8.1), while the polite declarative *-tey-yo* may be used along with the ender *-te-n-tey yo* or *-te-la-ko yo*. The ender *-te-nka* developed from the relative clause ender *-te-n* (RT-RL) + the defective noun *ka* 'whether'. Sentences with different forms of the retrospective suffix are illustrated in (162a). In addition to main and quotative clauses, relative clauses can also take the retrospective suffix, as in (162b).

(162)   a. *Mia ka   kukcang ey   ka-**te**-la/ka-**tey**-yo/ka-p-**ti**-ta.*
         Mia NM   theatre   to   go-RT-DC/go-RT-POL/go-AH-RT-DC
         'I saw Mia going to the movie.'

b. *culkew-ess-te-n*   *ttay*
   happy-PST-RT-RL   time
   'the time when (we) were happy'

Since the retrospective suffix denotes the speaker/hearer's past perception or experience, it usually does not occur in a construction where his own past action is described. Thus, *na nun kongpuha-te-la* 'I observed myself studying' is acceptable only if the speaker is talking about his dream or something. It can occur, however, in an adjective sentence where the speaker is the subject, as in *na nun muchek kippu-te-la* 'I was extremely happy', because it denotes the speaker/hearer's experience of his own feeling.

The requestive (subjunctive *à la* Martin 1954) mood is expressed by the suffix *-si* in blunt propositive and deferential imperative and propositive sentences (e.g., *ka(-si)-p-si-ta* 'Let's go', *cwumu-si-p-si-o*, 'Please go to sleep'), *-ke* (imperative) and *-se* (propositive) in the familiar level (e.g., *ese ca-ke-y* 'Please go to sleep' and *wuli ca-se-y* 'Let's go to sleep'), and ZERO in the other speech levels (8.4.3). In the plain-level imperative forms of some predicates (e.g., *issta* 'stay', *ancta* 'sit', *cata* 'sleep', *kata* 'go'), the fossilized requestive *-ke* (*-ne* after *o* 'come') occurs before *-la* as an allomorph of the regular ZERO, as in *anc-ke-la = anc-ala* 'Sit!', *yeki iss-ke-la = yeki iss-ela* 'Stay here!', and *o-ne-la = w-ala* 'Come!'

The suppositive (suspective *à la* Martin, et al. 1967) mood occurs in all four sentence types. Only two speech levels accept this suffix: the polite level in which the polite suffix *-yo* follows *-ci* and the intimate level in which no suffix follows *-ci*. This mood either denotes the speaker's supposition or makes a casual suggestion. In interrogatives, its function is to seek agreement as an English tag question does.

(163)   a. *Tongmin.i   nun   kongpuhay-ss-ci?*
            Tongmin   TC   study-PST-SUS
            'Tongmin studied, didn't he?'

         b. *ese   tul-e   o-si-ci-yo.*
            quickly   enter-INF   come-SH-SUS-POL
            'Please come in.'

9.8.3   *Modal elements: -keyss and -(u)l(i)*

The modal suffixes *-keyss* and *-(u)l(i)* denote the speaker/hearer's attitude or modality toward the content of the sentence. The suffix *-keyss* is termed the definite future suffix in Martin, et al. 1967 and the deductive-reasoning suffix in H.S. Lee 1991,

while *-(u)l(i)* is termed the prospective suffix in Martin, et al. and the presumptive
suffix in H.S. Lee. Their sharing of the same morphological slot is observed in *ka-ss-
keyss-nu-n ci* (go-PST-may-IN-RL whether) 'whether (he) might have gone' and *ka-
ss-ul-nu-n ci* (go-PST-PRS-IN-RL whether) 'whether (he) would have gone'.

Two basic meanings of *-keyss* are (a) the speaker/hearer's intention or volition
(164), and (b) the speaker's presumption or conjecture in declaratives and the hearer's
in interrogatives based on immediate information or circumstantial evidence (165).

(164)   a. *ce   nun   an   ka-keyss-e.yo.*
           I   TC   not   go-intend-POL
           'I don't intend to go.'

        b. *sensayng-nim   un   ka-si-keyss-e.yo?*
           teacher-HT   TC   go-SH-intend-POL
           'Do you intend to go?'

(165)   a. *nwun   i   w-ass-keyss-ta.*
           snow   NM   come-PST-think-DC
           'I presume that it (has) snowed.'

        b. *a-si-keyss-sup-ni-kka?*
           know-SH-think-AH-IN-Q
           'Do you think you know?; Do you understand?'

In rare cases, *-keyss* denotes immediate futurity when a sentence describes that an
animate subject referent is scheduled to take action.

(166)   *moksa-nim kkeyse selkyo ka iss-usi-keyss-sup-ni-ta.*
          pastor-HT NM   sermon NM exist-SH-will-AH-IN-DC
          'There will be a sermon by the pastor.'

The basic meaning of the so-called prospective modal suffix *-(u)l(i)* is probability
or predictability. The form *-(u)li* occurs in a quotative sentence, as in (167a), while the
form *-(u)l* occurs in a relative (i.e., adnominal) clause, as in (167b), *-l(i)* appearing
after a vowel or *l* and *-ul(i)* appearing after a consonant other than *l*.

(167)   a. *Cihwan.i nun o-li-la   ko sayngkak.hay-yo.*
           Cihwan TC   come-PRS-DC QT think-IN-POL
           'I think Cihwan will come.'

    b. *nay*   *ka*   *manna-l*   *salam*   *un*   *Mia*   *uy*   *apeci*   *ta.*
       I   NM   meet-PRS   person   TC   Mia   GN   father   is-DC
       'The person I will see is Mia's father.'

While the prospective suffix is used productively in relative clauses but rarely in main clauses, -*keyss* is used productively in main clauses but rarely in relative clauses. They are in complementary distribution to a considerable extent.

9.8.4   *Tense and aspect*

Tense and aspect interact closely with each other in their realization in syntactic and morphological forms. Tense is a grammatical category that locates the event (i.e., action, process, or state) denoted by a predicate on a time scale: past, present, or future, i.e., prior to, simultaneous with, or subsequent to a reference time, respectively. A reference time is usually the moment of speaking (utterance time), but may also be a past or future time. For instance, if an event is prior to a reference time which is prior to the moment of speaking, we can talk about past-past.

     While tense is defined with reference to points in time, aspect is usually defined in terms of the beginning, duration, completion, repetition, resulting, etc. of a verb and without reference to its position in time (e.g., S.O. Sohn 1995). That is, aspect is concerned with the internal temporal constituency of a situation. In Korean, aspect is observed not only in verbal suffixes but more frequently in complex predicates (9.10).

     When the reference time is the same as the utterance time, we can talk about absolute tense-aspect. There are two inflectional suffix slots that are relevant to tense and aspect. One or both slots may be filled with -*(e/a)ss* whose basic meaning is past but also includes perfect. If only one slot is filled, it refers to simple past or present perfect, depending on cooccurring time adverbials such as *ecey* 'yesterday', *i nyen cen ey* 'two years ago', and *cikum* 'now' or discourse contexts. If both slots are filled, they denote either past-past or past perfect. If no slot is filled, it is non-past, i.e., (generic) present, present progressive, or future, the interpretation of which again depends on time adverbials or discourse contexts, as illustrated in (168).

(168)   a. *Mia*   *ka*   *ecey*   *Mikwuk*   *ulo*   *ttena-ss-e.yo.*   (simple past)
           Mia   NM   yesterday   America   to   leave-PST-POL
           'Mia left for America yesterday.'

        b. *pom*   *i*   *ka-ko*   *icey*   *yelum*   *i*   *w-ass-e.*   (present perfect)
           spring   NM   go-and   now   summer   NM   come-PST-INT
           'Spring went and now summer has set in.'

    c. *nay   ka   cenhwahay-ss-ul   ttay Mia nun imi   Mikwuk*
       I   NM call-PST-PRS   when Mia TC   already America

       ulo   ttena-ss-ess-e.   (simple past; past-past)
       for   leave-PST-PST-INT

       'When I called, Mia had already left for America.'

    d. *ku   ttay   Milan.i   ka   mak   w-ass-ess-e.*   (past perfect)
       the time Milan   NM   just   come-PST-PST-INT

       'At that time, Milan had just come.'

    e. *wuli ye-tongsayng   un   yeypp-e.*   (generic present)
       our   girl-sister   TC   pretty-INT

       'My younger sister is pretty.'

    f. *Cihwan.i   nun   ceki   o-n-ta.*   (present progressive)
       Cihwan   TC   there   come-IN-DC

       'Cihwan is coming over there.'

    g. *apenim   un   nayil   Ilpon ulo   ttena-sey-yo.*   (future)
       father   TC   tomorrow   Japan to   leave-SH-POL

       'My father will leave for Japan tomorrow.'

The suffix *-(e/a)ss* which has historically derived from the resultative state *-e/-a issta* 'be in the state of . . .' denotes resultative state when it occurs with 'resultative' verbs such as *talmta* 'take after', *ipta* 'wear', and *nulkta* 'get old'. To indicate past in such cases, doubling of the suffix is necessary.

(169)   a. *hyeng   un   apeci   lul   talm-ass-e.*
       brother TC   father AC   resemble-PST-DC

       My brother takes after my father.'

    b. *ne   coh-un   os   ip-ess-kwun-a.*
       you good-RL   dress wear-PST-APP-DC

       'You are wearing a beautiful dress!'

    c. *na nun ely-ess-ul   ttay emeni lul talm-ass-ess-e.*
       I   TC young-PST-PRS when mother AC resemble-PST-PST-INT

       'When I was young, I took after my mother.'

Perfect meanings involved in the suffix -*(e/a)ss* are particularly distinct in so-called transferentive (TR) constructions in which the suffix -*taka* denotes transference from one event to another. (170a) denotes a situation in which the subject referent did not arrive at the church (an imperfect event) and (170b) a situation in which the subject referent did arrive at the church (a perfect event). Furthermore, in (170c), a threatening speech act, -*ess* is associated with future perfect.

(170)   a. *tongsayng   i   kyohoy   ey   ka-**taka**   w-ass-e.yo.*
              brother   NM   church   to   go-TR   come-PST-POL
              'My brother came back on his way to church.'

          b. *halmeni   nun   kyohoy   ey   ka-sy-**ess-taka**   o-sy-ess-e.yo.*
              grandma   TC   church   to   go-SH-PST-TR   come-SH-PST-POL
              'Grandma went to church and came back.'

          c. *ne   nayil   cwuk-**ess**-e!*
              you   tomorrow   die-PST-INT
              'You are a dead person tomorrow!'

In the conditional clause of an optative sentence, the past tense form is often used instead of the non-past ZERO form, as in *nayil pi ka w-**ass-umyen** coh-keyss-e* 'It would be nice if it rained tomorrow.'

The double-past form typically indicates that a past event situation no longer holds true at present. Notice the different implications in (171a) and (171b).

(171)   a. *ku   paywu   nun   Hongkhong   ulo   ttena-**ss**-ta.*
              the   actor   TC   Hong Kong   to   leave-PST-DC
              'The actor (has) left for Hong Kong (and he is no longer here).'

          b. *ku   paywu   nun   Hongkhong   ulo   ttena-**ss-ess**-ta.*
              the   actor   TC   Hong Kong   to   leave-PST-PST-DC
              'The actor had left for Hong Kong (but he may be here now).'

When the reference time is not the same as the utterance time, we can talk about relative tense-aspect, because the event time refers not to the utterance time but to a time that precedes or follows the utterance time. This is the case with many complex sentence constructions where the reference time of the embedded tense is the time denoted by the main clause tense.

(172)   a. *tongsayng un pap ul an mek-ko hak.kyo ey ka-ss-ta.*
          sister   TC meal AC not eat-and school to go-PST-DC
          'My sister did not eat her meal and went to school.'

     b. *ecey pam nwun i o-nu-n kes kath-**ass**-e.yo.*
          yesterday night snow NM come-IN-RL fact same-PST-POL
          'Last night, it seemed that it was snowing.'

In the above examples, the embedded tense is non-past (marked by ZERO), yet the embedded event took place in the past. The embedded event time takes the main clause event time, not the utterance time, as the reference point, hence the absence of the past tense suffix in embedded clauses.

Not all embedded clauses are required to have relative tense-aspect. For instance, coordinate clauses frequently manifest absolute tense-aspect in that they refer to the utterance time.

(173)   a. *Milan.i nun ca-**ss**-ko Tongmin.i nun kongpuhay-**ss**-e.yo.*
          Milan TC sleep-PST-and Tongmin TC study-PST-POL
          'Milan slept and Tongmin studied.'

     b. *na nun ku cha ka coh-**ass**-una sa-ci an-h-**ass**-ta.*
          I TC the car NM good-PST-but buy-NOM not-do-PST-DC
          'I liked the car but didn't buy it.'

While most complement clauses are subject to relative tense-aspect, relative and nominalized clauses are subject to both absolute and relative tense-aspect. The embedded tense in the following relative sentence may be interpreted as either absolute (i) or relative (ii).

(174)   *hyengsa ka pa eyse nolayha-nu-n yeca lul chayphohay-**ss**-ta.*
       detective NM bar at   sing-IN-RL   woman AC arrest-PST-DC
       i. 'The police detective arrested a woman who sings in a bar.'
       ii. 'The police detective arrested a woman who sang in a bar.'

The embedded clauses that require relative tense-aspect are of two general types: (a) those structurally not allowing any tense other than non-past tense and (b) those allowing either past or non-past tense. In both types, the embedded event may occur prior to, simultaneously with, or after the main clause event. The first type includes those embedded clauses which end in suffixes such as *-e/-a* (infinitive), *-key* 'so that',

-tolok 'to the point where', *-ca-maca* 'as soon as', and *-esel-ase* 'as, since', as illustrated in (175). When predicates are multiply embedded, as in (175a), only the tense of the last or main predicate is the reference point.

(175) a. *nam-un   pap   ul   mek-e   chiw-e   pely-ess-ni?*
remain-RL rice AC eat-INF remove-INF finish-PST-Q
'Did (you) finish up eating the left-over rice?'

b. *tongsayng   un   nalssi   ka   kayi-ca-maca   naka-ss-ta.*
brother   TC weather NM clear-as soon as go out-PST-DC
'My younger brother went out as soon as it cleared up.'

The second type includes those embedded clauses which end in conjunctive suffixes such as *-(u)myense* 'while' and *-taka* 'and then', nominalizers such as *-(u)m* and *-ki*, defective nouns such as *kes* 'fact', *tus* 'as if', and *cheylchek* 'pretence', and the quotative particle *ko*. In these constructions, the embedded past tense suffix occurs only when the embedded clause event takes place prior to the matrix clause event.

(176) a. *Mia nun   manh-i   ca-ss-umyense phikonhay hay-ss-e.*
Mia TC   much-AD sleep-PST-while be tired   show-PST-DC
'Mia felt tired even though she had slept a lot.'

b. *na   nun   Mia   ka   ttena-ss-um   ul   al-ass-ta.*
I   TC   Mia NM   leave-PST-NOM AC know-PST-DC
'I knew that Mia had left.'

c. *Milan.i nun   aph-ass-ta   ko   hay-ss-ta.*
Milan   TC   sick-PST-DC QT say-PST-DC
Milan said that she had been sick.'

Relative tense-aspect is observable even in a simple sentence with the retrospective mood suffix. The retrospective suffix inherently carries a past time feature, and the tense-aspect of the verb occurring with this suffix must have the retrospective past as the reference time.

(177) *ecey   Sewul ey nun pi   ka   o-te-lalw-ass-te-la.*
yesterday Seoul in TC rain NM come-RT-DC/come-PST-RT-DC
'I observed that it was raining/had rained in Seoul yesterday.'

9.9   **Passive and causative constructions**

Passives and causatives in Korean are expressed by derivational suffixes which take the same slot, as observed in the passive *mek-**hi**-keyss-ta* 'may be eaten' and the causative *mek-**i**-keyss-ta* 'may make (one) eat, feed'. The set of passive suffixes and that of causative suffixes are similar in form, and in some words both forms are identical, as in *po-ita* 'be seen; show', *ep-hita* 'be carried on the back; make (one) carry on the back', *cap-hita* 'be caught; cause to hold', *an-kita* 'be hugged, cause to hug', *ttut-kita* 'be torn off; cause to tear off', *kel-lita* 'be walked, cause to walk', and *mul-lita* 'be bitten; cause to bite'. Both sets of suffixes occur with a limited number of predicates. The difference usually appears in syntactic structure since a passive verb functions as an intransitive usually with a subject and a goal/agentive, whereas a causative verb functions as a transitive with a subject and an object or a ditransitive with a subject, a goal, and an object.

(178)   a. *ai   tul   eykey   pihayngki   ka   **po-y**-ess-ta.*   (passive)
             child PL   to   plane   NM see-PAS-PST-DC
             'The plane was seen by (lit. 'to') the children.'

     b. *na nun ai-tul   eykey   kulim   ul   **po-y**-ess-ta.*   (causative)
             I   TC   child-PL to   picture AC see-CAS-PST-DC
             'I showed a picture to the children.'

When a passive verb is accompanied by an object, ambiguity occurs in syntactic structure. The sentence in (179) is interpreted as both passive (i) and causative (ii).

(179)   *emeni   nun   aki   eykey   son   ul   **cap-hy**-ess-ta.*
             mother   TC   child   by/to   hand AC   hold-PAS/CAS-PST-DC
             i. 'Mother was caught by her hand by the child.'
             ii. 'Mother caused the child to hold her hand.'

From the shared properties such as the same morphological slot, similar forms, occurrence with limited predicates, and shared syntactic behaviour, it is proposed that Korean passive suffixes have developed from causative suffixes via functional shift (see H.M. Sohn 1996 for details). Furthermore, it is speculated that various allomorphs of causative suffixes developed from the ancient form of the phrasal causative construction *-key ha(y)* (-AD do) 'cause' via formal contraction and semantic reduction from indirect to direct causation.

9.9.1   *Passive sentences*

A construction is passive when the subject is acted upon. In general, an active transitive sentence is changed to a passive intransitive sentence, when (a) the object (accusative) of the active sentence is made the subject (nominative), (b) the active verb is replaced by the matching passive verb, (c) the subject (nominative) of the active sentence is made the agent with a locative/goal particle or otherwise omitted, and usually (d) the new subject is placed at the sentence-initial position. The locative-goal particles functioning as agentive are *kkey* 'by [human, deferential]', *eykey* 'by [animate, formal]', *hanthey* 'by [animate, informal]', and *ey* 'by [animal, inanimate]'.

(180)   a. *swunkyeng   i   ku   totwuk   ul   **cap**-ass-ta.*   (active)
            police   NM   the   thief   AC   catch-PST-DC
            'The police caught the thief.'

         a'. *ku   totwuk   i   swunkyeng   **hanthey   cap**-hy-ess-ta.*   (passive)
             the   thief   NM   police   by   catch-PAS-PST-DC
             'The thief was caught by the police.'

         b. *thayphung   i   ku   sem   ul   **hwipssul**-ess-ta.*   (active)
            typhoon   NM   the   island AC   devastate-PST-DC
            'The typhoon devastated the island.'

         b'. *ku   sem   i   thayphung   **ey   hwipssul-ly**-ess-ta.*   (passive)
             the   island NM   typhoon   by   devastate-PAS-PST-DC
             'The island was devastated by the typhoon.'

Only a limited set of transitive verbs can have passive forms with a passive suffix. For instance, verbs which do not allow a passive suffix include verbs ending in *ha* 'do' (e.g., *kongpuhata* 'study', *yaksok.hata* 'promise'), dative or benefactive verbs (e.g., *cwuta* 'give', *pat.ta* 'receive', *topta* 'help', *ipta* 'wear'), cognitive verbs (e.g., *alta* 'know', *moluta* 'do not know'), symmetrical verbs (e.g., *mannata* 'meet', *talmta* 'resemble', *ssawuta* 'fight'), and many others. Verbs whose stems end in the vowel *i* usually do not take a passive suffix (e.g., *kaluchita* 'teach', *ttaylita* 'hit', *tencita* 'throw', *mancita* 'touch', *nukkita* 'feel'), one exception being *chita* 'run over' vs. *chi-ita* 'be run over'.

There are four variants in the passive suffix, *-i*, *-hi*, *-li*, and *-ki*, whose occurrence is conditioned largely by the stem-final sound. The vowel *i* in each allomorph changes to *y* before the vowel *e* in casual speech (e.g., *po-y-ess-ta* 'was seen').

(181)

		Active (transitive) stems		Passive (intransitive) stems	
a.	*pha*	'dig'	*pha-i*	'be dug'
	noh	'put'	*noh-i*	'be put'
	mukk	'bind'	*mukk-i*	'be bound'
	camku	'lock'	*camk-i*	'be locked'
b.	*mek*	'eat'	*mek-hi*	'be eaten'
	ilk	'read'	*ilk-hi*	'be read'
	mut	'bury'	*mut-hi*	'be buried'
	palp	'step on'	*palp-hi*	'be stepped on'
c.	*kkul*	'pull'	*kkul-li*	'be pulled'
	phal	'sell'	*phal-li*	'be sold'
	nwulu	'press'	*nwul-li*	'be pressed'
	tut	'hear'	*tul-li*	'be heard'
d.	*ccoch*	'chase'	*ccoch-ki*	'be chased'
	tat	'close'	*tat-ki*	'be closed'
	ppayas	'deprive'	*ppayas-ki*	'be deprived'
	kam	'wind'	*kam-ki*	'be wound'

Notice in the above that the vowel *u* is deleted before the passive suffix (e.g., *camkuta* vs. *camk-ita*) and that *t*-irregular verbs have their *t* changed to *l* before the suffix *-li* (e.g., *tut.ta* 'hear' vs. *tul-lita* 'be heard').

There are some syntactic aspects rather peculiar to Korean passive constructions. First, if no passive form is available or the passive form is semantically or pragmatically inappropriate, an active construction is used with the focused or topicalized object placed in the sentence-initial position.

(182)   a. *ko.yangi   ka   cwi lul   cwuk-y-ess-e.yo.*
         cat   NM   rat AC   kill-CAS-PST-POL
         'A cat killed the rat.'

         b. *cwi   lul/nun   ko.yangi   ka   cwuk-y-ess-e.yo.*
         rat   AC/TC   cat   NM   kill-CAS-PST-DC
         'The rat, a cat killed it.'

Second, as inanimate agent subjects are pragmatically avoided except in metaphorical or personified expressions, passive constructions are preferred in such cases. Thus, *mos i os ul **ccic-ess-ta*** 'A nail tore my clothes' is an unnatural expression in favour of *os i mos ey **ccic-ky-ess-ta*** 'My clothes were torn by a nail.'

Third, when an object nominal is preceded by a possessive noun in an active sentence, two passive constructions can be made. One is obtained by making the object of the active sentence the subject (183b). The other is obtained by placing the possessor noun of the object in the active sentence as the subject of the passive sentence (183c). In the latter, the object of the active sentence remains unaffected.

(183)   a. *Ilpon   i   Hankwuk uy **yengtho lul   ppayas-ass-ta**.*
               Japan NM Korea   GN territory AC take-PST-DC
               'Japan occupied the Korean territory.'

          b. *Hankwuk uy **yengtho ka** Ilpon ey(key) **ppayas-ky-ess-ta**.*
               Korea   GN territory NM Japan by   take-PAS-PST-DC
               'The Korean territory was occupied by Japan.'

          c. *Hankwuk i   Ilpon ey(key) **yengtho lul ppayas-ky-ess-ta**.*
               Korea   NM Japan by   territory AC take-PAS-PST-DC
               'Korea had its territory occupied by Japan.'

Not all possessive constructions allow the passivization of the 'adversative' type (183c). Only those with an adversative passive verb do. Adversative passive verbs include *palp-hita* 'be stepped on', *ppayas-kita*, *cap-hita* 'be caught', *mul-lita* 'be bitten', *kkocip-hita* 'be pinched', *cha-ita* 'be kicked', and *cal-lita* 'be cut'. Thus, constructions with other passive verbs cannot be used as adversative, as in (184).

(184)   a. **Mia ka   Cihwan.i hanthey **sathang ul   mek-hy-ess-ta**.*
               Mia NM Cihwan   by   candy   AC eat-PAS-PST-DC
               'Mia had her candy eaten by Cihwan.'

          b. **Milan.i ka Yongho eykey **pay-kkop   ul   po-y-ess-ta**.*
               Milan NM Yongho by   belly-button AC see-PAS-PST-DC
               'Milan had her belly-button seen by Yongho.'

Fourth, there are certain passive constructions that do not allow a regular agentive particle to occur. This is the case when use of a regular agentive particle (*hanthey*, etc.) would be interpreted as locative or goal rather than agentive. In such constructions, the idiomatic phrase *ey uyha.ye(se)* or *ey uyhay(se)* 'by, owing to, in accordance with' (i.e., locative particle *ey* + *uyhata* 'depend, follow' + conjunctive suffix *-(e)se* ('and') is used. Use of the phrasal agentive form, however, renders the sentence very formal and sometimes unnatural.

(185) *ce kenmul un **cwuin ey uyhayse** hak.kyo ey **phal-ly-ess-ta.***
       that building TC owner by   school to sell-PAS-PST-DC
       'That building over there was sold to the school by the owner.'

Note in the above that replacement of *ey uyhayse* with a regular agentive particle *eykey* or *hanthey* will lead to either ungrammaticality or a different meaning, as *eykey* or *hanthey* will mean not 'by' but 'to' in such sentences.

Finally, certain passive constructions are considerably idiomatized, in which case their active counterparts do not convey the same meaning. Thus, sentences like the following lack corresponding active sentences.

(186) a. *nalssi   ka   **phul-ly-ess-e.yo.***
           weather   NM   clear-PAS-PST-POL
           'The weather has cleared up.' (lit. 'The weather was cleared.)

       b. *appa   ka   kamki   ey   **kel-ly-ess-e.yo.***
           dad   NM   cold   to   catch-PAS-PST-POL
           'My dad has caught a cold.' (lit. 'Dad was hooked by a cold.')

       c. *pap   i   an   **mek-hi-n-ta.***
           food   NM   not   eat-PAS-IN-DC
           'I have no appetite. (lit. 'Food is not eaten.')

Note, for instance, that (186a) is different from *X ka nalssi lul phul-ess-e.yo* 'X cleared up the weather' and (186b) from *kamki ka appa lul kel-ess-e.yo* 'A cold caught my dad'.

In addition to the suffixal passive verbs illustrated above, there are verbs that may be analysed as passive in terms of their meaning and syntactic behaviour and thus can be called lexical passive verbs. There are two general subtypes. One such type includes pure lexical passive verbs whose forms are entirely different from active verbs, as shown in *chita/ttaylita* 'hit' vs. *macta* 'be hit'.

(187) a. *Yongho nun Kihan ul   **ttayly-ess-ta.***
           Yongho TC Kihan AC   hit-PST-DC
           'Yongho hit Kihan.'

b. *Kihan   un   Yongho   hanthey   **mac-ass-ta.***
Kihan   TC   Yongho   by   get hit-PST-DC
'Kihan got hit by Yongho.'

The other lexical type includes verbs such as *tanghata* 'undergo', *pat.ta* 'receive (an action), suffer', *tut.ta* 'hear', *macta* 'receive', and *toyta* 'become', which combine with verbal nouns to form compound passive verbs. Examples include *kwutha-hata* 'assault' vs. *kwutha-tanghata* 'be assaulted'; *changphi-cwuta* 'insult' vs. *changphi-tanghata* 'be insulted'; *cemlyeng-hata* 'occupy' vs. *cemlyeng-tanghata* 'be occupied'; *conkyeng-hata* 'respect' vs. *conkyeng-pat.ta* 'be respected'; *cwumok-hata* 'pay attention to' vs. *cwumok-pat.ta* 'receive attention'; *salang-hata* 'love' vs. *salang-pat.ta* 'be loved'; *wiim-hata* 'entrust' vs. *wiim-toyta* 'be entrusted'; *kkwucwung-hata* 'scold' vs. *kkwucwung-tut.ta* 'be scolded'; *yatan-chita* 'scold' vs. *yatan-macta* 'be scolded'; *may-ttaylita* 'spank' vs. *may-macta* 'be spanked'; and *sa.yong-hata* 'use' vs. *sa.yong-toyta* 'be used'. Note that many of the verbal nouns involved are Sino-Korean, especially those occurring before *tanghata*, *pat.ta*, and *toyta*.

(188)   a. *wuli   kwun   un   cek   ul   **sasal-hay-ss-ta.***
our   army   TC   enemy   AC   killing-do-PST-DC
'Our soldiers killed the enemy.'

b. *cek   i   wuli   kwun   eykey   **sasal-toy-ess-ta.***
enemy   NM   our   soldier   by   killing-become-PST-DC
'The enemy was killed by our soldiers.'

In addition to the suffixal and lexical sets, there are also phrasal passives that consist of a verb stem followed by the infinitive suffix *-e/-a* and the inchoative verb *cita* 'get to be, become'. The basic meaning of *-e/-a cita* is change of state, as in *mul i malk-a ci-n-ta* 'The water is getting clear.' With the meaning of change of state intact, it can also convey passive meaning when it occurs with a transitive verb. Examples include *cwuta* 'give' vs. *cwu-e cita* 'be given'; *milwuta* 'postpone' vs. *milwu-e cita* 'be postponed'; *nwuluta* 'press' vs. *nwull-e cita* 'be pressed'; *mathkita* 'entrust' vs. *mathky-e cita* 'be entrusted'; and *nemkita* 'pass over to' vs. *nemky-e cita* 'be passed over'. Note that while the verb stem *toy* 'become' usually occurs with Sino-Korean verbal nouns, *ci* tends to occur with native verbs.

(189)   a. *kyengchal   i   cinsang   ul   palk-hy-ess-ta.*
police   NM   truth   AC   bright-CAS-PST-DC
'The police revealed the truth.'

b. *cinsang   i   kyengchal ey uyhay palk-hy-e   cy-ess-ta.*
   truth   NM police   by   bright-CAS-INF get-PST-DC
   'The truth was revealed by the police.'

cf. *cinsang i   kyengchal ey(key) palk-hy-e   cy-ess-ta.*
    truth   NM police   to   reveal-CAS-INF become-PST-DC
    'The truth was revealed to the police.'

Notice that the agentive in phrasal passive constructions is expressed by the complex agentive construction *ey uyhay* 'by', and not by *ey(key)* which has the dative/goal meaning 'to' due to the nature of the predicates which can take a dative/goal case. For an extensive survey of Korean passives, see I. Woo 1997.

9.9.2   Causative sentences

While passive constructions have the meaning of affectedness, causative constructions roughly mean (i) 'A causes something to B' or (ii) 'A causes (makes, lets, enables, permits, gets, or has) B (to) do something', where A is an agent and B is a patient in the meaning (i) or another agent in the meaning (ii). For an extensive recent study on Korean passives, see K. Kim 1994. Compare (190a), a basic sentence, with (190b) and (190c), its causative counterparts.

(190)   a. *ku   say   ka   cwuk-ess-ta.*
              the   bird   NM   die-PST-DC
              'That bird died.'

           b. *Yongho ka   ku   say   lul   cwuk-y-ess-ta.*
              Yongho NM the   bird AC   die-CAS-PST-DC
              'Yongho killed the bird.'

           c. *Yongho ka   ku   say   lul   cwuk-key   hay-ss-ta.*
              Yongho NM the   bird AC   die-AD   do-PST-DC
              'Yongho caused the bird to die.'

Notice in (190b, c) that the agent or causer is *Yongho* and the patient or causee is *ku say* 'that bird' and that what the agent did was to cause the patient to die.

Causative constructions are made by (a) introducing a new subject (agent) to a basic sentence, (b) changing the subject of the basic sentence into a direct or indirect object, i.e., to a direct object in the case of an intransitive basic sentence and to an indirect object in the case of a transitive basic sentence, and (c) replacing the basic sentence predicate with a causative verb or a causative verb phrase.

As alluded to in the above examples, there are two general types of formally distinct causative constructions in Korean. One type, usually called short-form causatives, comprises constructions in which a causative verb, such as *cwuk-ita* (die-CAS) 'kill' (cf. *cwukta* 'die'), occurs. The other type, usually called long-form (phrasal or periphrastic) causatives, consists of constructions where *-key ha(y)* 'cause (to do/be)' appears after a predicate, as in *cwuk-key hay-ss-ta* 'caused (it) to die'. In general, short-form causatives are associated with immediate or direct causation, while long-form causatives denote indirect causation.

Short-form causative verbs are either lexical or suffixal. Lexical ones are those which can be regarded as causative because of their meaning and syntactic behaviour. They are not numerous and include the following.

(191)	Basic		Causative	
	hata	'do'	*sikhita*	'cause to do, order'
	kata	'go'	*ponayta*	'send'
	calata	'grow'	*kiluta*	'raise, grow (something)'
	wumcikita	'move'	*wumcikita*	'move (something)'

There is a limited set of fossilized lexical causative verbs which have developed from sequences of an intransitive verb, the infinitive suffix *-e/-a*, and the fossilized auxiliary verb (or suffix) *(-)ttulita* which functions as an intensified causativizer. Examples include *nul-e-ttulita* (*nul* 'expand' + INF *-e* + *-ttulita*) 'dangle (something)' and *kiwul-e-ttulita* (*kiwul* 'tilt' + INF *-e* + *-ttulita*) 'tilt (something) forcefully'.

A much more productive set of short-form causative verbs are those derived from non-causative verbs through suffixation, that is, by attaching one of the causative suffixes *-y*, *-i*, *-hi*, *-li*, *-ki*, *-khi*, *-wu*, *-ywu*, *-iwu*, *-chwu*, and *-kwu*. These allomorphs are not completely predictable by phonological environments alone. As in passive suffixes, the stem-final vowel *i* becomes *y* before the vowel *e*. Some of these suffixes are homophonous with passive suffixes. A small number of adjectives and a large number of intransitive and transitive verbs are causativized in this way.

(192)	Basic stems		Causative stems	
	Adjectives			
	noph	'high'	*noph-i*	'heighten'
	nelp	'wide'	*nelp-hi*	'widen'
	cop	'narrow'	*cop-hi*	'narrow (something)'
	nac	'low'	*nac-chwu*	'lower'

Intransitive verbs

na	'come out'	na-y	'put out'
nok	'melt'	nok-i	'melt (something)'
cwul	'decrease'	cwul-i	'reduce'
nwup	'lie down'	nwup-hi	'lay'
al	'know'	al-li	'inform'
kwulu	'roll'	kwul-li	'roll (something)'
nam	'remain'	nam-ki	'leave (something)'
wus	'laugh'	wus-ki	'make (someone) laugh'
kkay	'wake up'	kkay-wu	'wake (someone) up'
ca	'sleep'	ca-ywu	'put to sleep'
tal	'get hot'	tal-kwu	'make hot'

Transitive verbs

po	'see'	po-i	'show'
ilk	'read'	ilk-hi	'cause to read'
ket/kel	'walk'	kel-li	'walk'
olu	'go up'	ol-li	'raise'
nem	'go over'	nem-ki	'pass (something) over'
tha	'ride'	tha-ywu	'cause to ride'
ssu	'put on'	ss-i.wu	'cause to put on'

When an adjective or intransitive verb is causativized, it becomes a transitive verb. When a transitive verb is causativized, the resulting sentence is ditransitive, with the original subject changed to the dative. As in other ditransitive constructions, the dative case can be changed to an accusative.

(193)   a. *kil   i   **nelp-ta**.*   (adjective)
             road NM   wide-DC
             'The road is wide.'

        a'. *inpu   ka   kil   ul   **nelph-i-n-ta**.*   (transitive verb)
            worker NM road AC   widen-CAS-IN-DC
            'Workers are widening the road.'

        b. *Mia ka   kil   eyse **wus-ess-ta**.*   (intransitive verb)
             Mia NM   road in   laugh-PST-DC
            'Mia laughed in the street.'

b'. *nay ka   Mia lul kil   eyse **wus-ky-ess-ta.*** (transitive verb)
    I   NM Mia AC road on   laugh-CAS-PST-DC
    'I made Mia laugh on the street.'

c. *ai   ka   os   ul   **ip**-ess-ta.* (transitive verb)
   child NM clothes AC wear-PST-DC
   'The child put on the clothes.'

c'. *nay ka **ai**   **eykey/lul** os   ul   **ip-hy**-ess-ta.* (ditransitive verb)
    I   NM child to/AC   clothes AC dress-PST-DC
    'I dressed the child.'

Long-form or phrasal (or periphrastic) causatives are formed with the verb stem *ha(y)* 'do, make, cause, let, permit, tell, arrange' preceded by a complement clause that ends in the adverbializer *-key* 'so that, to'. This type is very productive, in that *-key hata* can be used with any type of clause, including even a suffixal passive or causative construction.

(194)   a. *na nun Mia ka/eykey/lul kyengchal ey **cap-hi-key**   **hay**-ss-ta.*
          I TC Mia NM/to/AC police   by catch-PAS-to do-PST-DC
          'I caused/permitted Mia to be caught by the police.'

      b. *na nun enni eykey Mia eykey sacin ul **po-i-key**   **hay**-ss-ta.*
          I TC sister to   Mia to   photo AC see-CAS-to do-PST-DC
          'I had my older sister show the photo to Mia.'

There are many semantic and syntactic differences between a long-form causative and its corresponding short-form suffixal causative. One difference is that long-form causatives have two lexical items *-key* and *ha* that correspond to a causative suffix in short-form causatives. In particular, the verb stem *ha* denotes not only the 'cause' meaning but also other meanings such as 'do', 'make', 'force', 'order', 'ask', 'tell', 'enable', 'permit', and 'arrange'. Thus, the combined meanings of *-key* and *ha* result in various degrees of indirect causation, whereas a causative suffix is usually related to direct or immediate causation.

Another semantic difference arises when causatives occur with a negative element. Notice that (195a) and (195b) mean different things, because the scope of the negative adverbial *mos* 'cannot' covers only the immediately following verb and cannot go beyond *-key*.

(195) a. *tongsayng   i   ai   lul*   [*mos   **ca-yw**]-ess-e.yo.*
          sister   NM   child   AC   cannot   sleep-CAS-PST-POL
          'My younger sister was unable to put the child to sleep.'

       b. *tongsayng   i   ai   lul*   [*mos   **ca-key**]   **hay**-ss-e.yo.*
          sister   NM   child   AC   cannot   sleep-to   do-PST-POL
          'My younger sister did not let the child sleep.'

Still another semantic difference in the two causative types is observed in their presuppositional properties (C.M. Lee 1973:384). Thus, for instance, (196a) presupposes the prior existence of the road, but (196b) does not, since in (196b) the road may come about as a result of the action described. This may be due to the exclusive 'cause' meaning of a causative suffix and to the variety of meanings, including the 'creation' meaning, that the verb stem *ha* has.

(196) a. *inpu   ka   kil   ul   **cop-hy**-ess-ta.*
          worker NM   road   AC   narrow-CAS-PST-DC
          'The workers narrowed the road.'

       b. *inpu   ka   kil   ul   **cop-key**   **hay**-ss-ta.*
          worker NM   road   AC   narrow-to   do-PST-DC
          'The workers made the road narrow.'

Syntactically also, a long-form causative allows two nominatives in a sentence, one the main clause subject and the other the embedded clause subject, as in *Minho ka [Mia ka wus-key] hay-ss-e.yo* 'Minho caused Mia to laugh.' A short-form causative allows only one subject in the nominative case in a sentence, as in *Minho ka Mia lul/*ka wus-ky-ess-e.yo* 'Minho made Mia laugh.' This indicates that a long-form causative is a complex sentence, whereas a short-form causative is a simplex sentence.

Moreover, while short-form causatives do not allow any element to be inserted between the stem and the causative suffix (e.g., *wus(*-usi)-kita* 'make (someone) laugh'), long-form causatives allow the subject honorific suffix to be placed between the stem and *-key* and the accusative or any delimiter particle to be placed after *-key*.

(197) *Milan.i ka   hal.apeci lul   wus-**usi**-key (**lul**) (**kkaci**)   ha-n-ta.*
       Milan   NM   grandpa   AC   laugh-SH-to   AC   even   do-IN-DC
       'Milan (even) causes her grandpa to laugh.'

Short-form and long-form causatives have been a topic of great interest among generative linguists of Korean. Some relevant works are Cook (1968), B.S. Park (1972), I.S. Yang (1972), C.M. Lee (1973), Shibatani (1973), Patterson (1974), K. Park (1986), H.M. Sohn (1986, 1994), S.C. Song (1988), and K. Kim (1994).

9.10   Complex predicate constructions

In complex sentences with a relative or complement clause, the embedded predicate and its main clause predicate often become compounded so closely that they appear to form a complex predicate. This phenomenon is due to the fact that the head noun of a relative clause or the complementizer of a complement clause becomes fossilized with the following main clause predicate, expressing various aspectual and/or modality meanings.

There are three general types of such complex predicates depending on how the relative head noun or the complementizer is compounded with the following predicate: relative, serial, and auxiliary. The relative type consists of a relative clause predicate + a head noun + a main clause predicate, while the serial and auxiliary types consist of a complement clause predicate + a complementizer (e.g., the infinitive *-e/-a*, the conjunctive *-ko*, the adverbializer *-key*) + a main clause predicate. The difference between serial and auxiliary types is that in the former the complex predicates denote a series of actions or states, the first predicate modifying the second in terms of manner, while in the latter the first predicate is modified by the following auxiliary predicate in terms of aspect or modality.

A sentence with the complementizer *-ko* 'and' may be both serial and auxiliary. For instance, *moca lul ssu-ko iss-ta* (hat AC wear-and stay-DC) has two meanings: '(He) has a hat on' and '(He) is putting on a hat.' The first resultative-state interpretation is serial because the complex predicate involves wearing and stasis, whereas the second progressive interpretation is auxiliary because *-ko iss-ta* denotes progressiveness of the wearing action. This is due to the fact that the complementizer *-ko* denotes both simultaneity and sequentiality.

9.10.1   *Relative complex predicates*

Certain nouns, especially defective ones, that are preceded by a relative clause compound with a following main clause predicate. There are cooccurrence restrictions between such a noun and the following predicate. For instance, the adjective *kathta* 'same' occurs only with the defective noun *kes* 'fact, thing' to form the compound *kes kathta* 'seem, appear'. Many of the compounds of this type are grammaticalized forms and denote the speaker's (in statements) and the hearer's (in questions) modality (feeling, thinking, conjecture, etc.). These noun–predicate compounds frequently form complex predicates with the preceding embedded predicate, as illustrated in (198).

(198) a. *pi* *ka* ***o-n*** ***kes*** ***kath-a.yo.***
        rain NM come-RL fact same-POL
        'It seems that it has rained.'

    b. p*i* *ka* ***o-l/w-ass-ul*** ***kes*** *i-ta.*
        rain NM come-PRS/come-PST-PRS fact be-DC
        'It will probably rain/it has probably rained.'

    c. *pi* *ka* ***o-nu-n*** ***ka*** *po-ta.*
        rain NM come-IN-RL whether appear-DC
        'It seems to be raining.'

    d. *pi* *ka* ***o-l*** ***seng*** ***siph-ess-ta.***
        rain NM come-PRS appearance think-PST-DC
        'It appeared to be raining.'

    e. *pi* *ka* ***o-l*** ***tus*** ***hay-yo?***
        rain NM come-PRS look be-POL
        'Does it look as if it will rain?'

To denote exclusive activity or stativity, complex predicates with *-(u)l ppun i-ta* and *-(u)l ttalum i-ta* are used. Here, *ppun* 'being only' and *ttalum* 'nothing but' are defective head nouns.

(199) *na nun nay uymu lul ta **hay-ss-ul** **ppun/ttalum** i-eyyo.*
      I TC my duty AC all do-PST-PRS only be-POL
      'I have done nothing but my duty.'

Possibility and impossibility are expressed by the compound *-(u)l swu (ka) issta/epsta* 'can/cannot', where *-(u)l* is a prospective suffix, *swu* means 'way, method', and *issta/epsta* are existential predicates. An example sentence is *hal.apeci nun **talli-si-l swu (ka) eps-ess-e.yo*** 'My grandfather was unable to run.'

Experiential aspect is expressed by *-(u)n cek i issta/epsta* and *-(u)n il i issta/epsta*, where *-(u)n* is a past relative clause ender and *cek* 'time' and *il* 'thing, fact' function as the subject, whose predicate is the existential predicate *issta* 'exist, have' or *epsta* 'not exist, do not have'. This is illustrated in *Yongho nun Cwungkwuk ey **ka-n il/cek i eps-ta*** 'Yongho has never been to China.'

9.10.2   *Serial predicate constructions*

Serial predicate constructions consist of two or more predicates (flanked by a complementizer) which denote sequential actions or states that denote a single coextensive or extended event. As in auxiliary predicate constructions, a sentence with a serial predicate construction has a single subject, and the predicates constituting a serial construction cannot have separate tense-aspect or modality suffixes because they all share the main clause suffixes. Most serial predicate constructions take an infinitive suffix (*-e/-a*) as the complementizer. Rarely, some other complementizers such as the conjunctive *-ko* 'and' and the fossilized transferentive (TR) *-eta* (< infinitive *-e* + TR *-ta(ka)*) 'and (then)' are used. Notice in (200) that the first action modifies the second in terms of manner of action.

(200)   a. *Cihwan.i   nun   ttek   ul   son   ulo   **cip-e**   **mek-ess-e**.*
             Cihwan   TC   cake   AC   hand   with   pick up-INF   eat-PST-INT
             'Cihwan (picked up and) ate the rice cake with his fingers.'

         b. *mul-koki   ka   kom   eykey   **cap-hy-e**   **mek-hy-ess-ta**.*
             fish   NM   bear   by   catch-PAS-INF   eat-PAS-PST-DC
             'The fish was (caught and) eaten by the bear.'

         c. *Milan.i   nun   kapang   ul   an   **tul-ko**   **ka-ss-e**.*
             Milan   TC   bag   AC   not   hold-and   go-PST-INT
             'Milan didn't take her bag with her.'

         d. *wuli   nun   tongkwul   sok   ul   **tuly-eta**   **po-ass-ta**.*
             we   TC   cave   inside   AC   put in-TR   see-PST-DC
             'We looked into the cave.'

In the above examples, the actions of picking and eating, of holding and going, and of putting (one's head) in and seeing are each perceived as a single extended or coextensive event. That is, the two actions are subparts of a single overall event. The first action of each pair modifies the second, providing information as to in what manner the second action takes place. Thus, the two predicates constituting a serial construction may be treated as a single syntactic and semantic constituent in relation to the other constituents of the sentence.

Other examples with an infinitive complementizer include *kkakk-a mekta* (peel-INF eat) 'peel and eat', *kwuw-e mekta* (roast-INF eat) 'roast and eat', *cap-a mekta* (catch-INF eat) 'slaughter and eat', *ttal-a puthta* (follow-INF stick to) 'catch up with', *ttal-a cwukta* (follow-INF die) 'kill oneself with', *sa-a cwuta* (buy-INF give) 'buy and give', *cap-a kata* (hold-INF-go) 'take (a suspect) to', *cap-a tangkita* (hold-INF pull) 'pull, draw', *ki-e kata* (crawl-INF go) 'crawl away', *ttwi-e oluta* (jump-INF climb) 'jump up', *ttayly-e nwuphita* (hit-INF lay down) 'knock (someone) down', *ttayly-e puswuta* (hit-INF break) 'break down', *pha-a mekta* (dig-INF eat) 'eat into', *pha-a mutta* (dig-INF bury) 'bury', *mul-e cwukita* (bite-INF kill) 'bite to death', and *tul-e ota* (enter-INF come) 'come in'.

In a sequence of three predicates connected by infinitive suffixes, the most natural ordering is manner/cause predicate + path predicate + deictic predicate, as in *sumy-e tul-e kata* (penetrate-INF enter-INF go) 'penetrate into', *ki-e tul-e ota* (crawl-INF enter-INF come) 'crawl into', and *ttwi-e nayly-e ota* (jump-INF move down-INF come) 'jump down'.

One syntactic property of serial constructions with an infinitive suffix is that the suffix can be replaced with the conjunctive suffix *-ese* 'and then, by doing . . .' in many cases with concomitant change in meaning, as in *kwuw-e mekta* 'roast and eat' vs. *kwuw-ese mekta* 'roast and then eat'. This suggests that historically the infinitive suffix has developed from the conjunctive suffix *-ese* through syntactic, semantic, and phonological reduction.

Examples with the *ko*-complementizer include *pha-ko tulta* (dig-and enter) 'inquire into', *mul-ko kata* (bite-and go) 'carry by the mouth', *mul-ko nul.ecita* (bite-and hang on) 'bite at something and hang on to it, stick to', *kkwulh-ko ancta* (kneel-and sit) 'kneel down', and *nol-ko mekta* (play-and eat) 'idle away'. Examples with the transferentive *eta*-complementizer are *chy-eta pota* (lift-TR see) 'look up', *nayly-eta pota* (lower-TR see) 'look down', *nay-(e)ta pota* (take out-TR see) 'look out', and *tol-ata pota* (turn-TR see) 'look back'.

There are several recent works on serial predicate constructions in Korean: H.M. Sohn (1986), I.H. Jo (1990), S.Y. Kang (1992), S.H. Lee (1992), T.G. Chung (1993), S.H. You (1996), and Y.J. Kim (1997).

9.10.3   *Auxiliary predicate constructions*

In general, the first predicate in an auxiliary construction is semantically main and the second one auxiliary, although the second one is the syntactic head. The second predicate displays some aspectual and/or modality phenomena, by which we can distinguish auxiliary from serial constructions where the first predicate indicates the manner of action of the second predicate to a large extent. For instance, the auxiliary construction *nok-a kata* 'be melting away' shows a continuously melting aspectual phenomenon, whereas the serial construction *oll-a kata* 'go up' denotes going upward, where the action of going is semantically main.

The auxiliary predicate is defective in that it does not have a normal argument structure expected of its non-auxiliary usage. For instance, the full verb *pelita* 'throw away' has the argument structure <agent, theme, locative>, in which the agent is realized as the subject, the theme as the object, and the locative as an oblique case of the sentence, as in *na nun phyenci lul hyuci-thong ey pely-ess-ta* 'I threw away the letter in the waste basket.' Derived historically from the full verb *pelita*, the auxiliary verb *pelita* 'finish up' does not have the same argument structure. It shares the same subject with the preceding full predicate, as in *Mia nun ka-pely-ess-ta* 'Mia went away' where Mia is the subject of both the main verb *ka* and the auxiliary verb *peli*, and it has an aspectual meaning that the speaker perceived the event as being finished up once and for all. Thus, its argument structure contains only <agent> which is shared by the preceding verb, i.e., *kata* 'go' in the above sentence. An auxiliary predicate can even appear after its full predicate counterpart, as in *na nun phyenci lul hyuci-thong ey pely-e pely-ess-ta* 'I finished throwing away the letter in the waste basket.' As in serial constructions, the typical complementizer suffixes used are the infinitive suffix *-e/-a* and the conjunctive *-ko* 'and'.

One syntactic characteristic common to serial and auxiliary constructions is that the predicate preceding a complementizer suffix usually cannot be made in the past tense. For instance, we can say *ca-ko iss-ta* 'be sleeping' and *ca-ko iss-ess-ta* 'was sleeping', but not **ca-ss-ko iss-(ess)-ta*. This indicates that the predicates on both sides of a suffix syntactically form a closely knit unit in addition to being fused semantically. However, a delimiter can intervene between the two predicates, as in *ca-ko man iss-ta* '(He) is only sleeping.'

Many subsets of auxiliary constructions may be distinguished depending on different syntactic and semantic properties and the suffixes used, as illustrated below with typical constructions. Recent works on auxiliary constructions include I. Lee 1994, S. Rhee 1996, and S.S. Oh 1998.

9.10.3.1   Sensory constructions

Korean abounds with sensory adjectives which denote the speaker's emotions or sensations in declaratives and the hearer's in interrogatives. Since these adjectives denote unobservable internal feelings, they usually cannot be used to refer to a third person's emotion in the present time. Thus, *Mia nun kipp-e.yo* 'Mia is happy' is an unnatural utterance unless the speaker somehow already knows about *Mia*'s internal feeling. If a sentence with a sensory adjective refers to a past time, it becomes acceptable because the speaker could have had time to gain information about the referent's internal feeling after the event had taken place, as in *Mia nun kipp-ess-e.yo* 'Mia was happy.'

As a mechanism to express someone else's internal feeling, a sensory adjective is changed to a transitive verb with the attachment of an infinitive suffix and the verb *hata* 'show signs of being'. Thus, *kipputa* 'be happy' is changed to the auxiliary construction *kipp-e hata* 'show happiness', as illustrated in (201).

(201)   a. *na   nun   **kippu**-ta.*
            I   TC   happy-DC
            'I am happy.'

        b. *ne   nun   **kippu**-ni?*
            you TC   happy-Q
            'Are you happy?'

        c. *Milan.i nun **kipp-e**   **ha**-n-ta/**ha**-ni?*
            Milan   TC   happy-INF do-IN-DC/do-Q
            'Milan is happy./Is Milan happy?'

Intransitive and transitive sensory adjectives and corresponding verbs are illustrated in (202a) and (202b), respectively.

(202)   Adjectives   Verbs

	Adjectives	Verbs	
a.	*kipputa*	*kipp-e hata*	'feel happy'
	sulphuta	*sulph-e hata*	'feel sad'
	tepta	*tew-e hata*	'feel hot'
	phikonhata	*phikonhay hata*	'feel tired'
b.	*cohta*	*coh-a hata*	'like'
	pulepta	*pulew-e hata*	'envy'
	mipta	*miw-e hata*	'hate'
	silhta	*silh-e hata*	'dislike'
	musepta	*musew-e hata*	'fear, be afraid of'

In transitive constructions, the object is in the nominative case with the adjective, but in the accusative case with the verb, as shown in (203).

(203)   a. *na   nun   Tongmin.i **ka**   pulep-ta.*
            I   TC   Tongmin   NM   envy-DC
            'I envy Tongmin.'

    b. *Milan.i* *to*   *Tongmin.i* ***lul*** *pulew-e ha-n-ta.*

      Milan   also Tongmin AC   envy-INF do-IN-DC

      'Milan also envies Tongmin.'

The desiderative construction with the adjective *siphta* 'be wishful, be desirable, wish' is a peculiar type of sensory construction. First, the adjective must be preceded by a clause, which is its object. Second, this object clause is nominalized by the gerundive suffix *-ko*. Third, when the clause before *-ko siphta* is transitive, the object of the embedded verb may be marked with either a nominative or an accusative particle. When *siph-e hata* occurs, the object is always in the accusative case.

(204)   a. *na* *nun* ***kheyik i/ul***   *mek-ko*   *(ka/lul)*   *siph-ta.*

         I   TC   cake   NM/AC eat-NOM   NM/AC wish-DC

         'I want to eat cake.'

     b. *Mia nun* ***kheyik *i/ul***   *mek-ko (*ka/lul)* *siph-e*   *ha-n-ta.*

         Mia TC cake   NM/AC eat-NOM NM/AC wish-INF do-IN-DC

         'Mia wants to eat cake.'

9.10.3.2   Benefactive constructions

Benefactive constructions are formed by an action verb followed by the infinitive suffix *-e/-a* and a benefactive auxiliary verb which denotes benefaction towards the recipient. Benefactive auxiliary verbs are derived without formal change from donatory (i.e., giving) verbs, which are of three kinds: *cwuta* (plain), *tulita* (humble), and *ta(l)-* (reflexive). The reflexive form occurs mostly in the imperative quotative construction, and only when the benefaction is intended for the speaker. It may occur in the main clause (limited to the blunt speech level as in (205d)), along with *cwuta* or *tulita,* although this sounds old-fashioned. When used as an auxiliary, all these verbs of giving carry the benefactive meaning '(do) for (someone)'.

(205)   a. *Tongmin.i* *nun* *Milan.i* *lul* ***tow-a***   ***cwu-ess-ta.***

         Tongmin TC Milan   AC help-INF for-PST-DC

         'Tongmin helped Milan (for her).'

     b. *nwuna nun* *hal.apeci eykey phyenci* *lul* ***ilk-e***   ***tuly-ess-e.yo.***

         sister TC grandpa to   letter   AC read-INF for-PST-POL

         'Older sister read a letter to our grandpa (for him).'

c. *na n ku eykey sacin ul **po-y-e** tal-la ko hay-ss-ta.*
   I TC him to   photo AC see-CAS-INF for-IM QT say-PST-DC
   'I asked him to show me the picture (for me).'

d. *i phyenci lul **ilk-e** ta-o.*   (old-fashioned)
   this letter   AC   read-INF for-BL
   'Please read this letter for me.'

Grammaticalization of a benefactive auxiliary verb from a full donatory verb in complex predicate constructions manifests at least three stages. The first stage is that of a donatory verb which retains its original meaning of giving, as in (206a). In this function, it retains its full argument structure as <agent, theme, goal>. The second stage is that of a benefactive verb with argument structure <agent, goal> as in (206b). Notice that *chayk* is the theme of *phyeta*, and not of *tulita*. The third stage is that of constructions where the auxiliary verb cannot be related to a goal case, i.e., the stage of the argument structure <agent> as in (206c).

(206)   a. *na nun apeci kkey sikyey lul cip-e(se) **tuly-ess-ta.***
          I   TC father to   watch AC pick-and give-PST-DC
          'I picked up the watch and gave it to father.'

     b. *na nun apeci kkey chayk ul **phy-e** tuly-ess-ta.*
          I   TC father to book AC open-INF give/for-PST-DC
          'I opened the book for father.'
          (lit. 'I gave the benefit of opening the book to father.')

     c. *na nun (?apeci kkey) chayk ul **teph-e** tuly-ess-ta.*
          I   TC   father to   book AC close-INF for-PST-DC
          'I closed the book (for father).'

     d. *na nun (*emeni kkey) sicang ey **ka-a** tuly-ess-ta.*
          I   TC   mother to   market to go-INF for-PST-DC
          'I went to the market for mother.'

Notice that the benefactive auxiliary verb can no longer be associated with the goal case in (206d). In such cases, the benefactor is situationally or contextually understood, or can be expressed by a conjunctive structure such as *emeni lul wihay* 'for the sake of mother'. Development into this third stage is due to the nature of the embedded (first) verbs. For instance, certain transitive verbs (e.g., *phyeta* 'open') are more receptive to the goal case than others (e.g., *tat.ta* 'close') and, in general, intransitive verbs (e.g., *kata* 'go') are more readily grammaticalized than transitive verbs. For recent in-depth studies on Korean benefactive constructions, see Shibatani 1994 and S.H. You 1996.

9.10.3.3   Aspectual constructions: progressive, resultative, habitative, persistentive, terminative, sustentive, experiential, inchoative

Numerous types of auxiliary predicate constructions indicate various aspectual phenomena. Progressive aspect is associated with on-going actions, whereas resultative aspect denotes a state resulting from the completion of an action expressed by the predicate.

(207)   a. *Tongmin.i   nun   **kongpuha-ko**   **iss**-ta.*   (progressive)
                Tongmin   TC   study-and   stay-DC
                'Tongmin is studying.'

           b. *say   ka   **cwuk-e**   **iss**-e.yo.*   (resultative)
                bird   NM   die-INF   stay-POL
                'A bird is lying dead.'

Progressive and resultative aspects are expressed by *-ko issta* and *-e/-a issta*, respectively, where the conjunctive suffix *-ko* 'and' carries a simultaneity feature and the infinitive suffix *-e/-a* carries a resultative feature. The existential predicate *issta* 'stay, exist' should be replaced with *kyeysita* when deference towards the subject is called for. Neither formula ever occurs with an adjective, because stativity itself is an aspectual phenomenon which precludes any other aspect. While *-ko issta* occurs with any verb, *-e/-a issta* never occurs with a transitive verb and allows only intransitive verbs of the 'terminable' type (i.e., telic verbs). Thus, the transitive construction **al-a issta* 'be in the state of knowing' is not allowed. The intransitive construction *cwuk-e issta* 'be in the state of having died' is allowed, but **nol-a issta* 'be in the state of playing' is not, since *cwukta* 'die' denotes a terminable action but *nolta* 'play' does not. Both *cwuk-ko issta* 'be dying' and *nol-ko issta* 'be playing' are allowed since any verb can be made progressive.

Habitative aspect is typically expressed by the construction *-kon(un) hata*. The form *-kon(un)* is a fossilized compound consisting of the conjunctive suffix *-ko* 'and' and the topic-contrast (TC) particle *nun* 'as for', while *hata* is an action verb meaning 'do'.

(208)   *Mia nun tal   i   ttu-myen* **sulph-e ci-kon(un)**   **hay**-*ss-ta*.
          Mia TC moon NM rise-if   sad-INF become-habitually do-PST-DC
          'Mia became habitually sad, when the moon rose.'

The persistentive aspect is represented by *-e/-a kata* or *-e/-a ota*, where *-e/-a* is an
infinitive suffix, and *kata* 'go' and *ota* 'come' function semantically as auxiliary verbs
with meanings such as 'gradually, persistently, away/hither'. In some cases, *kata* and
ota tend to be associated with unfavourable and favourable events, respectively.

(209)   a. *Mia ka   na eykey coh-un   sosik ul   **cenhay** **w**-ass-ta*.
             Mia NM   me to   good-RL news AC   convey come-PST-DC
             'Mia brought good news to me.'

          b. *hal.apeci nun hay   mata   **nulk-e** **ka**-sey-yo*.
             grandpa   TC year every old-INF go-SH-POL
             'My grandpa becomes older every year.'

The typical auxiliary constructions for the terminative aspect are *-e/-a pelita* 'do
completely, get through' as in **mek-e pely**-*ess-ta* 'ate up', *-e/-a nayta* 'do thoroughly
all the way' as in **kyenti-e nay**-*ess-ta* 'endured to the end', and *-ko (ya) malta*
'(finally) end up doing, get around to doing' where *ya* 'finally, only' is a delimiter, as
in **cwuk-ko (ya) mal**-*ass-ta* '(finally) ended up dead'. The auxiliary verbs have
meanings deviant from their main verb counterparts: *pelita* 'throw away', *nayta* 'take
out', and *malta* 'stop doing'.

Sustentive aspect is expressed by *-e/-a twuta* 'get it done just in case' and *-e/-a
nohta* 'do for later, get it over with now (in anticipation of later use)'. The main verb
meanings of *twuta* 'put, place, put away, keep' and *nohta* 'put down, lay down'
become abstracted in auxiliary constructions.

(210)   a. *ku   chayk ul   **ilk-e**   **twu**-ess-e*.
             the   book   AC   read-INF get done-PST-INT
             'I have finished reading the book just in case.'

          b. *phyo lul mili   **sa**   **noh**-ass-e.yo*.
             ticket AC in advance buy do for later-PST-POL
             'I bought the ticket in advance.'

Experiential (or attemptive) aspect may be expressed by the auxiliary verb
construction *-e/-a pota* 'try to, have the experience that' as in *kaykwuli koki lul* **mek-e**

pota 'try eating frog meat'. This construction is widely used as a strategy to soften the speaker's assertion, as *ce nun ka po-keyss-sup-ni-ta* 'I think I better go.' The inchoative (change of state) aspect is expressed by an adjective + *-el-a cita* 'become, get to be', as in *mul i malk-a cy-ess-ta* 'The water became clear' and *ce kil i manh-i nelp-hy-e cy-ess-ta* 'That road has become considerably widened.' A sequence of aspectual auxiliary predicates may be attached to a main predicate, as in *ku chayk ul ilk-e pely-e po-a twu-ess-ta* '(I) tried to finish reading the book just in case.'

9.10.3.4   Permission, concession, prohibition, and obligation

Both permissive and concessive constructions are expressed by a verb followed by the conjunctive suffix *-to* 'even though' and the adjective *cohta* 'be good' or the verb *toyta* 'do, be okay'. Prohibition is represented by a verb followed by the conjunctive suffix *-myen* 'if' or *-(e)senun* 'if' and the negative verb *an toyta* 'not do, be not okay'. Obligation is made by a verb followed by the conjunctive suffix *-ya* 'if only' and the verb *hata* 'do'.

(211) a *ne*   *nun*   **ka-to**   *coh-ta.*
          you   TC   go-though   good-DC
          'You may go; It is okay with you even if you go.'

       b. *ne*   *nun*   **ka-myen/senun**   *an*   *toy-n-ta.*
           you   TC   go-if   not   okay-IN-DC
           'You shouldn't go; It won't do if you go.'

       c. *ne*   *nun*   **ka-ya**   *ha-n-ta.*
           you   TC   go-if only   do-IN-DC
           'You must go.'

9.11   Negation

Clauses or constituents of clauses are negated with negative elements. Two general types are sentential negation and constituent negation. The former is further subdivided into short-form negation and long-form (or periphrastic) negation. The latter can be further subclassified into predicate negation and nominal negation. In general, the scope of sentential negation may go over the word modified by the negative element while that of constituent negation is limited to the constituent (mainly a word) in question. For recent studies on Korean negation, see S.C. Song 1988 and J. Kim 1996, among other works.

9.11.1   *Sentential negation*

The most common way of negating a sentence is via a syntactic device, i.e., by placing a negative adverb immediately before the predicate. Negative adverbs used in declaratives and interrogatives are *an(i)* 'not' and *mos* 'not possibly, cannot, unable'. In general, simple negation or negative intent is expressed by *an(i)*, whereas inability or impossibility is expressed by *mos*. In speech, the contracted form *an* is usually used; in writing both *an* and *ani* are used. While *an(i)* is used widely with any predicate, *mos* usually does not occur with an adjective except in some idiomatized expressions such as *mos-hata* 'be inferior' and *mos-mattanghata* 'be unsatisfactory'.

(212)   *enni   nun   hak.kyo   ey   **an/mos**   ka-ss-e.yo.*
          sister   TC   school   to   not/cannot   go-PST-POL
          'My older sister didn't/couldn't go to school.'

In imperatives and propositives, the negative verb *malta* 'stop doing, don't do' is used after a clause nominalized with the suffix *-ci*. This verb is optionally contracted to *mata* before a vowel in a sentence-final position and obligatorily before *s*, *n*, *p*, and *o*, since this is an *l*-irregular verb.

(213)   a. *ne   nun   hak.kyo   ey   ka-ci   **ma(l-a)**.*
              you   TC   school   to   go-NOM   don't do-INT
              'As for you, don't go to school.'

          b. *sensayng-nim   un   ka-ci   **ma-si-p-si-o**.*
              teacher-HT   TC   go-NOM   don't do-SH-AH-RQ-IM
              'Please don't go, sir.'

          c. *ka-ci   **mal-ca**.*
              go-NOM   stop-PR
              'Let's not go.'

Occurrence of *an(i)* and *mos* in declaratives and interrogatives and of *malta* in imperatives and propositives applies to conjunctive constructions. That is, occurrences of these elements in non-final conjuncts are governed by the main sentence types.

(214)   a. *Tongmin.i   nun   ca-ci   **an-h-ko**   kongpuhay-yo.*
              Tongmin   TC   sleep-NOM not-do-and   study-POL
              'Tongmin is studying without sleeping.'

b. *ne*   *nun*   *ca-ci*   **mal-ko**   *kongpuhay-la.*
    you   TC   sleep-NOM   stop-and   study-IM
    'As for you, study without sleeping.'

The idiomatic expressions *malko* 'except for, not but' and *malko nun* 'except for' (derived from *mal-ko* 'stop-and' and TC *nun*) may occur in any type of sentence, as in *Minca malko Yongho ka ka-ss-ta* 'It's not Minca but Yongho who went' and *Minca malko nun amu to an w-ass-ta* 'Nobody came but Minca.'

The adverb *ani* is used as a sentential adverb in the sense of 'No' in response to a question, as in (215). Notice here that unlike in English, *ani* is not related to the truth of the event, but negates the semantic content of what the interlocutor is asking.

(215)   A: *Cihwan.i   an   ttena-ss-ni?*
             Cihwan   not leave-PST-Q
             'Didn't Cihwan leave?'

          B: **ani** *yo.*
             no POL
             'No. (She did.)'

The adverb *ani* also functions as an exclamatory in the sense of 'why, dear me, good heavens' showing surprise when something occurs unexpectedly, as in **ani**, *i salam i nwukwu ya?!* 'Dear me! Who is this person?'

Syntactic negation is expressed in two ways: a short form, as in (216a), and a long form, as in (216b). In general, the two forms share the same meaning, with slight stylistic difference – the former being slightly less formal than the latter.

(216)   a. *ape-nim   un   **an**   ka-sy-e.*
             father-HT   TC   not   go-SH-INT
             'Father is not going.'

          b. *ape-nim   un   **ka-ci**   (lul/to)   **an**-h-usy-e.*
             father-HT   TC   go-NOM   AC/even   not-do-SH-INT
             'Father is not (even) going.'

Notice in long form negation that the nominalizer suffix *-ci* is attached to the first predicate, producing a nominalized clause. A negative adverb is attached to the main clause verb *ha* (frequently contracted to *h*) 'do, be in the state of'. An option l accusative, nominative, or delimiter particle may intervene. The suffix *-ci* occurs only before a negative word, while the nominalizer *-ki* occurs only before a positive word. The predicate *hata* agrees in activity/stativity with the preceding predicate. Thus, compare (217a), where the verb *kata* 'go' appears, with (217b), where the adjective *cohta* 'good' occurs, and notice that the indicative suffix *nun* appears only in the former.

(217)   a. *Yongho nun hak.kyo ey ka-ci   **an-h-nun**-ta.*
              Yongho TC   school to   go-NOM not-do-IN-DC
              'Yongho does not go to school.'

        b. *Minca nun sengkyek i   coh-ci   **an-h**-ta.*
              Minca TC   personality NM good-NOM not-be-DC
              'Minca's personality is not good.'

There are several restrictions regarding the use of short and long negations. First, while verbs (except for some compounds to be discussed below) are relatively free to occur in both short and long forms, adjectives are more natural in long forms than in short forms. In particular, adjectives of three or more syllables usually are not acceptable in short forms. Thus, for instance, *alumtap-ci an-h-ta* 'be not beautiful' is natural while *an alumtap-ta* is not.

Second, the copula is not generally acceptable in long form if the complement is a noun. Thus, *haksayng i an ita* '(He) is not a student' is correct, while **haksayng i-ci an-h-ta* is not. If the complement ends in the Sino-Korean suffix *-cek* '-ic, -ive', however, long form negation is allowed with a copula, as in *hyokwa-cek i an ita* and *hyokwa-cek i-ci an-h-ta* '(It) is not effective.'

Third, when a verb is a compound one, as in *kongpu-hata* (study-do) 'study', *yathpota* (low-see) 'look down upon', and *nal-ttwita* (fly-jump) 'act violently', long-form negation is preferred to short-form negation, as in *kongpuha-ci an-h-nun-ta* and *yathpo-ci an-h-nun-ta*, but not **an kongpuha-n-ta* and **an yathpo-n-ta*. If, however, a verb compound is separable, a negative adverb can be placed between the component elements, as in *kongpu (lul) an ha-n-ta* 'does not study'. Compound adjectives cannot be separated in this way, as in **hayngpok an ha-ta* 'be not happy'.

Fourth, *mos* occurs with some adjectives but only in long forms. In this case, its basic meaning of negating ability becomes considerably diluted and behaves like an emphatic *an(i)*, as in *coh-ci mos ha-ta* 'be not good', *hayngpok.ha-ci mos ha-ta* 'be not happy', *kil-ci mos ha-ta* 'be not long', *neknek.ha-ci mos ha-ta* 'be not sufficient', and *kenkangha-ci mos ha-ta* 'be not healthy'.

Fifth, the negative verb *malta* occurs only as a long form negative, as in *o-ci ma(l-a)* 'Don't come.' In addition to imperatives and propositives, *malta* may occur in optative sentences such as *Mia ka o-ci mal-ass-umyen coh-keyss-e* 'I hope Mia won't come' and in idiomatized alternative constructions such as *ka-l kka ma-l kka* 'whether to go or not' and *pay ka po-i-l tus/lak ma-l tus/lak ha-n-ta* 'The ship is barely visible.'

Finally, only a long form can adjust the scope of negation. (218a) and (218b) have a wide scope, negating the whole sentence, whereas (218c) has a narrower scope, negating only the bracketed nominalized clause with the use of the topic-contrast delimiter *nun*. There is no such mechanism with short-form negation.

(218) a. ton   i   pantusi hayngpok ul   an   cwu-n-ta.
           money NM surely   happiness AC   not   give-IN-DC
           'Money surely does not give (you) happiness.'

       b. ton   i   pantusi [hayngpok ul   cwu-ci   an-h-nun-ta].
           money NM surely   happiness AC   give-NOM not-do-IN-DC
           'Money surely does not give (you) happiness.'

       c. ton   i   [pantusi hayngpok ul   cwu-ci   nun] an-h-nun-ta.
           money NM surely   happiness AC give-NOM TC   not-do-IN-DC
           'Money does not necessaily give (you) happiness.'

One aspect that deserves attention is the frequent occurrence of so-called negative polarity items. Many of them are adverbials such as *cenhye* 'at all', *kyelkho* 'after all', *yekan* 'ordinarily', *pyel-lo* 'particularly', *comchelem* 'rarely, seldom', *tomuci* 'utterly, at all', *iman ceman* 'in no small degree', *ilwu* 'by any means, (cannot) possibly', and *thong* 'in all, entirely, wholly'. Pronominal compounds like *amu to* 'anyone' and *amu kes to* 'anything', and delimiters like *pakkey* (developed from *pakk* 'outside' + *ey* 'at') 'except for' are also negative polarity items.

(219) a. *Minca   nun   cenhye   yeyppu-ci   an-h-a.*
           Minca   TC   at all   pretty-NOM   not-be-INT
           'Minca is not pretty at all.'

       b. *amu   to   an   w-ass-e.yo.*
           anyone even not   come-PST-POL
           'No one came.'

       c. *sensayng-nim   pakkey   o-si-ci   an-h-ass-e.*
           teacher-HT   except   come-SH-NOM   not-do-PST-INT
           'Nobody came except the professor.'

9.11.2   Constituent negation

Some verbs inherently incorporate negative features within themselves, the most typical ones being the existential predicate *epsta* 'not exist' (cf. *issta* 'exist') and the information verb *moluta* 'not know' (cf. *alta* 'know'). These are inherently negative predicates, in that sequences such as **an epsta* and **mos moluta* are ungrammatical.

Negative words idiomatized from syntactic negation with semantic shift belong to the class of constituent negation. Examples include *an-toyta* (not-become) 'be pitiful', *ansim-ch-an-h-ta* (from *ansim-ha-ci ani ha-ta* 'do not feel at rest') 'be uneasy', *kwaynch-an-h-ta* (from *kwankyey-ha-ci ani ha-ta* 'be not concerned) 'be all right', *kwi-ch-an-h-ta* (from *kwi-ha-ci ani ha-ta* 'be not valuable') 'be annoying', *phyen-ch-an-h-ta* (from *phyen-ha-ci ani ha-ta*) 'be sick', *mos-ssuta* (cannot-use) 'be useless', *mos-hata* (cannot-do) 'be inferior', *mos-sayngkita* (cannot-appear) 'be not good-looking', *mos-nata* (cannot-come up) 'look ugly', *mos-toyta* (cannot-become) 'be bad', and *cal-mos ita* (well-cannot be) 'be wrong'.

As discussed in 8.3.1, Sino-Korean nouns are negated by Sino-Korean negative prefixes such as *pi-, pul-, pu-, mu-, mol-*, and *mi-* that are comparable to English affixes *im-, in-, dis-, un-, non-, de-, ir-, -less*, etc. Cooccurrence of a prefix and a noun is not predictable. Thus, for instance, *pul-kanung* 'impossibility' cannot be replaced with forms like **pi-kanung, *pu-kanung, *mu-kanung, *mol-kanung*, or **mi-kanung*.

9.11.3   Double negation and rhetorical negation

Double negation is often used to achieve positive effect in an indirect way. The first negative is usually a short form, but the second negative must be in a long form, as in (220a). The adverb *mos* cannot occur in the second negative, as in (220b). Double negation cannot be used in imperative and propositive constructions. Thus, for instance, **an ka-ci mal-ca* (lit. 'Let's stop not going') is ungrammatical.

(220)   a. *Mia nun hak.kyo ey **an** ka-ci **an** h-ass-ta.*
             Mia TC   school   to not go-NOM not do-PST-DC
             'It is not the case that Mia didn't go to school.'

         b. **Mia nun **an** ka-ci **mos** hay-ss-ta.*
             Mia TC not go-NOM unable do-PST-DC
             'Mia was unable not to go.'

There are cases, such as rhetorical questions, in which a negative construction is interpreted as positive and a positive one as negative.

(221)   a. *Cihwan.i ka   **an**   o-keyss-ta!*
        Cihwan   NM   not   come-may-DC
        'I am pretty sure Cihwan will come.'

        b. *Milan.i   ka   w-ass-keyss-ni?!*
        Milan   NM   come-PST-may-Q
        'Do you think Milan has come? I don't think so.'

One productive rhetorical pattern is the confirmatory expression *-ci an-h?* and its contracted form *-c-an-h?* 'doesn't/didn't it?!, isn't/wasn't it?!' This pattern is similar in meaning to tag questions in English. The sentence has a falling intonation and the main clause is always in the present tense regardless of the embedded tense. Compare a regular negative expression in (222a) and the rhetorical expression in (222b).

(222)   a. *pi   ka   o-ci   an-h-ass-e.yo?*↑
        rain   NM   come-NOM   not-do-PST-POL
        'Didn't it rain?'

        b. *pi   ka   w-ass-ci   an-h-a.yo?*↓
        rain   NM   come-PST-NOM   not-do-PST-POL
        'It rained, didn't it?!'

In regular long-form negation, the embedded verb is always in the non-past tense, being controlled by the matrix tense. In rhetorical negation, however, *-ci an-h/-c-an-h* may be regarded as having been grammaticalized as a kind of modal suffix whose meaning is the speaker's seeking of the hearer's confirmation. Thus, the embedded predicate functions as if it is the only predicate in the sentence, taking a tense suffix of its own (cf. Kawanishi and S.O. Sohn 1993).

9.12   Adverbial constructions

Adverbials are those sentential constituents which modify a predicate, a clause, another adverbial, or even a nominal, in terms of negation, attribution (time, place, manner, degree), modality, conjunction, and discourse situations (cf. 8.1.1; 8.1.8). Some adverbials may belong to two or more of these subclasses. For instance, *palo* is a time adverbial in the sense of 'immediately', a manner adverbial in the sense of 'straightly, directly', and a modal adverbial in the sense of 'rightly, the very'.

Since adverbials are functionally defined notions, they include not only lexically inherent or derived adverbs, but also nouns, noun phrases, and clauses which function adverbially. In a broad sense, adverbials may include all case-marked nouns which modify predicates in one way or another. In the following description, however, case-marked nouns will not be discussed to avoid repetition, except for those which are fossilized as adverbs such as *ttayttay-lo* 'from time to time' (derived from *ttay* 'time' + *ttay* 'time' + *lo* 'with').

Adverbials can be followed by delimiters, such as *(n)un* 'as for', *to* 'even, also, indeed', and *man* 'only', which delimit or specify the adverbial meanings, as in ***ppalli man** ka-myen toy-n-ta* 'It will be fine if only (we) go fast'.

Adverbials always occur before the modified elements, preferably immediately before them. As long as they precede the modified element, adverbials can often be scrambled with clause-mate nominals for stylistic or connotational reasons. When the modified word is a copula, however, the adverbial cannot occur immediately before it, but must precede the complement since a copula and its complement are inseparable, as in *Mia nun **hangsang** haksayng i-ta* 'Mia is always a student.' In (223), the time adverbial *onul* can be freely scrambled with the nominals, the connotational differences being that *onul* modifies what follows it in each case.

(223)   a. ***onul** Milan.i nun   Yengkwuk ulo   ttena-ss-ta.*
            today Milan TC   England   to   leave-PST-DC
            'Milan left for England today.'

        b. *Milan.i nun **onul** Yengkwuk ulo ttena-ss-ta.*

        c. *Yengkwuk ulo Milan.i nun **onul** ttena-ss-ta.*

Adverbials occur recursively in a sentence. One or more adverbials may modify another adverbial or a predicate. When different types of adverbials cooccur, the natural order among them is modal, time, place, degree, and manner.

(224)   a. *kwa.yen Mia nun   nolay lul   [acwu] [cal] ha-n-ta.*
            indeed Mia TC   song   AC   very   well   do-IN-DC
            'Indeed, Mia sings very well.'

        b. *haksayng-tul un [tatal-i]   [hanpen ssik] [co.yonghi] mo.y-e.*
            student-PL   TC months-AD   once   each quietly   gather-INT
            'The students get together quietly once every month.'

Negative adverbials were discussed in the preceding section (9.11). Other adverbials will be taken up in the following subsections.

9.12.1   Attributive adverbials: time, place, manner, and degree

Attributive adverbials, as stated in Choy 1965:579, modify the attribute or property of the action or state of the predicate in terms of time, place, manner, or degree. Time adverbials indicate points of time (e.g., *onul* 'today', *cikum* 'now', *encey* 'when?'), duration (e.g., *nul* 'always', *olay* 'long', *yengyeng* 'forever'), relative time (e.g., *imi* 'already', *ilccik* 'early', *acik* 'yet, still'), and repetition/frequency (e.g., *ittakum* 'sometimes', *mayil* 'everyday', *congcong* 'often'). Place adverbials indicate location (e.g., *yeki* 'here', *kos-kos-i* 'every place', *eti* 'where?'), direction (e.g., *ili* 'this way', *celi* 'that way'), and distance (e.g., *melli* 'far away', *kakkai* 'near').

Manner adverbials denote various manners in which the action or state denoted by the predicate is to be manifested. They may be either lexical or clausal, the former being subdivided into those which are not onomatopoeic (e.g., *cal* 'well', *ecci* 'how?', *ese* 'quickly', *ppal-li* 'quickly, fast', *ilpule* 'on purpose', *makwu* 'carelessly', *manh-i* 'much', *kiph-i* 'deeply') and those which are (e.g., *ttok-ttok* 'with snaps', *thang-thang* 'bang-bang', *wulkus-pulkus* 'colourfully').

Lexical manner adverbials normally occur immediately before a modified predicate, but can be scrambled with nominals as in *Mia nun **ppal-li** cip ulo ka-ss-ta* 'Mia went home quickly', although it becomes unnatural if they precede the subject as in ?***ppal-li** Mia nun cip ulo ka-ss-ta*. Onomatopoeic adverbials were discussed in 5.3.

Clausal manner adverbials have several subtypes. First, the adverbializer *-i* may be suffixed to an embedded clause element, as in [*cwi cwuk-un tus-**i***] *co.yongha-ta* 'It is as quiet as if rats were dead', [*ca.yu ka eps-**i***] *nun mos sa-n-ta* '(We) cannot live without freedom', and [*nwun i o-l kes kath-**i***] *nalssi ka chwup-ta* 'It is cold, as if it is going to snow.' Second, the adverbial suffix *-key* 'so that' can be attached to an embedded clause predicate. In fact, all predicates (except for the copula) can be adverbialized with this suffix, some being more idiomatized than others.

(225)   *kam   i   [acwu pulk-**key**]   ik-ess-kwun.*
          persimmon NM   very   red-AD   ripe-PST-APP
          'The persimmons are red ripe.'

Third, the infinitive suffix *-e/-a* and the conjunctive suffix *-ko* 'and' also adverbialize the preceding clause to function as a complement clause, as in *Mia ka* [*ceyil cak-**a***] *po-i-n-ta* 'Mia looks the smallest' and *tongsayng i* [*ki lul tul-**ko***] *w-a.yo* 'My younger brother is coming holding a flag.'

Degree adverbials denote a qualitative or quantitative degree of the state or action indicated by the predicate. Lexical examples are *phek* 'very', *kkway* 'considerably', *keuy* 'almost', *kacang* 'most', *camos* 'exceedingly', *hato* 'excessively', *ssek* 'awfully, greatly', *maywu* 'very', *cham* 'truly, really', *acwu* 'very, quite, really', *hwelssin* 'by far', *nemu(-nemu)* 'overly, extremely', *ceyil* 'most', *cen-hye* 'entirely', *kuk-hi* 'extremely', and *taytan-hi* 'very'. All degree adverbials occur before an adjective, a manner adverb, or another degree adverb, as in **phek** *kiph-ta* '(It) is very deep' and **hwelssin** *te noph-i nall-ass-ta* '(It) flew much higher'. Some degree adverbials precede a verb if the verb is derived from an adjective as in *Mia lul* **cikuk-hi** *coh-a-ha-n-ta* '(He) likes Mia very much', if the adverb itself denotes quantity as in *yak.kan wumciki-n-ta* 'moves a little', or if a manner adverbial is understood, as in **nemu** *(ppal-li) talli-n-ta* 'runs overly (fast)'.

Degree adverbials such as *cen-hye* 'absolutely, at all', *kutaci/kuli* 'so much, particularly', *yekan* 'ordinarily', and *i-man ce-man* 'in no small degree' are negative polarity items (9.11.1). The 'projective' suffix *-tolok* 'so that, to the extent that' is a typical example that forms a clausal degree adverbial.

(226)   *enni nun* [*pyeng   i   na-tolok*] *yelsimhi   kongpuhay-ss-ta.*
        sister TC   sickness NM   occur-AD   hard   study-PST-DC
        'My older sister studied hard to the extent that she got sick.'

9.12.2   *Modal adverbials*

Modal adverbials are concerned with the speaker's feeling, opinion, or attitude. Accordingly, they usually modify a clause or sentence as a whole. Modal adverbials are different from attributive ones in that the latter are related to the property of the modified element whereas the former concerns the speaker's modality. They are however morphologically similar to each other. Sometimes, the same adverbial can be both attributive and modal. For instance, *hwaksil-hi* is a manner adverbial in the sense of 'for sure' (*Milan.i nun hwaksil-hi a-n-ta* 'Milan correctly knows (it)') and a modal adverbial in the sense of 'surely/certainly' (*hwaksil-hi Milan.i nun yeyppu-ta* 'Surely, Milan is pretty').

Modal adverbials may be classified into four general types: assertive (e.g., *ceypal* 'please', *kuyamallo* 'indeed, truly', *kwa.yen* 'indeed', *kyelkwuk* 'after all', *mullon* 'of course', *puti* 'at any cost', *sillo* 'indeed', *totaychey* 'on earth', *yeksi* 'after all'), exclusive (e.g., *kkok* 'surely', *ocik* 'only', *oloci* 'only', *taman* 'only', *tanci* 'merely, simply'), descriptive (e.g., *cayswu-eps-i* 'unluckily', *chalali* 'rather', *com* 'just, please', *eccayse* 'why', *machim* 'fortunately', *tahayng-hi* 'fortunately', *way* 'why'), and hypothetical (e.g., *ama* 'maybe', *hoksi* 'by any chance', *kulssey* 'well', *machi* 'as if', *manil* 'if', *selma* 'on no account', *selsa* 'even if').

Exclusive modal adverbials modify noun phrases, occurring immediately before them (9.12.3). The most natural syntactic position of the other modal adverbials is at the beginning of the clause or right after the subject, although they can be scrambled for stylistic reasons.

(227)   a. ***pulhaynghi to***   *totwuk i*   *cap-hi-ci*   *an-h-ass-ta.*
         unfortunately indeed thief NM catch-PAS-NOM not-do-PST-DC
         'Unfortunately, the thief has not been caught.'

        b. *Mia nun* ***kyelkho*** *sihap ey ci-ci*   *an-h-ul*   *kes*   *i-ta.*
           Mia TC ever   match in lose-NOM not-do-PRS fact be-DC
           'Mia will never lose in the match.'

Different modal adverbials manifest different syntactic peculiarities. For instance, *kyelkho* 'by any means' and *cokum-to* 'at all' are negative polarity items, thus occurring only with a negative construction; *machi* 'as if' occurs with suppositive predicates such as *tus-hata* 'it appears' and *kes kathta* 'it seems'; and *man.il/man.yak/kasa/kalyeng* 'if' occur only with a conditional or concessive clause ending in *-myen* 'if' or '*-(e)to* 'even if'.

While most negative polarity items occur with any negative construction, *ilwu* 'by any means, (cannot) possibly' occurs only with the impossibility formula *-(u)l swu epsta* 'cannot', as in *cwuk-un salam un* ***ilwu*** *ta sey-l* ***swu*** *eps-e.yo* 'The dead people are simply too numerous to count.'

9.12.3   Nominal-modifying adverbials

There are adverbials that modify a noun phrase, many of which are degree and modal adverbials. Degree adverbials such as *te* 'more', *kacang* 'most', *cokum* 'a little', *acwu* 'very', and *hwelssin* 'far more' can modify a noun phrase that contains a semantic component susceptible to degree, such as an adjectival meaning. For instance, in ***te/kacang*** *sin-hyeng ul sa-ss-ta* 'bought the newer/newest model' and ***acwu*** *papo ta* 'is a complete fool', *sin-hyeng* 'new model' has a semantic component [NEW] and *papo* 'fool' has a semantic component [FOOLISH]. In ***cokum*** *tong ulo ka-la* 'Go a little eastward!' and ***hwelssin*** *twi lul po-ala* 'Look far more backward!', *tong* 'east' means 'eastward direction' and *twi* 'back' means 'backward direction', and thus can be talked about in terms of degree.

Manner/degree adverbials like *kyewu* 'barely', *kocak* 'at most', and *keuy* 'almost' can occur not only with a numeral construction, as in *koki lul* ***keuy yel mali*** *cap-ass-ta* 'caught almost ten fish', but also with a noun phrase that denotes an object being implicitly compared with other objects, as in ***kyewu yenphil man*** *pat-ass-ta* 'received only pencils'.

Modal adverbials such as *kkok* 'surely', *palo* 'rightly, precisely', *oloci* 'only', *tanci* 'simply', *hankas* 'simply', *taman* 'only, merely', and *ocik* 'only' can occur with a noun phrase to refer to uniqueness, as in *Mia nun wuli cip palo iwus ey sal-a.yo* 'Mia lives right in our neighbourhood.'

9.12.4   Conjunctive adverbials

Conjunctive adverbials conjoin one sentence to another. Many of them have derived from conjunctive clauses with slight phonological change. For instance, *kuliko* 'and', *kulena* 'but', *kulemyen* 'then', and *kulayto* 'nevertheless' are fossilized respectively from the conjunctive clauses *kuli ha-ko* 'did it and', *kule ha-na* '(it) is so, but', *kule ha-myen* 'if (it) is so', and *kule hay-to* 'even if (we) do so'. The adverb *kulemulo* 'therefore' can be associated with *kule ha-mulo* 'since (it) is so', where *-mulo*, although currently used as a conjunctive suffix with the meaning 'since, as', is analysed into the nominalizer *-m* and the instrument case particle *ulo* 'with'. Other conjunctive words include *ku-lay-se* 'therefore', *ku-leh-ciman* 'however', *ku-leh-ta-myen* 'if so', *ku-le-na ce-le-na* 'at any rate', *ku-le-nikka* 'therefore', *ani-myen* 'if not', *cuk* 'that is', *hok-un* 'or', *tekwuntana* 'besides', *tewuki* 'moreover', *ttal-ase* 'accordingly', *tto-han* 'likewise', and *tto-nun* 'or'. Notice that demonstratives, especially *ku* 'that', are widely used to form lexical conjunctive adverbials.

Conjunctive adverbials are placed at the beginning of a sentence which is semantically conjoined to the preceding sentence, as in *hyeng i ttena-ss-e.* **kulayse** *hyengswu-nim i oylow-usy-e* 'My older brother left. So, his wife is lonely.'

9.12.5   Discoursal adverbials

Discoursal adverbials are so termed not only because they occur syntactically outside the boundary of a sentence but also because they are conditioned by discourse contexts or speech situations. Usually, they either occur alone, or precede a sentence, as a yes or no response, an address, or an interjection.

Yes/no responses are made by expressions like *onya* [plain], *ung* [intimate], *yey/ney* [polite] 'Yes'; *kuleh-ta* [plain], *kulay* [intimate], *kuleh-ney* [familiar], *kuleh-so* [blunt], *kulay-yo* [polite], *kuleh-sup-ni-ta* [deferential] 'Yes, that's right'; *ani-ta* [plain], *ani(-ya)* [intimate], *ani-ney* [familiar], *ani-(y)o* [blunt, polite], *ani-eyyo* [polite], *ani-p-ni-ta* [deferential] 'No'; and *chenman-ey* [intimate], *chenman-ey-yo* [polite] 'Not at all'. Notice that all of these words represent speech levels, some inherently and others with a sentence ender that reflects a speech level.

The most frequently used terms in the polite speech level are *yey/ney* 'yes' and *ani-(y)o* 'no', which do not mean 'yes' and 'no' in the English sense, but rather 'that's correct; I understand' and 'that's incorrect', respectively.

(228)   a. A: *hak.kyo ey an   ka-ni?*
                school to not go-Q
                'Aren't (you) going to school?'

         B: *ney. (an   ka-yo.)*
             yes not go-POL
             'No. (I am not going.)'

         b. A: *ne   ca-ni?*
                you sleep-Q
                'Are you sleeping?'

         B: *ani-(y)o. (an   ca-yo.)*
             no-POL   not sleep-POL
             'No. (I am not.)'

For addressing, an extensive set of address terms are used, which include not only personal names plus honorific titles but also professional titles and kinship terms. These address terms are closely interrelated with different speech levels, as in *Homin a* 'Homin!', *papo ya* 'Idiot!', *yay* 'Child!' [plain]; *ipwa* 'Hello!', *hyeng* 'Older Brother!', *nwuna ya* 'Older Sister!' [intimate]; *yepokey* 'Hello!', *haksayng* 'Student!', *Homin i* 'Homin!', *Kim-kwun* 'Mr Kim!', *i salam a* 'Hey!' (lit. 'this person!') [familiar]; *yepo/ipwa.yo* 'Hello!', *Kim-kwacang* 'Division Chief Kim!', *Dr Kim* 'Dr Kim!' [blunt]; *Kim-paksa(-nim)* 'Dr Kim!', *Kim sensayng(-nim)* 'Mr Kim!', *hal.apeci* 'grandfather [polite]; and *sensayng-nim* 'Sir, Professor!', *kwacang-nim* 'Division Chief!', *hal.ape-nim* 'grandfather!' [deferential] (see 9.14.1.2 for further discussion).

There are many interjections such as *acha* 'Heavens!, By Jove!, Shucks!', *emena* 'Good grief!' (used only by females), *pil-e mek-ul* 'Go to hell!', *ani* 'Oh My!, Why!, Good Heavens!', *a.yas* 'Ouch!', *celen* 'Good Heavens!', and *aiko/aikwu* 'Oh my!, Dear me!, Good heavens!, Alas!, Gosh!'. For an extensive list, see H.M. Sohn 1994.

The most frequently used interjection is *aiko* (or *aikwu*), as in ***aiko pay ya!*** 'Oh! My stomach aches!', ***aiko cwuk-keyss-ta*** 'Oh! I am really tired' (lit. 'I may die.'), ***aiko sikan i ta toy-ss-ney*** 'Oh my gosh! Time's up', and ***aiko kkamccak i-a*** 'God, you scared me!'

9.13   Reduction phenomena

Various parts of sentences may be reduced to pro-forms or ZERO. The reduced elements may be recoverable either from the discourse or situational context or from the sentential context of which they are a part. Although different kinds of reduction phenomena are interrelated, let us, for convenience's sake, use the term ellipsis to refer to the omission of a constituent attributable to the discourse or situational context, and terms like gapping, omission, pro-replacement, and reflexivization to refer to reductions attributable to sentential contexts.

9.13.1   *Ellipsis*

Being a situation-oriented language, Korean allows all major constituents of sentences, including noun phrases and predicates, to be left unexpressed if discoursally or situationally recoverable. In interpersonal encounters, the pronouns referring to the speaker and hearer are usually not expressed unless focused or delimited. Ellipsis is mostly optional, but there are considerably idiomatized expressions where omission is obligatory. To this group belong the 'expressive' formulae such as *sillyeyha-p-ni-ta* 'Excuse me', *komap-sup-ni-ta* 'Thank you', *coysongha-p-ni-ta* 'I am very sorry', *chwuk.hahay-yo* 'Congratulations!', *mian.hay-yo* 'I'm sorry', and *annyengha-sey-yo?* 'How are you?' In these expressions, words denoting the speaker and hearer are not easily expressible.

Optionality of ellipsis is illustrated in the following dialogue. Speaker A can freely omit *ne* 'you' and even *Cihwan* if he believes that B knows who A is talking about. In response to A, speaker B can choose any of the possible expressions without any particular constraint.

(229)   A: *(ne)*   *(Cihwan.i)*   *manna-ss-ni?*
                  you   Cihwan   meet-PST-Q
                  'Did you meet Cihwan?'

           B: *(na)*   *(Cihwan.i/ku-ay)*   *an*   *manna-ss-e.*
                  I   Cihwan/that-child   not   meet-PST-INT
                  'I didn't meet him.'

Such elements, however, must appear if they are to be focused or delimited in a certain way or if they introduce new information into the discourse, as in *Mia ka Cihwan.i man manna-ss-e* 'It's Mia who met only Cihwan.'

Predicates are also omittable if understood from the discoursal or situational context, as in *eti lul ilehkey ilccik?* 'Where (are you going) this early?' and its response *hak.kyo ey com* '(I am) just (going) to school.' One well-known type of discoursal ellipsis is the omission of a whole nominal clause that functions as a copulative sentence. The omitted clause can be inferred from a preceding utterance.

(230)   A: *ne   nun   mwel   mek-keyss-ni?*
             you   TC   what   eat-intend-Q
             'What do you want to eat?'

         B: *na   nun   pulkoki   y-a.*
             I   TC   roast meat   be-INT
             'As for me, (what I want to eat) is roasted meat.'

9.13.2   Gapping

Syntactic gapping optionally occurs in coordinate conjunctive clauses. Gapping in Korean applies from the left, unlike in English where it deletes verbs that would otherwise be repeated on the right.

(231)   *Milan.i nun Mikwuk ey (ka-ko), Mia nun Yengkwuk ey ka-ss-ta.*
          Milan TC   America to go-and Mia TC   England to go-PST-DC
          'Milan went to the United States and Mia (went) to England.'

9.13.3   Omission

Sentential elements may be omitted without being conditioned by any antecedent. One very productive pattern is the optional omission of certain case particles in colloquial speech when no particular focus of the nominal is needed and no ambiguity arises due to the normal word order or semantic transparency. Nominative *ka*/*i*, accusative *(l)ul*, genitive *uy*, and dative-goal-stative locative *ey*, *hanthey*, *eykey* are most frequently omitted in conversations.

(232)   a. *ne   (ka)   hal.apeci (eykey) ttek   (ul) tuly-ela.*
             you NM   grandpa   to   rice-cake AC   give-IM
             'Give some rice-cake to grandpa.'

         b. *Minho   (uy)   tongsayng   (i)   hak.kyo (ey)   ka-ss-e.yo.*
             Minho   GN   brother   NM   school   to   go-PST-POL
             'Minho's younger brother went to school.'

Optional omission of the quotative particle *ko*, often together with the following verb *ha* 'say', is exceptionless.

(233)   a. *Swuk.hi nun Milan.i lul   po-keyss-ta   **ko ha**-n-ta.*
             Swukhi TC   Milan AC   see-intend-DC QT say-IN-DC

→ *Swuk.hi nun Milan.i lul po-keyss-ta Ø ha-n-ta.*
→ *Swuk.hi nun Milan.i lul po-keyss-ta Ø Ø-nta.*
'Swukhi says that she will see Milan.'

b.	*ku*	*cip*	*ey*	*pul*	*i*	*na-ss-ta*	*ko*	*ha-y.*
	that	house	at	fire	NM	occur-PST-DC	QT	say-INT

→ *ku cip ey pul i na-ss-ta Ø Ø-y.*
'They say that a fire broke out at that house.'

Other minor optional contractions include *eyse* 'at, from' to *se*, *-ko na-se* 'and then' to *-ko-se* or *-ko*, *hanthey se* 'from' to *hanthey*, and *-ya ha-keyss-ta* 'should, must' to *-ya-keyss-ta*. Notice that upon deletion of elements, agglutination easily heals the wound by attaching the following orphaned elements to the preceding element.

There are fossilized (grammaticalized) expressions where the whole main predicate is omitted and not easily recoverable and the remaining subordinate clause behaves like the main clause (8.7; 9.8.1; 9.14.3). One motivation for such restructuring appears to be a pragmatic one, i.e., to mitigate the assertiveness of various speech acts. Native speakers tend to perceive such constructions as full-fledged main sentences.

(234)	a.	*Cihwan.i*	*ka*	*o-nu-n*	*ci*	*yo?*
		Cihwan	NM	come-IN-RL	whether	POL

      'I wonder if Cihwan is coming.'

	b.	*pi*	*ka*	*o-nu-n*	*tey*	*yo.*
		rain	NM	come-IN-RL	circumstance	POL

      'It's raining . **What shall we do?'**

	c.	*na*	*nun*	*an*	*ka-n-ta-nikka*	*yo!*
		I	TC	not	go-IN-DC-because	POL

      'I told you that I am not going.'

The omitted main clauses seem to be something like *moll-a.yo* 'I am not sure' in (234a), *etteh-key ha-l kka yo* 'What shall we do?' in (234b), and *tto mul-usey-yo* 'Are you asking again?' in (234c).

9.13.4 Pro-replacement

Pro-replacement refers to pronominal and pro-predicate replacement. Pronominal replacement is either reflexive (to be discussed in 9.13.5) or non-reflexive. Lacking authentic third person pronouns, Korean is generally parsimonious about non-reflexive pronominalization, and instead favours ellipsis or gapping or even repetition of the whole antecedent noun phrase. At best, some demonstrative compounds such as *i pun* 'this person', *ku i* 'that person', *ku ay* 'that child (over there)', *ku (i) tul* 'they' (lit. 'those persons'), *ku nye* 'that woman' (usually in literary writing), and *ku kes* 'that thing, fact' or the demonstrative *ku* 'he' (lit. 'that'; usually in literary writing) may be used for anaphoric pronominalization, in addition to their use as deictic pronominals.

(235)   a. *Minho eykey (kyay ka) eti   ka-nu-nya ko   mul-ess-e.yo.*
          Minho to   he   NM where go-IN-Q   QT   ask-PST-POL
          '(I) asked Minho where (he) is going.'

          b. *sacang-nim un sacang-nim/?ku pun cha lo o-sy-ess-e.yo.*
          president-HT TC president-HT/he   car by come-SH-PST-POL
          'Our (company) president came by his car.'

In (235a), use of the pronominal *kyay* or *ku ay* 'he/she, that child' in the embedded clause is somewhat unnatural, unless *Minho* is exclusively referred to in the sense of 'he and not others'. In (235b), use of *ku pun* 'he/she, that person' is unnatural because deferential third-person pronouns are rarely used to refer to an in-group member. Either the antecedent noun must be repeated or a deferential reflexive pronoun *tangsin* 'self' must be used, although the former usage is more natural.

The demonstrative compound *ku kes* 'it, that thing, that fact' can be used to pronominalize a clause.

(236)   *Mia ka chencay la ko ha-na, na nun (ku kes ul) an mit-e.*
          Mia NM genius   DC QT say-but I TC it   AC not believe-INT
          '(They) say that Mia is a genius, but I don't believe it.'

As for pro-predicate replacement, Korean does not have something like English *do*-auxiliary constructions (e.g., 'I did' in response to 'Did you go there?'), since no auxiliary predicate in Korean occurs independently without a main predicate. There are, however, other mechanisms. First, the adjective *kulehta* 'be so' is often used as a pro-predicate.

(237)   A: *pakk   ey pi ka   o-ni?*
          outside at rain NM come-Q
          'Is it raining outside?'

B: *kuleh-sup-ni-ta.*
be so-AH-IN-DC
'That's right.'

Second, only the predicate is repeated. An adverbial modifying the predicate, if any, usually appears with the predicate. When the predicate is a copula, the complement nominal must occur with the copula, since a copula cannot stand by itself.

(238) A: *Milan.i nun onul achim ilccik il-e na-ss-ni?*
Milan TC today morning early rise-INF appear-PST-Q
'Did Milan get up early this morning?'

B: *ilccik il-e na-ss-e.*
early rise-INF appear-PST-INT
'Yes, she did.'

Third, *hata* 'do, be in the state of' functions as a pro-predicate in limited cases. Compound verbs consisting of a verbal noun and *hata* are pro-verbalized as in (239).

(239) A: *Minho ka yelsim-hi kongpuha-ni?*
Minho NM diligent-ly study-Q
'Does Minho study diligently?'

B: *yesim-hi ha-y.*
diligent-ly do-INT
'Yes, he does diligently.'

When identical predicates are to be repeated, the second one is replaced with *hata* as in *Cihwan.i ka ka-ki nun ka-n-ta* → *Cihwan.i ka ka-ki nun ha-n-ta* 'Cihwan does go, but . . .' and *Mia ka hayngpok.ha-ki nun hayngpok.ha-ta* → *Mia ka hayngpok.ha-ki nun ha-ta* 'Mia is happy, but . . .'

9.13.5 *Reflexivization*

Korean has several third person reflexive forms with the meaning '(one)self': (a) the neutral Sino-Korean word *caki* (*ca* 'self', *ki* 'animate body') which can be used, in principle, for persons of all ages, (b) the deferential Sino-Korean word *tangsin* (*tang* 'proper', *sin* 'human body') which is used only for adult social superiors, (c) the plain native word *ce* 'himself' which is used only for social inferiors, children, or animals, and (d) the Sino-Korean word *cachey* (*ca* 'self', *chey* 'body') which is used for inanimate objects. There is yet another neutral Sino-Korean form *casin* (*ca* 'self', *sin* 'human body') which is used for all persons, either alone, or as part of a compound, as in *na casin* 'myself' (but not **na caki*), *ku yeca casin* 'the woman herself', *caki casin* 'one's own self', *tangsin casin* 'his own self', and *ce casin* 'his own self'. There is no gender distinction, but the plural suffix *-tul* is suffixed to *caki* or *casin*, as in *caki-tul* 'themselves', *casin-tul* 'selves', and *ce-tul* 'themselves'. In compounds, it is suffixed either to the element preceding *casin*, as in *wuli-tul casin* 'ourselves' and *caki-tul casin*, or to *casin*, as in *wuli casin-tul* 'ourselves' and *caki casin-tul*.

While the antecedents of *caki*, *tangsin*, and *ce* are sensitive to honorifics and are required to be in the third person, the antecedent of *casin* is free from these constraints, as in *na nun casin(/*caki/*tangsin/*ce) ey pulman i-ta* 'I am dissatisfied with myself', *apeci nun tangsin (/casin/?caki/*ce) ul koylophi-si-n-ta* 'My father tortures himself', and *Mia nun ce (casin) (/*tangsin (casin)/caki (casin)) ul miweha-n-ta* 'Mia hates herself.'

As for the scope of reflexivity, the most natural antecedent of a reflexive is the subject of a sentence/clause. However, other grammatical functions such as sentential topic, indirect or direct object, locative, and possessive may occasionally serve as antecedents as illustrated in (240).

(240)   a. *Minho nun* [*caki ka cikcep ka-ss-e.yo*].
              Minho TC self NM in person go-PST-POL
              'As for Minho, he went in person.'

      b. *Yongho nun Minca lul ce uy pang eyse po-ass-ta.*
              Yongho TC Minca AC self GN room at   see-PST-DC
              'Yongho saw Minca at self's (Yongho's/Minca's) room.'

      c. *Mia nun hal.apeci kkey tangsin (uy) chayk ul tuly-ess-ta.*
              Mia TC grandpa to   self   GN book AC give-PST-DC
              'Mia gave her grandpa self's (the grandfather's) book.'

      d. *na nun Tongmin.i sikyey lul caki cip eyse po-ass-e.*
              I TC Tongmin's watch AC self's house at   see-PST-INT
              'I saw Tongmin's watch at self's (his) house.'

When the reflexive is *casin* or one of its compounds, however, the antecedent is interpreted more definitely as the subject.

Between two coreferential elements, the one with higher topicality (i.e., taking a higher structural position) becomes the antecedent and the other the anaphor. That is, the antecedent must command the reflexive. Thus, only (241a) is grammatical despite the fact that the reflexive precedes its antecedent, because the antecedent structurally commands the reflexive occurring in a subordinate clause.

(241) a. ***caki** ka senthayk.ha-n namca wa **Mia** nun kyelhonhay-ss-ta.*
          self NM choose-RL man with Mia TC marry-PST-DC
          'Mia married a man whom she chose herself.'

       b. **Mia ka sentayk.ha-n namca wa caki nun kyelhonhay-ss-ta.*

Korean reflexivization applies across clause boundaries, as shown in (241a) and (242a). This is not true for English, where reflexivization is generally confined to a single clause, as in (242b).

(242) a. ***Tongmin.i** nun **Cihwan.i** eykey [**Milan.i** ka **caki** cip ulo*
          Tongmin TC Cihwan to Milan NM self's house to
          ka-ss-ta] ko malhay-ss-ta.
          go-PST-DC QT say-PST-DC
          'Tongmin told Cihwan that Milan went to self's (Tongmin's/Cihwan's/Milan's) house.'

       b. *Mary told Bill that [he should wash **himself**/***herself**].*

As shown in the above examples, Korean reflexives occur in the direct or indirect object position, copular complement position, and possessive and other case positions. Unlike in English, Korean reflexives may also occur as the subject of an embedded clause as in (240a) and (241a). In such cases, Korean reflexives usually correspond to English personal pronouns. For more on anaphoric phenomena in Korean, see W.C.M. Kim 1976, S.H. Park 1985, B.M. Kang 1988, S. Kang 1990, J.O. Choi 1992, H. Lee 1993, W.H. Kim 1994, and K. Lim 1998.

9.14   Honorifics and politeness strategies

Language has essentially two functions – transmission of information and knowledge on the one hand and establishment and maintenance of human relationships on the other. It is the function of establishing and maintaining human relationships that is relevant to linguistic politeness. Linguistic expressions of politeness are ubiquitous across all languages and cultures, although their forms are conditioned differently by respective linguistic structures and cultural variables, the latter including power variables such as age, kinship, gender, social status, and occupational rank, and solidarity variables such as different degrees of intimacy/distance and the formality of situation.

Many recent studies on linguistic politeness have identified two types of politeness: normative (or discernment) and strategic (or volitional). The function of normative politeness is social indexing, while that of strategic politeness is face-saving (cf. J. Koo 1995). In general, expression of normative politeness is bound by traditional and contemporary cultural norms of a society, while expression of strategic politeness is controlled by interlocutors in interactive speech act situations in performing their communicative goals. While the former is largely culture-bound, the latter is universal to a great extent. Both types of politeness expressions normally occur together in the same discourse.

By and large, normative politeness is expressed with grammatically and lexically encoded forms of politeness which are called honorifics, whereas strategic politeness is expressed with various assertion-softening or assertion-reinforcing measures such as phatic expressions, conversational formulae, lexical hedges, intonation, and direct and indirect speech acts. These two forms of politeness interact in the same discourse.

Non-verbal behaviour parallels the verbal expressions of normative and strategic politeness. For instance, one bows to a senior person such as one's professor when greeting or leave-taking. The senior person does not bow to his junior. A junior person is not supposed to smoke in front of an ingroup senior, since a junior is required to behave himself appropriately in the presence of an ingroup senior. Similarly, when asking for a favour, one should assume appropriate non-verbal behaviour in order to achieve one's communicative goals.

9.14.1   Lexico-suffixal patterns of honorifics

We define honorifics (indexical politeness forms) as grammatical and lexical forms encoding the speaker's socio-culturally appropriate regard towards the addressee (i.e., addressee honorification) and the referent (i.e., referent honorification). Relative interpersonal relationships are elaborately encoded in various linguistic forms to the extent that speech acts cannot be performed without taking the notion of honorifics into account. Sentences cannot be uttered without the speaker's approximate knowledge of his social relationship with the addressee and/or referent in terms of age category (adult, adolescent, or child), social status, kinship, and/or in- and outgroupness. The honorific system of Korean is the most systematic among all known languages. In this respect, Korean may be called an honorific language. In the following are presented the patterns of currently used honorifics many of which have already been presented here and there in relevant chapters.

9.14.1.1   Personal pronouns

Korean has a system of hierarchical personal pronouns, as presented in 8.1.3: first person *ce, na*; second person *elusin, tayk, tangsin, caki, caney, ne*; third person *D pun, D i, D salam, D ay* where D stands for a demonstrative. Recall that, in general, the first person humble form *ce* is used when talking to a senior or an adult equal and the plain form *na* when talking to a child or a younger adult. The second person *elusin* is often used to a respected person of over sixty years of age, while *tayk* 'you' (lit. 'honourable house') is used to refer to an adult stranger and cannot be used to a social superior. The blunt form *tangsin* is used to refer to an adult inferior, e.g., by a boss to his subordinate, except between husband and wife in which case the form carries an affectionate connotation. The familiar form *caney* is used by a superior to a much younger adult or adolescent inferior (e.g., one's adult student), or by a parent-in-law to a son-in-law, etc. The plain form *ne* is used to address or refer to a child or equivalent (e.g., one's own child or grandchild). Thus, except for the rarely used *elusin*, Korean does not have a second person pronoun to refer to a socially superior person. Consequently, Koreans make very extensive use of nominal substitutes such as *sensayng-nim* 'you' (lit. 'esteemed teacher') and *sacang-nim* 'you' (lit. 'esteemed company president').

Note that for third person pronouns, only demonstrative compounds are used, which consist of hierarchical nouns *pun* 'esteemed person', *i* 'person', *salam* 'person', and *ai/ay* 'child'. Between *i* and *salam*, the former is considered relatively higher. A husband refers to his wife with *ce salam* 'that person', whereas a wife refers to her husband with *ce i* 'that person'.

9.14.1.2   Address-reference terms

Korean has an extensive set of hierarchical adddress-reference terms which are sensitive to degrees of social stratification and solidarity between the speaker and the addressee and/or referents. While in English only military and police ranks and some other limited terms like *doctor, professor, father, Mr President, Mr Chairman, sir, madam*, etc. are used as address terms, in Korean all kinds of professional titles (including section chief, division chief, company president, nurse, and taxi or bus driver), as well as extensively diversified kinship terms, are used as address terms. In the following are ordered address-reference terms roughly in decreasing deference and/or distance: FN = full name; SN = surname; GN = given name; GT = general title (e.g., *sensayng* 'sir', *matam* 'madam', *senpay* 'senior', *puin* 'madam', *paksa* 'Dr', *yesa* 'lady', *chongkak* 'young man', *haksayng* 'young person, student'); KT = kinship term (e.g., *hyeng*' (male's) older brother'); PT = professional or occupational title (e.g., *sacang* 'company president', *kwukcang* 'division chief', *moksa* 'pastor'); HTa = highest honorific title (*-kak.ha* 'excellency'); HTb = second-level honorific title (*-nim* 'honourable'); HTc = third-level honorific title (*-ssi* 'Mr/Mrs/Ms'); HTd = fourth-level honorific title (*-kwun* 'Mr', *-yang* 'Miss'); and hon. = honourable.

(243)   Patterns   Examples
           (PT) + HTa: *taythonglyeng-kak.ha*
                                        'His Excellency President'
           GT/KT/PT + HTb: *ape-nim* 'hon. father'
                                        kyoswu-nim 'hon. professor'
           FN/SN + GT/PT + HTb: *Pak (Kinam) taysa-nim*
                                        'hon. ambassador (Kinam) Park'
           GT/KT/PT: *sensayng* 'sir' (lit. 'teacher')
                                        apeci 'father', *kwacang* 'Division Chief'
           FN/SN + GT/PT: *Kim matam* 'Madam Kim'
                                        Pak (Kinam) paksa 'Dr (Kinam) Park'
           takthe/misisu + SN: *takthe Li* 'Dr Lee', *misisu Pak* 'Mrs Park'
           FN + HTc: *Kim Minho-ssi* 'Mr Minho Kim'
                                        Pak Mia-ssi 'Ms Mia Park'
           misuthe/misu + SN: *misuthe Kim* 'Mr Kim', *misu Ko* 'Miss Ko'
           GN + HTc: *Minho-ssi* 'Mr Minho'
           SN + HTc: *Kim-ssi* 'Mr Kim'
           FN/SN + HTd: *Kim (Minho)-kwun* 'Mr (Minho) Kim'
                                        Pak (Mia)-yang 'Miss (Mia) Park '
           GN + HTd: *Minho-kwun* 'Mr Minho'
                                        Mia-yang 'Miss Mia'
           (SN) + GN: *(Kim) Minho* 'Minho (Kim)'
                                        (Pak) Mia 'Mia (Park)'
           GN + familiar vocative particle *i/ZERO*:
                                        Homin i 'Homin!', *Mia* 'Mia!'
           GN + plain vocative particle *a/ya*:
                                        Homin a 'Homin!', *Mia ya* 'Mia!'

Notice that while English honorific titles such as *Mr*, *Mrs*, *Miss*, and *Ms* are used primarily to indicate gender roles and marital status and are not hierachical, Korean HT's are definitely hierarchical. For instance, HTa is generally limited to the President of a nation (this usage is becoming obsolete in favour of HTb), while HTb is widely used for one's superiors or distant adult equals, HTc for colleagues or subordinates, and HTd for much younger inferiors or subordinates.

The most frequently used terms for a social superior or a distant adult equal are GT/KT/PT + HTb and FN/SN + GT/PT + HTb. When *-nim* is removed, no deference is shown, although in kinship terms, intimacy is thereby expressed. Thus, GT and PT without *-nim* are used to address or refer to a close colleague or an adult social inferior. Kinship terms like *puin* 'honourable wife', *oppa* '(female's) older brother', and *enni* '(female's) older sister' cannot take *-nim*. The term *puin* is equivalent to KT + HTb whereas *oppa* and *enni* are equivalent to KT. Noteworthy is the fact that, in speech, a married woman addresses and refers to her parents-in-law with *ape-nim* 'father' and *eme-nim* 'mother' and her own parents with *apeci* and *emeni*.

The title suffixes such as the Sino-Korean *-ssi*, *-kwun*, *-yang*, and loan *misuthe*, *misisu*, *misu*, *takthe*, as well as bare (SN) + GN, do not convey deference. In general, the gender-neutral suffix *-ssi* is extensively used among young company colleagues and college students, or to an adult junior member. The suffixes *-kwun* (to a male) and *-yang* (to a female), as well as (SN) + GN, are used by a senior person to a much younger adult, e.g., from a college professor to his student. Unlike in English, *Mr*, *Mrs*, *Miss*, and *Dr* in Korean are used to an adult equal or junior adult, and never to a senior person. SN + *-ssi* is used to an adult male whose occupation is socially very low, e.g., janitor. This may be because an SN without a GN does not carry any solidarity and *-ssi* does not carry deference. A similar case is that (FN) + *hyeng* 'older brother' is used to address or refer to one's (usually male's) male senior but SN + *hyeng* is used for one's equal or junior.

Personal names with the vocative particle (*i*) are generally used for addressing one's intimate adult friends or one's adult or adolescent students. Personal or other nouns with the particle *(y)a* are for addressing children, as in *Yongho ya* 'Yongho!', *papo ya* 'You fool!' and *apem a* '(child's) Dad!' (addressing one's adult son). Sometimes, *(y)a* is used as a diminutive marker without lowering the honorific level, as in *enni ya* 'Sis!' (female speaker) and *nwuna ya* 'Sis!' (male speaker). All the above terms are used for both address and reference, except for terms with a vocative particle which are used only as address terms.

9.14.1.3 Nouns, predicates, and particles

Korean has a limited set of nouns and predicates to refer to a superior or distant adult's family member, possession, and action, as well as some humble predicates to refer to one's own or an inferior person's action. Humble predicates are transitive, and their direct or indirect object is a superior person. In addition, three particles, nominative (limited to subject function), source, and dative-locative-goal, have corresponding honorific forms. Honorific nominative (subject) and source share the same form, suggesting a functional shift from source to subject. While the neutral ones are used for both children and adults without any particular deference, the honorific ones are used only for adults to indicate special deference.

(244)		Honorific	Plain	Gloss
	noun	*puin/samo-nim*	*che/anay/manwula*	'wife'
		tayk	*cip*	'house'
		atu-nim	*atul*	'son'
		olapeni(m)	*oppa*	'(female's) older brother'
		malssum	*mal*	'words'
		cinci	*pap*	'meal'
		sengham	*ilum*	'name'
		yensey	*nai*	'age'
	predicate	*kyeysita*	*issta*	'stay'
		capswusita	*mekta*	'eat'
		cwumusita	*cata*	'sleep'
		tolaka-sita	*cwukta*	'die'
		Humble	Plain	Gloss
	predicate	*tulita*	*cwuta*	'give'
		mosita	*teylita*	'accompany'
		poypta	*pota*	'see'
		aloyta	*allita*	'inform'
		yeccwuta	*mutta*	'ask'
		Honorific	Neutral	Case
	particle	*kkeyse*	*ka/i*	nominative (subject)
		kkeyse	*eykeyse/hantheyse*	source
		kkey	*eykey/hanthey*	dative/locative/goal

9.14.1.4   Subject- and addressee-honorific suffixes

Korean has a productive suffixal device for subject honorification, employing the inflectional suffix *-(u)si* (-*(u)sy* before a vowel in casual speech) that appears right after a predicate stem when the subject referent deserves the speaker's deference. This suffix has a variant form *-(u)sey* (from *-(u)si* + *-e* in -*e.yo*) before the polite ender *-yo*, as in *kyoswu-nim i ka-sey-yo/ka-sy-e.yo* 'The professor is going.'

Korean also has a suffixal device for addressee honorification. The addressee honorific suffix *-(su)p* (*-sup* after a consonant; *-p* after a vowel) appears only with the deferential speech level, as in *i kulim un coh-**sup**-ni-ta* 'This picture is good' and *ce nun ka-**p**-ni-ta* 'I am going.' In sentences like *Kim-sensayng-nim un ka-**si**-ess-**sup**-ni-kka?* 'Did Professor Kim go?', both the subject referent and the addressee are honorified.

9.14.1.5 Speech levels

Korean has a systematic set of six addressee honorific levels (styles, or 'registers') represented by sentence enders. As already indicated (8.4.3; 9.2.1), the six speech levels are interwoven with the four major sentence-types in suffixal realizations, as shown in (245) where morpheme boundaries are not marked. *-E* indicates the alternation between *-a* (after *a* and *o* in the preceding syllable) and *-e* (elsewhere).

(245)

		Declarative	Interrogative	Imperative	Propositive
	plain	*-ta*	*-ni?/-(nu)nya?*	*-kela/-Ela*	*-ca*
	intimate	*-E*	*-E?*	*-E*	*-E*
	familiar	*-ne-y*	*-na?/-nunka?*	*-key*	*-sey*
	blunt	*-(s)o/-(s)wu*	*-(s)o?/-(s)wu?*	*-(u)o/-wu*	*-(u)psita*
	polite	*-(E.)yo*	*-(E.)yo?*	*-(E.)yo*	*-(E.)yo*
	deferential	*-(su)pnita*	*-(su)pnikka?*	*-sipsio*	*-(u)sipsita*

The blunt-level forms *-(s)o* and *-(u)o* are disappearing from daily usage (probably due to its blunt connotation) or remain in the forms of the less blunt variants *-(s)wu* and *-wu* in the speech of some older generation speakers. The familiar level, typically used by a male adult to an adult inferior or adolescent such as a high school or college student or to one's son-in-law or to an old friend, is also becoming obsolete. Most younger generation speakers use only the deferential, polite, intimate, and plain levels.

The most popular level towards an adult is the polite one, a level less formal than the deferential one. This level is widely used by both males and females in daily conversations. While females predominantly use this level in all conversational situations, males use both the polite and deferential levels to address an equal or superior adult. Even in formal conversations, the deferential and polite levels are intermixed by the same interlocutors in the same discourse. In formal situations such as news reports and public lectures, only the deferential style is used.

The intimate level (polite-level form minus *-yo*), also called a half-talk style, is used by an adult to an adult junior such as a student, by a child of pre-school age to his or her family members including parents and grandparents, or between close friends whose friendship began in childhood or adolescence. This level is frequently intermixed with the plain or familiar level in the same discourse with the same person.

The plain level is used by any speaker to any child, to one's own younger siblings, children, nephews, nieces, or grandchildren regardless of age, to one's daughter-in-law, or between intimate adult friends whose friendship started in childhood, etc.

9.14.2   Syntactic patterns of honorifics

The honorific forms given in 9.14.1 cooccur in sentences. In order to see how, it is essential to distinguish two main dimensions: the dimension of referent honorifics (speaker–referent perspective) and that of addressee honorifics (speaker–addressee perspective). The former concerns the speaker's regard for a referent denoted by a nominal appearing overtly or covertly in a sentence, whereas the latter is associated with the speaker's regard for the addressee in a speech situation, which is usually reflected in the address term and predicate suffixes. In actual speech situations, addressee honorifics are more important and thus more finely segmented than referent honorifics in view of the subtlety of interpersonal feelings and 'face' involved in face-to-face interactions. The dimension of referent honorifics may be subclassified into subject, object, and oblique (e.g., dative, locative, goal, source) honorifics, in that the nominals in these grammatical functions may have deferential forms that trigger deferential or humble predicates. Subject honorifics are the most significant and therefore occur most productively. Many deferential predicates as well as the honorific suffix *-(u)si* are associated with the subject. The syntactic distribution of the two perspectives is llustrated in (246).

(246)   A daughter-in-law to her father-in-law

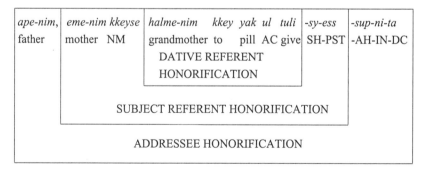

'Father, mother gave medicine to grandmother.'

Object honorification is irrelevant in (246) because *yak* 'pills, medicine' is non-human. Dative honorification is expressed by the honorific forms *halme-nim* 'grandmother' (cf. neutral *halmeni*) and *kkey* 'to' (cf. neutral *eykey* or *hanthey*) as well as by the humble verb *tulita* 'give (to a superior)' (cf. plain *cwuta*). Subject honorification is reflected in the honorific noun *eme-nim* 'mother' (cf. neutral *emeni*), honorific subject particle *kkeyse* (cf. neutral *ka/i*), and the subject honorific suffix *-si*. Addressee honorification is expressed by the honorific address term *ape-nim* 'father' (cf. neutral *apeci*), the addressee honorific suffix *-sup*, and the deferential declarative ender *-ni-ta* which consists of the deferential indicative mood suffix *-ni* and the declarative sentence type suffix *-ta*.

Compared to the honorific expression given in (246), the sentence in (247) is a non-honorific expression, uttered typically by an adult or a child to a child about another child.

(247)   A girl to her friend

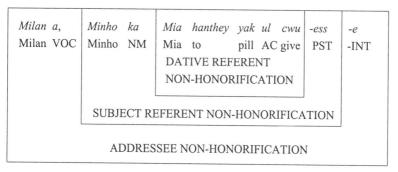

'Milan, Minho gave medicine to Mia.'

Notice in sentences (246) and (247) that honorific forms are spread throughout a sentence, rendering an honorific sentence to look markedly different from its plain counterpart. An honorific expression and its non-honorific counterpart may have the same truth values, but very distinct socio-cultural meanings and connotations. Further notice that addressee (non-)honorifics appear in the outermost layer of a sentence and referent honorifics in the inner layer, with subject honorifics taking a more outside position than dative and object honorifics. Since the addressee is a discoursal element and has no place in the sentential proposition, its honorific or non-honorific expression may occur as a vocative or address term preceding the proposition, with its syntactic reflexes limited to the last part of the predicate (e.g., *-sup-ni-ta*). The distinction between the perspectives of speaker–addressee and speaker–referent is structurally so tenacious that even when the addressee is coreferential to the subject referent, the two are grammatically differentiated, as in **sensayng-nim kkeyse encey** *ttena-si-keyss-sup-ni-kka?* 'When are you going to leave, Professor?', where both the subject honorific suffix and addressee honorific suffix occur.

There are cooccurrence restrictions between an address term and the addressee honorific form of the predicate on the one hand, and between a subject form (e.g., a pronominal or reference term) and the subject honorific form of the predicate on the other. This phenomenon may be termed honorific agreement. If an addressee is the same as the subject referent, agreement must range over the entire sentence, as roughly illustrated in (248). A subject honorific predicate form is either a predicate stem followed by the SH suffix *-(u)si* (or its variant *-(u)sey*) or a fossilized honorific predicate such as *cwumusita* 'sleep', *capswusita* 'eat', or *kyeysita* 'stay, exist'.

(248)	Address form	Subject 'you'	Predicate suffix	AH (speech) level
	elusin	*elusin*	*-(u)si*	def.
	(SN)-*sensayng-nim*	*sensayng-nim*	*-(u)si*	def./polite
	SN-*sensayng*	SN-*sensayng*	*-(u)si*/ZERO	polite/blunt
	yeposeyyo/*yeposio*	*tayk*	*-(u)si*	blunt
	FN-*ssi*	FN-*ssi*/*tangsin*	*-(u)si*/ZERO	polite/blunt
	GN-*kwun*/GN *(i)*	*caney*	ZERO	familiar/intimate
	GN-*ssi, caki (ya)*	GN-*ssi, caki*	ZERO	intimate
	GN *(y)a*	*ne*	ZERO	intimate/plain

Honorific agreement is particularly intriguing regarding the use of the honorific suffix *-(u)si* in relation to its trigger. It is widely held that this suffix is attached to the predicate if the subject of the predicate denotes an adult who deserves the speaker's deference, hence terms like subject honorification and the subject honorific suffix ensued. Thus, the sentence **Kim sensayng-nim kkeyse o-sy-ess-e.yo** 'Professor Kim came' shows that the subject noun phrase denoting a respected person triggers the honorific suffix in the predicate.

The honorific suffix is also triggered by a nominal which is not the subject of the predicate, as in *ce uy* **apeci** *nun khi ka khu-si-p-ni-ta* 'My father is tall', *ce uy* **apeci** *kkey kekceng i manh-***usey***-yo* 'My father has much worry', **apeci** *uy somay ka ccalp-***usey***-yo* 'The sleeves of your clothes are short, Dad', where **apeci**, rather than the subjects of the predicates (i.e., *khi*, *kekceng*, *somay*), triggers the honorific suffix. Notice that all the immediate subjects of the predicates are inanimate, whereas the noun *apeci* which deserves the speaker's deference is a higher subject, a locative, or a possessor. That is, a higher subject, a locative, and a possessor may trigger the honorific suffix *-(u)si* when the direct subject is inanimate. This non-subject honorification is blocked if the direct subject is animate, as in *apeci uy ko.yangi ka khu(*-si)-ta* 'My father's cat is big.' In possessive and locative constructions, there is a distinction between nominals denoting inalienably possessed entities such as body parts, ideas, and health and alienable nominals such as one's books, house, business, cars, clothes, money, flowers, etc. Appearance of the suffix -*(u)si* is obligatory in the former, and optional in the latter. There are many pragmatic factors that affect the presence or absence of the suffix in optional cases. For instance, the suffix is usually used if the person referred to is present in the speech situation, if the person is also the addressee, or if the speaker has a strong feeling of respect toward the referent. For further discussions on subject-honorific agreement, see H.M. Sohn 1992.

Use of propositive sentence enders including the deferential-level -*(u)si-p-si-ta* is generally avoided if the addressee is the speaker's senior adult. This is because the speaker cannot request a social superior to take an action together with himself. Thus, the utterance *sensayng-nim, ce wa hamkkey ttena-si-p-si-ta* 'Professor, let's leave together' sounds very rude when uttered to one's senior. Indirect speech strategies must be employed.

Studies on Korean honorifics include J.R. Hwang 1975; H.S. Wang 1984; C.S. Suh 1984, 1996; K. Sung 1985; H.S. Kim 1991; W.K. Lee 1991; M.R.P. Mun 1991; and S.K. Yun 1993, among many other works.

9.14.3   *Strategic politeness expressions*

In addition to the use of honorifics which are generally normative, linguistic politeness is expressed in many strategic ways. If a speech act is performed for the benefit of the addressee, the utterance is usually direct, often utilizing the imperative sentence type, as strong assertion is frequently needed for politeness. This is particularly true in Korean, as in *ese o-si-p-si-o* 'Welcome' (lit. 'Come quickly') and *annyenghi cwumu-sey-yo* 'Good night' (lit. 'Sleep peacefully').

If a speech act is not for the benefit of the addressee but for the speaker or somebody else, indirect speech acts are felicitous because direct speech acts are often 'face-threatening' to the addressee's positive self-esteem or to his freedom from imposition. Indirect utterances are used especially when the addressee is a senior or a distant equal or the utterances in question are made for the benefit of the speaker. Observe in (249) the decreasing degrees of indirectness which in turn denote decreasing degrees of politeness.

(249)   a. *sillyeyha-p-ni-ta   man, mun com yel-e   cwu-si-keyss-e.yo?*
              be rude-AH-IN-DC but   door just open-INF give-SH-may-POL
              'Excuse me, but would you kindly open the door for me?'

          b. *mun com yel-e cwu-si-keyss-e.yo?*
          c. *mun yel-e cwu-si-keyss-e.yo?*

    d. *mun com yel-e cwu-sey-yo.*

    e. *mun yel-e cwu-sey-yo.*

    f. *mun ye-sey-yo.*

       'Open the door.'

All the above sentences are in the polite speech level, and thus may be uttered to an adult. However, (249f) is a sheer command and thus impolite unless the act of opening the door is for the sake of the addressee. In general, the longer a sentence is, the more indirect and therefore the more polite it is, since more hedges are included. In (249a), several different hedging mechanisms are involved: the request-introducing formula *sillyeyha-p-ni-ta man* 'excuse me but'; the diminutive *com* 'just, a little'; the benefactive auxiliary verb *cwuta* 'do for'; the modal (conjectural) suffix *-keyss* 'may'; and the interrogative sentence type with rising intonation. Use of interrogative sentences for requests has become quite popular recently.

Omission of main clauses is a productive mechanism for performing indirect speech acts since main clauses usually carry the speaker's assertion. By omitting them, the speaker can give the addressee the option of making the final decision on the basis of the background information expressed in the unomitted clause (H.M. Sohn 1990a). Examples include *apeci ka cikum an kyeysi-nu-n tey yo* 'My father is not at home at the moment . . .' and *kulssey-yo, ce nun molu-keyss-sup-ni-ta man* 'Well, I don't think I know but . . .' In many cases, main clause omission has been fossilized to the extent that new sentence enders have developed from the expressed subordinate clause enders (cf. 8.7; 9.8.1; 9.13.3). For instance, the suppositive sentence *ku pun i o-si-l ci yo?* (the person NM come-SH-PRS whether POL) 'I wonder if he will come' must have developed from a negative construction something like *ku pun i o-si-l ci molu-keyss-e.yo* (the person NM come-SH-PRS whether not know-think-POL) 'I don't know whether he will come.' Similarly, the apologetic sentence *ce nun cikum aphu-ketun yo* (I TC now sick-given that POL) '(I am sorry to say but) I am sick now' where the provisional conjunctive suffix *-ketun* 'provided that, given that' occurs must have developed from a provisional construction such as *ce nun cikum aphu-ketun etteh-key ka-keyss-e.yo?* (I TC now sick-given that how go-may-POL) 'Given that I am sick now, how can I possibly go?'

There are many indirect speech acts which are idiomatized. One such case is posing a question to a social superior about his or her name, age, and other things. The formula is *etteh-key toy-sey-yo?* 'What is . . . ?' (lit. 'How does it become?'), as in *ilum i mwe yey-yo?* 'What is you name?' (to a child or a junior adult) vs. *sengham i etteh-key toy-sey-yo?* 'May I ask your name?' (lit. 'How does your name become?') (to a senior or distant adult). For extensive pragmatic studies on linguistic politeness in Korean, see C.H. Cho 1982 and J. Koo 1995.

SELECT BIBLIOGRAPHY

The names of Korean authors and other personal names in this bibliography are transcribed according to their individualized romanizations as much as possible, otherwise to the simplified McCune–Reischauer system *à la* Austerlitz, et al. (1980) or the Yale system. Titles of the journals, books, and articles written in Korean and names of Korean publishers are romanized following the Yale system. Names of all authors begin with a family name followed by a comma and a given name.

Major Korean-related periodicals

Bilingual Education for the Overseas Koreans. Published by the Korean Society of Bilingualism, Seoul.

En.e (*Linguistic Journal of Korea*). Published by the Linguistic Society of Korea, Seoul.

Gyoyug Han-geul. Published by Hankul Hak.hoy (Korean Language Society), Seoul.

Han-geul. Published by Hankul Hak.hoy (Korean Language Society), Seoul.

HSIKL = Harvard Studies in Korean Linguistics. Published by the Department of Linguistics, Harvard University, Boston, Massachusetts.

Hyengthaylon. Published by Pagijong Publishers, Seoul.

JKL = Japanese/Korean Linguistics. Published by the Center for the Study of Language and Information (CSLI), Stanford, California.

Journal of East Asian Linguistics. Published by Kluwer Academic Publishers, the Netherlands.

Korea Journal. Published by the Korean National Commission for UNESCO, Seoul.

Korean Language Education. Published by the International Association for Korean Language Education, Seoul.

Korean Language in America. Published by the American Association of Teachers of Korean.

Korean Linguistics. Published by the International Circle of Korean Linguistics.

Korean Studies. Published by the University of Hawaii Center for Korean Studies and the University of Hawaii Press, Honolulu, Hawaii.

Kwuk.e Kwukmunhak. Published by Kwuk.e Kwukmun Hak.hoy (Korean Language and Literature Society), Seoul.

Kwuk.ehak. Published by Kwuk.e Hak.hoy (Korean Language Association), Seoul.

Language Research. Published by the Language Research Institute of Seoul National University.

Mal. Published by the Yonsei University Korean Language Institute, Seoul.

Munpep Yenkwu. Published by Munpep Yenkwuhoy (Grammar Study Circle) and Tower Publisher, Seoul.

Say Kwuk.e Saynghwal. Published by the National Academy of Korean Language Research, Seoul.

The Sociolinguistic Journal of Korea. Published by the Sociolinguistic Society of Korea, Seoul.

Books, dissertations, and articles

Abasolo, R. 1974. *Basic Semantic Structures of Korean*. Seoul: Tower

Ahn, Hee-Don. 1991. Light verbs, VP-movement, negation and clausal architecture in Korean and English. Ph.D. dissertation. University of Wisconsin at Madison.

Ahn, Jeong Khun. 1987. *The Social Stratification of Umlaut in Korean*. Seoul: Hanshin.

Ahn, Joo-Hoh. 1994. Tongsa eyse phasayngtoyn ilunpa 'hwuchisalyu' uy munpephwa yenkwu (A study on the grammaticalization of so-called postpositions from verbs). *Mal* 19:133-54.

Ahn, Joo-Hoh. 1996. Myengsa phasayng uy munpephwa yenkwu: '*the.h*' lul cwungsim ulo (A study on grammaticalization in noun derivation: with reference to *the.h*). *Language Research* 32.1:101–35.

Ahn, Sang-Cheol. 1985. *The Interplay of Phonology and Morphology in Korean*. Seoul: Hanshin.

Ahn, Sung-Ho. 1990. Korean quantification and universal grammar. Ph.D. dissertation. University of Connecticut.

AKS (Academy of Korean Studies). 1986–94. *Hankwuk Pangen Calyocip* (Collections of Korean Dialectal Data).

An, Byong-Hi. 1971. Hankwuk.e paltalsa 2: Munpepsa (A history of Korean 2: grammar). *Hankwuk Munhwasa Taykyey* (An Outline of Korean Cultural History) 5:165–261. Seoul: Korea University Press.

An, Byong-Hi. 1992. *Kwuk.esa Yenkwu* (A Historical Study of Korean Linguistics). Seoul: Munhak kwa Cisengsa.

An, Byong-Hi and Kwang-Ho Lee. 1990. *Cwungsey Kwuk.e Munpeplon* (A Study of Middle Korean Grammar). Seoul: Hak.yensa.

An, Dong-Hwan. 1980. Semantics of tense markers. Ph.D. dissertation. Georgetown University.

An, Hwak. 1915. Cosen.e uy kachi (Values of Korean). *Hak ci Kwang* 3. Seoul.

An, Hwak. 1922. *Cosen.e Wenlon* (Principles of Korean). Seoul: Han.il Secem.

Aston, W.G. 1879. A comparative study of the Japanese and Korean languages. *Journal of the Royal Asiatic Society of Great Britain and Ireland*. New Series 11.3. (A shortened Japanese version appears in Ikeda and Ohno 1973:353–76.)

Austerlitz, R., Chin-W. Kim, S.E. Martin, S.R. Ramsey, Ho-min Sohn, Seok Choong Song, and E.W. Wagner. 1980. Report of the workshop conference on Korean romanization. *Korean Studies* 4:111–25.

Baek, Eung-Jin. 1984. *Modern Korean Syntax*. Seoul: Cengmin.

Baek, Eung-Jin (ed.). 1988. *Papers from the Sixth International Conference on Korean Linguistics*. Seoul: Hanshin.

Baek, Eung-Jin (ed.). 1990. *Papers from the Seventh International Conference on Korean Linguistics*. Toronto: University of Toronto Press.

Baik, Woonil. 1994. An electropalatographic study of coarticulation in Korean VCV and CVC sequences. Ph.D. dissertation. Georgetown University.

Bak, Sung-Yun. 1981. Studies in Korean syntax: ellipsis, topic and relative constructions. Ph.D. dissertation. University of Hawaii.

Bak, Sung-Yun. 1987. Conditionals in Korean. *HSIKL* II:163–73.

Bak, Sung-Yun. 1997. PAKK EY uy munpephwa hyensang (Grammaticalization in PAKK EY). *En.e* 22.1:57–70.

Barringer, H.R. and Sung-Nam Cho. 1989. *Koreans in the United States*. University of Hawaii Center for Korean Studies Monograph 15.

Bing, Li. 1996. Tungusic vowel harmony – description and analysis. Ph.D. dissertation. University of Amsterdam.

Blank, Lenore Kim. 1981. Language policies in South Korea since 1945 and their impact on education. Ed.D. dissertation. University of San Francisco.

Boller, A. 1857. Nachweis, dass das Japanische zum ural-altaischen Stamme gehort. *Sitzungsberichte der philos.-histor. Classe der kais* (Akademie der Wissenschaften, Wien) 33:393–481.

Burrow, T. and M.B. Emeneau. 1966. *A Dravidian Etymological Dictionary.* Oxford: Clarendon.

CEH (Caha Emun Hak.hoy) 1990. *Puk.han uy Cosen.ehak* (Korean Linguistics in North Korea). Seoul: Hanshin.

Ceng, Inci. 1446. *Hwunmin Cengum Haylyey* (Explanations and Examples of the *Hwunmin Cengum*).

Ceng, Yelmo. 1927–28. Cosen.ehak kayyo (An introduction to Korean linguistics). *Han-geul* 1.2 – 1.7 (1927); 2.1 (1928).

Chang, Kyung-Hee. 1985. *Hyentay Kwuk.e uy Yangsang Pemcwu Yenkwu* (A Study of Korean Mood Categories). Seoul: Tower.

Chang, Namgui. 1982. *Phonological Variations in 15th Century Korean. Journal of Chinese Linguistics* Monograph 1. University of California at Berkeley.

Chang, Suk-Jin. 1973. *A Generative Study of Discourse: Pragmatic Aspects of Korean with Reference to English. Language Research* 9.2 Supplement.

Chang, Suk-Jin. 1996. *Korean.* Amsterdam/Philadelphia: John Benjamins.

Cheun, Sang-Buom. 1975. *Phonological Aspects of Late Middle Korean.* Seoul: Pan Korea Book Corporation.

Cho, Choon-Hak. 1982. *A Study of Korean Pragmatics: Deixis and Politeness.* Seoul: Hanshin.

Cho, Dong-In. 1994. A comparative study of focus construction. Ph.D. dissertation. University of Southern California.

Cho, Euiyon. 1988. *Some Interactions of Grammar and Pragmatics in Korean.* Seoul: Hanshin.

Cho, Jai-Hyong. 1994. Scrambling in Korean: crossover, reconstruction and binding theory. Ph.D. dissertation. University of Connecticut.

Cho, Mi-Hui. 1994. Vowel harmony in Korean: a grounded phonology approach. Ph.D. dissertation. Indiana University. A shortened version appears in *JKL* 4:431–45.

Cho, Seung-Bok. 1967. *A Phonological Study of Korean.* Uppsala: Almqvist and Wiksells.

Cho, Sook Whan and Hyon Ho Lee (eds.). 1992. *A Festschrift for Tae-ok Kim.* Seoul: Hankwuk Munhwasa.

Cho, Sungdai. 1995. On verbal intransitivity in Korean: with special reference to middle constructions. Ph.D. dissertation. University of Hawaii.

Cho, Young-mee Yu. 1990. Parameters of consonantal assimilation. Ph.D. dissertation. Stanford University.

Cho, Young-mee Yu and S. Inkelas. 1994. Post-obstruent tensification in Korean and geminate inalterability. In Kim-Renaud 1994:45–60.

Cho, Young-mee Yu and P. Sells. 1995. A lexical account of inflectional suffixes in Korean. *Journal of East Asian Linguistics* 4:119–74.

Choe, Hyon Sook. 1988. *Restructuring Parameters and Complex Predicates: a Transformational Approach.* Seoul: Hanshin.

Choe, Jae-Woong. 1987. Anti-quantifiers and a theory of distributivity. Ph.D. dissertation. University of Massachusetts.

Choi, Eun Young. 1991. Postlexical phonology in Korean. Ph.D. dissertastion. University of Washington.

Choi, Jae Oh. 1992. Licensing in Korean: multiple case, predication, control, and anaphora. Ph.D. dissertation. New York University.

Choi, Soon-Ja. 1986. A cross-linguistic development study of negation in English, French, and Korean. Ph.D. dissertation. State University of New York at Buffalo.

Choi, Yeon Hee. 1988. Textual coherence in English and Korean: an analysis of argumentative writing by American and Korean students. Ph.D. dissertation, University of Illinois at Urbana-Champaign.

Choi, Young-Seok. 1988. A study of ascension constructions in Korean. Ph.D. dissertation. University of Hawaii.

Chon, Su-Tae and Hochol Choy. 1989. *Nampuk.han En.e Pikyo* (A Linguistic Comparison between South and North Korea). Seoul: Nokcin.

Chon, Yong-U. 1992. *Phyocwun Hankwuk.e Pal.um Sacen* (A Dictionary of Korean Pronunciation). Seoul: Cipmuntang.

Chong, Mi-Ja. 1987. A study of the function of tense and aspect in Korean narrative discourse. Ph.D. dissertation. Ball State University.

Choo, Miho. 1994. A unified account of null pronouns in Korean. Ph.D. dissertation. University of Hawaii.

Choe, Dong-Joo. 1999. 'i' kyey thukswu cosa uy munpephwa (Grammaticalization of the copula constructions). *Hyengthaylong* 1.1:43–60.

Choy, Hak-Kun. 1974. *Hankwuk Pangen Sacen* (A Dictionary of Korean Dialects). Seoul: Hyenmunsa.

Choy, Hyen-Pay 1929. *Wuli Malpon* (Our Grammar). Seoul: Yonsei University Press.

Choy, Hyen-Pay. 1937 (1959, 1965, 1971). *Wuli Malpon* (Our Grammar) Seoul: Cengumsa.

Choy, Hyen-Pay. 1942. *Hankulkal* (A Study of Hankul). Seoul: Cengumsa.

Choy, Hyen-Pay. 1961. *Kochin Hankulkal* (A Revised Study of Hankul). Seoul: Cengumsa.

Choy, Seycin. 1527. *Hwunmong Cahoy* (Explanations of Chinese Characters with Hankul).

Choy, Tae-Young. 1991. *Hankul Macchwumpep Kanghay* (Explications of Korean Spelling Conventions). Seoul: Sungsil University Press.

Choy, Ung-Gu. 1980. *Cosen.e Ehwilon* (Korean Lexicology). Sim.yang, China: Lyonyeng Inmin Chwulphansa.

Chung, Chan. 1995. A lexical approach to word order variation in Korean. Ph.D. dissertation. Ohio State University.

Chung, Gyeonghee. 1994. Case and its acquisition in Korean. Ph.D. dissertation. University of Texas at Austin.

Chung, Kook. 1980. Neutralization in Korean: a functional view. Ph.D. dissertation. University of Texas at Austin.

Chung, Taegoo. 1993. Argument structure and serial verbs in Korean. Ph.D. dissertation. University of Texas at Austin.

Chung, Young-Hee. 1991. The lexical tone system of North Kyungsang Korean. Ph.D. dissertation. Ohio State University.

Ci, Sekyeng. 1905. *Sinceng Kwukmun* (New Korean). Seoul: Kwanpo.

Clippinger, M.E. 1984. Korean and Dravidian: Lexical evidence for an old theory. *Korean Studies* 8:1–57.

CMS (*Cosen Munhwa.e Sacen*) (A Dictionary of Cultured Language). 1973. Phyengyang: Sahoykwahak Chwulphansa.

Cook, Eung-Do. 1968. Embedding transformations in Korean syntax. Ph.D. dissertation. University of Alberta.

Cwu, Sikyeng. 1905. *Kwukmun Munpep* (A Grammar of Korean Sentences). ms.

Cwu, Sikyeng. 1909. *Kwukmun Yenkwu* (A Study of Korean). ms.

Cwu, Sikyeng. 1910. *Kwuk.e Munpep* (A Korean Grammar). Seoul: Pakmun Sekwan.

Cwu, Sikyeng. 1914. *Mal uy Soli* (Speech Sounds). Seoul: Sinmunkwan.

Davis, S. and In-Seong Lee. 1994. Infixal reduplication in Korean ideophones. *JKL* 4:447–60.

Dempwolff, O. 1934. *Vergleichende Lautlehre des austronesischen Wortschatzes*, I. Berlin-Hamburg. 1937. II, ibid; 1938. III, ibid.

Dredge, C.P. 1977. Speech variation and social structure in a Korean village. Ph.D. dissertation. Harvard University.

Eckardt, A. 1966. *Koreanisch und Indogermanisch*. Heidelberg: Julius Groos.

Edkins, J. 1898. Etymology of Korean numerals. *The Korean Repository* V.9.

Eom, Ik-sang. 1991. A comparative phonology of Chinese and Sino-Paekche Korean. Ph.D. dissertation. Indiana University.

Fujioka, Katsuji. 1908. Nihongo no ichi (The position of Japanese). *Kokugakuin Zasshi* 14.8. Also in Ikeda and Ohno 1973:334–49.

Gale, J.S. 1894. *Korean Grammatical Forms*. Seoul: Trilingual.

Gale, J.S. 1897. *A Korean–English Dictionary*. Yokohama: Kelly and Walsh.

Gerdts, D.B. 1991. Case, chomage, and multipredicate domains in Korean. *HSIKL* IV:249–68.

Gim, Sheon-Gi. 1933. Kyengum uy poncil (The nature of tensification). *Han-geul* 1.

Gim, Sheon-Gi. 1938. *The Phonetics of Korean*. M.A. thesis. University of London. Seoul: Myongji University Press (1971).

Gim, Sheon-Gi. 1968a. Han, il, mong tan.e pikyo yenkwu (A comparative study of Korean, Japanese, and Mongolian words). *Han-geul* 142.

Gim, Sheon-Gi. 1968b. A comparative study of numerals of Korean, Japanese, and Altaic languages. *Myongji University Journal* 1.

Gim, Sheon -Gi. 1993. *Yeyscek Nolay uy Sayphul.i* (New Analyses of Old Songs). Seoul: Poseng Munhwasa.

Gyoyug Han-Geul 10. 1997. *Seykyey Kakkwuk uy Hankwuk.e Yenkwu Hyenhwang kwa Kyoyuk Panghyang* (Research Situations and Educational Directions of the Korean Language Worldwide). Seoul: Hankul Hak.hoy.

Haguenauer, C. 1956. *Origines de la civilisation japonaise: Introduction à l'étude de la préhistoire du Japon, première partie*. Paris: Imprimerie Nationale.

Hahn, Kyung-Ja Park. 1979. Development of negation in one Korean Child. Ph.D. dissertation. University of Hawaii.

Ham, Soonai. 1988. *A Study of Temporal Variables in English and Korean: Cross-linguistic, Developmental, and Native/Non-native Analyses*. Seoul: Hanshin.

Han, Eunjoo. 1990. Glide formation in Korean. *JKL* 1:173–86.

Han, Eunjoo. 1994. A prosodic analysis of Korean compounding. In Kim-Renaud 1994:61–76.

Han, Hak-Sung. 1987. *The Configurational Structure of the Korean Language*. Seoul: Hanshin.

Han, Mieko S. 1966. *Studies in the Phonology of Asian Languages* I: *Duration of Korean Vowels*. Acoustic Phonetics Research Lab. University of Southern California.

Han, Mieko S. and R.S. Weitzman. 1970. Acoustic features of Korean /P, T, K/, /p, t, k/ and /ph, th, kh/. *Phonetica* 22:112–28.

Hashimoto, Mantaro. 1973. Hankwuk.e accent uy um.wunlon (Phonology of Korean acent). *Han-geul* 151:3–34.

Hattori, Shiro. 1974. *Nihongo no Keito* (Geneaogy of Japanese). Tokyo: Iwanami Shoten.

Hong, Kimun. 1947. *Cengum Paltalsa* (A History of the Development of the Korean Alphabet). Seoul: Sewul Sinmunsa

Hong, Kimun. 1959. Cosen.e wa mongko.e wa uy kwankyey (The relationship between Korean and Mongolian). *Cosen Emun* 6:77–82.

Hong, Kimun. 1966. *Cosen.e Lyeksa Munpep* (A Historical Grammar of Korean). Phyengyang: Kwahak.wen.

Hong, Ki-Sun. 1991. Argument selection and case marking in Korean. Ph.D. dissertation. Stanford University.

Hong, Sungshim. 1985. *A and A' Binding in Korean and English: Government-Binding Parameters*. Seoul: Hanshin.

Hong, Yunsook. 1977. Hankwuk.e icilhwa uy kwucocek yenkwu (A structural study of Korean language divergence). *Thongil Cengchayk* 3.3:1–80.

Hong, Yunsook. 1988. *A Sociolinguistic Study of Seoul Korean*. Seoul: Hanshin.

Huh, Byok. 1994. Han-cwung yang kwuk.e uy ehwi pikyo yenkwu (A comparative study of Korean and Chinese vocabularies). *Mal* 19:5–26.

Huh, Woong. 1965. *Kwuk.e Um.wunhak* (Korean Phonology). Seoul: Cengumsa.

Huh, Woong. 1972. *Cwungsey Kwuk.e Yenkwu* (A Study of Middle Korean). Seoul: Cengumsa.

Huh, Woong. 1975. *Wuli Yeys Malpon: Hyengthaylon* (Middle Korean Morphology). Seoul: Saym Munhwasa.

Huh, Woong. 1983. Development of the Korean language. In Korean National Commission for UNESCO 1983:1–12.

Huh, Woong. 1984. *Kwuk.ehak* (Korean Linguistics). Seoul: Saym Munhwasa.

Huh, Woong. 1985. Tone in Kyongsang dialect. *Korea Journal* 25.6:19–32.

Huh, Woong. 1995. *20 Seyki Wulimal uy Hyengthaylon* (Morphology of 20th Century Korean). Seoul: Saym Munhwasa.

Hulbert, H.B. 1905. *A Comparative Grammar of the Korean Language and the Dravidian Languages of India.* Seoul: Methodist Publishing House.

Hur, Kwang Il. 1991. Tone in Middle Korean predicates. Ph.D. dissertation. Georgetown University.

Hwang, Huy-yeng. 1978. *Hankwuk Kwan.yong.e Yenkwu* (A Study of Korean Idioms). *Sengkok Nonchong* 9. Seoul: Sengkok Hakswul Munhwa Caytan.

Hwang, Juck-Ryoon. 1975. Role of sociolinguistics in foreign language education with reference to Korean and English: terms of address and levels of deference. Ph.D. dissertation. University of Texas at Austin.

Hyeklyen, Ceng. 1074–5. *Kyun.ye Cen* (Life of the Great Master Kyun.ye).

Hyengthaylon (Morphology) 1.1. 1999. Edited by Young-Gun Ko (Seoul National University Department of Korean Language and Literature).

Ihm, H.B., K.P. Hong, and S.I. Chang. 1988. *Korean Grammar for International Learners.* Seoul: Yonsei University Press.

Ikeda, Jiro and Susumu Ohno (eds.). 1973. *Ronshu, Nihon Bunka no Kigen* (Anthology on the Origin of Japanese Culture) V: *Nihonjinshuron, gengogaku* (Japanese Ethnology and Linguistics). Tokyo: Heibonsha.

Il.yen. 1285. *Samkwuk Yusa* (Memorabilia of the Three Kingdoms).

Itabashi, Yoshizo. 1987. Altaic evidence for the Japanese and Korean case suffix system. Ph.D. dissertation. University of Washington.

Iverson, G.K. and Hyang-Sook Sohn. 1994. Liquid representation in Korean. In Kim-Renaud 1994:77–100.

Izui, Hisanosuke. 1953. Nihongo to nanto shogo (Japanese and the languages of the Southern Islands). *Minzokugaku Kenkyu* 17.2.

Jeon, Jae-Ho. 1992. *Kwuk.e Ehwisa Yenkwu* (A Study of the History of the Korean Lexicon). Taykwu, Korea: Kyongbuk University Press.

Jeong, Dong-Bin. 1984. The effect of time compressed and time expanded English and Korean passages upon auditory comprehension by adult Korean listeners. Ph.D. dissertation. Wichita State University.

Jeong, Hy-Sook. 1992. A valency subcategorization of verbs in Korean and Russian: a lexicase dependency approach. Ph.D. dissertation. University of Hawaii.

Jeong, Weon-Don. 1992. Word formation and interface phenomena in the Korean lexicon. Ph.D. dissertation. University of Hawaii.

Jeong, Yeon-Chan. 1968. Antong cipang pangen uy sengco (Antong dialect tones). *Sengtay Munhak* 14:70–86.

Jeong, Yeon-Chan. 1971. Cwungsey sengco wa kyengsangto pangen sengco uy pikyo (A comparison between Middle Korean and Kyengsang province tones). *Hankul Hak.hoy 50 Tol Kinyem Nonmuncip,* 29–46. Seoul: Korean Language Society.

Jeong, Yeon-Chan. 1972. Cwungsey kwuk.e sengco uy pyentong kwa kiponhyeng (Variations in Middle Korean tones and their basic forms). *Han-geul* 150.

Jeong, Yeon-Chan. 1985. On the functional load of the tonemes in Korean phonology. *Korea Journal* 25.6:5–13.

Jhang, Sea-Eun. 1994. Headed nominalizations in Korean: relative clauses, clefts, and comparatives. Ph.D. dissertation. Simon Fraser University.

Jo, Mi-Jeung. 1986. Fixed word order and the theory of the pre-verbal focus position in Korean. Ph.D. dissertation. University of Washington.

Jones, G.H. 1892. Korean etymology. *The Korean Repository* I.11.

Joo, Yanghee Shim. 1989. A cross-linguistic approach to quantification in syntax. Ph.D. dissertation. University of Wisconsin at Madison.

Joo-Hwang, Shin-Ja. 1981. Aspects of Korean narration. Ph.D. dissertation. University of Texas at Arlington.

Jun, Sun-Ah. 1993. The phonetics and phonology of Korean prosody. Ph.D. dissertation. Ohio State University.

Jung, Yeon Chang, 1990. Discourse and recursive categorial syntax: a study of Korean particles with focus on subjects. Ph.D. dissertation. University of Washington.

Kanazawa, Shosaburo. 1910. *Nikkan Ryookokugo Dookeiron* (A Study of the Japanese–Korean Genetic Relationship). Tokyo: Sanseido.

Kang, Beom-mo. 1988. Functional inheritance, anaphora, and semantic interpretation in a generalized categorial grammar. Ph.D. dissertation. Brown University.

Kang, Hyunsook and Borim Lee. 1997. Generalized alignment and prosodic categorization in Korean. *JKL* 6:303–18.

Kang, Myung-Yoon. 1988. Topics in Korean syntax: phrase structure, variable and movement. Ph.D. dissertation. Massachusetts Institute of Technology.

Kang, Ongmi. 1993. Prosodic word-level rules in Korean. *JKL* 2:147–63.

Kang, Sahie. 1990. Discourse conditions and the Korean anaphora. Ph.D. dissertation. University of Florida.

Kang, Sun Young. 1992. Serial verb in Korean. In S.W. Cho and H.H. Lee 1992:513–31.

Kang, Yongsoon. 1991. Phonology of consonant–vowel interaction: with special reference to Korean and dependency phonology. Ph.D. dissertation. University of Illinois at Urbana-Champaign.

Kang, Young Eun. 1994. Weak and strong interpretations of quantifiers and definite NPs in English and Korean. Ph.D. dissertation. University of Texas at Austin.

Kang, Young-Se. 1986. Korean syntax and universal grammar. Ph.D. dissertation. Harvard University.

Kawamoto, Takao. 1974. Agreements and disagreements in morphology between Japanese and Austronesian (chiefly Melanesian) languages. *Minzokugaku Kenkyu* 39.2:113–29.

Kawamoto, Takao. 1977. Toward a comparative Japanese–ustronesian I. *Bulletin of Nara University of Education* 26.1:23–49.

Kawanishi, Y. and Sung-Ock Sohn. 1993. The grammaticalization of Korean negation: a semantic-pragmatic analysis of *-canh. HSIKL* V:552–61.

Kholodovich, A.A. 1939. *Grammatika Koreiskogo yazyka* (A Korean Grammar). Moscow.

Kim, Alan Hyun-Oak. 1985. *The Grammar of Focus of Korean Syntax and Its Typological Implications*. Seoul: Hanshin.

Kim, Andrew-Inseok. 1988. Iconicity as a constraint on first and second language acquisition: relativization in Korean and English. Ph.D. dissertation. Columbia University.

Kim, Bang-Han. 1981. The relationship between the Korean and Japanese languages. *Han-geul* 173/174.

Kim, Bang-Han. 1984. *Hankwuk.e uy Kyeythong* (Genealogy of Korean). Seoul: Min.umsa.

Kim, Cha-Kyun. 1970. Kyengnam pangen uy sengco yenkwu (A study of Kyengsang dialect tones). *Han-geul* 145:109–49.

Kim, Cha-Kyun. 1973. Kwuk.e sengcolon kwa sepu kyengnam pangen uy sengco (Korean tonology and Western Kyengnam tones). *Han-geul* 152:75–115.

Kim, Chang-Sop. 1996. *Kwuk.e uy Tan.e Hyengseng kwa Tan.e Kwuco Yenkwu* (A Study on Word Formation and Word Structure in Korean). Seoul: Thayhaksa.

Kim, Chang-Sop. 1998. Ceptwusa uy sacencek cheli (Lexicographic treatment of prefixes). *Say Kwuk.e Saynghwal* 8.1:5–22.

Kim, Chin-W. (ed.). 1978a. *Papers in Korean Linguistics.* Columbia, S.C.: Hornbeam.

Kim, Chin-W. 1978b. Linguistics and language policies in North Korea. *Korean Studies* 2:159–75.

Kim, Chin-W. 1988. *Sojourns in Language,* I and II. Seoul: Tower.

Kim, Chong-Taek. 1993. *Kwuk.e Ehwilon* (Korean Lexicology). Seoul: Tower.

Kim, D.W. 1987. Some phonetic aspects of intervocalic oral stop consonants in British English and Korean. Ph.D. dissertation. University of Reading.

Kim, Eunil. 1992. Voice in Korean. Ph.D. dissertation. University of Colorado at Boulder.

Kim, Gwee-Sook. 1993. On the distribution of the accusative marker in Korean: micro and macro analysis. Ph.D. dissertation. Columbia University.

Kim, Gyung-Ran. 1988. The pitch-accent system of the Taegu dialect of Korean with emphasis of tone sandhi at the phrasal level. Ph.D. dissertation. University of Hawaii.

Kim, Haeyeon. 1992. Clause combining in Korean discourse. Ph.D. dissertation. University of Hawaii.

Kim, Han-Kon. 1982. CAUSE as the deep semantic source of so-called 'causative' and 'passive'. *Language Research* 18.1:171–96.

Kim, Hye-sook. 1990. Reflexive relationship between address forms and context: a case study of Korean spouses. Ph.D. dissertation. University of Massachusetts.

Kim, Hyey-Suk. 1991. *Hyentay Kwuk.e uy Sahoy.en.ehakcek Yenkwu* (A Sociolinguistic Study of Contemporary Korean). Seoul: Thayhaksa.

Kim, Hyong-Joong. 1991. A unified set of features for Korean vowel harmony. *HSIKL* IV:107–18.

Kim, Hyong-Kyu. 1962. *Kwuk.esa Yenkwu* (A Historical Study of Korean). Seoul: Ilcokak.

Kim, Hyong-Kyu. 1972. *Kwuk.ehak kaylon* (An Introduction to Korean Linguistics). Seoul: Ilcokak.

Kim, Hyong-Kyu. 1982. *Hankwuk Pangen Yenkwu* (A Study of Korean Dialects), I and II. Seoul: Seoul National University Press.

Kim, Hyoung Youb. 1990. Voicing and tensification in Korean: a multi-face approach. Ph.D. dissertation. University of Illinois at Urbana-Champaign.

Kim, Hyung-Ok. 1994. A Descriptive analysis of errors and error patterns in consecutive interpretation from Korean to English. Ph.D. dissertation. Illinois State University.

Kim, Insoo. 1992. On the condition of syntactic recoverability of null arguments in Korean. Ph.D. dissertation. University of Florida.

Kim, Jae-Min. 1990. Coreference phenomena in Korean: a functional analysis. Ph.D. dissertation. University of Georgia.

Kim, Jee Eun. 1993. Semantic subcategorization of Korean for natural language processing. Ph.D. dissertation. Georgetown University.

Kim, Jeongdal. 1993. The serial verb construction in Korean. Ph.D. dissertation. University of Southern California.

Kim, Jeong-Ryeol. 1991. A lexical-functional grammar account of light verbs. Ph.D. dissertation. University of Hawaii.

Kim, Jinkyoung. 1996. *Negation in Korean: A Functional and Discourse Approach.* Seoul: Hankwuk Publishers.

Kim, Jong Shil. 1992. Word formation, the prosodic word, and word level phonology in Korean. Ph.D. dissertation. University of Texas at Austin.

Kim, Jong-Mi. 1986. Phonology and syntax of Korean morphology. Ph.D. dissertation. University of Southern California.

Kim, Jong-Yule. 1974. Basic structures and transformational derivations of complex sentences in Korean. Ph.D. dissertation. Columbia University.

Kim, Jung-Ran. 1994. Korean topic construction. Ph.D. dissertation. University of Maryland.

Kim, Kee-Ho. 1987. *The Phonological Representation of Distinctive Features: Korean Consonantal Phonology*. Seoul: Hanshin.

Kim, Kong-Chil. 1995. *Wensi Han.il Kongthong.e uy Yenkwu* (A Study on Ancient Korean–Japanese Cognates). Seoul: Hankwuk Munhwasa.

Kim, Kong-On. 1974. Temporal structure of spoken Korean: an acoustic phonetic study. Ph.D. dissertation. University of Southern California.

Kim, Kun-Su. 1961. Itwu yenkwu (A study of itwu). *Asey.a Yenkwu* 4.1:87–139.

Kim, Kwangjo. 1991. A phonological study of Middle Mandarin: reflected in Korean source of the mid-15th and early 16th centuries. Ph.D. dissertation. University of Washington.

Kim, Kyey-Gon. 1996. *Hyentay Kwuk.e uy Coepep Yenkwu* (A Study on Word Formation in Contemporary Korean). Seoul: Pagijong.

Kim, Kyunghwan. 1994. The syntax and semantics of causative construction in Korean. Ph.D. dissertation. University of Chicago.

Kim, Kyusik. 1912. *Cosen Munpep* (A Korean Grammar). mimeographed.

Kim, Mi-ran Cho. 1994. Acoustic characteristics of Korean stops and perception of English stop consonants. Ph.D. dissertation. University of Wisconsin at Madison.

Kim, Min-Su. 1957. *Cwuhay Hwunmin Cengum* (Annotated *Hwunmin Cengum*). Seoul: Thongmunkwan.

Kim, Min-Su. 1972. Pukhan uy en.e cengchayk (North Korean language policies). *Asey.a Yenkwu* 15.4:1–53.

Kim, Min-Su. 1983. *Sinkwuk.ehak* (A New Korean Grammar). Seoul: Ilcokak.

Kim, Min-Su (ed.). 1991. *Puk.han uy Cosen.e Yenkwusa* (*1945–1990*) (A History of Linguistic Studies of Korean in North Korea (1945–1990)). four volumes. Seoul: Nokcin.

Kim, Nam-Kil. 1984. *The Grammar of Korean Complementation*. University of Hawaii Center for Korean Studies Monograph 11.

Kim, Nam-Kil (ed.). 1986. *Studies in Korean Language and Linguistics*. Los Angeles: University of Southern California East Asian Studies Center.

Kim, No-Ju. 1994. Are there phonological contour tones in the North Kyungsang dialect of Korean? *JKL* 4:493–509.

Kim, No-Ju. 1996. Five types of segmental-prosodic rules that affect the tone bearing unit of North Kyungsang Korean. *JKL* 5:425–42.

Kim, Pokyem. 1960. Gehort die koreanische Sprache zur altaischen Sprachfamilie? *Hankwuk Munhwa Yenkwuwen Nonchong* 2.1:115–75. Seoul: Ewha Women's University Press.

Kim, Pusik. 1145. *Samkwuk Saki* (Historical Record of the Three Kingdoms).

Kim, Sayep. 1974. *Kodai Chosengo to Nihongo* (Old Korean and Old Japanese). Tokyo: Kodansha.

Kim, Seok-Duk (ed.). *Linguistics in the Morning Calm II*. Seoul: Hanshin.

Kim, Seongchan. 1995. The acquisition of WH-questions in English and Korean. Ph.D. dissertation. University of Hawaii.

Kim, Soo-Gon. 1976. *Palatalization in Korean*. Seoul: Tower.

Kim, Soon-Ham Park. 1967. A transformational analysis of negation in Korean. Ph.D. dissertation. University of Michigan.

Kim, Sung-Gon. 1989. *Wulimal Thossi uy Yenkwu* (A Study on Korean Particles). Seoul: Konguk University Press.

Kim, Sung-Uk. 1983. Topic realization in Korean: sentence-initial position of the particle *nun*. Ph.D. dissertation. University of Florida.

Kim, Tae Han. 1975. The grammar of Korean nominalizations and relativizations. Ph.D. dissertation. Claremont Graduate School.

Kim, Tong-Kug. 1995. Case realization and focus marker assignment in Korean and theory of morphological case. Ph.D. dissertation. University of North Carolina at Chapel Hill.

Kim, Twupong. 1916. *Cosen Malpon* (A Korean Grammar). Seoul: Sinmunkwan.

Kim, Twupong. 1924. *Kipte Cosen Malpon* (Revised Korean Grammar). Seoul: Cwungtong Sekwan.

Kim, Wan Jin. 1967. Hankwuk.e paltalsa 1: um.wunsa (A history of Korean 1: phonology). *Hankwuk Munhwasa Taykyey* (An Outline of Korean Cultural History) 5:113–64. Seoul: Korea University Press.

Kim, Wan Jin. 1971. *Kwuk.e Um.wunlon Cheykyey uy Yenkwu* (A Study of the Korean Phonological System). Seoul: Ilcokak.

Kim, Wan Jin. 1973. Cwungsey kwuk.e sengco uy yenkwu (A study on Middle Korean tones). Ph.D. dissertation. Seoul National University.

Kim, Wha-Chun M. 1976. The theory of anaphora in Korean syntax. Ph.D. dissertation. Massachusetts Institute of Technology.

Kim, Woo-che. 1995. Attitude and motivation of United States military personnel learning Korean as a foreign language. Ph.D. dissertation. University of San Francisco.

Kim, Woo-Ho. 1994. Grammatical relations and anaphora in Korean. Ph.D. dissertation. University of Colorado at Boulder.

Kim, Yang Soon. 1988. *Licencing Principles and Phrase Structure*. Seoul: Hanshin.

Kim, Yeong-Bae. 1977. *Phyengan Pangen uy Um.wun Cheykyey Yenkwu* (A Phonological Study of the Phyengan Dialect). Seoul: Dongguk University Institute of Korean Studies.

Kim, Yeong-Bae. 1992. *Nampuk.han uy Pangen Yenkwu* (A Dialectal Study of South and North Korea). Seoul: Kyengwun.

Kim, Yeong-Man. 1966. Kyengnam pangen uy sengco yenkwu (A study of Kyengnam dialect tones). *Kwuk.e Kwukmunhak* 31:21–51.

Kim, Yeong-Man. 1972. Kokum sengco pikyo caylon (A comparative study on old and contemporary tones revisited). *Han-geul* 149:43–76.

Kim, Yeong-Tae. 1975. *Kyengsang Namto Pangen Yenkwu* (A Study of the South Kyengsang Dialect). Seoul: Cinmyeng.

Kim, Yong-Bum. 1988. *A Fragment of Korean Phrase Structure Grammar*. Seoul: Hanshin.

Kim, Young-ja. 1981. A semantic study of transitivity in Korean: a cognitively based analysis. Ph.D. dissertation. Indiana University.

Kim, Young-Jin. 1990. Register variation in Korean: a corpus-based study. Ph.D. dissertation. University of Southern California.

Kim, Young-Joo. 1987. The acquisition of relative clauses in English and Korean: development in spontaneous production. Ph.D. dissertation. Harvard University.

Kim, Young-Joo. 1990. The syntax and semantics of Korean case: the interaction between lexical and syntactic levels of representation. Ph.D. dissertation. Harvard University.

Kim, Youngman. 1989. Middle Mandarin phonology: a study based on Korean data. Ph.D. dissertation. Ohio State University.

Kim, Young-Seok. 1985. *Aspects of Korean Morphology*. Seoul: Pan Korea Book Corporation..

Kim, Young-Wook. 1995. *Munpep Hyengthay uy Yeksacek Yenkwu*. Seoul: Pagijong.

Kim, Yunkyeng. 1938. *Cosen Munca kup Ehaksa* (A Linguistic History of Korean Writing and Language). Seoul: Cosen Kinyemtose Chwulphansa.

Kim-Cho, Sek Yen. 1999. *The Korean Alphabet of 1446: the Orthophonic Alphabet for the Instruction of the People*. ms. State University of New York at Buffalo.

Kim-Renaud, Young-Key. 1974. Korean consonantal phonology. Ph.D. dissertation. University of Hawaii.

Kim-Renaud, Young-Key. 1986. *Studies in Korean Linguistics*. Seoul: Hanshin.

Kim-Renaud, Young-Key (ed.). 1994. *Theoretical Issues in Korean Linguistics*. Stanford: CSLI Publications.

Kim-Renaud, Young-Key (ed.). 1997. *The Korean Alphabet: a Unique Invention*. Honolulu: University of Hawaii Press.

Kindaichi, Kyosuke, et al. 1951. Nihongo no keito ni tsuite (On the genealogy of Japanese). *Kokugogaku* 5:9–36.

King, J.R.P. 1991. Russian sources on Korean dialects. Ph.D. dissertation. Harvard University.

Kiyose, Gisaburo. 1986. Tunguz and other elements in the languages of the Three Kingdoms. *Korean Linguistics* 4:17–26.

KLA (Cosen.e Hak.hoy: Korean Language Association). 1933. *Hankul Macchwumpep Thongil.an* (A Proposition for Unified Hankul Spelling Conventions). Seoul: Cosen.e Hak.hoy.

KLA (Cosen.e Hak.hoy: Korean Language Association). 1936. *Cosen.e Phyocwunmal Moum* (A Collection of Korean Standard Words). Seoul: Cosen.e Hak.hoy.

KLAC (Kwuk.e Saceng Wiwenhoy: Korean Language Assessment Committee). 1988. *Kaycenghan Cosenmal Kyupemcip* (A Revised Collection of Korean Language Norms). Phyengyang: Sahoy Kwahak Chwulphansa.

Klein, E.F. 1979. Romanization of Korean: problems, experiments, suggestions. In McCann, Middleton, and Shultz 1979:174–99.

Ko, Do-Heung. 1988. Declarative intonation in Korean: an acoustic study of FO declination. Ph.D. dissertation. University of Kansas.

Ko, Young-Gun. 1983. *Kwuk.e Munpep uy Yenkwu* (A Study of Korean Grammar). Seoul: Tower.

Ko, Young-Gun. 1989. *Kwuk.e Hyengthaylon Yenkwu* (A Study of Korean Morphology). Seoul: Seoul National University Press.

Ko, Young-Gun and Kishim Nam (eds.). 1983. *Kwuk.e uy Thongsa Uymilon* (Syntax and Semantics of Korean). Seoul: Tower.

Ko, Young-Gun, Kwangsu Sung, Jaegi Shim, and Jongson Hong. 1992. *Kwuk.ehak Yenkwu Payk.nyensa* (One Hundred Year History of Korean Linguistics). I–IV. Seoul: Ilcokak.

Kokuritsu Kokugo Kenkyujo (National Language Research Institute, Japan). 1996. *Chosengo Kenkyu Bungen Mokuroku* (Bibliography of Korean Language Studies), 1945–93.

Kono, Rokuro. 1949. Nihongo to chosengo no nisan no ruiji (A few similarities between Japanese and Korean). *Jinbun Kagaku no Shomondai* (Issues in Humanities). Tokyo: Seki Shoin.

Koo, Hee San. 1986. *An Experimental Acoustic Study of the Phonetics of Intonation in Standard Korean*. Ph.D. dissertation. University of Texas at Austin.

Koo, Jasook. 1995. Politeness theory: universality and specificity. Ph.D. dissertation. Harvard University.

Koo, John H. and R.N. St Clair (eds.). 1980. *Bilingual Education for Asian Americans: Problems and Strategies*. Hiroshima, Japan: Bunka Hyoron.

Koppelmann, H. 1933. *Die eurasische Sprachfamilie, Indogermanische, koreanisch und Verwandtes*. Heidelberg: Winter.

Korean Language Society (Hankul Hak.hoy) 1991. *Wulimal Khun Sacen* (A Great Dictionary of the Korean Language). Seoul: Emunkak.

Korean National Commission for UNESCO (ed.). 1983. *The Korean Language*. Seoul: Sisa-yengesa.

Ku, Bon-Gwan. 1998. *15 Seyki Kwuk.e Phasayngpep ey Tayhan Yenkwu* (A Study on Derivation in 15th Century Korean). Seoul: Thayhaksa.

Ku, Bon-Gwan. 1998. Cepmisa uy sacencek cheli (Lexicographic treatment of suffixes). *Say Kwuk.e Saynghwal* 8.1:23–48.

Kwahak.wen (Academy of Sciences). 1960. *Cosen.e Munpep* (A Korean Grammar). Phyengyang: Kwahak.wen.

Kwen, Cey, et al. 1445–7. *Yongpi Echenka* (Songs of Flying Dragons).

Kwen, Tekkyu. 1923. *Cosen.emun Kyengwi* (Details of Korean Sentences). Seoul: Kwangmunsa.

Kwon, Hyongmyon. 1962. *Das koreanische Verbum verglichen mit dem altaischen und japanischen Verbum. Zur Typologie des Koreanischen.* Munich: author.

Kwon, Jae-Il. 1985. *Kwuk.e uy Pok.hapmun Kwuseng Yenkwu* (A Study of Korean Complex Sentence Structure). Seoul: Cipmuntang.

Kwon, Jae-Il. 1992. *Hankwuk.e Thongsalon* (Korean Syntax). Seoul: Min.umsa.

Kwon, Y.J. 1993. LF movement, licensing, and clausal structure in Korean. Ph.D. dissertation. University of Florida.

Ledyard, G.K. 1966. The Korean language reform of 1446: the origin, background, and early history of the Korean alphabet. Ph.D. dissertation. University of California at Berkeley.

Lee, Byung-Gun. 1973. Underlying segments in Korean phonology. Ph.D. dissertation. Indiana University.

Lee, Ceng-Ho. 1972. *Haysel Yekcwu Hwunmin Cengum* (Annotated and Translated *Hwunmin Cengum*). Seoul: Korean Library Science Research Institute.

Lee, Chang-Bong. 1995. A pragmatic study of Korean conditionals. Ph.D. dissertation. University of Pennsylvania.

Lee, Chungmin. 1974. *Abstract Syntax and Korean with Reference to English.* Seoul: Pan Korea Book Corporation.

Lee, Dong Jae. 1992. Korean verbal morphology: inflectional affixes are heads. Ph.D. dissertation. University of Hawaii.

Lee, Gunsoo. 1996. From referentiality to syntactic dependencies. Ph.D. dissertation. University of Wisconsin at Madison.

Lee, H.J. 1992. Logical relations in the child's grammar: relative scope, bound variables, and long-distance binding in Korean. Ph.D. dissertation. University of California at Irvine.

Lee, Hae Woo. 1994. An etymological comparison of Chinese dialects, Sino-Japanese, and Sino-Korean. Ph.D. dissertation. University of Hawaii.

Lee, Hi-Sung. 1938. Cosen.ehak uy pangpeplon sesel (A methodological introduction to Korean linguistics). *Han-geul* 7–9.

Lee, Hi-Sung and Byong-Hi An. 1991. *Hankul Macchwumpep Kanguy* (Lectures on Hankul Orthography). Seoul: Sinkwu Munhwasa.

Lee, Hong-Bae. 1970. A study of Korean syntax: performatives, complementation, negation, and causation. Ph.D. dissertation. Brown University.

Lee, Hyo Sang. 1991. Tense, aspect, and modality: a discourse-pragmatic analysis of verbal affixes in Korean. Ph.D. dissertation. University of California at Los Angeles.

Lee, Hyo Sang. 1993. Tense or aspect: the speaker's communicative goals and concerns as determinant, with reference to the anterior *-ŏss* in Korean. *Journal of Pragmatics* 20:327–58.

Lee, Hyun Bok. 1977. Nampuk.han.e uy umsenghak mich en.ehakcek pikyo yenkwu (A comparative phonetic and linguistic study of South and North Korea). *Thongil Cengchayk* 3.3:185–216.

Lee, Hyun Bok. 1989. *Korean Grammar.* Oxford: Oxford University Press.

Lee, Hyunoo. 1993. Categories, structure, and principles of anaphoric dependencies. Ph.D. dissertation. University of California at Los Angeles.

Lee, Ik-Hwan. 1978. *Korean Particles, Complements and Questions.* Seoul: Hanshin.

Lee, Ik-Seop and Hongbin Im. 1983. *Kwuk.e Munpep* (A Korean Grammar). Seoul: Hak.yensa.

Lee, Ik-Seop, Sang-Oak Lee, and Wan Chae. 1997. *Hankwuk uy En.e* (The Language of Korea). Seoul: Sinkwu Munhwasa.

Lee, In. 1994. *Analysis of Korean Complex Predicates: an Argument Structure Account.* Seoul: Hankuk Publishers.

Lee, Jeong-Shik. 1992. Case alternation in Korean: case minimality. Ph.D. dissertation. University of Connecticut at Storrs.

Lee, Jeyseon. 1996. Morphophonological reduction in Korean. Ph.D. dissertation. University of Hawaii.

Lee, Jin-Seong. 1992. Phonology and sound symbolism of Korean ideophones. Ph.D. dissertation. Indiana University.

Lee, Kay Won. 1984. Semantics of the Korean verb: a case grammar approach. Ph.D. dissertation. Georgetown University.

Lee, Keedong. 1993. *A Korean Grammar on Semantic-Pragmatic Principles.* Seoul: Hankwuk Munhwasa.

Lee, Keon Soo. 1991. Multiple accusative constructions in Korean and the stratal uniqueness law. Ph.D. dissertation. University of Hawaii.

Lee, Ki-baik. 1984. *A New History of Korea* (translated by E.W. Wagner with E.J. Shultz). Cambridge, Mass.: Harvard University Press.

Lee, Ki-moon. 1958. A comparative study of Manchu and Korean. *Ural–Altaische Jahrbucher* 30:104–20.

Lee, Ki-moon. 1963. A genetic view of Japanese. *Chosen Gakuho* 27:94–105.

Lee, Ki-moon. 1973. Hankwuk.e wa ilpon.e uy ehwi pikyo ey tayhan caykemtho (A lexical comparison of Korean and Japanese revisited). *Language Research* 9.2:1–19.

Lee, Ki-moon. 1976. *Kayceng Kwuk.esa Kaysel* (A Revised Introduction to the History of Korean). Seoul: Mincwung Sekwan.

Lee, Ki-moon. 1977. *Kwuk.e Um.wunsa Yenkwu* (A Study of Korean Historical Phonology). Seoul: Tower.

Lee, Ki-moon. 1991. *Kwuk.e Ehwisa Yenkwu* (A Study of the History of the Korean Lexicon). Seoul: Tong.a.

Lee, Kwee-Ock. 1991. On the first language acquisition of relative clauses in Korean: the universal structure of COMP. Ph.D. dissertation. Cornell University.

Lee, Maeng-Sung. 1968. *Nominalizations in Korean. Language Research* 4.1 Supplement.

Lee, Nam Duk. 1985–6. *Hankwuk.e Ewen Yenkwu* (A Study of Korean Etymology) I–IV. Seoul: Ewha Women's University Press.

Lee, Peter H. 1975. *Songs of Flying Dragons: a Critical Reading.* Cambridge, Mass.: Harvard University Press.

Lee, Peter H. (ed.). 1993, 1996. *Sourcebook of Korean Civilization* I and II. New York: Columbia University Press.

Lee, Pongwun. 1897. *Kwukmun Cengli* (A Korean Grammar). Seoul: Korean Language Bureau.

Lee, Sang-Cheol. 1986. Passive and causative in Korean: toward a universal characterization in terms of categorial grammar. Ph.D. dissertation. University of Texas at Austin.

Lee, Sang Do. 1987. A study of tone in Korean dialects. Ph.D. dissertation. Georgetown University.

Lee, Sang-Oak. 1979. *Middle Korean Tonology.* Seoul: Hanshin.

Lee, Sang-Oak and Duk-Soo Park (eds.). 1998. *Perspectives on Korea.* Sydney: Wild Poeny.

Lee, Shinsook. 1994. Theoretical issues in Korean and English phonology. Ph.D. dissertation. University of Wisconsin at Madison.

Lee, Sookhee. 1992. *The Syntax and Semantics of Serial Verb Constructions.* Seoul: Hankuk Publishers.

Lee, Sun Woo. 1983. *Syntax of Some Nominal Constructions in Korean.* Seoul: Hanshin.

Lee, Sung-Nyong. 1981. *Cwungsey Kwuk.e Munpep* (A Middle Korean Grammar). Seoul: Ul.yu Munhwasa.

Lee, Sung-Nyong, et al. 1971. *Kwuk.e Pangenhak* (Korean Dialectology). Seoul: Hyengsel.

Lee, Won-Pyo. 1989. Referential choice in Korean discourse: cognitive and social perspective. Ph.D. dissertation. University of Southern California.

Lee, Woo-Kyu. 1991. Honorifics and politeness in Korean. Ph.D. dissertation. University of Wisconsin at Madison.

Lee, Yong-Jae. 1978. Lenis obstruent fortition in Korean at different levels of acquisition. Ph.D. dissertation. University of Texas at Austin.

Lee, Yongsung. 1993. Topics in the vowel phonology of Korean. Ph.D. dissertation. Indiana University.

Lewin, Bruno. 1970. *Morphologie des koreanischen Verbs.* Wiesbaden: Otto Harrassowitz.

Lewin, Bruno. 1976. Japanese and Korean: the problems and history of a linguistic comparison. *Journal of Japanese Studies* 2.2:389–412.

Lim, Kihong. 1998. A split analysis of *caki*-binding in Korean. Ph.D. dissertation. University of Hawaii.

Lukoff, F. 1954. A grammar of Korean. Ph.D. dissertation. University of Pennsylvania.

Lukoff, F. 1978. Ceremonial and expressive uses of the styles of address of Korean. In C.W. Kim 1978a:269–96.

Maling, J. and Soowon Kim. 1992. Case assignment in the inalienable possession construction in Korean. *Journal of East Asian Linguistics* 1.1:37–68.

Martin, S.E. 1951. Korean phonemics. *Language* 27.4:519–33.

Martin, S.E. 1954. *Korean Morphophonemics.* W.D. Whitney Linguistic Series. Baltimore: Linguistic Society of America.

Martin, S.E. 1966. Lexical evidence relating Korean to Japanese. *Language* 42:185–251.

Martin, S.E. 1968a. Grammatical elements relating Korean to Japanese. *Proceedings of the 8th Congress of Anthropological and Ethnological Sciences* B.9:405–7.

Martin, S.E. 1968b. Korean standardization: problems, observations, and suggestions. *Ural-Altaische Jahrbucher* 40:85–114.

Martin, S.E. 1975. Problems in establishing the prehistoric relationships of Korean and Japanese. *Proceedings of the International Symposium Commemorating the 30th Anniversary of Korean Liberation.* Seoul: National Academy of Sciences.

Martin, S.E. 1992. *A Reference Grammar of Korean.* Rutland, Vermont and Tokyo: Charles E. Tuttle.

Martin, S.E. 1995. On the prehistory of Korean grammar: verb forms. *Korean Studies* 19:139–50.

Martin, S.E. 1996. *Consonant Lenition in Korean and the Macro-Altaic Question.* University of Hawaii Center for Korean Studies Monograph 19.

Martin, S.E., Yang-Ha Lee, and Sung-Un Chang. 1967. *A Korean–English Dictionary.* New Haven: Yale University Press.

Martin, S.E. and Young-Sook C. Lee. 1969. *Beginning Korean.* New Haven: Yale University Press.

Masterson, D. 1993. A comparison of grammaticality evaluation measurements: testing native speakers of English and Korean. Ph.D. dissertation. University of Hawaii.

Mathias, G.B. 1972. Review of Miller 1971. *Harvard Journal of Asiatic Studies* 32:284–9.

Mathias, G.B. 1973. On the modification of certain proto-Korean–Japanese reconstructions. *Papers in Japanese Linguistics* 2.1:31–47.

Matsumoto, Nobuhiro. 1928. *Le japonais et les langues austro-asiatiques: Etude de vocabulaire comparé. Austro-Asiatica* I. Paris: Librairie Orientaliste Paul Geuthner.

Matsumoto, Nobuhiro. 1948. Nihongo to nanpogo to no kankei (Relationship between Japanese and Southern languages). *Minzokugaku Kenkyu* 13.2:1–10.

McCann, D., J. Middleton, and E. Shultz (eds.). 1979. *Studies on Korea in transition.* University of Hawaii Center for Korean Studies Monograph 9.

Miller, R.A. 1967. *The Japanese Language.* Chicago: University of Chicago Press.

Miller, R.A. 1971. *Japanese and the other Altaic Languages.* Chicago: University of Chicago Press.

Miller, R.A. 1976. The relevance of historical linguistics for Japanese studies. *Journal of Japanese Studies* 2.2:335–88.

Miller, R.A. 1979. Some Old Paekche fragments. *Journal of Korean Studies.* 1:3–69.

MOE (Ministry of Education, South Korea). 1986. *Oylay.e Phyokipep* (Regulations on Loan Word Transcriptions). Seoul.

MOE. 1988a. *Hankul Macchwumpep* (Hankul Spelling Conventions). Seoul.

MOE. 1988b. *Phyocwun.e Kyuceng* (Standard Speech Regulations). Seoul.

Moon, Gui-Sun. 1989. *The Syntax of Null Arguments with Special Reference to Korean*. Seoul: Hanshin.

Moon, Yang-soo. 1974. A phonological history of Korean. Ph.D. dissertation. University of Texas at Austin.

Mun, Hyo-Kun. 1965. Sip.o seyki kwuk.e uy sengco yenkwu (A study of 15th century Korean tonology). *Inmwun Kwahak* (Seoul) 13: 25–66.

Mun, Hyo-Kun. 1966. Sip.o seyki kwuk.e uy sengco pyentong (Variations in 15th century Korean tones). *Inmwun Kwahak* (Seoul) 14/15:57–83.

Mun, Mae-Ran Park. 1991. Social variation and change in honorific usage among Korean adults in an urban setting. Ph.D. dissertation. University of Illinois at Urbana-Champaign.

Murayama, Shichiro. 1962. Nihongo oyobi kokurigo no sushi (Japanese and Kokwulye numerals). *Kokugogaku* 48:1–11.

Murayama, Shichiro. 1974. *Nihongo no Gogen* (Etymology of Japanese). Tokyo: Kobundo.

Murayama, Shichiro. 1976. The Malayo–Polynesian component in the Japanese language. *The Journal of Japanese Studies* 2.2:413–36.

Murayama, Shichiro. 1982. *Nihongo: Tamirugo Kigensetsu Hihan* (Against the Proposal Relating Japanese to Tamil). Tokyo: Sanichi Shobo.

Myong, Wol Bong. 1991. Icwung en.e wa cayso han.in uy mokwuk.e kyo.yuk muncey (Bilingualism and Korean language education for Soviet Koreans). *Bilingual Education for the Overseas Koreans* 8:1–10.

Na, Younghee. 1986. Syntactic and semantic interaction in Korean: theme, topic, and relative clause. Ph.D. dissertation. University of Chicago.

Nahm, Andrew C. 1993. *Introduction to Korean History and Culture*. Seoul: Hollym.

Nam, Kichun. 1995. Korean word recognition: are different orthographies recognized differently? Ph.D. dissertation. University of Texas at Austin.

Nam, Ki-Shim. 1978. *Kwuk.e Munpep uy Sicey Muncey ey Kwanhan Yenkwu* (Tense in Korean Grammar). Seoul: Tower.

Nam, Ki-Shim and Young-Gun Ko. 1985. *Phyocwun Kwuk.e Munpeplon* (Standard Korean Grammar). Seoul: Tower.

NAS (National Academy of Sciences). 1993. *Language Atlas of Korea*. Seoul: Sungci Munhwasa.

No, Taegyu. 1983. *Kwuk.e uy Kamthanmun Munpep* (A Grammar of Korean Exclamatory Sentences). Seoul: Poseng Munhwasa.

No, Yongkyoon. 1991. Case alternations on verb-phrase internal arguments. Ph.D. dissertation. Ohio State University.

Obayashi, Naoki. 1997. Kankokugo no daiiti onsetu ni okeru arutai sogo no *o ni tuite (On the proto-Altaic *o in Korean in the initial syllable). *Language and Literature* 32:1–16. University of Tsukuba, Japan.

O'Grady, W. 1991. *Categories and Case: the Sentence Structure of Korean*. Amsterdam and Philadelphia: John Benjamins.

Ogura, Shinpei. 1920. *Kokugo oyobi Chosengo no Tame* (For Japanese and Korean). Seoul: Utsuboya Shosekiten.

Ogura, Shinpei. 1929. *Kyoka oyobi Rito no Kenkyu* (A study on hyangka and itwu). *Keijo teikoku daigaku hobun gakuhu kiyo* I.

Ogura, Shinpei. 1935. Chosengo no keito (The lineage of Korean). *Iwanami Koza: Toyo Shicho* 7.

Ogura, Shinpei. 1944. *Chosengo Hogen no Kenkyu* (A Study of Korean Dialects). 2 vols. Tokyo: Iwanami Shoten.

Oh, Choon-Kyu. 1971. Aspects of Korean syntax. Ph.D. dissertation. University of Hawaii.

Oh, Sang-suk. 1998a. The Korean vowel shift revisisited. *Language Research* 34.2:445–63.

Oh, Sang-suk. 1998b. A syntactic and semantic study of Korean auxiliaries: a grammaticalization perspective. Ph.D. dissertation. University of Hawaii.

Ohno, Susumu. 1970. *The Origin of the Japanese Language*. Tokyo: Kokusai Bunka Shinkokai.

Ohno, Susumu. 1981. *Nihongo to Tamirugo* (Japanese and Tamil). Tokyo: Shinchosha.

Okagura, Yusaburo. 1889. Ritogenbungo (A study of itwu-Korean). *Tooyo Gakuei Zasshi* 144.

Ooya, Toru. 1889. Nihongo to chosengo to no ruiji (Similarities between Japanese and Korean). *Tokyo Jinrui Kagaku Zasshi* 4.37.

Osada, Natsuki. 1972. Genshi nihongo kenkyu, nihongo keitoron e no kokoromi (Remarks on Japanese genealogy). *Kobe Gakujutsu Sosho* 2.

Pae, Soyeong. 1993. Early vocabulary in Korean: are nouns easier to learn than verbs? Ph.D. dissertation. Kansas University.

Pae, Yang-So. 1970. *Hankwuk Oylay.e Sacen* (A Dictionary of Korean Loan Words). Seoul: Senmyeng.

Pak, Seymu. 1670. *Tongmong Sensup* (Children's Primer on Moral Rules).

Pak, Sungpin. 1931. *Cosen.ehak Kang.uy Yoci* (Essentials of Korean Linguistics). Seoul: Poseng College.

Pak, Sungpin. 1935. *Cosen.ehak* (Korean Linguistics). Seoul: Chosen.e Yenkwuhoy.

Pang, Cong-Hyen. 1946. *Hwunmin Cengum Thongsa* (A History of *Hwunmin Cengum*). Seoul: Ilsengtang.

Park, Byung-Chae. 1982. *Kotay Kwuk.e uy Yenkwu: Um.wun-phyen* (A Study of Ancient Korean: Phonology). Seoul: Korea University Press.

Park, Byung-Soo. 1972. A study of the Korean verb phrase and noun phrase complementation with special attention to the verb 'ha'. Ph.D. dissertation. University of Pittsburgh.

Park, Byung-Soo and James Hye Suk Yoon (eds.). 1998. *Selected Papers from the 11th International Conference on Korean Linguistics*. Seoul: Hankwuk Munhwasa.

Park, Duk-Soo. 1990. *Lexicon and Syntax in Korean Phonology*. Seoul: Hanshin.

Park, Jeong-Woon. 1994. Morphological causatives in Korean: problems in grammatical polysemy and constructional relations. Ph.D. dissertation. University of California at Berkeley.

Park, Jun-Eon. 1989. *Korean/English Intrasentential Code-Switching: Matrix Language Assignment and Linguistic Constraints*. Seoul: Hanshin.

Park, Kabyong. 1992. Light verb constructions in Korean and Japanese. Ph.D. dissertation. University of North Carolina.

Park, Myung-Kwan. 1994. A morpho-syntactic study of Korean verbal inflection. Ph.D. dissertation. University of Connecticut.

Park, Sayhyon. 1991. Analysis of Korean intonation. Ph.D. dissertation. University of Hawaii.

Park, Sung-Hyuk. 1985. Pronominal and anaphoric elements in Korean. Ph.D. dissertation. University of Texas at Austin.

Park, Yoen Mee. 1991. Head movement: inflectional morphology and complex predicates in Korean. Ph.D. dissertation. University of Wisconsin at Madison.

Park-Choi, Young-Soon. 1978. Aspects in the development of communicative competence with reference to the Korean deference system. Ph.D. dissertation. University of Illinois at Urbana-Champaign.

Patterson, B. Soon-Ju. 1974. A study of Korean causatives. *Working Papers in Linguistics* (University of Hawaii) 6.4:1–52.

Pei, M.A. 1954. *The World's Chief Languages*. London: George Allen and Urwin.

Polivanov, E.D. 1918. Odna iz japono–malajskich parallelej (One of the Japanese-Malay parallels). *Izvestija Rossijskoj Akademii nauk*, Ser. VI. 12.18: 2283–4.

Polivanov, E.D. 1927. K voprosu o rodstvennyx otnosenijax korejskogo i 'altajskix' jazykov (On the issue of the genetic relationship of Korean and Altaic languages). *Izvestja Akademia Nauk*, SSSR, Ser. VI, XXI. 15–17: 1195–204. Moscow.

Polivanov, E.D. 1960. Predvaritel'noe soobscenie ob etimologiceskom slovare japonskogo jazyka (The advance notice on the etymological dictionary of the Japanese language). *Problemy Vostokoved'enija* 3: 174–84.

Poppe, N. 1955. *Introduction to Mongolian Comparative Studies*. Helsinki: Suomalais-Ugrilainen Seura.

Poppe, N. 1960. *Vergleichende Grammatik der altaischen Sprachen, Teil 1, Vergleichende Lautlehre*. Wiesbaden: Otto Harrassowitz.

Prohle, W. 1916–7. Studien zur Vergleichung des Japanischen mit den uralischen und altaischen Sprachen. *Keleti Szemle* 17:147–83.

Pulleyblank, E. 1991. *Lexicon of Reconstructed Pronunciation in Early Middle Chinese, Late Middle Chinese, and Early Mandarin*. Canada: UBC Press.

Rahder, J. 1956. *Etymological vocabulary of Chinese, Korean, and Ainu* I. *Monumenta Nipponica* Monograph 16 (Tokyo). 1959–69. II and III, *Journal of Asiatic Studies* 2.1 and 2.2 (Seoul). 1961. IV, *Orbis* 10.1 (Louvain).

Ramsey, S.R. 1978. *Accent and Morphology in Korean Dialects: a Descriptive and Historical Study*. Seoul: Tower.

Ramstedt, G.J. 1924. A comparison of the Altaic languages with Japanese. *Transactions of the Asiatic Society of Japan*. Second Series 7.

Ramstedt, G.J. 1928. Remarks on the Korean language. *Mémoires de la Société Finno-Ougrienne* 58. Helsinki.

Ramstedt, G.J. 1939. *A Korean Grammar*. Helsinki: Suomalais-Ugrilainen Seura.

Ramstedt, G.J. 1949. *Studies in Korean Etymology*. Helsinki: Suomalais-Ugrilainen Seura.

Ramstedt, G.J. 1952. *Einführung in die altaische Sprachwissenschaft*, II, *Formenlehre*. *Mémoires de la Société Finno-Ougrienne* 104.2. Helsinki.

Ramstedt, G.J. 1957. *Einführung in die altaische Sprachwissenschaft*, I, *Lautlehre*. *Mémoires de la Société Finno-Ougrienne* 104.1. Helsinki.

Ree, Joe Jung-No. 1974. *Some Aspects of Korean Syntax*. Seoul: Yonsei University Press.

Rhee, Seongha. 1996. *Semantics of Verbs and Grammaticalization: the Development in Korean from a Cross-linguistic Perspective*. Seoul: Hankuk Publishers.

Sampson, G. 1985. *Writing Systems: a Linguistic Introduction*. London: Hutchinson.

Sasse, W. 1980. The 'Cultural Language': implementation of a policy in North Korea. *Korean Linguistics* 2:67–76.

Sato, Paul T. 1974. Origin of Korean *l* that corresponds to Japanese *t*. *Papers in Japanese Linguistics* 3.1:203–32.

Sato, Yutaka. 1993. Complex predicate formation with verbal nouns in Japanese and Korean: argument transfer at LF. Ph.D. dissertation. University of Hawaii.

Say Kwuk.e Saynghwal 1.2. 1991. *Oykwuk.in uy Hankwuk.e Haksup* (Korean Language Learning by Foreigners).

Say Kwuk.e Saynghwal 5.2. 1995. *Kwuk.e ey Nathanan Ilpon.e uy En.ecek Kansep* (Papers on Linguistic Interference of Japanese in Korean).

Say Kwuk.e Saynghwal 6.2. 1996. *21seyki uy Hankul* (Hankul in the Twenty First Century).

Say Kwuk.e Saynghwal 8.1. 1998. *Sacen Phyenchan ey Tayhan Kwuk.ehakcek Cepkun* (A Korean Linguistic Approach to Dictionary Compilation).

Sells, P. 1991. Complex verbs and argument structures in Korean. *HSIKL* IV:395–406.

Seong, Baeg-in. 1997. The present state and problems of genealogical studies of Korean. *Korea Journal* 37.3:166–225.

Serafim, L.A. 1994. A modification of the Whitman Proto-Koreo–Japonic vocalic hypothesis. *Korean Linguistics* 8:181–205.

Seycong. 1446. *Hwunmin Cengum* (Correct Sounds to Instruct the People).

Seycong. 1449. *Wel.in Chenkang-ci Kok* (Songs of the Moon's Reflection on a Thousand Rivers).

Shi, Chung-Kon. 1997. Two types of synthetic compounds and move-affix in Korean. *JKL* 6:369–80.

Shibatani, Masayoshi. 1976. Relational grammar and Korean syntax. *Language Research* 12.2:241–51.

Shibatani, Masayoshi. 1990. *The Languages of Japan*. Cambridge: Cambridge University Press.

Shibatani, Masayoshi. 1994. Benefactive constructions: a Japanese–Korean comparative perspective. *JKL* 4:39–74.

Shim, Jaegi. 1983. *Kwuk.e Ehwilon* (Korean Lexicology). Seoul: Cipmuntang.

Shim, Seok-ran. 1991. Word structure in Korean. Ph.D. dissertation. University of Illinois at Urbana-Champaign.

Shin, Chang-Soon. 1984. *Kwuk.e Munpep Yenkwu* (A Study of Korean Grammar). Seoul: Pak.yengsa.

Shin, Hyon-Sook. 1986. *Uymi Punsek uy Pangpep kwa Silcey* (Methodology and Practice of Semantic Analyses). Seoul: Hanshin.

Shin, Kyunggu. 1982. Passive constructions in Korean. *Linguistic Journal of Korea* 7.1:199–240.

Shin, Sang-Chul. 1987. A unifying theory of topic, conditional, and relative constructions in Korean: a case for archimorpheme across syntactic categories. Ph.D. dissertation. University of Michigan.

Shin, Seung-Hoon. 1997. Umlaut in Kyungsang Korean: the optimal domains theoretic account. *JKL* 6:283–302.

Shinmura, Izuru. 1935. Kokugo keitoron (Genealogy of Japanese). *Kokugo Kagaku Koza* 4. Tokyo: Meiji Shoin.

Shiratori, Kurakichi. 1897. Nihon no kogo to chosengo to no hikaku (A comparison between ancient Japanese and Korean). *Kokugakuin Zasshi* 4:4–12.

Shiratori, Kurakichi. 1914–6. Chosengo to Ural-Altai-go to no hikaku kenkyu (A comparative study of Korean and Ural-Altaic languages). Reprinted in *Shiratori Kurakichi Zenshu* 3. Tokyo: Iwanami Shoten (1970).

Silva, D.J. 1992. The phonetics and phonology of stop lenition in Korean. Ph.D. dissertation. Cornell University.

Sin, Kyengyey. 1750. *Hwunmin Cengum Wunhay* (Sound Explanations of *Hwunmin Cengum*). Seoul.

Sin, Swukcwu, et al. 1448. *Tongkwuk Cengwun* (Correct Rhymes of the Eastern Nation).

Sohn, Han. 1976. A cineradiographic study of selected Korean utterances and its implications. Ph.D. dissertation. University of Illinois at Urbana-Champaign.

Sohn, Ho-Min (ed.). 1975. *The Korean Language: its Structure and Social Projection*. University of Hawaii Center for Korean Studies Monograph 6.

Sohn, Ho-Min. 1986. *Linguistic Expeditions*. Seoul: Hanshin.

Sohn, Ho-Min. 1990a. Main clause deletion in Korean: politeness as a cause of linguistic change. ms. Presented at the 1990 Association for Asian Studies Meeting held in Chicago.

Sohn, Ho-Min. 1990b. Grammaticalization and semantic shift. In E.J. Baek 1990:425–35.

Sohn, Ho-Min. 1992. Honorific agreement in Korean. In S.W. Cho and H.H. Lee 1992:604–33.

Sohn, Ho-Min. 1994. *Korean*. Descriptive Grammars. London: Routledge.

Sohn, Ho-Min. 1996. Reanalysis in Korean complex predicate constructions: causative derivation. *JKL* 5:37–64.

Sohn, Ho-Min. 1997a. Mikwuk eyse uy hankwuk.e yenkwu wa hankwuk.e kyo.yuk: hyenhwang, hyen.an mich kwacey (Korean linguistics and Korean language education in America: status, issues, and tasks). *Gyoyug Han-geul* 10:55–90.

Sohn, Ho-Min. 1997b. Orthographic divergence in South and North Korea: toward a unified spelling system. In Kim-Renaud 1997:193–217.

Sohn, Ho-Min. 1998. Evolution of addressee honorifics in Korean. In S.O. Lee and D.S. Park 1998:480–90.

Sohn, Ho-Min and J. Haig (eds.). 1997. *JKL*: VI.

Sohn, Hyang-Sook. 1987. Underspecification in Korean phonology. Ph.D. dissertation. University of Illinois at Urbana-Champaign.

Sohn, John J. 1973. A study of grammatical cases of Korean, Japanese, and other major Altaic languages. Ph.D. dissertation. Indiana University.

Sohn, K.W. 1995. Negative polarity items, scope, and economy. Ph.D. dissertation. University of Connecticut.

Sohn, Sung-Ock Shin. 1992. Speaker-oriented and event-oriented causals: a comparative analysis of -*nikka* and -*ese*. *Korean Linguistics* 7:73–84.

Sohn, Sung-Ock Shin. 1995. *Tense and Aspect in Korean.* University of Hawaii Center for Korean Studies Monograph 18.

Sohn, Sung-Ock Shin. 1996. Contraction and restructuring in modern Korean: a case pf incipient grammaticalization. *Papers from the Chicago Linguistic Society Meetings* 30.1:139–58.

Sohn, Sung-Ock Shin. 1998. The grammaticalization of particles in Korean. In B.S. Park and J.H.S. Yoon 1998:871-80.

Song, Ki Joong. 1986. Remarks on modern Sino-Korean. *Language Research* 22.4:469–501.

Song, Kyung-sook. 1994. An international sociolinguistic analysis of argument strategies in Korean conversational discourse: negotiating disagreement and conflict. Ph.D. dissertation. Georgetown University.

Song, Nam Sun. 1993. *Thematic Relations and Transitivity in English, Japanese and Korean.* University of Hawaii Center for Korean Studies Monograph 17.

Song, Seok Choong. 1967. Some transformational rules in Korean. Ph.D. dissertation. Indiana University.

Song, Seok Choong. 1988. *Explorations in Korean Syntax and Semantics.* University of California at Berkeley (Institute of East Asian Studies).

Song, Zino. 1981. *Complex Noun Phrases in Japanese and Korean.* Ed.D. dissertation. University of San Francisco.

Starostin, S.A. 1991. *Altajskaja problema i proisxozdenie japonskogo jazyka* (The Altaic Problem and the Origin of the Japanese Language). Moscow.

Street, J.C. 1962. Review of Poppe 1960. *Language* 38:92–8.

Street, J.C. 1974. *On the Lexicon of Proto-Altaic: a Partial Index to Reconstructions.* Madison, Wis.: author.

Street, J.C. 1978. *Altaic elements in Old Japanese,* Part 2. Madison, Wis.: author.

Street, J.C. and R.A. Miller. 1975. *Altaic Elements in Old Japanese,* Part 1. Madison, Wis.: authors.

Suh, Cheong-Soo. 1975. *Tongsa 'ha-' uy Munpep* (A Grammar of the *ha* Verb). Seoul: Hyengsel.

Suh, Cheong-Soo. 1984. *Contaypep uy Yenkwu* (A Study of Korean Honorifics). Seoul: Hanshin.

Suh, Cheong-Soo. 1996. *Kwuk.e Munpep* (A Korean Grammar). Seoul: Hanyang University Press.

Suh, Jinhee. 1990. Scope phenomena and aspects of Korean syntax. Ph.D. dissertation. University of Southern California.

Suh, Sungki. 1994. The syntax of Korean and its implications for parsing theory. Ph.D. dissertation. University of Maryland.

Suk, Kyong-jing. 1975. Speech-act and syntactic regularity: a study of sentence enders in Korean. Ph.D. dissertation. University of Texas at Austin.

Sun, Mu. 1103–4. *Kyeylim Yusa* (Things on Korea). China.

Sung, Kwang-su. 1981. *Kwuk.e Cosa uy Yenkwu* (A Study of Korean Particles). Seoul: Hyengsel.

Sung, Kychul. 1985. *Hyentay Kwuk.e Taywupep Yenkwu* (A Study of Korean Honorifics). Seoul: Kaymunsa.

Swuyang. 1449. *Sekpo Sangcel* (Episodes from the Life of Buddha).

Toh, Soo-hee. 1984. *Paykcey.e Yenkwu.* (A Study on the Paykcey Language). Seoul: Hongmunkak.

Tyson, R.E. 1994. Korean color naming and Korean–English language contact: a study in linguistic variation and semantic change. Ph.D. dissertation. University of Arizona.

Underwood, H.G. 1890a. *A Concise Dictionary of the Korean Language.* Yokohama.

Underwood, H.G. 1890b. *Introduction to the Korean Spoken Language.* New York.

Vovin, A. 1997. Tungusic, Korean, and Japanese: the morphological evidence for genetic relationship. ms. University of Hawaii.

Wang, Hahn-Sok. 1984. Honorific speech behavior in a rural Korean village: structure and use. Ph.D. dissertation. University of California at Los Angeles.

Whitman, J.B. 1985. The phonological basis for the comparison of Japanese and Korean. Ph.D. dissertation. Harvard University.

Woo, Byong-koo. 1995. Interlanguage interference in adult acquisition of Korean as a second and a third language. Ph.D. dissertation. University of San Francisco.

Woo, Inhae. 1997. *Wuli Mal Phitong Yenkwu.* (A Study on Korean Passives). Seoul: Hankwuk Munhwasa.

Wymann, A.T. 1996. The expression of modality in Korean. Ph.D. dissertation. Universität Bern.

Yang, Byong-Seon. 1994. *Morphosyntactic Phenomena of Korean in Role and Reference Grammar.* Seoul: Hankuk Publishers.

Yang, Byunggon. 1990. Development of vowel normalization procedure: English and Korean. Ph.D. dissertation. University of Texas at Austin.

Yang, Cwudong. 1957. *Koka Yenkwu* (A Study of Old Songs). Seoul: Pakmun Chwulphansa.

Yang, Dong-Whee. 1975. Topicalization and relativization in Korean. Ph.D. dissertation. Indiana University.

Yang, Dong-Whee. 1988. *Hankwuk.e uy Tayyonghwa* (Pronominalizations in Korean). Seoul: Hankwuk Yenkwuwen.

Yang, Hyun-Kwon. 1990. Barriers and categories in Korean. Ph.D. dissertation. University of Texas at Austin.

Yang, In-Seok. 1972. *Korean Syntax: Case Markers, Delimiters, Complementation, and Relativization.* Seoul: Payk.hapsa.

Yang, In-Seok (ed.). 1982. *Linguistics in the Morning Calm.* Seoul: Hanshin.

Yang, Insun Kang. 1993. Clause linkage in Korean discourse. Ph.D. dissertation. Rice University at Houston.

Yenpyen En.e Yenkwuso (ed.). 1981. *Wulimal Uyseng Uythay.e Punlyu Sacen* (A Dictionary of Korean Sound Symbolic Words). Yenpyen, China: Yenpyen Inmin Chwulphansa.

Yeon, Jae-Hoon. 1994. Grammatical relation changing constructions in Korean: a functional-typological study. Ph.D. dissertation. SOAS. University of London.

Yi, Dong Lyong. 1982. Syntactic and semantic similarities in Turkic and Korean. Ph.D. dissertation. University of Washington.

Yom, Haeng-il. 1993. Topic-comment structure: a contrastive study of simultaneous interpretation from Korean into English. Ph.D. dissertation. Columbia University.

Yoon, Hang-Jin. 1991. Functional categories and complementation: in English, Korean, and Turkish. Ph.D. dissertation. University of Wisconsin at Madison.

Yoon, Hye Suk. 1989. *A Restrictive Theory of Morphosyntactic Interaction and its Consequences*. Seoul: Hanshin.

Yoon, Jong-Yurl. 1990. Korean syntax and generalized X-bar theory. Ph.D. dissertation. University of Texas at Austin.

You, Seok-Hoon. 1996. Argument licensing in complex verbal constructions. Ph.D. dissertation. University of Hawaii.

Youn, Cheong. 1989. A relational analysis of Korean multiple nominative constructions. Ph.D. dissertation. State University of New York at Buffalo.

Yu, Chang-Don. 1962. Sip.o seyki kwuk.e uy um.wun cheykyey (On the phonological system of 15th century Korean). *Kwuk.ehak* 1:5–24.

Yu, Huy. 1824. *Enmunci* (A Study of the Korean Native Script).

Yu, Kilcwun. 1909. *Tayhan Muncen* (A Korean Grammar). Seoul: Tongmunkwan.

Yun, Sung-Kyu. 1993. Honorific agreement. Ph.D. dissertation. University of Hawaii.

INDEX